4e

Human Relations

Marie Dalton
San Jacinto College

Dawn G. Hoyle
San Jacinto College

Marie W. Watts
Marie W. Watts and Associates

SOUTH-WESTERN
CENGAGE Learning™

Australia • Brazil • Japan • Korea • Mexico • Singapore • Spain • United Kingdom • United States

SOUTH-WESTERN
CENGAGE Learning

Human Relations, Fourth Edition
Marie Dalton, Dawn Hoyle, and Marie Watts

Vice President of Editorial, Business:
Jack W. Calhoun

Vice President/Editor-in-Chief: Karen Schmohe

Senior Acquisitions Editor: Jane Phelan

Senior Developmental Editor: Penny Shank

Editorial Assistant: Conor Allen

Contributing Editor: Elaine Langlois

Marketing Manager: Laura Stopa

Content Project Management:
Pre-PressPMG

Media Editor: Lysa Kosins

Production Technology Analyst: Starratt Alexander

Website Project Manager: Ed Stubenrauch

Manufacturing Coordinator: Kevin Kluck

Production Service: Pre-PressPMG

Copyeditor: Mark Mayell

Senior Art Director: Tippy McIntosh

Internal Designer: Joe Devine, Red Hangar Design

Cover Designer: Joe Devine, Red Hangar Design

Cover Image: ©Todd Davidson/
Getty Images

Photo Researcher: Darren Wright

For product information and technology assistance, contact us at
Cengage Learning Customer & Sales Support, 1-800-354-9706

For permission to use material from this text or product,
submit all requests online at **www.cengage.com/permissions**
Further permissions questions can be emailed to
permissionrequest@cengage.com

Exam*View*® is a registered trademark of eInstruction Corp. Windows is a registered trademark of the Microsoft Corporation used herein under license. Macintosh and Power Macintosh are registered trademarks of Apple Computer, Inc. used herein under license.

Library of Congress Control Number: 2009942154

Student Edition ISBN-13: 978-0-538-73108-9

Student Edition ISBN-10: 0-538-73108-7

South-Western Cengage Learning
5191 Natorp Boulevard
Mason, OH 45040
USA

Cengage Learning products are represented in Canada by Nelson Education, Ltd.

For your course and learning solutions, visit **school.cengage.com**

Printed in the United States of America
7 8 9 10 11 12 13 22 21 20 19 18

T he world is continually changing, and a major theme today is connection—electronic, social, personal, intellectual, global—and that is the way learning should occur. Increasingly, learners want more than just an understanding of the concepts of relating well to people; they want connections that will increase their effectiveness and employability. Today the challenge is to open your mind to conducting business and marketing products worldwide and serving new customers with unique needs and interests. Today's workers must learn to understand and work across differences. *Human Relations 4e* emphasizes the factors that are at the center of human relation issues such as communication, problem solving, customer service, and team dynamics. The authors' goal is help learners connect with critical every-day human relations issues.

Strong Pedagogy and New 21st Century Skills Focus

Human Relations 4e has been reorganized into four parts to present material in a logical manner.

Part 1 Focusing on You includes understanding the basics of human relations, strengthening emotional intelligence, motivating oneself, and using communication skills effectively.

Part 2 Focusing on Others addresses ethics, effective decision making, teams, conflict management, and leadership skills.

Part 3 Understanding Career Development tackles those topics that will increase career savvy such as intercultural competence, workplace etiquette, organizational culture, and career advancement strategies.

Part 4 Balancing Work and Life address embracing change, respecting rights of both employers and employees, and maintaining balance in one's work and home life.

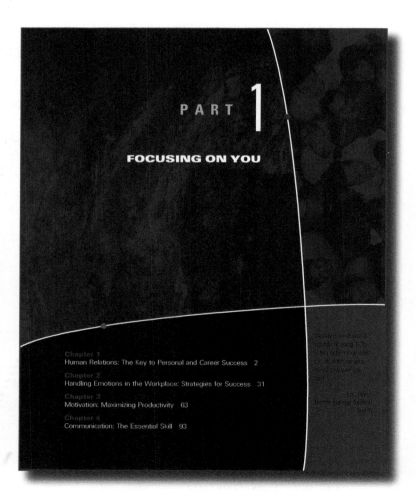

PART **1**

FOCUSING ON YOU

Each chapter is divided into smaller sections, making the content easy to master and reader friendly. Following each section, **Ask Yourself...** questions help readers create a personal connection with the concepts just presented. Since human relations means interaction among people, the more participative the class can become, the more students can learn from each activity. Chapters were revised and updated throughout with current examples from industry. This easy-to-use text will help the learner better understand not only themselves but the importance of developing healthy relationships in the workplace and prepare for successful employment.

The Partnership for 21st Century Skills has identified categories of skills and competencies that will help to ensure success on the job. **Chapter 1 introduces the 21st Century Skills**, and the scenarios, applications, and case studies in *Human Relations 4e* discuss and apply many of these skills, including the ability to:

- work creatively and seek innovative solutions

- apply critical-thinking and problem-solving skills

- communicate clearly and find opportunities to collaborate with others

- locate and use information effectively

- use appropriate media communicating and working

- work independently with limited supervision

- work effectively with diverse teams

KeyPoint
Statistical models are tools that help managers make decisions and plan and control activities.

Information Age and Creative Age—1990s to Present

Through its extensive research, the Partnership for 21st Century Skills[11] concluded that "over the last several decades, the industry economy based on manufacturing has shifted to a service economy driven by information, knowledge, and innovation." It added that "advanced economies, innovative industries and firms, and high-growth jobs require more educated workers with the ability to respond flexibly to complex problems, communicate effectively, manage information, work in teams and produce new knowledge."

> *I call the age we are entering the creative age because the key factor propelling us forward is the rise of creativity as the primary mover of our economy.*
> —Richard Florida, author of The Flight of the Creative Class, 2006

Pointing out that the United States is now more than 15 years into the information age (during which spending on information technology and use surpassed spending on production technology), the Partnership and others believe that the United States is now entering the creative age when collaboration and creativity will be essential.

Ask Yourself...

1. Do you have firsthand experience with the Hawthorne effect? Describe it. This might have resulted from the attention of a coach, teacher, boss, parent, or other person.

2. The classical school of management focused on organizational efficiency, the behavior on productivity, and the management science on solving complex problems. What do you think will be said of the "creative age"?

3. Do you agree with all of Mayo's conclusions? If yes, identify the ones with which you particularly agree. If not, identify the ones with which you most disagree and explain why.

1.4 21ST CENTURY SKILLS AND RESPONSIBILITIES

Researchers and writers point to certain personal characteristics and skills as being increasingly important for workers in today's organizations. The 21st century skills identified by the Partnership for 21st Century Skills[12] include a foundation of core subjects that "prepares students, workers, and citizens to

---

world languages, arts, mathematics, economics, science, geography, history, and government/civics. Beyond these, however, the Partnership identified three categories of skills that will increase your employability and effectiveness—learning and innovation skills; information, media, and technology skills; and life and career skills[13] (Figure 1.4). Each category includes both personal qualities and acquired skills. The Partnership believes that these sets of skills will withstand the test of time, fluctuations in the economy and the marketplace, and changing employment demands.

Figure 1.4

21st century skills.

Learning and Innovation Skills	Information, Media, and Technology Skills	Life and Career Skills
Creativity and innovation	Information literacy	Flexibility and adaptability
Critical thinking and problem solving	Media literacy	Initiative and self-direction
Communication and collaboration	Information and communications technology literacy	Social and cross-cultural skills
		Productivity and accountability

SOURCE: *21st Century Skills, Education & Competitiveness—A Resource and Policy Guide, Partnership for 21st Century Skills, 2008.* Used with permission.

KeyPoint
21st century skills include learning and innovation, information/media/technology, and life/career skills.

Related to the first two sets of skills (learning and innovation skills and information, media, and technology skills) are decision making, teamwork, and conflict resolution. Related to the third set of skills (life and career skills) are numerous other characteristics and behaviors. Some examples are effective management of emotions and attitudes (emotional intelligence), career advancement strategies, openness to change, work–life balance, motivation, etiquette, an understanding of organizational goals and culture, mutual respect, ethics, influence, negotiation, and goal setting. Each of these characteristics and behaviors will be discussed in appropriate chapters of this book.

As a member of an organization, you are expected to fulfill certain important responsibilities that call upon the skills and behaviors shown in Figure 1.4. Employees who don't help their organization grow and prosper by fulfilling their responsibilities won't be valued members. Your effectiveness in fulfilling the 16 responsibilities shown in Figure 1.5 will determine your impact, success, and satisfaction.

Special Features to Master the Concepts

- *NEW* **Jump Starts** are compelling, real-world scenarios that introduce each chapter; meaningful questions engage the learner right from the start.

- *NEW* **Ask Yourself...** questions are included after each section so that learners can check their understanding before continuing and connect with the content.

- **Connections—Technology, Global,** and **Ethical** address issues that workers face each day.

- *NEW* **In the News** scenarios straight from today's business headlines help learners relate the concepts to issues in today's market.

More End of Chapter Features:

- **Key Terms and Chapter Summary** provide an opportunity for quick review.

- **Review Questions** test students on conceptual points.

- **Critical Thinking** questions challenge students to apply the concepts.

- **Case Studies** challenge students to integrate the concepts to real-life situations and resolve the issues.

- **Human Relations in Action** applications combine research, oral presentations, team activities, and role playing, putting theory into practice.

New Updates in this Edition

- **Chapter 1** introduces the 21st Century Skills and provides a historical framework for the study of human relations.

- **Chapter 2** has a new focus—emotional intelligence. Students learn how to control their emotions at work through self-awareness and self regulation and focus on the behaviors that will get them ahead.

- **Chapter 6** includes a lively discussion of creativity, its importance to organizational survival, and ways to foster it in others and ourselves. Effective problem solving and improving decision-making is also addressed.

- *NEW* **Chapter 8** addresses conflict management, teaching students techniques for resolving and avoiding conflict.

- *NEW* **Chapter 11** stresses the importance of intercultural competence and working in diverse groups.

- **Chapter 16** expands the coverage of dealing with change in the workplace.

Experience Human Relations on the Web

www.cengage.com/management/dalton

Videos correlated to each chapter show how real companies build better performance and relationships. Video quizzes accompany each segment to check your comprehension. Also included are web activities, flash cards, and chapter quizzes.

Instructor's Resources

The Instructor's Resource CD provides extensive tools that make teaching and training easier.

- Chapter outlines
- Teaching suggestions
- Suggested responses to questions
- PowerPoint presentations
- Teaching Masters
- ExamView test banks

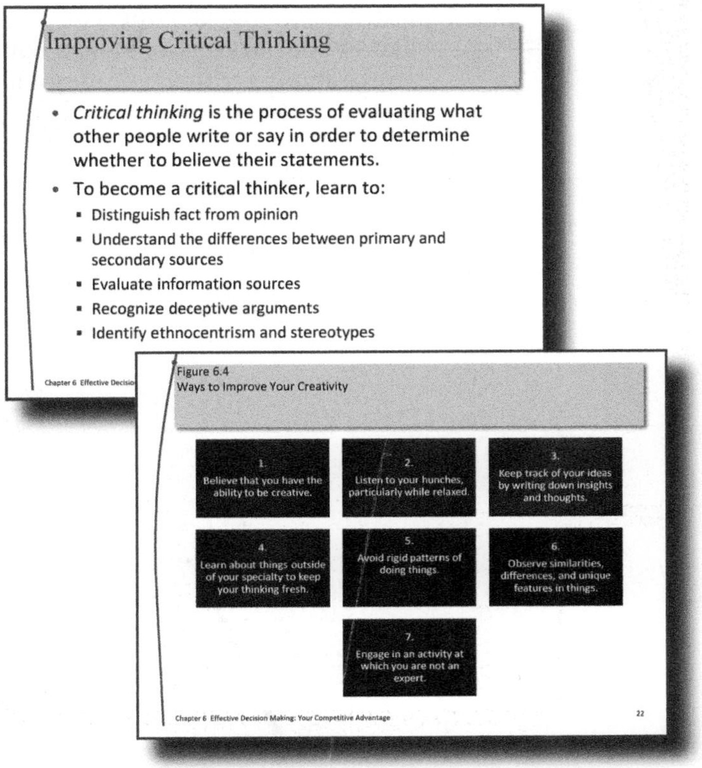

Improving Critical Thinking

- *Critical thinking* is the process of evaluating what other people write or say in order to determine whether to believe their statements.
- To become a critical thinker, learn to:
  - Distinguish fact from opinion
  - Understand the differences between primary and secondary sources
  - Evaluate information sources
  - Recognize deceptive arguments
  - Identify ethnocentrism and stereotypes

Chapter 6 Effective Decisio

Figure 6.4
Ways to Improve Your Creativity

1. Believe that you have the ability to be creative.
2. Listen to your hunches, particularly while relaxed.
3. Keep track of your ideas by writing down insights and thoughts.
4. Learn about things outside of your specialty to keep your thinking fresh.
5. Avoid rigid patterns of doing things.
6. Observe similarities, differences, and unique features in things.
7. Engage in an activity at which you are not an expert.

Chapter 6 Effective Decision Making: Your Competitive Advantage

22

Acknowledgments

Many people have contributed to the development of this text. The authors and publisher are grateful for the suggestions and feedback of the following reviewers who offered excellent suggestion and encouragement.

We offer our gratitude to our past and present students who helped clarify our thinking of what a human relations book should be and to future students and instructors who use this book as a reference and learning aid.

Helen Herbert
  Remington College

Ann Jordan
  Great Oaks Institute of Technology and Career Development

Beth Shewkenek
  Saskatoon Business College

Dottie Sutherland
  Pima Community College

Pam Uhlenhamp
  Iowa Central Community College

Karen Zempel
  Bryant & Stratton, Rochester

If this book makes your teaching-learning journey more pleasant, we would like to hear from you. Please contact us through Cengage.com if you have suggestions for how we might incorporate additional connections in future editions. Have a pleasant journey in getting to know yourselves and others!

Marie Dalton

Dawn Hoyle

Marie Watts

About the Authors

Dr. Marie Dalton is a consultant in workforce development, economic development, and grants development. Formerly Executive Vice President, San Jacinto College District in Houston, Texas, she was the founding head of the Aerospace and Biotechnology Academy, a unique multi-partner education/industry/government collaboration created to address workforce shortages. Her extensive professional experience includes positions as manager of business process reengineering, dean of continuing education, community college instructor, university professor, corporate trainer in the retail, petrochemical, and aerospace industries, and consultant to business and education in the areas of human relations, management, and communications. A successful author and popular speaker, Dr. Dalton has published five texts and numerous articles and has made dozens of presentations to international, national, state, and community groups.

Dawn G. Hoyle is a Human Relations Specialist and President of Hoyle and Associates. She has developed and conducted training seminars for major private industry and public sector organizations in the areas of human relations and supervisory skills. Ms. Hoyle also worked with NASA-Johnson Space Center for 37 years in various human resources, contract management, and program analysis positions. She has also been an instructor at San Jacinto College, teaching courses on Human Behavior and Motivation and Effective Supervision and has been an active public speaker specializing on those topics. She worked with the Aerospace and Biotechology Academy to help bring business, technology, and medical representatives together with educators and students to encourage education in science, technology, engineering, and math.

Marie Watts is the owner of her own human relations consulting firm, Marie W. Watts and Associates, that specializes in training in human relations skills, mediation, and discrimination investigations. Prior to starting her own business, she worked as a human resource director and manager and was with the Equal Employment Opportunity Commission (EEOC). At the EEOC, Ms. Watts investigated and supervised investigations of charges of discrimination in the workplace. From these activities, she developed a heightened awareness of how crucial human relations skills are to success in the workplace. Additionally, she is the coauthor of a novel about diversity and starting over called *An American Salad*.

Brief Contents

Contents

Part 3   **Career Development**

Part 4   Work and Life

PART 1

FOCUSING ON YOU

"Ability is what you're capable of doing. Motivation determines what you do. Attitude determines how well you do it."

—Lou Holtz, former college football coach

1

HUMAN RELATIONS:
THE KEY TO PERSONAL AND CAREER SUCCESS

OBJECTIVES

After studying this chapter, you should be able to:

1.1 Explain what human relations is.

1.2 Discuss the importance of human relations to organizations and careers.

1.3 Trace the development of human relations in business.

1.4 Discuss 21st century competencies and your responsibilities in a 21st century organization.

1.5 Explain which outside forces can affect organizations.

Jump Start

In January 2009, President Obama criticized Wall Street banks and other institutions for giving themselves nearly $20 billion in bonuses in the last year, spending money on exorbitant office decorations, and planning to buy a $550 million jet. These actions occurred as the economy was deteriorating and the government was spending billions to bail out financial institutions. Obama called their actions irresponsible and said institutions seeking financial assistance must exercise self-control.[1]

- What do the Wall Street institutions' expenditures have to do with human relations?
- Why do you think the president condemned these banks so harshly?

1.1   HUMAN RELATIONS DEFINITION AND SYSTEM

You may have the technical skills to do your job, but without effective human relations skills, you're heading straight into a career roadblock. Today's fast-paced, demanding workplace requires that you use diplomacy, tact, and many other human relations skills. Employees need a new mindset along with a solid set of concrete skills. What many people don't know is that effective interpersonal skills can be learned, like any other skill.

Human Relations Defined

Human relations is the study of relationships among people and how they interact. It looks at how this knowledge can be used to improve personal, job, and career effectiveness. Broadly, it includes all types of interactions, including conflicts, collaborations, and groups. Effective human relations is a combination of knowledge, experience, skills, and attributes. Collectively, these traits enable you to perform effectively. It involves cognitive skills, relationship skills, and personal capabilities. Examples of your cognitive skills are decision making, problem solving, critical thinking, creativity, and innovation. Your relationship skills include influence and negotiation, communication, listening, and trust building. Personal capabilities refer to your adaptability, flexibility, and resiliency, your degree of integrity and honesty, and your approach to self-development.

> **KeyPoint**
> Human relations, the study of relationships among people, will help you interact effectively with others.

People with strong human relations skills are better able to work with others and are more likely to succeed in their careers and in life. Studying human relations will help you understand why beliefs, attitudes, and behaviors can sometimes create relationship problems at work or in your personal life. When you have a good understanding of how your work habits, communication skills, and attitudes affect others, you'll be more prepared to avoid and manage these potential complications. Strengthening your human relations skills involves an understanding of your own psychology and that of others.

By studying human relations, you'll learn skills that will help you achieve your personal and professional goals and contribute to the success of organizations to which you belong. Away from work, your relationships may include parents, siblings, children, your spouse, and friends. On the job, your relationships may be with subordinates, coworkers, superiors, or clients. The study of human relations is helpful and interesting because it is about you and your interactions with others.

What Human Relations Is Not

Knowing what human relations isn't is as important to your success as knowing what it is. If you are practicing human relations effectively, you:

- Are strong and self-confident—but not overbearing
- Are modest—but not timid or self-effacing
- Are considerate of others—while keeping in mind both your own and your organization's needs
- Show an interest in other people and talk about topics that interest them—without prying into their personal life
- Listen—while still contributing your comments
- Are thoughtful—but not lazy or slow to action
- Are confident—but not unwilling to change or learn from errors
- Are able to relax—but remain focused

A Systems Approach to Studying Human Relations

Several factors influence how people interact and behave at work. You'll learn more about them throughout this book, which will use a systems approach in covering human relations in an organization. A *system* is a group of interrelated items or parts that act as a whole. In a system, all parts are connected to all other parts and are affected by at least one other part, and each part affects the whole.[2] For example, a company wanting to lower its production costs may attempt to reduce its faulty products. To do this, it would look at factors that can impact quality, such as its raw materials, technology, and manufacturing process; the skills and attitudes of its workers; their supervisor's management style; and other elements. In a systems approach, a company looks for connections among the different parts of the organization.

How individuals and groups interact affects the overall performance of the organization. With the systems approach, you'll be looking at the behaviors that are considered to have a significant systemic effect and how they impact individuals, groups, and the organization. Figure 1.1 depicts the key elements of the system this book calls "human relations and organizational productivity."

Note that the figure shows human relations and organizational productivity as the sum total of six parts. All of them are connected to each other, and each part affects the whole and at least one other part. Each part, in turn, is made up of a number of actions or behaviors:

- External factors—such as mergers, changing technology, and demographic shifts

Figure 1.1

Human relations and organizational productivity.

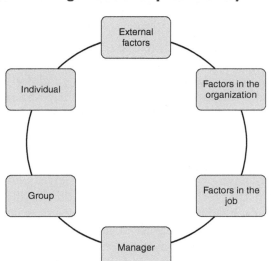

- Factors in the organization—such as leadership, power, diversity, goals, structure, and culture
- Factors in the job—such as adoption of new technology
- Manager—such as this person's managerial style
- Group—such as how the group approaches decision making, teamwork, or conflict management
- Individual—such as this person's learning and management of his or her feelings and those of others (emotional intelligence). His or her attitudes, perception, motivation, and communication ability/style. Ethics, etiquette, career advancement strategies, and goal setting. Openness to change, respect for employee rights, and work/life balance

KeyPoint
Numerous individual actions affect the system—such as emotional intelligence, attitudes, perception, motivation, communication, ethics, and openness to change.

Ask Yourself...

1. What is human relations? How can human relations skills help you at work? In your personal life?

2. Define a system and describe how your productivity at work might be affected by each of the following: (a) you work under a supportive supervisor; (b) you work with highly motivated and creative coworkers.

3. Give examples from your own experiences, movies, or TV shows of successful and unsuccessful human relations. What lessons can you learn from these?

1.2 WHY IS HUMAN RELATIONS IMPORTANT?

An article in *Today's Engineer*[3] highlighted the importance of human relations skills. A utility company in the middle of a merger reviewed a list of desirable skills and characteristics developed by managers and executives. The human resources director said those criteria would determine which employees to keep after the merger. Skills such as having a global perspective, being a team player, and exhibiting flexibility would help the remaining workers adapt to a changed work environment including global product and safety teams.

Effective human relations skills contribute to organizational and individual success. In fact, most people are fired because they cannot get along with others or they have poor work habits. Far fewer people lose their jobs because they lack actual technical knowledge. Additionally, managers spend hundreds of hours each year dealing with employee personality clashes.

The average worker will make 3 to 11 major career changes during his or her life. While different careers may require different technical skills, all positions require similar human relations skills. People with these human relations skills will always be in great demand.

©2009 Ted Goff

"All those who disagree with me, please raise your hands and say 'I resign.'"

Organizations seek human relations skills in the employees they hire, and many companies even provide training and development in these skills to their employees. Employers consider the time and money spent on the

In The News

Almost every day, items in the news highlight the importance of human relations skills in organizations. They emphasize that employees must respect the broad range of their responsibilities, no matter what their titles are. Today's organizations need and value employees who don't say "not my job" even when tasks may seem beneath their skill level (such as the CEO who hung his own window blinds[4]). Employees must be willing to show initiative and self-direction, collaborate, and—very importantly—put ego aside.

1. What human relations skills do you think would be helpful to you in a new job?
2. What conclusions can you draw about the importance to you and to your employer of continuing to develop your human relations skills?

training to be a wise investment because these skills give the company a competitive leg up through effective relations with customers and productive collaboration of coworkers. Employees see the value because training provides them with skills that help them professionally.

Importance of Human Relations to Organizations

In his book *Cybercorp,* James Martin[5] identified certain key characteristics of 21st century organizations (as shown in Figure 1.2). If you are to be a valued employee in an organization, you'll need a mix of technical skills (to help you perform specific tasks within your job), administrative skills (to help you cope with bureaucracy), and people skills (to enable you to work effectively with others). From an organizational standpoint, this means more cooperation; better communication; and more positive, productive attitudes. As a result, the company will usually have more collaboration, better worker attendance, better employee retention, and higher morale, which is more likely to produce higher quality products.

Employers want to feel confident that you'll treat customers and coworkers professionally; will speak, listen, and contribute in meetings; and will use etiquette and other aspects of human relations skills. Organizations today are faced with serious challenges that require effective use of their resources. People are their most important resource. Because jobs are becoming more interdependent, organizations need people who can cooperate, collaborate, and produce results by working with others. Today's workplace is made up of many different departments, and you'll probably be required to interact with many of them in your job. You'll play one main role at

KeyPoint
To be a valued employee, you will need a mix of technical kills, administrative skills, and people skills.

Figure 1.2

Characteristics of 21st century organizations.

Speed	Things happen fast, calling for quick decisions.
Turn-around time	Actions and results must occur quickly.
Uncertainty	Change and uncertainly create problems and opportunities.
Virtual corporation	Employees are not in one location.
Unique capabilities	An organization's unique abilities provide its competitive edge.
Agility	Flexibility is key.
Knowledge infrastructure	A base of knowledge is needed to capture, create, store, improve, clarify, disseminate, and use information.
Geographical diversity	Organizations focus on one product and are geographically diversified instead of geographically specific and focusing on many products.
Learning	The emphasis is on helping employees increase their skill and knowledge to contribute better to the organization.

your company, but consider the many other internal departments with which you may interact, such as accounting, purchasing, human resources, and marketing.

Increasingly, companies are taking into account employee needs and goals—personal and work related. Employers strive for win–win situations that allow both employees and the company to succeed. Organizations know they will be more productive and their employees more satisfied when effective human relations skills are used.

Successful companies do not focus solely on their own organizational goals. Companies that try to provide fair and just treatment for all employees, fulfill their employees' personal needs, and provide employee development programs that address the total person are more likely to enjoy greater success than organizations that do not.

Importance of Human Relations to Your Career

Working well with people whose personalities, attitudes, and goals are different from yours can sometimes be a challenge, one that requires diplomacy, tact, and other human relations skills. If you interact well in a variety of relationships, you're more likely to be able to influence others and achieve success. In fact, effective human relations skills may be the greatest contributor to the success or failure of your career. According to the Dale Carnegie

KeyPoint
Human relations skills give employers and employees a competitive leg up.

Digital Vision/Getty Images

Foundation, 85 percent of the factors contributing to job success are personal qualities, while technical knowledge contributes only 15 percent.[6]

As our economy evolves, organizations are increasingly aware of how human relations affects them and their workers. We are quickly moving from an economy that produces goods to one that provides services, is information and technology based, and expects speed. This kind of economy requires that you and other employees communicate and interact effectively and efficiently in complex situations.

Understanding human relations will enable you to gain valuable insight into how and why people think and act as they do, acquire skills for interacting with them, and develop skills for coping with potential job problems. Such skills will also help you build positive relationships, cope with job and personal problems, and develop career-enhancing strategies and personal and social competence.

> **"** *People don't care how much you know until they know how much you care.*
> —*Zig Ziglar, author, salesperson, and motivational speaker* **"**

Where Human Relations Starts

To help you start thinking about your human relations skills, rate yourself objectively on the following characteristics in column 1 (see next page). In column 2, indicate how you think your friends, families, and/or coworkers might rate you. In column 3, obtain ratings from someone who knows you well. Use S for strong, A for average, and N for needs improvement.

Human Relations Quiz

Category of Skills	How I Rate Myself	How I Think Someone Who Knows Me Well Might Rate Me	How Someone Who Knows Me Well Rates Me
Is self-confident			
Shows self-control (ethics, honesty, patience, tact)			
Is a creative problem solver			
Communicates well (speaking, listening, writing)			
Cooperates and collaborates			
Willing to learn from errors/change			
Shows self-initiative			
Is comfortable with other generations, races, and ethnic groups			
Is dependable, productive, and responsible			
Has good appearance (smile, grooming, dress)			
Totals			

In analyzing your overall ratings, you may find that you rated yourself higher or lower in column 1 than someone else rated you in column 3. Compare the ratings of each characteristic in the three columns and start thinking about your strengths and the areas in which you may need to improve. Keep in mind that everyone always has room for improvement.

Building your human relations skills starts with you—with understanding your own mental and emotional makeup and your effect on others. Knowing yourself, your values, and your principles will help you understand others, practice effective human relations, and achieve your goals.

This understanding can come through a variety of means. The easiest way to determine your effect on others is by listening and looking. What they say, how they say it, and how they react will provide feedback to you. If you are receptive, you will find that feedback from your friends, family, teachers, and coworkers can be informative and can help you grow and develop. Combined with close observation, feedback will enable you to determine how you are being perceived by others. For example, are you a good communicator who listens well and shares feelings and thoughts, or do you try to control communication and hide your thoughts and feelings? Do you demonstrate trust and respect for others, or do they try to avoid you or watch what they say around you? As you become more sensitive to feedback from others, you'll increase your self-understanding.

Self-help books, personality tests, and personal introspection can go a long way in helping you develop self-confidence. Trying to please everyone is a quick way to damage your self-concept and your relationships—almost as much a force in hurting relationships as the other extreme, not caring whether you please anyone. Self-understanding can help you develop self-confidence by identifying what your values and goals are and in what roles you want to succeed. Shakespeare said it best when he wrote, "To thine own self be true."

As you observe, receive feedback, and reach insights about yourself, you develop a strong inner core that can help you choose appropriate responses to problems or situations. You have three possible responses when faced with a human relations problem: change the other person, change the situation, or change yourself. In many cases, the third option will require you to stop doing what isn't working in order to succeed.

> " It is not the mountain we conquer, but ourselves.
> —Sir Edmund Hillary, mountain climber "

Ask Yourself...

1. Explain the statement, "Human relations skills may be the greatest contributor to your career success." Considering your present career plans, what human relations skills do you think will be most important to you and why?

2. Will human relations skills or technical skills be more important as you progress in your career? Do you think your career level at a particular time makes a difference in which is more important? Explain your responses.

3. Think about the career you envision for yourself over the next 5–10 years and discuss how human relations skills will be important to you and to your employer. Do you think some human relations skills will be more important than others at different stages of your career? Explain your responses.

1.3 DEVELOPMENT OF HUMAN RELATIONS

Human relations isn't a new idea. The American workplace has changed in striking ways over the years, from the farmers and craftsmen of the 1700s to the information age of today, and ways of managing workers for greater productivity have been studied closely. Over time, several distinct and important schools of thought on human relations have evolved: the classical school of management, the behavioral school, and the management science school.

The Classical School of Management — 1900s–1920s

The *classical school of management* focused on efficiency. Two branches of this school developed: scientific management theory promoted by Frederick W. Taylor and Frank and Lillian Gilbreth; and classical organization theory, based on the work of Henri Fayol.

Known as the father of scientific management, Taylor believed that tasks could be analyzed scientifically to make them more efficient. His work during the late 1800s and early 1900s led to the idea of mass production, and his scientific system influenced the development of every modern industrialized nation.[7]

Frank and Lillian Gilbreth, a husband-and-wife team, measured and improved the motion of work. They used photography to identify the distinct steps required to do a task, deleted the nonessential ones, and organized the steps in the most efficient way. The combination of the ideas of Taylor and the Gilbreths resulted in the famous time and motion studies that became a popular means of improving productivity.[8]

In 1916, Henri Fayol, a French industrialist, published his 14 principles of management, which included division of work, authority, discipline, chain of command, and other concepts still used in management today. His belief was that management could be viewed as a whole, with human relations, productivity, and the general administration of the organization being improved by applying basic principles.[9]

The Behavioral School of Management — 1920s–1950s

Disenchantment with the authoritarian, task-oriented approach of the classical school, increasing unionism, the Great Depression, World War II, and the post-war boom led to the *behavioral school of management*. This school of thought had two branches, the first of which was the human relations approach. In the mid-1920s to early 1930s, Elton Mayo and his associates from Harvard Business School conducted research at Western Electric's Hawthorne plant near Chicago. The Hawthorne studies considered how physical working conditions affect worker output.

Contrary to their expectations, the researchers found that regardless of changes—such as heating, humidity, lighting, work hours, rest periods, and supervisory styles—productivity levels increased significantly during the study. The researchers realized that productivity increased because the workers were

KeyPoint
Studies identified three ways of managing— classical school, behavioral school, and management science school.

receiving attention and felt that someone cared about them. This became known as the *Hawthorne effect,* the idea that the human element is more important to productivity than technical or physical aspects of the job. Mayo's work earned him recognition as the father of human relations and provided insights into the understanding of human relations in organizations. Figure 1.3 summarizes his conclusions.[10]

The second branch of the behavioral school was known as the behavioral science approach. In the mid to late 1950s, researchers began to use scientific methods to explore efficient management techniques. The studies included both workers and managers to get a total view of human behavior in the workplace and used psychology, sociology, and anthropology as tools for understanding the organizational environment.

KeyPoint
Key activities were the Hawthorne experiments, and key names are Frederick Taylor, the Gilbreths, and Elton Mayo.

Figure 1.3

Mayo's conclusions about human relations in organizations.

1. Giving people attention can change their productivity—the Hawthorne effect.

2. Employees have many needs beyond those satisfied by money.

3. Informal work groups can be very powerful within an organization, particularly through their ability to influence productivity levels.

4. The relationship between supervisors and employees is very important, affecting both quantity and quality of employee output. Good human relations is the key, not popularity.

5. Employees have many needs that are met away from the job. Therefore, managers cannot always control motivation.

6. Relations between coworkers affect their performance. These interactions allow employees to meet their social needs.

The Management Science School of Management—1960s–1990s

During World War II, both the British and the U.S. military needed to solve complex problems, such as coordinating massive troop movements and seeing that supplies arrived at appropriate places and in correct quantities. The military enlisted the help of mathematicians, physicists, and other scientists, leading to the *management science school*. The results were so successful that companies later used the techniques and models developed to solve complex business problems.

The computer made *statistical models* easier to use. Models are analytical tools that help managers make decisions and plan and control organizational activities. However, the computer is simply a tool; it is not perfect and cannot make decisions, and it does not reduce the need for effective human relations in the success of a project.

KeyPoint
Statistical models are tools that help managers make decisions and plan and control activities.

Information Age and Creative Age—1990s to Present

Through its extensive research, the Partnership for 21st Century Skills[11] concluded that "over the last several decades, the industry economy based on manufacturing has shifted to a service economy driven by information, knowledge, and innovation." It added that "advanced economies, innovative industries and firms, and high-growth jobs require more educated workers with the ability to respond flexibly to complex problems, communicate effectively, manage information, work in teams and produce new knowledge."

> " *I call the age we are entering the creative age because the key factor propelling us forward is the rise of creativity as the primary mover of our economy.*
> —Richard Florida, author of The Flight of the Creative Class, 2006 "

Pointing out that the United States is now more than 15 years into the information age (during which spending on information technology and use surpassed spending on production technology), the Partnership and others believe that the United States is now entering the creative age when collaboration and creativity will be essential.

Ask Yourself...

1. Do you have firsthand experience with the Hawthorne effect? Describe it. This might have resulted from the attention of a coach, teacher, boss, parent, or other person.

2. The classical school of management focused on organizational efficiency, the behavior on productivity, and the management science on solving complex problems. What do you think will be said of the "creative age"?

3. Do you agree with all of Mayo's conclusions? If yes, identify the ones with which you particularly agree. If not, identify the ones with which you most disagree and explain why.

1.4 21ST CENTURY SKILLS AND RESPONSIBILITIES

Researchers and writers point to certain personal characteristics and skills as being increasingly important for workers in today's organizations. The 21st century skills identified by the Partnership for 21st Century Skills[12] include a foundation of core subjects that "prepares students, workers and citizens to triumph in the global skills race." These include English/reading/language arts, world languages, arts, mathematics, economics, science, geography, history, and government/civics. Beyond these, however, the Partnership identified three categories of skills that will increase your employability and effectiveness—learning and innovation skills; information, media, and technology skills; and life and career skills[13] (Figure 1.4). Each category includes both personal qualities and acquired skills. The Partnership believes that these sets of skills will withstand the test of time, fluctuations in the economy and the marketplace, and changing employment demands.

Figure 1.4

21st century skills.

Learning and Innovation Skills	Information, Media, and Technology Skills	Life and Career Skills
Creativity and innovation	Information literacy	Flexibility and adaptability
Critical thinking and problem solving	Media literacy	Initiative and self-direction
Communication and collaboration	Information and communications technology literacy	Social and cross-cultural skills
		Productivity and accountability

SOURCE: *21st Century Skills, Education & Competitiveness—A Resource and Policy Guide*, Partnership for 21st Century Skills, 2008. Used with permission.

KeyPoint
21st century skills include learning and innovation, information/media/technology, and life/career skills.

Related to the first two sets of skills (learning and innovation skills and information, media, and technology skills) are decision making, teamwork, and conflict resolution. Related to the third set of skills (life and career skills) are numerous other characteristics and behaviors. Some examples are effective management of emotions and attitudes (emotional intelligence), career advancement strategies, openness to change, work–life balance, motivation, etiquette, an understanding of organizational goals and culture, mutual respect, ethics, influence, negotiation, and goal setting. Each of these characteristics and behaviors will be discussed in appropriate chapters of this book.

As a member of an organization, you are expected to fulfill certain important responsibilities that call upon the skills and behaviors shown in Figure 1.4. Employees who don't help their organization grow and prosper by fulfilling their responsibilities won't be valued members. Your effectiveness in fulfilling the 16 responsibilities shown in Figure 1.5 will determine your impact, success, and satisfaction.

Figure 1.5

Your responsibilities in the 21st century organization.

Responsibility	Importance
Demonstrate your emotional intelligence, positive attitude, and moral compass.	Demonstrates your character.
Be a motivated self-starter.	Shows your employers that they can depend on you to take initiative.
Be an effective communicator who contributes to the organization.	You spend an average of 10–11 hours a day communicating.
Make effective decisions.	A key to solving problems is the ability to identify problems and then make appropriate decisions.
Be a good team member.	Key to accomplishing group goals.
Understand and manage conflict.	Conflict can be excessive, disruptive, and dysfunctional.
Develop leadership ability.	Prepares you for additional responsibilities and higher-level positions.
Appreciate and use appropriate forms of power.	Helps you achieve personal and organizational goals.
Practice effective cross-cultural relations.	Increasingly important in the global economy and diverse workplace.
Practice effective etiquette.	Fosters good relations with peers, supervisors, and clients.
Demonstrate an understanding of organizational structure and climate.	Influence the kinds of interaction in an organization.
Take charge of your career advancement.	Important since the average worker will make 3–11 lifetime career changes.
Use skill in goal setting.	Provides direction and better chance of achievement.
Be open to change.	The main constant in today's world.
Demonstrate respect for employee rights.	Helps foster effective relationships and increase job satisfaction and performance.
Maintain work and life balance.	Necessary for health.

Ethics CONNECTION

During the bank bailouts and other economic problems of 2008–2009 and three weeks after his foundering brokerage firm was sold to Bank of America, John Thain, leader of Merrill Lynch, lost his job. Reportedly, Merrill Lynch paid billions of dollars in earlier-than-usual annual bonuses to executives just three days before the merger closed. Further, according to CNBC, Thain had supposedly spent $1.2 million to redecorate his office.[14] Because of the huge losses at Merrill Lynch, Bank of America sought a second financial package from Washington.

1. Do you consider it ethical for companies to provide executive bonuses when they are unable to reward investors or are even forced to request taxpayers' money from the government to survive? Why or why not?

2. Is your opinion affected by the fact that a few days after this news broke, Thain offered to reimburse Bank of America for the $1.2 million renovation? Or that he and four other executives did not accept the bonuses?

3. If you were one of the employees given a bonus when a company is in a financial situation similar to Merrill Lynch's, would you accept it? Why or why not?

KeyPoint
Employees who don't help their organization grow and prosper by fulfilling their responsibilities won't be valued members.

The responsibilities identified in Figure 1.5 are important to all members of an organization. Your willingness to accept these responsibilities and your skill in executing them will determine your success.

Ask Yourself...

1. Name the three categories of skills from the Partnership for 21st Century Skills and discuss where or how you plan to gain competence in these skills in your program of study or degree plan.

2. Is there one category of the 21st century skills that you perceive as being more important to you than the others? Why? In which category do you think you need to improve?

3. Why do you think initiative and self-direction are considered essential skills for the 21st century? How do you think you have done thus far in demonstrating these skills in your personal, academic, and/or professional life? Provide specific examples.

1.5 OUTSIDE FORCES AT WORK

All organizations are vulnerable to a number of outside forces, such as dual careers, divorce and single-parent households, multigenerational dependents, and increasing competition for jobs. If they don't adjust to a changing environment, they'll suffer financially or even go out of business. Generational differences alone are creating a major shakeup in the workforce: more generations are working simultaneously today than ever before, the over-55 workforce is growing rapidly, fewer young workers are entering the workforce, and the number of mid-career workers is declining.

At the same time, many organizations are merging, reorganizing, or downsizing and relying on outside consultants, temporary employees, and part-time workers. Simultaneously they are stressing the importance of service to clients and customers and watching in despair the growing instances of workplace incivility. Added to this is the daily stress resulting from a roller coaster economy, corporate scandals, income inequity, and other problems.

The frequency of changes within organizations requires that employees be open to change if they are to survive and thrive. In 2008 the management book *Who Moved My Cheese?* (on *The New York Times* and other best seller lists for ten years) became the best-selling business book ever with 22 million copies sold worldwide in 37 languages[15]—thus demonstrating the interest in openness to change. This simple story tells of two people and two mice who live in a maze with plenty of cheese. But one day their cheese disappears, and they must look for cheese elsewhere. The mice do this. However, one of the humans refuses to accept reality and adapt, demanding to know who moved his cheese. The other human, while initially resistant, realizes that he must leave his comfort zone and embrace change. Think of people you know who may have gone through corporate changes, layoffs, restructuring, or mergers. Do you think they acted like the mice or the resistant humans in the book?

Types of External Forces

Numerous types of external forces can affect organizations, as shown in Figure 1.6. In looking over the forces, note how interrelated these external environments are, demonstrating why forces outside the organization can have powerful effects on the organization, and on you and your coworkers. Many of these forces can't be controlled by the organization or its employees but can have a powerful effect on them. Think, for example, of ways in which you and your friends may have already felt the effects of the economy or competition.

Major events in 2009 showed how closely tied the world's economies are and the impact that the global economy can have on organizations and individuals. For example, on one day alone,[16] the following items appeared in the news:

- Delta Air Lines, already charging fees for first and second checked bags on domestic flights, will charge passengers $50 to check a second bag on

Figure 1.6

Types of external forces.

Competition (local, national, and international)

Globalization

Economic events—such as recessions

Legal–political events—such as an increase in taxes or political unrest in foreign countries

Macroconcerns—such as ones about the natural environment (going "green")

Mergers and management changes

Sociocultural events—such as demographic shifts

Unexpected natural disasters or acts of terrorism

Changing technology

---

international flights as a way of offsetting major losses in earnings. United Airlines, American Airlines, and U.S. Airways said they were studying Delta's decision and might need to follow suit.

- Heavy equipment maker Caterpillar, reflecting the depth of the global downturn, reported double digit sales declines in most of its businesses.

- The chemical company DuPont announced that it would boost efforts to cut costs and develop additional restructuring plans because of a sharp drop in global industrial demand.

- PepsiCo offered to buy its two largest bottlers, hoping to save money by combining the three companies.

- Because of escalating credit losses and setting aside more money for bad loans, Capital One Financial Corp. reported major quarterly losses, as did the banking company KeyCorp.

- With an industry-wide slump that is reshaping the print media and with advertising revenue plunging, the New York Times Co., owner of the *New York Times, Boston Globe, International Herald Tribune,* and 15 other daily newspapers, fell into a deeper financial hole.

> **KeyPoint**
> Because technology can assist companies, they must embrace it—and so must their employees.

At the same time, fewer people were buying homes and dining out because of the economy. The weakening economy led to numerous other problems:

- Stock market declines
- Corporate mergers
- A soaring jobless rate
- Concerns for home owners with mortgages
- Worries for retirees and those nearing retirement (through declines in stock values and retirement accounts)
- Increased taxation and recession fears

- Concerns about how businesses will afford needed infrastructure changes and technology upgrades

The one-day news summary suggests why today's businesses and individuals must be aware of what is happening locally, nationally, and globally. They must be flexible enough to develop strategies to try to adapt to changes and be willing to change as needed. Consider how the above items in the news could potentially affect businesses and individuals you know, how they could try to prepare themselves for some of these problems, and how they might respond. For example, business owners could assess how they might reduce costs, perhaps postpone expansion plans, or even reduce operations. Individuals might try to lower credit balances, maintain an emergency cash fund, delay major purchases and home mortgages, and even rethink retirement plans. Also consider how seriously interpersonal interactions might be affected by these changes and why the need for human relations skills increases in the face of changes and problems.

Examples of Two External Forces and Their Impacts

Organizational mergers and technology changes are frequent occurrences in the 21st century organization. They are also examples of two external forces that impact the organization and its employees.

Organizational Mergers Many organizations are merging today in an attempt to remain viable or to compete globally. These mergers offer a challenge for both employees and the organization, as they can affect thousands of people in various ways. A study of the many mergers occurring in the global banking industry indicated that employees suffered increased job insecurity and stress. Often, employees were learning about their company's merger or acquisition over breakfast while reading the morning newspaper before leaving for work. The study revealed that one of the main causes leading to failure of mergers was the neglect of human concerns.[17] Open communication between staff and management can help ensure a smooth transition, lessen insecurities, and dispel uncertainties. Although supporters of mergers tout increased efficiencies and an improved competitive edge, others say that mergers often fail to achieve those objectives. They attribute the failure to the difficulty of blending cultural and other human factors.

Technology Changes To accomplish tasks more efficiently and compete successfully, organizations are adding technologies that can have a profound impact on them and their employees. The Partnership for 21st Century Skills pointed out that as organizations incorporate technology, computers substitute for workers who perform routine tasks, but they complement workers who perform nonroutine problem solving.

To understand the ramifications of technology adoptions, consider them from a systems standpoint. Changes do not occur in isolation. For a company to get the most out of new technology, its employees may need to embrace new management styles, new office processes, and maybe even new organizational

KeyPoint
Organizational mergers and changing technology are examples of two external forces.

structures. The Partnership for 21st Century Skills emphasizes that increased computerization is creating tasks that require problem solving and communications. Workers need these skills when responding to discrepancies, improving production processes, and coordinating and managing the activities of others. These tasks affect how workers think, behave, and interact. As a result, employers are looking for workers with higher-level skills, particularly expert thinking and complex communications skills. If your business introduces new technology, you'll be expected to adapt to and participate in the change, work with others to help solve problems it may inadvertently create, and learn the most effective ways to use the new technology.

As technology develops, it makes possible a number of different ways of working. You may someday have a *virtual office*, which allows people in different (remote) locations to communicate online with one another as though they work in the same office. Or, you may be a telecommuter. *Telecommuters*, workers frequently based at home, use technology networks to send and receive work and information to and from different locations. Many companies offer the option of working at home to reduce employee gas usage, help employees with family responsibilities, or save office space. Businesses are experimenting with other work styles as well, such as *hoteling* (sharing an office space in your company's building through reservations) and flexible work schedules.

Yet many executives at companies that offer such workstyle options think that telecommuters do not advance as quickly professionally as office-based executives. One consequence of telecommuting and virtual teams is increased worker isolation. Another concern is that without in-person interaction, workers' social skills may deteriorate.

Technology affects everyone. It's not only changing how people do business but also how they live outside of work. Just today, you've probably already checked your e-mail, made calls and sent text messages with your cell phone, and updated your status on Facebook. As evident by the number of people addicted to their BlackBerry, the use of various technologies has grown tremendously in the last few years.

Because technology can enable companies to provide better products and to produce products more efficiently and perhaps less expensively, they must embrace it—and so must their employees. However, the increased reliance on technology often comes at a price for the individual. Scientists are becoming concerned about the ultimate effect on humans resulting from their reduced contact and interaction with other humans.

Further, some people are questioning the effect a heavy use of the digital technology will have on the wiring of human brains. Rewiring, the basis of learning and memory, occurs throughout development and even in adults after brain injuries. One study at UCLA's Semel Institute for Neuroscience and Human Behavior looked at how Internet searching activated the brain. The researchers concluded that mental activity differed between practiced searchers and those new to the Internet. The experienced group used additional areas of the brain that have to do with evaluation of information, decision making, conflict resolution, and rational thought. The research raised

> **"**
> *Apply yourself. Get all the education you can, but then ... do something. Don't just stand there, make it happen.*
> —*Lee Iacocca, former CEO of Chrysler Corporation*
> **"**

@ *Technology* CONNECTION

Technology innovation is changing the entertainment business today. Walt Disney Co., the world's largest media conglomerate, is using animatronic characteristics (advanced use of electronics and robotics) and new projection technology (projections that put the viewer into the environment). It has also acquired Pixar Films, thus bringing Apple's Steve Jobs onto the Disney board and his creative ideas into the mix. Disney CEO Bob Iger is described as someone who encourages risk taking and innovation.[18]

1. Technology is having an exciting impact on entertainment today. What examples do you consider particularly impressive?

2. What effect do you think Iger's leadership style might be having on technology innovation at Disney?

the question of whether humans let other parts of the brain kick in as we become fluent with the search page layout and the act of searching.[19]

A second concern is the increasing reliance on electronic information to the detriment of benefits from interacting face-to-face. Much is lost in the communication process when people are unable to see each other and obtain the instant feedback available in person. For example, brief comments in an e-mail may appear terse and even critical when not intended because of the lack of eye contact, tone of voice, and body language.

Third, some companies worry about employees spending too much company time on the Internet. While the benefits for everything from market research to business communication still outweigh the negatives for a company, make sure that the Internet is not a distraction for you at work.

Along with solutions, the increased use of electronic communication has produced security concerns. Companies and individuals must install and maintain anti-spam and anti-virus programs to ward off attacks that can destroy important and costly data.

Be careful what you do online and exercise caution with the information about yourself that you put into cyberspace. Employers have the ability and usually the right to monitor your e-mail, text messages, and the web sites you visit while at work. Additionally, a growing concern is the emerging field of collective intelligence, digital information that is being recorded by an increasing number of sensors, such as phones, GPS units, and tags in office ID badges that capture our movements and interactions.[20] A part of collective intelligence is information already gathered from web surfing, credit cards, and other sources.

Global CONNECTION

For foreign professionals in the United States, the economic meltdown and rising unemployment of 2008–2009 were particularly worrisome, as many of them faced having to leave the country. Some people expressed concern that this could result in less innovation in engineering and technology here and more business development in other countries.[21]

In other parts of the world, the impact of globalization on the local culture is a source of great concern. Some argue that globalization offers people of all cultures opportunities to enhance their lives and economies. By promoting increased interaction of people and ideas, globalization brings increased respect for an understanding of foreign cultures. By increasing international commerce and expanding the range of consumer choice, globalization promotes economic well-being that can help preserve local cultures.

1. In the United States, many people argue that globalization poses great risk to lower-skilled workers who could lose their jobs to intense global competition. Do you agree with this? Why or why not?

2. Do you think globalization is beneficial or damaging to other cultures? Explain your response.

The complexity of organizations, heightened expectations of employees, and new technologies have made your need for human relations skills more important than ever. This importance is increasing as world economies become more global and work forces more interactive. The effect of technology on work and employees will be discussed throughout this text.

Ask Yourself...

1. Think of an organization that has undergone significant recent change. What created that change? How did the organization respond? If you were a member of the organization, how do you think you would feel or act during and after the change?

2. Describe technological changes that you have experienced and the impact on your life. How do you react when your computer isn't working or you must deal with complicated automated answering services?

3. Imagine that you are part of a virtual office. How do you think you would feel initially? Over time? What could you do to remain connected with your coworkers?

KEY TERMS

human relations	management science school
system	statistical models
classical school of management	virtual office
behavioral school of management	telecommuters
Hawthorne effect	hoteling

CHAPTER SUMMARY

Human relations is the study of relationships among people, how they interact, and how this knowledge can be used to improve their personal, job, and career effectiveness. Human relations knowledge helps both the individual and the organization.

A system is a set of interrelated elements or parts that function as a whole. In a system, all parts are connected to all other parts and are affected by at least one other part, and each part affects the whole. In this text, human relations and organizational productivity are represented as the sum total of six parts (external factors, factors in the organization, factors in the job, the manager, the group, and the individual). Each part, in turn, is made up of a number of actions or behaviors.

Organizations for which you work will expect you to have a mix of technical skills (to help you perform specific tasks within your job), administrative skills (to help you cope with bureaucracy), and people skills (to enable you to work effectively with others).

Researchers identified three distinct ways of treating employees, called classical, behavioral, and management science, each developing at a different time in American history. Key activities were the Hawthorne experiments, and key names to remember are Frederick Taylor, the Gilbreths, and Elton Mayo.

The Partnership for 21st Century Skills emphasized that the U.S. economy is driven by information, knowledge, innovation, and collaboration. The 21st century skills they identified include learning and innovation skills, information/media/technology skills, and life/career skills. Learning and innovation skills include creativity and innovation, critical thinking and problem solving, and communication and collaboration. The second category includes information literacy, media literacy, and information and communications technology literacy. Life and career skills include flexibility and adaptability, initiative and self-direction, social and cross-cultural skills, and productivity and accountability. Along with these skills, employees are expected to fulfill certain responsibilities and should be aware of outside forces that can affect organizations.

REVIEW

1. Explain what human relations is and where it starts.

2. Why is human relations important in our personal and work lives? What do you think would happen to a business whose employees did not use effective human relations skills?

3. What are the three categories of skills identified by the Partnership for 21st Century Skills? Give examples of the personal qualities and skills in each category.

4. What are your human relations responsibilities in an organization?

5. What outside forces can affect organizations?

6. How is technology changing the world of work and affecting human relations?

CRITICAL THINKING

1. Jack Mitchell, chairman and CEO of Mitchell/Richards Clothing Store, recommends four simple hiring criteria to help ensure effective customer relations: people must be honest, be self-confident, have a positive attitude, and have a real passion to listen, learn, and grow to be the best.[22] A recent study found that an effective CEO needs to be a team builder, a communicator, open to new ideas, and a good listener if the organization is to be successful.[23] How do these personal characteristics and skills compare to the sets of skills in the 21st century list? How do you think human relations skills can help business owners? How will they help you?

2. Software license violations, music piracy, and copyright infringements are sometimes called victimless crimes. In actuality, piracy nurtures organized crime across the world, affects local economies, and stunts growth and jobs. How serious do you consider these actions to be? How do they relate to topics discussed in this chapter? What would you think of a friend who borrowed your recently purchased software or CD, made 20 copies, and distributed them to 20 friends for money? Would you respond differently if your friend gave away the copies? Why or why not? Identify other situations from home and work in which poor human relations skills were used. What happened? How could the situations have been improved?

3. Name the three schools of management theory and give examples of their impact in today's organizations.

4. Consider the following two anonymous quotations: "Some people dream of worthy accomplishments, while others stay awake and do them." "Isn't it amazing what can be accomplished when you don't care who gets the credit?" These quotations speak to at least two key skills and behaviors

discussed in this chapter. What are those two key skills and behaviors, and what do these quotations suggest about them?

5. What technology changes that affect local businesses are taking place in your community? Think of ways that technology can make businesses more productive. Give examples of changes and improvements that you have observed in some of the businesses with which you are familiar. How are they affecting your life? How are you using the Internet and how has your use changed over time?

6. An article in the *Houston Chronicle* pointed out that virtually all companies consider people skills essential if you are to progress in your career—and these skills become more important as you move up. The article added that many executives fail because of weaknesses in this area. Suggested behaviors included conducting productive conversations, reading body language, seeking feedback and criticism, and mastering listening skills.[24]

Doris Kearns Goodwin, biographer and historian, identified key characteristics of America's great presidents. These are related to courage, inspiring others, self-confidence, self-control, awareness of others, effective use of emotions, strong ethics, ability to learn from mistakes, willingness to change, and ability to relax.[25] What are the commonalities between the suggested business skills and the Goodwin characteristics?

CASE STUDIES

In small groups, analyze the following situations.

1 **Will Attitude Help?** You were excited to be hired right out of college three years ago by a well-respected architecture firm. You have always been willing to assume more assignments and work longer hours. As you look around, you realize that you frequently have better ideas and problem-solving skills than your coworkers. Yet your pay is no higher than that of your peers, asking for a raise is out of the question, and you don't really want to leave.[26]

1. Do you think this kind of situation happens very often? If so, provide examples from your own experience or that of a friend. How were these examples handled?

2. Is this kind of situation likely to create frustration or stress for you? Is it likely to impact your relationship with your boss? If so, how? With your coworkers? If so, how?

3. How can you stay positive if this workforce inequity starts creating stress or frustration for you?

2 Are You Personally Effective? The Houston-area aerospace industry, in an effort to help ensure safety and development in the space program, has been focusing on first-line supervisory skills. Its work has led to the identification of three major areas of personal effectiveness: (1) cognitive skills (decision making, problem solving, critical thinking, creativity, and innovation); (2) relating to others (influence, negotiation, communication, listening, and trust building); and (3) personal capabilities (adaptability, flexibility, integrity, honesty, resiliency, and self-development).[27]

1. Why do you think the aerospace employers identified each of these skills?

2. Do you consider yourself effective in these areas? Identify specific traits or behaviors you possess that support your answer. If you think you lack some of these skills, identify which ones and your plan for improvement.

3. What kinds of problems do you think poor skills in these areas could create for aerospace employers or any other organization? For you?

4. How do these skills relate to the skills discussed in this chapter?

3 What Now? Joan is the owner of an automobile parts supply company for American-made cars. Lately, the economy has tightened, sales of new cars have dropped, manufacturers of American-made cars have developed financial problems, and consumers are increasingly concerned about protecting the environment. Joan has become very concerned about the future of her business. She lies awake at night wondering if she will hear on the morning news that the manufacturers whose parts she handles have quit producing cars, thereby severely reducing her future sales.

1. What environments are affecting Joan's business?

2. What changes might Joan have to make to stay in business?

3. What human relations skills will Joan and her employees need to adapt to these changes?

HUMAN RELATIONS IN ACTION

Work in small groups and use your favorite Internet search engine to research the most frequent human relations skills requested of job applicants in five companies. Go to company web sites and look in their employment, human resources, or job opportunities sections. Look specifically at jobs that might be of interest to you and others in your group. In light of what you have learned in this chapter, the requested human relations skills may be varied and may range from basic and general to complex and specific.

Together write a one-page summary and analysis and share it with the class. In your report, briefly describe the major activities of your five selected businesses, tell what human relations skills were being sought, explain why you think these employers consider these specific skills to be important, and, because collaboration is a valued 21st century skill, explain what each member of your group contributed to this project. Format the report in an attractive, efficient, and effective informal memorandum style. It should include **TO:,** **FROM:, DATE:,** and **SUBJECT:** at the top of the page and topic headings to break up the paragraphs in the body. Give your recommendations and conclusions first, followed by your supporting evidence. Be sure to explain your decisions.

For additional resources, refer to the web site for this text:
www.cengage.com/management/dalton

RESOURCES

1. Stolberg, S. G., & Stephen, L. (2009, January 30). Obama goes after Wall Street. *Houston Chronicle* (from *New York Times*), pp. A1, A6.

2. Williams, C. (2008). *MGMT*. Mason, OH: South-Western, a part of Cengage Learning, 38.

3. Hissey, T. M. (2002, September). Enhanced skills for engineers. *Today's Engineer*.

4. Spolsky, J. (2008, December). Don't bother me, because I'm in the middle of my most important task as CEO—hanging window blinds. *Inc. Magazine*, 77.

5. Martin, J. (1996). *Cybercorp*. New York: Amacom.

6. Wray, R., Luft, R., & Highland, P. (1996). *Fundamentals of human relations*. Mason, OH: Thomson/South-Western.

7. Taylor, F. W. (1911). *Principles of management*. New York: Harper & Brothers.

8. Pioneers in improvement and our modern standard of living. IW/SI News, the newsletter of the International Work Simplication Institute, Inc. (1968, September), pp. 37–38. Retrieved August 13, 2009, from the Gilbreth Network, http://gilbrethnetwork.tripod.com/bio/html

9. Fayol, H. (1949). *General and industrial management*. (C. Storrf, Trans.). London: Sir Isaac Pitman & Sons, Ltd.

10. Mayo, E. (1934). *The human problems of an industrial civilization*. New York: MacMillan Publishing Company.

11. *21st century skills, education & competitiveness—a resource and policy guide, 2008*. Partnership for 21st Century Skills [online]. Available from http://www.21stcenturyskills.org

12. *Ibid.*

13. *Ibid.*

14. Creswell, J., & Louise, S. (2009, January 23). Merrill Lynch's leader gets the ax. *Houston Chronicle* (from *New York Times*), p. D1.

15. Sachs, A. (2008, December 4). Why is *Cheese* the best seller of all time? *Time*.

16. (2009, April 22). *Houston Chronicle*, p. D6.

17. Leonard, B. (2001, April). Bank mergers lead to job loss and insecurity. *HR Magazine*.

18. Siklos, R. (2009, January 19). Bob Iger rocks Disney. *Fortune*, 80–86.

19. Hotchkiss, G. (2009, March 6) Is Google rewiring our brains? [online]. *Search Engine Land*. Retrieved from http://searchengineland.com/dr-teena-moody-chatting-about-our-brains-on-google-16728

20. (2008, November 30). *Houston Chronicle*, p. DC.

21. Taxin, A. (January 3, 2009). Unemployment 'scary stuff' to foreign workers. *Houston Chronicle* (from Associated Press), p. D4.

22. Haley, F. (2003, December). Fast talkR: Smart shops. *Fast Company*.

23. Derocher, R. J. (2001, February/March). Can management style at the CEO level predict a company's success? *Insight*.

24. Weinstein, B. (2008, September 14). Improve your people skills to get ahead. *Houston Chronicle*, EE1.

25. Goodwin, D. K. (2008, September 14). The secrets of America's great presidents. *Parade*, 4–5.

26. The University of Texas Employee Assistance Programs (2006, March). Give your attitude a twist. Frontline Employee.

27. Dalton, M. (formerly) Executive Vice President, Aerospace Academy, San Jacinto College (2005). Personal observations during aerospace-industry committee work and service, Houston, TX.

HANDLING EMOTIONS IN THE WORKPLACE:
STRATEGIES FOR SUCCESS

OBJECTIVES

After studying this chapter, you should be able to:

2.1 Explain the importance of emotions and emotional intelligence.

2.2 Define self-awareness and describe its role in human relations.

2.3 Describe and use strategies for self-regulation at work.

2.4 Define the role of motivation and empathy in career success.

2.5 Use social skill to enhance work relationships.

2.6 Identify other emotional factors in human relations.

Jump Start

Inspired by the heroic acts of ordinary people after the September 11 attacks and Hurricane Katrina, Dave Girgenti of New Jersey founded Wish Upon a Hero in 2007. This website matches people with wants or needs to those willing to fulfill them. As of mid-2009, its mostly anonymous members had granted more than 33,000 of 50,000 wishes. Among those granted are money for special glasses for a three-year-old who lost an ear in a dog attack, reconnection of a birth mother with a child given up for adoption, and a trip to Pearl Harbor for the World War II veteran who lost much of his hearing during the war.[1]

- Think of times in your professional or personal life when you did something for someone else that made you feel good. Why did you take these actions?
- What emotions do you think were involved?
- Where do you think your motivation to take these actions originated: encouragement from others, role models, employer expectations, or elsewhere? Explain.

2.1 EMOTIONS AND EMOTIONAL INTELLIGENCE

Do you know how to calm yourself when you think you've been treated unfairly at work? How do you guard against risky decision making in a project that's behind schedule when your fears overcome your reason? Are you able to stop yourself from taking out your anger on coworkers or friends when you feel frustrated? Can you maintain a sense of optimism in the face of problems, such as a possible job layoff?

Chapter 1 presented human relations in terms of a system, in which each part affects the whole. People's emotions, of course, influence their actions. People's actions, in turn, affect other parts of the system. When employees are able to control their emotions and manage them effectively, the performance of the organization as a whole improves.

Emotions are your feelings, impulses to act, and mind and body reactions. They can simmer below the threshold of your awareness and have a powerful impact on how you perceive people and situations. Examples of emotions are anger, sadness, fear, enjoyment, love, surprise, disgust, and shame.

Emotions help shape our decisions, behavior, and actions. Being able to manage your emotions and to deal effectively with coworkers and their emotions is the basis of your emotional intelligence.

Definition of Emotional Intelligence

Simply put, *emotional intelligence* refers to your ability to recognize and manage your feelings and those of others.[2] It has to do not just with keeping your emotions in check but with using them in a thoughtful way. People with emotional intelligence have a thorough understanding of their own emotions, and they're good at understanding those of others. The nurse-anesthetist who can calm any pediatric patient, the brand-new engineering officer who quickly earns the respect and loyalty of crew members 30 years his senior, and the manager who never loses her cool and knows the right thing to say in any situation are all making use of their emotional intelligence.

For many years, researchers have tried to explain what intelligence is and to identify factors that predict success in work and life. In 1920, psychologist Edward Thorndike identified three different kinds of intelligence: abstract (thinking), mechanical (knowing how to do things, such as run a machine), and social. He described this new idea of social intelligence as the ability to understand and deal wisely with others.[3] Social intelligence was studied intermittently over the years, and then in 1990, psychologists John Mayer and Peter Salovey published a landmark paper on the concept of emotional intelligence.[4] Since then, it has been examined by neuroscientists, psychologists, and others and implemented by many businesses.

Daniel Goleman, a psychologist and writer for *The New York Times,* captured and popularized the concept in several books beginning in 1995. He asserts that being smart and having the expertise to do a job are not the best predictors of workplace success. They are basic requirements, but emotional intelligence is the factor that sets outstanding employees apart.

According to Goleman, emotional intelligence has five important components, shown in Figure 2.1.

Figure 2.1 ◑

Goleman's components of emotional intelligence.

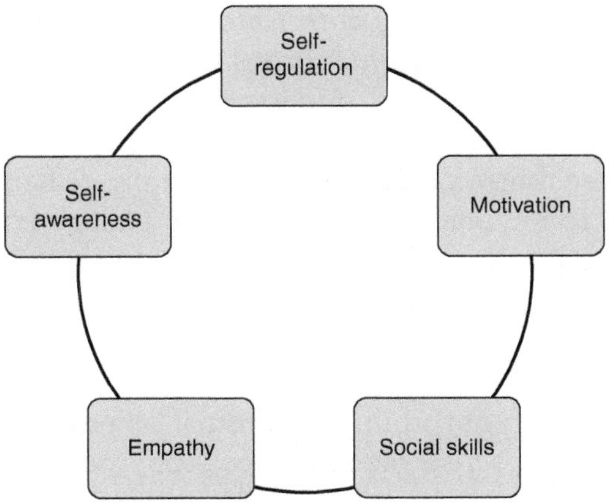

As shown in Figure 2.2, each of the five emotional intelligence components has several qualities, skills, and behaviors that lead to *competencies*—practical, useful ways in which we handle emotions on the job or in life. For example, being a good leader is a competency based on social skill, and a strong drive to achieve is a competency based on motivation.

KeyPoint
Emotional intelligence is composed of self-awareness, self-regulation, motivation, empathy, and social skills.

● **Figure 2.2**

The five components of emotional intelligence at work.[5,6]

Component	Definition	Qualities
Self-Awareness	the ability to recognize and understand your moods, emotions, and drives, as well as their effect on others	self-confidence; realistic self-assessment
Self-Regulation	the ability to control or redirect your disruptive impulses and moods; to think before acting	trustworthiness and integrity; comfort with ambiguity; openness to change
Motivation	a passion to work for reasons that go beyond money or status; to pursue goals with energy and persistence	strong drive to achieve; optimism, even in the face of failure; organizational commitment
Empathy	the ability to understand the emotional makeup of other people; skill in treating people according to their emotional reactions	cross-cultural sensitivity; service to clients and customers
Social Skill	proficiency in managing relationships and building networks	an ability to find common ground and build rapport

SOURCE: Adapted from "What Makes a Leader?" by D. Goleman, Winter 2008, *Harvard Business Review OnPoint*, pp. 38–47. Used with permission; and *Working with Emotional Intelligence*, by Daniel Goleman, 1998.

The following descriptions of components and competencies are based on those in Goleman's article "What Makes a Leader?" in *Harvard Business Review* and his book *Working with Emotional Intelligence*.[7,8]

The first component, *self-awareness*, means knowing yourself on an emotional level—recognizing and understanding your moods, emotions, and drives and how they affect you and others. For example, Javier, an emergency room nurse, knows that after an especially difficult shift, he's not going to want to talk to anyone for a while, so he plans some time alone. Raya, a graphic designer, knows to tone down the enthusiasm she's inclined to show when her group gets a new product because it's irritating to a few of the members. Self-confidence and the ability to assess yourself realistically are two competencies for self-awareness.

Self-regulation is your ability to control or redirect impulses and moods that are disruptive. It's also the ability to stop and think before acting. Sami, for example, has been having a lot of problems with his teenage son and often isn't in the best of moods when he arrives at work. But you'd never know it from the pleasant, professional way he talks with customers and coworkers. Barbara, a fifth-grade teacher, keeps a jar of candy on her desk for the stream of fifth graders and former students who trail into her room after school "just to talk." Though she's sometimes tempted to criticize, Barbara always holds herself back and listens. Competencies for self-regulation include self-control, trustworthiness, flexibility, and openness to change.

Motivation is a drive to achieve for the sake of achievement itself—not for money, for instance, or someone else's approval. Caleb is a minister who takes a deep and perpetual satisfaction in his work. Whatever his next assignment, he always approaches it with drive and enthusiasm. Competencies for motivation include a passion for one's work, a positive attitude, and commitment to the group or organization.

Empathy is the ability to understand other people's emotions and to respond appropriately to them. Kevin has a knack for knowing what will appeal to a particular customer and tailoring his approach to make a sale. The hotel desk staff values Vicki above all the other managers because of her ability to handle difficult guests. A service-oriented attitude toward customers and sensitivity to people of other cultures are two competencies for empathy.

Social skill is the ability to get along well with others—to manage relationships and build networks. It also means the ability to find things in common with others and to build rapport. When people occasionally start to argue at the monthly team meeting, Kazuo is the person who steps in and helps them resolve their differences. Cathy is liked and respected by people at every level in the courthouse, from the judges and attorneys to the secretaries and security staff. Two competencies for social skill are the ability to persuade people and to be a team leader.

> " *People who matter are most aware that everyone else does, too.*
> —*Malcolm S. Forbes, longtime publisher of Forbes magazine* "

Why Emotional Intelligence Matters

Many of the skills that employers look for in the employees they hire are emotional intelligence competencies, such as interpersonal skills, leadership ability, flexibility, and teamwork skills. Customer service skills, another emotional intelligence competency, are vital to almost any organization's success. Increasingly, organizations are finding that emotionally intelligent employees are better performers and more effective in their interactions with fellow employees. Also organizations that act toward their employees in an emotionally intelligent way become more satisfying and desirable places to work.

Emotional intelligence benefits you as well, both as an employee and as a person. It can help you cope with the disappointments and bad experiences that everyone has in life. It can keep you from saying and doing things that you will later regret and can improve your self-confidence and self-esteem. At work, employers have certain expectations of how you will behave. These expectations include actions such as displaying a positive attitude, getting along with fellow workers, and keeping your emotions in check. All of these behaviors have to do with handling emotions effectively and being professional.

As you develop your emotional competencies, you'll become better skilled at knowing and managing your own feelings. You'll also read and deal more effectively with other people's feelings in ways that contribute to healthy relationships and interactions. Most relationships can be capably managed if you use your strongest human relations skills. An effective beginning point is to remember that everyone wants to feel important.

Rating Yourself Emotionally

Start thinking about your emotional strengths. In Column 2, rate yourself on the five items shown (be objective). In Column 3, indicate how you think someone who knows you well might rate you. In Column 4, obtain ratings from someone who knows you well. Use S for strong, A for average, and N for needs improvement.

Emotional Strengths Quiz

	How I Rate Myself	How I Think Someone Who Knows Me Well Might Rate Me	How Someone Who Knows Me Well Rates Me
Knowing yourself on an emotional level			
Controlling your impulses and moods, not judging, and thinking before acting			
Striving to achieve for the sake of achievement			
Understanding other people's emotions and dealing with them accordingly			
Getting along well with others			
Totals (number of S, A, and N ratings in each column)			

In analyzing the totals, you will probably find that your ratings differ in the three columns. As you compare the ratings, start thinking about your strengths and the areas in which you may need to improve. Everyone always has room for improvement.

According to Goleman, emotional intelligence develops as people mature, but it can also be learned. The next few sections discuss the five key components of emotional intelligence and offer specific strategies for developing them. Some general suggestions are the following:[9]

- Know your strengths and weaknesses. Determine where you need to improve and whether you are willing to commit to changing.

- Define specifically how you want to improve—what habits you want to change and in what situations.

KeyPoint
Emotional intelligence develops as people mature, and it can be learned.

- Recognize how you feel and react in critical situations.
- Look for emotional role models whose behaviors you can try to follow.
- Seek feedback from trusted friends and coworkers.
- Track your changes, and treat lapses as learning opportunities to determine why you slipped.
- Keep practicing. It can take a long time to make a new behavior a habit.

Ask Yourself...

1. Discuss some emotional strengths that you've observed in friends or family members.
2. Based on the results of the Emotional Strengths Quiz, what areas have you identified for improvement? What actions can you take to improve?

2.2   SELF-AWARENESS

Self-awareness means recognizing your emotions, moods, and drives; truly understanding them; and knowing how they affect us and others.[10] When Michael's friend Julie said to him, "I think you're a very angry person," his first reaction was to dismiss the idea. He never shouted at anyone, never raised his voice. How could he be angry? But as he thought about that remark over the days that followed, Michael realized that he *was* angry, whenever things didn't go the way he thought they should, and that he expressed his anger by becoming cold and distant toward people. People who didn't know Michael were bewildered by his behavior. Friends and coworkers had learned to avoid him when he was that way.

Before we can control our emotions and use them in an effective manner, we need to understand them. Understanding our feelings gives us a clearer sense of who we are—what tends to engage us, for example, and why. It readies us to handle emotions when they arise, keep from being sidetracked, plan for them, and use them to our advantage. Seeing their effect on others can move us, when appropriate, to change our behavior so that the effect is a positive one.

> **KeyPoint**
> Self-awareness is recognizing our emotions, moods, and drives and understanding their effects on us and others.

Perceptions and Factors That Influence Them

An important step in becoming more self-aware is understanding how your perceptions affect you. *Perception* is the process by which you acquire mental images of your environment. Through perception, you organize, interpret, and give meaning to sensations or messages that you receive with your senses of sight, smell, touch, taste, and hearing.

Many factors influence perceptions. Culture, heredity, needs, peer pressure, interests, values, and expectations are a few examples. These factors contribute, in varying degrees, to the way you think and feel about people, situations, and events.[11] Stress, for instance, can distort your perception so that you are unable to evaluate situations objectively.

People develop certain attitudes and tend to make decisions based on those attitudes. Some of the things that influence perception and contribute to attitudes, such as culture, heredity, and interests, are so much a part of us that they are difficult to recognize. Others, such as peer pressure, needs, or conditions, are easier to identify.

Conditions and Characteristics That Influence Perception[12]

Time and place	Employees sometimes erroneously assume that an order from a supervisor is not as important when it takes place in the hall as when it occurs in the boss's office.
Emotional state	We are more receptive to ideas when we are relaxed than when we are feeling nervous or tired.
Age	A building or room that you thought was large when you were a child may seem small once you are an adult.
Frequency	If your supervisor starts including you in weekly planning sessions, you may feel uneasy at first but become comfortable after a while.

Among the many factors that can influence perception are the *halo effect* and the *reverse halo effect*. With the halo effect, you assume that if a person has one trait you view positively, all of that person's traits must be positive. For instance, imagine that you are the owner of an office supplies store. Tom has been a bookkeeper for you for several years, doing an excellent job in the back office, so you promote him to manager. You soon realize to your dismay, however, that he is not an effective manager because he lacks the necessary people skills to meet the public and supervise other employees. You were probably influenced by the halo effect.

Under the influence of the reverse halo effect, you allow one negative characteristic of a person to color your whole impression negatively. For example, again imagine that you are the owner of an office supplies store. Ruth Ann, a new hire, is having trouble learning one of the printing machines, and you've begun to think you'll have to replace her. However, you soon discover that she is excellent with customers in the front office, knows your accounting software better than any of your other workers, and is faster in designing business cards and other documents on the computer.

In The News

During the financial crisis in 2008, American International Group (AIG), which received an $85 billion taxpayer-funded loan, came under heavy criticism for spending $440,000 on a retreat for top insurance agents at a posh resort. Shortly thereafter it received additional aid, boosting its total to around $150 billion. On that same day, AIG spokesman Nick Ashooh defended the company against another media report of a sales meeting at a luxury resort. He said that while some of their past actions could be criticized, they felt this one was appropriate. Company officials said it was a sales training and education conference for about 150 independent financial advisers in its AIG Advisers Group.[13]

1. Would you consider this an ethical lapse on the part of AIG or a perceptual problem on the part of the public? Explain.
2. Do you think the reverse halo effect could be influencing the public's perception in this case? Why or why not?

Being aware of your own perceptions and what influences them is extremely important. With this awareness, you can withhold judgments until you've analyzed a situation. You can ask yourself why you're feeling the way you are, whether your feelings are justified, and whether you should act on those feelings.

Becoming attuned to your emotions means recognizing that you experience emotions constantly, from the moment you wake up in the morning until you go to bed at night. As you become attuned to your emotions, you can consider how they influence what you perceive, think, and do. Ginny found that she was arriving at work stressed and anxious because she didn't allow enough time to dress for work. Diego learned that tight deadlines filled him with anxiety and that a few minutes with a cynical coworker left him feeling dull and uninspired.

Analyzing your emotions may require you to step back for a while. Some people do this kind of thinking while they walk, exercise, or drive. Others like to set aside some time to do nothing but focus on what they've been feeling and why.

Once you understand how your feelings affect you, take some time to consider their effect on those around you. Sherry realized that her moodiness about her personal problems was causing coworkers to avoid her. Eric discovered that his stubbornness about refusing to compromise or consider others' ideas had resulted in people working around him and not including him in important decisions.

Self-Confidence

Remember that a competency is a practical, useful way in which we handle emotions on the job or in life. *Self-confidence* is a competency for self-awareness that is essential for success. To envision your goals, to strive, and to achieve, you need to have confidence in yourself and your abilities.

Self-confidence reflects how sure you are about your self-worth and capabilities. It's an attitude that allows you to have positive, yet realistic, views of yourself and situations. It can fluctuate depending on past performance and on your familiarity with the situation or task.

If you have self-confidence, you tend to believe in your own skills and abilities and to believe that, within reason, you'll be able to accomplish the goals you set. Because self-confident individuals trust in themselves, they tend to worry less about conforming to others' expectations and are more willing to take risks. Further, their self-confidence usually encourages others to have confidence in them.

People with low self-confidence often expect themselves to measure up to unrealistic expectations—their own, society's, their families', and those of their peers—thus setting themselves up for failure. These expectations may be real or imagined. People with low self-confidence often rely on the approval of others to feel good about themselves. They avoid taking risks because they're afraid of failing. Generally, such people don't view themselves as successful.

Related to self-confidence is *self-esteem*. Self-esteem refers to how you feel about yourself. If you see yourself as being good at something, this increases your self-esteem. People with healthy self-esteem feel emotions but don't let emotions overwhelm them. They're less likely to take things personally. They aren't overly concerned about past mistakes or failures, and they're better able to cope with problems and disappointments.

The benefits of feeling good about yourself extend to relationships with others. People with healthy self-esteem are better able to accept other people as unique, talented individuals. They tend to like others and exhibit social skill in ways such as showing appreciation and allowing others to be right.

Self-esteem is formed through our early life experiences by parents, other authority figures, and peers. It is related to our feelings of acceptability (the extent to which we perceive others as liking or accepting us) and adequacy (how well we perceive ourselves as performing in our various roles). Some people compensate or make up for perceived deficiencies in one area by becoming better in the other. For example, they may use knowledge and achievement to compensate for lack of people skills. Or they may focus on getting people to like or accept them to compensate for feelings of professional inadequacy.

Figure 2.3 provides some steps to help you if you want to improve your self-esteem.

> "He who is not courageous enough to take risks will accomplish nothing in life.
> —Muhammad Ali, American boxer"

Figure 2.3

Steps to improving self-esteem.[14]

- **Try to stop thinking negative thoughts about yourself**. When you catch yourself being too critical, counter it by saying something positive about yourself.

- **Aim for accomplishments rather than perfection**. Think about what you are good at and what you enjoy, and go for it.

- **View mistakes as learning opportunities**. Remind yourself that a person's talents are constantly developing, and everyone excels at different things—it's what makes people interesting.

- **Try new things**. Experiment with different activities that will help you get in touch with your talents.

- **Recognize what you can change and what you can't**. If you realize that you're unhappy with something about yourself that you can change, then start today. If it's something you can't change (like your height), then start to work toward loving yourself the way you are.

- **Set goals**. Think about what you'd like to accomplish, then make a plan for how to do it. Stick with your plan and keep track of your progress.

- **Take pride in your opinions and ideas**. Don't be afraid to voice them.

- **Make a contribution**. Volunteer your time in some way. Feeling like you're making a difference and that your help is valued can do wonders to improve self-esteem.

- **Exercise!** You'll relieve stress, and be healthier and happier.

- **Have fun**. Relax and have a good time—and avoid putting your life on hold.

SOURCE: *Adapted from ©1995–2009. The Nemours Foundation/KidsHealth and used with permission.*

> *A man can- not be comfort- able without his own approval.*
> —Mark Twain, writer and philosopher

Self-Disclosure and Feedback

The term used for healthy sharing of your perceptions, thoughts, feelings, opinions, and desires is *self-disclosure*, which means sharing them honestly, carefully, and appropriately. Needless to say, self-disclosure does not mean making rude or inappropriate comments and excusing that behavior by telling yourself that you're just being honest about your feelings.

Self-disclosure has many advantages. It can increase the accuracy of your communication. It may reduce stress because you no longer have to hide your feelings. It can also increase your self-awareness by helping you be open to both positive and negative feedback. *Feedback* is information given to a person that evaluates his or her actions or states what the receiver understood.

Finally, self-disclosure helps build good relationships with coworkers. When you disclose your true thoughts and feelings, you're demonstrating trust. Perceiving they are trusted helps people feel valued and encourages them to reciprocate.

KeyPoint
Self-disclosure is the sharing of perceptions, thoughts, feelings, opinions, and desires honestly, carefully, and appropriately.

Exercise care in making disclosures, particularly in the workplace. Telling too much about intimate matters or revealing personal information too soon or to the wrong person can detract from the professional image you wish to create. It can also be harmful to your career. We all know people who blurt out their personal problems to almost everyone they meet. Such behavior is inappropriate in most settings, but especially at work.

Ask Yourself...

1. List some emotions or moods that you've experienced today. What caused them? What was their effect on you and others?

2. Self-confidence is related to performance. What are some experiences you've had that have helped to build your self-confidence?

3. What are examples of topics that are inappropriate for disclosure at work? What might you do if someone disclosed inappropriate information about himself or herself? About coworkers? About your boss?

2.3 SELF-REGULATION

KeyPoint
Self-regulation is the ability to control or redirect disruptive impulses and to stop and think before acting.

Self-regulation is the second major component of emotional intelligence. It means being able to control or redirect impulses and moods that are disruptive. It's also the ability to stop and think before acting.[15] We can't stop ourselves from experiencing emotions. But we can control them, and we can even direct them in constructive ways.

Lily doesn't like criticism. When her supervisor or a coworker gives her feedback about her performance, she finds herself becoming instantly angry and defensive. Before becoming aware of the importance of self-regulation, she might have leapt to the conclusion that she was being attacked unfairly, and she might even have responded in kind. But instead, Lily makes a strong effort to control those emotions. She takes a few deep breaths to calm herself. Then she listens very carefully to what the other person has to say. It was hard to do at first. But with time, she became better at it. Now, Lily often finds that even if the criticism is somewhat unfounded, she can learn at least a little from it about how to improve her performance. Taking criticism gracefully also adds to Lily's image as a professional.

The ability to control and redirect your emotions is invaluable. It keeps you from being at their mercy. It prevents hasty, ill-considered words and actions. It puts you squarely in control of yourself, where you want to be. It enables you to display professionalism and to show people that you are responsible for your own behavior and actions.

Self-regulation doesn't mean stifling your feelings. People who exercise self-regulation acknowledge their feelings but make a choice about how and when to express them. When Jeff has a frustrating day at work, for example, he promises himself a long run that evening. When Susannah lost her son to cancer, she grieved, but she also channeled some of her feelings into creating a scholarship in his memory at his high school.

Improving Your Self-Regulation

To improve your self-regulation, try the following actions:

- Consciously manage potentially disruptive emotions and impulses when they arise. Different techniques work for different people. Some examples are taking a walk, talking with a trusted friend, counting to ten before acting, sleeping on a problem or decision, and getting a good night's rest. Additional ways are developing a written pros and cons list, scheduling work so that you are not overwhelmed by deadlines, and asking for help.

- Consistently maintain standards of honesty and integrity in your activities. Considering your own code of ethics ahead of time will help you take appropriate action when facing tough decisions.

- Take responsibility for your own performance, follow through, and be on time. These steps will help keep you focused and more organized. They'll also improve your self-esteem and gain respect from others.

- Be willing to listen, learn, and adapt. Telling yourself that you can be comfortable with new ideas will help you seek out information and try new ways of operating.

Self-regulation is a key measure of maturity. When you are able to control your feelings and actions effectively, you are better able to determine the outcome of your actions and are more likely to be personally and professionally successful.

> **KeyPoint**
> Self-regulation is a key measure of maturity and helps you determine the outcome of your actions.

Handling emotions effectively results in more productive interactions on the job.

Photodisc/Getty Images

Anxiety

A common emotion that people experience is anxiety, a normal reaction to stress. Karen feels anxious, for example, when she's torn between her parental and job responsibilities. When Pui's boss asked him to present his department's work at the next board meeting, something he'd never done before, Pui began to experience anxiety.

Individuals frequently cope with anxiety through the use of *defense mechanisms*. These unconscious strategies serve to protect our feelings of self-worth and to avoid or reduce threatening feelings. Sometimes, though, they may keep us from confronting the real problem. Figure 2.4 explains some common defense mechanisms.[16]

Figure 2.4

Common defense mechanisms.

Denial	Denying that anxiety exists
Repression	Pushing stressful thoughts, worries, or emotions out of mind
Rationalization	Explaining away unacceptable feelings, thoughts, or motives
Regression	Returning to previous, less mature types of behavior
Scapegoating	Blaming another person or group for a problem
Projection	Attributing an unacceptable thought or feeling about yourself to others
Displacement	Finding safe, less threatening people or objects and venting frustration on them
Sublimation	Directing unacceptable impulses into socially acceptable channels
Compensation	Attempting to relieve feelings of inadequacy or frustration by excelling in other areas

To deal with anxiety, accept that it won't disappear immediately and try the following suggestions:[17]

- Focus on only one problem at a time and try to determine what about it is creating your anxiety.
- Remind yourself of your strengths and what you like about yourself.
- Talk about your feelings with a trusted friend or counselor, or write them out on paper.
- Observe how others deal with similar experiences or situations.
- Decide what action, if any, you should and can take and develop an appropriate plan.
- Maintain a balanced lifestyle, including rest, diet, exercise, and recreation.

Global CONNECTION

In mid-2009, personal computer giant Dell formally banned the export of broken electronics (computers, monitors, and parts) to developing countries. Although Dell reported that it already prohibited its contractors from exporting e-waste to developing countries, the formal announcement was a clear, and public, policy statement. Environmental groups hoped that it would encourage other electronics manufacturers to adopt similar measures.

Groups that track e-waste intended for recycling in developing countries have found some disturbing results. In China, Ghana, Nigeria, and other countries, the equipment is smashed or burned, which exposes people to toxic chemicals.[18]

1. Do you view Dell's announcement as a helpful means of asking recycling contractors to regulate their behavior? Explain.

2. Do you think organizations have a social responsibility to regulate themselves, or should only individuals within organizations bear this responsibility? Explain.

Ask Yourself...

1. Do you ever feel that your emotions are controlling you or running away with you? What steps can you take to deal with them?

2. Think of situations that have created anxiety for you. How did you handle the anxiety? Would you manage it the same way today?

3. Examine your own thoughts and behaviors. Do you use any defense mechanisms? Which ones? Are they helpful, or would it be better to try something else?

2.4 MOTIVATION AND EMPATHY

The next two components of emotional intelligence are motivation and empathy.

Motivation

Motivation (discussed more fully in the next chapter) has a special meaning in terms of emotional intelligence. It is the desire to achieve for the sake of achievement itself. You may, for example, want to do a good job because you like the creative challenge, the stimulation of doing the work, or the chance to

> **KeyPoint**
> Motivation is the desire to achieve for the sake of achievement itself.

keep learning. Or you may be motivated by a sense of pride in getting things done, by the relationship you have with your coworkers, or even by the opportunity to mentor others on the job.[19]

Understanding what motivates you will help you identify the right kind of job for you. Likewise, if you can find a creative challenge, opportunity for learning, or other motivating factor in your current job or new tasks in that job, you are more likely to be a success. Actually, there are very few jobs that cannot be made more stimulating with a positive attitude.

A positive attitude is one of the competencies for motivation. It's also a very important quality that employers look for in job applicants. Your employer will expect you to demonstrate a positive attitude at all times, even when you are having a bad day at work or problems at home. A positive, enthusiastic attitude helps you be more creative and productive. It can improve your job security and put you in line for promotions and larger raises. When employees demonstrate a positive attitude, the company enjoys improved morale, increased productivity, and higher profits.[20]

Employers may not talk much about worker attitudes, but they notice them. Your employers will be looking for attitudes that say you're motivated and interested in the job, you understand how your work affects others, you aren't constantly complaining, and you're open to change. Demonstrating the right attitudes is especially important during weak economies when companies are downsizing or may use the economy as a reason for rightsizing.[21]

> " A pessimist sees the difficulty in every opportunity; an optimist sees the opportunity in every difficulty.
>
> —Sir Winston Churchill, prime minister of England during World War II "

Nine Ways to Demonstrate a Positive Attitude at Work[22]

1. Be a team player.
2. Don't act like a prima donna, always expecting to have your own way.
3. Don't make a habit of second-guessing decisions.
4. Come in earlier.
5. Be more productive.
6. Take on extra responsibilities without being asked.
7. Improve your relationship with your boss.
8. Volunteer for new assignments.
9. Don't be stubborn, arrogant, or inflexible.

Remaining positive is sometimes difficult, as all of us face challenges, obstacles, disappointments, and tough periods in our lives. We may be stressed by fatigue, tension, or illness. Other experiences, such as the death of a loved one or pet, divorce, or job loss, can also trigger stress. Even pleasant events can be stressful if they involve major changes, deadlines, or many details (such as a wedding). When these events occur, you may have difficulty remaining positive. Stress can distort your perception and your ability to view matters realistically.

While some people by nature tend to be more negative or more positive, you can develop a positive attitude. Three approaches that help are to (1) change your thought processes, (2) engage in positive self-talk, and (3) use visualization.

Change Your Thought Processes   Dr. David D. Burns, in his book *Feeling Good*, describes thought processes that prevent us from thinking positively. One is seeing things in black-and-white categories, so that you consider your performance a total failure if it isn't perfect. A second is exaggerating or minimizing the importance of your mistakes or someone else's achievements. Some other thought processes that interfere with positive thinking are over-generalizing, so that you see negative events as part of a pattern of failure; disqualifying positive experiences as "not counting"; and jumping to conclusions. Being aware of these processes and realizing when you are using them will help you develop positive thinking patterns.[23]

Engage in Positive Self-Talk   *Self-talk* consists of the characteristic comments you make to yourself about your performance. Positive self-talk involves making favorable statements, such as "I can do that job" or "I performed well." Part of your positive self-talk might be to say, "OK, I don't yet have faith in my ability to organize the entire sales promotion, but I can certainly contribute ideas, see what others have to say, and do some of the work."

Use Visualization   Taking time to practice visualization can help you develop a positive attitude and improve your motivation. *Visualization* is a technique used by many successful people to build self-confidence. It is the process of forming a picture in your mind, imagining yourself doing well.

Make time each day to picture yourself doing well. For example, if you have a test coming up, imagine yourself sitting at a desk, reading the questions, and writing the correct answers. If you are to make a presentation at work, visualize yourself successfully making the presentation and seeing your supervisor pleased. If you have studied hard or prepared thoroughly and are rested and healthy, visualization can enhance your performance.

> *Change your thoughts and you change the world.*
> —Norman Vincent Peale, minister and author

Visualization at the Olympics

Michael Phelps used visualization to help make Olympic history by winning a record eight gold medals in Beijing's 2008 Summer Olympics. While preparing, he imagined winning those eight medals. He then backed up his visualization with training. Just before the games, he wrote down what he hoped to achieve. After his amazing feat, a television interviewer asked him whether he had achieved what he had written down and Phelps answered, "Pretty much, yes."[24]

The following suggestions will help you maintain a positive attitude:

- While you won't be able to control everything in your job and how others act, you can control your attitude and how you respond.
- Avoid becoming entangled in office politics, gossip, and complaints.
- Show respect for your coworkers, customers, and supervisors and loyalty to your department and company.
- Accept change, challenges, and collaboration enthusiastically.

Empathy

Empathy is the ability to understand other people's emotions and to respond appropriately to them. It's essentially the ability to put yourself in others' shoes so that you sense their feelings and can see things from their perspective. Empathy can help you understand a customer's needs, sense the emotional currents in a meeting, or perceive who among the meeting attendees has the most influence on group decisions.[25]

Listening closely and watching for nonverbal cues (cues that aren't spoken, such as facial expressions and body language) will help you. Tune into the meaning behind the words being used and try to determine the speaker's feelings and intent.[26] Remarks such as "I see" and "I understand" communicate empathy, as do behaviors such as nodding, stopping what you are doing and truly listening, or paraphrasing the speakers' words and what you thought they meant.

Service to clients and customers is a competency for empathy. Employees who are good at customer service make a point of learning about their customers. They read a customer's body language, sense the person's mood, and relate to him or her accordingly. They ask questions. They listen carefully to what customers say and pick up quickly on what they want. People in service occupations, such as hairdressers, encourage customers to talk about themselves, and they remember personal information. They strike up relationships with these customers that often keep them coming back.

Sensitivity to people of other cultures is a second competency for empathy. When you are working with persons or groups from other cultures, whether they are across town or across the globe, empathy will help you make a real connection with them. Open your mind to understanding their culture, feelings, needs, and concerns. You can ask questions, for example, and you can read newspapers or books from that culture. You will learn more about diversity in Chapter 11.

Being aware of what may have influenced the perceptions and feelings of others is an important part of empathy. It will help you understand people and be more tolerant, even sympathetic. When you accept the fact that others have equal rights to their feelings or points of view, even if you don't agree with them, you can deal better with different situations.

Technology CONNECTION

A competency for empathy is service to clients and customers. For e-tailers, showing empathy can be a challenge because they can't interact with shoppers in person.

Live chat may be the most effective technology for surmounting that problem. A 2009 survey of regular Internet shoppers found that offering live chat on a site attracts customers who frequently shop online as well as those who typically spend more, and it builds customer loyalty. More than half of the shoppers said they were more likely to trust a web site that offered live chat and prefer to shop at sites with that option. The survey drew a direct connection between live chat and sales growth.[27]

Some sites are experimenting with ways to make the live chat interaction even more personal. One e-tailer increased the percentage of shoppers using the feature from 4 to 34 percent just by replacing a generic chat invitation such as "Do you want to chat?" with "Hi, I'm Mary. Do you have any questions?" Some sites post photos of real employees instead of stock photos.[28]

1. Have you ever used live chat with an online retailer? Were you satisfied with the outcome?
2. How does live chat increase opportunities to show empathy?

Ask Yourself...

1. Think of jobs you have had or tasks for which you were responsible (such as publicity for a club fundraiser). Did you feel motivated to do a good job? If so, why? Did the desire to achieve for achievement's sake have anything to do with it? If you didn't feel motivated, what held you back?
2. Think about one or two people you know who show empathy. In what ways do they do this?

> Great things are accomplished by talented people who believe they can accomplish them.
> —Warren Bennis, organizational consultant and writer

2.5 SOCIAL SKILL

When the multinational manufacturer that Harry worked for announced it was moving its headquarters, he started to receive calls from companies around town—people who had worked with him, or who'd heard about him from somebody who knew him, and wanted to offer him a job. And he had offers from the university where he was an adjunct faculty member, teaching a class each semester without pay, and from his old high school, where he kept active in various groups and any committee that was lucky enough to have him.

Harry is the kind of employee or team member that everybody wants. He can walk into a roomful of people he doesn't know and strike up a conversation with any of them. If you put him in charge of a team, you know that it will meet its goals and that everyone on the team will put in the work. Harry has a knack for getting people to do what needs to be done. He can move a meeting back on track, defuse a conflict, and ask tough questions without people taking offense.

Social skill, the fifth component of emotional intelligence, is the ability to get along well with other people—to manage relationships and build networks.[29] It's the culmination of all the other components. Clearly, to get along well with others, empathy is required. So are emotional steadiness and the ability to show emotion effectively, at the right moment. Being committed to a goal and having the inner motivation to reach it helps ready us for the personal engagements we'll make along the way.

Like the other components of emotional intelligence, social skill improves with experience and practice. The following general suggestions will help you develop and exercise your social skill:

- Be aware of how quickly emotional responses can occur and think before you act.
- Have a positive attitude.
- Show genuine interest in people and help them when you can (but be careful that you don't come across as trying too hard).
- Pay attention and provide genuine praise.
- Have a sense of humor and a ready smile.
- Sincerely listen to people and their ideas and concerns.
- Be sensitive to cultural differences.

A few examples of situations requiring social skill are giving and receiving compliments, playing roles, and working with a supervisor.

> **KeyPoint**
> Social skill is the ability to get along well with other people.

Giving and Receiving Compliments

Most people have a strong need for recognition and positive feedback. Equally important are recognizing others' happy occasions and achievements and thanking those who have helped you in your job or career.

Suggestions for giving a good compliment and gracefully handling compliments are shown in Figure 2.5.

Figure 2.5

Giving and receiving compliments.

To give a good compliment:[30]

- Be specific.
- Briefly state why you think this.
- To start a conversation, ask a related question with your compliment.

To receive a good compliment:[31]

- Don't make it about you. Talk about related matters instead.
- Don't discount the compliment. That would suggest the speaker made a mistake in judgment.
- Acknowledge the speaker's words and stop there, for example: "Thank you for saying that; it means a lot to hear it from you."

Understanding Your Roles

During your life, you'll fill many different roles. Employee, parent, church member, student, volunteer, and friend are examples. Usually, you'll fill several roles at the same time. Each role has its own acceptable behavior.

Part of social skill is understanding the various roles you play in life and then behaving appropriately for that role. People feel more comfortable dealing with individuals who fit roles as the roles are perceived. Be sensitive to the roles that you play and the perceptions and expectations that others have of you in those roles. Learn what the expected behaviors are and conform to them when appropriate.

Your comfort with different roles may vary. For example, if you have just started a new job, have been newly promoted to a supervisory position, or are returning to school after 12 years, you may feel ill at ease initially. Realize that being uncomfortable in a new role is natural. If you're aware of the behavior the role requires and remember that changing your behavior to conform to that role is expected and acceptable, you'll handle transitions into new roles better.

Being Assertive

Some people are uncomfortable about sharing their thoughts in classes, meetings, or even casual discussions. They may have significant ideas they could contribute, but they hold back because they're shy or unsure of themselves.

An effective approach in such situations is to be assertive. *Assertiveness* means expressing your thoughts and feelings while asking for what you want in an appropriate, calm, and confident manner. It is acting in a way that is neither too pushy nor too passive.

KeyPoint
Socially skilled people are assertive in expressing their thoughts and feelings.

People often confuse assertiveness with aggressiveness. An assertive approach shows respect for the contributions and feelings of others. An aggressive approach, on the other hand, fails to consider whether other people will be hurt by what you say.

Suppose one of your coworkers, Lucy, is suggesting a way of solving a problem that you think is a bad idea. You could respond in one of these ways:

- Interrupting Lucy to say: "That will never work. Here's what we should do."
- Waiting until Lucy has finished to say: "Those are good points. Perhaps we should also consider …"

The first response is inconsiderate of Lucy's feelings. The second shows respect for her ideas, while also asking others to consider your ideas. Some tips for speaking assertively follow:

- Make eye contact as you speak.
- Use nonjudgmental language.
- Speak in a strong, steady voice.
- Use appropriate gestures to reinforce what you have to say.

Being assertive takes practice. With practice, you will become more skilled and more comfortable. Chapter 12 continues the discussion of assertiveness.

Interacting Effectively with Your Boss

Having a good relationship with your supervisor is important in determining how your career progresses. The result can be faster promotions, increased flexibility in your assignments, and a greater understanding of how your work fits in with the overall organizational picture.

The most emotionally intelligent way to view bosses is as people with their own feelings and their own jobs to do. They have the same concerns, fears, and anxieties as others. They have their strengths and weaknesses, problems, good days, and bad days. You can help yourself by taking the time to understand your supervisor's personality and concerns.

Some key ways to make a good impression on your supervisor (without looking like the office apple polisher) include the following:

- Demonstrate a positive attitude.
- Have a strong work ethic. Do all your work on time and to the best of your ability.
- Be willing to assume additional responsibilities.
- Get involved in high-visibility projects and activities.
- Have a professional presence. Your dress, manners, speaking, and hygiene are important and will be noticed.

KeyPoint
The most emotionally intelligent way to view bosses is as people with their own feelings and their own jobs to do.

Be observant of day-to-day events that affect your supervisor's mood and adjust your approach accordingly. For instance, if you raise an issue when your supervisor is in a hurry or has just arrived late to work because of a flat tire, you can probably expect a less than enthusiastic reception. Also don't challenge your supervisor in front of others. Remember that most bosses appreciate tact and kindness just as much as you do.

Some additional strategies for managing your relationship with your boss include the following:[32,33]

- Communicate effectively. Keep your supervisor informed of the progress of your work.
- Be honest about problems. Most supervisors will tolerate some mistakes as part of the learning process.

"I'm in charge of making a great impression on upper management. You're in charge of everything else."

©2009 Ted Goff

- Don't try to change your supervisor. Study his or her preferences and try to conform to them.
- Try to make your supervisor and company look good. Build on your supervisor's strengths and compensate for his or her weaknesses.
- Know your supervisor's goals and understand how you can help meet them.
- Be sure your priorities are in agreement with your supervisor's and be aware of changing priorities.
- Recognize that you can learn from criticism. Learn how to ask for specific information and feedback.
- Try to see things from your supervisor's perspective. Supervisors may not always have the right perceptions, but they are in charge and do determine goals.

You will sometimes need to talk with your supervisor about problems (such as important material that has not arrived) or difficult situations (such as a complaining customer). To make the discussion productive, do some preparing beforehand. Try these steps for your discussion:

- Define the current problem or situation as you see it.
- State how you feel the situation should be and why.
- Suggest a solution.
- State specifically what you would like the supervisor to do.
- Affirm your support and offer your assistance.

Feeling intimidated by a new boss or other authority figures with whom you haven't had an opportunity to interact is natural. If you can't communicate comfortably, look for opportunities to interact in casual ways. For instance, you might speak briefly in the hall or, if appropriate, pop your head in their door for a quick hello. Take actions that will help you develop a good relationship right from the start. For example, be ready with suggestions if you are asked, offer to help, and don't prejudge. Realize that it will take some time for both of you to become comfortable with each other.

Ask Yourself...

1. Cite instances when you were assertive in expressing your desires. How did you handle the situations, and what were the outcomes? Would you handle them the same way today?

2. Think of the job you have now or a job you had in the past. Is (or was) it difficult to view your boss as a person? If so, why? What can you do (or what could you have done) to see your boss as more human?

3. Look back at the Emotional Strengths Quiz on page 36 and your answer to the second Ask Yourself question on page 37. Considering what you have learned about handling emotions in this chapter, what additional actions can you take to improve?

2.6 OTHER EMOTIONAL FACTORS

Other factors involving emotions can make a difference in how satisfactory your relationships at work are. They include keeping perfectionism under control and resolving to be happy. Some additional factors will be discussed in Chapter 18.

Perfectionism

You've probably observed or may have worked with someone who is hard to please or who can't let go of an assignment. The person keeps revising or tweaking, trying to attain perfection. Doing a good job is great, but being a perfectionist is sometimes not. While perfectionists and high achievers are similar, their actions can vary in significant ways.[34] Figure 2.6 describes some of those ways.

Perfectionism can result in striking outcomes. Because perfectionists are self-disciplined, they can accomplish a great deal. They have high standards and ethics, are responsible, and tend to be good problem solvers.

But perfectionism has a downside, particularly at work. Perfectionists frequently have impossibly high expectations of others as well as themselves. They may feel burdened by the responsibilities they impose on themselves, tend to think their work is never good enough, and believe they are not

KeyPoint
Perfectionists create problems for themselves and others with their behavior.

Figure 2.6

High achievers vs. perfectionists.

High Achievers	Perfectionists
Motivated by a desire to achieve	Motivated by a fear of failure
Set high goals	May set goals out of reach
Enjoy the pursuit of goals	Can't enjoy the process
Feel satisfaction from a good job	Satisfied only with perfection
Take pride in their accomplishments and those of others	Critical of themselves and others
Can rebound from disappointments	Beat themselves over the head if not perfect

appreciated. You can see that many of a perfectionist's qualities can make that person unpleasant company.

A perfectionist's attitude can also make life difficult for coworkers. Perfectionists expect fellow employees to share their unrealistic goals. They tend to be judgmental of others' work and critical of even the smallest mistakes. They often procrastinate about getting started (the fear of failure is too great), and they may neglect important parts of an assignment, such as deadlines, because they are focused on getting everything right. As a result, productivity suffers, and coworkers can feel resentful, frustrated, and stressed.

When you need to work with perfectionists, you can take several steps to lessen the effect of their attitude on your attitude and your work. First, think about why they behave as they do, and try not to take their attitude personally. Do your own work the way it should be done. Be firm in resisting unrealistic demands. When you see that efforts to make everything perfect are jeopardizing some of the goals of an assignment, point that out, and try to move things back on target. Showing perfectionists that you share their appreciation of quality work but can see a more realistic way of achieving it can be surprisingly effective.

If you see yourself in the above descriptions of perfectionists, the following suggestions may help:

- Think about what Pablo Casals, the great Spanish cellist and conductor, said: "The main thing in life is not to be afraid to be human." Human beings make mistakes. Accept yourself as human and forgive yourself for your mistakes.

- Accept that the ideal is a guideline or goal, not to be achieved 100 percent. Many jobs or tasks do require perfection, such as safely flying and landing a plane. However, some tasks need to be completed only in a satisfactory and timely fashion. The perfectionist is usually unable to differentiate between these two kinds of tasks.

- Set realistic and flexible time frames for achieving a goal or completing a task.

- Lighten up and allow others to catch up to your speed of doing things.
- Be responsive toward others' ideas.
- Strive to show patience, sincerity, acceptance, and liking in your voice and in nonverbal communication.[35]

Happiness and Job Satisfaction

KeyPoint
Studies show that people who are happy are more likely to be successful in many areas of life.

Your happiness is a very important factor in your relationships and your career and job success. But which comes first—happiness or success? One report, published in a professional psychology journal in 2005, concluded on the basis of 250 studies that success seems to follow happiness. The data found that happy people are more likely than less happy persons to have fulfilling relationships and marriages, high incomes, excellent work performance, community involvement, good health, and even a long life.[36]

Numerous researchers and writers have considered the question of what makes us happy. Their conclusions center on the actions shown in Figure 2.7.[37]

Figure 2.7

How to be happy.

- Make happiness a priority.
- Develop successful personal relationships and help others.
- Have high self-esteem and accept what you cannot change.
- Work hard at what you enjoy.
- Live in and enjoy the present and experience delight in your life.
- Face problems rather than running away from them or letting them overwhelm you.
- Engage in regular physical activity.
- Know and satisfy your most important values.
- Earn enough money to pay for necessities.
- Lead a meaningful life.

Ask Yourself...

1. Are you, or is someone you know, a perfectionist about some things? Think about the effects of these tendencies on you or others. How can you apply what you've read in this section to dealing with perfectionism?
2. What are some of the actions for being happy that you already take or that you might consider for your life? What steps will you take to accomplish them?

KEY TERMS

emotions	feedback
emotional intelligence	defense mechanisms
competency	denial
self-awareness	repression
self-regulation	rationalization
motivation	regression
empathy	scapegoating
social skill	projection
perception	displacement
halo effect	sublimation
reverse halo effect	compensation
self-confidence	self-talk
self-esteem	visualization
self-disclosure	assertiveness

CHAPTER SUMMARY

Emotions play a larger role than we sometimes realize in our behavior and actions. Being able to manage your emotions and to deal effectively with coworkers and their emotions is the basis of your emotional intelligence.

Emotional intelligence refers to your ability to recognize and manage your feelings and those of others.[38] It has five key components: self-awareness, self-regulation, motivation, empathy, and social skill. Each component has several competencies—practical, useful ways in which we handle emotions on the job or in life.

Gaining self-awareness requires understanding our perceptions, becoming attuned to our emotions, and analyzing them. We can take positive steps to build self-confidence. Self-disclosure can increase self-awareness by helping us be open to feedback.

Self-regulation is the ability to control disruptive impulses and moods and to stop and think before taking action.[39] With practice, we can control our emotions and even direct them in constructive ways. People often cope with anxiety through the use of defense mechanisms.

Motivation is the desire to achieve for the sake of achievement itself.[40] A positive attitude is one of the competencies for motivation and is a very important quality that employers look for in job applicants.

Empathy is the ability to understand other people's emotions and to respond to them appropriately. A service-oriented attitude toward customers and sensitivity to people of other cultures are competencies for empathy.[41]

Social skill is the ability to get along well with other people—to manage relationships and build networks.[42] It's the culmination of all the other components. It's important to understand our roles and to behave appropriately for them. People with social skill use assertiveness in expressing their opinions and ideas. The most emotionally intelligent way to view bosses is as people with their own feelings and their own jobs to do.

REVIEW

1. Explain what emotional intelligence is and why it is receiving attention today.

2. What are some strategies for improving emotional intelligence? Address all five components, naming two strategies for each.

3. What role does perception play in human relations? How can you tell when you're being influenced by the reverse halo effect? What steps can you take to change your perception so that it's more accurate?

4. Why is having a positive attitude at work important? Explain how shifts in thought processes, self-talk, and visualization can help in developing a positive attitude, and name five ways to demonstrate a positive attitude on the job.

5. What is assertiveness? How is it different from aggressiveness?

6. How can your perceptions of your supervisor affect your relationship? What are some ways to foster good interactions with your supervisor?

7. Discuss the pros and cons of being a perfectionist and ways to control the tendency to be a perfectionist.

CRITICAL THINKING

1. Harry Truman once said, "The president of the United States hears a hundred voices telling him that he is the greatest man in the world. He must listen carefully to hear the one voice that tells him he's not." Based on this quote, what do you think is the role of self-esteem in human relations? What are potential problems associated with too much or too little self-esteem? What is the importance of feedback in self-esteem?

2. Have you had a business transaction or personal interaction in which you felt you had been treated rudely? If not, imagine one. Describe the incident and your response. If you could relive the incident, would your response be the same?

3. You can find tests online to assess your emotional competencies. Locate one and complete it. Then consider the results. What do they tell you about possible areas for improvement? Based on your analysis, develop an action plan.

4. In early 2009, the Pharmaceutical Research and Manufacturers of America, a lobbying group for many large drug companies, enacted new voluntary rules that prohibit sales representatives from giving doctors free gifts and taking them out to eat.[43] A later article[44] reported safety concerns raised in a national study on distribution of free prescription samples for children. The study found that of the most frequently distributed samples in 2004, nearly 25 percent received new or revised FDA-required "black box" safety warnings over the next three years.

Do you think receiving a gift or free meal from a drug company makes a doctor more likely to prescribe the company's products? From the viewpoint of a doctor, what might be the costs and benefits to patients of giving out free samples? What do you think the news items have to do with human relations, emotions, and self-regulation?

CASE STUDIES

In small groups, analyze the following situations:

1 **Worst Employees of the Year**   Among those cited as the "10 worst employees of 2008" by Rachel Zupek, CareerBuilder.com writer,[45] were the following:

- The employee who, concerned that she was about to be fired, attempted to sabotage the company by destroying $2.5 million worth of computer files

- Four employees who collected more than $20,000 per person for hours they didn't work by clocking in for each other

- The judge who jailed all 46 people in a courtroom when a cell phone rang and no one admitted owning the phone

- The bank teller supervisor who stole $10,000 at a time over several years for vacations, bills, and her children's college tuition

- The transportation security agent who allegedly stole more than $200,000 worth of travelers' belongings

1. Considering these incidents from an emotional competency standpoint, what do you think the employees were thinking?
2. Which components of emotional intelligence are involved here?
3. Describe other examples of employees who could be cited as "worst." Which components of emotional intelligence did they seem to lack?

2 **Employee with an Attitude**   Carlos had begun discussion of technical problems on a current project with his project team when he noticed Roberta, the relatively new office manager, looking sour and uncommunicative—and not for the first time in these meetings. After covering the agenda and holding the related technical discussions, he went around the table and asked for questions or comments from each team member. All responded except Roberta. When Carlos queried her directly, she responded in a belligerent way, "You never give me a chance to speak!" and left the room.

After the meeting, Carlos stopped by Roberta's cubicle and asked privately if there was a problem. Roberta yelled, "I don't know what you want me to do in these meetings. You always pass me by in the discussions and let the others do all the talking."

Carlos was taken aback. He explained that the primary focus of the meetings was resolution of technical problems related to individual team members' parts of the project. He then assured Roberta that if she had suggestions, she was certainly welcome to contribute them.

1. Why do you think Roberta behaved this way? Was she using a defense mechanism? If so, which one?

2. Is Carlos at fault in any way? If so, how?

3. What do you think Carlos should do at this point? At the next meeting?

HUMAN RELATIONS IN ACTION

In two groups, use Internet resources and printed publications to find examples of methods employers have used to make work more personal for their employees or to build personal connections with their customers. As a group, prepare a one-page report to distribute at the next class meeting. Describe your findings and how they pertain to emotions and perceptions.

For additional resources, refer to the web site for this text:
www.cengage.com/management/dalton

RESOURCES

1. Bruno, L. (2009, April 24). Online genie: Site connects the needy to the charitable. *USA Today*, 6A. (Used with permission.)

2. Goleman, D. (2006). *Emotional intelligence: 10th anniversary edition*. New York: Bantam.

3. Thorndike, R. K. (1920). Intelligence and its uses. *Harper's Magazine 140*, 227–335.

4. Salovey, P. & Mayer, J. D. (1990). Emotional intelligence. *Imagination, Cognition, and Personality 9*, 185–211.

5. Goleman, D. (2008, Winter). What makes a leader? *Harvard Business Review OnPoint*, 36–47. (Originally published in November–December 1998, 95,99.)

6. Goleman, D. (1998). *Working with emotional intelligence*. New York: Bantam, 26, 27.

7. Goleman, What makes a leader? 95, 99.

8. Goleman, D. (1998). *Working with emotional intelligence*. 26, 27.

9. Schindler, Janine A. (2008). 7 steps to boosting your EI. *JAS Coaching & Training Newsletter*. [online]. Retrieved from http://www.jascoaching.com/newsletter0308.html

10. Goleman, What makes a leader? 95.

11. Baltus, R. K. (1998). *Personal psychology for life and work*. New York: McGraw-Hill.

12. *Ibid.*

13. Augstums, I. M. (Associated Press). (2008, November 12). AIG says sales meeting at luxury resort justified. *Houston Chronicle*, p. D3.

14. The Nemours Foundation/Kids Health. (©1995–2009). "How Can I Improve My Self-Esteem?" Available http://www.kidshealth.org/teen/your_mind/emotions/self_esteem. html#. Retrieved August 25, 2009. Adapted and used with permission.

15. Goleman, What makes a leader? 95.

16. Freud, A. (2001). *The ego and mechanisms of defense. Gale encyclopedia of psychology* (2nd ed.). Farmington Hills, MI: Thomson/Gale Group.

17. Scott, E. (2007, September 24). How to deal with stress and anxiety in four simple steps. *About.com: Stress Management*. [online]. Retrieved from http://stress.about.com/od/ fearandstres1/a/anxiety.htm

18. Mintz, J. (Associated Press). (2009, May 13). Dell makes e-waste policy formal. *Houston Chronicle*, p. D3.

19. Goleman, D. (1998). *Working with emotional intelligence*.

20. Humphrey, D. (2002). *Quick skills: What your employer expects*. Cincinnati, OH: South-Western Educational Publishing.

21. Sixel, L. M. (2009, January 29). Poor economy burns low performers. *Houston Chronicle*, pp. D1, D4.

22. *Ibid.*

23. Burns, D. D. (1999). *Feeling good: The new mood therapy*.

24. Bilanich, Bud. Formula for success. (2009). *Success Television*. [online]. Retrieved from http://www.successtelevision.com/index.php/Wisdom/Insights/Bedohave-and-visualization- of-success.html

25. Goleman, *Working with emotional intelligence.*

26. McCracken, P. (2000, January 16, *St. Louis Post-Dispatch). Using your EQ (emotional intelligence) to get ahead. The Impact Group.* [online]. Retrieved from http://www.impactgrouphr.com/who/article/OP0010.HTM

27. New research shows positive impact of live chat software on Internet retailers' sales. (2009, March). *BNET.* [online]. Retrieved from http://findarticles.com/p/articles/mi_pwwi/is_200903/ai_n31469784

28. When introducing live chat, retailers may want to introduce users to Mary. (2009, May 28). *Internet Retailer.* [online]. Retrieved from http://www.internetretailer.com/dailyNews.asp?id=30567

29. Goleman, What makes a leader? 95.

30. How to give a good compliment. (2009). *Life Coaches Blog.* [online]. Retrieved from http://lifecoachesblog.com/2007/02/13/how-to-give-a-good-compliment

31. Strause, Liz. How to receive a compliment without being a self-centered idiot. (2007). *Successful and Outstanding Bloggers.* [online]. Retrieved from http://www.successful-blog.com/1/how- to-receive-a-compliment-without-being-a-self-centered-idiot

32. Gabarro, J. J., & John P. K. (2005, January). Managing your boss. *Harvard Business Review, 83*(1), 92–99.

33. Reeves, S. (2006, March 9). The boss and you. *Forbes.* [online]. Retrieved from http://www.rediff.com/money/2006/mar/17forbes.htm

34. Scott, E. (2008, January 9). Perfectionist traits: Do these sound familiar? *About.com: Stress Management.* [online]. Retrieved from http://stress.about.com/od/understanding stress/a/perfectionist.htm

35. Baron, R., & Elizabeth W. (1994). *The enneagram made easy.* New York: HarperCollins.

36. Lyubomirsky, S., King, L., & Diener, E. (2005). The benefits of frequent positive affect: Does happiness lead to success? *Psychological Bulletin, 131*(6), 803–855.

37. DuBrin, A. J. (2008). *Human relations for career and personal success.* Upper Saddle River, NJ: Pearson Education, Inc.

38. Goleman, *Emotional intelligence: 10th anniversary edition.*

39. Goleman, What makes a leader? 95.

40. *Ibid.* 99.

41. *Ibid.* 95.

42. *Ibid.*

43. Cook, L. (2009, January 2). Code puts cap on drug companies. *Houston Chronicle,* pp. A1, A6.

44. Paying a price. (2009, January 14). *Houston Chronicle,* p. B8.

45. Zupek, R. (2008, November 23). 10 worst employees of 2008. [online]. *CareerBuilder.com.* Retrieved from http://www.careerbuilder.com/Article/CB-1067-The-Workplace-10-Worst-Employees-of-2008

MOTIVATION:
MAXIMIZING PRODUCTIVITY

OBJECTIVES

After studying this chapter, you should be able to:

3.1 Explain why motivation is important to your success and describe the basic behavior model.

3.2 Explain the difference between needs and wants.

3.3 Describe the contributions of four major theorists to the study of human motivation.

3.4 Explain the application of motivation theories.

3.5 Describe how motivators are changing in the current work environment.

Jump Start

Computerized Facility Integration (CFI), a top-performing Fortune 500 company, is the nation's largest consulting and systems integration firm. It focuses on facilities management and corporate real estate. Management at CFI has developed some effective motivational techniques.

CEO Robert Verdun says, "What gets rewarded gets done." Bonuses are given every month to all employees, from clerks to senior managers, for hitting their specific performance goals. The company expects everyone to be an achiever, and employees are rewarded. He feels the biggest advantage of the bonus system is that it keeps communications flowing among employees at all levels. This has created an overall company growth rate of about 30 percent each year since 1990.

Another reason staffers remain loyal is the many unusual job opportunities provided within the company. If employees aren't happy in their current role, management will find them something of interest. CFI also splurges on perks and fun activities such as a birthday party celebration for everybody and MP3 player giveaways. "We try to keep it fun," says Verdun.[1]

- Would you like to work for CFI? Why or why not?
- What motivational techniques do you think would gain your loyalty and motivate you the most?
- Describe some ways an employer, parent, or other person has tried to motivate you.

3.1 IMPORTANCE OF MOTIVATION

Motivation is the emotional stimulus that causes you to act. The stimulus may be a need or a drive that energizes certain behaviors. At work, motivation is a combination of all factors in your working environment that lead to positive or negative efforts. If you understand what motivates you, you are more likely to achieve your personal and professional goals.

Likewise, if organizations know how to motivate employees, they can increase productivity. This ability to boost production is increasingly important as U.S. organizations compete in the global market. A growing number of organizations are introducing new strategies to motivate today's workers.

In the systems approach to human relations and organization productivity used in this book, motivation is associated with the individual as a 21st century responsibility. It is also an important life and career skill related to initiative, self-direction, productivity, and accountability.

To predict what motivates people most effectively, you must guess what physiological and psychological processes underlie their behavior. For example, if Allen works much harder than Sid, it's logical to assume that Allen is more highly motivated than Sid to achieve some goal—perhaps a bonus, a promotion, or the prestige associated with being the top producer in the organization. However, unless Allen explains why he's working harder, one can only guess what his motivation or need may be.

In The News

Kip Tindell, president and CEO of The Container Store, is often seen dusting shelves or helping customers with their packages. This kind of positive attitude is why The Container Store has been the only retail business listed on *Fortune* magazine's annual "Best Company to Work for in the USA" for two straight years, and near the top for eight years.

Tindell believes that employees are a company's most valued assets. This conviction is reflected in an annual turnover rate of only 24 percent compared to an industry average of 73.6 percent. The Container Store has an aggressive hiring policy, recruiting only top performers who believe in customer service.

Training and communication rank high as employee motivators. In their first year, employees receive 241 hours of training compared to an industry average of only 7 hours. Training is customized to the individual employee and his/her specific job. The company encourages open communication through daily sales information and financial data provided to each employee. In addition, its six-month performance reviews prompt frequent discussion and feedback.

Additional perks include wages that are considerably above the industry average, flexible parental shifts as needed, and a 40 percent discount on store merchandise. Employees respond to this kind of positive atmosphere by believing that The Container Store is like working with a big family.[2]

1. What do you think The Container Store looks for in selecting top performers as new hires?

2. Why do you think training would be a motivator?

3. What makes good communication an effective motivator?

Through studies of motivation and behavior, psychologists have generally concluded that all human behavior is directed toward satisfying a need. Figure 3.1 on page 66. illustrates a basic behavior model with an unsatisfied need as the starting point in the process of motivation. An unsatisfied need causes inner tension (physical or psychological). The individual engages in some action to reduce or relieve the tension. The individual wants to do something that will satisfy the perceived need. For example, a thirsty man needs water, is driven by his thirst, and is motivated to drink.

All humans have needs. People need to be accepted, fulfilled, recognized, and appreciated. They need to dream, aspire, desire, and acquire. Understanding the complexity of these motives or needs—our own as well as those of others—is essential in establishing and maintaining good human relations.

Figure 3.1

A basic behavioral model.

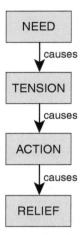

Your behavior, like everyone else's, is clearly motivated by needs, and yet you may often not understand the complexities and subtleties of your motives and needs. How often have you done something and then asked yourself, "Why did I just do that?" To experience the full range of activities involved in the motivation, try a simple exercise: Think of something you are sure you need and the reason for needing it. What will you do to satisfy your need? Could the action you take actually cause you to be dissatisfied? An awareness of these actions will help you better understand your behavior.

Ask Yourself...

1. What is motivating you most today?
2. What actions might you take to satisfy the needs behind that motivation?
3. How do you think the basic behavioral model applies to you?

3.2 WANTS VERSUS NEEDS

Your wants may be different from your needs, as in the following scenario:

> Wimberley just graduated from college and is about to start her first big job. Her new workplace is located 20 miles from her apartment, so she will need reliable transportation. As Wimberley shops for a car to satisfy this need, she finds one she really likes. However, the car costs far more than her budget will allow.
>
> Wimberley reasons, "I want this convertible with the deluxe option package, but all I need is an economical gas-saver. I need safe transportation from point A to point B and that doesn't require deluxe extras. Besides, the economy car fits my budget and will be easy on gas, and I can afford the insurance, too."

Often we are conditioned to think that our wants are our needs, when, in fact, a need can be satisfied much more simply. We all have needs, which differ greatly in origin and occur in varying degrees of intensity. Needs are divided into two categories: primary (physiological) and secondary (psychological).

Primary needs are required to sustain life. These include food, water, air, sleep, and shelter (for individual survival) and sex/reproduction (for survival of a societal group). Because these needs are basic to survival, we can easily understand why and how they affect a person's behavior.

Secondary needs are psychological and are far more complex. They include the need for security, affiliation or love, respect, and autonomy. Secondary needs are a result of our values and beliefs. These needs are not identical for everyone, and neither is the value or priority placed on satisfying them.

Gary Applegate, in his book *Happiness, It's Your Choice,* states that we have eight secondary needs: security, faith, worth, freedom, belonging, fun, knowledge, and health. Everything else, according to Applegate, is a want. He suggests that wants can be seen as pathways to meeting our needs.[3]

As you learned in Chapter 1, Elton Mayo determined early in the development of human relations theory that people have many needs, both on and off the job. The individual must take personal responsibility for satisfying these needs to assure that good human relations are maintained. Managers cannot always control motivation if the need is not work related, but can have strong influence if the employee is driven by money or work group assignments.

Ask Yourself...

1. Describe several primary needs you may have satisfied today.
2. What are some of your current secondary needs? How are you satisfying them?
3. Describe times when you may have confused your wants and your needs. What happened?

3.3 FOUR THEORIES OF MOTIVATION

KeyPoint
Maslow, Herzberg, McClelland, and Vroom explained motivation in the workplace.

Many theories have been developed about motivation. Four of these theories apply to individual behaviors in the work setting. Abraham Maslow, Frederick Herzberg, David McClelland, and Victor Vroom contributed the most to understanding motivation in the workplace.

Maslow's Hierarchy of Needs

Like many other psychologists, Abraham Maslow agreed that only a felt need motivates and that once a need is satisfied it ceases to motivate. However, he went on to identify a hierarchy of needs. Figure 3.2 illustrates Maslow's five need levels and briefly describes the needs associated with each level. The five levels are physiological needs, safety and security, social needs,

Figure 3.2
Maslow's hierarchy of needs.

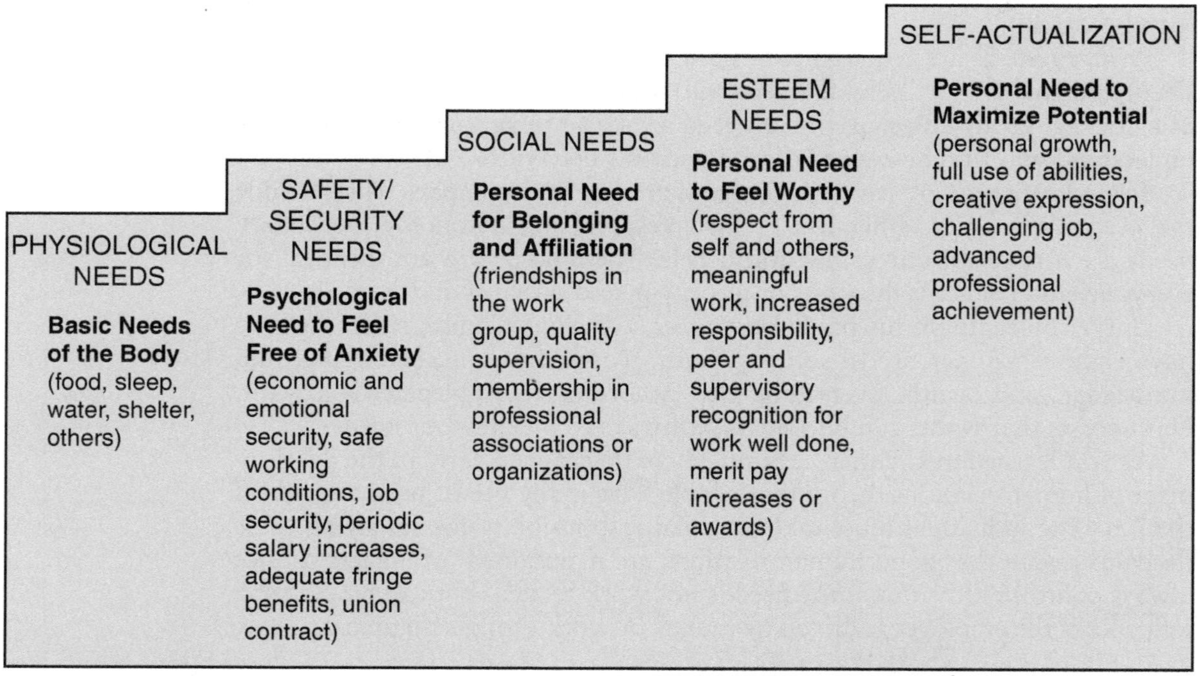
PHYSIOLOGICAL NEEDS
Basic Needs of the Body
(food, sleep, water, shelter, others)
SAFETY/ SECURITY NEEDS
Psychological Need to Feel Free of Anxiety
(economic and emotional security, safe working conditions, job security, periodic salary increases, adequate fringe benefits, union contract)
SOCIAL NEEDS
Personal Need for Belonging and Affiliation
(friendships in the work group, quality supervision, membership in professional associations or organizations)
ESTEEM NEEDS
Personal Need to Feel Worthy
(respect from self and others, meaningful work, increased responsibility, peer and supervisory recognition for work well done, merit pay increases or awards)
SELF-ACTUALIZATION
Personal Need to Maximize Potential
(personal growth, full use of abilities, creative expression, challenging job, advanced professional achievement)

Digital Vision/Getty Images

esteem, and self-actualization. *Maslow's hierarchy of needs* was presented in 1954 in his book *Motivation and Personality*. The theory became an important building block in the understanding of human behavior, laying a foundation for the work of other theorists.[4]

Physiological Needs   Your *physiological needs* include your desire for food, sleep, water, shelter, and other satisfiers of physiological drives. These are your most basic needs and, until they are satisfied, other needs are of little or no importance. In the workplace, adequate air conditioning and heating, water fountains, cafeteria or snack machines, and other satisfactory working conditions are designed to meet some of these needs.

Safety and Security Needs   Today, *safety and security needs* are more often reflected in your need for economic and emotional security than for physical safety. At work, safe working conditions, job security, periodic salary increases, adequate fringe benefits, or a union contract may fulfill these needs.

Social Needs   Your *social needs* center around your desire for love, affection, acceptance in society, and meaningful affiliation with others. These needs are often satisfied in the workplace by compatible friendships in the work group, quality supervision, and membership in professional association or organizations.

For most people, the need for satisfactory relations with others and a place in society is so important that its lack is often a cause of emotional problems and general maladjustment.

Esteem Needs   Often called ego needs, your *esteem needs* include your need for respect from yourself and others. Fulfilling these needs gives you a feeling of competence, control, and usefulness. In the workplace, these needs are generally met through meaningful work, increased responsibility, peer and supervisory recognition for work well done, and merit pay increases or awards. People whose esteem needs are not met often experience feelings of inferiority and hopelessness.

Self-Actualization Needs   Your *self-actualization needs* refer to your desire to become everything of which you are capable, to reach your full potential. These needs include the desire to grow personally, to use your abilities to the greatest extent, and to engage in creative expression. In the workplace, these needs are most often met through a challenging job, the opportunity to be creative, and advanced professional achievement.

A common question asked about self-actualization is whether we ever fully actualize. The answer lies in the individual. People actualize at different levels.

Some people, for example, are satisfied with a bachelor's degree from a local college, whereas others feel a need for a master's or doctoral degree from a prominent university. Some individuals have their needs fulfilled at a lower-level job; others are more career-focused and feel a need to climb the corporate ladder.

Technology CONNECTION

An article in the November 2008 issue of *Entrepreneur* magazine hails Rick Alden, the CEO of Skullcandy, Inc., as a step ahead of his target audience and the technology it needs. A few years ago, while riding on a subway in London, Rick noticed headphone-wearing passengers struggling to answer their cell phones. He noticed the same thing on several other occasions and again while on a ski trip to Utah. Alden realized there was a need in the market, and he was motivated to give it a try. In 2002, he came up with a basic design for headphones that would work interchangeably with a cell phone and music devices. From that success, he was able to launch a company of audio products soon after.

Skullcandy caters to the needs of the edgy consumer. Speaker-clad helmets and backpacks with speakers hidden near the iPod holder appeal to the more youthful surfers and skateboarders. Those sitting behind a desk wishing they were on a ski slope or a mountain bike also use the products. Alden says, "If they put stuff on their heads, we want to be the guys providing it."[5]

1. Which of Maslow's need levels are being satisfied by Skullcandy's consumers?
2. What do you think motivated Alden to begin Skullcandy, other than financial gain? How would you have gone about doing this?
3. Have you felt or had similar ideas and not acted on them? Besides money, what would you need to act on them?

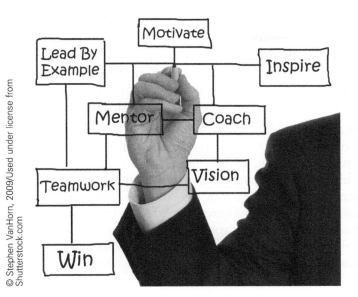

© Stephen VanHorn, 2009/Used under license from Shutterstock.com

Some individuals tend to be creative with what they do and will thrive on the feedback from their product or outcomes. The ego satisfaction level may be very simple or may be very high for these individuals, illustrating the wide range and complexity of actualizing. Satisfying your self-actualization need level is influenced by many factors and only you can determine what these are for you.

Maslow believed that we generally satisfy these needs in a hierarchical order, fulfilling basic needs first before moving on to the higher-order needs. However, he added that we can move up and down the hierarchy, depending on the situation at hand.

For example, in recent years many companies have merged, downsized, and streamlined to become more competitive in the global marketplace. With mergers and downsizing, jobs are often eliminated or greatly reduced in level of importance. Successful, often long-term employees who may have been operating at the esteem and self-actualization levels may suddenly be without a job. These people are compelled to return to the more basic levels of safety and security needs—they simply need a job and an income. Most likely, these people will resume their natural progression through the need levels once the security of a paying job satisfies their lower-order needs.

Herzberg's Two-Factor Theory of Motivation

In 1959, Frederick Herzberg presented his two-factor theory of motivation. He asked over 200 accountants and engineers about what in their work led to extreme satisfaction or extreme dissatisfaction. Herzberg concluded that two sets of factors or conditions influence the behavior of individuals at work. He called the first set hygiene factors and the second set motivational factors.[6]

Hygiene Factors   *Hygiene factors*, also known as maintenance factors, are factors in your job that are necessary for you to maintain a reasonable level of satisfaction. These factors include company policies and procedures,

KeyPoint
Individuals can move up and down the hierarchy of need levels.

KeyPoint
Herzberg defines two major sets of behavioral factors in the workplace.

working conditions and job security, salary and employee benefits, the quality of supervision, and relationships with supervisors, peers, and subordinates. Although the absence of these factors may cause you considerable dissatisfaction, their presence will not necessarily make you more motivated. Generally, these factors prevent employees from being unhappy in their jobs. However, happy employees are not necessarily motivated workers.

Motivational Factors   According to Herzberg, *motivational factors* in your job build high levels of motivation and job satisfaction. These factors include achievement, advancement, recognition, responsibility, and the work itself. Herzberg found that highly motivated employees have a high tolerance for dissatisfaction if adequate maintenance factors are absent. This has to do with employees' perceptions of motivational factors. A factor that motivates one individual may be perceived as a mere maintenance factor by another. The two-factor theory compares sets of satisfiers and dissatisfiers and their effects on job attitudes as shown in Figure 3.3.

Figure 3.3

Herzberg's two-factor theory of motivation.[7]

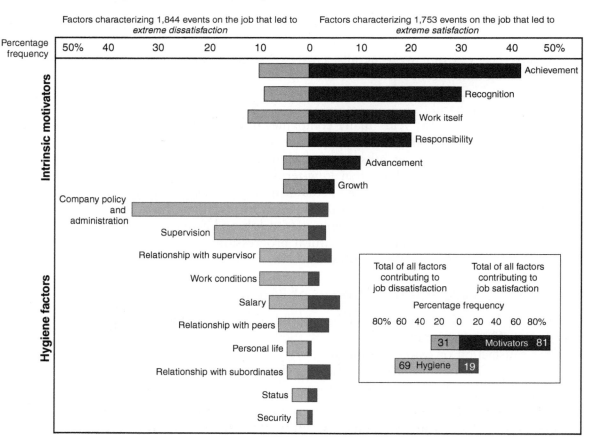

Herzberg's theory extended Maslow's ideas and made them more specifically applicable to the workplace. Additionally, it reinforced the concept that while some factors tend to motivate employees, others have little effect on worker productivity. We tend to be motivated by what we are seeking rather than by what we already have. Figure 3.4 compares Maslow's hierarchy of needs theory to Herzberg's two-factor theory.

Figure 3.4

Similarities in the Maslow and Herzberg theories.

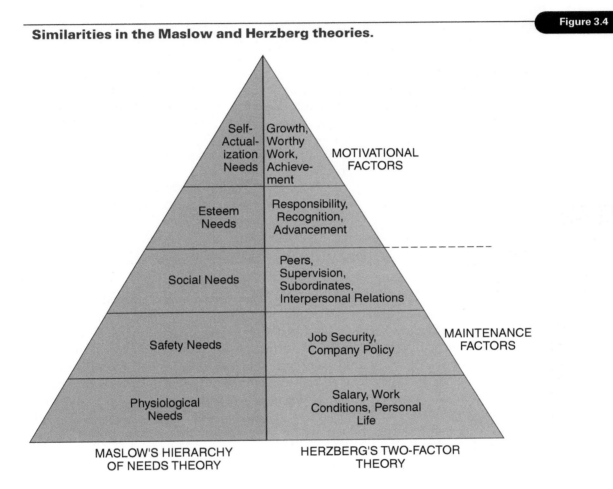

MASLOW'S HIERARCHY
OF NEEDS THEORY

HERZBERG'S TWO-FACTOR
THEORY

McClelland's Acquired Needs Theory

In 1955, David McClelland developed a theory of motivation that says your needs are the result of your early personality development. Calling it the acquired needs theory, he wrote that through cultural exposure, people acquire a framework of three basic needs: achievement, power, and affiliation. McClelland's premise was that these three needs are the primary motives for behavior.[8]

Following McClelland's theory, if you recognize which of the needs is most important to others, you can create the right environment for them. For

KeyPoint
McClelland says most people are motivated by achievement, affiliation, or power.

McClelland's Acquired Needs Theory

High need for:	Personality trait tendencies
Achievement	• Seek and assume responsibility • Take calculated risks • Set challenging but realistic goals • Develop plans to achieve goals • Seek and use feedback in their actions
Affiliation	• Seek and find friendly relationships • Are not overly concerned with "getting ahead" • Seek jobs that are people intensive • Require high degrees of interpersonal action
Power	• Seek positions of influence • Enjoy jobs with high degrees of authority and power • Are concerned with reaching top-level, decision-making positions • Need autonomy

example, people with a high need for achievement have a natural tendency to become leaders or managers. Planning, setting goals and objectives, and controlling the methods of reaching those goals are a basic part of their work style.

People with a strong need for affiliation are less concerned with getting ahead than they are with developing close relationships and friendships with others at work. They tend to enjoy jobs that require a variety of interpersonal contacts. People with a strong need for power naturally seek positions with a great deal of authority and influence. McClelland found that people who are highly successful tend to be motivated by the need for power.[9]

McClelland's acquired needs theory provides additional insight into the kinds of needs and motives that drive individual behavior and strengthens our knowledge of how to influence the behavior of others. The theory also helps to determine our own motives and understand our behavior.

Vroom's Expectancy Theory

KeyPoint
According to Vroom, we are motivated by expected results or actions.

Victor Vroom, another motivational theorist, took the basic ideas of Maslow, Herzberg, and McClelland one step further. His expectancy theory views motivation as a process of choices. According to this theory, you behave in certain ways because you expect certain results from that behavior. For example, you may perceive that if you study hard for an upcoming examination, you stand a strong chance of getting an "A" in the course. If you have a need for the prestige or achievement inherent in making an "A," you're more likely to work for it, expecting to receive the high grade to fulfill your need.[10]

A leader works to assure maximum output from the group.

Image Source/Getty Images

Vroom was careful to emphasize the importance of the individual's perceptions and assessments of organizational behavior. Not all workers in an organization place the same value on factors associated with job performance. What individual workers perceive as important is far more critical to their choices than what their supervisors view as important. This idea still intrigues researchers, and further work is being done in the area of the expectancy theory of motivation.

The most persistent theme in motivational theories is that all behavior is directed toward some goal to satisfy a need. If the action you take leads to positive outcomes, you will probably repeat the behavior. If the action you take leads to negative results, you will usually not repeat the behavior.

New Methods of Motivation

Managers and supervisors in today's workforce are faced with motivating a diverse group of employees. Making people of all ages and cultural backgrounds feel important, connected, useful, and motivated is a major challenge. In these highly competitive times of shrinking budgets, some unconventional and cost-effective means are necessary to increase staff motivation and retention. Retention is a key player in corporate costs with some estimates to replace a departing employee ranging as high as 250 percent of that person's annual salary. Turnover losses are said to impose a $5 trillion annual drain on the U.S. economy and are often the most ignored business expense. The workers leaving may be the very employees you don't want to lose, making the loss even more painful.[11]

Employers tend to think increased pay, extra holidays, more benefits, and longer vacations will motivate their employees. Repeated studies over time have told us these incentives are not what people want most. A recent survey of 614 employers performed by a Watson Wyatt Reward Plan Survey indicated that recognition is the preferred motivator, and turnover is lower when a recognition or rewards program exists in an organization. Additionally, a Gallup study of nearly 5 million employees revealed lower turnover, higher productivity, and greater customer loyalty resulted in organizations that increased praise and recognition.

Similarly, statistics from the U.S. Department of Labor reveal that feeling unappreciated is the number-one reason that employees leave. This sentiment seems to be global in nature. For example, in a study done by HRM Singapore, 3,000 employees were asked about their most important "want" from their job. The most popular response was career training followed by recognition. Good pay came in third, followed by a better relationship with the manager. It is a simple truth that employees work harder when they feel valued for their contributions. One of the best indicators of a great manager and a very good organization is their willingness to understand their employees' needs, maintain open communication in working toward meeting those needs, and reward and recognize accomplishments along the way. Recognition is confirmation of achievement and says others believe in us. Plus, it simply feels good.[12]

One of the most frequently overlooked methods of motivating employee is the use of applied attention. Managers can provide motivation simply by talking with employees to ensure life on the job complements their professional and personal interests, acknowledging outstanding employee contributions in front of peers, regularly complimenting and thanking staff members, and occasionally holding meetings with staff to encourage networking and camaraderie. These small investments can bring huge returns in benefits to the organization and the employee.

> *After climbing a great hill, one only finds that there are many more hills to climb.*
> —Nelson Mandela, former president of South Africa

Ask Yourself...

1. Have you ever experienced moving both up and down Maslow's Hierarchy of Needs? Do you think this made you a stronger person? Why or why not?

2. Think about a job you've had. Which of Herzberg's hygiene factors influenced your satisfaction level and which would have caused you to become dissatisfied if they had been removed?

3. Which of McClelland's personality tendencies do you most strongly exhibit and in which need group do you believe you belong?

4. How would you use Vroom's Expectancy Theory to identify your own motivation for behavior?

3.4   APPLYING MOTIVATIONAL THEORIES

Knowledge of motivational theory can help us as individuals in a variety of ways. Understanding the differences between a want and a need, recognizing what motivates us, learning alternative ways to fulfill needs, and learning how to motivate others when we are in leadership situations can help us reach our personal and professional goals. Learning to recognize the difference between wants and needs can help us be satisfied with what we have. This lesson can also assist us in being patient and planning alternative ways to fulfill our needs and wants.

Finding Fulfillment

Figure 3.5 expands the behavior model discussed in the beginning of the chapter to show possible reactions. Here again, an unsatisfied need creates tension and motivates a search for ways to relieve that tension. If the goal is achieved, the individual will usually engage in some form of constructive behavior. If the goal is not achieved, the individual has a choice of behaviors with positive or negative results.

Recognizing possible outcomes and realizing that you have choices in your behavior can help you turn difficult situations into positive ones. By avoiding negative behaviors and by considering which behaviors might benefit you in the long run, you can often find the need fulfillment you desire.

Two situations are described on page 80. Determine the types of behaviors that may result from each of these real-world situations. Once you have identified the behaviors, discuss what would motivate you to react in such ways.

You can choose and apply positive behaviors that result in the outcomes you prefer. You can also realize the negative effects that poor choices may

Figure 3.5

A basic motivation model.

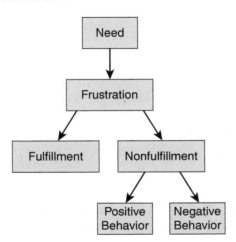

Motivation Theory Applications

You hope to receive an A on a term paper that took a great deal of time and effort to prepare. You need the high grade to improve your semester grade for the class. Your paper is returned to you with a "C" appearing at the top of the page.

You can choose to react in the following ways:

POSITIVE   **NEGATIVE**

a. _____   _____

b. _____   _____

c. _____   _____

d. _____   _____

As an employee, you really want the supervisory position that is open in your work unit. You are very qualified to do the job and you need the extra money to help with the expenses of a new baby. You have always been a team player and the boss seems to like you. Unfortunately, you get word on Friday that Jose was chosen for the position instead of you.

You can choose to react in the following ways:

POSITIVE   **NEGATIVE**

a. _____   _____

b. _____   _____

c. _____   _____

d. _____   _____

have. Understanding why you act and react to any given situation may often help you avoid destructive behaviors that limit future opportunities.

Motivating Others

Both at work and in your personal life, you may be placed in positions of leadership and held responsible for accomplishing a goal. For example, you may be elected president of your local civic group or you may be selected for a supervisory job at work. In either of these two leadership roles, understanding motivation is important.

As a leader, you are likely to be judged by the performance of your group. The output of followers usually depends on their motivation to do what they are asked to do. Performance and motivation are closely linked, so a large part of your job as the leader is to obtain maximum output from your group—and that's not always easy. Encouraging others to maximize their potential and contribute their enthusiasm and energies at peak levels requires that you have a sound understanding of motivational concepts and techniques. When you are sensitive to what increases motivation and you understand the behavior of others, you are better able to make the group more productive.

Although motivating your group members is one of your functions as the leader, you cannot do it alone. Because the decision to act comes from within people, all of them have a shared responsibility whether they are the leader or the follower. However, as the leader, you do have some influence over the follower's level of motivation. Psychological research has identified three *motivational source fields* that are believed to influence individual behavior. Figure 3.6 illustrates the fields and their degrees of influence.[13]

Figure 3.6

Motivational source fields.

SOURCES OF FOLLOWER MOTIVATION

DEGREE OF POSSIBLE LEADER INFLUENCE

Outside Forces
- Supervisory Style
- Organizational Culture, Goals and Structure
- Type of Work
- Recognition (Promotion/Awards)
- Environment (Furniture, Equipment, Tools, Supplies)

HIGH

Inside Forces
- Willingness
- Desires
- Values
- Personal Goals
- Ambitions

MEDIUM

Early Forces
- Genetic Influence
- Family Size
- Childhood Experiences
- Siblings
- Parents

LOW

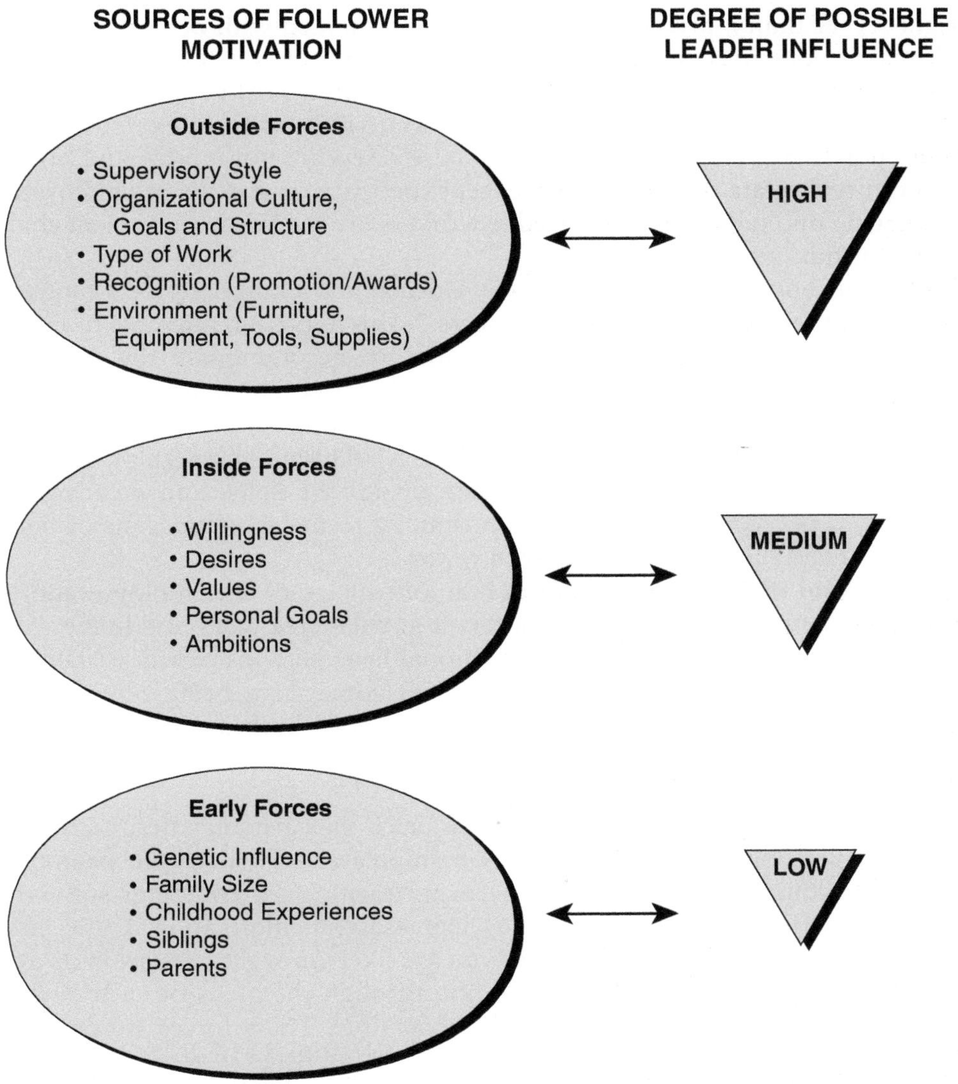

Outside forces, such as praise, variation of tasks, and financial rewards, influence motivation the most. Praise involves positive reinforcement for tasks that are completed properly. Task variation can occur through enlargement or enrichment of a job, assignment to special task forces, or rotation through different work assignments.

Financial rewards, which include raises, bonuses, and stock options, are the most misunderstood outside motivators. Our society is increasingly materialistic, and we are constantly bombarded by advertising telling us what we need.

According to Peter Drucker in *Management: Tasks, Responsibilities, Practices,* people are generally driven to want so much that their income is never large enough to satisfy their needs. For some people, especially knowledge workers (people who earn their living by what they know rather than what they produce), money is a form of feedback, representing their value to the organization. If organizations paid us what we think we should be paid, they would not be able to function. We begin to see raises and bonuses as a right rather than a privilege and become discontented with our salaries and, ultimately, our jobs. Organizations, then, cannot rely on financial rewards alone to satisfy employees. Other outside motivators must be used.[14]

In a *Harvard Business Review* article, Manville and Ober explained that in a knowledge economy, a company's core assets are not mortar and bricks or even real estate. It is the intelligence, experience, and skills of employees. Managing and motivating knowledge workers are the key management challenge for this century.

In their book *The Carrot Principle,* Gostick and Elton describe a motivational approach called "whole-life success." This approach attempts to blend on-the-job duties and off-the-job activities to accommodate the interests of the individual and maximize the motivational potential. For example, a security guard with a passion for conservation was given the new title of "Security and Energy Conservation Officer." During his regular security round, he's now responsible for turning off all the lights and securing all doors to conserve energy, thereby contributing to the green interests of both the guard and the facility—a win–win reward.

This kind of motivation requires real knowledge of the employee and is not just a simple rehash of the old attempt at balancing work and home. It is motivating on a much deeper and emotional level perhaps best described by a manager when she said, "Success doesn't come from being powerful; it comes from empowering others to achieve success." In these turbulent times, using other means of motivating is essential. Money is not always the best motivator.[15]

Inside forces (as shown in Figure 3.6) such as a person's desires, ambitions, or personal goals are less easily manipulated. Consider, for example, that your company wants its employees to learn a new computer software program. Offering training on it may increase your motivation. If the new ability promotes some personal goal, you are likely to want to excel in its application. Influencing people's motivation through the areas of early forces (also shown in Figure 3.6) is virtually impossible. These forces were established early in life and firmly fixed within value and belief systems.

> " Never confuse movement with action.
> —Ernest Hemingway, author "

In The News

The folks at Globoforce, an employee recognition specialist group, have defined "psychic income" as the need for social acceptance, increased self-esteem, and enhanced self-realization. In lean economic times, employees will often feel some sense of sadness and depression and will need that valuable stroke of "thank you." Organizations are seeking cost-effective and creative ways to show appreciation for their workers' jobs well done. A recent study from Japan found that a simple compliment creates a chemical reaction in the brain similar to that caused by a cash award. An additional study completed by Watson Wyatt Worldwide, a major consulting firm, found that 48 percent of employees surveyed preferred "improved communication" as a best way to reduce employee stress. Psychic income, spreading goodwill and appreciation among employees, gets big results and saves big dollars.[16]

1. What types of "psychic income" efforts would work with you rather than a cash award? Give some examples that you think would be reasonable in your current or past work environment and explain why these would be suitable replacements for the alternatives usually offered.

2. Why do you think communication consistently makes the top of the list as a motivator? How do you feel it motivates you and in what way?

Understanding the sources of motivation that are available to them gives leaders a framework to develop steps that may energize followers. Albert Bernstein and Sydney Rozen conducted research on successful methods that corporate leaders use to create environments that will motivate employees. They concluded that the steps shown in Figure 3.7 could enhance motivation. You may recognize some of these methods and choose to apply them in your role as a leader at work and elsewhere.[17]

Sam Walton, founder of Wal-Mart, was a master of applying these motivation methods. Nothing says "You are important to me!" louder than paying attention to some of these details. For example, listening is often the key to making others feel important, and Sam Walton would often pull out a scrap of paper and turn a fleeting thought or suggestion from an employee into a concrete opportunity. Both the company and the employee would benefit. He motivated many employees by validating their worth and letting them know that the company was listening, cared about their ideas, and would follow through on promises made. Adopting some of these methods for enhancing motivation will boost your leadership effectiveness.

Figure 3.7

Methods for enhancing motivation.

1. *Sell, don't tell.* Selling a course of action by explaining the benefits and the reasons for doing it is more likely to persuade employees to act than simply ordering, "do it."

2. *Let your followers make their own decisions.* Employees must feel some control and authority over their own jobs.

3. *Delegate, don't dump.* Delegating only unpleasant tasks is called dumping and is considered an abuse of power. When delegating, give challenges that will develop a subordinate's abilities—and delegate authority with the responsibility.

4. *Set goals with your followers.* Regular goal setting improves performance. Define subordinates' work in terms of goals and objectives.

5. *Listen to your followers and let them know that you are listening.* Schedule regular meetings to let them express what is on their minds. Followers tend to work harder if they feel that you care.

6. *Follow through.* Effective leaders take action to make their promises happen and keep their followers informed on what is happening.

7. *Don't change course midstream.* Followers need continuity. Be consistent.

8. *Build in a monitoring system.* Check with your group daily. You should be aware of possible problems to prevent disruption to the work environment. Encourage employees to report problems without being asked.

9. *Give criticism gracefully.* Reprimanding or ridiculing followers in public can cause problems. If criticism must be given, it should be done in private and in a constructive manner.

10. *Have a plan for employees' future.* People who cannot envision career growth will probably leave. People are more likely to work hard if they see a possibility of growth in their jobs.

11. *Avoid hasty judgments about work style.* Individuals will handle tasks differently than you expect. Allow the freedom of personal choice as long as the task is completed in an acceptable manner.

12. *Use rewards and incentives.* Use praise immediately when a task is done well. Praise is an important method of motivating some individuals.

13. *Encourage camaraderie and friendship.* Allowing employees time to socialize in the workplace can create a team atmosphere. Given a chance to be sociable, employees can form essential networks and expand their means of being creative and productive.[15]

Ask Yourself...

1. Which of the outside forces have had the greatest influence in motivating you in the workplace? The least?

2. Reviewing the Methods for Enhancing Motivation, which would you consider the top five most important of those methods and why?

3. Which would be the most difficult for you personally and why? How would you try to overcome your fear or discomfort with that method and execute its use?

3.5   HOW MOTIVATORS ARE CHANGING

Managers and supervisors are recognizing significant changes in what motivates employees in today's workplace. The changes have come about because four generations are now fully engaged in the workplace: the Traditionalists, born before 1946; the Baby Boomers, born between 1946 and 1964; Generation X, born between 1965 and 1979; and Generation Y (or Millennials) and its subset, born after 1979. Each brings different values and expectations into the workplace, described in the following paragraphs. While each generation has certain characteristics, not every member of a generation will share these values and characteristics.

> **KeyPoint**
> Effective leaders develop an atmosphere conducive to motivation.

Generational Expectations

Traditionalists were influenced by the Great Depression and World War II. Increasingly, these workers are remaining in the workforce well past the traditional retirement age. They're working longer because of their personal financial situation, because they are physically and mentally healthy, because they like what they do, and because of a personal/family situation. Some may have to continue while others clearly just want to extend their work life.[18] Deeply patriotic, they are loyal and have faith in institutions. Fiscal restraint and a strong work ethic characterize this generation.

Baby boomers, on the other hand, are more motivated by work that provides a sense of identity—interesting and challenging work, recognition and appreciation for a job well done, more participation in decision making, and more leisure time. Their entry into the workplace brought with it demands for a flexible work environment. Employers responded by devoting more time to the development of their employees through training, job enrichment, and job enlargement.

Generations X and Y have untraditional mindsets when compared to their baby boomer parents. They tend to have a confident attitude, and statistically they may be weaker in written and oral skills than the boomer generation. Sometimes described as cynical about the future and unwilling to conform, members of Generation X are known to jump from job to job if the work bores them or is not fun. Generation X workers are quick thinkers and risk takers, want immediate gratification, and often have advanced technical skills.

Generation X is entrepreneurial. Individuals in this age group create new businesses faster than all other age groups and maintain successful start-up companies at a rate three times higher than any other age group. They want to control their destiny, make all the decisions, and keep all the money. Some of them deliver a challenge to supervisors who must motivate this cynical, nonconformist group. They are completely at ease using the Internet as a tool for solving problems, researching issues, and communicating through advanced technologies.[19]

Ralph Schomburg, a training leader and manager in the aerospace industry, has spent many hours learning what it takes to motivate Generation X. He believes employers must look at the factors that influenced their values and belief systems. Unlike the baby boomer generation, many of these younger workers grew up as latch-key kids with divorced parents and with crooked politicians, pollution, and other ecological concerns looming large in their lives. Schomburg believes these workers place different priorities and values on traditional motivational tools and are more loyal to their personal careers than to the company. The box that follows represents Schomburg's view of Generation X motivators.

> *If you don't think every day is a good day, just try missing one.*
> —Zig Zigler, author and motivational speaker

Motivating Generation X Workers

MONEY: Money can be a strong motivating force for Generation X. The desire for "stuff" moves this group to work for reward. Money is a measure of their sense of accomplishment. It also provides independence and identity.

TRAINING: This means of increasing their skills and abilities is important to Generation X. It makes them more marketable and mobile—and appeals to their need for self-fulfillment.

FEEDBACK: The need to know how they're doing is strong. Providing positive (or negative) feedback helps Generation X plan their next move.

REWARDS: Traditional "employee of the month" recognitions won't work. To motivate this group, hand them free tickets to the movies or sports events after they've done good work.

More than 60 million strong, Generation Y (Millennials) is the second largest workforce in America's history, and members are viewed as loyal and hardworking if they see value in what they're doing.

Technology (e-mail, cell phones, and instant messaging) is a central focus in the daily activities of this generation. It has considerable influence on their personalities, attitudes, expectations, and learning strategies. They multitask easily, expect constant access to information and have zero tolerance for delays, and have a strong need for continual stimulation and challenge. Members of Generation Y have been told since birth that they can be and do anything they can imagine. Hence, they seem determined to live their best life ever at all times.[20]

A smaller subset of Generation Y is a group called the Gen Why's, with ages ranging in the very early teens to people in their twenties. Eric Chester first identified the Gen Why's in his book, *Employing Generation Why—Understanding, Managing, and Motivating Your New Workforce.* Chester believes that this group feels their services are in high demand and employers need to be mindful of their time and needs. Like any other group, they like to be shown respect and want their contributions to be valued. Their appearance may be noticeable in the workplace—perhaps by a colorful or "statement" T-shirt, flip-flops, MP3 players, cell phones, or other electronics. While Traditionalists and Boomers may not understand these differences in the workplace, generational differences need not be a distraction from getting a good job done.[21]

Motivating Generation Y Workers

MONEY: Generation Y expects and believes that, in spite of economic blips, they will be better off than their parents. They have a very optimistic outlook on life, work, and the future, and that carries into their pay expectations. They have lofty financial and personal goals.

TRAINING: Generation Y is the most education-minded generation in history. Influenced by baby boomer parents who value education and a workplace that demands it, they realize the key to their success lies in advanced learning and continuing education.

FEEDBACK: Generation Y prefers to work with highly motivated teams of committed people and want immediate feedback on their performance.

REWARDS: Managers must figure out a way to offer incentives at work that some competitors are willing or able to offer. Money matters, but Generation Y is willing to meet specific work standards—goals, deadlines, and parameters—in exchange for financial and nonfinancial rewards.

New Methods for Motivating Workers

The challenge of managing, motivating, and retaining workers from varied generations requires a new set of attitudes and skills. The assumptions that money alone motivates and that the workplace is of prime importance in workers' lives are no longer valid. In order to develop interesting and challenging work, employers must devote more time to employee development in the form of education and training, job enrichment, and job enlargement. As an employee, you will need continuous training to acquire new skills and knowledge. This training can include classroom as well as on-the-job training.

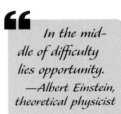

In the middle of difficulty lies opportunity.
—Albert Einstein, theoretical physicist

Rotating jobs will continue to be another way to motivate employees. In a job rotation, you move from a current position to a new position of your choice or need. You also receive training and exposure that can provide future career opportunities for you. This additional experience and training will empower you with the tools needed for your success.

Few organizations actually train their managers on the importance of personal recognition in motivating their employees. In a survey reported by Bernstein and Rozen, great disparity was found between what people say motivates them and what their companies are actually providing. For example, although 91 percent of the individuals in the survey stated that recognition for good work is important, only 54 percent felt that they were actually receiving appropriate recognition. A Gallup poll disclosed that 65 percent of Americans had received no praise or recognition in the workplace in the past year. These findings point out that the old "Way to go!" still works and that today's managers often fall short by adopting a management style known as management by exception.[22] Under this technique, the boss gives attention to you only when you do something wrong.

A key concept in Ken Blanchard's *One Minute Manager* is that the fastest way to motivate employees is by applying a little praise. In fact, the book's advice is to "catch them doing something right!" It stresses that praise should be specific, appropriate, and immediate.[23] The Hilton hotel chain has adopted a program based loosely on this concept and has had good results from its implementation. The program is described below as follows.

> *Where the needs of the world and your talents cross, there lies your vocation.*
> —*Aristotle, ancient Greek philosopher*

Catch Me At My Best

If you are a guest at Hilton properties such as Hampton Inns, Doubletree, or Embassy Suites, you may see colorful comment cards at the front check-in desk. These "Catch Me at My Best" cards are provided for customers who want to leave a brief note of praise for the general manager about some special deed one of the hotel employees has performed. The cards have several blank lines so that you can describe what you may have caught the employee doing right. You may use these cards for any hotel employee during your stay at the facility. Your words of praise and recognition are then presented to that staff member with a perk or award of some type. They go a very long way toward motivating employees on a daily basis and encouraging better service.[24]

Smart leaders have discovered that words of encouragement given to a person who has done an outstanding job pay real dividends. By contrast, an old adage states, "Label a man a loser and he'll start acting like one." These practices illustrate the self-fulfilling concept that people tend to act in accordance with their self-image. If they see themselves as successful, respected, and contributing members of the work force, their behavior is likely to reflect this perception.

A strong motivational factor influencing worker behavior today is the desire for more leisure time. Increasingly, employers are finding their workplaces deserted by mid-afternoon on Friday; employees are slipping away for an early start on their weekend. Though this practice affects productivity through lost work time, it can also have a positive effect on employee morale. However, dedicated employees who stay on the job until closing time resent having to handle the work left by those who skip out.

Some methods used by organizations to cope with employees' desire for more leisure time include changing work shifts to four 10-hour work days and instituting flexible work hours on Fridays to accommodate earlier arrival and departure times. Other employers allow individuals to choose which two days of the week they prefer as their "weekend." For some employees, this choice satisfies a desire for leisure time that is less crowded and ends the "skip out early" syndrome.

More and more of these innovative approaches to motivating today's workers may be seen as employers adjust to the changing needs of a multigenerational, multiethnic, multicultural workforce.

Ask Yourself...

1. What are the five generational groups in the workforce today and to which group do you belong? What challenges have you seen employers face in motivating this new generational mix of workers?

2. Which of the new methods of motivating employees across the generational gap appeal to you most and what is the main benefit to you? What methods do you think work best for motivating today's workforce?

3. Mr. Schomburg identified four major methods of motivating Generation X workers. From your personal viewpoint, how would you rank these four motivators? Which of these motivators is most important to you and why? What would you add to his list, if anything?

KEY TERMS

motivation
primary needs
secondary needs
Maslow's hierarchy of needs theory
physiological needs
safety and security needs
social needs
esteem needs

self-actualization needs
Herzberg's two-factor theory
hygiene factors
motivational factors
McClelland's acquired needs theory
Vroom's expectancy theory
motivational source fields

CHAPTER SUMMARY

The study of motivation is an ongoing attempt to understand a complex aspect of human behavior. A significant relationship exists between needs and motivation. Motivation is defined as the needs or drives within individuals that energize certain behaviors. Only a felt need motivates. Once that need is satisfied, it will no longer be a motivator.

Maslow developed a hierarchy of needs arranged in a specific order. He believed that individuals normally address these needs in a natural order, fulfilling lower-order needs first before moving on to higher-order needs. Herzberg believed that hygiene factors are necessary to maintain satisfaction among employees, whereas motivational factors build high levels of motivation. McClelland's theory states that individuals acquire needs for achievement, affiliation, or power through cultural exposure during early personality development. Vroom believed that people behave in certain ways based on expected results from that behavior.

The most persistent theme in motivational theories is that all behavior is directed toward satisfying some need. If an action leads to positive outcomes, it will probably be repeated. If it leads to negative results, the behavior will usually not be repeated. Needs vary in importance and intensity with each individual but generally fall into one of two basic categories, primary or secondary. Primary needs are basic to physical survival, and secondary needs are psychological. By understanding the difference between wants and needs, individuals can learn how to make constructive choices. Outside, inside, and early motivational source fields influence behavior, and leaders can influence motivation by working with the source fields.

Today's unique mix of age groups in the workforce creates challenges for managers and requires applying new methods of motivation for best results. Interesting and challenging work, recognition and appreciation for work well done, being included in key decision making, and having more leisure time have replaced some of the traditional motivators, such as money and job security.

REVIEW

1. Explain why understanding motivation is important to organizations and to individuals.

2. What is the basic motivational behavior model from its point of origin through its completion?

3. Who are the four major motivational theorists and what are each of their major contributions to the study of human relations?

4. What are some of the newer methods being used to motivate employees? Give examples.

5. What outside forces can affect an employee's motivation?

6. Why is it important to understand the multigenerational relationships in the workplace today? Give examples of qualities in each of the groups.

7. Which of the motivational techniques are becoming increasingly important? Why?

CRITICAL THINKING

1. Describe a recent personal situation in which a basic motivational behavior model was evident. Which of the needs did you feel you had to satisfy and what action did you take to relieve the tension? Once fulfilled, did you have a sense of moving on to the next level of need satisfaction? At what level are you currently operating and are you feeling motivated to advance or do you feel actualized?

2. From the above-mentioned scenario, describe whether the action you took resulted in constructive or destructive behavior. Might you have handled it differently? If so, how?

3. Identify a situation in which you were able to apply one or more of the motivational source fields to influence the behavior of a coworker. Which source did you use and why did you choose that source? Why do you feel your choice was effective?

4. One of the most frequently and preferred methods used today for motivating employees is better communication between supervisor and employee coupled with recognition and praise for a job well done. What major study, done early in the development of human relations studies described in Chapter 1, first identified the benefits that recognition has on the motivation and productivity of employees? What are the similarities in the two ideas and the resulting outcomes? How have things changed in motivation methods today, or have they?

5. With an understanding of the generational diversity in the workforce, what kind of problems do you think might arise in a work group consisting of

three senior Vietnam War veterans and two members of Generation Y with degrees in computer science? What motivational methods would best suit this group? How would you keep this group focused and on task?

CASE STUDIES

In small groups, analyze the following situations.

1 **Mr. Lazy** Carolyn has supervised Bob for seven years, and Bob is eligible for retirement in two more years. There are four junior analysts in the office with only two years of experience, but they are highly motivated and eager to do a good job. Bob is 52, financially comfortable, and happily married with no children at home. He's become known as Mr. Lazy because he has openly stated to Carolyn that he doesn't want new job assignments, avoids any overtime, and doesn't desire a promotion. The younger analysts have begun to resent Bob's attitude and having to carry his workload.

1. According to Maslow's theory, at which need level is Bob operating?

2. How can Carolyn motivate Bob to assume more of the job assignments as they come in?

3. Do you think there may be a generational issue in this situation? If so, how will Carolyn resolve this motivational dilemma? Do you think Carolyn should just allow Bob to do his job as it is and work around him for his short remaining tenure and resolve the problem later?

4. What do you think will happen to Bob if his behavior does not change?

5. What do you think the others will do if things remain the same much longer?

2 **Flickering Lights** Billie hurried into a local department store just before closing time when all the clerks were clearing their registers and flickering the lights to signal customers it was time to go. It was important that she have a camera first thing in the morning so she was trying to hurry. Gary, a clerk in the camera department, looked up and asked if she needed help, walked her several aisles over, and discussed features of several different models to help her choose the camera best suited to her needs. He then selected the appropriate batteries and memory card for the camera. His cordial behavior and help with her problem eased her anxiety and made the sale pleasant. Gary's charm, manners, and enthusiasm indicate a high level of inner motivation and self assurance.

1. What do you think motivates Gary to show the interest and care about his customers when others might be annoyed and anxious to leave for the day?

2. How do you think Billie will feel about Gary and the store the next time she has any camera-related items to purchase? Will she be motivated to return to this store for other items as well? Why, and for what reasons related to the motivational theories presented in this chapter?

3. Which of the motivational source fields do you think may be in use here? Do you think Gary routinely operates at this level or do you think he may be unusually motivated to satisfy some particular need with the company?

HUMAN RELATIONS IN ACTION

Using any Internet search engine or job search site, browse through job listings to find one that would motivate you to apply for that job. Prepare a written report on how you selected your new job and what motivated you to choose that job field. Present your report in an attractive, interesting, and informative format. You might include a copy of the application or other indicators of why you were motivated to make this choice.

For additional resources, refer to the web site for this text:
www.cengage.com/management/dalton

RESOURCES

1. Fisher, A. "Staying power." *Fortune Magazine*, June 2008. Retrieved May 12, 2009, from http://money.cnn.com/galleries/2008/fortune/0806/gallery.Fortune40_retention.fortune/3.html.

2. Sekula, R. D. Outside the box: How Kip Tindell analyzes his customers, employees and limits to lead the container store to double-digit growth. *Smart Business*, 2009. Retrieved May 12, 2009, from http://www.sbnonline.com/Classes/Article/PrinterFriendly/ArticleDraw_P.aspx.

3. Applegate, G. *Happiness, It's Your Choice*. Sherman Oaks, CA: Berriner Publishing, 1985.

4. Maslow, A. H. *Motivation and Personality*. New York: Harper & Row, 1954.

5. Alden, R. "The sound rattles your head and bleeds through your eyes." *Inc. Magazine*, September 2008, 111.

6. Herzberg, F. *Work and the Nature of Man*. New York: HarperCollins, Inc., 1966.

7. Herzberg, F. One more time: How do you motivate employees? *Harvard Business Review Classic*, January 2003, 112.

8. McClelland, D. C. *Studies in Motivation*. New York: Appleton-Century Croft, 1955.

9. McClelland, D. C., and Burnham, D. H. Power is the great motivator. *Harvard Business Review Classic*, January 2003, 123–139.

10. Vroom, V. H. *Work and Motivation*. New York: John Wiley & Sons, 1964.

11. Gostick, A., and Elton, C. *The Carrot Principle*. New York: Free Press, 2007.

12. *ibid.*

13. Massie, J. L., and Douglas, J. *Managing—A Contemporary Introduction*. Englewood Cliffs, NJ: Prentice-Hall, Inc., 1992.

14. Drucker, P. F. *Management, Tasks, Responsibilities, Practices*. Dexter, MI: Transaction Publishers, 2007.

15. Gostick, A., and Elton, C. *The Carrot Principle*.

16. Frauenheim, Ed. Say anything (nice). Workforce Management, November 21, 2008. Retrieved May 5, 2009, from http://workforce.com/wpmu/globalwork/2008/11.

17. Bernstein, A. J., and Rozen, S. C. How to re-energize your staff. *Working Woman*, April 1989, 45–46.

18. Plotczyk, P. Boomers and X-ers and Y-ers—oh my! Worksystems Affiliate International, Inc., 2007. Retrieved May 5, 2009, from http://www.wsa-intl.com/pages/241_boomers_and_x_ers_and_y_ers_oh_my_.cfm?

19. Gravett, L., and Throckmorton, R. *Bridging the Gap: How to Get Radio Babies, Boomers, Gen X-ers, & Gen Y-ers to Work Together and Achieve More*. Franklin Lakes, NJ: The Career Press, Inc., 2007.

20. *ibid.*

21. Chester, E. *Employing Generation Y*. Vacaville, CA: Chess Press, Inc., 2002.

22. Bernstein, A. J., and Rozen, S. C. How to re-energize your staff.

23. Blanchard, K., and Johnson, S. *The One Minute Manager*. New York: William Morrow and Company, 1983.

24. Chester, E. *Getting Them to Give a Damn*. New York: Kaplan Publishing, 2005.

COMMUNICATION:
THE ESSENTIAL SKILL

OBJECTIVES

After studying this chapter, you should be able to:

4.1 Explain the communication process.

4.2 Discuss the factors that impact communication.

4.3 Make your communication skills work for you.

4.4 Describe how technology is changing worker communication.

Jump Start

Communication technology is quickly catching up with science fiction as depicted in comic books and movies of the past, and it is impacting how people work. Wrist-sized telephones were once thought impossible—but today they're reality. Working with and actually seeing employees—and their visitors—in offices in far parts of the world seemed to be wishful thinking—but today it's happening, allowing workers to interact with video screens rather than the physical persons.

An example of such interaction via video screens is the executive assistant at a Cisco Systems office in Texas working with an executive at a Cisco office in Silicon Valley who did not want to lose her when she moved. Through the use of Cisco's telepresence video-conferencing, they are able to see and talk with each other, and she handles his calls, arranges meetings, and even greets his visitors.[1]

However, many people believe that technology will never take the place of face-to-face communication.

- What benefits and drawbacks do you see with the use of distance communication technologies in such situations described here?
- What do you think is the future impact of such technologies?

4.1 THE IMPORTANCE OF COMMUNICATION

Today's demanding workplace requires that you communicate with clarity, tact, and confidence. As shown in the systems approach discussed in Chapter 1, communication ability and other individual skills influence how people perform. Further, communication is a learning and innovation skill, an important responsibility in the 21st century, and an integral part of emotional intelligence.

Definition of Communication

Communication is the process by which people exchange information through a common system of symbols, signs, or behavior. This process sends messages from one person to another. Symbols can be written or spoken words. Signs can be shapes and colors. Behavior can be any nonverbal communication, such as body movements or facial expressions.

Listening, speaking, writing, and reading are the four basic skills used in communicating. Of these skills, listening and speaking are the most frequently used. They're also the two in which we receive the least training. However, you can sharpen any communication skills through experience, training, or both. This chapter will help you learn to listen, speak, and write more effectively at work. It will also help you combine these skills to make effective professional presentations. Finally, it will discuss communication technologies you are likely to use in your work.

Some Forms of Communication on the Way Out[2]

Yellow Pages	Answering Machines
Classified Ads	Cameras That Use Film
Movie Rental Stores	Drive-In Theaters
Dial-Up Internet	News Magazines
Landline-Based Phones	VCRs

- Why do you think Yellow Pages and classified ads are decreasing in use?
- How do you rent or obtain movies?
- Do you have a landline phone at your house? If not, why not? If so, do you think you will keep it for the foreseeable future?

Today's world is information based, and every technological advance seems to bring us into contact with more people. We spend the majority of our waking hours communicating in person, by phone, through e-mail, and by other electronic means. It's not surprising, then, that communication problems occur often. In fact, estimates are that:

- People hear incorrectly 75 percent of the time.
- They don't accurately remember 75 percent of what they hear within three weeks.
- Communication problems account for as much as 80 percent of problems at work.

KeyPoint
To communicate effectively, focus on sharpening your listening, speaking, writing, and nonverbal skills.

Employers look for strong communications skills in their new employees.[3] In fact, in survey after survey, year after year, communications skills rank among the top skills employers desire most.

Four examples will demonstrate the role effective communication plays in human relations at work. First is the employee who asks the boss for clarification of a written work order. This will prevent doing a job incorrectly and causing a problem. Another example is the boss who calls employees together to discuss a major company change and answer questions. This way, they will not learn about the change through gossip or an impersonal memo.

The third example is the employee who waits for the right time to ask the boss for a raise. When the boss has just returned from a budget-cutting meeting, this request might be especially awkward. The fourth example is the employee who learns to use communication technologies. Tools such as web conferences can facilitate interaction with coworkers and customers, make the company more productive, and save money.

Effective communicators understand when to use impersonal, interpersonal, and personal communication. In so doing, you can more easily determine how formal you should be.

Impersonal communication normally refers to items such as reports. These use varying degrees of one-way communication. They also require a more formal writing style.

Interpersonal communication involves communicating or networking with other individuals, groups, or even organizations. This communication helps you fulfill your responsibilities.

While you will also use personal communication at work, exercise caution in what you share, where and when you share it, and with whom.

The more sensitive and knowledgeable you are about communication, the stronger your human relations skills will be. To help you start thinking about your communication competencies, rate yourself objectively on the following skills in column 2. In column 3, indicate how you think someone who knows you well might rate you. In column 4, obtain ratings from someone who knows you well. Use S for strong, A for average, and N for needs improvement.

In analyzing the totals, you will probably find that your ratings differ in the three columns. Compare the ratings of each competence and start

Communication Competency Quiz

Competence	How I Rate Myself	How I Think Someone Who Knows Me Well Might Rate Me	How Someone Who Knows Me Well Rates Me
Uses tact			
Encourages honest communication			
Listens effectively			
Reads nonverbal cues			
Masters communication technology			
Writes clearly and concisely			
Prepares professional look-ing/sounding correspondence			
Limits jargon to those who understand			
Totals (number of S, A, and N in each column)			

thinking about your strengths and the areas in which you may need to improve. Everyone will have an area for improvement.

Communication Flow

In any organization, communication will flow upward, downward, or horizontally. In each instance, the communication process includes three elements. The *message* is the content of the communication. The *sender* is the person who transmits the message. The *receiver* is the person to whom the message is sent.

Communication can be verbal or nonverbal. Verbal communication is either spoken or written, such as questions and responses. Nonverbal examples are nodding, smiling, or frowning. In addition, communication can be one way or two way. An example of one-way communication is a formal speech, bulletin, or report. A discussion with your boss and an instant message conversation are examples of two-way communication.

Whether you are the sender or the receiver, you are responsible for determining that the correct message has been received. This is normally done using feedback (discussed in Chapter 2). *Feedback* is information given back to a sender that evaluates the message and states what the receiver understood. It helps clarify communication, verify understanding, and overcome communication barriers (distortions and blockages). To be most effective, feedback should be timely, often, and precise.

Figure 4.1 depicts the communication process and the relationship of feedback to the sender and the receiver.

> **KeyPoint**
> The elements of the communication process are the sender, the receiver, the message, and feedback.

Figure 4.1

Communication process.

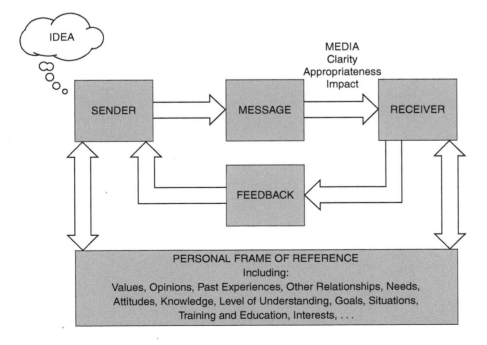

Feedback improves communication and saves time. It can also reduce errors and human relations problems. In face-to-face communication, feedback can be fast, with both the listener and the speaker continuously giving feedback to each other verbally and nonverbally. This happens through frowns, nods, verbal expressions of agreement or disagreement, questions, statements, and other means. Even silence can be a surprisingly powerful form of feedback. It can, for example, communicate power, uncertainty, agreement, or disapproval.

Feedback can also be provided electronically. You've no doubt received receipts at fast food restaurants, office supply stores, discounters, and elsewhere asking you to evaluate their service or products online or over the phone.

Pay close attention to the feedback you receive to determine whether your recipients interpret your message correctly. Figure 4.2 shows some ways that you can make sure you are obtaining feedback effectively.

Figure 4.2

Ways of obtaining feedback effectively.

When Face to Face with the Receiver	When Not Face to Face with the Receiver
Ask questions that determine whether the receiver understands your message.	Ask questions that determine whether the receiver understands your message.
Ask the receiver to restate what you've said.	Ask the receiver to restate what you've said.
Watch for signs of understanding (such as nods) or confusion (such as frowns).	If you've sent a memo or letter, request a written answer/estimate of when you may expect an oral or written answer.
	If you do not receive a written or oral answer, follow up and check for compliance. (Repeat your request or see whether the action you requested has been taken.)

Ask Yourself...

1. Which of the four basic communication skills are you most comfortable using? Why?

2. Which communication skill do you think you need to improve? How are you planning to improve it?

3. What have you seen in the movies or on TV that you consider to be effective communication? What made it effective?

4.2   FACTORS THAT HINDER GOOD COMMUNICATION

Numerous factors can cause distortions and blocks in communication. These factors can create problems for you. Figure 4.3 describes some barriers to communication and how to overcome them.

> **"** *Truly great leaders spend as much effort collecting and acting upon feedback as they do providing it.*
>
> —*Alexander Lucia, communications author* **"**

𝓔𝓽𝓱𝓲𝓬𝓼 CONNECTION

In 2009, Facebook received the strong negative feedback possible when communication isn't clear. Facebook quietly updated its terms of use, creating great concern among users. The fear was that Facebook would forever control the information they shared on the social networking site, even were users to cancel their account. When thousands of users joined protest groups creating a virtual riot, the company decided to reinstate its previous terms. Founder Mark Zuckerberg assured users that they own and control their information. A few days later Facebook added that when it considers future changes, it will ask users for comments and, if the concerns are significant, will make decisions by user vote. Soon after, Facebook offered two options, which it said were created from input from users and experts.[4,5,6]

1. Do you view this incident as a potential ethical lapse, merely a communication error, or a wakeup call to be careful with personal information you share online?

2. Have you ever provided feedback online? If so, for what purpose?

3. What personal information are you sharing online and what measures do you think are in place to secure your information?

Figure 4.3

Barriers to communication.

Barrier	Possible Problem	Potential Solution
Semantics (study of word meanings)	Words with multiple meanings, abstract terms, poor word choice.	Use feedback; ask questions.
Emotions	Distortions, overreactions, preconceived ideas, attitudes.	Calm down; have an open mind; withhold judgment until you have adequate information.
Role expectations (how we expect ourselves/others to act in various roles)	Discounting others' opinions, not allowing others to change their roles	Try to separate people from roles; allow others to change; be aware of the effect that power may have on perceptions.
Personality and appearance	A message may be rejected on the basis of the appearance of the sender or the message.	Make appearance appropriate for the role and image you wish to present.
Prejudice	Can alter our perception of the message.	Recognize contributions; evaluate communication on the basis of the message itself rather than the appearance of the sender.
Failure to recognize changes	Can cause confusion, fear, or mistrust.	Recognize people, objects, and situations, which can change and interpret communication in that light.
Poor organization of ideas	Listeners/readers have difficulty understanding or lose interest.	Outline before writing; organize and revise for clarity; consider classes and workshops to help.
Information overload (more messages coming at us than we can process successfully)	Loss of ability to continue processing and remembering information, failure to listen carefully, forget information, communication break-down, stress, loss of job satisfaction.	Develop coping strategies (notes, group activities, recognize overload and relax, reduce noise, focus, get enough rest/sleep, eat healthily, delegate, say no, prioritize)

> *The art of communication is the language of leadership.*
> —James Humes, author and former White House speechwriter

Notice that some of the communication barriers shown in Figure 4.3 lie in your senses, in word meanings, and in the emotions and attitudes of the sender and receiver. Several additional factors can make a difference in the success or failure of your communication.

Time

The way you use time is important. Frequent tardiness will cause others to view you as disorganized, disrespectful, and even rude. Using tardiness as a manipulative ploy to put yourself in a higher-status position will simply cause frustration and anger and will cost you respect. Further, because you risk losing credibility, people may be less likely to listen and accept your ideas. At work, tardiness may result in your being disciplined or even fired. Developing the habit of punctuality can enhance your communication, relationships, and professional image.

Timing

To be effective in your communication, remember that at times everyone needs to be left alone or at least have fewer interruptions. Your supervisors or coworkers may be tired, preoccupied, rushed, angry, or frustrated. If you try to force communication with them at those times, don't be surprised or hurt if they seem uninterested.

> **KeyPoint**
> Time, timing, context, medium, and humor are barriers that can impact communication.

    On the other hand, keeping your supervisor informed in a timely manner is important. Since supervisors don't always ask for information, you must use your own judgment in determining what to tell them and when. Keep your supervisor informed about the work you're doing, potential problems, and concerns. If you know that you won't be able to meet a required deadline, let the person in charge know as soon as possible. Doing your work in the manner and timing that your supervisor wants is also important. Most organizations have room for honest discussion on the best way to approach a task. However, when your supervisor makes a decision following discussion, comply immediately.

"Got half a minute for a few hundred questions?"

© 2009 Ted Goff

Context

Context refers to the conditions in which something occurs that can throw light on its meaning. For example, if your boss says that the company is considering a reorganization, you could draw a number of different conclusions. If this statement is made during a poor economy, you may fear losing your job. However, if it is made during an economic boom and the company is enlarging the area you service, your job may be more secure than ever. Therefore, consider the context of a message along with its other components to interpret it more accurately.

Medium

The *medium* is the form in which a message is communicated. For example, if you receive an express or registered letter from an attorney, it may create more anxiety than one through regular mail.

Another point to consider is not only what medium is suitable, but also what medium the receiver prefers. For example, if your boss likes brief memos regarding the status of your projects, don't give her a four-page, overly detailed account. If you know that a customer never reads e-mail, call him instead. If your product team members like to talk through new ideas, don't send them a written proposal and expect them to give it their full consideration.

Ethics CONNECTION

Steve Jobs, Apple cofounder and former CEO of Pixar Animation Studios, is considered a nonconformist who never settles and an innovator who shook up the computer, music, and entertainment industries. He's viewed as always working on another industry-changing innovation that combines function and elegance. He is also described as a smart and charismatic leader with a devoted following. His skill at persuasion and salesmanship—evident in his keynote speeches at technical conferences—has added to his image.[7]

When Jobs took a leave of absence from Apple for health reasons in January 2009, the company's stock dropped. Speculation concerned the impact Jobs has had on Apple in particular and on technology in general. One newspaper likened his following to that of a rock star and suggested that he should be more open about his illness.[8]

1. Do you agree with the newspaper's statement? Why or why not?
2. Where do you think the right of investors for information and the right of individuals for privacy start and end?
3. Do you think that Jobs's reputation and following or the timing of this incident during the 2009 economic bust should be factors in what information is communicated? Why or why not?

Humor

President Dwight Eisenhower once said, "A sense of humor is part of the art of leadership, of getting along with people, of getting things done." Having and displaying a healthy sense of humor can help you create a favorable long-term impression, as people usually like others with whom they can share a laugh.

Humor can be a helpful part of your communication. However, if you use it inappropriately or thoughtlessly, you risk causing offense, embarrassment, and misunderstanding. Here are some quick tips for using humor at work:

> **KeyPoint**
> Humor can assist communication but must be used carefully to avoid causing offense, embarrassment, and misunderstanding.

Quick Tips for Using Humor at Work

- Avoid humor associated with politics, religion, race, gender, ethnicity, and weight or other physical characteristics.
- Avoid humor until you understand a coworker's personality and sensitivities.
- Avoid sarcasm and cynical humor.
- Don't make humorous comments about emotionally painful situations.
- Don't use crude or offensive humor with coworkers, even in informal or social settings outside work.

Remember, also, that sometimes what you may carelessly say away from the job can find its way into your workplace and hurt you.

Ask Yourself...

1. Think about barriers in communication that you have observed or experienced. How might these barriers have been minimized?

2. Give examples from your own experience of when you misunderstood a message. What can be done to avoid the problem in the future?

3. Describe a time when your message was misunderstood by the receiver. What should you have done to make your message clearer?

4. Describe a time when humor helped clarify communication you received or sent. Can you think of a time when humor made a message unclear? What happened?

4.3 MAKING YOUR COMMUNICATION SKILLS WORK

To communicate effectively, focus on sharpening your basic skills. These include listening, speaking, writing, nonverbal communication, and presentation skills.

Listening Skills

Perhaps the most important communication skill is the ability to listen. In fact, we spend 45 percent of our time doing it. Good listening skills are required at every level of an organization, particularly the higher levels. Showing a genuine interest in what others are saying to you is a good way to build a strong, long-term working relationship. Yet only 2 percent of us have had any formal training in it.

Figure 4.4 shows the barriers to listening identified by communications experts.[9]

> *Wisdom is the reward you get for a lifetime of listening when you'd have preferred to talk.*
> —Doug Larson, newspaper columnist

Figure 4.4

Barriers to listening.

- Inattention, preoccupation, or lack of interest in the subject or the speaker.
- Internal "noise" within your mind or outside noises or distractions.
- Your emotional or physical state, such as anger, depression, or fatigue.
- Prejudices, listening for what you want to hear, thinking ahead or back.
- Language or knowledge differences, semantics, or poor delivery of the message (which means you will need to ask for more information).

You can become a better listener by using *active listening*. This is a conscious effort to hear what someone is saying to you and to be aware of what that person is communicating nonverbally.

To strengthen your active listening skills, follow these suggestions:

- Set aside whatever else you are doing and give the speaker your undivided attention.
- Keep your thoughts in the present. Don't anticipate or plan what you're going to say next, and don't jump to conclusions.
- Be aware of your biases and prejudices, and avoid prejudging the speaker.
- If possible, eliminate distractions by using a quiet, private location for communication. For face-to-face communication, look at the person speaking to you to help you concentrate.

- Ask for clarifications, restate important points ("so you're saying that ..."), and ask questions, especially who, what, when, where, or why questions that invite a more thoughtful response.
- Be ready to give feedback.
- Pay attention to the speaker's nonverbal communication (discussed later in this section).
- While some note taking can be helpful and may even be necessary, avoid letting it divert your attention from the speaker.
- Listen for major ideas, but don't try to remember everything.
- Don't fake attention, as it takes too much work and is distracting. Besides, it's hard to disguise feigned interest.

> *Knowledge speaks, but wisdom listens.*
> —Jimi Hendrix, guitarist, singer, and songwriter

Speaking Skills

Spoken communication is any message sent or received through oral words. We talk to our coworkers all day long, but we may not always give enough thought to what we're saying. How many times have you heard or said, "That's not what I meant to say"? Effective spoken communication is clear, direct, and to the point. And like other skills, it requires practice.

Figure 4.5 provides some guidelines for making your spoken communication more effective.

Figure 4.5 ◑

Guidelines for effective spoken communication.

Voice	Your voice should be pleasant and appropriate for the situation. (Try recording yourself to learn how your voice sounds.)
Respect for the listener	Avoid wasting the listener's time. Plan ahead what you are going to say, even in telephone calls. Avoid vague or rambling sentences.
Clear word choice	Use descriptive, specific verbs, adverbs, and adjectives. Choose words that you are sure your audience will understand. Use slang and jargon (terms unique to particular industries or offices) sparingly and carefully.
Grammar	Always use correct grammar.
"I" phrases	When expressing your opinion, beginning your message with "I think," "I believe," "I feel," or "I don't understand" is more effective than comments such as "You made me angry," or "You are wrong," or "You are confusing me."

If you provide oral directives or complex instructions, follow them up in writing. People usually recall only 50 percent of what is said to them immediately after, and their recall drops as time passes. Parts of a message are lost or distorted after passing through two people.[10]

Don't worry excessively about what others will think. Ask questions to show you're paying attention and want to contribute.

> Great leaders are almost always great simplifiers, who can cut through argument, debate, and doubt to offer a solution everybody can understand.
> —Colin Powell, U.S. Army general and former Secretary of State

Two additional points are important in making your spoken communication effective: choose the right level of communication and respect confidentiality.

Remember that you communicate on many levels and must choose the right level for the situation or relationship.[11] The first level is the conventional, cliché, or cocktail conversation. This communication with casual acquaintances at work is fairly impersonal. An example is "How are you?" Fine, how are you?"

The second level is exploratory. It is communication about facts or other people. For example, you may report, "John is handling the Mercer account." Notice that on this level you are not sharing information about yourself. Rather, you are "exploring" your relationship with another by sharing neutral information.

Level three is participative. On this level, you start talking about yourself. For example, you might say, "I'm having fun with the Austin project." This talk can evolve into self-disclosure, in which you start to express your ideas and feelings.

Free sharing makes up the last level. At this deepest level, which involves some risk, you share your more personal thoughts and feelings. For example, you may say to your boss, "I'm having fun with the Austin project, unlike the nightmare I had with the Dempsey work."

People who are emotionally healthy and socially adept are able to use all levels and know when each is appropriate. You can't go through life being impersonal in all of your interactions. Nor can you share your thoughts and feelings with everyone you meet. Common sense is your best guide in deciding what to say, to whom, and in how much detail.

Regarding confidentialities, remember that being discreet is important in human relations at work, as well as in personal relationships. In fact, its importance cannot be overemphasized. When millionaire developer Donald Trump was asked about another CEO's most admirable traits, he specifically named the person's ability to keep a secret. During your career, you'll no doubt come in possession of confidential information that can make or break

> Leaders can do everything right with their teams and still fail if they don't deliver their message to each member as an individual.
> —Bill Parcells, Super Bowl Coach

the success of projects, partnerships, or other relationships. Knowing when not to speak will help identify you as a person who understands and respects confidences.

In addition to working on the mechanics of good spoken communication (from grammar to voice control), you'll benefit by following these suggestions for improving your spoken communication:

- Know when to just listen. Sometimes you need to be patient and supportive and wait before speaking.

- Question assumptions, as appearances of the person or situation can be deceiving. Keep in mind that you are communicating with another distinctly individual human being who feels the need to like and be liked.

- Tell the truth. You might never consider telling a big lie, but even small white lies such as "I like it" (if untrue) or "I'll get back to you soon" (when you don't intend to) can create hurt, confusion, and resentment.

- Think before speaking. Ask yourself, "What does the listener want/need/expect to hear and what do I want to communicate?" The key to communication is truly understanding what must be communicated and then doing so in a way that is on point and will hold the listener's interest.

- If you're an unhappy customer, use expressions such as "I'm not upset or angry at you, but I am very upset," "What I want from you is …," and "What would you do if you were in my shoes?"

> "
> *Our lives begin to end the day we become silent about things that matter.*
> —Dr. Martin Luther King, Jr., civil rights leader
> "

Ethics CONNECTION

In its first wide-scale layoff, Microsoft[12] mistakenly gave more severance money than it intended to some laid-off workers and less to others. The company sent a letter asking the ex-workers who received overpayments to return them. The letter then surfaced on the Internet. Microsoft quickly reversed its decision and called the laid-off workers to tell them they could keep the money. It also corrected the underpayments with a letter and a check.

1. If you were one of the affected laid-off workers, how would you feel about the company after this mistake had been rectified?

2. Do you think that Microsoft handled this matter appropriately? If not, how do you think it might have handled it more effectively?

Written Communication Skills

Good writing skills are essential to your career success, as writing is a basic and frequent form of communication, whether in formal letters and reports or in less formal e-mails. The purpose of writing, like speech, is to communicate, not impress. Inexperienced writers sometimes think that they must change their personalities and write in a showy, stilted, unnatural manner, but this is neither necessary nor desirable. The following suggestions will help you make your writing a positive reflection of you:

While Preparing　Think about your recipients, what they may already know and may still need to know, and what you want to communicate. Take the time to organize your thoughts before writing. Make an outline or just a short, simple list.

While Writing　Keep your average sentence length between 15 and 20 words. Cut down on long sentences, and vary the length of your sentences. Be succinct and to the point—strive to use as few words as possible to say what you need to say. Use active and passive voice appropriately. For example, in a sales message when you want to stimulate interest, you might use active voice to say, "This software will save your company time and money." In a refusal message when you want to buffer the bad news through passive voice, you might say, "Your shipment can be made as soon as we receive your check."

After Writing　Check yourself on the *5 Cs of communication* rule: written communication should be clear, correct, concise, complete, and courteous. Ask yourself these questions:

- *Clear.* Is my writing clear? Can the reader easily understand the message? Is my message factually accurate? Does it agree with company policy?

- *Correct.* Are my grammar, spelling, punctuation, and format correct?

- *Concise.* Have I avoided trite or confusing words or phrases? Have I deleted unnecessary words? Do my sentences and paragraphs say what needs to be said in as brief a way as possible?

- *Complete.* Have I included all the information the reader will need to understand my message?

- *Courteous.* Is the tone of my message courteous and respectful of the reader?

For any type of formal communication such as a letter, memo, or report, use a standard business format appropriate for the document. This will add to your message's appeal and make it easier to read. Allow adequate time to review, revise, and proof your work. You may want to put aside the first draft of the document and come back to it a little later. This frequently

KeyPoint
In writing, you should follow the 5 Cs of communication: Writing should be clear, correct, concise, complete, and courteous.

makes errors and needed changes more obvious. In your review and revision, look for errors in format, grammar, spelling, punctuation, word choice, and content.

In any written communication, including e-mail, use your software's spelling and grammar checker. However, don't rely solely on it, as it will not differentiate, for example, between "there" and "their." Nor will it let you know if you have erroneously deleted or repeated content. Proofread again carefully after spellchecking. By proofing, you ensure that the document is error free and ready to go out. As a last check, consider having someone else proof your important pieces of correspondence.

Don't make the mistake of thinking that strong communication skills aren't important in e-mails. Keep in mind that every written communication creates a mental image of the sender. To be an effective communicator, you'll want your writing style in e-mails and other correspondence to show that you are an intelligent, clear thinker with a sense of purpose.

The following suggestions will help you attain that image through your written communications:

- Include a brief subject line to announce your message and help your reader prioritize it.

- Use a greeting, such as "Dear Dr. Hennessey."

- Use standard capitalization, punctuation, and spelling and write clearly and briefly.

- Be courteous and cordial but avoid jokes.

- Avoid sending information that could damage someone's career or reputation, including your own.

- When e-mailing, avoid an unintended "Reply all" so that you don't inadvertently send your message to the wrong persons.

- Don't use all capital letters in e-mails.

- In multiple e-mail conversations, delete older messages to keep the e-mail short and clear.

- Know and respect your company policies regarding the use of e-mail for personal communications.

- Don't forward junk e-mail simply because you think it is interesting.

An important reminder in human relations is not to send e-mail when you're angry. If you've received an e-mail from a coworker that upsets you, you'll only make the situation worse by responding with harsh words in the heat of the moment. Lashing out may bring you temporary satisfaction but no long-term benefits. Instead, take a deep breath and a break, organize your thoughts, and compose a response that is professional and appropriate.

KeyPoint
To be an effective communicator, make your writing style in e-mails and other correspondence show that you are an intelligent, clear thinker with a sense of purpose.

Global CONNECTION

If not now, you may soon be a part of a worldwide workforce. Through digital communication technology, you—like many people already—may be able to work without a particular employer, perhaps from your home. Such work usually involves narrow, specific tasks.

Examples include the following:[13]

- Researchers at a major university tested the possibility of having players in online role-playing games view real medical scans in the game and find signs of cancer. Out of this grew a new company that is using game psychology in business applications.

- A major online book retailer is experimenting with a digital workplace involving people around the world. The workers receive a few cents per minute for tasks such as labeling photos or transcribing podcasts.

- Another company is handling telesales calls for businesses by using thousands of home agents, rather than employees.

1. What has been your experience with global digital communication?
2. Would you enjoy being involved with any of the processes of the companies described above? Why or why not?
3. Do you think countries with a higher use of the Internet have an obligation to assist countries that are still behind in order to help grow a worldwide supply chain of talent? Why or why not?

KeyPoint
Nonverbal communication is any meaning conveyed through body language, through the way the voice is used, and through the way people position themselves in relation to others.

Nonverbal Communication

Nonverbal communication—communication without words—is any meaning conveyed through body language, through the way the voice is used, and through the way people position themselves in relation to others.

How you say something is frequently just as important as what you say. Your tone of voice, facial expression, gestures, or haste may determine how listeners interpret your words and may even overshadow them.

People with strong human relations skills are usually good at reading others' body language and in using nonverbal communication. In a well-known study, Dr. Albert Mehrabian, an expert in nonverbal communication, found that nonverbal communication accounts for at least 93 percent of the impact of our communication and words account for only 7 percent.[14]

Effective Communication Among Workers

In advocating effective communication between civil servants and contract employees, the Houston-area aerospace industry[15] defined a set of supporting behaviors that would be helpful anywhere (and particularly when you are participating in or chairing committees): be respectful, demonstrate consideration or appreciation, respect yourself and each other, and appreciate the creativity and broader perspective of a diverse team.

To monitor how you are doing, ask yourself the following questions:

- Do I actively solicit contributions from the people with whom I work?
- Do I use the term "team" rather than "I"?
- Do I treat others as I wish to be treated?
- Do I share praise in public and constructive criticism in private?
- Do I give others the benefit of the doubt and understand a situation before responding?
- Do I value all constructive input and use this to make a decision?
- Do I credit others for their work?
- Am I aware of nonverbal cues, whether my own or others?

Understanding others' nonverbal communication is important because people often show their feelings and attitudes by their actions rather than their words. If you appreciate others' thoughts and feelings, you can interact more effectively with them.

However, don't rely on one clue by itself. Instead, consider it in the context of what is happening or being said. For example, during a conversation with a coworker, you notice that she suddenly frowns. You assume that means she disagrees with what you just said. However, she appears to be listening, continues the discussion, and even expresses agreement. Soon she mentions that she has a sudden splitting headache.

Figure 4.6 shows some of the common means of communicating nonverbally. Be aware of them in yourself and others. Try to convey the message you intend and receive a complete message from others.

KeyPoint
Recognizing nonverbal communication is an important human relations skill, as people often show their feelings and attitudes by their action rather than their words.

Figure 4.6

Common means of communicating nonverbally.

Nonverbal Transmitters	Examples
Posture	Individuals in high-status positions (such as upper management and politicians) may display their status through relaxed positions. Those in lower-status position (such as subordinates) may tend to keep their heads down and hands together or at their sides.
Facial expressions	Smiling can detract from a serious message. Because women tend to smile more than men, this can create misunderstandings for them at work and in their personal relationships.
Eye contact	We generally use eye contact to signal we want communication (for example, when you try to make eye contact with a waiter in a restaurant). When we wish to avoid talking to someone, we look away and avoid eye contact (for example, when your instructor asks a question you cannot answer or when you approach someone in the hall).
Voice	People generally view a fast but not excessive rate of speaking as more persuasive, trustworthy, and enthusiastic.
Body movements	Jerky head movements or excessive hand gestures may be associated with nervousness.
Personal space	In general, people in the United States tend to prefer more personal space than people in other cultures.
Seating	High-status or dominant individuals (such as formal or informal leaders) tend to sit in the head table position and participate more than those who sit along the side. Conflict is more likely between people sitting across from each other than between people sitting next to each other.

KeyPoint
Common nonverbal transmitters are posture, facial expressions, eye contact, voice, body movements, personal space, and seating.

The following two suggestions can make your nonverbal communication work for you:

- Act confident. Look people in the eye, stand straight, hold your head high, move with determination, speak loudly (within reason) and distinctly, and avoid nervous gestures. Act upbeat and smile.

- Get people to open up to you. Listen well, lean forward when listening, look people in the eye, sit with arms and legs uncrossed, and nod occasionally. Smile, have a relaxed posture and movements, and shake hands in a firm but not overpowering way. Mirror the other person's posture or match the voice tempo of the other person to build rapport.

When using nonverbal communication, keep in mind that nonverbal behaviors such as closeness or touching may be misinterpreted at work. Also remember that nonverbal communication varies from culture to culture (as will be discussed in a later chapter).

Professional Presentation Skills

Another communication skill growing in importance is the ability to make effective professional presentations to individuals or to groups, whether for sales or for information sharing. For example, your boss may ask you to present a concept for a project to your coworkers, explain a product to potential buyers, or speak to your local Chamber of Commerce about some aspect of your work.

Making an effective presentation requires your best speaking, listening, and nonverbal skills. You'll even need sharp writing and technology skills to organize your presentation and create effective presentations or visual aids.

The following suggestions will help you make presentations that accomplish your goals.[16]

- Consider your audience: who they are, what they want to know, and how much time you have to present and answer questions.

- Decide on your goal or reason for making this presentation (for example, to inform, persuade, request action, or build a relationship). Be prepared to state what you want at the beginning and end of your comments.

- Prepare your presentation, its parts, format, and visual aids.

- Build self-confidence through your personal appearance, belief in your message, careful preparation, positive self-talk, and visualization.

- Consider your delivery and involvement of the audience. Be enthusiastic and avoid nonwords such as "ah" or "uh."

Prior to and during your presentation, consider nonverbal aspects of your message. During your preparation, practice visualization or even try out your presentation in front of a mirror to increase your confidence. These may help you eliminate excessive head and hand movements, keep your hands out of your pockets, stand confidently and relaxed, smile naturally, and relax your voice. During the first half minute of your presentation, smile, walk confidently to the podium or front, establish eye contact by scanning the group, and thank your introducer and audience. Take a deep breath, relax, smile, and start your speech slowly, using a confident, energetic tone of voice. Begin with a humorous or light remark or just a friendly "Hello, how are you today?" Vary your distances from sections of the audience to stop their talking or to encourage them to participate. Lean forward when asked a question and look at all people in the group. Draw in nonattentive or nonresponsive people by looking at them or asking them a question.

Have fun. If you're enjoying yourself, your audience is more likely to enjoy themselves.

KeyPoint
Making effective presentations, growing in importance, requires your best speaking, listening, and nonverbal skills and even sharp writing and technology skills.

Ask Yourself...

1. Review the aspects of spoken communication and determine where your skills are strongest. Explain.

2. Think of a situation in which you had trouble completing a task because of poor communication. What happened, and how might you have improved it?

3. Have you ever received an e-mail that was so poorly written you had difficulty understanding it? How might it have been improved?

4. Do you communicate well nonverbally? How might you improve this form of communication?

4.4 TECHNOLOGY AND WORKER COMMUNICATION

Technology is changing how we communicate in our work. Wireless and integrated technologies allow sending images, text, and sound from virtually anywhere. Voice mail, e-mail, faxes, text messaging via cell phone and BlackBerry, instant messaging, web conferencing, and other technologies permit us to communicate more quickly, frequently, and efficiently. Phones are smarter and more useful, the Internet pervasive, touch interfaces more sophisticated, and hardware more powerful and less expensive. Even newspapers provide multimedia search options.

Increases in computer power and Internet connection speed will bring even more changes in how we work.[17] We're told to expect iPhones the size of a credit card that can connect to billions of pea-sized wireless sensors attached to buildings, streets, retail products, and clothes, all sending data over the Internet. These sensors will enable you to track and manage events in the physical world, use hand and arm gestures to control commands, and view results with special glasses.

> **"** *The wireless music box has no imaginable commercial value. Who would pay for a message sent to nobody in particular?*
>
> —*David Sarnoff's associates in response to his urgings for investment in the radio in the 1920s* **"**

In The News

With the volume of messages by e-mail, texting, and so on, some people feel they have to eliminate some form of communication to make room for others. What they are giving up is voice mail. In an age of instant information, they view it as too time-consuming. Introduced in the early 1980s and hailed as a miracle then, today it's being avoided or ignored by many people. In fact, research shows that people take significantly longer to reply to voice messages than text messages, and some rarely dial in. If, as some people believe, voice mail is heading toward obsolescence, this trend seems to be driven by young people. Others disagree that voice mail is going away, liking the sound of the human voice.[18]

1. What has been your experience with the relative use of voice mail and text messages in your personal and work life? What do you think are the benefits of each?

2. Do you think that voice mail obsolescence in work is inevitable? Why or why not?

3. Do you agree that young people under 25 are driving communication technology changes? If so, why do you think this is happening?

Some of the technologies you are likely to use at work are discussed as follows. Keep in mind that most of them have security concerns associated with them.

Concerns About Cybersecurity[19]

Concerns about cybersecurity are producing calls for increased efforts to secure and protect privately owned and government infrastructures from criminals, foreign intelligence agencies and militaries, and others. Both the chair and the ranking member of the U.S. House Subcommittee on Emerging Threats, Cybersecurity, Science, and Technology have pointed out that today's hackers are organized crime syndicates and national militaries that commit espionage. With increasingly sophisticated equipment, they are able to electronically infiltrate sensitive U.S. computer networks to obtain military technologies and steal trade secrets from American companies.

Voice Mail   In its simplest form, voice mail is a system that extends the cap-abilities of your telephone. While it offers more options than the traditional answering machine, it also does the job of an answering machine, receiving and storing incoming messages for you.

However, voice mail is also capable of responding to messages or transmit-ting the same message by telephone to different groups on the voice mail sys-tem. For example, you may want to give one or more coworkers some information but not necessarily talk with them. To do this, you would call the voicemail system (rather than the coworkers' telephones), log on with your number and password, record the message in your own voice, and tell the sys-tem to send the message to your coworkers by keying in their extensions or names. Your message immediately goes to your coworkers' voice mailboxes without their phones ringing. They know they have a message because their message-waiting light comes on.

You could also send the message to group lists of any size (preprogrammed names and numbers). Further, you could mark the message as private or urgent or request notification that the message has been accessed.

Voice over Internet Protocol (VOIP) or other technologies will allow you to forward messages on your computer system to another system. With this, you are using the Internet as the transmission medium for your phone calls. Your voice is converted into a digital signal that travels over the Internet. If you are calling a regular number, this signal is converted to a regular tele-phone signal on the other end for the persons you are calling.

Text-Based Messaging (Smart Phones, Instant Messaging, and Text Messaging)   You probably have first-hand experience with one or more of the following examples of smart phones: Apple's iPhone, Google's Android, Microsoft's Windows Mobile, Nokia's Symbian, and RIM's BlackBerry. Ways in which you and other businesspersons may be using them on the go include managing contacts and documents, searching the Internet, or locating physical locations.

Instant messaging is common in business today because of its speed and ease of use. Requiring only Internet access and software, it allows you to send and respond to brief written messages in real time. With a webcam, you may enhance your message to have sound and pictures.

With text messaging, you may use your cellular telephones or other integrated voice and data devices to send text messages rather than voice messages. This is helpful when talking is inconvenient, you want to send group messages, or other technologies are not available. For example, for many businesspersons and other individuals, this was the sole means of communication immediately after Hurricane Ike struck the Gulf Coast area.

E-mail   With its ease of use and speed, e-mail is the most frequently used form of electronic communication in business today. All you need is a computer, keyboard, and Internet service provider. Your message then appears in text rather than voice.

A frequent e-mail application is the quick transmittal of large or small attachments, such as reports, proposals, pictures, worksheets, and charts with your message. If your documents are not already available electronically, you can first scan them and then attach them to your e-mail message.

Technology CONNECTION

When the White House Press Office e-mailed President Obama's schedule to the media, its contents became a news item for an unexpected reason. Daily schedules to the media are routine. What was unusual about this one was that at the bottom it included a series of exchanges from the press team, as well as a draft of the schedule. Staffer comments shown in the e-mail demonstrated much collaboration of contents and included recommendations to emphasize certain factors and to delete an item.

The White House explained that a sleep-deprived staffer made the erroneous release of the draft schedule with comments.[20]

1. Why must the President's staff take extreme care when communicating electronically?

2. Should the President's staff be able to communicate privately without having to worry about outsiders reading what they're saying? Should the media members who received the draft have recognized it as a mistake and treated it confidentially? Why or why not?

3. Why do so many people have to collaborate over something as simple as the wording of a daily schedule? What factors should be taken into consideration when deciding on that wording?

4. What lessons can you draw about your own e-mails from this incident?

Fax   While e-mail use has outpaced faxes in today's business world, they are still helpful for quick transfer of document copies. They're especially useful when, for example, you need to send someone a letter with a signature on it.

Teleconference/Videoconference/Web Conference   To reduce travel costs and save time, your boss may ask you to participate in teleconferences, videoconferences, and web conferences in place of face-to-face meetings. In fact, in 2009, when President Obama's budget deleted the Department of Education's attaché to a United Nations agency in Paris, the president declared that the

United States could save this money and still participate using e-mail and teleconferencing.[21]

Teleconferences, videoconferences, and web conferences involve the live exchange of information among persons and machines remote from each other. They are linked through a telecommunications system, usually over a phone line and/or the Internet using technologies such as VOIP (discussed earlier). They may incorporate audio, video, and data services. Skype, Google Talk, Windows Live Messenger, and Yahoo Messenger are popular forms.

With these, you are able to communicate with people across town or across the world from your desk or home. With web conferencing, which requires no special software or hardware, you may share documents, make presentations, demonstrate products and services, and collaborate on projects using your computer and telephone.

In web conferences, you are able to communicate with people across town or across the world from the comfort of your desk or home.

Blend Images/Getty Images

Social Computing   "Twittering" (or "tweeting") via cell phones revolutionized political communication and fundraising during the Obama Presidential campaign and gained national visibility. Many people believe that social computing, such as Twitter, LinkedIn, and Facebook, will gain in use in business as ways of staying connected for professional reasons. According to MC Press Online, with more people using these networks, they will find ways to expand opportunities and benefits for their companies.[22]

Business Intelligence   As discussed further in the decision-making chapter, computer software can assist businesspersons in making business decisions and communicating information. For example, your employer may ask you to help obtain information to make difficult decisions in a tough economic climate. Using business intelligence software, you may develop a more accurate picture of the company's economic health by combining data from multiple sources into easy-to-interpret reports.

Technology CONNECTION

If you thought a camera was watching you as you view a kiosk screen, how would you feel or react? This is happening in marketing communication. Leaders in developing marketing technology describe the new possibilities as ways to reach targeted groups of people through smart ads. Cameras imbedded in an ad kiosk screen or hidden near it can track who looks and for how long, determine the viewer's gender, approximate age range, and, in some cases, ethnicity—and change the ads accordingly.

A video screen might show an ad for a man's product for a group of men at the kiosk and then switch to a woman's product when women walk up. The manufacturers say that nothing is ever stored and no identifying information is associated with the pictures. Critics fear erosion of privacy and use of this technology on consumers without their knowledge.[23]

1. How do you feel about this marketing strategy?
2. What do you see as its potential benefits? Potential problems?
3. Are you willing to give up some of your privacy in return for ads more in line with your interests? Why or why not? Under what conditions?

Speed and frequency made possible through today's technologies may mean that less thought goes into the tone and meaning of messages, leading to potential problems in human relations and communication. When using electronic communication, both the sender and the receiver are responsible for heading off miscommunication and ill will. The etiquette of using various technologies will be discussed in another chapter. However, consider these general suggestions:

Telephone—A Human Relations Tool   Whether you are the caller or the one being called, make your telephone a human relations tool for you. Remember that you are representing your company. During your phone conversations, vary your tone, loudness, and speed. Smile, as a smile can be heard over the phone. When leaving a telephone message, either with a person or through voice mail, make it clear, concise, correct, and courteous. Leave only the

> **KeyPoint**
> When using electronic communication, both the sender and the receiver are responsible for heading off miscommunication and ill will.

necessary information to keep your message brief. End calls gracefully, summarizing key points and thanking the other person, using a rising, upbeat tone of voice.

Consider recording a daily telephone and e-mail message to let others know whether you're in that day or not and when you might return phone calls or e-mails. Some offices require that this be done.

E-mail Considerations   E-mail may be quick and convenient, but be aware of situations when using the telephone or face-to-face communication would be more appropriate. Keep your messages brief. This will not only save your receivers' time, but will also increase the chances that they will read the entire message and respond to all questions you may have raised. All too often readers quickly respond to one question and overlook others, creating the need for additional communication. Accuracy and proofreading are important in all business-related communications, even e-mails and instant messages.

Your company may have standards for electronic file organization and file naming. If not, create an easy, straightforward system for yourself. This will simplify storing and retrieving your work, even months down the road.

Double check that your important e-mail messages have reached their intended recipients. Anti-spam and anti-virus filters and blocking mechanisms may derail them or discard your attachments.

Electronic Cautions   Because of the speed of communication technology, the temptation to respond quickly is high. However, one angry response on your part could cause you or your company to lose valuable clients, customers, or good will.

Remember that anything you send electronically could be broadly distributed or reach unintended recipients. Be especially careful with personnel data, patient records, student information, and financial information.

Also, think twice about the appropriateness of your personal information and photos you post in social networks. Prospective employers are beginning to use these postings to gain a more complete picture of who you are and how you might perform as an employee.

Further, be careful of your behavior around others—at work or otherwise. With the popularity of cameras in cell phones, many people have come to regret their actions.

Along the same line, if you are using your e-mail for professional reasons, be sure your e-mail address reflects your professionalism. Avoid cute or suggestive addresses.

Use communication technologies prudently and safely. Paying bills online while driving your car or a work-related vehicle can and has caused accidents, injuries, and deaths. Be aware of other persons and your situation when using your communication technologies. Reading messages on your BlackBerry while in a meeting can damage your image.

KeyPoint
Be cautious with technology. Think before responding, consider what you share or post, watch your behavior, use a professional e-mail address, and exercise safety.

Understand and respect the idea that everyone needs downtime. Being able to be connected at all times does not mean that we should be. A growing concern is that the widespread use of technology and information overload are making the United States less connected, creative, and productive and more stressed than ever.[24] Respect others' and your own time. Try for brief, accurate messages and only when they are needed.

Ask Yourself...

1. Name four forms of electronic communication that you use. What are the positive and negative aspects of each type of communication?

2. What are some techniques you have used to make your communication more effective?

3. What do you think will be the impact of future communication technology on human relations?

KEY TERMS

communication
message
sender
receiver
feedback
semantics
information overload

context
medium
active listening
spoken communication
5 Cs of communication
nonverbal communication

CHAPTER SUMMARY

Communication is the process by which we exchange information through a common system of symbols, signs, or behavior. This process sends messages from one person to another. Symbols can be written or spoken words. Signs can be shapes and colors. Behavior can be any nonverbal communication, such as body movements or facial expressions.

Listening, speaking, writing, and reading are the four basic skills used in communicating. Of these skills, listening and speaking are the most frequently used. Unfortunately, they are the two in which we receive the least training. However, any communication skill can be sharpened, through experience, training, or both.

Communication is important today because we live in an information society and we must interact with a variety of people. Communication can flow up, down, or horizontally in an organization. It can also be one-way or two-way. It includes three elements: the sender, the receiver, and the message. Feedback helps the receiver understand the message as the sender intended it.

Communication can be distorted or blocked because of barriers. Verbal communication can be a strong part of our human relations skills if we develop good listening skills and an ability to use the written and spoken word.

Nonverbal communication is any meaning conveyed through body language, the way the voice is used, and the way people position themselves in relation to others. It accounts for at least 93 percent of the impact of our communication.

Time, timing, context, medium, and humor contribute additional dimensions of meaning to messages and communicators.

Electronic forms of communication are emerging rapidly and continue to alter how we interact and work. Examples of these are voice mail, text-based messaging (smart phones, instant messaging, text messaging), e-mail, faxes, business intelligence, teleconference/videoconference/web conference), and social computing.

REVIEW

1. Define communication, its flow, and its role in human relations.

2. Describe common communication barriers and strategies for overcoming them.

3. What is information overload? What are some effective ways of avoiding it?

4. How can listening skills be improved?

5. What are some guidelines to make your verbal messages and presentations more effective?

6. Why is an understanding of nonverbal communication important in organizations? What are the different components of nonverbal communication?

7. Name four common forms of electronic communication and provide examples of their use by workers.

CRITICAL THINKING

1. Think of situations at work in which nonverbal communication can be used to enhance communication, both as a sender and as a receiver. Share these instances with your classmates.

2. Think of business-related communications that you have received through various technologies. Describe these to your classmates, along with your appraisal of the effectiveness of these communications. If you think they could have been improved, explain how.

3. Compare this hypothetical rough draft to how it reads in its final form:

   Rough draft: *"Things are just horrible, but I don't know what I should do. I have to decide if I can go on like this, and if I can't go on, should I end it all? I just don't know."*

   Final draft: Shakespeare, Hamlet, Act II, Scene 1, *"To be, or not to be, that is the question."*

   Now with your classmates think of other long statements you have heard or read and shorten them while still retaining their point and clarity.

4. Go online to locate and complete a communications quiz to assess your abilities and receive an in-depth analysis. After completion, consider what you have learned and how you will address any weak areas.

CASE STUDIES

In small groups, analyze the following situations.

1 **Mike's Missed Step**   Today was going to be a big day for Mike. He finally had a chance to show management that he had some good ideas about how the company could be improved. Because of a new policy allowing employees to submit written suggestions for changes to top management, he planned to send a memo to the president for consideration. Having worked in the stockroom for three years, he had seen the great amount of time wasted by pulling supplies on numerous orders and handing them to individual employees at the front window. He thought that if the departments obtained all supplies at the same time on one order, the company could save stockroom personnel time, speed up distribution of supplies, reduce paperwork, and lessen the need for overtime.

Knowing that his suggestion had to be received before the 9 a.m. management meeting, Mike hurriedly prepared an e-mail and sent it without proofing it or asking someone else to read it. After he sent it, he called the president's secretary to make sure she gave it to the president before the meeting. The e-mail the president received said, *"Want to save a lot of money? Have everyone come get their supplies at the same time and not waste so much of my time."*

Mike eagerly waited for some response to his recommendation. Finally, he received a brief written memo thanking him for his suggestion and stating that, after consideration, management had decided not to make a change. He later learned that management didn't consider his proposal because they didn't understand it. They thought he was recommending that everyone, including managers, go to the supply room at a certain time to retrieve whatever supplies they needed (rather than, as Mike intended, having one departmental staff member pick up supplies for all department members on one order).

Amazed, Mike said, "What? I told them what I thought would work. Why didn't they understand?"

1. What happened? Why didn't the managers understand what Mike was recommending?

2. How could he have handled this situation better?

3. Rewrite Mike's message so that it is complete, concise, correct, clear, and courteous.

2 **Jumping to Conclusions**   It was the morning of New Year's Eve at Gloria's Gourmet Goods. The employees were exhausted after putting in 12-hour days during the holidays. Sleet was beginning to fall outside, which caused Gloria, the store's owner, to be late arriving. As she entered the store, she noticed that it was extremely crowded. Shoppers nudged one another in the aisles, fighting over goodies and jockeying for positions in the checkout line. The telephones were ringing, and a cash register was malfunctioning.

Suddenly Gloria heard loud voices arguing. As she moved closer, she saw that the cheese clerk, Robert, and a customer had raised their voices and were waving their hands excitedly.

"Wait your turn!" Robert yelled at the customer. "That Robert," thought Gloria. "He's always causing trouble."

Gloria walked up to Robert and whispered in his ear, "You're fired. Leave." Robert looked up at Gloria in surprise and began to protest.

"I don't want to hear it," said Gloria, softly but firmly.

"Yeah?" responded Robert, as he stomped off. "And a happy new year to you, too." The customers around them looked confused.

A bit later, Charles, the assistant manager, came into Gloria's booth where she was filling out Robert's termination papers.

"You know, Gloria, Robert didn't start that. The woman yelled at him and demanded that he quit helping an elderly lady with two grandchildren. When he didn't, the younger lady came over and grabbed him by the arm and jerked him away. That's why Robert reacted as he did."

1. Identify all the communication barriers in this scenario.

2. How should Gloria have handled the situation?

3. What communication skills should Robert have used?

4. What about the customer?

5. What do you think the outcome would have been if they had used better communication skills?

HUMAN RELATIONS IN ACTION

1. When you search for information online, Microsoft retains data identifying your search (words and sites you searched and time and date) for 18 months, and Google and Yahoo keep it for nine months.[25,26]

   1. In small groups research collective intelligence online, including individual experiences with its collection and use.

   2. As a class, discuss how you feel about collective intelligence and identify two beneficial ways you think it might be used and two potentially harmful ways it might be used. Would you feel different if this information was maintained only from your online searches at work rather than at home also? Why or why not? Would you care if your supervisor knew what searches you make at work? Why or why not?

2. The technologies discussed in this chapter were in use in 2009. You are studying this chapter at a point beyond 2009, and new developments have no doubt been made in communication technologies.

    1. To update your knowledge, working in small groups, go online and research what new and emerging technologies may provide assistance to you and fellow workers during the next three to five years.

    2. As a class, discuss your findings and identify what potential impact these technologies may have on how you perform your work.

3. In the library or online, find three recent articles regarding the increasing use of communication technologies and suggestions for their effective use.

    - In a small group of two or three classmates, write and prepare a five-minute lesson based on your findings.

    - Follow these steps:

    1. Relate the articles to communication suggestions in this chapter.

    2. Follow the suggestions for improving written and verbal communication given in this chapter.

    3. Determine who will teach what information

    4. Deliver the presentation to your classmates.

    5. After the presentation, discuss verbal and nonverbal communication used during the presentation by both the speaker and the listeners, feedback you observed or heard during the presentation, and problems in listening you may have observed during the presentation.

For additional resources, refer to the web site for this text:
www.cengage.com/management/dalton

RESOURCES

1. Hof, R. D. (2007, August 20 & 27). Technology on the march. *BusinessWeek*, 80–83.

2. 24 things about to become extinct in America. (2009) *Care2*. [online]. Retrieved on February 2, 2009, from http://www.care2.com

3. Alsop, R. (2002, September 9). Playing well with others. *The Wall Street Journal*, R11.

4. Ortutay, B. (Associated Press). (2009, February 19). Facebook reverses course on policy of use change. *Houston Chronicle*, p. D3.

5. St. Louis Post-Dispatch. (2009, February 21). About Facebook: Hoisted on its own e-petard. *Houston Chronicle*, p. B6.

6. Zuckerberg, Mark. (2009, February 12). Update on terms. Facebook Blog. [online]. Retrieved October 29, 2009, from http://blog.facebook.com/blog.php?post=54746167130. Otherwise locate through web search using words "Facebook's terms of use."

7. Starr, A. (2008, September 4). Never settle: Secrets of an innovator—Apple CEO Steve Jobs exemplifies lifelong learning and creativity. *AARP.org.* [on-line]. Retrieved on May 2, 2009, from http://www.aarp.org/aarp/live_and_learn/Cover_Stories/articles/Never_Settle__Secrets_of_an_Innovator.html. Otherwise locate through web search using words "AARP article on Steve Jobs."

8. Philadelphia Inquirer. (2009, January 17). Steve Jobs: Apple's core visionary. *Houston Chronicle*, p. B6.

9. Schilling, Dianne. (nd). Be an effective listener! Women's Media. [online]. Retrieved October 29, 2009, from http://www.womensmedia.com/new/self-improvement-listening.stml. Otherwise locate through web search using words "how to listen."

10. *Ibid.*

11. Powell, J. (1969). *Why am I afraid to tell you who I am.* Chicago: Argus Communications.

12. Mintz, J. (Associated Press). (2009, February 24). Ex-workers at Microsoft told to keep the cash. *Houston Chronicle*, p. D3.

13. Hof, Technology on the march, 80–83.

14. Mehrabian, A., & Ferris, S. R. (1974). Inferences of attitudes from nonverbal communication in two channels. *Nonverbal Communication*. New York: Oxford University Press.

15. Houston area aerospace industry. (2005). Leadership Training Materials. From e-mails from Joint Leadership Team to Local Aerospace Industry.

16. How to deliver an effective presentation at work. E-HOW. [online]. Retrieved October 29, 2009, from http://www.ehow.com/how_5204199_deliver-effective-presentation-work.html.

17. Hof, Technology on the march, 80–83.

18. Colvin, J. (*New York Times* News Service). (2009, April 5). You've got voice mail, but do you care? *Houston Chronicle*, p. G6.

19. Langevin, J., & Michael M. (2008, December 21). U.S. must update laws on defending computers from foreign hackers. *Houston Chronicle*, p. E1.

20. Oops! Obama's press office has an e-mail snafu. (2009, April 9). *CNN Politics.com*. [online]. Retrieved on May 4, 2009, from http://www.cnn.com/2009/POLITICS/04/09/press.office.email/index.html. Otherwise locate through web search using words "Obama email snafu."

21. Education office in Paris dropped. (2009, May 9). *Houston Chronicle*, p. A2.

22. Exler, R. (2009, January 5). MC Press Online. The Top Ten Things to Watch Out for in Midrange Technologies in 2009. [online]. Retrieved on May 4, 2009, from http://www.mcpressonline.com/analysis/analysis-of-news-events/the-top-ten-things-to-watch-out-for-in-midrange-technologies-in-2009.html09. Otherwise locate through web search using words "MC Press Online top ten things to watch out for."

23. Ramde, D. (Associated Press). (2009, February 3). As you watch the screen, it may watch you back. *Houston Chronicle*, p. D3.

24. Parker, K. (The Washington Post Writers Group). (2009, April 2). Time for overstimulated Americans to take a break? *Houston Chronicle*, p. B11.

25. Markoff, J. (*New York Times*). (2008, November 30). You're leaving a digital trail—do you care? *Houston Chronicle*, p. D3.

26. How web searches can destroy your privacy. (2009, February 8) *Parade*, 8.

PART 2

FOCUSING ON OTHERS

"I suppose leadership at one time meant muscles; but today it means getting along with people."

—Mohandas Gandhi

5

ETHICS AT WORK:
YOUR ATTITUDE AND RESPONSIBILITIES

OBJECTIVES

After studying this chapter, you should be able to:

5.1 Define ethics.

5.2 Discuss ethical issues at work.

5.3 Describe how companies are addressing business ethics.

5.4 Discuss ways to manage yourself ethically at work.

5.5 Discuss ways to solve ethical dilemmas.

Jump Start

The Peanut Corporation of America (PCA) filed for Chapter 7 bankruptcy after closing its Georgia and Texas plants following what could be one of the Food and Drug Administration's (FDA) most high profile tainted food cases in U.S. history. The epidemic salmonella outbreak caused over 600 cases of illness and was linked to nine deaths across 44 states. Federal investigators claimed the company's executives shipped tainted food even after internal tests showed they were contaminated. One internal e-mail depicts a company driven by profits urging employees to ship out products with "Turn them loose" as the directive. The company sent peanut supplies to schools, nursing homes, and food processors primarily for use in cookies and snacks across the country.

Filing Chapter 7 allows the PCA to sell off its assets to pay any debts. The company's executives have refused to testify at Senate subcommittee hearings citing the Fifth Amendment right against self-incrimination on advice from their lawyers. Some legal experts have suggested the question is not whether significant charges will be brought, but what the charges will ultimately be.[1]

- How and why do you think the chief executive continued to get away with this kind of unethical behavior? Why do you think no one raised the issue of this being unethical?
- What would you have done if faced with this situation? What would you like to see happen as an outcome of this case?

5.1 KNOWING YOUR PERSONAL ETHICS

You are faced with decisions every day that require you to draw on your sense of right and wrong. You make choices based on a set of values instilled early in life. The process of choosing can be complicated by many factors, so you may find yourself facing difficult situations with questions not easily answered.

Ethics is a set of moral values separating right from wrong. For example, the West Point Cadets have a Cadet Honor Code that says, "A cadet will not lie, cheat, or steal or tolerate those who do."[2] This is a very clear statement of what they consider to be right or wrong. A violation of this Code is considered unethical behavior and may cause a cadet's immediate dismissal from the academy.

Ethics can be as important to you in the workplace. Most people and businesses operate in an ethical manner with all parties following the rules of sound business practices. However, when unethical behavior violates the law, you can usually expect legal consequences. Ethics are values we "ought" to follow, while laws are rules we must legally follow.

You will face ethical issues every day on your job, whether you are just beginning your career or are a senior-level manager about to retire. Making sound ethical choices early on will establish you as trustworthy and responsible. This will demonstrate your strong work ethic that may be of help in future job or project assignments. Your ethical behavior is important because it can significantly impact your success in life.

> **KeyPoint**
> Ethics is a set of moral values separating right from wrong.

Values are frequently linked with ethics but are actually a part of what collectively makes up your ethics. Values are principles, standards, or guidelines you consider desirable and important. They may include but are not limited to the following examples:

- Integrity
- Honesty
- Loyalty
- Trust
- Respect
- Dependability
- Punctuality
- Hard work
- Fairness
- Kindness
- Sincerity

These beliefs or qualities generally develop during your formative years and are heavily influenced by your family, friends, religion, and schools. Your values will determine how you will behave in certain situations. For example, were you to get your first job as a bank teller at the local bank, you'd want to be dependable, punctual, trustworthy, and honest to impress your employer and to begin your job résumé with favorable references.

Business ethics, on the other hand, are rules of conduct that apply to businesses and their employees. They are a way of putting many of your values into play in the business setting. However, while you may allow your decision making at work to be influenced by your boss, your team members, or coworkers, ultimately your decisions about your conduct rest with you. If you are true to your values, you realize that your decision making may affect others personally, reflects on you personally, and you will make the right decision based on your personal ethics.

You may remember from your youthful years rules such as "If you borrow Tommie's toy, take good care of it," or "Don't break your father's tools; they're too expensive to replace," and "Don't you take (or break) anything in this store; it doesn't belong to you." These same rules should have followed you into the workplace. They are now called business ethics. Taking good care of your office equipment, using the company's car for business purposes only, or not taking office supplies home from the supply cabinet are similar actions. How you treat each of these situations is important. These rules will guide you in caring about the company's assets and demonstrate your moral and ethical code. Ethical guidelines don't age or become obsolete.

Often in certain businesses or professions, you may experience conflict with your principles and ethics. Doctors may not be able to share information about a patient's illness that would be important to another family member's health or well-being. Criminal defense lawyers sometimes have to defend a client in court when they are in ethical conflict with the requirement. A corporate

> *We are the people our mothers warned us about.*
> —Jimmy Buffett, American songwriter

attorney may have to defend a client company that is dumping waste in bay waters knowing the environmental damage is wrong. Before entering a field, you may want to consider potential ethical conflict down the road.

Ethics has an overarching impact on organizational productivity and the human relations system identified in this text. It is closely related to life and career skills, self-direction, and accountability. Ethics play a strong role in your everyday decisions no matter whether they are personal or business related.

> **KeyPoint**
> Ethics has an overarching impact on organizational productivity and the human relations system identified in this text.

Ask Yourself...

1. What other values can you think of that make up part of your ethical standards? Which of these values are the strongest of your beliefs and why?

2. Name some other types of jobs or professions that you feel might present ethical dilemmas for you. How would you respond to a job offer from one of these companies, especially if the pay rate was above what you had expected?

5.2 UNDERSTANDING ETHICS AT WORK

Ethics is a complex issue in today's workplace. People may arrive on the job with different morals and values based on previous influencing factors in their lives. Some will be more easily influenced by the behavior of those around them, even if that behavior is unethical. It is important, therefore, that you set your own standards based on your personal beliefs and values, keeping in mind that you are developing and protecting your own reputation for which you will be held accountable.

Understanding Ethical Issues

Ethics is not only an individual issue but also an organizational one. The longer you spend in a workplace, the more you'll see how a company's ethics affect an organization's employees, its customers, and the public in general. You may be affected by issues with which you are unfamiliar. The following topics cover issues you may encounter in your workplace and give a brief description of their purpose.

> *Ethics is a code of values which guide or choices and actions and determine the purpose and course of our lives.*
>
> —*Ayn Rand, novelist and philosopher*

Code of Conduct   In the interest of the company and its employees, more than 80 percent of American companies have developed a *code of conduct* by which they expect all employees to abide. A code of conduct is a set of rules for required behaviors and responsibilities expected of a company and its employees or members of a group. British Petroleum (BP) has an extensive code of conduct for its employees largely because of the multinational nature of its business and past unethical encounters with communities. The chief executive states on the front of the current document, "The BP code of conduct summarizes our standards for the way we behave. All our employees must follow the code of conduct. It clearly defines what we expect of our business and our people, regardless of location and background. Ultimately, it is about helping BP people to do the right thing."[3] A code of conduct leaves no doubt about what is expected of employees.

Many organizations institutionalize ethical policies by adopting a code of ethics for members of the organization. This is especially true for professional groups including doctors, lawyers, purchasing agents, procurement professionals, nurses, real estate sales people, and corporate leaders. Figure 5.1 illustrates the code of ethics of a well-known professional organization, the National Management Association[4]. Employees can be dismissed, demoted, or reprimanded if they intentionally violate these codes. Codes may not actually change people's behaviors, but proponents argue that they do communicate to employees that the company is committed to its standards and is asking employees to adopt them. You should find out if your company or organization has a code of conduct or a code of ethics and become familiar with its rules.

Intellectual Properties   In today's environment, a company's most valuable asset may be its intellectual property (IP), and special steps are usually taken to protect it as if it were physical assets. *Intellectual property* is the knowledge or confidential business information an employee may have about that company. Examples might include protecting a prototype design of a new aerospace vehicle before it goes into production; keeping the names

Figure 5.1

The National Management Association's Code of Ethics.[4]

- I will recognize that all individuals inherently desire to practice their occupations to the best of their ability.
- I will assume that all individuals want to do their best.
- I will maintain a broad and balanced outlook and will recognize value in the ideas and opinions of others.
- I will be guided in all my activities by truth, accuracy, fair dealing, and good taste.
- I will keep informed on the latest developments in techniques, equipment, and processes. I will recommend or initiate methods to increase productivity and efficiency.
- I will support efforts to strengthen the management profession through training and education.
- I will help my associates reach personal and professional fulfillment.
- I will earn and carefully guard my reputation for good moral character and good citizenship.
- I will promote the principles of our American Enterprise System to others by highlighting its accomplishments and displaying confidence in its future.
- I will recognize that leadership is a call to service.

SOURCE: The National Management Association
Reprinted by permission of the National Management Association

of a client list for a prominent plastic surgeon from his competitors; making certain a new invention is safely guarded until the patent lawyers can register the item; or assuring that the financial records of your company aren't given to your competitor. Be aware of your company's policies regarding IPs and how they may affect you in your work environment.

Non-Disclosure Agreements (NDAs)   These are sometimes called confidentiality agreements. *Non-disclosure agreements* are legal contracts between you and the company that forbid you from disclosing certain information defined in the document. Such agreements allow companies to hire individuals, expose them to sensitive data on projects, and then feel comfortable that their IPs will be safe and not passed on to unauthorized persons when that employee leaves. Be careful not to violate an NDA should you work in one of these situations because of the legal implications.

Trade Secrets   *Trade secrets* are certain types of confidential business information that are protected by law under the Uniform Trade Secrets Act (UTSA).[5] Most states have adopted the use of UTSA in their corporate proceedings. Similar to intellectual property, a trade secret is anything valuable or secret enough to give another business a competitive advantage. Examples include designs, recipes, or business plans for a new start up. Trade secrets are very sensitive areas for companies. Many young entrepreneurs today guard their company start-up plans and operations and expect employee loyalty. Divulging trade secrets is a legal and ethical issue and is punishable under the UTSA.

Additional items are currently causing ethical concerns that are worth mentioning in this section. Again, this information is provided to give you an awareness of the issues involved and how they may affect you in the workplace.

Internet and Cell Phone Use While at Work   Your company may already have policies or codes on Internet and cell phone use while at work. Roughly 40 percent of employers have established rules governing these activities to curb the loss of time and waste of activity. According to a recent survey done by the American Management Association[6] (AMA), 65 percent of companies block certain web sites with commercial software, and three quarters of all companies surveyed are monitoring employee web site activity, often retaining and reviewing e-mail messages. Some companies do allow reasonable amounts of time for Internet use to conduct personal business while at work. Be prudent with your use of the Internet, visiting only those sites you think are appropriate while on company time.

Cell phones create mixed problems for employees and the company. They are no longer used simply to make phone calls. Some companies issue phones to their employees and then are able to track their whereabouts via GPS tracking systems.[7] Some employers ban the use of cell phones while on their property. One big issue is employees sending text messages at inappropriate times. Recently an employee at the National Aeronautics and Space Administration (NASA) was fired for texting during a meeting meant as orientation for new hires and answering text messages while engaged in office conversation with coworkers about job responsibilities. Ironically, the meeting content was covering company procedures and policies.[8] Applying common sense to the use of your cell phone and being courteous to others at all times when using your cell phone are the best means of making a good impression while at work.

Social Networking Follow the same rules as Internet use while at work: limit the use and do only at appropriate times. The larger problems here are the use the companies are making of these networks. Often a company will check a potential employee's account to validate or verify application information prior to employment. Sometimes the personal or social account information has not been exactly the professional "best foot forward," and in some cases the employee has actually lost the job opportunity. For example, two employees were recently fired from their jobs when a supervisor overheard their off duty online network discussion about their dislike of that supervisor and the job.[9] On the other hand, these same networks are beneficial to companies in many ways. Corporate networking forums bring employees together and can quickly "buzz" internal information. This is an

Ethics CONNECTION

A news release from Reuters[10] reported that a Swiss insurance worker was fired after being caught posting on Facebook when she should have been at work. The worker called in sick claiming she had a migraine headache that would require her to lie still in the dark. She would, therefore, be unable to sit in front of her computer and do her job. The problem arose when the employer discovered she was active on Facebook that same day.

Nationale Suisse, her employer, cited "abuse of trust" as the reason for her dismissal, rather than the activity on Facebook. The company felt that if she was well enough to be active on Facebook, she could have been active at work.

Facebook and similar applications are raising ethical concerns in the workplace and have been involved in workplace controversy on several occasions. Some companies have completely banned their use, and in other situations employees have been fired over comments they make about work-related matters while online.

1. How do you feel about the Nationale Suisse worker being fired? How do you think you might have handled this dilemma if you had been her supervisor? Do you think it is ethically appropriate for employers to check social networks to see what employees do during non-work hours? Why or why not?

2. Do you agree or disagree with employers prohibiting social networks in the workplace? Why or why not? How do you feel about employees losing their jobs over comments made after hours?

area that is still developing and may see many changes before specific "rules" can be established. Caution with these activities should be your approach at present.

Be aware of how you may be involved in these activities and the effects they may have on you. Your behavior and attitude should reflect positively on the company as well as on yourself.

The company must share the responsibility with you for upholding its ethical standards and social responsibility within the community. You can feel good about the company, what it does, and what you do for it. Such actions become a winning situation for you, the organization, customers, and the public in general.

Seeing Our Ethical Future

The Josephson Institute is a nationally known organization that promotes ethical behavior in industry, education, sportsmanship, and other fields of human behavior. One of the contributions the institute makes is performing reputable surveys spanning multiple years, collecting data for comparisons and trend analyses for anticipated or expected behaviors in the workforce of the future. The following information sheds some light on its most recent activities and concerns.

Michael Josephson, head of the Josephson Institute of Ethics, recently commented, "One only has to watch the very popular reality TV shows *The Apprentice, Survivor,* and *The House* (*Big Brother* in America) to realize that those who win deceive the others without getting caught. It is a cunning game of false alliances, cheating, and ruthless behaviors to win. No one seems offended by the activities; indeed, most of these shows are now in multi-year seasons. This speaks loudly of our nation's moral and ethical dilemma."[11] Josephson believes the lessons being learned by today's youth, who are watching these shows, will help shape the values that will carry directly into the workforce of the near future. The ideas of cheating and ruthless behavior to win, depicted in the reality shows, are the wrong values to instill or condone, no matter the age.

Josephson tries to keep a finger on America's ethical pulse. His institute frequently runs surveys on thousands of high school students to assess the habits of dishonesty in the workforce of the future. His latest press release to *The New York Times* read, "Josephson Institute's Report Card on American Youth: There's a Hole in Our Moral Ozone and It's Getting Bigger." *The New York Times*[12] reported that the nearly 30,000 students surveyed revealed entrenched habits of dishonesty. "They lie, cheat, and steal and they are doing it more and more often."

What's worse is that 93 percent reported they were satisfied with their personal ethics and character. Seventy-seven percent said, "When it comes to doing what is right, I am better than most people I know." This survey data addresses honesty and integrity as it translates to the workforce of the future. This group of students will be the next group of workers bringing this set of

> *We are made wise not by the recollection of our past, but by the responsibility for our future.*
>
> —*George Bernard Shaw, poet and author*

Ethics CONNECTION

An article in *Business Week*[13] described Dove's "Campaign for Real Beauty" ads as being fake when it paraded larger ladies with images described as "real women" before the American public. Dove was denouncing pencil-thin, airbrushed, unrealistic fashion models, berating the damage done to the developing self-images of young women. It was learned later that Dove's photos with love handles and visible cellulite might have been digitally enhanced for the fashion spread. One of the leading photo specialists for *Vogue* and Dior said after working on this campaign, "Do you have any idea how much retouching was done on that ad? It was a challenge to keep everyone's face showing the mileage but not looking unattractive." This news came only after Dove ran the ad.

The ad agency ran the video on YouTube calling it "Dove Evolution." The video revealed time-lapse photography of a thin model showing her first arriving for a photo shoot with a blemished, unmade face and ending in a billboard glamour shot. Amazing changes were made to her hair, makeup, and the shape of her face by editing the photo heavily. Dove's ad line was, "No wonder our perception of beauty is distorted. Take part in the Dove Campaign for Real Beauty." The final shot was of the "real women" again, in contrast to the thin model.

1. Do you feel this ad is socially acceptable? Why or why not?
2. Why would some people consider the ad unethical and why do you agree or disagree?

values and ethical behavior into the workplace to be trained and supervised and to eventually run our businesses.

Authors Kenneth Blanchard and Norman Vincent Peale provide a simple four-step approach to resolving ethical dilemmas. In their book *The Power of Ethical Management*, they offer the following questions to be used in an ethics check of behavior:[14]

1. Is it legal? Will you be violating any laws or company policies?
2. Is it balanced? Will your decision be fair to all parties concerned, and will it promote a win-win situation?
3. How will your decision make you feel about yourself? Will you be proud of your choice?
4. Would you feel good if your family were to read about your decision in the local newspaper?

Blanchard and Peale think that ethical behavior is strongly related to self-esteem and that people who feel good about themselves are better able to make ethical decisions and withstand the pressures against those choices.

Ask Yourself...

1. Think of recent stories in the news where problems resulted from unethical decisions. Discuss ways these situations may have been avoided and the ethical dilemmas the people in these problematic situations are now facing.

2. Do you think the American culture has experienced a change in ethical standards in the past few years? If so, how do you think the trend began and what were its most significant influencing factors?

5.3   ADDRESSING BUSINESS ETHICS

Today, corporations are concerned with trying to do the right thing. There are legal influences in place to help protect missteps that have plagued corporations. Daily headlines describe situations that raise ethical questions. In some cases, laws may have been broken, and in other situations organizations or individuals have not been socially responsible in some way.

Social Responsibility

> **KeyPoint**
> The classical, accountability, and public perspectives explain how society views levels of social responsibility and degrees of involvement by corporations in environmental issues.

One of the more prominent concerns in business and industry is *social responsibility*, the obligation we have to make choices or decisions that are beneficial to the whole of society. Both the Generations X and Y workforce and the general public have a genuine interest in what corporations are doing today to protect the environment and other social issues affecting their communities. Of considerable importance today is *corporate social responsibility*, the idea that corporations have an ethical obligation beyond their economic, profit-driven purpose to stockholders and owners. This is a broader concept and includes not being able to hide under contracts or laws to protect them. It is mutually beneficial to the corporation and the community to establish these working relationships to solve a wide range of problems from medical experiments, air pollution, poverty, environmental cleanups to many others. Toyota's WhyNot.com web site gives detailed descriptions of the company's areas of interest in the environment and its communities and shows its deep commitment to corporate social responsibility.[15]

In his article "The Paradox of Business as Do Gooders," Joe Nocera states, "The degree to which a company is considered successful may well depend on how ethically they conduct their business or how socially responsible to

> *We have a Bill of Rights. What we need is a Bill of Responsibilities.*
> —*Bill Maher, TV commentator*

Social responsibility is the obligation to make choices or decisions that are mutually beneficial to the whole of society.

Photodisc/Getty Images

the environment they may have become."[16] Corporate social responsibility may be viewed from one of three perspectives: classical, accountability, and public.

The *classical perspective* holds that businesses need not feel responsible for social issues and should concentrate on being profitable, as an economy based on strong businesses best serves society overall. This view suggests that profit is the bottom line and that ethics has a lesser role in the situation.

The *accountability perspective* holds businesses accountable for their actions, with a responsibility to be fair and considerate in their business practices. This view requires sensitivity to environmental and social issues and prevents unethical decisions in such matters as toxic waste disposal and discrimination against minorities, women, older employees, or workers with disabilities.

The *public perspective* links businesses with the government and other groups to solve social and environmental problems actively. This view requires involvement by all parties in improving the general quality of life. Decisions are made with the goal of profit for the business but also with consideration of impact on pollution or unemployment. Starbucks is a successful model of this perspective. Its web site shows the variety of its programs.[17]

From any of these perspectives, ethics plays a role in decision making to some degree. Should a company pollute the air or water because control devices are expensive to install and would reduce profits? Should the company install expensive pollution-control devices that may reduce the budget and cause employee layoffs, affecting local unemployment problems? Considering these questions makes more obvious the relationships of values, integrity, and ethics at play.

KeyPoint

Many companies are addressing business ethics by developing sophisticated written standards guiding their ethical obligations and corporate responsibility.

In The News

TerraChoice, North America's premier environmental marketing firm, recently sent researchers into a large retail store to validate the green advertising claims of over one thousand products. The group was surprised when only one product passed the criteria for a legitimate eco-friendly product. Some "non-toxic" products were in fact toxic, and some boasting "energy certification" had no certificates. The findings were so disappointing that the group decided to rerun the research on a new batch of products to rule out any human errors made in the first evaluation process. The results were the same.

TerraChoice reported a practice known as "greenwashing," where the environmental benefits of a product are intentionally misleading to the consumer. The sales of organic and eco-friendly products recently exceeded $20 billion in the United States and are expected to increase steadily with little to no Federal Trade Commission controls on the advertising of the products. A Green Guide for consumers is being developed that will help define green in advertising much the way "low fat" and "low calorie" are now understood. But for now, Scot Case, the president of TerraChoice, says that by buying these products to support a greener industry, you may only lose the green in your wallet.[18]

1. Can you think of any product manufacturer guilty of greenwashing? List and discuss a few of the different product varieties you have chosen. Why have you chosen these products, and how could the manufacturers improve their message to the consumer?

2. Why do you think the public continues to buy damaging products and do you think customers will continue to do so without some requirement for change?

Many companies are addressing business ethics by developing sophisticated written standards guiding their ethical obligations and corporate social responsibility. The American Society for Quality is leading international efforts to standardize methods in recycling initiatives, energy management, green cleaning, and fresh water initiatives. Ben & Jerry's cofounder, Jerry Greenfield,[19] is proud of his ice cream company's deep commitment to social responsibility. In a recent Internet podcast interview, he said that "customers today expect you to be environmentally responsible and they don't mind asking you right out what you are doing about it. Social responsibility and quality are very closely related and we strongly believe in both."

Legal Influences on Ethics

Relying on our value system to guide us in our decision making will most often result in ethically sound judgments. We may, however, experience conflicts with this method when we operate in an environment that does not share similar values. Operating in certain other ethnic cultures, for example, may create difficulties. What may be considered unethical in one culture may be perfectly acceptable in another. In some cultures, for example, expectations are that government officials will be given "gratuities" for services rendered. In the United States, this is considered not only unethical but also illegal.

The *Foreign Corrupt Policy Act* of 1977 was passed to guard against such conflicts. This law requires U.S. companies to operate ethically in their worldwide business dealings, and the U.S. Justice Department polices activities of U.S. companies overseas to prevent unethical actions. Specifically, the act makes it illegal for a U.S. citizen and certain foreign issuers of securities to make a corrupt payment to a foreign official for the purpose of obtaining business with, or directing business to, any person. The provisions also apply to foreign firms and persons who take any form of a corrupt payment while in the United States.

Several laws have been enacted to assist companies in determining accepted principles of right and wrong. The U.S. Sentencing Commission Guidelines for Organizations[20] was established to hold companies responsible for unethical behavior resulting from employee activities, whether the management was aware of the activity or not. An amendment was added in 2004 to strengthen ethics training and boost ethical environments in all areas of concern. According to an article in *HR Magazine,* "All businesses are subject to these guidelines and the guidelines provide incentives to comply, cooperate, and

> *Always Do Right! This will gratify some people, and astonish the rest.*
>
> —*Mark Twain, American author*

Global CONNECTION

According to a *Business Week*[21] article, IBM and Boeing both announced plans to bring some of their outsourcing back home. In fact, IBM recently opened two new global service delivery centers in Michigan and Iowa.

After looking at 72 countries, an IT research firm selected China as the next best location for outsourcing. But IBM and Boeing both agree low cost is not the only decision factor. Access to good skills in the local area and the cooperation of a local university willing to adjust its curricula helped influence the choice as well. The school would work with businesses to develop and include course requirements helpful to the developing job skills market.

1. What skills do companies need to return outsourced IT jobs back to the United States? What do you think is being done to prepare employees for skills companies seek? Is this effort succeeding?

2. Do you think this gives any unfair advantage to college towns? Why or why not? Which of the responsibility perspectives is influencing this action? Discuss the variety of groups and individuals that stand to benefit from this action. What ethical outcomes will be most beneficial to all groups involved?

disclose illegal activities to authorities."[22] Fines for noncompliance can be heavy. The fines may be greatly reduced if a company has compliance programs in place before the illegal activity occurs and is reported. A complex formula determines the amount of the fine, which can range from $500 to nearly $3 million.

The recent results of a National Business Ethics Survey done by the Ethics Resources Center (ERC)[23] provide an inside look at corporate ethics in America. The ERC surveyed nearly 4,000 employees to benchmark current beliefs and behaviors within organizations. Overall, misconduct in organizations is very high with more than one half of the employees seeing, but not necessarily reporting, unethical behavior. Many employees won't report wrongdoings because they fear retaliation or because they feel it won't be taken seriously and acted upon.

Only 9 percent of the companies surveyed had strong ethical cultures established with solid ethical programs and reporting systems available at their facilities. The major indications were that establishing and maintaining a strong ethical culture happens only when the top management leaders embed strong ethics as a part of the company's core values and personally demonstrate their importance in company operations.

This same attitude about ethics must pass down the chain of command through the first line supervisor to direct reports at all levels. Some companies involve all employees in the development of their code of ethics and make it a living document with any revisions communicated throughout the

Global CONNECTION

Former Wal-Mart CEO Lee Scott pledged to build serious corporate social responsibilities and strengthen ethical values globally. While addressing a group of over 1,000 Chinese suppliers at a meeting in Beijing, China, he was asked if social and environmental responsibility should still be a top priority with all that's going on in the global economy. Scott replied, "You're darn right social responsibility should be a priority, more now than ever before."

Some might be skeptical when hearing this statement from Wal-Mart, which has suffered smudges on its reputation in certain ethical areas. However, Scott firmly stated a new corporate pledge in hopes that thousands of other companies will take it seriously and follow with similar programs. He told the suppliers, "Companies who cheat through toxic waste dumping, cheat on the age of its employees, don't pay their taxes, don't honor their contracts or cheat on overtime charges will ultimately cheat on the quality of their products."[24]

1. How do you think Wal-Mart will address these issues with stores and help implement new programs aimed at assuring compliance?

2. Why do you think Scott made this position very clear to the Chinese delegation and what effect do you think it will have, if any?

robynmac/iStockphoto.com

organization. The codes are incorporated into performance appraisals and used as performance incentives when possible.

Even the most detailed, well-constructed ethics program will not be successful without commitment, communication, and mutual trust with the tone set by top management. The keys are the CEO, a board with independent members, a system of checks and balances on management in place throughout the company, and a mechanism to allow complaints to surface. A strong code of ethics, written rules, and corporate procedures are important, but without strong commitment and enforcement from senior management, they are merely words on paper. Communicating expectations through continuous training programs for all employees may serve to build the mutual trust required in an effective ethics program.

Publicly traded companies must comply with federal regulations. In 2002, Congress enacted an important business reform act. *The Sarbanes-Oxley Act*[25] is a set of complex regulations that protects investors and enforces corporate accountability and responsibility by requiring accuracy and reliability of corporate accounting and disclosures. Also known as the Corporate and Criminal Fraud Accountability Act of 2002, the bill was passed quickly as a response to increased corporate fraud, accounting scandals, and record-breaking bankruptcies. The act grants the Securities and Exchange Commission increased regulatory control and imposes greater criminal and compensatory punishment on executives and companies that do not comply. It also establishes procedures for handling whistleblower complaints.

A *whistleblower* is a person who identifies organizational wrongdoing or illegal practices to officials who have the authority to enforce appropriate actions on any inappropriate behavior. The Sarbanes-Oxley Act made it a crime for a corporation to retaliate against a whistleblower, and

In The News

Business ethics aren't the same everywhere! Warren Osburne, CEO of Seastone LC, has worked with thousands of companies during his 20 years of experience in China and has encountered some interesting interfaces with international associates. He will tell you it depends on where you are and with whom you're dealing. He has encountered some of his Asian counterparts violating his company's code of ethics and the Foreign Corrupt Practice Act without ever knowing what happened to create the problem. It's not at all unusual to receive an offer of a substantial bribe, sometimes called "facilitation payments" to help clearing goods through customs or processing government paperwork. Osburne makes certain that all partners and associates know that Seastone won't tolerate that kind of behavior. By screening potential suppliers and establishing his ethical rules, he minimizes the potential for ethical conflict.[26]

1. What do you think Osburne is looking for when he screens his potential clients list and does interviews? Do you think Osburne has developed his own code of ethics? What do you think might be some of the steps?

2. How do you think the Asian associates feel about all the laws and codes in our Western culture's way of doing business? How would you feel if you encountered similar ethical issues with your business associates?

managers found guilty can go to prison for up to ten years. Additionally, the company might incur substantial monetary fines.

With the rise of unethical practices in recent years, we are left wondering whether we are living in a mindless, valueless society on a path of destruction or whether we are simply overexposed to excessive media coverage of unethical behavior and corporate greed. In either case, individuals and organizations now have a greater obligation to improve current ethical practices.

Ask Yourself...

1. If you had a start-up company anxious to get into multinational markets, how would you go about learning and then introducing all the laws that affect those operations to your new clients?

2. Do you feel your personal ethics have become more relaxed or more rigid? Discuss the reasons why.

3. In what areas do you think companies can or should offer ethical guidance to their employees? Would you accept and use this type of help? Why or why not?

5.4 MANAGING YOURSELF ETHICALLY AT WORK

Behaving ethically and responsibly enhances your life, makes human interactions less stressful, and boosts self-esteem. Additionally, understanding ethics can make or break your career. Anyone working today needs to take the following measures:

- *Learn about and respect the value systems of others.* Remember that others grew up in different circumstances and may have developed a different set of values. Aim to respect those values.

- *Learn about the ethics and the norms of your place of business.* If your business has a written ethics policy or set of guidelines, be sure you are familiar with it. If there is no written code, then ask questions to determine how management views certain behavior. For instance, before giving a gift to a supervisor, inquire of others around you if this is an accepted practice.

Technology CONNECTION

The Wall Street Journal [27] reported that while the use of cameras in law enforcement to catch speeders and other law offenders is spreading, so is anger towards lawmakers. When cameras in Schaumberg, IL, collected nearly $1 million in fines in only three months, townspeople were outraged. The tickets were issued for failing to come to a complete stop before turning right at a red light. The right turn led into the town's primary shopping center. Many vowed to stop shopping at the mall unless the cameras were turned off. Right-hand turns at that intersection are no longer monitored.

In Britton, CT, an infrared camera, "Plate Hunter," is mounted on police cars. The camera automatically reads license plates for delinquent parking ticket violations. Police can impound the car and add another fine. The township collected more than $2.8 million in less than three months. Soon after, an Arizona State Trooper arrested a man while he was attacking a camera with a pickaxe. A few months later, cameras recorded four men dressed as Santa Claus placing wrapped presents over the cameras to block their views. People across America are finding ways to counteract what they feel is an unethical and unregulated means of gathering monies for public funds.

1. How do you feel about the use of these cameras? Have you seen them in locations around where you live or work? What has been the reaction by others you know?

2. Do you think using these cameras is ethically fair to the town population? Do you think they will become a permanent part of our law enforcement process?

- *When confronted with something that feels uncomfortable, take time to think.* Use some of the techniques suggested in this chapter in order to sort out how you wish to handle the situation. Make a list of your options and the pros and cons of the consequences before you decide what to do.

Trustworthiness is a core value and important in setting our ethical standards. In a recent Zogby International[28] poll of more than 8,000 adults, 97 percent described themselves as trustworthy. However, only 75 percent of that group considered the people they live and work with as trustworthy. Being trustworthy may play a role in your future success efforts—whether you are chosen for certain positions or given certain assignments that may lead to promotions. It is important to maintain this as part of your personal ethical standards and disregard temptations that may come along.

You will find that employees vary in their perceptions of situations and may not always see things the same way. We are reminded from our understanding of emotional intelligence, discussed earlier in Chapter 2, that what may seem ideal to you may not seem so to others. We should always be aware of the many ways we influence the behavior of those around us.

Ask Yourself...

1. When faced with a situation where your perception vastly differs from the other person on what really happened, how would you resolve the situation?

2. How would you think understanding ethics might affect your career? Why would you think behaving ethically would boost your self-esteem?

5.5 SOLVING ETHICAL DILEMMAS

Ethical dilemmas arise when our sense of values or social responsibility is questioned internally or challenged externally. Figure 5.2 on page 148 provides some possible unethical behaviors in personal and business settings. How to handle most of these is likely covered in a company's code of conduct, office procedures manual, or government law regulation. You are responsible for knowing how these affect you in your work setting and what to do to reach a quick resolution, if possible. Know what steps to take.

The following scenarios offer you some examples of ethical dilemmas that others have found themselves facing. They are meant to help you think about your behavior if you are ever faced with a similar situation.

- Your first job is with a marketing firm and you're excited about getting your first large account. You're handed an account for a well-known alcoholic beverage very popular with young people. You don't drink and have some very strong personal feelings against alcohol. You are very uncomfortable promoting this product but are tempted to stay with

Figure 5.2

Examples of unethical behaviors.

Personal	Business
Cheating on exams/tests	Intimidating or abusive behavior
Accepting credit for work/favors not performed	Accepting gifts from subordinates and vendors
Falsifying employment application information	Falsifying time/expense reports
Betraying personal confidences	Keeping unauthorized materials/monies
Plagiarizing papers and projects, borrowing content	Doing personal business on company time
Pirating software	Violating safety regulations
Making unauthorized copies of corporate information/records	Polluting the environment
Being involved in office gossip	

the account to appease your new boss. This presents you with an ethical business dilemma. The right thing to do would be to request a different account assignment and openly and honestly discuss the reasons for your request. Your honesty and candor about the subject will uphold your ethical standards, and you will be able to feel good about yourself. The company should appreciate your honesty and respect your request for a different account if at all possible. It becomes a winning situation for you, the organization, and the account customer.

- Your best friend called Sunday and asked you to go to church with her. You politely declined, saying you had to go to the library to work on a project due on Monday. Your friend was disappointed but understood. You went back to bed, then spent the rest of the day in front of the TV watching your favorite ball team in an important game. What's the moral dilemma and how would you solve it?

- You are at a restaurant celebrating your dad's 50th birthday. When the bill comes, you pick up the tab and go to pay the bill. You notice the waiter has not applied the tax to the already large amount and is ready to check you out. You are tempted to ignore the error, thinking that the restaurant will never miss it. What will you do?

- You're responsible for the government credit card issued in the agency's name to you for buying office supplies and certain other items allowable with your limited budget. The items are clearly defined and records are kept on what is purchased on your card. You are running late to go home one evening, need gas, and realize you have no money and your bank is closed. You could put the gasoline purchase on your government card and your agency would never know the gas charge wasn't for one of the government cars used by the field auditors from the office. How would you handle this?

At the heart of ethical dilemmas is not whether you know what is right or wrong, but whether you will choose the right behavior.

The Ethics Resources Center (ERC) is an organization that offers decision-making tools and training covering many business topics, a newsletter, and other business-related ethical guides. They offer the following guidelines for making good decisions.

1. Define the standards. Inquire about company standards, the code of ethics, or accepted norms and how they relate to this request.

2. Perform risk assessment. What degree of risk is involved with an action? What may be the consequences of your decision?

3. Make the decision. Be willing to take responsibility for your actions. Proceed with caution.

4. Re-evaluate the situation. If there is still some discomfort with the decision you made, seek help from a trusted resource. Approach with caution but clarity about what you want to do next or solicit their suggestions.

5. Check your moral compass. You may be in the wrong job, department, or working for the wrong supervisor and may choose to make a move to an area more in line with your ethical standards or work preferences.

Ethics is a complex subject that should be taken seriously in today's work environment. Knowing and understanding this subject will help you manage a successful career.

KeyPoint
At the heart of ethical dilemmas is not whether you know what is right or wrong, but whether you will choose the right behavior.

Ask Yourself...

1. When faced with a situation where your perception vastly differs from the other persons involved, how would you resolve the dilemma to the satisfaction of both of you?

2. Think of a significant question that has been bothering you and that you have been unable to fully resolve. Relate it to the questions listed on page 138. Do these help you come to a resolution? Discuss your findings and share how you arrived at the resolution.

KEY TERMS

ethics
values
business ethics
code of conduct
intellectual properties
non-disclosure agreement
trade secret
social responsibility

corporate social responsibility
classical perspective
accountability perspective
public perspective
Foreign Corrupt Policy Act
Sarbanes-Oxley Act
whistleblower
ethical dilemma

CHAPTER SUMMARY

Ethics is a set of moral values separating right from wrong. Business ethics are rules of conduct that apply to business and their employees. Personal ethics involve decisions outside work, whereas business ethics apply to work-related decisions.

Codes of conduct define the intent of the corporation. Intellectual properties, non-disclosure agreements, and trade secrets are important terms to know when dealing with ethical issues.

Knowing how to handle Internet access, cell phone usage, and social networking in the workplace is important.

Many companies have put tremendous effort towards social responsibility—protecting the environment and volunteering in the communities. Whole communities and industries come together to work out issues and engage in programs to benefit people and the environment.

Corporate social responsibility can be viewed from three perspectives—classical, accountability, and public. To improve business practices at publicly traded companies, the U.S. government passed several laws to uphold ethical business practices. The Sarbanes-Oxley Act protects whistleblowers from retaliation and safeguards financial and accounting practices.

Dilemmas involve making decisions on issues that question our value system. Several steps guide ethical decision-making: validate the situation, assess the risk, decide, get help as needed, and if necessary, change positions.

In order to deal more effectively with ethical issues, you need to know yourself and your values, know and respect the values of others, be aware of your company's code of ethics, and explore situations before acting.

REVIEW

1. Explain the differences among ethics, values, and social responsibility.

2. What are some of the methods used in determining ethical standards?

3. What is meant by ethical dilemmas?

4. What methods can you use in dealing with ethical dilemmas?

5. What steps are companies and the federal government taking to improve the standards of ethics within companies?

CRITICAL THINKING

1. Think of at least three events that recently appeared in the news that you think have had a profound effect on ethics in business. Why did you pick these three events and what will the effects be?

2. Review the lists in Figure 5.2, "Unethical Behaviors." Which of the behaviors in the chart have you witnessed? Do you feel you responded in the most ethical manner? Would you respond differently today?

3. If you work, does your company have a code of ethics or some other form of ethics program? If you don't work, find one from another company. Discuss that program and its effectiveness.

4. You are a supervisor in the Last Chance Corporation. You have been in talks with the management of your company and know that a large layoff is about to take place. You are aware that one of your employees is about to close on the purchase of a new house. Shortly after the close, he will be laid off. You have been told that everything is strictly confidential and you are not to tell anyone about the layoff. Should you warn your employee about the coming layoff? What is the ethical thing to do, and why?

5. You and your best friend work at a fast food restaurant. Your friend has been giving free meals to his girlfriend who comes into the restaurant. Your friend feels that he doesn't get paid enough for what he does, and, since the company is so big, the meals will never be missed. Your friend is off today and you are behind the counter when the girlfriend comes in. She expects you to give her a free meal. What are your options? What should you do?

CASE STUDIES

In small groups, analyze the following situations:

1 **All Money Is Green** Guy Walters is the chief executive officer of a major engineering firm. He has been appointed committee chair for the High Speed Transportation System (HSTS). This group is expected to develop a viable method of transporting mass quantities of products safely and quickly to major distribution points around the world. Funding for this project has come from many companies interested in rapidly moving their products into global marketplaces. Guy feels strongly about making a success of this project and believes that it will greatly benefit the transportation industry, his company, and his personal career.

In a meeting with Glenda, his chief financial officer, Guy discovers that his budget is too limited to complete the project. Glenda explains that they are confined by the company's accounting policies to using the HSTS's funds and that getting approval for additional funding will be difficult. "We will have to bring the matter before the executive board and request additional funds before we can go on," Glenda told him.

Guy was frustrated. "You know how they feel about budget overruns. Why can't we just divert some of the leftover funds from other study programs to wrap this up? What's the big deal anyway? All money is green! We are all working toward the same end—profits for the company. We're so near completion on this job that I don't want to slow progress by begging for dollars. Do some of that 'creative accounting' for which you budget people are so famous. They'll never know the difference."

1. What is the ethical issue in this situation?

2. What does Guy mean by "All money is green"? Is he correct?

3. How should Glenda respond to Guy's request?

4. How would you resolve the ethical dilemma Glenda faces?

2 **Anxious Alan** Alan was excited about his new job with the local pharmacy. His family had always used the pharmacy, and he had many memories from his childhood about what good and reliable business practices it seemed to have. He would be able to live in the same neighborhood, walk to work, and be home for dinner with his family. It was too good to be true.

Alan was six months into his new job when he realized there was a problem. In his position in the finance office, he learned that the company had designed a billing system to cheat both customers and their insurance companies. The system overcharged for services and had been in effect for almost five years now. The company actually had a tutorial for the software it had developed and trained employees on its use. When employees complained, they were told to "use it or lose it"—their job, that is.

Alan was very uncomfortable with this process and felt these unethical practices were unfair and unjust. After much thought, he decided to take matters into his own hands and followed the company procedures for whistleblowers. He hired an attorney experienced in the government's False Claims Acts and filed a suit. Alan won his case; the pharmacy had to pay out nearly $1 million as a result. The company's financial procedures were corrected to reflect more responsible and ethical methods of dealing with their customers and the insurance companies.

1. How would you feel if you were an employee there and had been asked to use this financial system? What would you do about the situation?

2. What else might Alan have tried to remedy the situation? Would it have been as effective?

3. Why do you think it took five years before anyone actually took action to stop the unethical practices?

HUMAN RELATIONS IN ACTION

As an additional project, form groups of three of more; assume the role of Company XYZ. Develop a code of ethics for your company (as if you were the company management). Prioritize your code statements in order of importance. Go to www.ethics.org and select any number of other company samples to use as guidelines if necessary. Don't just copy another company's codes. Explain why you made the choices you did. Do your choices reflect personal, social, or corporate interests? Why do you think these are important guidelines to follow? What were some of the deciding factors that led you to the final set? Prepare a one-page summary of your findings and present them to the class for discussion.

For additional resources, refer to the web site for this text:
www.cengage.com/management/dalton

RESOURCES

1. Bluestein, G. (2009, February 14). Feds mount evidence in salmonella outbreak probe. *The Seattle Times*.

2. Kellogg, D. (2009). Cadet codes of conduct and what they mean for you. Retrieved May 26, 2009, from Cadetstuff.org web site: http://www.cadetstuff.org/archives/p000204.html.

3. (1999–2009). Complying with laws, regulations and our internal code of conduct is central to our sustainability as a business. Retrieved May 26, 2009, from BP web site: http://www.bp.com/sectiongenericarticle.do?categoryId=9027892&contentId=7050805.

4. National Management Association's Code of Ethics. (2009). [Online]. Available: http://nma1.org/About_Us/Vision_Mission_Statement_Code_Ethics.html#Code_of_Ethics.

5. Marrs, S. D. (2005, June 20). It's Monday morning. Do you know where your trade secrets are? Retrieved May 26, 2009, from Beirne, Maynard & Parsons, L.L.P. Web site: http://www.beirnemaynardparsons.com/publications/articles.php?action=display_publication&publication_id=9.

6. Amour, S. (2008). Companies keep an eye on workers' Internet use. *USA Today*.

7. Alaniz, R. (2008, July). The advantages and pitfalls of employee monitoring. Retrieved May 26, 2009, from Fleet Financials web site: http://www.fleetfinancials.com/Article/Print/Story/2008/07/The-Advantages-of-Employee-Monitoring.aspx.

8. Schomburg, R. (2009). Personal Communication.

9. Searcey, D. (2009, April 23). Employers watching workers online spurs privacy debate. *The Wall Street Journal*.

10. Thomasson, Emma. (Retrieved 2009, April 28). Facebook surfing while sick costs Swiss woman job. [Online]. Available: http://www.Reuters.com.

11. Character counts. (2009). [Online]. Available: http://www.charactercounts.org/programs/reportcard/index.html

12. Dirty rotten teenage scoundrels. (2008). [Online]. Available: http://www.parenting.blogs.nytimes.com/2008/12/03/dirty-rotten-teenage-scoundrels.

13. Dove real women campaign. (2009). Businessweek.com [Online]. Available: www.businessweek.com/the_thread/brandnewday/archive/2008/surprise_ doves.html.

14. Blanchard, Kenneth, and Norman Vincent Peale. (1988). *The Power of Ethical Management*. New York: William Morrow and Company, Inc.

15. Toyota's social responsibility. (2009). [Online]. Available: http://www.toyotawhynot.com/gclid,CNglxull25Kcfrmuagodt3-wVQ#/community/togethergreen.

16. Nocera, J. (2007, February). The paradox of business is do gooders. *The New York Times*.

17. (2009). Starbucks and the environment. Retrieved May 26, 2009, from Starbucks web site: http://www.starbucks.com/retail/spring_environment.asp.

18. (2007, November 30). Eco-friendly product claims often misleading. Retrieved May 26, 2009, from NPR Web site: http://npr.org/templates/story/story.php?storyId=16754919.

19. (2009, March 6). Ben & Jerry's co-founder Jerry Greenfield talks social responsibility. Retrieved May 26, 2009, from The SRO web site: http://thesro.org/ben-jerrys-co-founder-jerry-greenfield-talks-social-responsibility/.

20. Dalton, D.R., M.B. Metzger and J.W. Hill. (1994). *The New U.S. Sentencing Commission Guidelines and Wake Up Call for Corporate America!* New York: Academy of Management Executives.

21. IBM and Boeing bring work closer to home. (2009). [Online]. Available: http://www.seekingalpha.com/article/116148-IBM-and-boeing-work-closer-to-home-bad-news-for-outsourcing?

22. Tyler, K. (2005). Do the right thing: ethics training program helps employees deal with ethical dilemmas. *HR Magazine*. [Online]. Available: http://www.shrm.org/Publications/hrmagazine/Pages/default.aspx.

23. (2009). ERC Surveys & Benchmarking. Retrieved May 26, 2009, from ERC web site: http://www.ethics.org/page/benchmarking-services.

24. Wal-Mart on ethics in China. (2008). China Challenger Blog. [Online]. Available: http://www.chinacallenger.blogs.com/2008/10/30/wal-mart-on-ethics.html.

25. The Sarbanes Oxley Ruling Summary. 2009. [Online]. Available: http://www.sox-online.com/act.

26. Dutton, G. (2008, May). Do the right thing. (Cover story). *Entrepreneur*, 36(5), 92. Available: http://www.smartusa.com/smart-car-FAQ-ASPX.

27. Buckley, William M. (2009, March 27). Get the feeling you're being watched? If you're driving, you just might be. *Wall Street Journal*.

28. Zogby international poll: Zogby Poll, U.S. public widely distributes its leaders. (2006, May). [Online]. Available: http://www.zogby.com/search/readnews.cfm?ID=1116.

EFFECTIVE DECISION MAKING:
YOUR COMPETITIVE ADVANTAGE

OBJECTIVES

After studying this chapter, you should be able to:

6.1 Understand why effective decision making is important and how to make good decisions.

6.2 Connect critical thinking skills to effective decision making and be able to devise a plan to strengthen your critical thinking.

6.3 Understand why creativity is important when making decisions.

6.4 Recognize problems and understand why resolving them can be complicated.

Jump Start

Long known for its innovation, 3M was founded in 1902 as the Minnesota Mining and Manufacturing Company and brought us products such as Post-it® notes, Scotch® tape, masking tape, and Thinsulate™. But by 2001, when James McNerney became CEO of 3M, the company had become unwieldy and listless, its stock unattractive. McNerney immediately began to identify problems in work processes, cut staff, and introduce efficiency into the organization through the use of Six Sigma, a continuous process and quality improvement tool. The result? While profits soared and stock price rose, creativity and innovation fell. 3M went from being ranked first in the Business Week/Boston Consulting Group's most innovative companies list in 2004 to twenty-second in 2008.

The problem plaguing 3M and other companies like it was how to remain efficient while not stifling creativity and innovation. Efficiency entails demanding an environment of accuracy, reliability, and repetition, while creativity flourishes in an environment of contradictions, failure, and coincidence. While efficiency helps businesses stay competitive with current products and services, creativity and innovation are vital for product and service development, which is essential in a rapidly changing, global economy.[1]

- Do you believe that McNerney's decision to improve processes and quality was effective? Why or why not?
- Can you think of an instance when creativity at work would be more important than productivity?

6.1 IMPORTANCE OF EFFECTIVE DECISION MAKING

Throughout your personal and professional lives, you are forced to make decisions. In fact, you make dozens of them daily, from what to wear to which e-mail to answer first. Whenever you have more than one way of doing something, you must make a decision. Sometimes the decisions you make include problem solving. At other times, you must choose among a number of opportunities facing you. For example, at some point you may have considered whether to go to college, to go to work, or to combine the two. If you decided to go to college, you then had to consider your major field of study. You may have then considered several occupations with different rewards such as travel, money, or flexibility.

Sometimes we feel more comfortable not making a decision and "just seeing what happens." Keep in mind, though, that *no decision* is a decision! By not making a choice, we have, in effect, decided to let things remain as they are.

Effective decision making greatly impacts the organization and human relations system. Leadership, the manager's style, and how the group and

KeyPoint
Effective decision making is a key 21st century skill.

individual approach decision making are particularly affected within the organization. Likewise, decision making is related to learning and innovation skills and is a part of your response in a 21st century organization.

A 2007 study by the Partnership for 21st Century Skills found that 99 percent of U.S. corporations surveyed agreed that critical thinking and problem-solving skills will be necessary if the United States is to compete economically in the future. Furthermore, economic innovation is expected to be driven increasingly by creativity and new ways of approaching and solving problems.[2]

For this reason, effective decision making is a must for a successful career. Many factors enter into play when making good decisions. First, you need confidence in your ability to make decisions. Self-confidence can be boosted by thinking critically, being creative, and knowing effective problem-solving approaches. Knowing about available decision-making tools is important. Even deciding which decision to make first is important! Additionally, you must be able to judge when a decision should be made in a group or individually.

Making Better Decisions

An orderly approach will help when making decisions. The first order of business is deciding what decisions should be made first. Then, decide whether the decision should be made by an individual or a group. If the group will make the decision, certain protocols should be followed. Once these choices are made, the next course of action is determining whether utilizing decision-making tools will improve the effectiveness of the decision.

Determine What Decisions Should Be Made First   Put simply, prioritize. Because you are faced with a multitude of decisions every day, you just can't devote much time, thought, or effort to all of them, nor should you want to do so. Economists point out that only about 20 percent of problems are vital.

This is called the *"80-20 rule,"* meaning that 20 percent of your problems will account for 80 percent of your losses or gains. The value of the 80-20 rule is that it reminds us to focus our time, efforts, and resources on the 20 percent that matters. (In the ABC analysis identified in Figure 6.3, this 20 percent would be the "A" items.) This rule is also sometimes referred to as "Pareto's Principle" because it uses the 80–20 ratio that Italian economist Vilfredo Pareto used to explain distribution of wealth in his country.[3]

Determine Whether an Individual or Group Should Decide   Whatever decision-making technique is used, most work-related problems and many personal ones require that decisions be made by groups of people rather than by individuals alone. Such situations require strong human relations skills, skills that can be enhanced by knowledge of group decision making. In general, groups make better decisions than individuals because of the increased input and suggestions. However, pitfalls exist, such as wasting time and engaging in *groupthink* (in which group members may go along with an idea simply because the majority likes it). The first step, then, is deciding whether a group should be used in making a decision. Factors to be considered are listed in Figure 6.1.

Figure 6.1

Individual vs. group decision making.

Situational Factors Supportive of Individual Decision Making[4]	Situational Factors Supportive of Group Decision Making[5]
1. When time is short.	1. When creativity is needed.
2. When the decision is relatively unimportant.	2. When data for the solution rest within the group.
3. When the leader has all the data needed to make the decision.	3. When acceptance of a solution by group members is important.
4. When one or two group members are likely to dominate the discussion.	4. When understanding of a solution by group members is important.
5. When destructive conflict is likely to erupt among group members.	5. When the problem is complex or requires a broad range of knowledge for solution.
6. When people feel they attend too many meetings, don't feel they should be involved, or are pessimistic about the value of group meetings.	6. When the manager wants subordinates to feel part of a democratic process or wants to build their confidence.
7. When the relevant decision-making data are confidential and cannot be shared with all group members.	7. When more risk taking in considering solutions is needed.
8. When group members aren't capable or qualified to decide.	8. When better group member understanding of each other is desirable.
9. When the leader is dominant or intimidates group members.	9. When the group as a whole is ultimately responsible for the decision.
10. When the decision doesn't affect the group directly.	10. When the leader wants to get feedback on the validity of his or her ideas and opinions.

Review the factors carefully. Notice that group decision making assumes that members are knowledgeable, will participate, can be creative in their solutions, and are likely to support what they help create. Human relations skills can help groups arrive at healthy decisions.

The goal of group problem solving is to reach *consensus*—to develop a solution that all members can support, even if it's not each member's first choice. The Merriam-Webster Online Dictionary defines consensus as "group solidarity in sentiment and belief" and "the judgment arrived at by most of those concerned."[6] It does not mean that the final solution is the one each member thinks is the best one, but rather that the solution is one that all members can at least support. If group decision making is not approached

> One thing is sure. We have to do something. We have to do the best we know how at the moment ... If it doesn't turn out right, we can modify it as we go along.
>
> —*Franklin D. Roosevelt, U.S. President*

carefully and the process is not monitored for real input, a potential risk is that a consensus decision is a "watered down" decision that tries too hard to make everyone happy.

For a group to have the greatest likelihood of reaching consensus, certain guidelines should be followed. Consider the recommendations shown in Figure 6.2 when you are working with a decision-making group.

Figure 6.2

Recommendations for group decision making.

1. State the idea or proposal in the clearest terms possible. Writing it on a chalkboard or flip chart will help.

2. Poll each member for opinions by asking, "What do you think of the idea (or proposal)?" Use an open-ended question such as this one rather than "do you agree?"

3. If everyone expresses positive opinions for the idea or proposal, you have total consensus.

4. If someone disagrees, ask why and ask for an alternative idea or proposal.

5. Restate any opposing ideas or proposals to ensure understanding.

6. Use problem-solving techniques to resolve the differences. For example:

   a. Find common ground and work toward another suitable alternative.

   b. Use a best-estimate approach to weigh alternatives.

   c. Strive for a substantial agreement among group members and encourage willingness to try the idea or proposal for a limited time.

   d. Use negotiation that results in a "win–win" situation. Negotiation is discussion that leads to a decision acceptable to all.

7. Avoid forcing unanimity, voting, "averaging," "majority rule," or horse trading ("I'll do this if you do that"). Voting divides the group into a win–lose situation.

8. If one group member changes his or her mind, poll opinions from each member again.

9. If someone still disagrees, return to step 4.

10. If only one person, or a small subgroup, continues to disagree, get that person or group to give permission to try the idea or proposal for a limited time period. The permission might include the stipulation to test the counter idea or proposal if the first one fails to accomplish its objective.

11. If all parties now agree to support the decision, consensus has been achieved.

KeyPoint
Intuition is an important part of decision making.

Choose Decision-Making Tools   Once you are ready to make a decision, numerous tools are available. Jonah Lehrer, author of *How We Decide,* says that when important complex decisions such as buying a house, leaving a job, or purchasing furniture are made, you should listen to your emotions.

Neuroscientists, in fact, have discovered that the emotional brain is useful at helping make hard decisions. The brain constantly learns from mistakes, acquiring knowledge and wisdom about a situation through trial and error. You are not consciously aware of this process. Some call this ability intuition, gut reaction, or feeling. While emotions are not completely accurate, you should take them into account when making complex decisions.[7]

Other decisions, Lehrer points out, require reason. For instance, daily mundane decisions, such as picking out bath soap, green beans, or socks, can benefit from rational analysis. When the details of the product aren't that important or when the decision does not matter that much, a rational decision based on price, for instance, is probably the best choice. Additionally, decisions involving novel problems require reason.[8]

Most scientists believe the human brain can only consciously process between five and nine pieces of information at a time.[9] Because of the limitation of the brain and the wide variety of information available, decision makers are increasingly using computing power in the decision-making process.

Decision support systems (DSS) are generally computer applications that help sort through large amounts of data and pick among a variety of choices. This field is rapidly expanding and no universally accepted model of DSS exists.[10]

Some DSS models consider the relationship to the user. A passive system simply collects and organizes data while an active system actually processes data and shows solutions. A cooperative system collects data and performs analyses, allowing the human component to revise or refine the system.[11]

Another popular DSS model takes into account the type of assistance given. Common types are:[12,13]

> *Garbage in, garbage out.*
> —*Anonymous*

- Model Driven—Decision makers use statistical, simulations, or financial models to develop a solution or strategy. These systems don't necessarily have to be extremely data intensive. For instance, companies can input different variables such as interest rate and expenses to determine what their return on investment of a particular project would be.

- Communications Driven—Collaborators work together to come up with a series of decisions to develop a solution or strategy. These models can be within an office structure or initiated online and can include groupware, video conferencing, and computer-based bulletin boards. Global teams can use these tools to collaborate on projects.

- Data Driven—Emphasis is placed on collected data that is then manipulated to fit the decision maker's needs. Generally the data forms a sequence, such as daily sales, operating budgets from one quarter to the next, or inventory levels over the sales cycle. A company might use this information to determine when and how much new product to produce.

- Document Driven—Documents in a variety of data types such as text documents, spreadsheets, database records, images, sounds, and video are used to develop decisions or further manipulate the information to refine strategies. Examples of documents that might be accessed by a document-driven DSS are policies and procedures, catalogs, and corporate minutes of meetings.

Technology CONNECTION

Scottish researchers have determined that one radiologist assisted by a computer-aided detection system was able to spot breast cancer as well as two different radiologists reading the same mammogram. The computer-aided detection program highlights areas on the mammogram that may be abnormal. The radiologist then examines the area highlighted and determines whether further tests are needed. Both methods detect approximately 87 percent of breast cancer.[14]

1. How important do you believe it is to understand what factors computer models analyze when using them to assist you in making decisions? Explain your answer.

2. Do you believe computers will eventually replace humans for complex decision making? Why or why not?

3. How do you feel about trusting your health to a computer?

• Knowledge Driven—Special rules are stored in a computer or used by a human to determine whether a decision should be made. Companies, for instance, may sort resumes for a position using rules that identify minimum skills for the job.

Many decision-making tools exist and more are being developed as computer power and sophistication increase. Figure 6.3 illustrates a variety of tools commonly used in business to assist in decision making.

> *Tell me what you know. Tell me what you don't know. And then, based on what you really know and what you really don't know, tell me what you think is most likely to happen.*
>
> —Colin Powell, American statesman and a former four-star general in the United States Army

Ask Yourself...

1. What was the last significant decision you made? How did you determine whether to make it alone or with input from others?

2. What human relations skills did you use in implementing the decision? Did you use any computer-driven tools to assist in your decision making? If so, which?

3. Was your resolution effective? Could improved human relations skills have helped you develop a better outcome to the decision?

Figure 6.3

Commonly used decision-making tools.

1. **Decision tree**—graphic depiction of how alternative solutions lead to various possibilities.

   Helps people and organizations see the implications that certain choices have for the future. Can be used formally by actually drawing a tree or informally in our heads.

2. **Cost–benefit analysis**—examination of the pros and cons of each proposed solution.

   Popular in the public sector, frequently used for evaluating proposals to provide a nonprofit service to the community, such as hospitals or child care. Involves comparison of all costs against value of the service to the community.

3. **ABC analysis**—concentration of decisions where the potential for payoff is greatest.

   Involves concentration on the vital few items ("A" items), not the trivial many ("C" items). Example: In choosing a builder for your home or office, the quality of the construction would be considered an "A" item, paint color a "C" item, and brand of appliances probably a "B" item.

4. **PERT chart** (Program Evaluation and Review Technique chart)—a graphic technique for planning projects in which a great number of tasks must be coordinated.

   Shows the relationships between tasks and helps identify critical bottlenecks that may delay progress toward a project's completion. The critical path is the sequence of activities that must be done one after another and that requires the longest time for completion.

5. **Quality circle**—committee of 6 to 15 employees, generally volunteers from the same work area, which meets regularly to examine and suggest solutions to common problems of quality. Committee usually receives training in group processes, problem solving, brainstorming, and statistical quality control.

   A form of participative management that encourages employees to provide input on key decisions. Widely used in Japan beginning in the 1950s and in the United States beginning in the 1970s and 1980s; still used but not as widely.

6. **Six Sigma**—sophisticated method of continuous process improvement that uses a structured statistical approach to improve bottom-line results. Involves statistically measuring baseline performance to improve performance processes, product quality, and process engineering.

   A disciplined, data-driven method on which to base decisions about process defects and errors. Can be used in manufacturing and service industries. When implemented strategically, can help companies improve bottom-line results by minimizing waste and non-value-adding tasks.[15]

7. **Six Thinking Hats**—A form of group decision making designed by Edward de Bono that gives each person a role to play in wearing the six hats of intelligence. Each "hat" represents a different way of viewing the situation or issue. White hat presents the facts; red hat says how one feels about the issue; black hat is the pessimist looking at the negative side; yellow hat is the optimist looking at the positive effects; green hat offers alternatives and what ifs; and blue hat is the coordinator and facilitator.

   Encourages participation and open communication, and gives validation to the many different ways a problem can be solved. Postpones judgment so more ideas can emerge. Claims to reduce time spent in meetings by 20–90 percent.[16]

6.2 IMPROVING CRITICAL THINKING

Unless you follow certain principles, your thinking will most likely be biased and distorted, resulting in poor decisions.[17] Thinking critically enables you to have a more realistic picture of the issues. *Critical thinking* is the process of evaluating what other people write or say in order to determine whether to believe their statements.[18] Critical thinkers gather all available information and take into consideration what others have stated or discovered about the issue as well as their own observation, experience, reasoning, and reflection. Without this crucial skill, we cannot reliably determine what to believe or do, which will likely lead to poor decision making.

A critical thinker defines vital questions and problems, and gathers and assesses relevant information. Then, he or she comes to well reasoned conclusions and solutions, testing these conclusions and solutions with an open mind to determine their effectiveness and consequences. A critical thinker is able to communicate with others while working on complex problems without being unduly influenced by them.[19] Anyone can greatly improve the quality of the thought processes that go into making a decision by learning to do the following:[20]

- Distinguish fact from opinion
- Understand the differences between primary and secondary sources
- Evaluate information sources
- Recognize deceptive arguments
- Identify ethnocentrism and stereotypes

Distinguishing Fact from Opinion

An effective critical thinker will listen carefully with an open mind and weigh what is stated, distinguishing fact from opinion.[21] A *fact* is a thing that is known to be true, to exist, or to have occurred while an *opinion* is a view about a particular issue and is not necessarily true.[22] Important to remember is that a statement presented as fact may, in reality, be untrue. For instance, e-mails and news stories began to circulate stating that the United Kingdom would stop teaching about the Holocaust to avoid offending Muslim students. The country's frustrated schools secretary took the unprecedented action of sending statements to embassies and the "world media" refuting the report.[23,24]

Additionally, facts may be misleading when taken out of context. *Context* refers to the interrelated situation in which an event occurs. For instance, an employee complained to his supervisor that his coworker shoved him, demanding action be taken. Shoving did actually occur. However, an investigation determined that the individual complaining had baited the other man by calling him names and then blocking his exit from the work area. A critical thinker is aware that examining context can assist in evaluating facts.

Opinions can't be dismissed out of hand and need to be taken seriously because individuals frequently act on opinion. Shoppers, for instance, may believe that name brand canned goods are of better quality than store brands. Their opinion will influence the way they shop even if their opinion is not backed up by fact.

While analyzing some statements and separating fact from opinion may be easy, you may find that others are more difficult to evaluate, especially when they are stated in such a way as to imply there can be no argument. For example, an air freshener manufacturer may make the statement that its product captures the essence of "an incredible field of flowers." To determine whether this is indeed fact, you would need to decide what different varieties of flowers would make up an incredible field of flowers and then conduct a smell test to see whether the product indeed captured its essence.

Understanding Primary and Secondary Sources

A primary source is original material that has not been interpreted by anyone else.[25] Examples of primary sources include court records, letters, and government documents. Original research and position papers of organizations are also considered primary sources.

While an eyewitness account is a primary source, realize that the person's account might be colored by personal experience and potential stake in the situation. For instance, the eyewitness account of an industrial accident might be different if told by the employee accused of ignoring safety regulations than by a person standing nearby who witnessed the accident.

A secondary source consists of information collected from primary sources and then interpreted by the collector. Many magazine articles, critical analyses, and histories are considered secondary sources. When collecting secondary sources, you have the advantage of being able to put objective distance into your analyses and to look at several different primary sources. However, biased views can still occur.[26]

When thinking critically about the information presented by a secondary source, ask these questions:

- What types of primary sources did the author use?
- Can you be sure the sources are accurate?
- Is it possible that the author's information is colored by his or her personal views?

Evaluating Information Sources

Realize that all information has a point of view no matter how objectively you attempt to present it. When evaluating sources, try to determine the writer's point of view and whether his or her view affects the accuracy of the topic coverage.

Ask yourself these questions:

- Who is the source of this information?
- What is his or her point of view?
- When was this written? The writer's opinion might have changed over time.
- Is this source useful to me?[27]

> *For every expert there is an equal and opposite expert; but for every fact there is not necessarily an equal and opposite fact.*
> —Thomas Sowell, American writer and economist

In The News

Years ago executives at Fannie Mae and Freddie Mac, two large mortgage lenders, were warned by their own employees that they were offering chancy mortgages that could pose a long-term danger to the firm. They were giving out loans without verification of income, assets, or employment. Despite the warnings, these companies continued to take risks, which ultimately led to seizure by federal regulators.[29]

Executives most likely ignored the warnings because the human brain has a bias towards certainty. When you receive information that does not fit into the way you see things, you have the ability to dismiss the information. Doing this can lead to bad decisions.[30]

1. Recall a time when you ignored warning signs that indicated your view of a situation was wrong. What happened? Could you have made a better decision if you had listened to the warning signs? Explain your answer.

2. What can you do to be sure that you spend time looking at the other pieces of information that cause you to be uncomfortable or disturb your way of thinking?

> *If you can't answer a man's arguments, all is not lost; you can still call him vile names.*
> —*Elbert Hubbard, American publisher and writer*

Recognizing Deceptive Arguments

The ability to recognize deceptive arguments is crucial to critical thinking because you can easily be misled and swayed to a particular point of view unless you listen critically and recognize where you are being distracted from the real issues. Listening to the opposite opinion can help you learn to better recognize deceptive arguments. Some of the types of deceptive arguments are as follows:[28]

- *Bandwagon*—the idea that "everybody" does this or believes this. Commonly held beliefs are not necessarily correct beliefs.

- *Scare tactics*—the threat that something terrible will happen if you don't do or don't believe this. Many organizations try to subtly frighten us into using their product or service. If you don't dye your hair, you won't be hired for a job. If you don't take their pill, you'll fall deathly ill. One particular restaurant is where the in-crowd eats and if you do not eat there, you will be unpopular.

- *Personal attack*—criticizing an opponent personally instead of debating his or her ideas rationally. If you have a problem with someone at work, make sure your complaints are about their policies or harmful work habits, and not personal things that aren't directly affecting your ability to do your job.

- *Testimonial*—quoting or paraphrasing an authority or celebrity to support one's own viewpoint. While testimonials can legitimately further an argument, they often come from people who have no expertise in the area of debate. Celebrities, for instance, are frequently spokespersons for companies selling anything from shampoo to cars. Their knowledge of the topic matter should be taken into account when listening to their arguments. Furthermore, realize that a quote used to support an argument may be taken out of context or used in a manner not intended by the speaker.

- *Straw person*—exaggerating or distorting an opponent's ideas to make one's own seem stronger. For example, one of the company's sales managers makes a 30-minute presentation regarding a new computer system she wants the company to purchase. She has carefully detailed the good and bad points of the system. At the end of her presentation, she remarks that sales should greatly increase with the system. The next day another sales manager, who prefers a different system, goes on full attack. He ignores all of the presentation except the last remark when discussing the issue with his boss. He emphasizes the system will not increase sales, that the other sales manager is naïve, and that she does not know what she is talking about. He then begins to tell how great his preferred system is.

- *Slanting*—persuading through inflammatory and exaggerated language instead of reason. A business owner finds that the county wants to turn a road near his facility into a toll road, which would greatly increase his shipping costs. He speaks to a local business advocate group about the problem. Ranting, he complains that civil liberties are being taken away, the community is being required to pay again for something it has already paid for, and that county leaders are stupid and will raise taxes anyway.

> **KeyPoint**
> No individual can be 100% objective.

Identifying Ethnocentrism and Stereotypes

At times arguments are bound in stereotypes and ethnocentrism.[31] *Stereotypes* are attitudes which assume all members of a group share the same set of characteristics. A specific form of stereotyping, *ethnocentrism*, holds that one's own nationality, religion, or cultural traditions and customs are superior to others. Often ethnocentrism and stereotypes are found in arguments that generalize.[32] "Illegal immigrants need to be deported because they take jobs unemployed citizens could do" is an argument steeped in stereotypes and generalizations. By recognizing stereotypes and looking for generalizations, critical thinkers can better evaluate information presented.

Lastly, when thinking critically, remember the following:

- All people have subconscious biases.
- Stay humble and realize your own potential for fallibility.
- Everyone has a tendency towards groupthink, and a certain amount of an individual's belief system is based on what others say instead of what he or she has personally witnessed.[33]
- No matter how good we believe our critical thinking skills are, we always have room for improvement.[34]

Effective decision makers spend time analyzing their thinking skills, learning to recognize their own faulty thoughts and emotions. By making adjustments for these deficiencies, they improve their decision-making abilities.

Ethics CONNECTION

Federal immigration agents raided a kosher meat-processing plant in Iowa and detained 389 workers, nearly a third of the workforce. Several immigrants recounted stories of family poverty and ill health in their native countries to the judge, asking him to reduce their jail time. The plant, the largest employer in the town, was eventually forced into bankruptcy.[35,36]

When considering a solution to these types of moral issues, ask yourself these five questions:[37]

- What benefit and harm will each course of action produce, and which alternative will lead to the best overall consequences?
- What moral rights do the parties involved have, and which course of action best respects those rights?
- Which course of action treats everyone the same (except when there is a morally justifiable reason not to) and does not show favoritism or discrimination?
- Which course of action advances the common good?
- Which course of action develops moral virtues?

1. Name an ethical decision with which you are struggling and ask the five questions above.
2. Explain whether you are closer to a decision on the issue, and, if so, how.

> *Everything that can be invented has been invented.*
> —Charles H. Duell, Commissioner, U.S. Office of Patents 1899

Additionally, these individuals accept ambiguity and rely on the element of doubt, listening to a variety of sources. They push themselves by reminding themselves of what they don't know and not becoming over confident.[38]

Ask Yourself...

1. How do you evaluate whether information on a web site could is biased?
2. Give one fact and one opinion about a recent movie you saw.
3. Describe a time when you or someone else used slanting or scare tactics to bolster your side of the argument? Were they effective?

6.3 NURTURING CREATIVITY AND INNOVATION

Creativity is a thinking process that solves a problem or achieves a goal in an original and useful way. Simply stated, it is the ability to come up with new and unique solutions to problems. Turning these creative solutions into products and services, *innovation*, is growing in importance in the global economy. Professor Richard Florida of the University of Toronto estimates that in 1900 only about 10 percent of the U.S. workforce worked in creative occupations. By 2005 that number was 30 percent.[39]

Many business forecasters believe that creativity and innovation are an important source of future jobs as routine jobs are being moved offshore. Florida believes that the creative sector is responsible for most new wealth generation. Because creativity and innovation are becoming essential in keeping a competitive advantage, both individuals and organizations need to foster these skills.[40]

Everyone has the potential for creativity. Some people simply develop their potential more than others. Being creative does not require genius. Cultivating the vivid imagination that we have as children allows creativity to occur later in life. Being open to new ideas and responding to intuition are important characteristics of creative individuals. Creative types will also investigate ideas that interest them without immediately judging the ideas too harshly.

Further, creative people:[41]

- Are sensitive to problems and deficiencies.
- Possess flexibility, openness, and a tolerance for ambiguity.
- Are self-confident, independent, and willing to risk failure.
- Can make leaps of reasoning from one fact to another similarly unrelated one.
- View nature as fundamentally orderly.
- Use divergent thinking to search for answers, going in many directions, and convergent thinking to make choices based on analysis, reason, and experience.

> "
> *Creativity requires the courage to let go of certainties.*
> —Erich Fromm, social psychologist and philosopher
> "

The Five Stages of the Creative Process

Although the creative process is still somewhat mysterious, experts on creativity generally agree that a person goes through five stages in the creative process. These stages are not necessarily distinct and usually involve a complex recycling of the process.[42]

1. *Preparation*—acquiring skills, background information, and resources; sensing and defining a problem. This stage requires a creative and different viewpoint. Sometimes it simply involves looking for relationships; at other times it means questioning accepted answers.

2. *Concentration*—focusing intensely on the problem to the exclusion of other demands. This is a trial-and-error phase that includes false starts and frustration.

3. *Incubation*—withdrawing from the problem; sorting, integrating, and clarifying at an unconscious level. This stage often includes reverie, relaxation, or solitude. Incubation is the most mysterious part of the creative process. People have compared it to a bird sitting quietly on a nest of eggs waiting for them to hatch. Although not much action can be observed, a person in this stage may be mentally reviewing many ideas and much information, even in dreams. This stage can range in length from a few hours to many years. Several important global concerns are now in the incubation stage, including how to deal with terrorism, cope with trade deficits, solve food and water shortages, find new sources of fuel, reduce production costs, and develop effective mass transit systems.

4. *Illumination*—the "Aha!" stage; often sudden, involving the emergence of an image, idea, or perspective that suggests a solution or direction for further work. Its occurrence is unpredictable and can come at totally unexpected times.

5. *Verification* or *Elaboration*—testing out the idea, evaluating, developing, implementing, and convincing others of its worth. Thomas Edison once said, "Genius is 1 percent inspiration and 99 percent perspiration." This stage often requires working closely with others, using finely tuned human relations skills.

Unleashing Your Creativity

Creativity can be developed and nurtured by using the techniques listed in Figure 6.4. It can also be hampered in a variety of ways. Researchers have identified different ways that creativity is blocked. Information overload, unproductive thought processes, emotional blocks, cultural blocks, and environmental blocks are some of the obstacles you need to overcome to be creative.

Information Overload   Sometimes our minds are cluttered with trivia that we are unable to clear away. This clutter can interfere with your creativity. Changing your activities or environment can help overcome this block. For example, if you have been working in your office, you might go to the library for a short period. If you are searching for the solution to a particular problem, you might temporarily put the problem out of your mind only to have the solution come to you when you are out walking that evening.

Failing to use all of your senses is a third way that thought processes block creativity. Using sight, sound, smell, taste, and touch as inputs into the creative process can help. Many people, for example, find that watching playful kittens or happy children stimulates their creativity. The sights, sounds, and smells of nature inspire others.

Unproductive Thought Processes   To stimulate creativity, learn to modify your problem-solving habits and develop new ways of thinking that enhance creativity. The first block to overcome is the inability to isolate the real source of a problem. People often stereotype a dilemma and see only what

> *A lot of people have dreams and never do anything about them. When you have ideas and dreams, do something about it.*
> —Paul Newman, actor

they expect to see. To overcome this limit, develop the habit of taking a "big picture" perspective. Look at every angle and take a wide view of the dilemma.

Figure 6.4

Ways to improve your creativity.[43,44]

1. Believe that you have the ability to be creative.

2. Listen to your hunches, particularly while relaxed.

3. Keep track of your ideas by writing down your insights and thoughts. Keep a pad somewhere handy in which to record your ideas as they occur.

4. Learn about things outside of your specialty to keep your thinking fresh.

5. Avoid rigid patterns of doing things. Change your rhythms. Draw your problems instead of writing them down. Change your scene or environment by taking a trip or walking. Try a different route to work occasionally.

6. Observe similarities, differences, and unique features in things, whether they are situations, processes, or ideas.

7. Engage in an activity at which you are not an expert and that puts you outside of your comfort zone.

8. Engage in hobbies, especially those involving your hands. Keep your brain trim by playing games and doing puzzles and exercises.

9. Take the other side occasionally in order to challenge and scrutinize your own beliefs.

10. Have a sense of humor and learn to laugh easily. Humor helps put you and your problems into perspective and relieves tension, allowing you to be more creative.

11. Adopt a risk-taking attitude. Nothing is more fatal to creativity than fear of failure or resistance to change.

12. Think positive! Believe that a solution is possible and that you will find it.

13. Turn your ideas into action; follow through. Use positive reinforcement with yourself and reward yourself as a payoff for completing a project.

KeyPoint
Creative individuals are comfortable with uncertainty.

Emotional Blocks Fear of taking a risk or making a mistake is one of the biggest emotional blocks to creativity. Not all ideas are successful, and the creative individual must be willing to risk negative outcomes. Therefore, refrain from letting others (or yourself) engender such fear in you.

Being overly critical will also kill creativity. Most people would rather judge an idea than generate one. Many ideas die because they are judged too early, before they have been fully developed. Review the steps in the creative process and recall that generation of ideas and evaluation of them are two different parts of the process.

Assess Your Creative Thought Processes

Think about your own thought processes.

- Do you look at the big picture?
- What settings inspire your creativity?
- Are you more creative when you are alone or when you are around other people?
- Do you tend to be more creative in the mornings or evenings?
- Have you developed habits for remembering your ideas?

Concentrate on these aspects of your own creativity to see it increase.

The ability to tolerate ambiguity is essential in the creative process. When something is ambiguous, it can be understood in more than one way. That is precisely what you want in creativity. If you are able to look at a problem in a different way, you are closer to coming up with a novel solution. Black and white, either/or thinking is a communication barrier. If such thinking impedes communication, it will certainly inhibit creativity. Most people have an overriding desire for order and predictability, but the creative process can be a messy one. New ideas or projects are not orderly or predictable, and people working on them can become frustrated if they cannot tolerate ambiguity. Being aware of this emotional block may help you overcome it.

If you are to be creative, you must unlock your unconscious mind. When you are tense or preoccupied, you are unable to be creative. Relaxation and the ability to "sleep on it" are helpful. Many excellent ideas have been conceived on the golf course, in the shower, on the way to work, or during routine chores.

Another emotional block is fear of change. Some people find tradition more comfortable. Because creativity by its nature is newness and change, you should develop a positive attitude toward change if you wish to be more creative. Engaging in new activities, sports, or hobbies can help stimulate your creativity.

Finally, some people are unable to distinguish fantasy from reality. The creative individual needs to be able to distinguish what is feasible from what is not. Remember that an important step in the problem-solving process is the evaluation of ideas for practicality.

Cultural Blocks   Some cultural taboos stand in the way of creativity. In some cultures, conformity is valued. The Japanese have a saying that "the nail that sticks up will be hammered down." New ideas do not develop in a conforming environment, though.[45] In other cultures idleness is not valued. In the United States we have a saying that "idle hands are the devil's workshop." However, the creative process is not always visible, and time spent gazing out the window may seem wasteful and might make an individual appear lazy. Playing is seen as an activity for children, and pleasure is considered unproductive and inefficient. To be creative, you must rid yourself of

KeyPoint
The American culture values "busyness" which can stifle creativity.

such notions and allow your mind to float in a random fashion sometimes, to see figures in clouds. Of course, this only works if you have done the real work first of filling your mind with ideas and information with which your mind can build and create when you do let it float.

Other cultural biases lock out the use of intuition and qualitative judgment in favor of logic, reason, numbers, and practicality. Reality, however, dictates that a balance be maintained between these two sets of forces. Another cultural block is the idea that problem solving must always be a serious business. Humor not only relieves stress, it can also unlock creativity. Studies have suggested that laughter enhances creativity because it frees up the childlike part of us. It also can help to strengthen team relationships. And, if used appropriately, humor can deflect anger and reduce tension.[46]

Environmental Blocks   A lack of trust and cooperation among colleagues can short-circuit creativity. Group interactions are particularly vulnerable when members of rival groups are thrown together to resolve a problem. Autocratic bosses and those who provide little or no feedback can also hinder creativity. They may value their own ideas and not support those of subordinates, blocking the contribution of ideas. In some situations, groups become merely a rubber stamp and approve ideas without exploring them. This block may happen for two reasons. Sometimes, people are afraid to speak up and present opposing views. At other times, they fear jeopardizing harmony, so they make a decision that satisfies both sides but that is not the most practical or realistic.

> ## Nine Supervisory Steps toward a Creative Workplace[47]
>
> 1. Help people see the purpose of what they do.
> 2. Expect a lot.
> 3. Tell employees what you expect, not how to do it.
> 4. Realize that people are different.
> 5. Be available to your employees.
> 6. Get the word out in 24 hours or less.
> 7. Provide the proper tools.
> 8. Say "thank you" and mean it.
> 9. Have fun.

Turning Creativity into Innovation

No matter how creative you are, your creativity is useless to organizations unless innovation occurs. Knowing how to present ideas successfully and get others to act on them is a crucial skill for you. New ideas are not usually immediately embraced in a company. They must be cultivated and supported from conception to implementation. The idea must have a champion, someone who is willing to speak up for it, and to commit to it.

Figure 6.5

Are you an intelligent risk taker?

Would you	Yes	No
Try a dish you've never had at an ethnic restaurant?		
Volunteer to test a new piece of equipment at work before any of your coworkers?		
Ask for a promotion or a raise?		
Go roller-skating or try some other sport you've never done before?		
Join a local volunteer group if you do not know any of the members?		
Take a class to learn a new skill like auto repair or flower arranging?		
Ask someone out on a date?		

If you answer *yes* to most or all of these questions you are probably an intelligent risk taker. You are willing to try things that have a limited downside and a positive expected outcome.

Being a champion of an idea takes enthusiasm and the willingness to take risks. After all, the idea may prove to be fruitless. The champion, who may be you or someone else such as your supervisor, must put together a team to develop the idea. Few ideas and projects are implemented by one person alone. Working as part of a creative team will require not only creativity but also well-developed skills in human relations, including problem solving, decision making, and communication.

If you are trying to move an idea through an organization, be prepared to persist. Ideas must be sold to others. Even the most successful projects have their downsides when the going is tough and participants become discouraged. As the champion of an idea or as a member of a team developing an idea, you should be emotionally prepared for these periods. Having supportive family, friends, or coworkers can help tremendously. Effective communication and networking skills will help you develop a coalition and gather others who are willing to support the idea. You or the person serving as the champion must then work to maintain their support.

Creative people have a much better chance of bringing their ideas to fruition if they are able to work effectively with others. A strong trait in people with effective human relations skills is the willingness to share credit. When a creative group project or idea is successful, the person in charge must be

> **KeyPoint**
> While creativity is important, human relations skills are necessary to make the idea reality.

Global CONNECTION

GE Healthcare's Wisconsin clinical system unit combined technology and creativity to introduce an innovative portable electrocardiograph (ECG) into the market in India in just 22 months. A global team, which included eight engineers based in India, assisted. They took GE's 15-pound ECG machine and reduced it to less than three pounds. By using off-the-shelf parts, they reduced the wholesale cost 60 percent.

Creativity included using a printer adapted from bus terminal kiosks in India that is designed to work in dusty environments. The team learned about a low-cost source for technology that cut the plastic mold prototypes far earlier in the process. This allowed them to get feedback from doctors early in the process before changes became expensive. The team also simplified the battery to reduce its memory use.

The new machine will cut patient costs in half, and GE is expecting their $5 million outlay for the project to be recouped in less than 18 months.[48]

1. Do you believe developing the new machine would have been as effective without the input of Indian engineers? Why or why not?
2. Recall a time you were involved in solving a problem. How thoroughly did you analyze issues and obtain feedback from those involved? Could you have done a better job of defining the problem? If so, how?

sure to share the credit. While patents and copyrights exist to protect individuals' creations, taking individual credit for a group project only ensures that group members will be less inclined to work with you on future projects. Learning and sharing information can contribute to a creative atmosphere.

If you are a supervisor in an organization, you have a responsibility to stimulate creativity among your employees. Several methods for accomplishing this are: [49,50]

- Suspending judgment
- Accepting a reasonable amount of failure
- Offering constructive criticism
- Tolerating some different behavior

The National Institute of Business Management has pointed out that managers skilled in stimulating creativity among workers make it to the top faster than those who aren't.[51]

Ask Yourself...

1. What can you do immediately to improve your creativity?
2. Do you have a risk-taking attitude? Are you ready to fail?
3. Have you had an "Aha!" moment recently about a problem or opportunity? What were you doing when that moment occurred?

6.4 PROBLEMS AND SOLUTIONS

> The problem is not that there are problems. The problem is expecting otherwise and thinking that having problems is a problem.
>
> — Theodore Rubin, American psychiatrist and author

A popular definition of a *problem* is a puzzle looking for an answer. Whether the problem is an organizational one or a personal one, it can be defined as a disturbance or unsettled matter that requires a solution if the organization or person is to function effectively. Sometimes problems are obvious. Other problems only become evident when expected results are compared to actual results. In that case, the gap is the problem that needs solving. Determining that solution involves decision making.

Types of Problems and their Resolution

Problems may be of three types, as shown in Figure 6.6. In looking at the problem of a project that is behind schedule, for example, follow the helpful maxim that says, "A problem well defined is a problem half solved."

Identify the Problem   First, identify the problem, defining it clearly and specifically. Instead of saying, "We are behind schedule," say, "We have only two weeks in which to complete this project." Collect and analyze all information pertinent to the problem—people, processes, materials, equipment, or other matters. Try to uncover all relevant data. Be objective. See the situation as it actually is, not as you think it is. Don't let emotions color your perception. Quantify the problem if possible. Examine all facets of the issue and identify the source of the problem. List possible causes and then select most likely cause(s). For instance, you might find that absenteeism has been high, materials have been late in arriving, and a new computer system used on the project has had start-up difficulties.

Figure 6.6

Three types of problems.

Types of Problems	Examples
1. Occurring now and must be addressed now	• The economy is forcing the XYZ Company to lay off several employees.
	• You have returned to school, requiring you to allocate part of your budget to school expenses.
2. Expected in the future and plans must be made for dealing with them when they do occur	• The ABC Company has a deadline of May 1 to complete a project and is now behind schedule.
	• You have a major paper due in two weeks and have not started writing it.
3. Foreseen for the future but so serious that actions must be taken immediately to prevent their development	• Earnings projected for a company reveal that it will be unable to meet its payroll by the middle of the fourth quarter.
	• The term paper that you have not yet started and that is due next week is a minimum requirement to pass the course.

Generate Ideas   The second step is to generate ideas. This is particularly important if the problem is hard because hard problems rarely have easy solutions. As part of a group involved in finding a solution to the problem, consider using brainstorming to develop as many alternative solutions as possible for removing the causes of the problem. *Brainstorming* is a problem-solving technique that involves the spontaneous contribution of ideas from all members of the group. The goal is to generate as many ideas as possible—more ideas mean better results. Reserve judgment—no ideas should be eliminated initially. An idea that seems ridiculous may trigger a feasible idea in someone else. By throwing ideas back and forth and adding to them, members can form a plan. Brainstorming is a freewheeling, fun activity that encourages creativity.[52]

Evaluate Ideas for Practicality   The next part of the problem-solving process is to evaluate alternatives for practicality. Analyze the implications of each alternative by evaluating the pros and cons. Rather than just saying that one solution is better than another, define "better." Develop criteria such as cost and speed. Consider the information gathered while generating the ideas and, if possible, discuss the criteria with experts. Try to anticipate problems

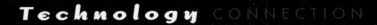

Technology CONNECTION

Because today's silicon-based solar cells are only about 20 percent efficient, IBM Corporation and Harvard University want to improve them and, in turn, lower the cost per watt of electricity they generate. To do so, they need to test organic materials to find one that can be used in low-cost, high efficiency current generation. Unfortunately, examining each potential compound would take 100 days of computer time under normal circumstances and the entire project could take as many as 22 years to complete. Project co-ordinators have resolved their problem by asking the World Community Grid (WCG) for help. The WCG is a humanitarian computing grid with over 413,000 members in 200 countries. Members lend their computing power to the WCG when their computers are not in use. Project organizers estimate that by using this virtual grid the project can be completed in two years.[53]

1. What other problems do you know that have been solved by technology?
2. Do you believe technology can solve all problems? Why or why not?
3. The atomic bomb was hailed as a technological solution that forced a quick end to World War II. Discuss the positive and negative effects this technology has had on the world.

that some alternatives might create. Consider what factors caused the gap between the expected and actual results.

In this example, try to imagine the impact of each change—the absenteeism, late materials, and new computer system. Using a process of elimination, imagine what difference returning a changed factor to its original condition would make. If that does not solve the problem, keep checking. Would the project be on time if absenteeism had been at its usual rate, or if materials had arrived on time, or if the computer system had not been changed? After considering these options, you might decide that the most likely cause was the late materials.

What can you do, in this example, to ensure the timely arrival of materials in the future? You might consider ordering earlier, or ordering from a different source, or even changing the design so that other materials can be substituted for those you might have trouble obtaining.

Then, anticipate the likely results of each alternative. You may discover that some alternatives create more problems than they solve. If you choose to substitute materials in our example, you may create design problems. Although ordering from another source seems reasonable, you may find that the second source is more expensive. You may decide that ordering earlier is the best alternative, but you may not always have advance notice of the need. The basic question is whether your projects are being completed on time using the specific plan for ordering supplies.

Determine a Plan of Action   Select your best solution. This step is the decision phase in the problem-solving process. Weigh all the chances of success against the risks of failure. The strengths of your solution should exceed its weaknesses. Develop a plan of action for carrying out your solution. What will be done, how, by whom, where, when, and at what cost?

Implement the Plan   Implement the idea by carrying out your best solution. Consider that you may have to alter your plans and be ready.

Evaluate the Effectiveness of Your Plan   The last step involves evaluating results. Follow up and modify actions when necessary. Make sure that your actions accomplish your objectives by examining the situation carefully. If your goals are not being met, you may have to study the problem further and explore other alternatives.

"Shoot. I meant to correct this problem after the last time it happened."

© 2009 Ted Goff

When trying to solve a problem, be alert to pitfalls or problem areas. Common ones are:

- Overanalyzing, which can lead to inaction
- Not taking necessary action, or acting too quickly
- Erring in judgment or execution
- Not having a backup plan
- Not involving others in the problem-solving process
- Perceiving the problem incorrectly

Ask Yourself...

1. Name a recent problem you had to resolve. Did you follow the steps indicated in reaching a resolution? If not, would resolution have been easier if you had?

2. Have you ever acted too quickly when taking action on a problem? If so, what happened? What can you do in the future to ensure you take time to analyze it appropriately?

KEY TERMS

80-20 rule
groupthink
consensus
DSS (decision support systems)
critical thinking
fact
opinion
context
stereotypes
ethnocentrism

creativity
innovation
preparation
concentration
incubation
illumination
verification or elaboration
problem
brainstorming

CHAPTER SUMMARY

Making decisions effectively is a key skill. You are constantly forced to make choices among actions, opportunities, or solutions. Several well-known techniques can be effective for making personal and work decisions. Decision making may be done by individuals or by groups. The goal of group decision making is to develop a solution that all members can support.

Critical thinking is an important skill in decision making. Unless you take steps to think critically, your thought processes may lead to a biased, ineffective decision. A critical thinker is able to gather information regarding a situation and to evaluate it to determine its validity. He or she is able to distinguish fact from opinion, primary sources from secondary sources, and is able to recognize deceptive arguments. A critical thinker is also skilled at evaluating sources of information as well as recognizing when ethnocentrism and stereotypes are being utilized.

Creativity, along with innovation, is an increasingly important work skill. Creativity involves several steps, and creative ideas can come from many sources. Blocks to creativity include information overload, unproductive thought processes, emotional blocks, cultural blocks, and environmental blocks. You can take several steps to overcome blocks and develop your own creativity, starting with believing that you can be creative.

Problems are disturbances or unsettled matters that require solutions if organizations or individuals are to function effectively. Problems become evident when expected results are compared to actual results. They can best be solved by following specific steps beginning with defining the problem and ending with following up and modifying the chosen solution when necessary.

REVIEW

1. What steps should you take to make better decisions?

2. What is critical thinking and why is it more important than ever before in today's workplace?

3. How can you improve your creativity?

4. What is a problem and what are the steps in solving a problem?

CRITICAL THINKING

1. Think of a problem you faced recently. Apply the problem-solving process to it. Would you take the same action now that you did at the time? Share your answer with the class.

2. Add up the number of decisions you made in the last three days and the number of decisions you have put off. Did you use any of the tools discussed to make your decisions? Should you have put off your decisions? Why or why not?

3. Find an article in a magazine, newspaper, or online about a current hot topic. Analyze the article using the critical thinking skills presented in this chapter. Can you identify any deceptive arguments? What is your evaluation of the objectivity of the source and the strength of the sources of information?

4. Review the different blocks to creativity. Name examples of each kind and consider them in relation to yourself. Are these blocks hampering your own creativity? Identify what you can do to overcome each block.

CASE STUDIES

In small groups, analyze the following situations:

1 **The 80-20 Rule** Jorge is a medical imaging technician at a small company. When he arrived at work on Wednesday, the 15th, he found the following on a to-do list from his supervisor:

1. Dr. Salinas has asked you to squeeze in an extra patient. Work her in around 3 p.m.

2. Call patients to remind them of their appointment tomorrow.

3. Take your annual TB test before the end of the month.

4. Complete the required blood borne pathogens training before the end of the month.

5. Stock the supply cabinet for next week's work.

Jorge already has seven patients on his schedule and, with the emergency patient, he will have eight. It takes him 50 minutes to run the test on each patient, and he has to change the linens and assure that hazardous waste such as used needles or other supplies are disposed of properly. Additionally, Jorge's supervisor has told him that all overtime allotted for the week has been used so he is not allowed to stay late to complete any of the assigned tasks.

1. Apply ABC analysis to Jorge's dilemma. Categorize each task; label it A, B, or C, and explain your reasoning.

2. Based on your ABC analysis, what recommendation would you make to Jorge about his priorities for the day?

2 Help! Help!   Three years ago, Yolanda started a home decorating business. Most of her customers are homeowners. Her business has been so successful that six months ago she hired an employee to help her. She was lucky enough then to find someone who was experienced and fast.

Last month, Yolanda hired a second person when she found that deadlines were not being met. The second employee is not experienced but is eager to learn and, in fact, seems to be a quick study. However, because of all the rush projects, Yolanda has not had much time to train her, so the employee has spent a good deal of time standing around and watching Yolanda work.

Yolanda feels overwhelmed. One of her vans has been malfunctioning, resulting in downtime. Her staff frequently runs out of needed supplies in the middle of a job. Another problem is that the local supplier she uses does not keep needed materials in stock.

Additionally, Yolanda has not promptly responded to those seeking quotes, ultimately losing business. Currently, Yolanda is trying to handle quotes, consulting with customers, overseeing the work, and completing the bookkeeping herself. Unfortunately, she does not have sufficient cash flow to hire new employees.

1. Identify Yolanda's problems, possible solutions, and how they would be implemented. Do this on your own without consultation with others.

2. Then, in a group, use the suggestions in Figure 6.2 to identify the problems, the possible solutions, and how they should be implemented.

3. Compare the results. Did the group make a better decision than you did by yourself? Did it take longer for the group to reach consensus?

HUMAN RELATIONS IN ACTION

Do an Internet search on the decision tree, a decision-making model described briefly in Figure 6.3. Using the decision tree, map out the following problem—your employees have too much work to complete in a 40-hour week. Show possible solutions and the potential consequences of each possible solution in your decision tree.

For additional resources, refer to the web site for this text:
www.cengage.com/management/dalton

RESOURCES

1. Hindo, B. (2007, June). At 3M, a struggle between efficiency and creativity. *IN*, 8–16.

2. Society for Human Resource Management. (2008). Workforce readiness and the new essential skills. *Workplace Visions, 2,* 4–6.

3. Reh, J. F. *Pareto's principle—The 80–20 rule.* (n.d.). Retrieved on April 20, 2004, from http://management.about.com/cs/generalmanagement/a/Pareto081202.htm

4. Consensus. (2009). *Merriam-Webster Online Dictionary.* Retrieved on March 24, 2009, from http://www.merriam-webster.com/dictionary/consensus

5. Sussman, L. & Deep, S. D. (1997). *COMEX: The communication experience in human relations.* Mason, OH: Thomson/South-Western.

6. *Ibid.*

7. Lehrer, J. (2009). *How we decide.* New York: Houghton Mifflin Harcourt.

8. *Ibid.*

9. *Ibid.*

10. *What is a decision support system?* Retrieved on April 13, 2009, from http://www.tech-faq.com/decision-support-system.shtml

11. *Ibid.*

12. *Ibid.*

13. Power, D. J. (2007, March 10). *A brief history of decision support systems version 4.0.* Retrieved on April 24, 2009, from http://dssresources.com/history/dsshistory.html

14. Bankhead, C. (2008, October 01). *Computer-aided mammography matches accuracy of double reading.* Retrieved on April 14, 2009, from http://www.breastcancer.org/symptoms/testing/new_research/20081001b.jsp

15. *New to six sigma: A six sigma guide for both novice and experienced quality practitioners.* (n.d.). Retrieved on April 20, 2004, from http://www.isixsigma.com/library/content/six-sigma-newbie.asp

16. De Bono, E. (1999). *Six thinking hats.* Boston: Back Bay Books.

17. *Critical thinking: Where to begin.* (n.d.). Retrieved on October 8, 2008, from critical-thinking.org http://www.criticalthinking.org/starting/index.cfm

18. Cengage Learning-InfoTrac College Edition. (n.d.). *Critical thinking.* Retrieved on October 23, 2008, from http://infotrac.thomsonlearning.com/infowrite/critical.html

19. *Critical thinking: Where to begin.* (n.d.)

20. Cengage Learning-InfoTrac College Edition. (n.d.). *Critical thinking.*

21. *Ibid.*

22. *Evaluating the information—fact vs opinion.* Retrieved on November 10, 2009, from Rhodes University Library web site: http://www.ru.ac.za/static/library/infolit/fact.html

23. Holocaust 'ban' e-mail confusion. (2007, April 17). *BBC News.* Retrieved on November 10, 2009, from http://news.bbc.co.uk/2/hi/uk_news/education/6563429.stm

24. UK government acts on hoax e-mail. (2008, February 4). *BBC News.* Retrieved on March 17, 2008, from http://news.bbc.co.uk/2/hi/uk_news/education/7226778.stm

25. Cengage Learning-InfoTrac College Edition. (n.d.). *Critical thinking.*

26. *Ibid.*

27. *Ibid.*

28. *Ibid.*

29. *Fannie, Freddie execs were warned of problems: report.* Retrieved on December 9, 2008, from http://www.reuters.com/article/newsOne/idUSTRE4B80XJ20081209

30. Lehrer, J. (2009). *How we decide.*

31. Cengage Learning-InfoTrac College Edition. (n.d.). *Critical thinking.*

32. *Ibid.*

33. *Critical thinking: Where to begin.* (n.d.)

34. *Ibid.*

35. Schulte, G. (2008, May 20). Detainees to be jailed, then deported in deal. *Des Moines Register.* Retrieved on March 28, 2009, from http://www.desmoinesregister.com/article/20080520/NEWS/805200402

36. Schulte, G. (2009, March 25). Attempts to sell Agriprocessors' assets collapse. *Des Moines Register.* Retrieved on March 28, 2009, from http://m.dmregister.com/news.jsp?key=434211

37. Velasquez, M., Andre, C., Shanks, T., & Meyer, S. J. & Michel J. (n.d.). *Thinking ethically: A framework for moral decision making.* Retrieved on December 8, 2008, from Santa Clara University, The Markkula Center for Applied Ethics web site: http://www.scu.edu/ethics/practicing/decision/thinking.html

38. Lehrer, J. (2009). *How we decide.*

39. Society for Human Resource Management. (2007). Creativity and innovation. *Workplace Visions, 1,* 2–8.

40. *Ibid.*

41. Creativity and counseling. Highlights: An ERIC/CAPS fact sheet. (1984). *ERIC Digest.* Retrieved on August 14, 2009, from http://www.ericdigests.org/pre-922/creativity.htm

42. Creativity and counseling. Highlights: An ERIC/CAPS fact sheet, *ERIC Digest.*

43. Calano, J. & Salzman, J. (1989, July). Ten ways to fire up your creativity. *Working Woman,* 94–95.

44. Raudsepp, E. (1985, June). How creative are you? *Nation's Business,* 25–26.

45. Oech, R. von. (1992). *A whack on the side of the head.* Menlo, CA: Creative Think.

46. Axtell, R. E. (1998). *Do's and taboos of humor around the world.* Hoboken, NJ: John Wiley & Sons.

47. Barlow, J. (1999, April 11). Nine steps toward a great workplace. *Houston Chronicle.*

48. McGregor, J. (2008, April 17). GE: Reinventing tech for the emerging world. *BusinessWeek: IN Focus.* Retrieved on December 8, 2008, from http://www.businessweek.com/magazine/content/08_17/b4081068884259.htm

49. *Brainstorming: Generating many radical ideas.* Retrieved on April 20, 2004, from http://www.mindtools.com/pages/article/newCT_04.htm

50. Warner, C. *How to manage creative people.* Retrieved on April 20, 2004, from http://www.mindtools.com/pages/article/newCT_04.htm

51. National Institute of Business Management. (1989, July 1). Personal report for the executive: How to harness creativity.

52. *Brainstorming: Generating many radical ideas.* Retrieved on April 20, 2004, from http://www.mindtools.com/pages/article/newCT_04.htm

53. IBM. (2008, December 8). Harvard to use home computers to make better solar cells. *Journal of New England Technology.* Retrieved on December 8, 2008, from http://www.masshightech.com/stories/2008/12/08/daily3-IBM-Harvard-to-use-home-computers-to-make-better-solar-cells.html

GROUPS AND TEAMS:
WORKING WELL WITH OTHERS

OBJECTIVES

After studying this chapter, you should be able to:

7.1 Explain the structure and function of groups in the workplace.

7.2 Identify benefits and types of workplace teams.

7.3 List roles and characteristics of effective team members.

7.4 Explain the stages of team development.

7.5 Describe strategies for creating and leading teams.

Jump Start

Since its 2002 founding, Chicago-based Total Attorneys had grown into a $24 million business, providing small law firms with customized software and practice management services. But there were problems. Development had slowed, to the point that sometimes, by the time a product was ready, the client's needs had changed. And morale was down. Employees didn't feel connected to projects or one another.

CEO Ed Scanlan turned to a new software development model called *agile development.* In place of the old system, in which software passed from developers to coders to quality assurance testers, he installed smaller teams that crossed departments, usually a project leader, designer, coder, and quality assurance tester. Big projects were broken into miniprojects with short deadlines. Teams set daily goals, reviewed progress, and were empowered to make decisions.

When productivity rose and employee satisfaction with it, Scanlan applied agile development across the company. Now Total Attorneys can run projects, change strategies, and innovate more quickly, like the small startup it once was. The shift in strategy has paid big benefits. In 2008, *Inc.* ranked Total Attorneys 169th in the 500 fastest-growing U.S. companies, 8th in the Top 100 Businesses in the Chicago area, and 23rd in the Top 100 Business Services Companies in the nation.[1]

- How did teamwork change the software development process at Total Attorneys?
- Why do you think employee morale rose after the change?

7.1 GROUPS AT WORK

You are probably a member of several groups. They can be as small as your immediate family or as large as a military battalion. Scarcely a day goes by when we do not interact with one or more groups.

A *group* is two or more individuals who are aware of one another, interact on a regular basis, and perceive themselves to be a group. Regardless of a group's size or type, the ability to work well with others is the most important requirement for being an effective group member.

Most groups have a common thread: the purpose of satisfying organizational or individual needs. Group members tend to receive some degree of satisfaction from their association, or they will leave the group and seek another for fulfillment or satisfaction.

Work groups are important because they influence the overall behavior and performance of individuals in the workplace. In the systems approach used in this book, a group's actions and behaviors—how it makes decisions, works together, and solves problems, for example—affects the other parts of the system and the organization's overall performance. Figure 7.1 illustrates the relation of group behavior and morale to performance and productivity. As you can see, a positively motivated group can increase productivity. Unfortunately, a negative group can create roadblocks to an organization's success.

The groups we belong to at work fall into two general categories: formal and informal (Figure 7.2).

> **KeyPoint**
> Groups influence behavior and performance at work.

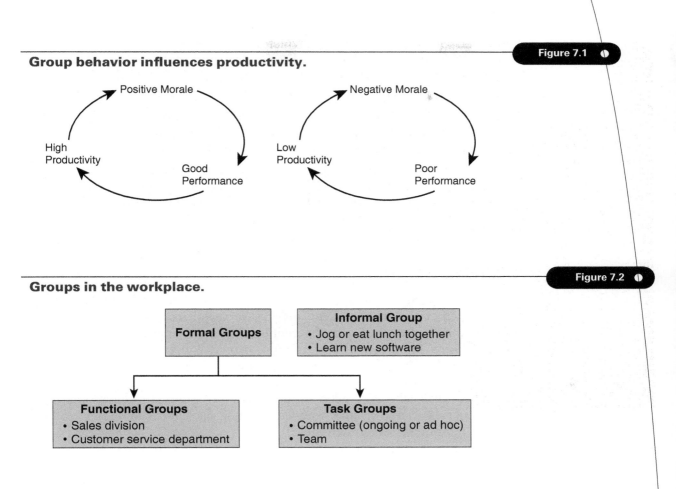

Figure 7.1

Group behavior influences productivity.

Figure 7.2

Groups in the workplace.

Formal Groups

A *formal group* is designated by an organization to fulfill specific tasks or accomplish certain organizational objectives. Group members may have similar or complementary skills, responsibilities, or goals clearly related to the organizational purpose. Positions within the formal group are officially identified, usually assigned to individuals, and meant to provide order and predictability in the organization.

There are two kinds of formal groups. The first is the *functional group*, which is made up of managers and subordinates assigned to certain positions in the organizational hierarchy that together fulfill a specific, ongoing function. For example, a sales division is a functional group whose purpose (function) is to sell products or services. If you have ever held a job and reported to a supervisor, you have been a member of a functional group. Group positions or assignments in functional groups are usually permanent and serve as the skeleton of the organizational structure.

The second kind of formal group is the *task group*, which is formed for a specific reason with members drawn from various parts of the organization to accomplish a specific purpose. A task group may consist of individuals representing various functional specialties across the organization. An example

> *Alone we
> can do so little;
> together we can
> do so much.*
> —Helen Keller,
> American author
> and activist

of a task group is a committee, which may be formed to develop procedures, solve a short-term problem, exchange ideas and information, or make recommendations for a decision. (Group problem solving and decision making were discussed in Chapter 6.)

- *Ongoing committees* are relatively permanent groups that address organizational issues on a continuous basis. Two examples are plant safety committees and employee promotion boards.

- *Ad hoc committees*, on the other hand, have a limited life, serving only a one-time purpose and disbanding after accomplishing it. Two examples are a committee formed to create a new corporate logo or a committee charged with recommending ways to address staff shortages.

Informal Groups

Informal groups form spontaneously when members with similar interests get together voluntarily. They may share social interests, such as politics, sports, and other recreational activities. Other informal groups satisfy members' needs for informal job training, provide opportunities for status, or help members gain information concerning the organization.

The formation of informal groups in the workplace is natural. Groups tend to form whenever people are in close proximity and have occasion to see and talk to one another frequently. They share ideas, opinions, and feelings, and pursue similar activities.

There are a few important facts to know about informal groups. First, they satisfy individual needs, something that might not happen in a formal group. Second, although informal groups do not appear on the company's formal organization chart, they have a powerful influence on members' behavior. Third, informal groups exist in all organizations and do not necessarily indicate that the formal group is inadequate or ineffective.

Why People Join Groups

The reasons that people join groups vary depending on their needs and which needs are strongest at any given time. Studies have identified the four most common reasons for joining groups as social connection, power, self-esteem, and goal accomplishment.

Social Connection   Groups can provide us with a sense of belonging and reduce feelings of isolation. Being a member of a social group gives us an opportunity to share ideas or exchange information, making us feel needed and increasing our sense of worth. People tend to feel a stronger sense of affiliation when they join a group voluntarily than when they are assigned to a group.

Power   There is power in numbers. Groups can give us the confidence to speak out and make requests. This sense of power and security can also provide us with the courage to tackle difficult tasks by reminding us that we're not working alone.

Self-Esteem   People frequently join groups for self-esteem, as membership in some groups can raise our sense of belonging. This is especially true if the group is a prestigious one.

Goal Accomplishment   Joining a group may enable us to accomplish goals more easily because we can learn skills and acquire knowledge from other members. Group membership might allow us to complete individual goals at the same time that we're completing group objectives.

While working in an organization, you can have relationships on both personal and professional levels that fulfill your needs within the organization. Furthermore, the wider your circle of acquaintances, the easier it will be for you to fulfill your needs.

Ask Yourself...

1. What groups do you interact with in a typical day?
2. How have groups affected your performance at work or school?

In The News

Every Tuesday morning, three retired housemates in red, white, and blue stand along Main Street in a village in coastal Maine, waving American flags as passing drivers honk their horns in support. The "flag ladies" started the practice shortly after September 11 to honor those who died in the attacks and to be of service. When U.S. troops went to Afghanistan and Iraq, the women expanded their activities, seeing troops off and greeting them on their return. Each trip involves a two-hour drive each way to airports in Bangor, Maine, and Portsmouth, New Hampshire. The flag ladies snap pictures of the soldiers they greet and post them on their web site for families. They send packages to troops, sometimes slipping in school supplies for Afghan children, and to combat support hospitals. The flag ladies raise the spirits of many, both in the United States and abroad.[2]

1. Which, if any, of the four common reasons that people join groups do you think motivated the flag ladies to form theirs? What needs might belonging to the group meet for them, and how?

2. List the various groups the flag ladies encounter, and describe the effects you think their activities have on these groups.

7.2   TEAMS AT WORK

Throughout your life, you will be a member of many different teams, some at work and some in other areas of your life. We commonly think of a team as a group of individuals doing the same activity or task, such as playing a sport. In today's work environment, however, teams may include representatives from a variety of disciplines, departments, or even different lines of business who come together to achieve a common objective. When an identifiable group of people are working together toward a common goal and are dependent upon one another to realize that goal, they may be referred to as a *team*.

Major corporations in the United States began experimenting with team concepts on a small scale as early as the 1920s, with their popularity increasing in the late 1960s. However, it wasn't until the 1980s that teams gained importance in the workplace as companies began to realize the benefits derived from their use.

Benefits of Teams

Teams have many benefits for organizations. They include improved decision making and problem solving, a greater reservoir of ideas and information, increased sharing of individual skills, increased productivity, and improved quality and quantity output. Studies have shown that workers like participating in team activities and having greater responsibility, and they appreciate opportunities to contribute their ideas and knowledge toward improving operations. Allowing employees to serve on an effective team translates directly into greater job satisfaction (which improves performance) and loyalty.

Teams benefit employees as well. As a member of an effective team, you have a sense of making real, direct, and appreciated contributions. This

KeyPoint
Throughout your career, you will be a member of many different teams.

KeyPoint
Teams have many important benefits for organizations and employees.

Image Source/Getty Images

increased feeling of worth improves your commitment to the goals and objectives of the team and the organization. Teams also offer valuable opportunities for networking. And being part of a successful team gains you recognition and improves your chances for better assignments and promotions.

Types of Teams

Many types of teams exist today, and an organization may have several types operating at the same time. The following are five common types of teams.

Project Teams   *Project teams* come together to complete a specific project. When the project is over, the team disbands. Project teams are frequently used in the engineering and construction industries to design and construct buildings or plants. Once the project is completed, the team disbands and the team members are generally assigned to other teams.[3]

Self-Directed Work Teams   *Self-directed work teams* are teams that, to a certain extent, manage themselves. They plan their own work, make their own decisions, and solve problems that arise in the course of their activities. Examples are a production line responsible for packaging products and a faculty team from several departments that develops a new cross-disciplinary academic program.[4]

Functional Work Teams   *Functional work teams* involve employees from one particular function, such as accounting or human resources, who work together to serve various clients either inside or outside the organization. For example, a team consisting of computer programmers, network specialists, and hardware installation experts may work together to install a computer system for an outside client or for a new location of their own organization.[5]

Cross-Functional Work Teams   *Cross-functional work teams* are composed of individuals from two or more different functional areas. They are commonly used to design and bring a new product to market and to help ensure its success. The teams at Total Attorneys in this chapter's Jump Start are cross-functional work teams. Another example is the cross-functional team that developed the iPhone for Apple. The members who designed the iPhone's graphical interface have skills and backgrounds different from those who engineered its functionality. After the iPhone's release in 2007, other teams continued to work on improvements and new applications.

Virtual Teams   *Virtual teams* are usually task- or project-focused teams that meet without all members being present in the same location or at the same time. They often meet using *groupware*, software designed to support work groups at remote locations with data sharing, audio and video conferencing, virtual white boards, chat, e-mail, and other features. Virtual teams have become increasingly popular as companies move into multinational markets, invest in communications and networks, seek to save costs, and bring together far-flung talent after downsizing.

Technology CONNECTION

Samsung, a leading electronics and appliance manufacturer, stays competitive by using collaborative design and communication systems to help meet the high demand for its products. A few years ago, with the help of a leading software company, it successfully developed a multi-use, web-based system to manage and track the work of its dozens of product development teams.

A key feature of the system is versatility. Team members use it to enter data about their work. Project leaders and managers use it to set schedules, assign tasks, and make progress reports. Resource managers can access the data they need to allocate resources quickly and appropriately. The executive team uses the system to analyze project data rapidly and make good strategic decisions.[6]

1. Previously, projects were managed and reported on in different ways (and with different software), and information was stored on 45 different servers. What problems do you think that created for the various leaders and managers described in the feature?

2. What features might be added to the system for use within a product development team? For sharing questions, methods, discoveries, and solutions among teams?

Teams Don't Fit All Situations

Not every organization is suited to teamwork. Some structures and operating styles do not lend themselves readily to the universal use of teams. For the team concept to be successful, management must be fully supportive and have a clear mission and values that sustain this approach.

Another issue is the work itself. There are times when individual effort might be more effective to resolve a particular issue.

Lastly, participants must buy into the premise that in order to succeed, they must commit to helping those around them succeed and that all the team members will be held personally responsible for the outcome. This adjustment can be difficult for some individuals, particularly if they are accustomed to succeeding on their own.

Ask Yourself...

1. Think of ways you've benefited from being involved in teams. What did you learn through your experiences?

2. Suppose you were asked to work on a team whose members are halfway around the globe. What problems do you think might occur and how would you handle them? What benefits might there be?

7.3   WORKING AS A TEAM

One of the first actions a team should take is to agree on its goals. Even if the team's mission seems obvious, everyone benefits from discussing it, even for a few minutes. An open discussion will help clarify the mission for all members and build commitment to the team's work.[7] Then the team can begin to plan how its goals will be achieved.

A second task is to begin to fill roles. In many teams, some roles, such as leader and secretary, are assigned. People in these roles have a specific, recognized set of responsibilities. But usually, these *formal roles* aren't the only ones operating on a team. Most teams also have *informal roles* that members take on themselves when they perceive a need.[8] It may become clear, for instance, that some valuable ideas raised in a team's brainstorming sessions are being missed because members aren't articulating them clearly. Seeing this, Alécia may decide to step in after the sessions and restate these ideas. Figure 7.3 lists several common informal roles.

> " *Teamwork divides the task and multiplies the success.*
> —Unknown "

Figure 7.3

Informal roles.	
Information seeker	Asks for facts, feelings, suggestions, and ideas about the team's concerns.
Information giver	Gives information about the team's concerns, stating facts and feelings; gives ideas and makes suggestions.
Coordinator	Pulls together group ideas and suggestions; recommends a decision or conclusion for the team to consider.
Harmonizer	Reduces tension and reconciles differences.
Supporter	Praises others' efforts and helps build group solidarity.

The need for someone to fill an informal role often emerges as the team continues to do its work. Filling informal roles is important in making the team effective and productive. Members may find themselves filling more than one role, often roles they're good at but also roles that are new to them. On a successful team, many such opportunities will arise for everyone to be a leader.

Role ambiguity occurs when individuals are uncertain about what role they are to fill or what is expected of them. All of us experience some initial feelings of role ambiguity when we join new teams or groups.

KeyPoint
Filling both formal and informal roles is essential for a team's success.

Being a Good Team Member

When you are a member of a team, you can help make the team effective and the experience pleasant if you remember certain suggestions:

- Know your role(s) and the team's goals. Be aware of your strengths and weaknesses and what you can contribute to the team.

- Be a willing team player. At times you may be asked to perform tasks that you dislike or with which you disagree. Realize how performing these assignments will contribute to the group's productivity and do them willingly (unless you disagree on ethical or moral grounds).

- Cooperate with other team members. Using open communication and solid human relations skills enhances harmony.

- Support other team members by giving them encouragement and assisting them when necessary with their tasks.

- Share praise. Do not claim credit for yourself if a team effort was involved.

Figure 7.4 identifies characteristics of a good team player.

Figure 7.4

Characteristics of a good team player.

A good team member generally:

- Thinks in "we/us/our" terms versus "I/me/mine" terms.
- Is flexible and willing to share information, ideas, and recognition.
- Gets along well with others.
- Exhibits interest and enthusiasm.
- Remains loyal to the team purpose and team members.

Importance of Human Relations Skills

Once team members understand their mission and roles, communication and other human relations skills become important.

A key ingredient for any team effort is open communication. It enhances creativity, camaraderie, and productivity. Speaking assertively and listening actively are two valuable skills. Speaking clearly, calmly, and firmly and displaying confidence and good body posture are also important. Even in unpleasant situations, an assertive person will remain calm and in control, which goes a long way toward establishing the trust and confidence needed in team members.

On an effective team, good human relations skills are on constant display. They include applying emotional intelligence in managing oneself and one's relationships with others, handling confrontations or problems fairly, and resolving issues in a satisfactory way. Organizations often deliberately select people from different backgrounds for team membership. Being comfortable with diversity and open to others' ideas and practices are important. Chapter 11 talks more about diversity.

Working in Virtual Teams

Some considerations that require attention with virtual teams are sensitivity to cultural diversity when team members are from different nations, and time variances when scheduling meetings. Team experts Jon Katzenbach and Douglas Smith offer these pointers for working as a virtual team:[9]

- Hold a face-to-face meeting early to confirm your goals, agree on a working approach, and establish rules for using groupware.

- Select groupware features as a team and practice them together so all members will be familiar with the technology.

- Agree on team netiquette; for example, agree that members will answer e-mail within 24 hours, record vacation days on the team calendar, and let other members know when they will be on site.

- Continue to hold face-to-face meetings as often as needed.

Ask Yourself...

1. Think of a role you've played, or are currently playing, on a team. How did you come to be in that role, and how did (or do) you feel playing it?

2. Based on your own experiences and observations, what are some other roles of effective team members?

7.4 TEAM GROWTH

Initially, team members go through a feeling-out stage, learning what each has to contribute and how to interact with one another. As they continue to work together, they become more comfortable with the team effort, and their performance improves. A team is considered mature when its members help one another and address problems that impede its work. Eventually, the team becomes highly effective and focused on the common purpose of achieving team goals. Five factors that influence a team's effectiveness are behavior and interest, synergy, cohesiveness, norms, and status.

The Four Stages of Team Development

In 1965, psychologist Bruce W. Tuckman put forward a model of team development that is still widely accepted today. According to this model, a team will typically pass through four stages of development: forming, storming, norming, and performing.[10]

Forming   Individuals identify the team's goals and how their own goals may fit with the team's. They decide how much time, energy, and effort they wish to commit to the team and become acquainted with other team members. Everyone behaves politely, and individuals seldom take strong stands at this stage.

> **KeyPoint**
> A typical team passes through four stages of development: forming, storming, norming, and performing.

Storming   Members may engage in constructive conflicts and disagreements. Individuals may question the team's direction and progress, and some will resist task assignments or attempt power plays to gain control. Some may display frustration with the team's activities. Others become stronger through listening and handling challenges and complaints. Members learn how to deal effectively with disagreements and establish a better balance and clear direction. Real progress occurs.

Norming   Team members pursue responsibilities and work toward team goals. The team works as a whole to resolve problems, establish action plans, and focus on getting things done. Individuals develop negotiation skills, deal with ambiguity, cooperate, and communicate effectively. Not all teams reach this stage.

Performing   Individuals actively help one another complete assignments and tasks in order to achieve team goals. Team members develop a sense of trust and commitment at both individual and team levels. Members acknowledge cooperation and performance, value learning, and imagine future objectives. Again, not all teams reach the performing stage.

Behavior and Interest

> **KeyPoint**
> A team's effectiveness is influenced by behavior and interest, synergy, cohesiveness, norms, and status.

People's behavior changes constantly. Changes in behavior may occur for a number of reasons, such as changing perceptions, the influence of family or peers, continued education, acquisition of new skills, or reassignment within the organization. These behavior changes may have a positive or negative effect on the team.

The team itself can cause an individual to behave differently. Some people are more comfortable in a one-on-one situation than in a team atmosphere.

Finally, the level of interest that members have in the team's goals and activities may change over time. For example, you may have once been a member of a group of friends that made up the company softball team and socialized together every weekend. Eventually, the team grew smaller or broke up as individual members became involved in new personal activities or other job and school responsibilities.

Synergy

Synergy is the cooperative interaction of two or more individuals to achieve a result they wouldn't have been able to achieve on their own. When the individual talents of team members come together to achieve a group goal, that team has found synergy. Put simply, synergy means that the whole of the group is greater than the sum of its parts.

Teams can take advantage of synergy to develop more and better ideas and to make superior decisions through brainstorming. Studies have shown that the collective creativity of the group increases the number of alternative solutions or ideas that are generated, and a group consensus helps ensure commitment from all team members. Decisions made by effective groups generally produce better results.

Cohesiveness

Another factor influencing a team's behavior is cohesiveness. *Cohesiveness* is the degree to which a team "sticks together" and acts as one. In general, the more cohesive a group is, the more effective it is. As the team becomes more successful, it becomes even more inseparable. This effect occurs because cohesive team members stay close, supporting and encouraging one another. This support and encouragement helps reduce stress, leading to greater job satisfaction.

Cohesiveness develops through a number of factors, one of which is team size. Smaller groups tend to be more cohesive because they can communicate readily. Similarity of the individuals in a group is also a factor. The more individuals share similar values, backgrounds, and ages, the more cohesive they tend to be.

Sometimes teams become more cohesive because of outside pressures. The "It's you and me against the world!" attitude draws members together to support and assist one another.

Group Norms

Group norms are shared values about the kinds of behaviors that are acceptable to the team. These norms are standards of behavior that each member is expected to follow—similar to rules that apply to members of sports teams. Some norms are formally stated, but most are not. Group norms generally develop over time and usually relate to those matters of most importance to the group as a whole.

We learn about norms in various ways. For example, we learn about formally stated norms in orientation programs, classroom training, and on-the-job training. We grasp norms that aren't formally stated through conversations with other group members and observations of their behavior.

Often group norms enhance group effectiveness. For instance, when the members of Billie's graphic design team are having trouble coming up with a new design, they always go out to a particular Thai restaurant for lunch. They stuff themselves and relax, joke, and laugh. After a while, they start sketching on the place mats, and the idea they've been looking for generally comes along. The lunches also boost the team members' commitment, stoke their enthusiasm, and build cohesiveness.

Unfortunately, group norms sometimes prevent members from working toward the goals of the organization. For instance, a factory might judge an assembly line worker's performance purely on speed and output. But if that worker is pressured by coworkers to work more slowly so they don't look bad, then group norms are having more influence on the worker than the goals of the company. In this case, the sanctions and rewards of the informal group are stronger than those of the formal organization.

Failure to conform to group norms is known as *deviance*. Some examples of deviance are missing meetings, showing up late, having a poor attitude, or not completing one's share of the work. If the infraction is minor or members don't consider it important, deviance isn't punished. If it involves breaking company rules, punishment can be formal and might include poor reviews, reduced pay, reprimands, and even termination.

In smaller groups, punishment, if any, is more likely to take the form of informal *sanctions*. Two typical sanctions are talking to the member about how that person's actions are affecting the group and tending to avoid or exclude the member. Sanctions may also include gossip, criticism, and even more severe actions such as harassment. The type of sanction may depend on how important other members perceive the violation to be.

Status of Group Members

The status of group members sometimes influences a group's chemistry negatively. In some groups, social class, economic success, and higher education may confer higher status. Members with these attributes may be given more respect, and other group members may pay more attention to them. In a well-functioning group, though, members set status aside and focus on their goal.

Ask Yourself...

1. Consider a group or team of which you're currently a member. In what stage of development is it? How can you tell?

2. Think about a team to which you've belonged. What are (or were) its norms?

Ethics CONNECTION

A Texas high school basketball coach was fired when his team won a game 100–0. The head of Dallas Covenant School and its board chair issued this statement: "It is shameful and an embarrassment that this happened. This clearly does not reflect a Christlike and honorable approach to competition."

The coach, Micah Grimes, wrote in reply, "We played the game as it was meant to be played. My values and my beliefs would not allow me to run up the score on any opponent, and it will not allow me to apologize for a wide-margin victory when my girls played with honor and integrity."

Girls basketball does not have a mercy rule that says a team leading by a wide margin should reduce the intensity of its play or simply let the clock run out to avoid embarrassing the other team. The winning team's spectators cheered their team on as they continued to score.

The opposing team's school, Dallas Academy, specializes in teaching students with learning disabilities. Its high school had 20 students, and 8 girls were on the varsity basketball team. It was recognized nationally for hanging in and refusing to give up.[11]

   1. List all the group norms in this situation.

   2. Were any norms violated? Why, or why not?

7.5   CREATING EFFECTIVE TEAMS

Creating effective teams from the ground up requires both organizational support and good leadership. Organizations support teams through actions such as encouraging employee involvement, granting authority, supplying resources, and accepting team decisions. Leaders of workplace teams may have widely different styles, but all of them must fulfill similar responsibilities. Teams and their leaders should be prepared to deal with challenges such as negative behavior, conflict, and groupthink.

Team Building

Many organizations make a conscious effort to develop competent teams through team building. *Teambuilding* is a series of activities designed to help work groups solve problems, accomplish work goals, and function more effectively through teamwork. Constructive team building requires that each participant accept the team goals and objectives and take ownership of the results. Because of this, a high degree of cohesion develops within the group, and the open environment improves the quality of problem solving and decision making. Team building enables teams to reach high levels of performance.

> *If everyone is moving forward together, then success takes care of itself.*
> —Henry Ford, automobile manufacturer

Leadership

> *Leaders don't create followers; they create more leaders.*
> —*Tom Peters, management consultant*

During your career, you are likely to have opportunities to lead a group or team. According to Warren Bennis in his article "The Secrets of Great Groups," leaders of successful groups "vary widely in style and personality." Some are doers; others are facilitators, ensuring the team runs smoothly and members have the resources they need. But all these leaders have several things in common. For example, they share leadership responsibilities with members who assume informal roles. And they take on any role necessary for the team to achieve its overall goal. Bennis writes that effective group leaders "understand the chemistry of the group and the dynamics of the work process" and "provide direction and meaning."[12]

In some workplace teams, the team leader is chosen by the members. And in others that have a formal leader, another leader may emerge over time. The choice of an informal or ***emergent leader*** in an effective team is made by consensus. The team will usually select this leader based on his or her strengths and abilities.

Figure 7.5 lists some responsibilities of a team leader.

Figure 7.5

Responsibilities of a team leader.

- Assign the right people to the right tasks and make expectations clear.
- Encourage participation by nudging, assisting, encouraging, and answering questions.
- See the big picture and plan.
- Involve new employees in the team to bring a fresh outlook or approach.
- Provide encouragement, motivation, and spirit.
- Administer rewards for performance, including positive reinforcement and acknowledgement of contributions.
- Teach, assist, and answer questions.
- Remove obstacles that keep the team from performing.
- Keep things on track and moving forward.

Setting the Group Size Studies have shown that the preferred group size for maximum effectiveness in problem solving and decision making is five or seven members. (Having an odd number of members prevents tie votes.) Groups of fewer than five offer a number of advantages due to their small size. A significant disadvantage, however, is that there are fewer people to share task responsibilities. In groups larger than seven, more diverse opinions are shared. But larger groups tend to have a host of problems, including difficulties in communication and coordination.[13]

Identifying Effective Team Members   If you are able to select the members of your team, aim for a cross section of talents with each member representing expertise in a separate discipline. When drawing a team from an existing group, rely on the strengths of certain individuals and develop abilities in others. When appropriate, a good team leader will cross-train employees in different job responsibilities or rotate them to different departments or functions to enhance their knowledge of operations.

Strive to recognize valuable traits in individuals and encourage them to flourish. The freedom to make mistakes allows growth through trial and error. Leadership skills are discussed in fuller detail in Chapter 9.

Leading Virtual Teams

Experts offer these pointers for leading virtual teams:

- An important step is to establish trust among all team members. Trust is a major challenge for virtual teams and may require a little time and effort from the group.
- Often, the leader must adjust to letting go of the traditional overseeing of onsite workers.
- Reliability and accuracy of others' work is important, as is knowing that all members are carrying their fair share of the workload.
- Virtual teams have many leadership roles; assign some to members. The roles of facilitator, note keeper, and discussion leader are especially important but sometimes undervalued when teams don't meet in person.[14]

Challenges

The challenges facing a team don't have to do merely with attaining the goal the organization has set them. Teams and team leaders will also encounter and deal with challenges to the team process itself.

Negative Behavior   While many of the behaviors that team members exhibit are positive ones, a few create problems and should be managed by the group leader, a facilitator, or other team members. Two examples are blocking and dominating.

- Blocking   Resisting any suggestions or ideas of the team; acting negatively toward the group purpose and members
- Dominating   Forcing opinions, ideas, and desires on other team members; manipulating team behavior by asserting status or authority; using flattery, interruptions, or other aggressive measures

Sometimes an emergent leader has purposes and goals that differ from those of the team and team leader. When that happens, conflict will arise.

"There are some egos in here gumming it up."

In *Quick Skills: Teamwork,* Douglas Gordon suggests that as the leader, your role may be to talk to the offending member and if necessary apply some form of discipline. An alternative is to restructure tasks to reduce that person's interactions with the group.[15]

Conflict Although conflict is often regarded as a barrier to teamwork, constructive conflict is actually an essential part of the process, part of the storming stage of team development. It can stimulate team members to resolve issues and improve performance. Conflict, however, can also be disruptive or destructive. Chapter 8 discusses managing conflict in work groups.

Groupthink A third challenge that teams sometimes face is groupthink. Mentioned briefly in Chapter 6, groupthink occurs when members of a group tend to suppress their own ideas and to make their opinions and decisions conform to those of other members. Through groupthink, a group may be led to a conclusion without fully exploring or even considering alternatives.

A phenomenon identified by psychologist Irving Janis, groupthink can have some negative results. It was identified, for example, as a factor in the disastrous decision to launch the space shuttle *Challenger* the day it exploded.

Douglas Gordon offers several suggestions for reversing the process of groupthink, including the following:

• Break a large team into smaller groups for discussion and then compare their results.

• Solicit opinions and information from qualified people who aren't on the team.

• Select a member to be a devil's advocate, challenging team assumptions.[16]

Ask Yourself...

1. Compare the level of individual participation in classes with many students to those with fewer students. Are you more likely to participate in class discussion when you're in a small class? Why?

2. Think of a time when you were part of a group or team in which negative behavior, conflict, or groupthink was a problem. What was the effect on the group or team? How, if at all, was the problem resolved?

KEY TERMS

group	virtual teams
formal group	groupware
functional group	formal roles
task group	informal roles
ongoing committees	role ambiguity
ad hoc committees	synergy
informal groups	cohesiveness
team	group norms
project teams	deviance
self-directed work teams	sanctions
functional work teams	team building
cross-functional work teams	emergent leader

CHAPTER SUMMARY

Most of us interact with a variety of groups every day. Most groups exist to satisfy organizational or individual needs. Work groups are important because they influence the overall behavior and performance of individuals in the workplace.

Workplaces include both formal and informal groups. Formal groups may be functional groups (part of the organizational hierarchy) or task groups (such as committees and teams). Informal groups, formed by members who share similar interests, can exert a powerful influence on members' behavior.

Throughout your career, you will be a member of many different teams. Teams benefit both organizations and employees. Five common types of teams are project teams, self-directed work teams, functional work teams, cross-functional work teams, and virtual teams. Though popular, the team approach doesn't fit every organization or situation.

Early tasks of teams are to agree on goals and begin to fill roles. Many teams have both formal, assigned roles, and informal roles that members take on themselves when they perceive a need. Certain behaviors, actions, attitudes, and characteristics make for effective team members. Team members also need good human relations skills, especially communication.

Teams typically pass through four stages of development: forming, storming, norming, and performing. A team's effectiveness is influenced by its members' behavior and level of interest, synergy, cohesiveness, group norms, and member status.

Creating effective teams requires both organizational support and good leadership. Team building activities help work groups solve problems, accomplish work goals, and function more effectively through teamwork. Many of us are likely to have opportunities for group or team leadership in our careers. Successful leaders have different styles but share similar responsibilities, and they share leadership responsibilities with team members. Three challenges teams may encounter are negative behavior, conflict, and groupthink.

REVIEW

1. Why should we study group and team dynamics?

2. What are the benefits of teams for organizations and employees?

3. What can you do to become an effective team member?

4. What happens during the stages of team development?

5. What are some factors that influence group and team effectiveness?

6. As the leader of a group or team, what would your responsibilities be?

CRITICAL THINKING

1. Think of a group with which you are associated, such as a social club, church group, civic group, or work group. What kind of group is it? Who is the formal leader? Is there an emergent leader? Why is this individual recognized as the emergent leader? Why did you become a member of this group?

2. Give some examples of group norms and describe the groups to which they belong. How might these norms be violated? What do you think would happen if the norms were violated?

3. Identify some important informal group roles. Which, if any, of these roles do you play or have you played most often? Which have you observed other people playing? What made them so recognizable to you?

4. Identify a problem within your community. If you were the formal leader of a group assigned to correct the problem, what qualities, skills, and background would you look for in choosing team members? How would you approach the task of team formation?

5. Think of a team to which you've belonged and discuss the stages of team development as they occurred. Were the stages readily identifiable, and what prompted each transition?

CASE STUDIES

In small groups, analyze the following situations:

1 **A Company Crisis** Anita Magill took over as chief executive officer at Magill Manufacturing after her father retired from running the business. Magill Manufacturing is a keystone company in Lisbon, Ohio, and provides jobs to a large number of citizens in the community. Anita takes great pride in continuing the family business but knows that she'll need to run the operation differently than her father has.

After only a short time, Anita has realized that the company is suffering from high absenteeism, chronic tardiness, and low morale. Frequent complaints are filed, employee attitudes are poor, and there's a general sense of discontent among the workers. Management is viewed as coercive, with "little dictators" running isolated kingdoms throughout the company. Employees feel that managers give little support to their ideas or suggestions. Working at Magill Manufacturing has become a way to earn a paycheck and little more. These conditions are reflected in slumping productivity and the declining quality of products. Anita knows she needs to act quickly if she's going to turn this situation around and improve quality, increase productivity, and reestablish company loyalty.

1. How can Anita use team concepts to improve conditions at Magill Manufacturing?

2. What types of team dynamics do you see happening within the company? Support your answers with examples from the chapter.

3. What different types of teams can Anita form to help solve the company's problems? Discuss how they may be successful and why.

2 Who's the Boss?   Robert has just been promoted into his first supervisory position. His team has been pulled together to help get the designs completed and construction started on a new bank remodeling and expansion. Initially, a high degree of camaraderie existed among the eight engineers on the team. The lead engineer, Kendra, has a longstanding record of good performance, knowledge of how the teams work, and loyalty to the organization. Kendra often helps train new employees, offering advice and showing them established procedures for the jobs.

Robert is somewhat uneasy with the guidance being given by Kendra. He frequently challenges her decisions and questions the approaches that she recommends to the junior engineers. Rather than relying on her knowledge and experience, Robert sets out to gain absolute control and change the workflow methods.

It doesn't take long for the junior engineers to get the picture. After all, they don't want to do a job twice—the way Kendra tells them and then again the way Robert requires it. Now Kendra feels ostracized from the group. The feeling of being an outcast is uncomfortable. After a few months of seeing the situation deteriorate further, Kendra asks to be moved to another project to prevent any loss of her opportunities for career advancement.

1. Into what type of team has Robert been promoted? Was there an emergent leader on this team? Who and why?

2. What factors influence this team's effectiveness? What were the effects when that effectiveness weakened?

3. What could Robert do differently to minimize the team's disharmony? What could Kendra do to ensure continued team cohesiveness?

HUMAN RELATIONS IN ACTION

In groups, choose a movie that you feel demonstrates aspects of large and small group or team interactions discussed in this chapter. Be certain the movie illustrates a variety of group characteristics. Examples are war films with groups ranging from squadrons to close personal friendships, films about sports teams or musical groups, or films about explorers or survivors of a disaster.

While you watch the film, take notes about the different types of team interactions, roles, stages of team development, group norms that are accepted (or not accepted), and any other factors you recognize as relevant to the chapter material.

Together, prepare a written description and analysis of these findings. Be prepared to present your findings to other class members. Share and compare your findings. If you need suggestions for movie selections, your teacher has a list of possible choices.

For additional resources, refer to the web site for this text:
www.cengage.com/management/dalton

RESOURCES

1. Dahl, D. (2009, May). Managing: Fast, flexible, and full of team spirit. How to work more like a start-up. *Inc.*, *31*(4), 95–97; and Total Attorneys web site: http://www.totalattorneys.com

2. Monroe, B. (2008, July). The flag ladies of freeport, Maine. *Reader's Digest*, 21; and History of the flag ladies. Retrieved on July 30, 2009, from Freeport Flag Ladies web site: http://www.freeportflagladies.com

3. Morgeson, F. P. (2005). The external leadership of self-managed teams: Interviews in the context of novel and disruptive events. *Journal of Applied Psychology*, *90*(3), 497.

4. Nelson, N. (2002). The HR generalist's guide to teambuilding. Society for Human Resource Management White Papers, August.

5. *Ibid.*

6. Samsung uses project management solution to streamline research and development. Microsoft Case Studies. Retrieved on July 31, 2009, from http://www.microsoft.com/casestudies/Case_Study_Detail.aspx?CaseStudyID=53153

7. Gordon, D. (2001). *Quick skills: Teamwork*. Cincinnati, OH: South-Western Educational Publishing, 12.

8. Gordon, *Quick skills: Teamwork*, 16.

9. Katzenbach, J., Smith, D. K. (2001, fall). The discipline of virtual teams. *Leader to Leader*, *22*. Retrieved on July 30, 2009, from http://www.pfdf.org/knowledgecenter/journal.aspx?ArticleID=112

10. Tuckman, B., Jensen, B. M. (1977). Stages of small group development revisited. *Group and Organizational Studies*, *2*, 419–427.

11. Coach says team played with honor. (2009, January 26). Retrieved on August 2, 2009, from ESPN Rise: Girls Basketball web site: http://sports.espn.go.com/highschool/rise/basketball/girls/news/story?id=3859935

12. Bennis, W. (1997, winter). The secrets of great groups. *Leader to Leader*, *3*, 29–33. Retrieved on from http://www.leadertoleader.org/knowledgecenter/journal.aspx?ArticleID=140

13. Likert, R. (1961). *New patterns of management*. New York: McGraw-Hill.

14. Duarte, D., Smith, N. (2006). *Mastering virtual teams: Strategies, tools, and techniques that succeed*. San Francisco, CA: Jossey-Bass; and Katzenbach, The discipline of virtual teams.

15. Gordon, *Quick skills: Teamwork*, 86.

16. Gordon, *Quick skills: Teamwork*, 79.

CONFLICT MANAGEMENT:
TECHNIQUES FOR RESOLUTION

OBJECTIVES

After studying this chapter, you should be able to:

8.1 Define conflicts, explain why they are increasing in the workplace, and identify techniques to manage them.

8.2 Explain emotional intelligence as well as the problem-solving and communication skills needed to manage conflict.

8.3 Manage angry and hostile individuals.

8.4 Manage conflict within work groups.

8.5 Understand the methods organizations use to manage conflict.

Jump Start

A reporter for a major metropolitan newspaper was being pressured by her boss to stay for a meeting even though she had made a commitment to go to her son's school play. The conflict escalated verbally; an argument ensued. The reporter screamed, "I quit!" and left in tears. She eventually returned, however, when another employee stepped in to help resolve the issue.[1]

Conflict in the workplace is a common occurrence. Americans spend approximately 2.8 hours per week at work dealing with it. Compared with other countries, 36 percent of U.S. employees report having to deal with conflict always or frequently while globally the percentage is 29 percent.[2]

- Have you ever been in conflict with someone at work? If so, how was it resolved?
- Have you ever intervened in a conflict? Was your intervention successful? Why or why not?

8.1   CONFLICT DEFINED

The *Merriam-Webster Online Dictionary* defines **conflict** as a mental struggle resulting from incompatible or opposing needs, drives, wishes, or external or internal demands.[3] Conflict in the workplace is inevitable, but you can take steps to control and resolve it. People have differences at work every day involving:[4]

- Personality clashes
- Complaints from customers
- Disputes with superiors
- Disagreements about methods of work
- Differences over pay and working conditions
- Workplace responsibilities

Conflict exists in today's workplace for a variety of reasons. Some of these are rapid change, the increasing complexity of work, an economy that pushes companies to do more with less, the vast diversity of employees in the workforce, and the availability of more options and information with which to make decisions.

Workplace conflict can be positive if channeled in a healthy, open, and positive way. It can:[5]

- Result in a better understanding of other people.
- Lead to an improved solution to some problem or challenge.
- Force the development of a major innovation or new idea.

In fact, a lack of conflict can indicate problems within the organization. Employees are most likely not expressing their opinions or contributing ideas. Groupthink may be occurring. An organization not looking at issues from a number of viewpoints will most likely fall behind the competition.

> **KeyPoint**
> Unresolved conflict can negatively impact an organization's bottom line.

An organization that successfully promotes healthy conflict will:[6]

- Set clear expectations for it.
- Encourage conflict around ideas and issues.
- Expect people to use data and facts to support opinions and recommendations.
- Not tolerate personal attacks.
- Reward, recognize, and thank people who are willing to take a stand.

However, unresolved conflict can be destructive. Employees can develop feelings of hurt, anger, fear, confusion, stress, and anxiety. These feelings can lead to strained relationships, defensiveness, jockeying for position, and even meltdowns.[7,8] Morale plummets. After a disagreement 76 percent of workers will go out of their way to avoid one another, diminishing team cooperation.[9]

Organizations soon begin to be affected by the emotions and actions of their employees in conflict. Signs of unresolved conflict within organizations can be:[10]

- Loss of productivity
- Increased absenteeism
- Workplace bullying
- Injury and accidents
- Employee turnover
- Grievances and litigation
- Increased customer complaints

If unmanaged conflict is such a hindrance and managed conflict can lead to big breakthroughs, why doesn't someone move quickly to handle it? The biggest reason is that managing it requires courage. Avoiding and minimizing conflict is easier than tackling it head on. Additionally, our society tends to reward competition rather than collaboration.[11] This is particularly true in the workplace where performance appraisals often focus on individual—rather than group—achievement.

To handle conflict, individuals and organizations are increasingly relying on the principles of conflict management. ***Conflict management*** is a process in which the parties cooperate and work together to reach a solution that is agreeable to all. Most conflicts can be managed so that they don't become a destructive force at work.[12]

Because conflict has the potential to be pervasive, you must do your part to minimize it. The following suggestions will help minimize conflict:

- Use strong communication skills so that you lessen the possibility you are causing conflict.
- Listen carefully for areas of agreement and build on them.
- Use conflict management skills to defuse conflict between yourself and others, regardless of who is responsible for escalating the conflict.
- Use conflict management skills to help others who are in conflict defuse and resolve it. This role is called a ***third-party conflict manager.***

The ability to manage conflict greatly impacts the organization and human relations system. How conflict is managed affects organizational factors such as leadership, managerial style, power, culture, and the group's ability to make decisions. Likewise, conflict management is related to communication and collaboration and is a part of your response in the 21st century organization.

Conflict management requires strong emotional intelligence.[13] A strong range of communication and problem-solving skills are also required.[14] While anyone can learn conflict management, it takes practice. No set formula exists. Your ability to manage conflict hinges on your attitudes toward others, the image others have of you, and your mastery of various communication and conflict resolution skills.

Ask Yourself...

1. Describe a time when you saw conflict in an organization handled successfully.

2. After it was resolved, did the conflict make your organization more effective or less effective? Explain your answer.

8.2 EMOTIONAL INTELLIGENCE AND SKILL SETS

Self-regulation and empathy are two components of emotional intelligence vital to successful conflict management.[15] Additionally, you need an array of skills at your disposal. Think of these skills as tools you might employ depending on the situation. As you practice these skills, you will become more adept at using them. Skills that are particularly valuable include active listening, focusing on needs rather than wants, and formulating and expressing desired outcomes.

Emotional Intelligence

Self-Regulation   Trustworthiness is one of the self-regulation skills Daniel Goleman indentifies in *Working with Emotional Intelligence*.[16] If others do not view you as trustworthy, any attempts you make to resolve issues will be ignored.

You can't force others to trust you. A human's ability to trust is based, in part, on past experiences with trust and betrayal. You can, however, develop and use behaviors that encourage others to trust you. These behaviors are ability, integrity, and benevolence.[17]

Does the other party see you as competent and skillful? For others to see you as able, you need more than just the skills required for the task at hand—you must project self-confidence. Your coworkers must have as much belief in your abilities as you do.

KeyPoint
While you cannot force others to trust you, you can display behaviors that will encourage trust.

Integrity is displayed by the extent to which you walk the talk. Do you stand for fairness? Do your actions back up your words? Do you follow through on what you say?

To project fairness, you must be as objective as possible. This means that you are as free as possible from self-interest, prejudice, and favoritism.[18] While no one can be entirely objective, you can increase your objectivity by following these suggestions:[19]

> **KeyPoint**
> You can increase the odds of appearing fair by thoroughly understanding the issues, gathering as much accurate information as possible, and constantly monitoring your own objectivity.

- Ensure you understand the problem and what constitutes a solution. To do this, listen to the other side of the story and be sure you know how the other person thinks the issue should be resolved.

- Obtain as much accurate and comprehensive information from unbiased sources as possible. You may need to consult with a mentor or other person who has had experience with the problem you are attempting to resolve. You may need to read or research the topic, particularly if the question in conflict is how to proceed with a technical problem.

- Maintain objectivity in evaluating ideas to minimize personal bias. Spend time thinking about the issue and asking yourself whether you have let your personal bias interfere with how you are seeing the situation.

Lastly, your coworkers need to feel you are willing to advance their interests or at least not to block them. This is called benevolence. You can show you are benevolent by communicating honestly and openly and by not always having to be in control.[20]

Other self-regulation abilities important to conflict management are conscientiousness, adaptability, flexibility, and a willingness to admit when you are wrong and apologize.[21]

Rate Your Empathy

1. Are you affected when you see a stranger suffering?
2. Are you excited in movies when the main characters overcome hardship?
3. Are you able to pinpoint quickly the moods of your friends and coworkers?
4. Are you frequently moved to help someone who is having problems?
5. Are you at ease talking about your feelings or emotions?

If you answered "yes" to four or more of these questions, you most likely have a good sense of empathy. If you answered "yes" to two or fewer of the questions, you need to work on becoming more empathetic.

Empathy When you're displaying empathy, you're respecting the differences and sensing the feelings and perspectives of others. You develop empathy by listening carefully to others and imagining yourself in their shoes. A healthy and sincere ability to empathize enables you to separate the person from the problem, which is a hallmark of a good conflict manager.[22]

Empathizing with someone does not mean you agree with him or her.[23] The importance is in understanding others' viewpoint and feelings.

Ethics CONNECTION

Is using violence to resolve conflict ever acceptable? Mohandas K. Gandhi (1869–1948), a spiritual leader in India, opposed using violence as a means to resolve conflict. He practiced nonviolence of conflict resolution while protesting British imperial rule in India. He preferred to win over the hearts and minds of his opponents to his point of view, give them a way to save face, and seek a win–win resolution wherever possible. He felt that nonviolence was a way of taking positive action to resist oppression or bring about change.

While most everyone would agree that violence should never be used at work to resolve issues, it does happen. Psychological violence such as bullying, use of profanity, and put-downs as well as hostile and aggressive behavior occur. Occasionally violence turns physical, resulting in shouting, throwing objects in anger, spitting, rude gestures, shoving, fist fights, or even stalking. None of these behaviors are ever appropriate at work.

1. Why do you believe violence occurs in the workplace?
2. Have you ever witnessed violence being used to resolve conflict at work? If so, describe your experience.
3. If you had been responsible for resolving the conflict you witnessed, how would you have handled it? Explain your answer.

❝ *Some people think only intellect counts: Knowing how to solve problems, knowing how to get by, knowing how to identify an advantage and seize it. But the functions of intellect are insufficient without courage, love, friendship, compassion and empathy.*
—*Dean Koontz, American Author* **❞**

Skill Sets for Resolving Conflict

Active Listening In his book *Conflict Management Skills*,[24] Gregorio Billikopf describes two skills that are extremely important in resolving conflict. The first is listening. Good active listening skills will allow you to focus on the other individuals' wants and needs without judging or interrupting and to display empathy. If you listen to the other person's side of the argument, he or she is more likely to listen to yours.

Focusing on Needs   The second skill Billikopf considers important is the ability to focus on needs rather than positions.[25] Needs are not always obvious.

For example, an employee who had been terminated called the company's human resource (HR) manager requesting a copy of his personnel file. His position was that he wanted a copy of the file. Since company policy did not allow files to be released, an argument ensued. However, after some questioning, his need was uncovered. He needed to be sure that nothing in his file would keep him from being hired at another company.

As a conflict manager, don't assume you know the needs of the other party. Make an effort to discover them. Remember that the emotions of the other person are real. He or she is entitled to his or her feelings even if you don't agree. Additionally, be honest about your own interests and fears and share your needs with the opposing party.[26]

To be sure you're not making assumptions:[27]

- Analyze your assumption and determine how much of it is based on fact.
- Present your understanding of the conflict and allow open discussion.
- Put yourself in their shoes. Take your assumption and argue the other side of it for the sake of argument.

A helpful step in identifying needs is to take big problems and break them down into small ones.[28] By closely examining and understanding the small pieces of the problem and its underlying emotions, you can more effectively seek resolution.

Developing and Analyzing Options   Developing and analyzing options takes time. Be patient and allow everyone an opportunity to consider the ideas presented. Good options are developed through active participation by the parties, meet the needs of all parties, allow the parties to save face, and are based on objective standards.[29,30]

Defining and analyzing options takes creativity. The steps are:[31]

1. Define the problem.
2. Actively consider different solutions.
3. Think through each solution as if you were actually going to implement it. Look for unexpected benefits as well as problems.
4. Set aside the problem and wait for a sudden flash of inspiration that needs to be tested carefully. You may need to repeat this step several times.

You've heard the expression, "Be careful what you wish for because you just might get it." Unfortunately, in the heat of conflict we frequently fail to think carefully about what we want.[32] For instance, suppose you are having trouble with a coworker and tell your supervisor you don't want to deal with her anymore. Are you ready to deal with the consequences of your request?

What if your supervisor gives you what you want—not having to deal with your coworker—by transferring you to another unit or terminating you?

Reality checking is a way to explore the consequences of possible solutions. Develop and honestly answer probing questions about what you want as a resolution and what might happen if you chose that option.[33] Only by doing this can you arrive at solid options that are in the best interests of both parties.

Win–win options are those that satisfy the interests of both parties. While the parties may not have gotten everything they wanted, they are satisfied with the agreement and can live with it.

Good options help the parties save face. *Saving face* refers to maintaining a good image. Many times people who are involved in conflict do not want to admit they were wrong or have backed down. You can help the other party save face by granting minor concessions or simply stating your feelings or wishes without making a judgment about the other person.[34] Never brag or gloat over your victory.

© 2009 Ted Goff

"Could you hire some other employees? The ones you have just can't get along with me."

Techniques for moving toward resolution[35]

Ask questions

Why? Why not? What if?

Offer alternative solutions

A possibility is…. What do you think about…?

Reframe

Help the other party look at the situation from a new perspective. For example, being transferred to a new unit can be reframed as an opportunity to do something more enjoyable.

Share experiences

Disclose experiences so that the affected persons will realize they are not the only ones to go through these types of situations.

Discuss costs

Explore both emotional and financial costs.

Focus on the future

Work to put the past behind you and look to the future.

Global CONNECTION[36]

While conflict is difficult enough to resolve in U.S. workplaces, issues are even more complex in the global workplace. Not only must you possess strong communication skills, you must also have cultural intelligence. Cultural intelligence means you have knowledge concerning the appropriateness of behaviors and motivation in the culture in which you are attempting to resolve conflict. This ability to negotiate across cultures is increasingly important as corporations expand globally.

For example, business negotiations in China can be frustrating for Americans for several reasons. In Chinese society, developing personal connections is very important. Time must be allotted to allow these connections to develop. Because China has a strict social hierarchical system that favors centralized decision making, communication styles tend to be indirect and group harmony valued. In addition, research shows that the Chinese favor trust over law (for example, formal contracts) as well as respect the status of superiors, elders, and parents.

1. If you were sent to another country to negotiate a contract, how could you make sure you had enough cultural intelligence?
2. Do you believe many Americans lack the patience to build personal connections? If so, why do you think this is? How can America become a more patient society?

KeyPoint
Not allowing the other side to save face can derail a resolution.

Lastly, base good options on objective standards. Objective standards are rules of thumb you can use for your settlement that are developed by others who are not involved in the conflict. For instance, if you are an insurance adjuster and are negotiating with a customer over the value of an aircraft that has been destroyed, you might look at objective criteria such as (1) the original price minus depreciation, (2) replacement costs, (3) market value prior to its destruction, or (4) what a court of law might award as its value.[37]

> *When you are in deep conflict about something, sometimes the most trivial thing can tip the scales.*
>
> —Ethel Merman, American actress and singer

Ask Yourself...

1. Would others describe you as trustworthy? Can you be trustworthy and still change your position on issues? Explain your responses.
2. Why is it so hard to resist telling our side of the story first rather than concentrating on understanding what the other side has to say?
3. When you are involved in conflict, how important is saving face? Why do we, at times, wish to humiliate those with whom we have been at odds?

8.3 MANAGING ANGRY CONFRONTATIONS

Angry confrontations with customers or coworkers can erupt at any time in the workplace. Knowing how to deal effectively with someone else's anger and aggression is crucial. If a customer or coworker becomes loud and aggressive, do the following:

1. *Try not to take the confrontation personally.* If you do not know the individual, he or she is most likely displaying the perceptual defense mechanism of displacement, as discussed in Chapter 2. If you are dealing with someone you know, realize that the anger directed at you may not be totally justified and some displacement is most likely occurring. Whether the anger is justified or not, taking it personally and lashing back will only make the situation worse.

2. *Speak softly.* If you raise your voice, the other individual will raise his or hers. Use body language that indicates you are paying attention.

3. *Deal with emotions first.* Until the person calms down, he or she will not be able to enter into a problem-solving mode. Realize that the individual owns the emotions and they are real to that individual even if you feel the emotions are unjustified.

4. *Listen actively.* Continue to listen actively and acknowledge feelings as the individual vents. Make statements such as, "I can see why you're angry," or, "I'm sorry we've let you down." Continue to listen actively until the anger has run its course. If you have made a mistake, apologize. If you are dealing with a customer and the company has made a mistake (even if you did not), apologize.

5. *Don't inflame the situation.* Becoming defensive or trying to jump into the problem-solving mode before the individual's emotional outburst has run its course will only frustrate him or her and cause more anger and aggression.

> **KeyPoint**
> Never try to problem solve until you have dealt with emotions.

In The News

Actor Christian Bale became intensely angry on the set of *Terminator Salvation* when the cinematography director accidentally ruined a scene by walking onto the set. Bale went into a four-minute frenzy, which included explicit language and threats. Because he threatened to halt production, movie executives sent a tape of his ranting to their insurance company in case Bale left the project. Bale later apologized, stating his behavior was "inexcusable" and "deeply embarrassing."[38,39]

1. What do you imagine was going on inside Bale that caused him to behave the way he did?

2. If this type of rage was directed at you, how would you handle it?

In most instances the angry individual will calm down within minutes. You may need to remind the individual that you want to help but that he or she must calm down first. If the person does not compose himself or herself fairly quickly, or if you feel threatened, leave the area.

While these steps may seem simple to follow, they take practice. Generally you're caught off guard by someone's anger and you may need a minute to assume the right mindset to deal with it. Then, too, it's hard to concentrate when anger is directed at you. A good dose of self-confidence and strong self-esteem as well as practice will pay off in the long run.

Ask Yourself...

1. Have you ever been on the receiving end of a hostile confrontation? If so, what happened? Could you have handled it better? If so, how?

2. Why is it so hard not to take anger directed at you personally?

8.4 MANAGING CONFLICT IN GROUPS

Conflict in work groups can be experienced by single team members or by the team as a whole. The causes may be mutual antagonism, organizational reliance, goal ambiguity, labor–management disputes, and unclear roles.

Causes of Conflict in Groups

Mutual Antagonism   Conflicts may arise within the team or even between teams. Within the team, a conflict may occur between a supervisor and a subordinate or between any two or more team members. Between teams, ill feelings may exist for a variety of reasons. For example, plant operators may resent corporate engineers who design and implement changes that do not work well. The engineers may look down on the plant operators whom they perceive to have less education and knowledge. Such conflict may create considerable tension.

> " The easiest, the most tempting, and the least creative response to conflict within an organization is to pretend it does not exist.
>
> —Lyle E. Schaller, author and consultant "

Organizational Reliance   In most organizations, teams rely on one another. For example, machine operators depend on the maintenance crews to perform periodic maintenance on equipment. A production team may rely on the sales team to provide orders from customers to keep the production line in full operation. Conflict may arise between the teams if maintenance is inadequate or if sales orders force production into overtime to meet unrealistic schedules.

Technology CONNECTION[40,41]

Cybersettle, Inc., went online in 1998 and by 2009 had handled over 220,000 transactions. Legal professionals, insurance carriers, and governmental entities use it to settle a variety of disputes such as personal injury and property damage, with the largest settlement so far being $12.5 million. The company claims to have settled more insurance claims online than any other company in the world.

Here's how the process works: Parties submit settlement offers and demands confidentially online. The case automatically settles when the demand is less than the offer. However, if the offer and the demand are within a specific range of each other, the case is automatically settled by splitting the difference.

1. In what situations might you use a computer to settle a complaint?
2. Will this type of resolution technique work for all types of complaints? Explain your answer.

Goal Ambiguity   Team goals may differ from the goals of the organization. For example, the organization may want to hurry processes and jeopardize a product's quality to save time and money, while the work teams may want to take time to ensure quality.

Labor–Management Disputes   Labor and management have long had disagreements over work conditions, hours, and wages. However, the trouble often goes deeper. Conflict may be based on roles that each feels necessary to portray. Management representatives may believe that taking a tough, inflexible stance with union representatives just prior to contract negotiations is necessary to set the stage. This situation occurs frequently when union and management have opposing views.

Unclear Roles   The uncertainty brought on by constant changes in roles and missions breeds conflict. These environmental changes cause instability among team members, and conflict may occur. Good communication among team members helps control this type of conflict.

> " A permanent division of labor inevitably creates occupational and class inequality and conflict.
>
> —Robert Shea, novelist and journalist "

Options for Dealing with Group Conflict

The techniques listed in Figure 8.1 give you some options for dealing with conflict in groups to which you belong. When confronted with confusion or disagreements among team members, be alert and aware that the conflict exists, look for the causes, and understand the reasons as much as possible. The best option for group effectiveness is to acknowledge the conflict and attempt to resolve it using your human relations skills. You can assist your group in this process by developing strong facilitation skills.

At some point in your career, you may be responsible for facilitating or resolving a group conflict. A good facilitator works to keep trust, openness, and informality as a foundation for conflict resolution. The facilitator:[42]

- Teaches people to think of alternative ways to share information and resources.
- Encourages brainstorming sessions to allow all ideas to flow.
- Helps tie together various comments, questions, and concerns raised in discussion.
- Ensures all participants are aware of decisions being reached.
- Involves all participants, even those who do not frequently speak up.
- Stays process and goal oriented by keeping the meetings and discussions focused on group objectives.
- Remains alert and sensitive to the fine line between discussion that distracts from the topic and related helpful discussion.
- Discusses controversial issues thoroughly and attempts to reach a win–win resolution.
- Is skilled in decision making and aware of techniques favored by other group members.

You don't have to be a formal group leader in order to facilitate. All you need is strong human relations skills and a willingness to step forward.

© Marcin Balcerzak 2009/Used under license from Shutterstock.com

Group conflict resolution options.

Figure 8.1

Resolution Style	Characteristics	When to Use
Competing[43]	Highly goal oriented, relationships are low priority, has a need to win, can use aggressive behavior to resolve conflicts	An unpopular decision needs to be made, there is no likelihood of change, or resolution is needed immediately
Accommodating[44]	Smoothes over and gives in, ignores own goals	Maintaining relationship outweighs everything else, time is limited and harmony is of utmost importance, changes or suggestions are not important
Avoiding[45]	Withdraw, hide, and ignore conflict; give up personal goals and remain passive	Issue is trivial, stakes not high, little chance of getting what you want, disruption outweighs the benefit of conflict resolution, or others can more effectively resolve conflict
Compromising[46]	Sacrifice some goals and persuade others to give up some of theirs, assertive and cooperative but neither side is satisfied	Important/complex issues with no clear or simple solutions, conflicting people are equal in power and have strong interests in different solutions, no time restraints
Forcing[47]	Forcing results when two groups reach an impasse and allow an authoritative figure to choose one preference	Important/complex issues with no clear or simple solutions, conflicting people are equal in power and have strong interests in different solutions, time restraints
Collaborating[48]	Seeks resolution by looking for solutions agreeable to all sides	Maintaining a relationship is important, time is not a concern, peer conflict involved, working to gain commitment through consensus building

Ask Yourself...

1. While collaborating at work to manage conflict may be the best approach, when might you use the avoiding technique?

2. Have you ever been in a conflict in an organization where the parties were told how the situation was to be resolved without being allowed any input? What happened? Were the parties satisfied? Why or why not?

3. Think about a group in which you participate. Does someone act as the facilitator? If so, how effective do you believe that person's facilitation skills are? How could his or her skills be improved?

8.5 ORGANIZATIONAL SOLUTIONS TO CONFLICT

Organizations use a wide variety of methods to deal with conflicts that employees are not able to resolve on their own. These methods are known as *internal dispute resolution (IDR)* because they address disputes outside the courtroom. Organizations are not legally obligated to offer any form of IDR so you should become familiar with whether and how your employer deals with conflict. IDR may be informal or formal.[49]

Informal IDR

Open Door Policies   Many companies have a policy that encourages open communication. *An open door policy* means you are free to talk with any level of management at any time.[50] The open door method is the one most often used to resolve conflict. As a practical matter, you should start with the lowest level of management possible.

Human Resource Departments   One of the functions of an HR department is to listen and respond to employees. Many departments will take note of complaints and work to resolve them in a variety of ways. The department may launch a formal investigation, speak informally with the parties, or simply coach you on ways you can handle the situation.

Remember that complaints of harassment based on race, religion, sex, national origin, age, and disability cannot be kept confidential by HR or management. Harassment is illegal and complaints about it will be handled differently than other reports of conflict.

Ombuds   *Ombuds* (also known as ombudsmen or ombudspeople) provide informal, confidential help for those who want their problems addressed but not advertised. Ombuds generally report directly to the head of the organization and maintain a neutral stance. They work to ensure the process is fair and does not take sides. Keep in mind that you may still need to use the organization's formal grievance procedure even if you've spoken to the ombuds.[51]

KeyPoint
Attempt to handle conflict on your own before you use company-sponsored methods.

Telephone or Web Hotlines   Many organizations have hotlines either via telephone or web to report problems or conflicts as well as ethical or legal violations. Depending on the system, you will either speak to a live operator or leave a message. If you leave a message, be sure you provide enough information to allow the organization to investigate the issue.[52]

Formal IDR

Grievance Procedures   The *grievance procedure* provides formal structure and outlines the steps an employee should take to resolve an issue. Generally, it gives timelines for lodging a complaint and receiving a response. The formal grievance procedure is usually outlined in the employee handbook or policy manual for nonunionized employees and in the collective bargaining agreement for unionized employees.[53]

Peer Review   The *peer review process* generally involves volunteer employees who sit on a panel and determine whether a policy or procedure was properly and fairly applied. The panel normally cannot change company policy, pay rates, or work rules. They may have the authority to render a final decision.[54]

Mediation   *Mediation* is a voluntary process whereby a neutral third party presides over a formal resolution session. Mediations have the following components:[55]

- Opening statement by the mediator, which sets the ground rules for the session.

- A chance for each party to make an uninterrupted statement expressing the concerns and feelings.

- Interchange where parties discuss and work to a resolution. The parties may remain in the same room or the mediator may shuttle back and forth between the parties. Additionally, the mediator may hold what is called a caucus. In a *caucus*, the mediator discusses issues with one party in private.

- If successful, parties write an agreement.

In mediation, discussions held are confidential and cannot be used in any future formal hearings or procedures. The parties in the dispute are responsible for crafting a resolution and the mediator assists.[56]

In organizations the mediators can be peers trained in the process or an internal or external third party.[57]

Arbitration   In *arbitration*, the employment dispute is submitted to an impartial person or panel that makes the final decision and may either be voluntary or involuntary.[58] Many times parties agree in advance to resolve future issues through arbitration. The written decision may or may not be **binding** and enforceable in court.[59] A binding decision is one that the parties must follow and cannot appeal. In a unionized workplace, the arbitration procedure is negotiated as part of the collective bargaining agreement. For union and management, arbitration is usually the only way to resolve job-related disputes.[60]

> **KeyPoint**
> Because companies may offer a variety of ways to resolve issues, you should be aware of all of them and pick the one that best fits your issue.

> " *I am a woman in process. I'm just trying like everybody else. I try to take every conflict, every experience, and learn from it. Life is never dull.*
> —*Oprah Winfrey American television personality* "

In The News[61]

While working in Iraq in 2005, Jamie Leigh Jones, a contractor for Halliburton, claims that she was sexually assaulted after a fellow employee gave her a drink that caused her to pass out. The company insists the case must go through arbitration, but Jones is fighting desperately to have her case heard in U.S. criminal court.

Predispute mandatory binding arbitration is a staple in the United States in resolving everything from consumer to workplace disputes. Frequently contracts outline that you must agree to binding arbitration upon signing. Most of the time the arbitration process is private and records are not made available to the public.

The arbitration industry agrees that corporations win their arbitrations more of the time. However, the industry says that is because the company will only take a case to arbitration it feels it can win. Opponents say arbitrators who frequently rule against companies are not picked to serve on future panels. Opponents are calling for arbitration to be voluntary. However, arbitration advocates argue that if arbitration is voluntary, it wouldn't be used as often, and courts would be overwhelmed with unnecessary litigation.

1. In court you frequently present your case to the judge and a jury of your peers. Would you agree to arbitration rather than taking a dispute in which you were involved to court? Why or why not?

2. Taking a case to court is much more expensive and time consuming than arbitration. Do you believe more workplace disputes should be forced into arbitration? Why or why not?

The arbitration process is more informal and more confidential than a court setting. Arbitration follows these steps:[62]

- Parties submit statements.
- Parties attend a hearing and plead their side.
- The arbitrator(s) may ask questions.
- The arbitrator(s) generates a written decision.

Ask Yourself...

1. Have you ever used an organization's formal or informal system to resolve a conflict? If so, what happened? How did you feel about it?

2. Would you rather have a conflict resolved through mediation or arbitration? Please explain your answer.

KEY TERMS

conflict	ombuds
conflict management	grievance procedure
third-party conflict manager	peer review process
reality checking	mediation
win–win options	caucus
saving face	arbitration
internal dispute resolution (IDR)	binding
open door policy	

CHAPTER SUMMARY

Conflict in organizations is on the rise today because of rapid change, the increasing complexity of work, an economy that pushes companies to do more with less, the vast diversity of employees, and the availability of more options and information with which to make decisions. It can take the form of personality clashes, complaints from customers, disputes with superiors, disagreements about methods of work, disputes over pay and working conditions, and arguments about who does what and who is accountable to whom. While conflict that is channeled into a healthy, open, and positive working relationship can lead to positive results, unresolved conflict can be destructive.

You need strong emotional intelligence as well as communication and problem-solving skills to manage conflict effectively. Self-regulation, empathy, active listening, focusing on needs, and developing options are essential abilities. Lastly, mastering the skills necessary to deal with angry confrontations takes practice.

Groups at work can have conflict either within the group or with other work groups. The causes of conflict can be mutual antagonism, organizational reliance, goal ambiguity, labor–management disputes, and unclear roles. A number of options for dealing with group conflict are available, including collaboration. Additionally any group member can develop and utilize facilitation skills that assist the collaboration process.

Organizations have developed a variety of ways to handle conflict both informally and formally, ranging from open door policies and grievance procedures to mediation and arbitration.

REVIEW

1. What is conflict and what factors bring it about in the workplace?

2. What emotional intelligence attitudes are important in managing conflict?

3. What emotional intelligence skills are important in managing conflict?

4. What are the steps in handling angry confrontations?

5. What causes conflict in and between work groups?

6. What techniques can you use to resolve conflicts in work groups?

7. What is IDR and what are the common techniques employed in IDR?

CRITICAL THINKING

1. Describe a conflict you have experienced within a group setting. What were the causes of the conflict? Was it resolved effectively? If so, how was it resolved? If not, what techniques could have been used?

2. How important is forgiveness to resolving conflict? Why is this so hard?

3. Objectivity is a must in resolving conflict. Can we ever be totally objective? Why or why not?

4. Think of something that happened to you recently that made you angry or upset you. How can you reframe the incident?

5. Discuss a time when you used avoidance during a conflict. Was this technique effective for the situation? Why or why not?

6. Have you ever been in a group meeting only to discover later that some individuals thought a decision had been made while others did not? How can you ensure this does not happen?

CASE STUDIES

In small groups analyze the following situations:

1 **Quick to Anger**   Jacqueline slammed her lunch sack on the table and sat down in a huff.

"What's wrong?" Selina asked.

"I didn't get the promotion to executive assistant," she complained. "I've had it up to here. I always get passed over."

"I'm sorry to hear that," Selina said. "Who'd they promote?"

Jacqueline said, "Archie got the job. I've been here longer than he has so I should've gotten it. I called an attorney and I plan to sue the company. They've got it coming. I should have that job."

"Archie's the new guy who used to work for Transtower, isn't he?" Selina said. "Wasn't he an executive assistant over there?"

"Maybe he was," Jacqueline asked. "So what?"

"He may be more qualified than you," Selina explained. "Have you talked to human resources to find out why you didn't get the job? Don't you think you should do that before you see the attorney?"

"Maybe you're right. I'll think about it," Jacqueline said.

1. What did Jacqueline fail to do in the midst of her anger?

2. What do you believe the consequences could be for her if she goes ahead with contacting an attorney before thinking things through?

3. What technique is Selina using?

4. If Selina had told Jacqueline the other person was more qualified and she should not take any action, do you believe Jacqueline would have listened? Why or why not?

2 **Throwing Her Weight Around** Monique is new in the office. She works closely with Wanda, a long-time employee who has a reputation for being bossy and rude. A month into her new job, Monique noticed that Wanda has been taking office supplies home with her. At first it was small items like paperclips and pens, so Monique tried to ignore what she saw. Lately, though, Wanda has been getting bolder. Last week Monique saw her take a computer mouse, and today Wanda took a toner cartridge for her printer at home.

Being new, Monique is hesitant to confront Wanda about what she's been doing. But Monique can't keep this to herself any longer. She summons her courage and tells Wanda, "I've seen what you've been doing. You need to stop immediately or I'll have to tell someone higher up."

Wanda scoffs. "No one's going to miss these things. Mind your own business. Or I promise, I can make things miserable for you here." Monique has no doubt that Wanda means what she says.

1. Was it okay for Monique to ignore Wanda's theft of small items to avoid a conflict?

2. Should Monique now report the theft to someone else?

3. Have you ever confronted someone at work over an ethical issue? Are you glad you did?

HUMAN RELATIONS IN ACTION

1. Watch the 1957 movie *12 Angry Men*.

   Then, discuss the following:

   - Describe some positions that are displayed.

   - Name some underlying needs.

   - Name several standards or benchmarks jurors utilized to base guilt or innocence. What influenced using those standards?

   - What emotional intelligence was displayed?

   - What communication skills were displayed?

   - How were options developed?

   - What techniques were used to help jurors move toward resolution?

   - Did juror #8 help others save face? If so, how?

   - What facilitation skills were used?

2. Read the following scenario as a group.

   You and a coworker are responsible for making a presentation to upper management. You have tried to get with the coworker on several occasions to go over your parts of the presentation but have not been able to connect. When you arrive for the presentation, the equipment is not set up properly and the handouts, which were your partner's responsibility, are incomplete. During the presentation your coworker monopolizes the time, forcing you to rush through your part. You fear you did not emphasize the key points appropriately. Afterward your partner said, "The presentation could have been better, but I think they liked it."

   Discuss the following:

   - What emotions would you feel in this situation?

   - What thoughts would go through your mind?

   - How would you handle the situation?

   - What skills in this chapter would you find particularly helpful in handling your coworker?

   For additional resources, refer to the web site for this text:
   www.cengage.com/management/dalton

RESOURCES

1. How to avoid a major meltdown at work. (2008, September 17). Retrieved on March 11, 2009, from http://www.cnn.com/2008/LIVING/worklife/09/17/cb.work.meltdowns

2. CPP Global human capital report. (2008, June). Workplace conflict and how businesses can harness it to thrive. Mountain View, CA: Author.

3. Conflict. (2009). *Merriam-Webster Online Dictionary*. Retrieved on February 22, 2009, from http://www.merriam-webster.com/dictionary/conflict

4. Crawley, J. (1994). Constructive conflict management, managing to make a difference. San Diego, CA: Pfeiffer & Company.

5. Gurchiek, K. (2008, December 9). Report: Managed right, conflict can benefit organizations. Retrieved on December 18, 2008, from http://www.shrm.org/hrnews_published/articles/CMS_027332.asp#P-8_0

6. Heathfield, S. M. (n.d.). Fight for what's right: Ten tips to encourage meaningful conflict. Retrieved on May 4, 2009, from http://humanresources.about.com/od/conflictresolution/a/fightforright.htm

7. Crawley, *Constructive conflict management, managing to make a difference.*

8. *Coping.org: Tools for coping with life's stressors, tools for relationships, handling conflict.* (n.d.). Retrieved on October 9, 2008, from http://www.coping.org/relations/conflict.htm

9. CPP Global human capital report, Workplace conflict and how businesses can harness it to thrive.

10. The cost of conflict. (n.d.). About Workplace Conflict. Centre for Conflict Resolution. Retrieved on February 9, 2009, from http://www.conflictatwork.com/conflict/cost_e.cfm

11. *Why do we tend to avoid conflict?* (n.d.). Retrieved on October 9, 2008, from http://www.ohrd.wisc.edu/onlinetraining/resolution/aboutwhatisit.htm#avoidconflict

12. CPP Global human capital report, Workplace conflict and how businesses can harness it to thrive.

13. Goleman, D. (1998). *Working with emotional intelligence*. New York: Bantam Books.

14. Crawley, *Constructive conflict management, managing to make a difference.*

15. Goleman, *Working with emotional intelligence.*

16. *Ibid.*

17. *Ibid.*

18. Lewicki, R. J., & Tomlinson, E. C. (2003, December). *Trust and trust building*. Retrieved on February 20, 2009, from http://www.beyondintractability.org/essay/trust_building/

19. Philadelphia University. (n.d.). Problem-solving. Textile teaching & learning initiative. Retrieved on February 22, 2009, from http://fibers.philau.edu/ntc/I99P01/Problem%20Solving.html

20. Lewicki & Tomlinson, Trust and trust building.

21. Billikopf, G. (2008). *Conflict management skills*. Retrieved on October 9, 2008, from http://www.cnr.berkeley.edu/ucce50/ag-labor/7labor/13.htm

22. Fisher, R., & Ury, W. (1991). *Getting to yes*. New York: Penguin Books.

23. Goleman, *Working with emotional intelligence*.

24. Billikopf, *Conflict management skills*.

25. *Ibid*.

26. *Ibid*.

27. University of Houston Clear Lake. (n.d.). Basic mediation training. Houston, TX: Author.

28. Billikopf, *Conflict management skills*.

29. Campus-adr. Retrieved on October 9, 2008, from http://www.campus-adr.org/CMHER/ReportArticles/Edition1_4/Corecomp1_4.html

30. University of Houston Clear Lake, Basic mediation training.

31. Billikopf, *Conflict management skills*.

32. *Ibid*.

33. *Fact sheets: Dealing with impasse*. (n.d.). Retrieved on February 11, 2009, from http://www.adr.af.mil/factsheets/factsheet.asp?id=7365

34. *Face saving*. (n.d.). Conflict Research Consortium, University of Colorado, Retrieved on May 2, 2009, from http://www.colorado.edu/conflict/peace/treatment/facesavr.htm

35. University of Houston Clear Lake, Basic mediation training.

36. SHRM briefly stated: *Cross-Cultural negotiation: When science and art work together*. (2008, December 1). Retrieved on February 11, 2009, from http://moss07.shrm.org/Research/Articles/Articles/Pages/When%20Science%20and%20Art%20Work%20Together.aspx

37. Fisher & Ury, *Getting to yes*.

38. *Christian Bale goes ballistic on set*. Retrieved on February 9, 2009, from http://www.hollyscoop.com/christian-bale/christian-bale-goes-ballistic-o

39. *Apologetic Christian Bale calls f-Bomb tirade 'inexcusable.'* Retrieved on February 9, 2009, from http://www.people.com/people/article/0,,20257508,00.html

40. *New York city to "Cybersettle" more cases online*. (n.d.) Retrieved on February 9, 2009, from http://www.cybersettle.com/info/news/pressreleases.aspx?id=36

41. *Cybersettle Fact Sheet*. (n.d.). Retrieved on February 9, 2009, from http://www.cybersettle.com/info/about/factsheet.aspx

42. *Building coalitions*. (2002, April). Florida Cooperative Extension Service, Institute of Food and Agricultural Sciences, University of Florida. Gainesville, FL: Author.

43. Falikowski, A. (2002). *Mastering human relations* (3rd ed.). Toronto, Canada: Pearson Education.

44. *Ibid*.

45. *Why do we tend to avoid conflict?*

46. Falikowski, *Mastering Human Relations*.

47. Burke, R. J., & Cooper, C. L. (2003). *Leading in turbulent times: Managing in the new world of work*. Boston: Blackwell Publishers.

48. Falikowski, *Mastering Human Relations*.

49. *Resolving workplace disputes internally.* (2009, March 1). Retrieved on May 5, 2009, from http://moss07.shrm.org/Research/Articles/Articles/Pages/ResolvingDisputesInternally.aspx

50. Open door policy: Definition for the human resources glossary. (n.d.). Retrieved on May 5, 2009, from http://humanresources.about.com/od/glossaryo/g/open_door.htm

51. Hirschman, C. (2003, January 1). Someone to listen. *HR magazine.* Retrieved on May 5, 2009, from http://www.shrm.org/Publications/hrmagazine/EditorialContent/Pages/01

52. *Resolving workplace disputes internally.*

53. *Ibid.*

54. *Ibid.*

55. Crawley, *Constructive conflict management, managing to make a difference.*

56. *Ibid.*

57. *Alternative dispute resolution.* (2004, February 1). SHRM Briefly Stated. Retrieved on May 10, 2009, from http://moss07.shrm.org/Research/Articles/Articles/Pages/Alternative_20

58. Crawley, *Constructive conflict management, managing to make a difference.*

59. *Resolving workplace disputes internally.*

60. *Ibid.*

61. Goodwin, W. (2009, June 9). *Rape case highlights arbitration debate.* Retrieved on August 6, 2009, from http://www.npr.org/templates/story/story.php?storyId=105153315

62. *Introductory guide to AAA arbitration and mediation.* (n.d.). Retrieved on February 11, 2009, from http://www.adr.org/searchRes.asp

9

LEADERSHIP:
WHAT MAKES AN EFFECTIVE LEADER?

OBJECTIVES

After studying this chapter, you should be able to:

9.1 Describe the roles of leaders, managers, and followers.

9.2 Discuss leadership theories over time.

9.3 Identify leadership styles.

9.4 List skills required of leaders at different organizational levels.

9.5 Name basic characteristics and behaviors of effective leaders.

9.6 Explain leadership needs for the future.

Jump Start

Jim Sinegal, CEO of Costco, the fourth largest retailer in the United States, is a devout believer in servant leadership, feeling that leadership is about how well you serve others, mainly your customers and employees, and not how far you advance yourself or how much money you make. This belief is reflected in his humble office space, which has only folding chairs and tables, where he answers his own phone and wears a plain employee badge that just says "Jim." The real show is how he takes care of his employees. He pays 42 percent higher wages than his closest rival, provides health benefits coverage for both full- and part-time employees, and donates a matching percentage of savings toward their 401(k) accounts. He consistently promotes from within the organization, visits every store at least once each year, knows most people on a first-name basis, and maintains an open-door policy for anyone who needs or wants to see him. Because his employees feel good about themselves and their jobs, turnover is one-fifth that of his closest competitor and the lowest in the retailing industry. He has 462 stores in 37 states and 8 countries, yet he doesn't spend a single dollar on advertising. More than 120,000 satisfied employees and many happy customers spread the word for him.[1]

- Which of Sinegal's leadership actions do you feel is the most important and why?
- What other things do you think he could do to create an even stronger leadership role with his employees, if any?

9.1   UNDERSTANDING LEADERSHIP

There is always going to be someone in charge. Whether that person is appointed by officials or anointed by friends, a leader will be present in every group. This person largely contributes to the success or failure of whatever effort he or she is leading. In this chapter, you will learn the important role leadership plays in organizations and the critical skills that will help prepare you to be an effective leader in the 21st century. With lapses of integrity and unethical behaviors headlining the news each week, the need for leaders who can restore confidence and reassure people of the integrity and quality of organizations is important. Understanding leadership and how it works will be helpful to you.

> " Leadership is influencing—nothing more, nothing less.
> —John Maxwell, management consultant and author "

Becoming a Manager or a Leader

Often the terms *leadership* and *management* are used interchangeably. However, distinct differences can be drawn between the two. A person can be a leader without being in an officially appointed management or supervisory position. Similarly, a person can be a manager without being a leader. Understanding the subtle differences in these two roles will be very helpful and important to you.

The manager asks how and when; the leader asks what and why.
—*Warren Bennis, management leader and author*

In the revised edition of Peter Drucker's book *Management*, the first 17 pages are devoted to defining management and managers with little reference to leaders or leadership.[2] From those pages, and many other sources, we learn that management is the use of resources, including human resources, to accomplish goals. It is mostly what we do and how we do it—planning, ordering, controlling, budgeting, organizing, and other similar activities. While managing is usually legitimized through official positions with formal titles in an organization, it may occur in many settings. For example, you may be the manager of a small floral shop or a local bookstore, both requiring meticulous management of inventory and sales. Or you may be the manager of an NFL team with lots of human resources to manage and still not be a leader. You may lack the ability to inspire or influence others. Managers can be leaders only if employees allow them to influence their attitudes and behaviors.

Influence is a key component of leadership. *Influence* is your ability to change the attitude or behavior of an individual or group. This ability may result from the use of your power (discussed in Chapter 10) that can come from any number of sources. For example, a manager may use his or her legitimate title or position to influence others to follow his or her lead on a special project. Simply knowing how to do a job well or being promoted may get you into a manager's position, but you will still need the skills and ability to influence others if you are to become their leader.

Leadership is the process of influencing the activities of individuals or organized groups so that they follow and do willingly what the leader wants them to do. To be a leader, you must deal directly with people, develop rapport with them, apply appropriate persuasion, inspire them, and thus influence them to cooperate in pursuing your goals and vision. Being a leader requires more than vocational or professional competence. Leaders must also establish and maintain positive relationships with their followers to achieve their goals. Successful leaders often develop empathy, trust, and mutual respect with their followers. Developing such skills help leaders understand how people feel, what motivates them, and the best ways to influence them.

Leadership skills are useful to everyone. Almost daily we face situations that call on our ability to lead in some way. Whether we are parenting, teaching, meeting with academic or social groups at the college, working with charity events, planning a garden club meeting, attending a Chamber of Commerce meeting or a sports team meeting, or planning a family reunion, we may be called upon to put our leadership skills to use or find that they come in handy to understand the interactions with others in these situations.

To attain your goals, whether personal or organizational, you must be effective in directing and coordinating the behaviors of others to assist you in achieving those goals. For example, suppose your work group has a goal to increase sales by 15 percent. You could use leadership skills to influence your coworkers to sell more to win the bonus prize. Or imagine a group of concerned neighbors have come together to lobby for an additional stoplight at a dangerous corner in your neighborhood. You have been asked to lead

KeyPoint
Managers can be leaders only if employees allow them to influence their attitudes and behaviors.

Example is not the main thing in influencing others, it is the only thing.
—*Albert Schweitzer, Pulitzer Prize winning scientist*

the effort because they trust your judgment and respect your influence with contacts at the mayor's office. You will find many situations that require leadership skills. A solid understanding of and a conscientious effort to acquire these skills and abilities can be beneficial to you.

In both of the previous cases, the leader emerged from within the group. This person is called an emergent leader, first mentioned in Chapter 7 in the discussion about team leaders. Emergent leaders play an important role in any group activity because of the strong influence they may have on the group members. For example, an emergent leader may cause dissention among assembly line workers before the company's management has a chance to get a new contract agreement fully negotiated. Or an emergent leader may help sway the vote on accepting that company contract. Emergent leaders need no official or appointed position because their leadership comes from their ability to influence their followers, and this degree of influence may well be stronger than that of the official position leader. An effective official leader will seek out the emergent ones to know their purpose and goals, to lessen any opportunity for conflict, and to increase the probability of harmony.

> "
> *If your actions inspire others to dream more, learn more, do more and become more, you are a leader.*
> —John Quincy Adams, American president
> "

In The News

Delta CEO Richard Anderson embodies the spirit of a leader. A few years back, Delta Airlines plunged into bankruptcy and teetered on total dissolution until Anderson rallied its rebirth. Anderson led Delta's merger with Northwest Airlines, which strengthened Delta's presence in Europe and South America. He established 37 committees within the organization to involve employees in activities that would affect them personally to help make the transition a smooth one. These committees planned everything from how to merge warehouse plane parts to new designs for the flight attendant uniforms. To remain in touch with the people he leads and hear their suggestions and concerns, Anderson flies at least once a month in a Delta cockpit to visit firsthand with his pilots for candid information on how they think things might improve. He also makes frequent cross-country visits to job sites to get employee input on how to do things better at Delta.[3]

1. How would you feel if you were the pilot and Anderson showed up in your cockpit with questions about job satisfaction? Would you be open and provide constructive feedback, or would you be uncomfortable with this approach?

2. Based on our previous discussion of managers and leaders, which do you think Anderson is, and why?

Evolving Roles of Managers and Leaders

Many changes in today's business environment have created the need for a different kind of manager. Peter Drucker, the world-renowned management consultant and author, tells us that the period from 1970 to 2010 experienced more change than the world has ever seen and there's much more coming at an even faster pace, creating an ever-changing work environment.[4] The wider generational workforce expectations create a unique challenge for any leader and in some cases may require rethinking many of the old managerial philosophies. At times there can be major disconnects that give rise to conflict or discomfort. For example, courtesy and good manners may be lacking in some younger employees. Dan Cathy, president and CEO of Chick-fil-A, currently offers etiquette classes to his employees to expand their knowledge on appropriate behaviors in dealing with customers. Cathy feels customer satisfaction is the company's key to success in his specialty business and is helping his employees know how to keep the customer happy.[5]

Another of the many changes has to do with the rapid transitions in technology that both managers and employees have experienced. Some of the traditional and boomer managers have had to adjust considerably to survive with their limitations while trying to keep pace or fully understand some of the electronic creativity and expertise many younger employees demonstrate. This can often stretch the application of emotional intelligence to its limits.

Today's business environment is also changing, which will affect leadership styles. Employees may not have a cubicle, a desk, or a wired phone. Some people work from home. They may not have regular 9–5 work hours, and some don't even have to report their hours worked as long as the job gets done. Performance may be measured purely on results. Managers have had to adapt their styles and techniques to deal with these changing times. These new management styles have encouraged creativity, risk taking, healthy conflict, and learning from errors made along the way. Good human relations skills have been helpful in making these transitions.

Figure 9.1 illustrates the traditional levels of management in a typical organizational hierarchy. Although many of these new work arrangements and continuous management changes will somewhat flatten the structure of the hierarchy in many organizations, this arrangement is likely to survive in many cases. Leadership, however, can exist at any level within an organization, and as the many changes continue to occur, the roles of managers will continue to evolve. These challenges will test the skills and abilities of the organizational leader.

Follow the Leader

Your success as a leader may depend on how well you develop your followers. Often leaders think they have to be in control all the time and do it all themselves. But the most effective leader will learn to let go and become the follower in some situations, allowing followers to take the lead and begin to transform themselves into a leader. In this dynamic relationship, leaders and followers can learn from each other, and both strengthen their skills and abilities. As a leader, take the opportunity to develop leadership talent among followers, so they will

> Even if you are on the right track, you'll get run over if you just sit there.
> —Will Rogers, author, actor

Figure 9.1 ●

Levels of management within a typical hierarchy.

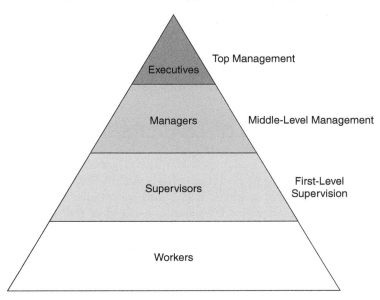

Top Management — Executives

Middle-Level Management — Managers

First-Level Supervision — Supervisors

Workers

take the initiative at appropriate times. Your success is largely dependent upon those around you—make sure to lead them well and develop them even better so they are ready to assume your job when you are ready to move on.

A valuable part of becoming a leader is being an effective follower, a role all of us play throughout our lives. Whether or not we are in the ranks of management yet, all of us must be followers at some point. Learn to "manage up," realizing that the people above us have certain expectations of us no matter where we are in the work group. Learning effective methods of being a good follower will improve opportunities for demonstrating our leadership capabilities.

Leadership Learning

1. Support your organization's goals. Be clear on the overall direction and ask questions if you are unclear about anything.

2. Approach any assignment as an opportunity to learn and grow. After all, you will have a chance to hear various points of view, see different parts of the organization, interact with different people, and observe new skills.

3. Take responsibility for any assignment and display that attitude and commitment toward others.

4. Handle problems rapidly. Discuss any major crisis with your supervisor to keep him or her aware.

5. Handle changes smoothly. Try to accept changes as quickly as possible and make them a part of your routine with minimal disruption.

Ask Yourself...

1. Why do you think people skills are so vital to the success of a leader and what are some ways you learn these skills?

2. What is the difference between a manager and a leader and what are some ways to make the transition?

9.2   THE EVOLUTION OF LEADERSHIP THEORIES

Ideas about leadership have changed significantly over the years and have influenced how organizations and individuals within them operate. The *great man theory*, the first of these ideas, was based on a belief that certain people are born to become leaders and will emerge in that role when their time comes. Today we know that people can learn to be leaders. Whether it happens through education, observation, or hands-on experience, leadership is primarily a learned ability. Theories of leadership generally fall under one of three broad categories—trait, behavioral, or situational theories. Each of these ideas has evolved over time yet remains in some way linked to its predecessor.[6]

Do Common Leadership Traits Exist?

Wondering whether leaders have certain traits in common, researchers studied the physical, personality, and intelligence traits of prominent leaders in business, military, medical, and other fields. Looking at height, weight, personal appearance, and physique, they found no conclusive common traits.[7] They also looked at degrees of confidence, independence, and perception, and while a list of desirable traits was formed, it too became confusing once the effects of outside influences were introduced. This idea gave way to a belief that perhaps the success of leaders is based on their behavior rather than their traits.

> " *Leaders are made, they are not born. They are made by hard effort, which is the price all of us must pay to achieve any goal that is worthwhile.*
>
> —*Vince Lombardi, former NFL coach* "

Behavioral Theories

Behavioral theorists believed that successful leaders could be identified by what they do rather than what they have. In trying to understand certain behavioral patterns or styles of leadership, researchers measured behaviors such as degree of control or authority, degree of flexibility, concern about getting the job done (task accomplishment), and concerns for subordinates or others. Several landmark management studies from this period are still used today in identifying the styles of leaders.[8]

In his classic 1960s book *The Human Side of Enterprise*, Douglas McGregor suggested that leaders treat followers according to the assumptions they hold about what motivates those followers. As can be seen in Figure 9.2, the traditional view—known as *Theory X*—exhibits a fairly dim view of workers' attitudes and motivation, while the second set of assumptions, *Theory Y*, takes a much more optimistic view of human nature.[9]

Figure 9.2

McGregor's Theory X and Y.

Theory X contends that people	Theory Y contends that
• have an inherent dislike of work, considering it necessary only for survival	• the expenditure of physical and mental effort in work is as natural as play or rest
• are not ambitious	• people will direct themselves toward objectives if their efforts are rewarded
• will avoid work if they can	• most people are eager to work and have the capacity to accept, or even seek, responsibility as well as to use imagination, ingenuity, and creativity in solving problems
• prefer to be directed, wanting to avoid responsibility	• under the right circumstances, people derive much satisfaction from work and are capable of doing a good job

Leaders that subscribe to Theory X believe that workers have to be controlled, highly directed, and threatened to make them work, which results in a strict, authoritarian leadership style. The Theory Y style leader believes in being more supportive of the worker and less directive and uses a more democratic or participative approach to leading.[10]

Another of the well-known theories of this period is the two-dimensional *Managerial Grid* developed by Robert Blake and Jane Mouton. A grid is used to plot the degree to which leaders show concern for people and production (or getting the job done), with 1 being the least concern and 9 being the most concern. Figure 9.3 illustrates the five specific leadership styles identified by Blake and Mouton.[11]

This theory suggests that the best leadership style is the 9,9 Team Management approach because it results in high productivity and positive

● **Figure 9.3**

Blake and Mouton's Managerial Grid identified five specific leadership styles with varying degrees of concern for the tasks and the employees.

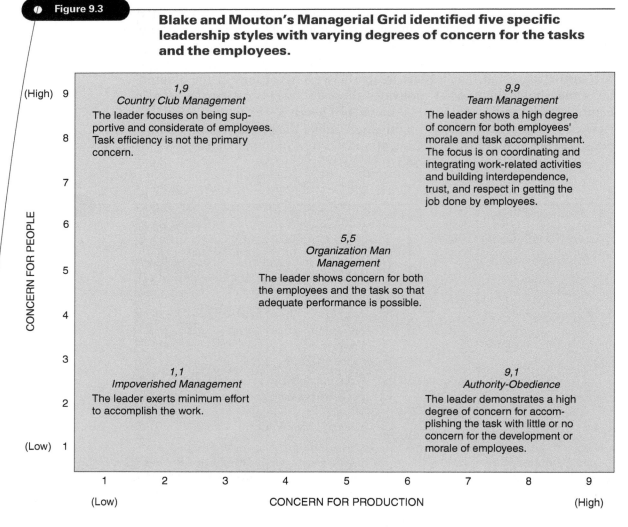

SOURCE: Robert Blake and Jane Srygley Mouton, *The Managerial Grid III: The Key to Leadership Excellence* (Houston: Gulf Publishing Company, 1985), 12. Reproduced by permission.

outcomes. It is a goal-directed team approach. However, using a 9,9 team leadership style in every situation is difficult if not impossible because of the many variables that can occur. For example, a call for an emergency job may require a jump to the 9,1 authority style to get the job done with high direction in a short time. Fluctuations in leader–follower situations gave rise to the next group of theories that focus on assessing the situations at hand.

Your leadership style should allow employees to develop with confidence

Digital Vision/Getty Images

Situational or Contingency Theories

As theorists continued their research of leadership styles, they realized that in most cases, leaders needed to adapt their styles to the situations at hand. Fred E. Fiedler developed one of the more important theories from this era in his 1967 book *A Theory of Leadership Effectiveness*. He suggested that some leaders function best in highly directive situations while others are more permissive. Therefore, organizations should consider each situation before assigning leaders because the same person may be effective in one situation but not in another.[12]

Following Fiedler's logic, Paul Hersey and Ken Blanchard developed a blend of the ideas of Blake and Mouton and Fiedler, using the grid method of measuring how a person may behave differently depending on the nature of the task to be done. Unlike the Managerial Grid concept, which stresses one best way to influence others, their model says that the leadership style used with followers will vary, depending on the job to be done, where it's to be done, how it's to be done, and when it's to be done (job situation). Hersey and Blanchard suggest that leaders should vary their style as followers, whether individuals or groups, develop and mature in their abilities to do their jobs. For example, when a task is new, the leader must start with more direction to show followers how to do the job. As they begin to learn the job, the leader can offer support only as needed, but continue to monitor their development. Once a follower is fully able to do the job, the leader can delegate the task and offer support only if needed at all.

> **"**
> *Some leaders develop followers. Other leaders develop other leaders.*
>
> —*Zig Ziglar, author, motivational speaker*
> **"**

Remember, however, that as followers assume additional new tasks, their confidence level may fall. This will require a leadership style adjustment to match the situation. The leader's style will return to more basic learning, telling, and showing techniques, becoming supportive and providing encouragement until the followers are again confident that they can do the job. Then you can provide less-direct supervision and allow them the freedom to follow through. Groups and teams may go through the same changes in maturity as they progress through the forming, storming, and norming phases discussed in Chapter 7. The Hersey and Blanchard model has been a long-lasting learning tool for understanding the shifts in human behavior in work-related situations.

Ask Yourself...

1. Think about some supervisors you have had. Did they exhibit more Theory X or Theory Y behaviors in their management style? Why do you categorize them as such? Which did you feel was more effective and why?

2. Have you, or someone you know, experienced being more effective doing a job in one situation versus another? Explain and discuss. (For example, working in one department versus another, working for one supervisor versus another, selling shoes versus being a nurse, etc.)

3. From your current position, what additional helpful ideas would you have for followers who are learning to be an effective leader? Do you have any additional helpful ideas on managing upward to your supervisors?

9.3 LEADERSHIP STYLES

KeyPoint
Democratic leaders tend to share authority with their employees and involve them in decision making and organizational planning.

A leadership style is a leader's pattern of behavior, and most leaders have a style they prefer to use. Studies of leadership behavior patterns have identified three traditional leadership styles: autocratic, democratic, and free rein.

The *autocratic leadership* style is also described as authoritarian or directive. Leaders using this style are usually concerned with just getting the job done, using close supervision, and they are not at all comfortable with delegating their authority to anyone. A close match to this style is the Theory X leader described earlier in the chapter. Historical examples of individuals exhibiting this leadership style that you might recognize would be Attila the Hun, Henry Ford, George S. Patton, and perhaps Donald Trump and Martha Stewart.

The *democratic leadership* style is often described as participative and easy going. The democratic style is generally preferred by managers and employees. Democratic leaders tend to share authority with their employees, involving them in decision making and organizational planning. These leaders show concern for their employees and closely match the Theory Y leader mentioned earlier. Examples of this leadership style would include Martin Luther King Jr., former president Jimmy Carter, successful entrepreneur Russell Simmons, popular TV host Oprah Winfrey, and Costco CEO Jim Sinegal.

Free-rein leaders allow employees to more or less lead themselves. They may integrate some activity or close out some assignment with a signature, but for the most part, they are uninvolved with directing or controlling tasks. This style can be highly effective if the tasks are clearly defined and the employees are skilled and responsible. An example might be the supervisor of a group of research scientists working on a new disease cure or the leader of a group of advanced doctors working on a research grant to stop global warming. These two groups know their tasks and are skilled enough to need little to no direction on how to do their jobs. The assigned leaders of these groups may or may not be a member of the group at all. They may only monitor their progress on a periodic basis or respond to calls for assistance on an as-needed basis. For the most part, the groups are allowed to lead themselves with minimal direction or support from any leader.

> *One person can live on a desert island without leadership. Two people, if they are totally compatible, could probably get along and even progress. If there are three or more, someone has to take the lead. Otherwise, chaos erupts.*
> —Warren Bennis, business professor, author, and leadership expert

You may be most comfortable working under people with a particular leadership style. You should, however, be able to adapt to changes in leadership styles or different leaders as situations demand. One of the new work models being introduced to companies and producing popular results is the Results Only Work Environment (ROWE), and it is definitely an example of the free-rein leadership style. ROWE is a work method that gives employees complete control over their time and can bring about complete work–life balance. Two former HR managers with Best Buy, Cali Ressler and Jody Thompson, developed the idea and began its implementation in most departments at the Best Buy headquarters in Minneapolis.[13] ROWE works best for work groups whose work is project or task based. It requires mature, experienced managers who can articulate what they want done in their departments, and employees need to be highly productive and self-motivated to survive in this environment. Employees are allowed to set their own work schedule and do whatever they want, whenever they want, from wherever they want to do it. As long as the work is done, it doesn't matter how else they spend their time (within reason). This focus on results requires managers and employees to be very clear about job requirements and expectations. The new work model is dramatically changing old work belief systems dating back to the 1950s that no longer apply in the technologically advanced work environments of today. Some of the larger technology companies, such as IBM, AT&T, and Sun Microsystems, have up to 50 percent of their employees working without a permanent office space—they telecommute. Adopting these new work environments creates complete cultural changes in some cases. Management and employees have to rethink how they will do business, and so far the results have been positive. Managers set the tasks and measure only the results. This is an example of a free-rein manager and management changes occurring in the workplace.

Ask Yourself...

1. Would you like to work for a company using the ROWE? Why or why not? How does that style differ from methods you may have already experienced?

2. As a leader or a follower, which of these management styles do you think will be more comfortable for you (or is already) and why do you think it's best for you? Will you have any problems changing as situations or people change?

9.4 EFFECTIVE LEADERSHIP SKILLS

Leaders must demonstrate adequate skills to be effective. Fortunately, good leadership skills can be learned or developed. Chapter 1 identified three basic types of skills for good employees, which are also beneficial to a good leader. If you aspire to be a formal leader in any legitimate organization, you need to pay particular attention to developing your technical, conceptual, and human relations skills.

Technical skills are those skills required to perform a particular task—to get the job done. For example, a first-line supervisor may need the knowledge and ability to step into the production line and assemble a part or tear down a mechanism to solve a problem or train employees on the process. Obviously, this skill is more important at levels of leadership closest to the actual work being done. On a personal level, you would use these skills because you are the best at what you do and that's why you are leading others.

Conceptual skills are often referred to as administrative or big picture skills. They include the ability to think abstractly, analyze problems, and deal with bureaucracy. At work, conceptual skills become even more important as you rise into ever-increasing levels of greater responsibility or into management ranks. Planning and coordinating the overall activities of an organization and its resources requires an ability to view the operations from an overall perspective and anticipate as well as solve problems. You may also use these conceptual skills on a personal level when planning a charity event involving a cross section of civic groups, for example.

Human relations skills cut evenly across all levels of leadership. These are people skills—the ability to communicate effectively, inspire and motivate, be perceptive, and apply empathy and fair judgment when dealing with those you lead. As discussed in Chapter 1, some of the more positive results of developing these skills are having a more cooperative and collaborative

> "
> *The most important single ingredient in the formula of success is knowing how to get along with people.*
> —*Theodore Roosevelt, American president*
> "

group, producing higher-quality products, realizing higher morale, and retaining more employees. These skills are also used in the workplace when just two or more people are interacting. Strengthening your skills in communications, group dynamics, problem solving, motivation, goal-setting, and leading will, of course, help prepare you for success in any setting, professional or personal. Roosevelt's quotation (see margin) on knowing how to get along with people supports the importance of developing good human relations skills.

Global CONNECTION

As of 2009, the lagging U.S. economy had taken a toll on many retailers. Liz Claiborne's New York fashion design office is a recent American company outsourcing its operations. Li & Fung, a Hong Kong company, is ready to take on the full range of the fashion design office's activities—locating factories, finding raw materials, hiring employees, and assuming all manufacturing and delivery details. In this way, they are finding sources for the company's operations.

Talbots, Hello Kitty, and Toys 'R' Us have similar agreements with Li & Fung. The two brothers are praised for their efficiency and global savvy. Fung is a Princeton graduate and his brother, Victor, has a degree from MIT. Their strategy is to take over a company, then bid out the work globally for the best quality and cheapest price to accomplish the job more efficiently. The company has doubled its revenue in only three years and has 80 offices in 40 countries with hopes of much greater expansion.[14]

1. Based on the types of business and work done by Li & Fung, which leadership style do you think would best fit the activities? Explain your answer.

2. What leadership skills do Fung and Victor most likely use in the line of manufacturing and delivery work described above?

Technical, conceptual, and human relations skills can be acquired or developed through observation, education, and experience. Consider investing in yourself and pursuing any of the many opportunities for lifelong learning or continuing education that are available to you. Jack Kahl, in his book *Leading from the Heart*, says that the effective leader yearns for knowledge and learning to increase the odds that the best decisions will be made and the hopes for success are increased.[15] It's important that you continue to grow, as learning is never finished.

The following list provides some advice on ways in which you may develop your leadership skills. Remembering that leadership can be learned, it's never too late, or too early, to begin the process.

> **"**
> *Leadership and learning are indispensable to each other.*
> —*John F. Kennedy, American president*
> **"**

Developing Leadership Skills

- Take advantage of leadership training classes offered by your employer or other sources available to you.
- Listen to audio tapes written by well-known leaders.
- Join professional groups and attend their meetings to learn more about a subject of your choice.
- Attend seminars on leadership skills subjects led by reputable presenters.
- Network with other aspiring leaders in your community and ask questions that will benefit your knowledge base.
- Take a public speaking class to improve your communications skills.
- Learn from a mentor. Find one who has already been through this learning process and is willing to share some wisdom with you.
- Read books, continuously sharpening your skills in your area of expertise and expanding your knowledge of leadership skills.
- Start your own leadership learning library. Save quotes, training materials, books of interest that you have read or ones you want to read, gather reference materials to answer questions that may arise. The library will grow along with your competence.
- Become a good listener.

Leadership classes are important and are offered in many places. Many companies offer training classes that prepare employees for leadership positions. Starbucks, the Seattle-based coffee company, has a three-level program for its leading potentials. It's called Learning to Lead, which develops leadership skills, basic store operations skills, and some basic management skills, such as the use of their internal computer systems. This program provides excellent beginning leadership skills training for those beginning career hopefuls.[16]

Starting a learning library is an excellent idea and you may already be working on one of your own. John Maxwell, a writer on leadership, tells an interesting story of how he began his library just after taking his first leadership position. He wrote a note to the top ten leaders in his area of interest and offered to pay them $100 for half an hour of their time. You might call this extreme mentorship, but it was an effective beginning that certainly seems to have paid off in the long run. When one of the leaders answered granting the half-hour interview but lived far away from Maxwell, Maxwell would arrange his family vacation that summer near the interview. The family had some interesting points of vacation, and Maxwell amassed an unmatched volume of knowledge shared with him by these outstanding leaders that helped to guide him through his leadership years.[17] Listening is one of the more important skills to develop. Only through listening can you learn what you need to know. You may someday be able to share what you have learned with others and influence their journey.

Technology CONNECTION

CEO Kevin Plank started Under Armour Performance Apparel in 1995 while he was playing football for the University of Maryland. Unhappy with the very uncomfortable, hot, sweaty, heavy, cotton T-shirts players wore, he set a goal of building a better shirt—one that would remain dry, fit comfortably, and ultimately help him perform better. From the beginning, better performance has been the mantra for Under Armour. Plank set out to use the most innovative science and technology available to design and manufacture his products. His success plan started with high-performance undershirts for men, moved into sports apparel for women, and recently expanded into the hi-tech footwear arena. Plank follows all the current athletic trends and monitors important global industry news to stay on the leading edge of athletics. He listens to athletes' needs and then applies the right science and technology to respond to those needs. Today, as the leader of his team, Plank applies the same leadership to help his team operate and execute his ultimate goal. They "huddle" for meetings and the "Offensive Sales Team" plans to make Under Armour number one in performance apparel. With offices in Maryland, Denver, Amsterdam, Hong Kong, Toronto, and China, he's well on his way. His earned revenue in 2008 approached $775 million.[18]

1. Why do you think Plank has been successful in this new venture?
2. What leadership qualities has he exhibited throughout the operations of his company?

Coaching and mentoring will also help you develop leadership skills. Early in his career, Alan Flynt, a young, highly successful executive in the aerospace industry, deliberately chose a high-ranking, intelligent, and respected executive to be his mentor. He scheduled a meeting with this individual and asked him if he would be willing to share his knowledge and experience as a mentor. They then formed a long and lasting relationship. Alan's mentor was Randy Stone, later chosen to be the Center Director of NASA's Johnson Space Center. Following the guidance and counsel of his mentor over the years, Alan found that he followed a similar path on his way to a highly successful career with the Space Center.

Ask Yourself...

1. Which items in the Developing Leadership Skills list have you already experienced? If none, which one will you choose? Discuss the benefit(s) to you.
2. Why do you think listening is such an important leadership skill? What other skill(s) or activities would you select as being equally important?

9.5 CHARACTERISTICS AND BEHAVIORS OF LEADERS

Aside from the skills already described in this chapter, certain other elements have proven to be critical to effective leadership. These elements include the satisfactory performance of the basic job functions, common behavioral characteristics, and certain attitudes and behaviors.

Functional Abilities

As a member of the classical school of management researching the basic functions of managing and leading, Luther Gulick coined an acronym that has held through time as a quick reference identifying each of the basic functions of business leadership: *PODSCORB*. The functions are planning, organizing, directing, staffing, coordinating, reporting, and budgeting.[19] Planning is the function of determining what needs to be done and how best to get it done. Organizing establishes the formal structure of authority and sets objectives. Staffing is the HR department activities—hiring, training, and keeping staff happy. Directing is giving the orders and serving as the leader. Coordinating is the integration of all the functions. Reporting is assuring basic communication through systems and records, and budgeting encompasses all the accounting and control activities, the fiscal systems. You will need these basic skills to operate effectively in the business environment at any level.

Characteristics

> " No man will make a great leader who wants to do it all himself or get all the credit for doing it.
> —Andrew Carnegie, industrialist "

A characteristic is a distinguishing feature or attribute that may set you apart from the norm. Studies that began during the behavioral sciences school of management identified behaviors and abilities to be considered key characteristics of effective leaders. Figure 9.4 identifies these characteristics and provides clear definitions of each.

Motivating employees means getting commitments through the gentle art of persuasion and setting examples of excellence. Empathy helps give leaders power. That power comes from the company's success and the leader's staff working well together. A follower's trust of the leader is essential to motivation. Leaders can develop trust by "walking their talk," being reliable and supportive, and honoring their commitments and promises.

Leaders often find delegating the single most difficult thing to do. Sometimes it may seem quicker to do a job yourself rather than explaining to someone else how to do it. Or perhaps you worry that no one could possibly do the task as well as you, so you prefer to do it yourself. However, one of the true measures of an effective leader is how well-trained his followers are to step in and do his job when necessary. The smart thing to do is to let go, delegate, and develop someone to be ready to step into your role so you can move on when the next opportunity presents itself.

Figure 9.4

Leadership characteristics.

Communication

Leaders express themselves effectively. Certainly this ability includes good oral and written communication skills but goes far beyond that. It is a different kind of communication that says you have a presence, an air of confidence, an outward display of knowledge, charisma, or enthusiasm that clearly demonstrates that you are in fact the leader. It is a different kind of communication, often referred to as body language or silent communication, as discussed in Chapter 4. It means that as a leader you know who you are, what your strengths and weaknesses are, and how to use them to their full advantage. You also know what you want, why you want it, and how to get it. You set goals and achieve those goals by communicating to others. You obtain the support and cooperation of others by making sure they're aware of your goals.

Good Decision Making

As a decision maker, you are able to gather facts, organize information, and apply good judgment in your choice of action. Your willingness to make a choice after considering all possible alternatives is essential. Depending upon the complexity of the decision to be made, you may use decision-making models. You may want to refer to Chapter 6 for additional information on decision making.

Taking Risks

Effective leaders often take responsible risks and are willing to try everything that may bring desired results. The willingness to take risks seems to set them apart from the crowd. Being a risk taker, you don't fear failure. You view it as a temporary setback and feel that failure today does not rule out success tomorrow. Some U.S. companies are deliberately making risk-taking part of their corporate culture. Risk takers tend to be achievement-oriented, goal-directed, and self-confident. The willingness to try new ideas often reaps great rewards for the individual and the company.

Motivation

To be an effective leader, you must be able to influence others to produce good results. In the climate of the 21st century workplace, motivation of employees will lean away from the autocratic methods of the past toward the new style of inspiring and empowering employees. John P. Kotter, author of *The Leadership Factor,* says that leadership is "the process of moving people in some direction mostly through non-coercive means." A good leader recognizes that people are a key resource to the success of the organization, project, or vision.[20]

Delegation

Delegation means assigning tasks to subordinates and following up to ensure that they are completed properly and on time. As an effective leader, you will delegate tasks to others to develop their skills and build a stronger team.

Ethics CONNECTION

Cracker Barrel restaurants offer every new employee the opportunity to become a leader from the very beginning. The Personal Achievement Responsibility (PAR) program provides training in basic job and leadership skills, preparing employees for management positions. As employees progress through the program, they receive raises based on their performance. They also earn perks like raises, insurance benefits, and store discounts. Once they reach the top level of PAR, they are eligible to join an internship program that puts them on a fast track to a management position.

Cracker Barrel's only requirement for this program is a high school diploma or the equivalent. The program opens many opportunities for workers who choose to participate. The company believes that "if you grow your workers, your workers will grow your business—it's a partnership."[21]

1. What's your impression of this kind of partnership? Would you want to work for Cracker Barrel? How ethically committed would you feel toward this company once they had provided you with such a positive start to a career?

2. If you were in the PAR program, do you think the program could benefit you in other jobs later in life? How else do you think this program might be of benefit to you?

Following these steps will help you delegate successfully:

1. Select the most qualified person to perform the task.
2. Give good instructions.
3. Ask for feedback to make sure instructions are understood.
4. Don't constantly look over workers' shoulders. Assign the task and leave the worker alone to complete the job.

As the leader, you should follow up to offer support if needed and to ensure the job gets done, but don't interfere with that individual's methods of doing the job. While delegating and letting go may be a difficult skill to develop, it is probably one of the smartest and best steps to becoming an effective leader.

Attitudes and Behaviors

Attitudes and behaviors play an important role in the workplace. Followers are affected by the example you set as a leader and will react to your enthusiasm and dedication. A showing of empathy toward followers will gain you their respect. Figure 9.5 lists some of the most expected and respected behaviors of an effective leader. Each of these behaviors has a direct bearing on

Figure 9.5

Behaviors of effective leaders.

- Being passionate
- Being open-minded
- Being enthusiastic
- Being empathetic
- Being ethical
- Being competent
- Being courteous
- Being considerate
- Being fair
- Being honest
- Being trustworthy

your success as a leader. The most highly rated and recurring behavior in the surveys and discussions reported in recent research documents was being trustworthy. Followers tended to feel strongly that trust and honesty were the very foundation of a good leader–follower relationship and without them, there wasn't much to build on.

These are desired behaviors of effective leaders and behaviors that you should develop and cultivate. As discussed in the earlier chapters, your behavior reflects predispositions, mental states, emotions, and moods. Be aware when you bring them with you to the office or workplace. Displaying a sense of humor can be a way to maximize good human relationships. That's not to say that you need to be the office clown, but you can express feelings and enjoy your time at work. It is, however, important to maintain a proper business or professional face when interacting with others.

Ask Yourself...

1. Think of an example when a supervisor's attitude may have affected your job performance (positively or negatively) and discuss the effects it had.

2. Which of the leadership characteristics do you think might be your strongest and why?

9.6 LEADERSHIP TODAY

Researcher Bernard Bass suggested two ways to categorize leadership—transactional and transformational. And in recent years, another category has been added called the servant leader.

Transactional Leadership

Transactional leadership requires that leaders determine what followers need to achieve their own and organizational goals, classify those needs, and help followers gain confidence that they can reach their objectives. It involves hierarchies and structures and followers directed by leaders. While this style is still with us, a move toward more human-relations-oriented styles has become increasingly popular.

Transformational Leadership

Transformational leadership motivates followers to do more than they originally expected by raising the perceived value of the task and by getting them to transcend self-interest for the sake of the group goal, make positive changes, and strive toward self-actualization.[22] This leadership style encourages more and better everything for the greater good of the group. The result can be very beneficial if you are trying to revitalize a flat or sagging organization, if you need to rev up the energies of your sales force to hit higher quotas, or if you just need to inspire a lagging team. Prime examples of transformational leaders may be President John Kennedy, Dr. Martin Luther King Jr., and President Barack Obama.

Servant Leadership

Described in *The Servant Leader* by James A. Autry, the servant leader believes his or her mission is to serve the needs of others. This idea has caught the attention of company owners and has in some cases been adopted as a company credo.[23] This philosophy says that the servant leader should lead and develop employees for the mutual benefit of the group, employee, and company. Servant leaders have qualities such as honesty, good listening skills, patience, and gratitude and are more concerned about the needs of others than their own. They use their talents to benefit the group. In their book *Leading with Kindness*, William Baker and Michael O'Malley believe that leadership is achieved through helping others become successful and feel that gratitude is the most important theme of servant leadership.[24]

Leadership with Emotional Intelligence

According to research by Daniel Goleman, whose work with emotional intelligence was introduced in Chapter 2, effective leaders have a high degree of emotional intelligence. They understand and manage their own feelings and have empathy for others. They have a passion to work for the sake of work itself and pursue goals with energy and persistence. They're good at managing relationships and building networks and are skilled at finding common ground and building rapport. Some of the qualities you will recognize are self-confidence, trustworthiness, openness to change and effectiveness in leading, positive attitude, persuasiveness, and building and leading teams.[25]

Leadership Differences in Men and Women

Men and women are sometimes perceived as acting differently in leadership positions, with men being more task oriented and women more relationship oriented. However, some evidence supports the idea that the perceived gaps between the leadership styles of men and those of women are closing as rigid structures and authoritarian management fade. In a recent MSNBC poll, the best attributes of female leaders match those that are most desired by the "younger talent," ages 16–30, of both genders.[26] These Gen Y employees expressed a high preference for female leadership. This group wants greater flexibility, more collaboration in decision making that may impact their work life, and more open communication about the organization's activities. These are the most frequently cited traits associated with women in the workplace. Betty Spence, president of the National Association for Female Executives, says, "Women are what the 21st century needs. They are good for business."

> **"** *People with humility don't think less of themselves, they just think of themselves less.*
> —Ken Blanchard and Norman Vincent Peale, authors **"**

Some management thinkers believe the similarities between male and female leaders outweigh the differences. Individuals who choose leadership-intensive careers (law enforcement, corporate management, military, politics, and education) have common leadership traits and come by them through experience and education. A study done by a Dallas-based management firm The Innis Company found integrity was considered the best attribute, followed closely by flexibility and then people skills.[27] Both males and females can make these skills a part of their leadership style.

One gender's style is not better or more correct than the other's. Having a different management style can work as long as you demonstrate similar skills. Both men and women bring unique and desirable skills to the workplace. As discussed in the earlier sections, leadership is often situational, actually requiring different styles ranging from task oriented to relaxed and relationship oriented. Some of the styles may indicate intergenerational influences. Remembering that an important part of the definition of leadership is "influencing the behavior of others" makes a good leader one who listens, motivates, and provides support to their followers.

Other Considerations

As the masses of baby boomers begin to retire, the workforce will be made of the Gen X, Gen Y, and Gen Why's. This makes for a decisively different mix of attitudes and desires. Chapter 3 described the characteristics of these groups and how they interact. These younger workers have a different attitude about how long they'll remain in any one job. They aren't looking for

40 years with a company and a gold watch when they retire. Leaders have to gain their respect, keep them challenged, and draw on their many talents.

Most new leadership models still deal heavily with human relations skills. As technology advances and economies change, you'll need to constantly work on your human relations skills. As a worker and leader, rather than taking or giving orders, you will be working in a more collaborative and co-operative environment mutually beneficial to the organization and the employee.

The next generation of leaders will be more intellectually and emotionally aware and anticipate and accept change, seeing it as an opportunity. Many of the same qualities required of leaders in the past, such as vision, integrity, and honesty, will still be required, and the effective leader of the future will continue helping others perform to their highest standards.

Ask Yourself...

1. What are your thoughts on the servant leader? Would you be comfortable using this style of leadership? For what kinds of jobs do you think it may be best suited?

2. Describe similarities, in terms of leadership, between the components of emotional intelligence and human relations skills. How many of these components or skills have you used to your benefit in a job situation and how did they benefit you?

KEY TERMS

influence

leadership

great man theory

Theory X

Theory Y

Managerial Grid

autocratic leadership

democratic leadership

free-rein leaders

technical skills

conceptual skills

human relations skills

PODSCORB

transactional leadership

transformational leadership

delegation

CHAPTER SUMMARY

Leaders, people who influence the behavior of others, may be found at all levels of the organizational hierarchy and in personal life. You can be a leader without being a formal manager. Leadership has long been a subject of research to define its origin and identify traits or behaviors that may single out leaders. From the great man theory, researchers moved on to other theories for identifying and developing leaders. Some of the best known of these theories are Theories X and Y, the Managerial Grid, and the Hersey and Blanchard model.

Several distinctive styles of leadership have also been identified. They are autocratic, democratic, and free rein. Good leaders have a preferred style but change their approach to fit the needs of the situation. An effective leader in any organization must be able to apply technical, conceptual, and human relations skills. These skills can be acquired or developed through observation, experience, and continuing education. Mentoring is another effective means for acquiring leadership skills. Successful leaders will also display certain functional abilities, characteristics, attitudes, and behaviors known to be critical to effective leadership. Future leaders will be transformational, motivating their followers to transcend self-interests for the sake of the group goal, and they will self-actualize with servant leadership. Experts predict that the next generation of leaders will acquire or develop the skills and abilities required to meet the unique needs of the new generations of followers.

REVIEW

1. Define leadership. What is the difference between a leader and a manager?

2. Discuss the leadership theories described in this chapter and name and define the three traditional leadership styles.

3. What are the three categories of skills required of leaders? How do they vary with the leader's level?

4. What methods of developing leadership skills are described in chapter? Why is lifelong learning even more important today?

5. Name some of the basic characteristics and behaviors of an effective leader.

6. How do transactional and transformational leadership differ? Will servant leadership be a more important style in the future? Why, or why not?

CRITICAL THINKING

1. Describe the leadership style, from a situational perspective, that should be applied to you in your present job or in an organization to which you belong. Is that style being used? Why, or why not?

2. Cite examples from your experience of leaders you perceive to be transformational or servant leaders. What skills and special characteristics do they demonstrate?

3. Think of a leadership style under which you've worked. Was that style appropriate for the situation? What other style would you have recommended if a change needed to be made and why?

4. Do you think organizations will train their leaders to become servant leaders, and how will they measure the outcomes? Is this style more intuitive?

5. Why do you think emotional intelligence has emerged as a key characteristic of effective leaders? Do the leaders or the followers make the real difference in its popularity?

CASE STUDIES

In small groups, analyze the following situations:

1 **The Rebirth of a Clinic**   Cheryl was a state-certified midwifery nurse and ran the for-profit birthing clinic with an iron fist. The company that owned the clinic expected maximum efficiencies from its operation and monitored productivity, tracking how long the doctors spent with each patient in consultation, how long people took to pay their bills, even how many employees took a little too long at lunch. The company held Cheryl responsible for running the clinic and she had strict expectations to meet. The office staff knew the rules and followed closely—nobody wanted to be without a job.

The clinic eventually closed and Cheryl found a job with a not-for-profit organization whose clients were of low income. After several weeks the clinic's chairperson asked her to use a kinder, gentler approach—a little less formal—in dealing with the office staff and the local patrons. The chairperson spoke to her in a gentle and empathetic way, praising her abilities and past efforts. He said he was sure she would do a fine job for the clinic in the future and she would be doing less of the office management function and more baby deliveries and patient care skills. Cheryl realized that she needed to adapt her leadership style to fit in with her new managers. She left the meeting feeling good about the transition and highly motivated to perform her new duties.

1. What leadership style do you think Cheryl was applying to the clinic staff when it was owned and operated by the business management company? Why was it so effective at that time?

2. What effect do you think the clinic becoming a charity-run operation had on the leadership style used? Why would that have had an effect at all?

3. What leadership style did the minister use in his interaction with Cheryl? What results can you imagine their talk had on the office operations?

2 **"How Is It Today?"**   Edna was a very hard worker—no one could match her output. She had always been good at what she did, and she represented her company to the public with style and class. However, she had a "Jekyll and Hyde" personality that revealed itself to the office staff of seven clerks performing administrative types of duties that were key to the success of the office operations. The group operated at a maximum workload capacity, handling large numbers of projects—more than some offices would even begin to tackle. The stress level was extremely high, yet the staff remained close, good-natured, and laughed among themselves to relieve the tension. Edna, on the other hand, carried her stress internally and took much of her work home at night. This trademark took its toll on her health and the nerves of the office staff. Each day, they waited on edge for her arrival, in fear of the "mood of the day" and what impact it would have on office personnel and operations.

The staff turnover ratio was extremely high. There were complaints by employees who felt that the negative behaviors were too extreme.

Edna's reputation was well known throughout the company. When people in other departments learned that a coworker reported to her, they would roll their eyes in sympathy. The office was successful overall, but it was not as effective as it could be.

1. Which leadership style do you think Edna applied in her office operations? Do you see evidence of more than one? If so, which ones and why?

2. How might Edna have benefited from applying emotional intelligence to her situation in this high-stress office? How might her office have benefitted from the application of more human relation skills?

3. What specific attitudes and behaviors might Edna have demonstrated toward her followers to ease the tensions that might eventually cause costly turnovers and more formal complaint filings?

HUMAN RELATIONS IN ACTION

Working in small groups, design a brochure for a professional training course aimed at preparing employees to be effective leaders in the 21st century. Your professional looking brochure should contain course content presented in the chapter and any other human relations course content from other chapters that you may want to cover. Collectively, assume you are the company owner and will be the course leader making the presentation. You may choose to explore some of the collaborative communications software available to share ideas and graphics through the Internet source searches. In your brochure, outline and discuss the topics you plan to cover, explain why these topics are important, and identify the benefits of this course for the participants. Discuss your topic content choices before beginning your search. Enhance your brochure with any other items of interest that add to its professional appeal. These may include Internet downloads, graphic depictions, and photos and videos available from net sources. Your teacher may want to give final approval of your topic choices before your research begins or review your final project presentations before class time. Check with your teacher for any additional special instructions.

Present your brochure to the class, selling your company's superior leadership skills knowledge. Be persuasive; make the reader want to take your course(s).

For additional resources, refer to the web site for this text:
www.cengage.com/management/dalton

RESOURCES

1. Maxwell, J.C. (2007). *The 21 Irrefutable Laws of Leadership*. Nashville, TN: Thomas Nelson.

2. Drucker, P.R. (2008). *Management* (Rev.ed.). New York: HarperCollins.

3. Foust, D. (2009, May). "Pulling Delta Out of a Nose Dive." *Business Week*. 37.

4. Miller, D. (2008). *No More Mondays*. New York: Doubleday.

5. Maxwell, J.C. (2007). *The 21 Irrefutable Laws of Leadership*.

6. Massie, J. L., & Douglas, J. (1992). *Managing: A Contemporary Introduction*. Upper Saddle River, NJ: Prentice Hall.

7. Ibid.

8. Ibid.

9. McGregor, D. (1960). *The Human Side of Enterprise*. New York: McGraw-Hill.

10. Ibid.

11. Blake, R., & Mouton, J. (1985). *The Managerial Grid: The Key to Leadership Excellence*. Houston, TX: Gulf Publishing.

12. Fiedler, F. E. (1967). *A Theory of Leadership Effectiveness*. New York: McGraw-Hill.

13. Ressler, C., & Thompson, J. (2008). *Work Sucks and How to Fix It*. New York: Penguin Group.

14. Einhorn, B. (2009, May). "How Not to Sweat the Details." *Managing*. 52–53.

15. Kahl, J. (2004). *Leading from the Heart: Choosing to be a Servant Leader*. Austin, TX: Green Leaf Book Group.

16. Chester, E. (2005). *Getting Them to Give a Damn*. New York: Kaplan Publishing.

17. Maxwell, J. C. (1999). *The 21 Indispensable Qualities of a Leader*. Nashville, TN: Thomas Nelson.

18. Plank, K. (2003, December). "How I Did It: Kevin Plank." *Inc. Magazine*. Retrieved from www.inc.com/magazine/20031201/howididit

19. Douglas, J., & Massie, J. L. (1992). *Managing: A Contemporary Introduction*. Upper Saddle River, NJ: Prentice Hall.

20. Ibid.

21. Cottrell, D. (2007). *Monday Morning Choices*. New York: HarperCollins.

22. Bass, B. M. (1990). *Bass & Stogdill's Handbook of Leadership*. New York: The Free Press.

23. Autry, J. (2006). *The Servant Leader*. Roseville, CA: Prima Publishing.

24. Baker, W. F., & O'Malley, M. (2008). *Leading with Kindness: How Good People Consistently Get Superior Results*. New York: Amacom.

25. Goleman, D. "What Makes a Leader?" *Harvard Business Review*. 76(6), November–December 1998, p. 95.

26. Tahmincloglu, E. (2007, March 8). "Men rule—at least in workplace attitudes." MSNBC Retrieved from http://www.msnbc.msn.com/id/17345308/

27. Innis Company. (2009, July). "Do men and women lead differently?" Dallas: TX. Retrieved from www.inniscompany.com

10

APPRECIATING POWER:
POSITIONING AND POLITICS

OBJECTIVES

After studying this chapter, you should be able to:

10.1 Define power and explain why developing power is necessary.

10.2 Identify and discuss the basic power sources available to you.

10.3 Name and discuss the three basic power personalities.

10.4 Discuss techniques used in power positioning and power politics.

10.5 Explain why empowering others is important.

10.6 Discuss the pitfalls of developing power.

Jump Start

Oprah Winfrey is known as "the queen of talk." She is a cultural icon, a financial power-house who can have a dramatic effect on businesses. An author's work can be a guaranteed success if it is selected to be part of Oprah's Book Club. This impact on business has not gone unnoticed. In May 2009, CNBC premiered its original documentary "The Oprah Effect," which follows the aftermath of businesses once highlighted on Winfrey's "My Favorite Things." Web sites crash, phone lines jam, and lines form immediately after a company's product or service is featured on Winfrey's show. Winfrey's power to influence others is undeniable. She has utilized it to develop a successful magazine and a cable channel and to launch other successful television talk-style shows.[1]

- How do you think Oprah has generated such influence in today's society?
- Can you name other people who've become influential because of her? How are they influential?
- If Oprah were to leave her talk show, would her ability to influence others go with her? Why, or why not?

10.1 DEFINING POWER

Power is the ability to influence others to do what you want them to do. It involves changing the attitudes or behaviors of individuals or groups. Power is exercised by all levels of employees in their work and by people in their personal lives.

Power gives you the means to accomplish tasks and can help you reach your goals. Many experts point out that people can't succeed in organizations today without acquiring some power and learning how to use it. Also, an understanding of power can help you recognize when those around you are attempting to influence you through the exercise of power. The appropriate use of power can be a strong factor in how effective your human relations skills are.

A fine distinction exists between influence and power. *Influence* is the application of power through actions we take or examples we set that cause others to change their attitudes or behaviors. People must possess power from some source before they can influence the behaviors of others. Sources of power can often be found by utilizing 21st century skills. Communication and collaboration with others provide connections that can lead to powerful impacts and new alliances that can result in the ability to influence others.

Often, the term power brings to mind negative images. Terms such as manipulation, control, domination, exploitation, corruption, and coercion are frequently associated with power. Because of the tarnished image of abusive power, many individuals tend to shy away from learning about and practicing

In The News

Powerful businesses can be the result of a chance meeting. Bob McKnight, the CEO of Quicksilver, has been called "the Surfin' CEO." Throughout college, McKnight helped pay his expenses by showing surfing movies he had filmed up and down the California coast. His rise to success began when he met well-known surfer Jeff Hackman. Hackman knew of surfer shorts coming out of Australia. He also knew designer Alan Green. McKnight and Hackman acquired the rights to manufacture and sell the surfer shorts in America and began selling the shorts out of the back of a van to local surf shops. That was the beginning of Quicksilver, which grew to become a surfware giant and a well-known sports brand.[2]

1. What lesson could be learned about networking with persons who share similar interests?
2. Do you think other successful businesses could result from the partnering of persons with similar passions? Why, or why not?

> *Nearly all men can stand adversity, but if you want to test a man's character, give him power.*
> —Abraham Lincoln, U.S. president

positive power. The effective use of emotional intelligence can counter these negative associations. For example, self-regulation assists in using power positively in ways that incorporate trustworthiness, integrity, and openness to change.

Patricia Russo has confessed that while at AT&T it was her taste of power that made her want to run a big corporation. Russo's position at AT&T was the first time she was the top leader at a corporation. She had the power to make decisions and changes and plan a company's path—and she liked it. She liked being in control, watching the results of her own leadership and seeing what worked and what did not.

After 20 years at AT&T, Russo moved to the number two slot at Kodak, then returned as CEO of AT&T spin-off Lucent Technologies.[3] In July 2008 she left Lucent, and in 2009 she was selected to be on the board of directors of the new General Motors Corp.[4] Russo has used her power positively to advance her career.

Power can be a healthy, desirable attribute when channeled appropriately. It is most effective when its use is not obvious. Positive uses of power include influence, leadership, control, authority, and direction. These strong behaviors are necessary in both your personal and professional lives.

Acquiring some power and learning how to use it, then, is essential to your achievement of personal and organizational goals. An understanding of the sources of power available to you and techniques for drawing upon them will assist you in strengthening your power base.

Ask Yourself...

1. Why is power a necessary tool?
2. How have you had power exercised over you, and how did you feel about it?
3. Describe instances when you have used power in a positive way.

10.2   THE SOURCES OF POWER

John French and Bertram Raven, who study and research power, identified five basic power sources: reward, coercive, legitimate, expert, and referent. The first three sources are derived from your position within an organization; the second two are generated from your personal characteristics. Other theorists add derivative power and passive power to the list.[5]

Reward Power

Reward power is the ability to give something of material or personal value to others. The rewards may be in the form of promotions, bonuses, supplies and equipment, highly desirable job assignments, or reserved parking places. The reward may also take the form of valued information, praise for a job well done, or a desired position title. At home, reward power may come in the form of an unexpected gift, an allowance, a night to eat out, or a trip to the movies.

Reward power is considered to be the most important source of power by French and Raven because it places the reward seeker almost totally at the mercy of the reward giver. Only by submitting to the desired behavior can the seeker hope to obtain the reward from the giver. The strength of this power source varies with the amount or value of the rewards controlled by the giver. From the corporate chief executive to the unit secretary who controls the distribution of supplies, a full range of individuals can hold this power source.

> **KeyPoint**
> Developing or acquiring power sources is a necessary step in gaining power.

Coercive Power

Coercive power is based on fear and punishment. Demotions, dismissals, reprimands, assignments of unpleasant tasks, and public embarrassment are examples of coercive power. This form of power can be directed toward superiors, coworkers, or subordinates. For example, a supervisor may be successful in getting employees to work longer hours for less pay through fear of losing their job if they don't. At home, coercive power may come in the form of a threat of possible divorce if a behavior or situation change does not occur.

Coercive power can be used in a positive manner, such as in an emergency, to let others know that you mean business. When an employee's performance is slipping, being firm and pointing out the consequences of continued nonperformance can have a positive effect.

However, open use of coercive power is generally considered unacceptable in the work environment, and the user may risk retaliation, sabotage, or malicious obedience—where employees do exactly what they are told even though they know that it will result in an undesirable outcome, and then wait for it to blow up in their supervisor's face. Those subjected to coercive power may develop low morale because coercive power is a negative motivator. This counterproductive use of power also places the user at a greater risk of being removed from any position of power. Because of its potential for harm, coercive power should be used with caution.

An important tool available to organizations, yet seldom used, is an employee's evaluation of his or her supervisor. Normally, supervisors are given a top-down evaluation, when in fact the more beneficial information may stem from a bottom-up evaluation. For example, when two top-level executives of a major computer firm were rated by their employees as remote, opinionated, poor listeners, and unappreciative, they were shocked—enough to work with training coaches to change those behaviors and to improve rapport with their employees.

Legitimate Power

Legitimate power is derived from formal rank or position within an organizational hierarchy. A company president holds greater legitimate power than a regional vice president, and a general department manager will hold more legitimate power than a first-line supervisor or a technician on an assembly line. This power source is dependent on the formal, established chain of command within the organization and the perceived authority of the individual in that position of power. Examples away from work include a team captain and a committee chairperson. These individuals are perceived to have an "appointed" power.

Often, individuals have titles that set them apart from the crowd—General Colin Powell, Secretary of State Hillary Clinton, Dr. Oz (a doctor known through his media appearances), or chairman and CEO of Microsoft. These titles are not meant to be intimidating, but they do give the owner a certain earned or entitled presence of power.

However, just because you are ranked higher in an organization doesn't mean that you hold total power over those under you. An example is the security guard who has the legitimate power to request the president of the company to present identification to enter a secured facility.

Expert Power

Expert power develops when an individual possesses specialized skills, knowledge, or expertise. This power source is limited in that it is useful only when the knowledge is of value to the seeker. This power source is not dependent on appointed rank or position. Expert power may be demonstrated by individuals ranging from the CEO to the night janitor or any individual with "special" expertise. For instance, when the building heat is malfunctioning, employees will turn to the HVAC expert rather than the company's CEO, who probably has no knowledge of how to fix the building's heat.

Expert power can also be found off the job. You may, for example, defer to a neighbor with extensive mechanical experience when dealing with an automobile that won't start or a dishwasher that doesn't work. An example in today's environment is the computer expert who visits your home to help with computer problems that you may never have been able to solve on your own. Or the certified public accountant who does your complicated tax returns so you don't have to try to figure out tax codes and other complicated rules. You may have some particular skill or talent that affords you this power source.

Referent Power

Referent power is based on respect or admiration for the individual. This respect or admiration may result from personal charisma and "likable" personal traits. Sports heroes, political leaders, and dynamic religious or business leaders can influence the behavior of others who have a desire to emulate their heroes' perceived success. Corporate officers and politicians engulfed in scandal may retain their legitimate power but lose their referent power with some of the public. Persons who will probably always retain their place of prestige include newsman Walter Cronkite, basketball star Magic Johnson, Reverend Billy Graham, Dr. Martin Luther King Jr., and astronaut Neil Armstrong. These individuals are respected and admired by most Americans and hold a place of power for their accomplishments.

Derivative Power and Passive Power

Derivative power comes from close association with a powerful person. All of us are familiar with signs and symbols of people using this power technique. Examples of using derivative power to gain advantages are name-dropping and use of social networking cliques such as "good old boy" systems that favor insiders to the exclusion of others.

Passive power, the last of the power sources, stems from a display of helplessness. A child often uses this power source effectively on a parent to gain attention or solicit help with some undesirable task. Unfortunately, we sometimes see the same technique carried into adulthood and used in the workplace. For example, an employee will act incapable in order to gain help in accomplishing a task or to escape it altogether. A simple statement that says, "I cannot possibly manage this all by myself and, besides, you are so much better at this sort of thing than I am," will often subtly but powerfully gain the desired results.

Derivative and passive power sources are not dependable over a long period of time. They tend to damage the image and credibility of the user. Recognizing that these power sources exist and avoiding their use will aid you in developing more desirable power sources. Additionally, being knowledgeable will help you avoid being the pawn that is duped in the game of passive power.

Power Source Linking

Power sources may be highly linked and tend to occur in combinations. An example of power source linking is the prominent sports figure Peyton Manning. He has expert power because he possesses special skills and expertise in the sport of football, and he has referent power due to the admiration and respect of his strong character and ethics, as clearly demonstrated by the amount of confidence advertisers have put in him through numerous product endorsements. He also has legitimate power as a high-profile competitor in his sport who has won the Super Bowl, been named the NFL MVP several times, and holds many NFL passing records.

With some individuals, we don't have to guess or be told which power sources they use or possess. The names or faces of certain individuals are easily recognized because of the impact they have had on us or on our world. We immediately acknowledge and can often easily identify the power sources of people such as those in these photos.

What are the power sources for these individuals?

Figure 10.1 provides an illustration of power source linking. As you read the example, note the various sources of power that are used and how they are linked.

Figure 10.1

Power source linking.

Thomas, the head of the accounting department, glared at the young staff accountant who sat nervously in the chair beside him. He was angry at the accountant's antics and felt that he had to show him that he couldn't get away with foolishness that reflected negatively on the company. Thomas's brow was furrowed, reflecting a scowl. He showed his anger by speaking in harsh tones and short phrases. He was the department chief with full authority to administer the punishment due for the embarrassment caused the company and to delay any promotion until the staff accountant's behavior matured.

> "
> *Being powerful is like being a lady. If you have to tell people you are, you aren't.*
> —*Margaret Thatcher, former British prime minister*
> "

In this example, Thomas has legitimate power given to him through his position in the organization. Additionally, he is exercising coercive power through his intimidating body language and threats of consequences.

The type of behavior response from individuals will vary in different situations depending on what the receiver perceives the power source of the sender to be. For example, individuals with a high degree of expert power are usually admired and respected and, therefore, have a high degree of referent power. Similarly, individuals with a high degree of legitimate power may wield strong reward and coercive power over others.

Many combinations of power can be developed. A particularly powerful combination to acquire is expert, legitimate, and reward power sources. Obviously, the more power sources you acquire, the stronger your influence will be in the work environment and on a personal level.

Your ability to use these power sources individually or in combination relies heavily on the perception of those involved. They must believe that your power source is genuine. John P. Kotter has stated that, in order to develop the perception in others that you are truly powerful, you must use your power sources wisely and appropriately. Recognize what sources you don't have and avoid their use. Using undeveloped sources or abusing your power sources weakens your credibility and strips you of what power you do have. Understand the risks and benefits of using each of your power sources and develop your skills accordingly.[6]

Ask Yourself...

1. How were the power sources of the individuals pictured on the previous page developed? How are those sources linked?

2. Which of the power sources do you think link in your personal activities?

3. Have you ever seen or heard about someone who used linked power sources unwisely and inappropriately? What was the outcome?

4. Which of these power sources do you have?

10.3   THE PERSONALITY OF POWER

Some behavioral theorists believe that a person's use of power is based more on individual characteristics, charisma, and acquired personality traits than on other factors. These traits vary in intensity in different people, resulting in three basic power personalities: the power-shy, the power-positive, and the power-compulsive.

Power-shy individuals tend to avoid being placed in positions that require overt use of power. They quickly sidestep or totally shun responsibility and leadership, feeling extremely uncomfortable with decision making and influencing or controlling the behavior of others. Power-shy individuals make excellent followers and will usually excel in positions that require them to operate independently and rely on individual skills and abilities. You may recognize why Oprah Winfrey was once considered a power-shy individual. Early in her career, Oprah had feelings of insecurity and image issues based on her weight and race. Breaking into the television reporting industry was not easy then. She relied on her skills and abilities to become a more power-positive person.

Power-positive people genuinely enjoy accepting responsibility and thrive on the use of power. Highly power-motivated, these individuals enjoy controlling situations and directing and influencing the behavior of others. They express strong views and opinions and are usually risk takers and adventurers. Power-positive individuals can be valuable resources when placed in leadership roles requiring the described qualities. Tyra Banks has hosted one of the most successful talk shows on television and she has produced other successful media projects. However, Banks has stated that as a teenager she was skinny and tall, and unkind comments from other students would send her to her room crying. At 17, the fashion industry discovered her and she became a supermodel. How do you think Banks' success in her field helped her transform from being a power-shy to a power-positive person? Only when the need or desire for power becomes compulsive and is a driving force directing all actions toward selfish goals does it take on negative overtones.

Power-compulsive individuals have a lust for power and are seldom satisfied with the amount of power they have. These individuals constantly seek increased levels of control and influence over others and have a strong need to display power plays for personal gain in all situations. This use of power is destructive and intimidating, seldom benefiting the organization or the individual.

Fortunately, the need and desire for power varies greatly in individuals. A work environment needs both power-shy and power-positive personalities to create balance. We acquire power in varying amounts, from different sources, and at different times in life. How we choose to use it reflects our positive or negative motive.

The short self-inventory presented in Figure 10.2 will rate your power personality. Does the need for power control you, or do you constructively use the power that you have for growth and advancement? Be honest in

> **KeyPoint**
> Power-positive people enjoy responsibility, controlling situations, and influencing the behavior of others.

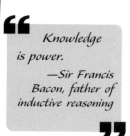

> *Knowledge is power.*
>
> —Sir Francis Bacon, father of inductive reasoning

Figure 10.2 ◑

Power personality test.

INSTRUCTIONS: Rate yourself on each statement using the following scale:
1 = seldom or never true, 2 = sometimes true, 3 = always or often true.

1. I always make my point of view known, both in personal and in business situations.
2. If I don't achieve my career goals, I won't feel like a success.
3. I never feel subordinate to others in business matters.
4. It is important to me to be the leader in my workplace or office.
5. I would only accept a new position that had more power and prestige than my current position.
6. I would feel angry if asked to do subordinate tasks.
7. I become frustrated when upstaged at work.
8. Demonstrating authority is necessary, even if others are sometimes humiliated.
9. At work, I always get my way.
10. I feel a sense of importance when others adhere to my schedule or must wait for me.
11. I fear being humiliated by others.
12. If others take advantage of me, I feel angry or humiliated.
13. A real career has power; otherwise it is just a job.

SCORING

Total score of:	1–9	Low need for power
	10–19	Moderate need for power
	20 and above	High need for power

your responses to obtain a true reflection of yourself. You may also want to have your spouse, close friend, or coworker answer the questions about you. Seeing yourself as others see you is an excellent method of gaining insight.

A high score on the scale could indicate a need to evaluate your power motives. You may want to examine and better understand your interactions with others both at home and at work. Questions you will want to ask yourself may be:

• Do you need to dominate situations? Does this apply to home and work?

• Do you need to have power over others to feel effective or successful?

• How does the need for power impact situations at home and work?

Use your knowledge of the components of emotional intelligence to create a plan to improve your use of power.

Ask Yourself...

1. If you are power shy, how might you change that power personality?
2. Was your score on the power personality test what you expected? Are you happy with the results? Why or why not?

10.4 SUCCESSFULLY DEVELOPING YOUR POWER

Building power is a complex process and requires an understanding of the responsibilities of power, power sources, and knowledge of the ethical use of power. Some individuals may operate from a totally subconscious level in their quest for power, whereas others consciously and methodically plan their steps to the top. Building and maintaining a strong power base usually requires a thorough understanding of power positioning, power politics, and power symbols.

In The News

Indra Nooyi, CEO of PepsiCo, has been in the number one spot of *Fortune* Magazine's "50 Most Powerful Women" list in both 2008 and 2009. Nooyi's company revenues posted $39 billion in 2008. The criteria used to judge who makes this list include the size and importance of the woman's business, her clout inside the company, the arc of her career, and her influence on mass culture and society. After Nooyi joined PepsiCo in 1994, she helped the company make tough decisions, such as shedding KFC, Pizza Hut, and Taco Bell. She engineered the $3 billion acquisition of Tropicana and the $14 billion takeover of Quaker Oats, the makers of Gatorade.[7]

Indra Nooyi began her schooling in Kathmandu. She received a bachelor's degree in chemistry from Madras Christian College and earned an MBA at the Indian Institute of Management in Calcutta. She also earned a masters degree in public and private management at Yale.[8]

1. What power sources do you think Indra Nooyi possesses?
2. What do you think Nooyi's power personality is?

Power Positioning

Power positioning is the conscientious use of techniques designed to position yourself for maximum personal growth or gain. Achieving success is sometimes attributed to luck or being at the right place at the right time. (How often have you heard the cliché, "It's not what you know, but whom you know"?) However, you can apply specific techniques of power positioning that don't rely on luck or influencing others.

Some 20 years of research by behavioral scientists has resulted in the identification of techniques that strongly influence the degree of personal power we attain. Position power is less effective without personal power. The techniques in Figure 10.3 will greatly increase your power and enhance your chances of success.

Individuals are seldom fully proficient in all these techniques. Effective power positioning requires skillful planning and careful implementation. If you are a well-grounded person applying emotional intelligence in your day-to-day human relations activities, you'll be able to handle most difficult situations you face. Self-assessment is an important first step in identifying which technique needs attention and which already is fully developed in you.

> *To know the pains of power, we must go to those who have it; to know its pleasures, we must go to those who are seeking it.*
> —Charles Caleb Colten, author and English cleric

Figure 10.3

Techniques to strengthen your personal power.

1. Communicate well. Influencing others strengthens power.
2. Be decisive. Stand behind issues you have thought through.
3. Learn to lead. Build a reputation for being trustworthy and ethical.
4. Know your organization. Learn its history and internal politics.
5. Choose a mentor. Pick a successful person to advise and guide you.
6. Be an authority. Owners of resources and information hold the power.
7. Be a team player. Assist others in achieving goals and objectives.
8. Become highly visible. Volunteer for special projects and activities.
9. Learn to network. Meet many people and build useful networks.
10. Become confident. Project a positive self-image.
11. Develop advanced skills. Expand your education, skills, and abilities.
12. Be committed. Demonstrate determined dedication to excellence.

> *Power always has to be kept in check; power exercised in secret, especially under the cloak of national security, is doubly dangerous.*
> —John Stewart Mill, philosopher and economist

Power Politics

In his book *Unlimited Power,* Anthony Robbins states that preparation and opportunity will generate luck. Success is not an accident, and *power politics* allows us to develop opportunities for success.[9] Generally, power politics is a concept that refers to interacting with those in pursuit of one's own self interests.

Not all decisions for promotion and rewards are made on the basis of merit, fair play, rationality, or even ethics. The only defense you may have against unfair practices is becoming politically astute. This means developing an awareness of power politics, understanding how it works, and applying those techniques with which you are most comfortable.

A first step in this process is to determine how politically inclined you are. The checklist in Figure 10.4 is a quick self-test that will give you some insight into your political inclination. It is an abbreviated version of the Organizational Politics Scale developed by business and psychology author Andrew J. DuBrin in *Winning Office Politics*. DuBrin's complete test consists of 100 comprehensive questions that provide an in-depth index of an individual's political tendencies. He places the scores in five categories that illustrate a person's identity as a politician. This shortened test version may help you determine where you would fall in the category scale.[10]

In his *Winning Office Politics,* DuBrin goes on to explain the following five categories of power.[11] As you read the definitions and the categories of the people they describe, you may recognize yourself or others with whom you come in contact. The importance here is to recognize that at times power source usage will fluctuate so that accommodating and controlling the changes is important.

- *Machiavellian.* The Machiavellian is a power-hungry, power-grabbing individual. Often ruthless, devious, and power-crazed, he or she will try to succeed at any cost to others.

- *Company Politician.* This individual is a bureaucrat who maneuvers shrewdly. Most successful individuals fall into this category. Company politicians desire power, but it is not an all-consuming preoccupation for them. They will do whatever is necessary to address their cause except deliberately defame or injure others.

- *Survivalist.* The survivalist practices enough power politics to take advantage of good opportunities. Not concerned about making obvious political blunders, he or she will stay out of trouble with others of a higher rank.

- *Straight Arrow.* This person is not particularly perceived as a politician. The straight arrow fundamentally believes that most people are honest, hardworking, and trustworthy. The favorite career advancement strategy is to display job competence, but he or she may neglect other important career-advancement strategies.

- *Innocent Lamb.* The innocent lamb believes fully that good people are rewarded for their efforts and will rise to the top. This individual remains focused on the tasks at hand, hoping that hard work will be rewarded.

Obviously, some individuals are well suited to applying whatever methods and techniques that will advance them toward their goals. The Machiavellian

Figure 10.4

How political are you?

Directions: Answer each question "mostly agree" or "mostly disagree," even if it is difficult for you to decide which alternative best describes your opinion.

1. Only a fool would correct a boss's mistakes.
2. If I have certain confidential information, I release it to my advantage.
3. I would be careful not to hire a subordinate with more formal education than myself.
4. If I do somebody a favor, I remember to cash in on it.
5. Given the opportunity, I would cultivate friendships with power people.
6. I like the idea of saying nice things about a rival in order to get that person transferred from my department.
7. Why not take credit for someone else's work? They would do the same to me.
8. Given the chance, I would offer to help my boss build some shelves for his or her den.
9. I laugh heartily at my boss's jokes, even when they are not funny.
10. I would be sure to attend a company picnic even if I had the chance to do something I enjoyed more that day.
11. If I knew an executive in my company was stealing money, I would use that against him or her in asking for favors.
12. I would first find out my boss's political preferences before discussing politics with him or her.
13. I think using memos to zap somebody for his or her mistakes is a good idea (especially when I want to show that person up).
14. If I wanted something done by a coworker, I would be willing to say "If you don't get this done, our boss might be very unhappy."
15. I would invite my boss to a party at my house, even if I didn't like him or her.
16. When I'm in a position to, I would have lunch with the "right people" at least twice a week.
17. Richard M. Nixon's bugging the Democratic Headquarters would have been a clever idea if he hadn't been caught.
18. Power for its own sake is one of life's most precious commodities.
19. Having a high school named after me would be an incredible thrill.
20. Reading about job politics is as much fun as reading an adventure story.

Interpretation of Scores. Each statement you check "mostly agree" is worth one point toward your political orientation score. If you score 16 or over, it suggests that you have a strong inclination toward playing politics. A high score of this nature would also suggest that you have strong needs for power. Scores of 5 or less would suggest that you are not inclined toward political maneuvering and that you are not strongly power-driven.

SOURCE: Andrew J. DuBrin, *Winning Office Politics* (Englewood Cliffs, NJ: Prentice-Hall, 1990).

and Innocent Lamb types are extremes to avoid, but falling somewhere in the middle of these categories may prove valuable in power politics.

Organizational politics are unavoidable. The political implications of your actions, and the actions of others, must be taken into consideration whenever operating within an organization, be it large or small. Playing power politics can be negative or positive. Negative methods are manipulative, coercive, exploitative, and destructive. Positive methods are used to achieve common goals, empower others, build cooperation, develop effective personal contacts, and gain credibility and leadership.

The political power checklist itemized in Figure 10.5 provides a quick reference to methods that you may use to become politically powerful. It can be used to check your personal progress or map your strategies.

Figure 10.5

Political power checklist.

Use this checklist to assess your progress in building a power base.

_____ Do you have a mentor?
_____ Are you sought out for advice or information?
_____ Are your achievements visible?
_____ Are you presenting your major accomplishments at appraisal time?
_____ Are you setting mid- and long-range goals and following through?
_____ Are you outpacing your competition?
_____ Are you paying attention to power dynamics?
_____ Are you attempting to influence others?
_____ Are you getting credit and recognition for your ideas?
_____ Are you developing and increasing your power sources?
_____ Do people enjoy working with you?

Perhaps one of the most notable political and personal power people in our nation's history is Eleanor Roosevelt. Most people liked her either very much or not at all—seldom was there room for middle ground with her personal traits and characteristics. However, she became a strong icon of power with her untiring devotion to human rights: support of the United Nations formation, delegate to the UN General Assembly, and chair of the committee that drafted and approved the Universal Declaration of Human Rights. Her personal and political power made a lasting difference.

Networking

As discussed in the previous chapters, networking is often used as a means to exchange favors and information and as a means of building sources of talent and friendship for help in the future. Treat your network much the same as you would treat a team, involving people with a wide variety of skills, diversities of topic knowledge, and cultural foundations. Your network over time will become a means of obtaining and giving information and assistance.

Networking can be a source of power, as seen in the beginning of this chapter with Bob McKnight, CEO of Quicksilver. McKnight's business success began directly from his networking with people with similar interests. He has now gained legitimate power from the business that he developed and that continues to thrive.

You should revise and update your network occasionally, ever widening your scope of contacts. Conversely, be certain to return your time, skills, and knowledge to other members when required—and always with a kind word of thanks.

Power Symbols

Power symbols come in the form of physical traits or personality characteristics as well as external physical factors, such as clothes or cars. Power symbols are present everywhere. We turn on soap operas and watch as the rich, handsome tycoon and his ex-model wife, who is draped in jewels, are driven in their Rolls Royce to a romantic weekend on their 80-foot yacht. We then pick up the paper only to see that another corporation has built an even larger building designed by a popular architect. Or it may be something as simple as a big floppy-brimmed hat and dark sunglasses that give an exotic vision of mystery and power.

Do individuals acquire these power symbols after they obtain power? Do some people with little power use them to portray the illusion of power? If you don't have power, will the use of power symbols speed your ability to obtain it? One thing is certain—our perceptions are influenced by these symbols. Understanding power symbols will help you decide how you wish to use them and recognize their use by others.

Traits and Characteristics   Do some characteristics identify the potential of an individual to hold power over others? High achievers are generally perceived as powerful, and their traits have been associated with power. These individuals are seen as self-confident, ambitious, dominant, attractive, selfish, ruthless, decisive, strong-willed, determined, accomplished, and goal-directed.

Whether individuals start with these traits or acquire them is undetermined. However, most theorists believe that they are learned abilities nurtured from infancy. Individuals gain these strengths through exposure and experience and cultivate them because of benefits that they derive from their use. The desire for some of these traits is no doubt strengthened through the constant reinforcement by the media that these are the dynamic traits of success and power.

Some studies have supported the idea that certain physical traits make a more powerful impression. For example, people do make a mental connection between height and power, reported Wayne Hensley, a scientist who has done research on whether height provides any real advantage. Through a

KeyPoint
Power symbols influence perceptions and come in the form of physical traits or personality characteristics.

survey of some 243 executives, Hensley found that 90 percent of them were taller than the average five-foot-nine-inch male. He also found through a sampling of male university professors that the taller the teacher, the higher the academic ranking. Full professors averaged a two-or-more-inch advantage. The same pattern held true in his research on the last 21 U.S. presidential elections. The taller candidate was chosen to be the chief executive in 17 of the 21 elections.[12]

In The News

Nancy Lublin founded Dress for Success in 1996 as a nonprofit organization to help disadvantaged women obtain economic independence by providing professional attire for job interviews. The nonprofit accepted clients only through referrals from other public service programs. Once a client found a job, they could return and receive additional workplace-appropriate clothing. Lublin's concept worked. Soon other communities were contacting her to help start programs in their own areas. Lublin trademarked the name and licensed it to over 20 affiliates. The organization soon added a Professional Women's Group program to provide career training skills and professional coaching. Today, Dress for Success has grown to include four countries and has been featured on The Oprah Winfrey Show, 60 Minutes, The Today Show, CNN, and in many print magazines.[13,14]

1. How do you think clothing and appearance make a difference in business?
2. How many smart business principles do you see applied in Lublin's decisions? Discuss any other growth potential you see.

Additionally, some studies have shown that specific nonverbal behavior patterns differ between high- and low-power individuals. These behaviors deal with direct eye contact, facial expressions, body gestures, and body positioning. For example, a less powerful person is more likely to be touched, whereas the more powerful person is far more likely to do the touching.

External Physical Factors   Clothing is an external physical factor that may send power signals. The famous adage "Clothes do not make the man" does not hold completely true. Certainly, the idea of "dressing for success" has merit.

Personal appearance seems to carry importance in most cases. From our hairstyle down to our shoes, our appearance makes a statement about the degree of power we either hold or seek. Stylish appearance makes a perceived difference and will let others know you are serious about your career choices. The best approach is to dress for the job you want to have.

> It is an interesting question how far men would retain their relative rank if they were divested of their clothes.
>
> —Henry David Thoreau, author

Entrepreneurs in fitted suits, board members in the "corporate uniform," and power brokers in the "right kind of suit" all understand the psychological advantages gained from dressing for the part. It is important to make your statement, but know what statement you are making.

To some, style is also the very nature of executive power. Individuals often believe that attire plays a key role in workplace outcomes. Clothing can have a strategic use for managing professional impressions. Many believe that they can influence others and gain greater power depending on what they wear. Understanding the value of workplace attire can be seen as essential to gaining workplace success.[15]

Power is also communicated through use of space. In some cases, powerful people will enjoy zones of personal space. For example, the corporate CEO may be seated behind a large, executive-style desk, issuing orders to a subordinate standing on the opposite side of the desk. A less powerful person will usually make an appointment and wait to be ushered in by invitation to see the power holder, whereas the more powerful person is far more likely to walk right into the smaller office area of a subordinate and be given immediate recognition and respect. Although these cues are subtle, they do leave the impression that an individual is powerful.

KeyPoint
Clothing is an external factor that sends powerful signals and can be an essential tool in your workplace success.

In The News

University of Connecticut President Michael J. Hogan gave advice during his 2009 commencement speech that graduates should say "yes" to job offers. Hogan was referring to a trend seen in new graduates of turning down jobs. New graduates had spent their college years in a booming economy and had never experienced a downturn. So while these graduates were presenting the right image to obtain the job offer, many ultimately refused to accept. The reasons ranged from wanting higher compensation to not getting a good "vibe" from the prospective employer.

At the University of Oregon, career counselor Clarice Wilsey worries about students' futures. Employer participation at the university's job fairs is down, and she feels that after a few months of not finding the job they want, students will panic. President Hogan concluded that saying "yes" to a job offer will help start a career.[16]

1. Do you agree with new graduates who turn down job offers in a slow job market? Why or why not?

2. Describe an "image" or professional appearance that would make a new graduate a strong job candidate.

On the other hand, some symbols of power are being challenged. The recent decline in the economy can be seen in the pay packages being offered to CEOs questioned by the public. In fact, in 2008 CEO pay packages fell 6.8 percent. This marks the first time since 2002 that CEOs have seen their pay drop and is a sharp contrast from 2007 when a similar study reported a 1.3 percent increase in pay packages.[17]

Not all companies are yielding to public indignation for large CEO compensation packages or power. The Royal Bank of Scotland defended its decision to provide a large compensation package to its new CEO, even with a recent scandal regarding the outgoing CEO's golden parachute pension. The package given to incoming CEO Stephen Hester is valued at $15.7 million. The bank stated that the package is justified and is based largely on performance and will benefit shareholders.[18]

> *It isn't a mistake to have strong views. The mistake is to have nothing else.*
> —Anthony Westin, ethicist and author

Based on how they're dressed, which of these two women is most likely the boss? What external factors are sending power signals?

Thoughts today about what is the appropriate use of symbols seem to move in extremes from one end of a spectrum to the other. This can be attributed in part to the rise of the baby boomers, who have moved away from tradition in many areas, and to the dramatic changes in business itself, as advances in technology alter the way we work. Our work and personal environments will continue to evolve throughout the 21st century.

Technology CONNECTION

President Obama is an enthusiastic user of a Blackberry, a traditional business standard of implied power. Letting the president keep his Blackberry presented a problem after he was elected, though. It raised a question of security. Some argued that a "connected" president would be better for the country. After all, the president's ability to reach beyond his inner circle gives him access to fresh ideas and constructive critics. Ultimately, Obama was able to keep his Blackberry, with special technology being implemented to ensure security. This issue will most certainly come up again. Technology itself demonstrates power, and with each new president, we are likely to have a new technology or device used by millions that must now be made secure for one person.[19]

1. What do you identify as symbols of power?
2. How might high-tech perks affect the attitudes of business associates?
3. Do you think the importance of high technology and the ability to obtain it is overemphasized today? Why or why not?

> *The ego trip is something that never really gets you anywhere.*
>
> —*Suzan L. Wiesner, author*

Regardless of how the world changes, the powerful person will always acquire benefits. As an individual rises to a position of power, certain symbols will set that person apart from others. Today, power symbols provided by organizations may include a company car, a personal assistant, opportunities to travel, or advanced personal technological devices.

Ask Yourself...

1. Do you agree with the "casual Friday" concept for corporate settings? What effect do you think this idea has had on work environments?
2. Were you surprised or comfortable with your power category based on DuBrin's political assessment instrument? How will you use this information?

10.5 EMPOWERMENT OF OTHERS

Empowerment became a trendy management catch phrase in the 1990s, but the trend has carried over into the 21st century. *Empowerment* is allowing others to make decisions and have influence in desired outcomes. Now organizations continue to reduce the layers of decision making to lower levels. The need for a leaner operation naturally requires passing the power to those most qualified to make the right decision. It involves not only the delegation of tasks, but also assigning the appropriate authority and supplying the necessary information and training with the task so that the individual has considerable likelihood of being successful. It is the giving of power to others and helping them develop their own power sources. The ability to empower others is a sign of an accomplished leader.

Kenneth Blanchard is a world-renowned consultant and author of many books, including *The 3 Keys to Empowerment: Release the Power within People for Astonishing Results*. The title speaks to his strong support of empowering others. Blanchard feels managers must start practicing empowerment by sharing information with others and allowing them the autonomy to use that information. The decision-making process must be flattened and the freedom to do that pushed down to the lowest levels at which a competent decision can be made. If these steps are taken, organizations may expect to get remarkable results from subordinates.[20]

KeyPoint
Empowerment is allowing others to make decisions and influence others.

Global CONNECTION

Bill Gates, cofounder of Microsoft, is out to make a difference in the world with his Bill and Melinda Gates Foundation. HIV prevention programs have been a global focus of the foundation. While many know of the Gates Foundation HIV work in Africa, a recent focus has been on India. In 2003, the Gates Foundation committed $258 million to the Avahan program. Avahan provides funding to HIV prevention programs in six Indian states. In 2009, Bill Gates contributed an additional $80 million to the program. Although criticized in a recent *Forbes* article as not being very effective—because of Gates' tendency to apply business and technological solutions to global health issues and the agencies not achieving all of their goals—supporters argue it is too early to tell. However, soon the Indian government will be taking the reins of the prevention programs from Avahan to ensure their longevity. Regardless of the issues with Avahan, Gates was honored in New Delhi and received the Indira Gandhi Prize for Peace, Disarmament, and Development on behalf of his foundation.[21]

1. Have you found areas in your life where you feel that, if you were empowered with the authority, you would be able to reach a goal successfully?
2. How do you feel about the outreach work Gates' foundation performs? What other ways would you like to see the foundation put its contributions to good use?

> *Growth demands a temporary surrender of security.*
> —Gail Sheehy, author

Blanchard points out that many people will be uncomfortable with newly acquired power, but given the opportunity to use their power and the freedom to make mistakes, they will mature in confidence. This approach is a winning one for all those who involved. He believes that the rewards will be more involved employees with less turnover and a more diverse pool of expertise and brainpower to utilize. With the trend toward larger, global businesses, empowerment may become an increasingly important element of successful human relations and effective business.[22]

Knowledge work, with its reliance on project teams and cross-functional collaboration, is naturally resistant to the old forms of authoritarian leadership. Relinquishing power and giving it away will be a method of survival. Companies cannot be fast or global unless people in the field are empowered to make judgment calls and make decisions in a timely manner.

Authoritarian managers who see empowerment as giving up their own personal power are missing the point. You actually gain more power by giving some of yours away. The Ritz-Carlton hotel chain management experienced this when it empowered its front-line employees to resolve customer service problems for any amount less than $1,000. The employees felt good about their jobs and themselves in those jobs. The hotel management greatly reduced the amount of paperwork and labor spent processing minor claims resolving customer complaints.[23]

One final testament on behalf of empowerment comes from Warren Bennis in his workbook *Learning to Lead*. He says that in organizations with effective leaders, empowerment is used widely. The organizations are successful and the leaders are fulfilled. Bennis stated that people who are empowered will feel more significant and find their work more exciting.[24] Empowerment can strengthen leaders' operation and improve operational efficiencies.

Ask Yourself...

1. Does empowerment differ from delegation? How?
2. Do you think that empowerment is just a trend in the workplace or a real asset in leadership? Explain.
3. What other benefits do you think might come from empowering others?

10.6 POWER PITFALLS

The more power you are able to exert, the more easily you will accomplish your goals. With each goal accomplishment, some degree of additional power is gained that enhances further accomplishments. Each cycle increases the ability to go beyond the previous level.

A number of behaviors, however, can block the development of power. Individuals who are so eager to be liked that they bend over backward to please others will find the development of power difficult. Being eager to please includes being unwilling to face a conflict for fear of offending others or refusing to take some action that will displease them.

On the other side of the coin, being aggressive and coming on too strong at inappropriate times can reduce your power. Refusing to share power by being unwilling to delegate is also viewed negatively.

In an executive coaching session, founder and owner of RW Cuddy & Associates Bob Cuddy recommends methods of using power more effectively. He advises participants to force themselves to speak for no more than two minutes in any meeting. Other people have many good ideas and thoughts that should be heard.[25]

Ethics CONNECTION

In a paper released by the National Bureau of Economic Research, CEO gender was examined as related to women being under-represented among senior management and how this reflects on any unobserved differences in productivity. Examining financial data on S&P 1500 firms, the report found no differences between the stock returns of companies that were headed by women and those headed by men. These results support that gender does not impact the job performance of CEOs.[26] However, a "glass ceiling" still exists regarding CEO compensation. In fact, a report from the Corporate Library indicated that CEO compensation packages offered to women averaged only 85 percent of those offered to men. This difference worsens at the largest companies, where CEO packages to women were less than two-thirds of their male counterparts.[27]

1. Do you think there is or can be a "gender advantage" when leading a major company? Why or why not?

2. Why do you think women lose ground in compensation packages when data demonstrates good job performance?

A major pitfall of power gaming is overconfidence and arrogance. It is easy to be carried away with the exhilaration that power can bring. Care should be taken to guard against becoming too fond of your own abilities and basking too long in the glow of the spotlight. Remembering that others may know how to play the power game indicates a certain amount of wisdom and maturity.

Individual arrogance exists today as evidenced many times in politics, sports, entertainment, and business figures. One example is the former CEO of Tyco currently serving 25 years in prison for defrauding company shareholders. He was convicted of grand larceny, conspiracy, falsifying business records, and violating general business law. The court found that he abused an employee loan program and misrepresented the company's financial condition to investors to boost the stock price, then quickly selling $575 million in stock. His arrogance tipped the scale when he threw a lavish $1 million birthday party for his wife on a Mediterranean island and then wrote the costs off his taxes as a company shareholders meeting.[28]

A truly powerful person has the ability to recruit allies and harness resources to accomplish a mission or goal. Power use is least effective when it is abused for selfish or personal gain and most efficient when it is an exercise of strength that enables you to achieve your goals and objectives without harm or damage to others.

Ask Yourself...

1. Describe some ways you might lose your power. How can you safeguard against this?
2. In meetings you have attended, who did the most talking? Was the speaker perceived to be more or less powerful?
3. How can you guard against becoming arrogant or self-centered?

KEY TERMS

power	passive power
influence	power-shy
reward power	power-positive
coercive power	power-compulsive
legitimate power	power positioning
expert power	power politics
referent power	power symbols
derivative power	empowerment

CHAPTER SUMMARY

Power is the ability to influence others to do what you want them to do. Despite its sometimes negative connotation, experts agree that the acquisition and appropriate use of power is necessary for individuals at all levels of an organization if they are to accomplish goals and objectives.

Many sources of power are available and need to be cultivated for maximum effectiveness. These sources include reward, coercive, legitimate, expert, and referent powers. Derivative and passive powers are sources that are best left uncultivated. In addition to these power sources, research has defined three basic power personalities: the power-shy, the power-positive, and the power-compulsive personalities.

Developing power is not a matter of luck. It must be planned. Part of this planning and development involves a thorough understanding and respect for power positioning, power politics, and power symbols. Empowering others is also a method of acquiring power and can be beneficial for all parties involved. Avoiding the power pitfalls and ensuring that you have used power in a positive manner are crucial to power development.

REVIEW

1. What is power, and why is developing it necessary?

2. Which basic power sources are available to you?

3. What are the three basic power personalities?

4. What techniques can you use in the planning and implementation of power positioning?

5. Why is empowering others important?

6. What are the pitfalls in developing power?

CRITICAL THINKING

1. Think of individuals who are powerful or have power over you. Which power sources do they possess? Which ones are most effective?

2. Review the power sources available to you. Which is your strongest source, and which is your weakest? Do you have linkages?

3. Do you effectively plan the use of your power to gain personal advantages? How, and why?

4. Which of the power personalities best fits you? Are you comfortable with your assessment? Why, or why not?

5. What power symbols do you possess? How do you use these symbols in your power building?

6. How many of the power techniques have you cultivated? How have they benefited your power positioning?

7. Do you agree that playing power politics is an unavoidable means of assuring personal and professional success? Why, or why not?

CASE STUDIES

In small groups, analyze the following situations.

1 **Tom Goodman, Effective Supervisor**   Tom is a supervisor in a large call center whose accounts are for outbound bill collection for credit card companies. He is known as a good supervisor. Turnover at the center is high, and management has adjusted and maintains a constant recruitment effort. Although the working environment is often tense because of the nature of the business, Tom's department beats the odds. There is little turnover in his area. In fact, Tom has many employees who have been with the company for more than five years. He maintains several routines that he believes contribute to employee longevity. First, Tom has instigated a flex time program that allows employees to have some control of their schedule. Next, he maintains a break room that is stocked with snacks and drinks. Tom also has a "chill-out" policy, in which employees may get off the phone and take a few minutes to regroup after an especially frustrating telephone conversation. He also holds weekly roundtable meetings in which employees can share difficult calls and give each other advice. The employees respect Tom and often comment on his leadership skills.

1. What sources of power has Tom developed? How are they linked?

2. What behaviors or activities do you feel most add to Tom's power? Which activities do you feel add the least power?

2 **Mary on the Dock**   Mary works on the loading dock of a large national package delivery service. The shifts are strenuous and work moves quickly. Mary supervises the department that handles loading outbound trucks. Being small in stature, Mary has to work hard to be effective in her job. Often she must correct employees when they are not handling tasks in an effective manner. At times she has even stepped in and made employees watch her to learn how to correctly do a task—with coworkers watching. Mary takes her job seriously and is known for firing people on the spot. Many employees in the past have transferred out of her department. Mary feels that she is very successful in her position and is proud of her accomplishments.

1. What type of power do you think Mary believes she has? Are there other possible power sources?

2. What type of power do you think the employees believe Mary has?

3. What new behaviors or activities could Mary do to gain power from other sources?

HUMAN RELATIONS IN ACTION

As a group, collectively pool your resources and decide on a prominent person from somewhere in your community whom you may interview about how he or she became successful. This person should hold a reasonably powerful position. Based on the chapter topics, prepare a written report on how you believe this individual became and remains powerful. Describe traits, characteristics, power plays, and others. Be prepared to show and discuss your findings in class.

For additional resources, refer to the web site for this text:
www.cengage.com/management/dalton

RESOURCES

1. Schaeffer, C. (Producer). (2009, May 28). *The Oprah effect* [Television documentary]. Englewood, CA: CNBC.

2. Abkowitz, A. (2009, July 20). The surfin' CEO. *Fortune, 2,* 18. Retrieved on July 24, 2009, from http://money.cnn.com/2009/07/09/news/companies/quiksilver_surfing_ceo_bob_mcknight.fortune/index.htm

3. Sellers, P. (2003, October 13). The 50 most powerful women in American business. *Fortune,* 148. Retrieved on July 24, 2009, from http://money.cnn.com/magazines/fortune/fortune_archive/2003/10/13/350927/index.htm

4. Corkery, M. (2009, July 24). [Weblog] GM's new board members: Up to the tasks? *Wall Street Journal, Deal Journal.* Retrieved on July 24, 2009, from http://blogs.wsj.com/deals/2009/07/24/gms-new-board-members-a-scorecard-of-their-deals/

5. French, J., & Raven, B. (1968). The bases of social power. In D. Cartwright & A. Zander (Eds.), *Group dynamics* (3rd ed.). New York: Harper & Row.

6. Stoner, J., & Freeman, E. (1991). *Management.* Upper Saddle River, NJ: Pearson Higher Education.

7. Sellers, P. (2003, October 13). The 50 most powerful women in American business. *Fortune,* 148. Retrieved on July 24, 2009, from http://money.cnn.com/magazines/fortune/fortune_archive/2003/10/13/350927/index.htm

8. Useen, M. (2008, November 19). America's best leaders: Indra Nooyi, PepsiCo CEO. U.S. News and World Report, Retrieved on July 24, 2009, from http://www.usnews.com/articles/news/best-leaders/2008/11/19/americas-best-leaders-indra-nooyi-pepsico-ceo.html

9. Robbins, A. (1997). *Unlimited power.* New York, NY: The Free Press.

10. DuBrin, A. (1990). *Winning office politics.* Englewood Cliffs, NJ: Prentice-Hall.

11. DuBrin, A. (1990). *Winning office politics.* Englewood Cliffs, NJ: Prentice-Hall.

12. Hensley, W. (1998). The measurement of height. *Adolescence, 33*(131), 629–636.

13. Dress for Success. (2009). *What we do.* Retrieved on July 24, 2009, from http://www.dressforsuccess.org

14. Huffington Post (2009). Biographies. Retrieved on July 24, 2009, from http://www.huffingtonpost.com/nancy-lublin

15. Peluchette, J., Karl, K., & Rust, K. (2006). Dressing to impress: Beliefs and attitudes regarding workplace attire. *Journal of Business and Psychology, 21,* 45–63.

16. Friess, S. (2009, July 25). In recession, optimistic college graduates turn down jobs. *The New York Times.* Retrieved on July 26, 2009, from http://www.nytimes.com/2009/07/25/us/25students.html

17. Median CEO pay packages fall 6.8 percent (2009, April 8). *Phoenix Business Journal.* Retrieved on July 26, 2009, from http://www.bizjournals.com/phoenix/stories/2009/04/06/daily36.html

18. RBS defends CEO's pay package (2009, June 24). *Wall Street Journal* (In brief). Retrieved on July 26, 2009, from http://online.wsj.com/article/SB124581627991145659.html

19. Podesta, J. (2009, January 20). Obama's link to America: His Blackberry. *Las Angeles Times,* Opinion.

20. Blanchard, J., & Carlos, J. (1999). *The 3 keys to empowerment: Release the power within people for astonishing results*. San Francisco, CA: Berrett-Koehler Publishers, Inc.

21. Heim, K. (2009, July 23). Gates foundation increases funding, defends AIDS initiative in India. *The Seattle Times*. Retrieved on July 26, 2009, from http://seattletimes.nwsource.com/html/thebusinessofgiving/2009526034_gates_foundation_increases_fun.html

22. Blanchard, J., & Carlos, J. (1999). *The 3 keys to empowerment: Release the power within people for astonishing results*. San Francisco, CA: Berrett-Koehler Publishers, Inc.

23. Hesselbein, F. Working smart newsletter. National Institute of Business Management. Retrieved on July 30, 2004, from http://www.nibm.net/newsletter.asp?pub=PRE

24. Bennis, W. (1989). *On becoming a leader*. Reading, MA: Addison-Wesley Publishing Company.

25. Cuddy, R. W. (2009). *Executive leadership coaching*. Retrieved on July 26, 2009, from http://www.rwcuddy.com

26. Wolfers, J. (2006). Diagnosing discrimination: Stock returns and CEO gender. National Bureau of Economic Research.

27. Female CEOs receive lower total compensation than male counterparts (2008, November). The Corporate Library.

28. Forbes, S., & Prevas, J. (2009). *Power ambition glory: Stunning parallels between great leaders of the ancient world and today*. New York, NY: Random House, Inc.

PART 3

CAREER DEVELOPMENT

"If people knew how hard I worked to get my mastery, it wouldn't seem so wonderful after all."

— Michelangelo

11

INTERCULTURAL COMPETENCE:
A 21ST CENTURY IMPERATIVE

OBJECTIVES

After studying this chapter, you should be able to:

11.1 Define intercultural competence and explain its importance in the emerging economy.

11.2 Understand what internal factors contribute to conflict in diverse environments.

11.3 Recognize linguistic styles and how they affect interactions in a diverse workplace.

11.4 Appreciate the opportunities of cross-cultural diversity.

11.5 Know how to thrive in a diverse environment.

Jump Start

The Johns Hopkins Health System received a national equal opportunity employment award from the U.S. Department of Labor in 2008, marking the first time a hospital has been honored. The Department of Labor award is made to a federal contractor or non-profit organization that has established and instituted comprehensive workforce strategies to ensure equal employment opportunity and that exemplifies best corporate practices of nondiscrimination. The efforts of the system's Bayview unit were cited.

To achieve this recognition, programs to assist females, minorities, and people with disabilities were implemented, including providing training to its staff to enhance their skills and prepare them for advancement within the organization. Additionally, Bayview formed a diversity counsel, bringing staff together to develop and implement programs that successfully recruit, engage, and retain a diverse workforce at all levels of the organization. "Team Bayview has worked diligently to implement practices and create a culture where our diverse workforce is celebrated," said Gregory F. Schaffer, president of Johns Hopkins Bayview Medical Center. "We are committed to equal opportunity and affirmative action. We believe in our strong plans to recruit, attract, and retain female and minority candidates as well as veterans and people with disabilities."[1]

- Why do you think Johns Hopkins Health System is so committed to developing an inclusive work culture?
- Would you want to work at a company that is committed to including employees who are different? Why, or why not?

11.1   INTERCULTURAL COMPETENCE AND DIVERSITY

Diversity refers to differences. In people, these differences can be thought of in four layers, as shown in Figure 11.1. The sum of your individual differences affects how you view others and how others view you. *Intercultural competence* is the measure of your effectiveness when you interact with people who are different from you. This includes not only people who live in different parts of the world but also those who work next to you.[2]

The business world is paying increased attention to the issue of intercultural competence. The global economy and the rapidly changing composition of our population have opened many markets to American businesses. To capitalize on these opportunities, organizations must understand the consumers and their needs. An interculturally competent workforce is now a competitive necessity—it can help a business create new and more innovative products as well as better meet the needs of customers and clients.

Without input from an interculturally competent staff that understands the consumers and their needs, some American companies have made major mistakes. American Motors, for instance, tried to sell an automobile named "Matador" in Puerto Rico. However, it did not sell well because "matador" carries the connotation of "killer." Pepsodent's efforts to sell teeth-whitening toothpaste in Southeast Asia was disappointing because many cultures in

KeyPoint
Strong intercultural competence is the key to a successful career.

Figure 11.1

Dimensions of diversity.[3]

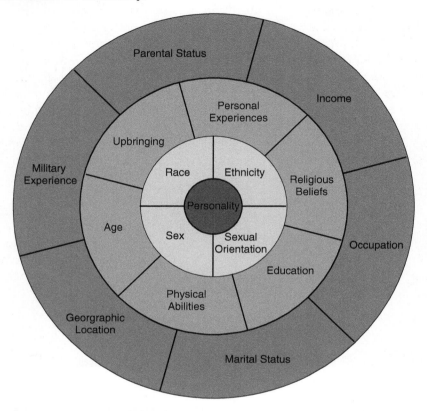

Each employee brings many dimensions of diversity to the workplace.

that area value the habit of chewing betel nuts, which darken the teeth. Some believe this habit strengthens teeth, sweetens breath, aids digestion, and even cures tapeworms. Historically, stained teeth were desirable as a sign of marriageability or "coming of age."[4]

Additionally, the pool from which organizations draw employees has become ever more diverse. The percentage of white non-Hispanic-Americans, who accounted for nearly 75 percent of the U.S. labor market in 1996, is expected to fall to nearly 65 percent by 2016. African-Americans, Hispanic-Americans, and Asian-Americans are projected to increase their labor force participation at faster rates than white non-Hispanic-Americans and constitute a larger share of the labor force in 2016. By that year Hispanic-Americans will make up 16 percent of the workforce, African-Americans 12 percent, and Asian-Americans 5.3 percent.[5]

Lastly, the nature of work is changing. The need for a highly skilled workforce will make diverse groups an increasingly important source of labor. Organizations that fail to utilize the best and brightest from the talent available run the risk of falling behind their competitors. Michael Lewis, the author of *Moneyball: The Art of Winning an Unfair Game,* says that the inability to envision a certain kind of person doing a certain kind of thing because you've never seen someone who looks like him do it before is not just a vice—it's a luxury. What begins as a failure of imagination ends as market inefficiency. When you rule out an entire class of people from doing a job simply because of their appearance, you are less likely to find the best person for the job.[6]

Given these changes, it is not surprising that employers across the United States view strong intercultural competence—your ability to communicate and collaborate with teams of people across cultural, geographic, and language boundaries—as essential.[7] You can increase your skill at interacting competently and respectfully with others by understanding what is driving diversity, recognizing factors that cause conflict, being attuned to different linguistic styles, and developing skills that will help you thrive in a diverse environment.

Changing Makeup of the Workforce

Employers are increasingly expected to accommodate the needs of a complex and diverse workforce that is changing. Women in the workforce have unique needs. More minorities and people with disabilities are entering the workforce while older workers are staying longer or returning in increasing numbers. Also, more employees are revealing their sexual orientation.

Women   Women now make up approximately half of the workforce and more than half of college enrollments.[8,9] Despite gains, a woman's salary is, on average, 76 percent of a man's across all industries.[10] Women are more likely than men to have family care responsibilities, which significantly impact women's employment choices, security, and advancement.[11]

Despite comprising about half of the workforce, in 2008 women held just 15.2 percent of director positions at Fortune 500 companies. Only 92 of the companies had three or more women board members while 159 of these companies had just one woman. Women of color fared poorly, holding only 3.2 percent of the board of director positions. Additionally, only 15.7 percent of women held corporate officer positions in 2008, and just 6.2 percent held top earner positions.[12]

Older Workers   Baby boomers are those Americans born between 1946 and 1964, during the "baby boom" that followed World War II. For decades, whatever boomers were doing became the most significant factor in demographic studies of U.S. trends. Today, the boomers are getting older. The Bureau of Labor Statistics states that by 2016, 22.7 percent of the nation's workforce will be comprised of adults aged 55 and older. Of these older workers, 16.6 percent will be 55 to 64, 4.9 percent will be 65 to 74, and 1.2 percent will be 75 and older.[13]

A survey by the American Association of Retired People polled Americans between 45 and 74 who were working or looking for work and found that, of those interviewed, 70 percent planned to work for pay during their retirement. Roughly half planned to work on a part-time basis. Not only did those surveyed need extra money, but they also wanted to work for enjoyment, to have something interesting and challenging to do, and to stay physically active.[14]

> *Human diversity makes tolerance more than a virtue; it makes it a requirement for survival.*
> —Rene Dubos, French-American microbiologist and humanist

KeyPoint
Developing intercultural competencies in dealing with others who are decades older or younger than you is a reality in today's workforce.

In The News[15]

Mildred Heath, 100, was America's Oldest Worker for 2008. She began her career in the newspaper business 85 years ago at the age of 15, where she worked alongside her sweetheart, Blair Heath. Eventually the two married and continued to work in journalism. In 1938 they founded the *Overton Observer* in Overton, Nebraska. Today the newspaper is owned by Heath's daughter and son-in-law, employing three generations. Heath works 30 hours a week. She files, takes classified ads and photographs, and seeks local news. Even at her 100th birthday party, she kept a notepad and pen handy to gather news for the week's paper. Heath has seen dramatic changes in technology during her career. She first taught herself to operate a Linotype, a machine that turned hot lead into lines of type for the printing press. When the computer came along, she sat down and taught herself how to use it.

1. Does Heath fit your concept of an older worker? Why, or why not?
2. What conflicts have you seen arise as different age groups attempt to coexist in organizations?
3. What can you do to relate to workers who are significantly older or younger than yourself?

Race and Ethnicity   The Bureau of Labor Statistics states that the workforce will become increasingly diverse racially and ethnically. Minorities, now roughly one-third of the U.S. population, are expected to become the majority in 2042, with the nation projected to be 54 percent minority in 2050. By 2023, minorities will comprise more than half of all children.[16]

International migration has played a vital role in the composition and size of the U.S. population. By 2007, 12.6 percent of the U.S. population was foreign born. In fact, almost 20 percent of the U.S. population aged 5 and over spoke a language other than English at home in 2007.[17]

Workers with Disabilities   People with disabilities are the nation's largest minority and cross all racial, gender, educational, socioeconomic, and generational lines. As of 2006, almost one-eighth of all working-age Americans had at least one disability. They are only half as likely as Americans without disabilities to be employed (38 percent compared with 78 percent), and only 17 percent of those with more severe disabilities are employed. The disabled who are employed earn less—median annual earnings for full-time, year-round workers is $30,000 for those with disabilities, compared with $36,000 for those without disabilities.[18]

As the growth in the traditional labor pool slows, the workforce ages, and disability rates rise, more organizations will be forced to hire from this

KeyPoint
All employees have the potential to be a member of the nation's largest minority group—workers with disabilities.

group.[19] The good news is that technology (such as screen readers and voice recognition systems) is helping compensate for disabilities. Additionally, telecommuting and flex time arrangements are easing the pressure on the disabled who have transportation difficulties or need to stay close to home because of treatment issues.[20]

Lesbian, Gay, Bisexual, and Transgender (LGBT) Estimates of the LGBT population in the United States vary but are projected to be anywhere from 3 to 10 percent of the total population.[21] While federal law does not protect LGBTs from being terminated from their jobs because of their sexual preference, many state and local governments are moving to give this population civil rights, and many companies are including them in their diversity initiatives. Nine of the Fortune 10 Companies, for instance, prohibit discrimination based on sexual orientation, five prohibit discrimination based on gender identity, and eight provide benefits to same-sex couples.[22]

> *Let us put our minds together and see what life we can make for our children.*
> —Sitting Bull, Sioux chief

Understanding Diverse Needs

While the diverse groups discussed in this section offer many advantages for organizations, they can also be a source of conflict and loss of productivity. Disagreement can evolve from internal factors such as biases and prejudices as well as differences in values. Linguistic styles also contribute to misunderstandings. In order to thrive in a diverse environment, workers must understand these issues.

Ask Yourself...

1. On a scale of 1 to 10 with 10 being the highest, rate your intercultural competence. Identify areas in which you feel uncomfortable.
2. Have you ever been in a situation where intercultural differences caused friction? Describe your experience.

> *Ultimately, America's answer to the intolerant man is diversity, the very diversity which our heritage of religious freedom has inspired.*
> —Robert F. Kennedy, U.S. senator and civil rights advocate

11.2 FACTORS CAUSING CONFLICT

Biases, prejudices, and value systems are ingrained in all of us, and we base our daily actions on them, often unconsciously. The more diverse a group, the more diverse the internal factors are, thus increasing the likelihood for conflict. By understanding these factors, you can improve your understanding of others and yourself and work to reduce conflict.

A *bias* is an inclination or preference either for or against an individual or group that interferes with impartial judgment. We begin developing biases early in life, influenced by our family, personal and educational experiences, the media, and peers. Often, preferences are not spoken but rather are learned by watching and viewing what happens in the world around us. By the age of five, many children have definite and entrenched stereotypes about people of other races, women, and other social groups. They have acquired these beliefs from various sources well before they have the ability or experiences to form their own beliefs.[23]

Prejudice is prejudging or making a decision about a person or group of people without sufficient knowledge. Prejudicial thinking is frequently based on stereotypes. A stereotype is a fixed or distorted generalization made about members of a particular group. When stereotyping is used, individual differences are not taken into account. Because people tend to grow up with people like themselves, they may develop prejudices about people they do not know—views that are full of inaccuracies and distortions. The goal of diversity is to increase trust among groups who do not know enough about each other. You will benefit from knowing how to control biases and prejudices and not letting them interfere with your ability to interact with others. Use the quiz on the next page to explore your biases.

"You're not so bad for someone who's different."

© 2009 Ted Goff

Once you have explored your biases, you need to deal with them. In *Workforce America!* Marilyn Loden and Judy B. Rosener offer these tips:[24]

- Acknowledge the existence of bias and prejudice and accept responsibility for it.
- Identify problem behaviors and assess the impact of behaviors on others.
- Modify your behavior.
- Obtain feedback on changes.
- Repeat steps when necessary.

Values, according to *Merriam-Webster's Online Dictionary*[25] are those things (such as a principle or quality) that are intrinsically valuable or desirable. All individuals develop a set of values, or *value systems*, which provide a road map for their behavior in a variety of situations. Your values evolve from the influences of your family, society, religious training, and personal experiences. Not only do individuals have their own value systems, but organizations do as well. Underlying every decision made at work is a corresponding value. Because these values may be so ingrained in you, you are usually not aware of them as you make decisions. In diverse groups, many more value systems are at work, which can cause conflict in decision making.

KeyPoint
Differing value systems can cause conflict at work.

Rating Your Behavior[26]

Directions
Answer the following questions by rating your behavior on a scale of 1 (never) to 5 (always). Circle the appropriate answer.

How often do you:	never				always
Interrupt someone who is telling a racial or ethnic joke?	1	2	3	4	5
Read about the achievements of people with physical or mental disabilities?	1	2	3	4	5
Challenge friends expressing a gender stereotype?	1	2	3	4	5
Send e-mails to TV or radio stations that broadcast news stories with cultural or racial biases?	1	2	3	4	5
Examine your own language for unconscious bias or stereotypes?	1	2	3	4	5
Ask exchange students questions about their countries of origin?	1	2	3	4	5
Recognize compulsory heterosexuality in the media?	1	2	3	4	5
Volunteer your time for a cause you support?	1	2	3	4	5
Donate goods or money to shelters for battered women or homeless people?	1	2	3	4	5
Intervene when a person or group is sexually harassing someone?	1	2	3	4	5
Think about the definition of rape?	1	2	3	4	5
Truly appreciate a friend's differences from you?	1	2	3	4	5
Take the lead in welcoming people of color to your class, club, job site, or living situation?	1	2	3	4	5
Challenge the cultural expectation of slimness in women?	1	2	3	4	5
Protest unfair or exclusionary practices in an organization?	1	2	3	4	5
Ask a member of an ethnic group different from yours how that person prefers to be referred to?	1	2	3	4	5
Think about ways you belong to oppressor and oppressed groups?	1	2	3	4	5
Identify and challenge "tokenism"?	1	2	3	4	5
Examine your own level of comfort around issues of sexual orientation and sexual practices?	1	2	3	4	5
Celebrate your uniqueness?	1	2	3	4	5

Variation
After you have rated your behaviors, examine your responses for patterns. Did you surprise yourself in any regard?

Are there any behaviors you would like to engage in less frequently? More frequently? How will you implement those changes?

Source: Janet Lockhart, M.A.I.S. and Susan M. Shaw, Ph.D. Used with permission.

As a society, for example, Americans tend to expect individuals to speak up for themselves. Americans value those who speak their minds and do not let themselves be taken advantage of. Have you heard the expression, "the squeaky wheel gets the grease"? On the other hand, the Turks, who tend to value harmony over individuality, have a saying that "one who speaks truth would be expelled from nine villages."

Differing Generational Values[27]

Traditionalists (born before 1946)
Tend to value work before play, following the rules, loyalty, and patriotism.

Baby Boomers (born between 1946 and 1964)
Tend to value working hard and playing hard, personal accomplishment, and a participative workplace.

Generation X (born between 1965 and 1980)
Tend to value self-sufficiency, pragmatism, flexibility, and technology.

Generation Y (born after 1980)
Tend to value work-life balance, tolerance, and multi-tasking.

It's important to note that while certain groups may tend to value certain behaviors, not all members of that group necessarily hold those values. Also, no right or wrong value systems exist. Diverse value systems cause us to define problems and develop solutions to those problems differently. For example, generational values and national values can affect the way people work together in an organization.

Ask Yourself...

1. Think of three celebrities. Do they fit the stereotypes you grew up with regarding persons of color, older people, females, or persons from certain areas of the country? Why, or why not?

2. Identify some decisions you have made in the past week, such as whether to study, whether to go out to eat, or what television show to watch. What were the values behind those decisions?

11.3 LINGUISTIC STYLES AND INTERACTIONS

Linguistic styles refer to characteristic speaking patterns. Directness or indirectness, pacing and pausing, word choice, and the use of elements such as jokes, figures of speech, stories, questions, and apologies are also included.[28] Differing linguistic styles can cause conflict and misunderstandings.

Understanding your linguistic style and that of others is extremely important when dealing with a diverse group of individuals. By understanding style differences, you can focus on the message rather than letting the way the message is delivered influence the way you interpret it.

Important factors to consider when dealing with linguistic styles are that they are norms. Variations exist, and individuals do not always follow the linguistic norm of their group. Individual personality, culture, class, and sexual orientation can cause these variations. No style is right or wrong—they are just different ways of delivering communication. The more you understand your own style and the styles of others, the more comfortable you will be communicating in diverse groups.

Direct–Indirect Communication Styles

Direct and indirect communication styles can be a source of conflict in communication. A *direct communication style* reflects a goal orientation and a desire to get down to business and get to the point, while an *indirect communication style* reflects a focus on the relationship and is used to develop a rapport before getting down to business.

A supervisor who is an indirect communicator may say something like, "You might consider adding another paragraph to your report explaining the history behind the project." To the supervisor, this is a nice way to say "do it" when he or she does not want to appear rude or abrupt. When two communicators have an indirect style, there is usually not a problem.

However, if the recipient operates in a direct manner, he or she may ignore an indirect message, much to the frustration of the supervisor. The supervisor will think the employee does not follow directions, and the employee will see the supervisor as "wishy-washy," indecisive, or unclear.

On the other hand, a direct supervisor who hands a subordinate an assignment and simply says, "Get this back to me by 4:00 this afternoon," without engaging in any additional conversation may be seen as cold, uncaring, and callous.

Listen to yourself and to those around you to identify styles. If you have a direct communication style and someone speaks indirectly, you may need to ask questions to ensure you understand exactly what he or she wants you to do. If you have an indirect style, you may need to speak more directly to ensure that your wishes are followed.

The important point to remember is that no one style is correct. Concentrate on the message and clarifying your understanding of the message rather than on the way it's delivered. At times, you may need to adapt your style to match those with whom you are interacting.

High and Low Context Modes

Cultures and groups can operate in a low context or a high context communication mode. *Low context groups* value the written or spoken word. They are task oriented and results driven and generally adopt a direct linguistic style. In low context situations, knowledge is more transferable and available to the public. Examples of low context situations are in sports and activities

> **KeyPoint**
> Because linguistic styles differ, it is important to concentrate on the message rather than on the way it is delivered.

> **KeyPoint**
> You can improve your ability to communicate by altering your style to fit the individual receiving the message.

in which rules are clearly laid out and in restaurants, grocery stores, hotels, and airports.[29] Overall, modes in the United States tend to be low context.

High context groups, however, are more difficult to penetrate. Long-term relationships are important, and communication is less verbally explicit. Strong boundaries define who is accepted and who is considered an outsider. Many times, decisions and activities focus on face-to-face relationships and often around one person who has authority. Some examples are small religious congregations, family events, small businesses, regular "pick-up" games, and groups of friends.[30] Modes in many cultures such as Saudi Arabia and Japan tend to be high context.

Entering low context groups is easier than entering high context groups. Many situations have both high and low context aspects. For example, membership in a nonprofit organization may be open to anyone, but the group may have a high context core group in charge of the organization.

Assess your circumstances and, if you find yourself in a high context situation, be patient. You may need to seek input from an established member of the group in order to learn the unwritten rules and the way the group functions. Lastly, make it a point to assist newcomers in assimilating into high context cultures in which you operate.

Conversational Rituals and Styles

Conversational rituals are things we say without considering the literal meaning of our words. The purpose is to make interactions as pleasant as possible.[31] For instance, many of us say, "How are you?" and do not expect or want the other person to tell us about his or her aches and pains. This is just a way to be nice.

> " *To effectively communicate, we must realize that we are all different in the way we perceive the world and use this understanding as a guide to our communication with others.*
>
> —Anthony Robbins, self-help writer, entrepreneur, and professional speaker "

However, if others do not understand conversational rituals and take them literally, problems can occur. For instance, some people may say, "I'm sorry," but do not mean this literally. While the statement may be seen as an apology or taking blame, many times it's intended as an expression of understanding and caring about the other person's situation. Other conversational rituals include saying thanks as a conversational closer when there is nothing to thank, asking for input from many different individuals before making decisions, and giving praise.

Some individuals, on the other hand, use conversational rituals such as fighting. They may argue heatedly to explore ideas and not take the exchange personally. This group may also tend to engage in razzing, teasing, and mock-hostile attacks.

Ethics CONNECTIONS [32,33]

Do you ever feel the political correctness police are out to get you? Do you avoid interacting with others who are different because you are afraid you might say something that might embarrass or hurt them or get you in trouble? If so, you're not alone.

Fear of not being politically correct can paralyze the workplace. Valda Boyd Ford of the Center for Human Diversity defines this paralysis as the fear that keeps you from communicating in culturally or linguistically awkward situations.

Unfortunately, these feelings can make you avoid communicating honestly and can dampen work productivity and creativity. The right thing to do is to engage in open and honest communication.

You can improve your self-confidence in these situations by learning more about others, expanding your life experiences (including interacting with people who are different from you), and using effective communication skills.

1. Did you ever have a situation when you said something that offended another person? What happened?
2. How can you learn more about what might embarrass or hurt others?
3. Do you think an apology in awkward situations helps? Why or why not?

Learning to communicate openly and honestly in a culturally diverse situation can improve your effectiveness.

Digital Vision/Getty Images

KeyPoint
Regional
conversational
style
differences can
cause us to
misread others.

Regional Differences

Regional differences in conversational styles also occur. According to social scientists, the number of U.S. dialects range from a basic three—New England, Southern America, and Western/General America—to 24 or more. Regional variations include differences in pacing, accents, pronunciations, tone of voice, loudness, when you start and stop talking, what you talk about and to whom. Variations are not only influenced by geographical location, but also by ethnicity, social class, and gender.[34]

Regional differences can cause misinterpretations. For instance, someone from the southern part of the United States may view someone from the north who speaks rapidly and gets to the point without first conducting some small chat as rude, while a northerner may find a southerner's attempt to say "Hi, how'ya doin?" to every stranger he passes on the street alarming.

Contrasting Linguistic Styles[35]

Style A	Style B
Direct	Indirect
Talk about things	Talk about relationships
Convey facts	Convey feelings and details
Compete; one-up	Gain rapport; speak to save face; buffer comments to avoid insults
Solve problems	Look for discussion
Goal oriented	Relationship oriented
Hierarchy, competition	Level playing field
Conversation to give information	Conversation to give information, connect, and compete
Minimize doubts	Downplay certainty
Razz, tease, mock-hostile attacks	Self-mocking

Style A elements are often used by males while Style B elements are often used by females. Note, however, that linguistic styles are affected by a number of cultural and societal factors, and many individuals of either gender may use a mix of these elements.

To improve your communication in a diverse group, follow these tips from Marilyn Loden and Judy B. Rosener in *Workforce America!*[36]

- Identify your own personal communication style.
- Recognize your own personal filters, and test assumptions you have with other, neutral parties.
- Acknowledge your own personal style of communication and how it might be perceived as threatening or confusing to others. Disclose personal styles to ease communication.
- Become aware of whether you are in a low context or high context culture to reduce your frustration.

Ask Yourself...

1. Do you currently work with anyone whose linguistic style is different from yours? What can you do to make your communication more effective?

2. Have you ever tried to enter high and low context situations? How did the experiences differ?

11.4   GLOBAL INTERCULTURAL COMPETENCE

In today's global organization you may find yourself working in a virtual global team or interacting face to face with workers from other countries, either here or abroad. In these situations, you will be expected to show a high degree of intercultural competence at the global level. In fact, Janet Reid of the consulting firm Global Lead predicts that by 2019 every leader will need to be competent at the global level.[37] This area of competency is not limited to learning other languages, but also includes understanding how cultural patterns and core values impact the communication process—even when everyone is speaking English.[38] By understanding how people from different cultures communicate with one another, you can raise your intercultural competency.

An important first step in sharpening your global intercultural competency is realizing that people from different cultures express their thoughts in different ways and words alone are not enough to discern meaning. Important but complex variables are time and space, fate and personal responsibility, face and face-saving, and nonverbal communication.[39]

Time and Space

The use of time and space is a key cultural difference. In the West, time is viewed as quantitative, measured in units that reflect the march of progress. Time is logical, sequential, and present-focused, moving incrementally toward a future. In the East, time is viewed as having unlimited continuity, endlessly moving through various cycles.[40]

> *If you can speak three languages you're trilingual. If you can speak two languages you're bilingual. If you can speak only one language you're an American.*
>
> — *Author unknown*

These differing views of time can cause problems because those who see time as having unlimited continuity may not have the same sense of urgency as those who see it as logical and sequential. For instance, punctuality is not rigidly observed in many Middle Eastern and North African countries.[41] In Latin America the concept of mañana (tomorrow) is prevalent. Work promised may not be completed as agreed.[42]

Individual work styles also vary greatly along with perceptions of time and priorities. Some people work in a *monochronic* style. They do one thing at a time and follow plans closely. *Polychronic* workers may do many things at once, change plans easily, and tolerate interruptions.[43] Respect work style differences and concentrate on meeting goals. Focus on completing tasks in a timely fashion rather than dwelling on how tasks are completed.

The use of space, particularly in conversations and negotiations, varies greatly. North Americans tend to prefer a large amount of space, while Europeans tend to stand more closely when talking. To Europeans, the North Americans can seem cold or disinterested. To North Americans the Europeans can seem pushy and disrespectful.[44]

The use of space also frequently shows itself in how people arrange their offices, particularly during negotiations, and how they wait in lines in group settings such as stores and offices. The English and Americans prefer that people respect the line, whereas some groups, such as the French and Armenians, believe that line jumping or saving places is acceptable.[45]

Fate and Personal Responsibility

"Fate and personal responsibility" refers to the degree to which individuals and groups feel they are the masters of their lives as opposed to seeing themselves as subject to forces outside their control. Areas of the world with a relatively small territory, repeated conquests, and harsh struggles, such as Northern Ireland, Mexico, Israel, and Palestine, are more likely to see struggles as inevitable. When people with a more free will concept interact with someone who is more fatalistic in orientation, miscommunication is likely.[46]

Suppose you are a project lead of a virtual global team. You have a completion deadline less than a week away when a natural disaster hits the island where your Filipino coworker lives, causing a project delay. While you still feel the deadline can be met with extensive overtime, your colleague sees no reason to worry. Fate has caused the project deadline to be missed.

Global CONNECTION[47]

According to recent reports by the British Council, English is the first/native language of less than 10 percent of the world's population, but it's the most significant second language spoken worldwide. Non-native speakers of English now outnumber native speakers three-to-one, and within a decade, more than 2 billion people are expected to speak it.

Interestingly and importantly, however, International English is not the same language that is spoken in Australia, Canada, New Zealand, the United Kingdom, and the United States, where English is the first language. Cautions the British Council: People from English-speaking countries have the most to lose as the world adopts an international form of English. These speakers will need to replace local expressive terms, local metaphors, short cuts, sayings, and clichés such as "We can't miss," "It's a home run," and "What's up?"

The Society for Human Resource Management points out that to be an effective communicator in International English, you must use it correctly in dialog, phone conferencing, videoconferencing, written and verbal presentations, e-mails, reports, training, knowledge transfer, cross-functional team activities, business travel, relocation, and more.

1. In your interaction with people from other cultures, what kinds of communication challenges have you encountered?

2. Do you know anyone who has been trained in International English? If so, what benefits have they identified?

Face and Face-Saving

While face is important in all cultures, how a particular culture handles ideas of status, power, courtesy, outsider relations, humor, and respect may vary greatly. Face and face-saving are tied to the concepts of fate and personal responsibility; that is, if you see yourself as a self-determining individual, then you are more likely to work to preserve your image with others and yourself. If, however, you see yourself as a group member, then considerations about face involve your group, and you would attempt to avoid potential damage to your relationships by avoiding direct confrontation and problem solving.[48]

As an example, a Malaysian team member received a performance appraisal in an e-mail from his American boss that contained constructive criticism. The Malaysian team member immediately asked for a transfer. The American boss had drawn from his American culture when giving the performance appraisal, emphasizing individual responsibility. For the Malaysian employee, the individual criticism caused him to suffer a loss of face for his team. Had the supervisor had stronger intercultural competence, he would have given feedback in an indirect, subtle, and nonconfrontational manner.[49]

Nonverbal Communication

As discussed in Chapter 4, nonverbal communication is important in any interaction with others. Its importance is multiplied across cultures with their different systems of understanding and using gestures, postures, silence, spatial relations, emotional expressions, touch, physical appearance, and other nonverbal cues.[50] People in the United States and Canada place more importance on the meaning of words, while those in Japan and Colombia consider nonverbal communication more important in the total meaning of a message.

Some elements of nonverbal communication and how they are expressed are consistent across cultures, such as enjoyment, anger, fear, sadness, disgust, and surprise.[51] However, differences occur regarding which emotions may be displayed acceptably in various cultural settings and by whom, thus leading to miscommunication and even mistrust. For example, in China and Japan, where most people find it unacceptable to show anger or sadness, bad news may be delivered with a smile to hide those feelings.

Another problem is that the same verbal cue can convey different messages and social skills in different cultures. For example, pointing your finger in the air may summon a server at a restaurant in Austria but earn you an impolite image in Belgium. Nodding your head up and down means no in Bulgaria and side to side means yes.[52]

The handshake is common in the United States between men, women, and men and women, while in many other countries customs differ about who shakes hands with whom. In Australia, for example, women do not usually shake hands with other women. In India, men and women do not usually shake hands with each other. And in South Korea, women usually do not shake hands at all. Even a seemingly innocuous act such as handing out business cards varies among cultures. For this reason, Americans who will work abroad are frequently given training in cultural differences, particularly if they will be working with people who may have had little previous interaction with Americans.

Because so many differences exist in intercultural competency, developing fluency and functioning effectively requires that you observe, study, and cultivate relationships across cultures. While the Internet and e-mail are beginning to change perceptions and erase communication barriers that have existed across different cultures worldwide,[53] the following general guidelines will help you:[54]

- Be aware of settings and situations that are uncomfortable for those with whom you are communicating, and try to reduce power dynamics.

- Focus on understanding, and don't express disagreement or conflicting ideas immediately.

- Explore the possibility that what is presented may not be the main issue. Listen, work on trust, and be patient.

- Acknowledge differences and different experiences and avoid saying "I know how you feel."

- Focus on similarities or common ground, such as work, families, leisure, and basic human concerns.

- Treat all people with dignity and respect regardless of diversity issues. Keep an open mind, and keep the discussion simple. Speak politely. Avoid making judgments and assumptions, and avoid ethnic, racial, and gender jokes.

- Respect all people as adults who have the right to make decisions freely. Avoid dictating, giving orders, giving commands, and using slang terms.

- Keep a sense of humor.

Ask Yourself...

1. Think of instances when you have interacted with persons from another culture. What were some of the communication differences you observed?

2. Do you think you will handle your next interaction with someone from another culture differently? If so, what will you do differently?

3. How difficult do you think it is to avoid local expressions? What expressions do you use frequently that might pose problems for non-native speakers of English?

11.5 THRIVING IN A DIVERSE ENVIRONMENT

To thrive in a diverse workforce, you must not only explore and deal with your own biases and prejudices and understand your own value systems, but you must also develop empathy, engage in positive self-talk, treat others with dignity and respect, be flexible and learn to deal with ambiguity, and use inclusive language.

Empathy

Empathy is detailed in Chapter 8. Cultural coach Linda Wallace suggests the following activities to increase your empathy and raise your comfort level with those who are different:[55]

- Take advantage of cultural offerings at colleges.

- Shop in a new part of town.

- Volunteer for a community-based initiative that works with people who make you feel the most uncomfortable.

> *It starts with your heart and radiates out.*
>
> —Cesar Chavez, American migrant worker and labor leader

- Seek others to act as advisors on cultural issues.
- Develop a learning plan using books and films.
- Talk to a child who has not yet learned to be judgmental.
- Learn a foreign language and experience the culture.
- Listen to a radio talk show of a host who angers you and try to understand his or her viewpoint.

Positive Self-Talk

The *Pygmalion effect* is a psychological phenomenon whose premise is "you get what you expect." Make it a regular practice to tell yourself that you will get along with and understand others who are different—it will become a self-fulfilling prophecy.[56] If you train your "inner voice" to expect the best and avoid negativity, you will build self-esteem and be more likely to respect yourself and others.

Dignity and Respect

Most individuals want to have more authentic, honest, and respectful relationships with others. Remembering that others may see dignity and respect differently, try to find out what that means for each individual and act accordingly. This may involve being sensitive to physical needs, work/family needs, language barriers, and cultural taboos and customs. Remember, respecting others' values and viewpoints doesn't mean you must accept or adopt their way of thinking. You may simply need to respectfully agree to disagree.

You can communicate dignity and respect by encouraging open communication—share a part of yourself and be open to the differences in others. Listen actively and be other-oriented, showing interest in what other people have to say. Additionally, speak to others as you would speak to your peers to help create a sense of equality. Body language and tone can help create a genuine, sincere style.

Flexibility and Ambiguity

Expect ambiguity and learn to deal with it. What you think you see may not be reality to others if they have different viewpoints and perspectives. Observe and analyze situations carefully before taking actions. For example, your boss's behavior may create ambiguity because it can be interpreted in two or more ways. Use the Rolling the D.I.E. suggestions in Figure 11.2 to help you evaluate your perceptions of a situation.

> **KeyPoint**
> Treating others with dignity and respect is the key in developing authentic and honest relationships.

> " *Integrity is doing the right thing even if nobody is watching.*
> —Jim Stovall, motivational speaker and author "

Figure 11.2

Checking your perceptions.

William Sonnenschein, author of *The Diversity Toolkit,* suggests using the Rolling the D.I.E. self-awareness tool to check your perceptions of a situation.[57]

1. **D**escribe the experience. (My supervisor snapped at me.)

2. **I**nterpret it in as many different ways as you can. (She doesn't like me; she is having a bad day because her mother is in the hospital; she is frustrated because her boss has given her a difficult deadline.)

3. **E**valuate the interpretations to determine which one is the most accurate.

You may need to think on your feet, be flexible, and adapt to the communication style of the individual with whom you are speaking in order to operate effectively.

Technology CONNECTION

Technology is now helping the disabled perform tasks at work that were once thought impossible. A hand-held device helps the blind identify the denomination of paper money. A variety of emergency alerting systems use flashing lights or vibrations to warn the hearing impaired of anything from telephone calls to fire alarms. Environmental control units enable users to easily turn off and on lights and appliances, adjust thermostats, or control switch-operated battery-powered devices. Many are operated by remote control, voice activation, touch buttons, or timers. Even alternatives to the traditional computer mouse have been developed for those with various fine motor limitations, spasticity, or other gripping limitation.

1. Have you been exposed to any assistive devices for the disabled? If so, describe them.

2. Do you ever use any assistive devices developed for the disabled? If so, which ones?

Inclusivity

Make a conscientious effort to use language and actions that include others. For example, when sending an invitation to a function, you might say that employees may bring significant others rather than husbands and wives. Because many religions and cultures have prohibitions on consuming certain food products, offer food that is acceptable for everyone. Additionally, make certain that entrances and facilities are accessible and comfortable to everyone. Deliver information in alternate formats if needed, such as braille or captioning.

Handling Offenses

If someone has said something to offend you, try the following techniques to resolve the issue:[58]

- Be clear about your goals for challenging the individual.
- Try to assume goodwill—the other person did not realize what he or she said was offensive.
- Talk to the person privately.
- Be honest and direct when explaining how the comments made you feel.
- Use "I" phrases (see Chapter 4).
- Give examples of the comments and behaviors that offended you.

If you have been told you've offended someone, do the following:

- Listen carefully and reserve judgment.
- Ask questions to clarify the other person's concerns.
- Apologize if you had no intention of offending that individual.
- Do not use the phrase or word that was offensive in the future out of respect for the individual.

If you are unable to resolve the issue yourself, seek assistance from your supervisor or the human resources department.

KeyPoint
You can handle many offenses yourself by assuming good will and listening actively.

Ask Yourself...

1. Have you ever been in an environment where you felt excluded? What could others have done to make you feel included?

2. Make a list of five things you can do in your daily life and work to show empathy and be more respectful of the needs of others.

3. Why is it important to recognize and analyze ambiguity? How should you deal with it?

KEY TERMS

diversity
intercultural competence
bias
prejudice
values
value systems
linguistic styles
direct communication style

indirect communication style
low context groups
high context groups
conversational rituals
monochronic style
polychronic style
Pygmalion effect

CHAPTER SUMMARY

Intercultural competence refers to your effectiveness in dealing with those who are different from you. As our economy becomes increasingly global and our workplace more diverse, organizations are demanding that their employees have a high degree of intercultural competence. While a diverse workforce allows organizations to be competitive and to attract the best and brightest employees, it can also be a significant source of conflict.

Understanding how biases and prejudices affect our ability to deal with those who are different from us is imperative if the conflict diversity brings is to be minimized. Other sources of conflict include value systems and linguistic styles.

Intercultural competence at the global level brings additional challenge. People from other cultures express their thoughts in different ways. To communicate effectively, be aware of the variables of time and space, fate and personal responsibility, face and face-saving, and nonverbal communication.

Skills to thrive in a diverse environment include developing empathy, positive self-talk, treating others with dignity and respect, being flexible and learning to deal with ambiguity, acting in an inclusive fashion, and handling offensive behavior.

REVIEW

1. What is intercultural competence, and why is developing it important?

2. What are biases and prejudices? How do they interfere with our interactions with others who are different from us?

3. What are linguistic styles, and how can different linguistic styles cause conflict?

4. Explain the challenges global intercultural competence represents.

5. What actions can improve your ability to thrive in a diverse environment?

CRITICAL THINKING

1. Has the racial and ethnic composition of your community changed in the last decade? If so, how?

2. Do you believe you have a responsibility to share information about yourself in order to facilitate better understanding? Give an example of a situation in which sharing information about yourself was helpful.

3. Recall a conflict you have either seen or been a part of at work that you feel may have been caused by different linguistic styles. How could the conflict have been resolved?

4. Have you ever been in a group with an individual who was born in another country and had recently arrived in the United States? Describe some cultural differences you noticed.

5. How can you learn about other cultures? Identify at least five things you could do or resources or people you could consult for more information.

6. Consider this advice: "We should treat others as they like to be treated." How do you like to be treated? Do different members of your group have different ideas about how they would like to be treated? What lessons can you learn from this?

CASE STUDIES

In small groups, analyze the following situations.

1 **Hey, Didn't I Say That?**   Jack, the team leader for Axel Corporation's production team, was beginning to panic. Good ideas for resolving their dilemma just weren't coming. Then, Hannah raised her hand. Jack opened the floor for her to speak.

"Uh, I don't know if this would work or not, but..." Hannah proceeded in a low, tentative voice to suggest a resolution to their current problem. She was ignored and the discussion moved to other areas.

Fifteen minutes later, Ashton spoke up in a clear, confident voice. "This is what we should do..." He proceeded to expound on Hannah's idea. The team became animated and started a lively discussion. Within 30 minutes, the team had developed an action plan for solving their production problem. As the team members left the conference room, other team members congratulated Ashton on his contributions to the group.

1. Why didn't the team members acknowledge Hannah for her idea?

2. Why did the team members acknowledge Ashton's contributions?

3. What could Hannah have done differently to get the members of the group to listen to her? What do you think she learned from this experience?

4. Does Jack have an obligation to ensure that team members get credit for their contributions and that the group is aware of these contributions? Why, or why not?

2 **In the Eye of the Beholder**   Jane glanced at her watch. Huo and Wang were supposed to be at her office 15 minutes ago. Frustrated, she called the production department only to be told they had left 20 minutes ago. After a search she found they had been waiting in the reception area instead.

The next morning, frustrated, Jane went to see Fernando, the human resource manager.

"I'm at my wits end," she complained. "I give those guys an assignment and they act like they understand perfectly what to do. Half the time they mess it up. Then, to top it off, when I ask them to come to my office, they just sit in the waiting room and never tell me they're here. We're going to have to let them go."

1. Why do you believe Huo and Wang do not ask Jane for clarification on assignments or tell her when they arrive at her office?

2. What could Jane do to improve communication with Huo and Wang?

3. If you were the human resource manager, what would you do to repair this situation?

HUMAN RELATIONS IN ACTION

The Internet contains a wealth of information on intercultural competency. Locate at least three relevant web sites, and identify five new tips for dealing with differences in the workplace. Carefully analyze the web sites to make sure they are reputable, up-to-date, and unbiased.

Write an action plan no more than one page in length to improve your own ability to interact in a diverse environment. The action plan should:

- State an explanation of a goal or problem and give a rationale for your decision or recommendation.

- Indicate what resources, tools, or people you will need to use to implement your plan.

- Identify any issues or barriers that need to be considered and explain how you can overcome them.

- Give a schedule or timeline for completing the steps in your plan with deadlines for each step.

- Identify what alternative steps (contingency plans) will be taken if your plan does not work.

For additional resources, refer to the web site for this text:
www.cengage.com/management/dalton

RESOURCES

1. Award celebrates best corporate practices of equal employment opportunity with ceremony on October 16 in Washington, D.C. (2008, September 25). Retrieved October 28, 2008, from http://www.hopkinsbayview.org/news/080930laboraward.html.

2. Intercultural competence as a key enabler of organizational growth and success. (2008, November 1). Society for Human Resource Management Research Article. Retrieved May 14, 2009, from http://moss07.shrm.org/Research/Articles/Articles/Pages/InterculturalCo.

3. How should my organization define diversity? (n.d.). Society for Human Resource Management. Retrieved July 13, 2004, from http://shrm.org/diversity/definingdiversity.asp.

4. Texin, Tex. (n.d.). Marketing translation mistakes. Internationalization, localization, standards, and amusements. Retrieved July 13, 2004, from www.i18nguy.com.

5. Toossi, Mitra. (2007, November). Employment outlook: 2006–16 Labor force projections to 2016: More workers in their golden years. *Monthly Labor Review*, 33–52.

6. Lewis, Michael. (2003). *Moneyball: The art of winning an unfair game.* New York: W.W. Norton & Company.

7. 21st century skills, education & competitiveness: A resource and policy guide. (2008). Partnership for 21st Century Skills. Tucson, AZ: Author.

8. Toossi, Mitra. (2007, November). Employment outlook: 2006–16 Labor force projections to 2016: More workers in their golden years.

9. School enrollment in the United States: 2006. (2008, August). U.S. Department of Commerce Economics and Statistics Administration, U.S. Census Bureau. Washington, D.C.: Author.

10. Industry male median earnings (dollars) by subject vs. women's wages as percentage of male wages, United States category industry total median earnings (dollars) vs. women's wages as percentage of male wages, United States category industry female media U.S. Census Bureau (2007, August 8). Retrieved January 5, 2009, from http://www.swivel.com/graphs/show/22519323.

11. Creating Gender Parity in Sector Initiatives Women Work! The National Network for Women's Employment. (n.d.). Retrieved January 5, 2009, from http://www.womenwork.org.

12. Hastings, Rebecca R. (2009, January 26). Women make slow progress toward top, studies report. Retrieved February 10, 2009, from http://moss07.shrm.org/hrdisciplines/Diversity/Articles/Pages/WomenM.

13. Toossi, Mitra. (2007, November). Employment outlook: 2006–16 Labor force projections to 2016: More workers in their golden years.

14. Staying Ahead of the Curve 2007: The AARP Work and Career Study. (2008, September). Washington, D.C.: American Association of Retired People.

15. Mildred Heath, 100, is America's oldest worker for 2008. (2008, September 24). Retrieved October 28, 2008, from http://www.prweb.com/releases/2008/09/prweb1372914.htm.

16. An older and more diverse nation by midcentury. (2008, August 14). Retrieved January 5, 2009, from http://www.census.gov/Press-Release/www/releases/archives/population/012496.html.

17. One-in-Five Speak Spanish in Four States: New Census Bureau Data Show How America Lives (2008, September 23). Retrieved January 5, 2009, from http://www.census.gov/Press-Release/www/releases/archives/american_community_survey_acs/012634.html.

18. Empowerment for Americans with disabilities: Breaking barriers to careers and full employment. (2007, October 1). Washington, D.C.: National Council on Disability.

19. Wells, Susan J. (2008, April). Counting on workers with disabilities: The nation's largest minority remains an underused resource. *HR Magazine*, 45–49.

20. Empowerment for Americans with disabilities: Breaking barriers to careers and full employment. (2007, October 1). Washington, D.C.: National Council on Disability.

21. Lesbian, gay, bisexual & transgender workplace issues. (2007, December). Retrieved October 28, 2008, from http://www.catalyst.org/publication/203/lesbian-gay-bisexual-transgender-workplace-issues.

22. Ibid.

23. Paul, Annie M. (1998, May/June). Where bias begins: The truth about stereotypes. *Psychology Today*.

24. Loden, Marilyn, and Rosener, Judy B. (1990). *Workforce America! Managing employee diversity as a vital resource.* New York: McGraw-Hill.

25. Value. (2009). In Merriam-Webster Online Dictionary. Retrieved May 14, 2009, from http://www.merriam-webster.com/dictionary/value.

26. Lockhart, Janet & Shaw, Susan M. (n.d.). Rating your behavior handout. Writing for change: Raising awareness of difference, power, and discrimination. Retrieved July 13, 2004, from http://www.toleranceusa.net/teach/expand/wfc/pdf/section_1/1_03_rating_behavior.pdf.

27. Guss, Elizabeth, and Miller, Mary C. (2008, July 1). Ethics and generational differences: Interplay between values and ethical business decisions. Retrieved May 15, 2009 from http://moss07.shrm.org/Research/Articles/Articles/Pages/EthicsandGener.

28. Tannen, Deborah. (2002). *The power of talk: Who gets heard and why.* Boston: Harvard Business School Press.

29. Beer, Jennifer E. "High and Low Context," Culture at Work: Communicating Across Cultures, 1997–2003. Retrieved July 13, 2004, from http://www.culture-at-work.com/highlow.html.

30. Ibid.

31. Tannen, Deborah. (1994). *Talking from 9 to 5: How women's and men's conversational styles affect who gets heard, who gets credit, and what gets done at work.* New York: HarperCollins.

32. Ford, Valda B. (2007, November). The paralysis of political correctness. *HR Magazine.* 69–71.

33. Hastings, Rebecca R. (2009, April 7). Political correctness stifles conversations about race. Retrieved April 10, 2009, from http://www.shrm.org/hrdisciplines/Diversity/Articles/Pages/PoliticalCorr.

34. Do you speak American? From Sea to Shining sea. (n.d.) Retrieved January 5, 2009, from http://www.pbs.org/speak/seatosea/americanvarieties/.

35. Tannen, Deborah. (1994). *Talking from 9 to 5: How women's and men's conversational styles affect who gets heard, who gets credit, and what gets done at work.* New York: HarperCollins.

36. Loden, Marilyn, and Rosener, Judy B. (1990). *Workforce America! Managing employee diversity as a vital resource.* New York: McGraw-Hill.

37. Fisher, Anne. (2009, May 25). When gen x runs the show. *Time Magazine*, 48–49.

38. Why is cross-cultural communication important? (2006, March 9). University of the Pacific School of International Studies. [on-line]. Available: http://www.pacific.edu/sis/mair/cross-cultural-communication.htm. Retrieved 2009, February 15.

39. Cross-cultural communication. (2003, July). Beyond Intractability.org. [on-line]. Available: http://www.beyondintractability.org/essay/cross-cultural-communication/. Retrieved 2009, February 15.

40. Dahl, Stephan. (n.d.) Communications and Culture Transformation. Retrieved May 18, 2009, from http://www.stephweb.com/capstone/.

41. Kenig, Graciela. (2006, December 6). Time management in other cultures. Retrieved May 16, 2009, from http://network.latpro.com/profiles/blogs/time-management-in-other

42. Harris, Philip R., and Moran, Robert T. (1991). *Managing cultural differences*. Houston, TX: Gulf Publishing Company.

43. Dahl, Stephan. (n.d.). Hall's Classic Patterns: An overview of intercultural research. Retrieved July 14, 2004, from http://stephan.dahl.at/intercultural/hall.html.

44. Cross-cultural communication. (2003, July). Beyond Intractability.org. [on-line]. Available: http://www.beyondintractability.org/essay/cross-cultural-communication/. Retrieved 2009, February 15.

45. Ibid.

46. Ibid.

47. 'International English' helps redefine global communication. (2005, April). Society for Human Resource management Global HR Library – Organizational Development. [on-line]. Available: http://www.shrm.org/global/library_published/subject/nonlC/CMS_012223.asp# TopOfPage. Retrieved 2008, December 30.

48. Cross-cultural communication. (2003, July). Beyond Intractability.org. [on-line]. Available: Retrieved, February 15, 2009 from http://www.beyondintractability.org/essay/cross-cultural-communication/.

49. Society for Human Resource Management, Research Quarterly. (2008, Third Quarter). "Selected cross-cultural factors in human resource management." Alexandria, VA: Author.

50. Cross-cultural communication. (2003, July). Beyond Intractability.org. Retrieved February 15, 2009, from http://www.beyondintractability.org/essay/cross-cultural-communication/.

51. Ibid.

52. Cross-cultural communications. (2000, September 10). International Real Estate Digest. February 15, 2009, from http://www.ired.com/news/2000/0009/cross-culture.htm.

53. Graham, Jeffrey P. (2000, February). A new era in cross-cultural communications. Gateway Newsletter at Trade Compass. [on-line]. Retrieved February 15, 2009, from http://www.going-global.com/articles/a_new_era_in_cross-culturalcommunications.htm.

54. Strategies for cross-cultural communication. (ND). Cultural Competency. Retrieved February 15, 2009, from https://www.dshs.state.tx.us/thsteps/cultural/strategies.shtm.

55. Wallace, Linda S. (2003, May 23). 10 Practical ways to increase an individual's cultural IQ. *Houston Chronicle*.

56. HRZone, "The Pygmalion effect: Belief in potential creates potential," from Brian D. McNatt, "Ancient Pygmalion joins contemporary management: A meta-analysis of the result," *Journal of Applied Psychology*, 200 85, no. 2, pp. 314–322. Retrieved July 14, 2004, from http://www.hrzone.com/articles/pygmalion_effect.html.

57. Sonnenschein, William. (1999). *The diversity toolkit*. (Chicago: Contemporary Books).

58. Stern-LaRosa, Caryl & Bettmann, Ellen H. (2000). *Hate hurts: How children learn and unlearn prejudice*. New York: Scholastic, Inc.

WORKPLACE ETIQUETTE:
RULES FOR BEHAVIOR

OBJECTIVES

After studying this chapter, you should be able to:

12.1 Define workplace etiquette and its connection to assertiveness.

12.2 Explain the importance of workplace etiquette.

12.3 Use etiquette to make a good impression.

12.4 Use correct etiquette with customers and associates.

12.5 Apply etiquette in electronic communications.

Jump Start

A survey by the Society for Human Resource Management found most companies agree that employers have the right to monitor employee use of the following technologies in the workplace: Internet, computer, instant message, telephone, e-mail, cell phone camera, and cell phone calls. Additionally, 53 percent agreed that they have the right to read employee e-mails and 41 percent to listen to employee telephone conversations.[1]

- Do these findings surprise you? Why or why not?
- Why do you think companies want to monitor these forms of communication?
- Now that you know that the majority of companies are in favor of such monitoring, will this modify what you think you can communicate at work? Why or why not? If so, how?

12.1 ETIQUETTE

Many problems at workplace are the direct result of lapses in etiquette. Have you ever observed any of these offensive workplace behaviors?

- Not greeting customers or coworkers
- Disturbing others by speaking or laughing loudly
- Swearing
- Taking personal calls on cell phones
- Asking customers or coworkers about their personal lives

Judgments are often quickly made about your competence, credibility, professionalism, and character based on your behavior and appearance. A well-known adage is that you never get a second chance to make a first impression. Knowledge of social skills and etiquette is, therefore, increasingly important.

We are all born charming, fresh, and spontaneous, and must be civilized before we are fit to participate in society.

—Miss Manners, Judith Martin, American etiquette authority

Workplace Etiquette

Workplace etiquette deals with commonly accepted rules for good behavior in workplace interactions. Put simply, when you use correct etiquette, you act appropriately, are considerate, make other people feel comfortable in your presence, and try not to embarrass others. Etiquette has been called the oil that prevents friction in business and social settings.

Knowledge of etiquette contributes to the social skill component of emotional intelligence. Your effective use of social skills will help you develop positive and productive relationships with others.

Knowledge of etiquette provides you with a code of behavior in different settings, much as rulebooks provide you with a set of directions for playing

KeyPoint
Workplace etiquette deals with commonly accepted rules for good behavior in workplace interactions.

"We'd like you to change your email address from LittleHoneyDoodle to something more professional."

©2009 Ted Goff

golf, tennis, and other games. If you know the rules, you can play the game better and enjoy it more. When you walk into a situation and are sure that you know how to handle yourself, your self-confidence will be obvious to others.

In The News

Concerns about the spread of the H1N1 virus have resulted in numerous etiquette reminders aimed at reducing its spread. Appropriate coughing and sneezing behaviors are mentioned frequently, reminding people to cover their mouths, not to spit in public, to discard used tissues immediately, and to wash hands with soap and water. Asked whether they have modified their usual interactions, many people report a decline in shaking hands with others (or at least sanitizing their hands afterward).[2]

1. Have you ever had a "good manners" class or discussed etiquette in school? If so, how was it helpful to you?

2. Have you ever been in an interaction where you felt uncertain about what to do or how to act, particularly in light of health concerns? How did you feel? How did you overcome the feelings of uncertainty?

3. If you were provided an opportunity to take an etiquette class at work, would you? What would you hope to learn?

Rules, then, are an important component of etiquette, but they aren't the only one. Knowledge of etiquette rules alone will not strengthen your human relations skills. You must also use courtesy.

Workplace Etiquette and Courtesy

Typifying effective workplace etiquette and courtesy in a high productivity setting, Gene Kranz, head of Mission Operations Directorate during some of NASA's most exciting early space explorations, suggests that managers should use one or more of the following, every day and in every conversation, to get the most from their workers:[3]

- You did a good job.
- What is your opinion?
- I made a mistake.
- Will you please…
- Thank you.
- We…

When you act with courtesy, you're combining kindness and politeness. An unkind act is never a courteous one, no matter how correct it may be, and impolite acts are neither courteous nor correct. Being courteous involves being thoughtful and considerate of others, even in little ways, and using a friendly voice and facial expression.

Assertive Behavior

How well you put etiquette into practice depends on your usual behavior. As discussed in Chapter 2, *assertiveness* is the process of expressing your thoughts and feelings while asking for what you want in an appropriate, calm, and confident manner. It is acting in a way that is neither too pushy nor too passive.

Using your best human relations skills and workplace etiquette enables you to use appropriate assertive behaviors for best outcomes. Understanding the additional information here will assist you.[4]

The line between assertive and aggressive behaviors can be hard to judge. When you use assertiveness appropriately, you show that you respect the ideas and feelings of others. When you act aggressively, though, you fail to consider whether people are hurt by what you say. For example, if you need to repeat a message because another person didn't pay attention the first time, you would repeat the message with firmness and respect, but not with critical comments or a caustic tone.

> *We are responsible for what we do, no matter how we feel.*
>
> —*Unknown*

Assertive People...

- Demonstrate respect for themselves and others
- Feel they are equal to others
- Make their own choices
- Are comfortable using proper etiquette
- Use nonverbal communication that shows confidence but does not intimidate
- Speak clearly, calmly, and firmly
- Maintain eye contact without staring
- Have a relaxed facial expression and body, with shoulders back and posture erect
- Tend to remain calm, pleasant, and in control
- Are able to say no without feeling guilty

If you have found yourself overloaded, taken advantage of, or talked into doing tasks you would prefer not to do, try analyzing situations when you have trouble saying no and order them by difficulty (saying no to someone soliciting money on the phone? a friend wanting to borrow your new camera?). Write down what you consider to be appropriate responses to the various situations. You don't have to apologize for saying no, explain your feelings, or provide reasons, but you should be tactful.

If You're the Target of an Overly Aggressive Person

If you're the target of an overly aggressive or rude person, you don't have to tolerate it.

Calmly saying "Please lower your voice" or "Why are you speaking to me that way?" is usually enough to set boundaries and let the person know what you're willing to accept.

If you are an assertive person, you'll find that others respect and value you. This can often help you get what you want. To strengthen your assertiveness skills, consider the following:

1. Take small steps in the beginning, perhaps starting in smaller groups, with persons with whom you feel comfortable, or with noncontroversial topics.

2. State your position or needs in ways that don't violate the rights of others. Use assertive phrases such as "I think…," "I feel…," "I don't understand…," "I would like/need…," and "No, I won't be able to…" Practice this phrasing and other communication techniques to become familiar and comfortable with them.

3. When you speak, use a modulated, enthusiastic voice; make eye contact; avoid phrases such as "I guess"; and avoid ending sentences that sound like questions.

4. Think win–win: don't feel that every idea you put forth has to be accepted. Be willing to listen to other ideas and strive for a decision that everyone can support.

Using Assertive Behavior If You're an Unhappy Customer

Using effective human relations and etiquette can help you win a fast and happy resolution. These words can serve you well in any negotiation situation:

1. Acknowledge your feelings while remaining detached, professional, and nonaccusatory: "I'm not upset or angry at you—but I am upset."

2. Remembering that this business transaction is a negotiation, think of a remedy that makes sense and say what you want: "What I want from you is…"

Your goal is to break through the other person's shell and help him or her see your point of view: "What would you do if you were in my shoes?"

With practice, you will become more skilled with your assertiveness skills. Remember that it will take some time for everyone (including you) to become comfortable with your behavior. If you're a passive person, those around you may be uncomfortable when you first become assertive. Be careful that you don't go overboard and become aggressive while trying to become comfortable with your new behavior.

> *Sometimes when I'm angry I have the right to be angry, but that doesn't give me the right to be cruel.*
>
> —*Unknown*

Ask Yourself…

1. Think of friends who may be particularly skilled in using correct etiquette. Describe instances when these skills were helpful.

2. Among your acquaintances, can you think of individuals who have effective assertiveness skills? Give examples of their behavior and how it helped.

3. Which of the characteristics of assertive people do you think will be most helpful to you? Which do you think you need to develop further? How might you do this?

12.2 IMPORTANCE OF WORKPLACE ETIQUETTE

Companies view etiquette as a way of giving them a competitive edge in winning and retaining a solid market share. They fear losing customers who aren't treated well and are embarrassed by employees who may be technically brilliant but lack basic manners and social graces.

Knowledge of the finer points of good manners can help you build long-term relationships with coworkers, customers, and clients. Often, the ability to engage in small talk over dinner or in small groups, listen effectively, and make introductions—all in a natural and sincere way—is a part of many companies' marketing strategies.

Etiquette is more important than ever today for a variety of reasons:

- In the 1960s and early 1970s, "doing your own thing" became the norm, and many children weren't taught etiquette, resulting in a generation of business people who may feel awkward and ill at ease, particularly with the increasing use of teams and group decision making.

- The heavy use of computers may result in people frequently working in isolation or being treated impersonally, which can leave them desiring human connection. This need can be at least partially met through socially correct interpersonal behaviors.

- Electronic communication requires specific etiquette skills.

- The growth of the global economy and an increasingly diverse population requires that workers interact with people of all cultures, being careful not to offend them by violating their communication or behavioral norms.

- Because of workforce changes (multigenerations, disabled workers, underrepresented populations, and others), old behavioral rules are being reexamined and new ones created. Some of these behaviors are being determined legally; others fall outside of the legal domain and are less specific. Just because something is legal doesn't make it ethical or appropriate—for example, older workers making jokes at the expense of younger workers, younger workers excluding older workers from lunch tables, or supervisors yelling at all workers equally. These are not illegal behaviors, but they are certainly inappropriate.

Knowledge of etiquette, then, is a key ingredient in human relations and in business and personal success. Such knowledge can help you feel comfortable because you know what to do and can do it with grace, style, and ease. Work situations that call for effective etiquette include relationships with coworkers, managers above you, people below you in the hierarchy, customers and clients, and the public where you are seen as representing your organization. Away from work, you will enhance your chances for satisfactory relationships with people if your behavior says that you respect them.

KeyPoint
Mastering workplace etiquette is important to any person who wants to be successful, and what is appropriate behavior depends on where you are, when, and with whom.

Good manners will open doors that the best education cannot.

—Clarence Thomas, Associate Justice of the U.S. Supreme Court

Global CONNECTION

As the world becomes increasingly global, understanding the effects of good manners in all cultures becomes more important. Even though the world seems to be getting smaller, etiquette for greetings, communications, meetings, and negotiations still varies globally.

Many global, cross-cultural companies are recognizing the important need for etiquette training. They know that what may be considered appropriate behavior in one culture may be considered rude in another. For example, handshakes vary around the world. In Italy, they may include grasping the arm with the other hand. You may even receive a kiss on both cheeks if you have developed a very good working rapport. In West Africa, your hand may be held far longer than is usually done in the United States.[5]

Other global differences involve greetings. For example, in Hong Kong you are expected to extend greetings to the most senior member first and usually address people with a title and surname. Also common are gift giving and lengthy meals and negotiations.

1. Think of interactions involving persons from other cultures—some that you may have experienced or seen in a movie or on television. Were certain etiquette rules obviously observed or violated? If so, what?

2. What do you think might have happened if a misunderstanding occurred during these interactions?

3. How might the interactions have been improved?

Appropriate etiquette depends to a certain extent on where, when, and with whom the interaction occurs. Behavior considered appropriate with one group or individual might be considered offensive with someone else. Often, etiquette will come down to learning a person's preferences and then respecting them.

Because etiquette depends on timing and setting, you must develop good judgment and sensitivity to people around you. This awareness will give you the best chance of success in your relationships, in business situations such as negotiations and sales, in leadership positions, and in any situation requiring cooperation and teamwork.

The remainder of this chapter will discuss etiquette as a typical worker might use it on a normal workday. As you read the following sections, imagine yourself in the example situations and apply the suggestions to your own life and work situation.

Ask Yourself...

1. Which one of the reasons given for the importance of etiquette do you think is most important and why?

2. Think of reasons why etiquette is important to you. Cite examples of when you need these skills in your life.

3. How can proper etiquette be used to demonstrate respect? Give examples of effective etiquette and etiquette blunders you have witnessed in the workplace.

12.3 PROFESSIONAL PRESENCE

KeyPoint
Professional presence is a combination of your poise, self-confidence, control, and style that empowers you to command respect in any situation.

Susan Bixler and Lisa Scherrer Dugan, authors of *5 Steps to Professional Presence*,[6] define **professional presence** as a combination of your poise, self-confidence, control, and style that empowers you to command respect in any situation. As suggested earlier, people form their impressions of you in the first few seconds they meet you, and initial impressions can be difficult to change. They may form these initial impressions from a variety of factors, such as your appearance, manners, self-confidence, voice, posture, facial expression, attitude, and handshake.

Self-confidence, voice, posture, facial expressions, and attitude were discussed in earlier chapters. This section will provide you with information about your appearance (clothes and grooming) and manners (general manners, table manners, introductions, hugging, and swearing).

Appearance

Your clothes, grooming, and hygiene say a lot about you. Think about what you wore to work or class today and your overall appearance. When dressing this morning, did you consider the statement your clothes would make? Whether your appearance would indicate that you fit in with the environment in which you function? How your appearance made you feel about yourself? How your appearance would reflect on your company? Would your boss have been proud to take you to a meeting with a client?

If etiquette pertains to appropriate behaviors, certainly it must be extended to include appropriate dress, hygiene, and grooming. If you dress inappropriately, others may perceive this as a lack of respect for the situation and the people involved. They make assumptions about how you feel about yourself and how you will work, perform, or behave based on your appearance and dress. In fact, studies suggest that people are more productive when they dress professionally.[7]

People who take their careers seriously (and want to hold onto their jobs during weak economic times) know that image is important. You'll be a poor representative for your company if your appearance is making a statement that doesn't agree with the image of your company.

Additionally, your clothing and accessories can help you feel better about yourself, which can, in turn, make you feel more comfortable interacting with others. If you can forget about your appearance because you're satisfied with it, you're free to concentrate on the other person.

The most important rule of dress for work is to dress appropriately for your organization and profession. Some organizations are conservative in nature and expect their employees to dress accordingly. Many other organizations allow less conservative dress, although good taste is still expected.

The moment people look at you, they begin to form an opinion about your education and economic level, your social position, and your level of success. Tight, revealing, or outdated clothes in most kinds of jobs are considered inappropriate, as are strong colognes, flashy jewelry, unnatural hairdos (for example, garish multicolors) and makeup, or extreme tattoos and piercings. Clothes and shoes should fit well and be clean. Many experts still suggest following the adage "Dress for the position you want."

Building a career wardrobe doesn't have to be expensive. Quality, fit, and cleanliness are the most important factors—not quantity, price, or the latest fashion fad. Choose classic pieces that won't go out of style, add separates, and accessorize with conservative, tasteful items.

Beyond these items, remember the following points in the importance of grooming:

- Clean, well-groomed hair, styled neatly
- Shower, deodorant, clean teeth and breath
- Clean, trimmed fingernails
- Minimal cologne or perfume
- No gum, candy, or tobacco products
- All clothing cleaned and pressed and in good condition (no missing buttons)
- Clean, polished, conservative shoes with heels that aren't worn down
- For women, conservative makeup in neutral colors
- For men, freshly shaved face

> **"**
> *A person with class is someone you want to be around—all the time.*
>
> —*Clare Booth Luce, American playwright*
> **"**

In the 1990s, many organizations began permitting business casual dress. However, because of blatant violations in dress, increasing sloppiness, and a more competitive economy, this trend seems to be slowing down or reversing.

Business casual means dressing in a professional yet relaxed manner appropriate for the occasion and location. For men, this may mean khakis or dress trousers and a button-down or polo shirt. For women, it may mean conservative slacks with a sweater or blouse.

If you're meeting with customers or clients, wear your dressier business clothes. And if you go to several out-of-office meetings in one day, a classic, neutral look is usually best, with a jacket you can shed if needed.

Because fashions change and dress codes vary in different organizations, become familiar with the office attire policies outlined in your organization's employee handbook. Observe what your coworkers wear, and dress in a manner that makes you feel confident and will make others take you seriously.

Manners

Having good manners means that you:

- Know how to behave when dining.
- Make smooth introductions.
- Avoid obscenities and offensive comments or stories.
- Can use correct meeting etiquette.
- Are familiar with technology etiquette.

Table Manners "I was embarrassed!" said a manager after observing one of her junior employees display dreadful manners at a business dinner with a major client. The employee spoke with a mouthful of food, waved his fork in the air while talking, dragged his bread through the sauce on his plate, and downed it all with a big gulp of wine. Of course, the client was unimpressed.

Correct table manners make business luncheons more comfortable and enjoyable.

©Yuri Arcurs, 2009/Used under license from Shutterstock.com

Practically everyone shares meals with others at some time as a part of the workday. Whether you're eating in the company cafeteria with coworkers or attending a business luncheon outside the company, you can make these times more relaxed and enjoyable by understanding certain basic rules of etiquette. In general, the manners shown in Figure 12.1 should be used in any setting.

> **"** *The truth of the matter is that you always know the right thing to do. The hard part is doing it.*
>
> —*General H. Norman Schwarzkopf* **"**

Figure 12.1

Basic table manners.

- Sit down from the left side of the chair when possible. (This rule keeps people from bumping into each other.)
- Wait until all people at the table are seated and have their food before beginning to eat. (Exceptions: When people are on different schedules or dishes will lose their flavor if cooled or heated.)
- Place your napkin in your lap as soon as you're seated, and sit with both feet on the floor.
- Avoid playing with your silverware or food.
- Keep the hand not holding the fork in your lap (unless you need to use a knife).
- Don't place your elbows on the table while eating. Sit straight but not rigid throughout the meal.
- Never reach for food or condiments across the table. Pass both salt and pepper together. Ask the person nearest the item you want to "please pass the…" Bowls are passed to the right when initially served.
- Don't smack or slurp while eating or talk with your mouth full.
- Don't groom at the table. If women need to add lipstick or men or women need to smooth wind-blown hair, they should go elsewhere to do so.
- Excuse yourself to people on each side if you need to leave the table.
- Place your napkin in your chair if you temporarily leave the table during the meal.
- When finished eating, lay your silverware in your plate placed in a 5:20 position and your napkin on the table to the left of the plate. Don't shove your plate away from you or comment about how full you are.
- Cocktails before or after dinner may be appropriate in a social setting, but alcohol is best avoided at most work-related meals.

Introductions and Remembering Names Most jobs require you to meet new people and at times introduce people to one another. The latter situation is more likely to create anxiety. You can reduce your anxiety, be more comfortable, and create a gracious atmosphere if you remember the overriding goals of putting people at ease and showing them proper respect.

In introductions, if you remember the general rules shown in Figure 12.2, you'll be demonstrating your human relations skills and manners.

Figure 12.2

General rules for introductions.

Organizational hierarchy	Introduce younger people or people lower on the organizational hierarchy to older people (those appearing to be 15 years older) and superiors, respectively. Address the older person or person higher on the hierarchy first: "Dr. Rutherford, I would like you to meet Rhonda Elliott, the new associate in our office."
Gender	Introduce a man to a woman if they are about the same age and on the same level of the hierarchy. Address the woman first: "Ms. Salinas, I would like you to meet Mr. Freedman. He handles the new product line in the San Francisco office."
If you forget names	Simply say, "I'm sorry; I've forgotten your name" or "I'm sorry; I'm terrible with names. Please introduce yourselves."
If your name is mispronounced	Give the correct pronunciation when acknowledging the person to whom you are introduced. For example, if your name is Dalton and you are introduced as Dawson, you may correct this mistake simply by saying, "Sam Dalton. I'm glad to meet you."
If no one introduces you	Politely smile and say something like, "I'm Danielle Muster from Accounting." Be gracious and friendly in order to put the group at ease.

During introductions, a handshake is the usual greeting. If done correctly, it will help you make a connection with the person. Use a firm grip, perhaps with one or two gentle pumps, and then release. Accompany the handshake with a smile, eye contact, a slight forward lean, and a brief remark such as, "I'm happy to meet you."

Hugging in the Workplace While hugging is becoming more common as a greeting in the United States and many other countries even in the workplace, do it respectfully while being mindful of cultural differences. While a quick hug may be acceptable, long hugs or prolonged embraces are not appropriate.

In 2009 when President Obama and First Lady Michelle Obama met with Queen Elizabeth of England, some people in the media wondered whether etiquette had been breached when the queen put her hand on Mrs. Obama's back and the first lady responded in kind. Such an act by the queen is unusual, and touching the queen is normally viewed as inappropriate by many people. When asked, etiquette expert Anna Post said that this wasn't wrong at all, as good manners suggest that when someone reaches out (whether with a handshake or a hand on your back), you automatically do the same.[8]

Many people still frown on hugging in work-related situations. Use caution in putting an arm around coworkers of either sex, placing a hand on their shoulder, or touching a coworker in any way.

Swearing on the Job   While language that was once forbidden is routinely heard in the media and numerous settings, its use could be a career breaker in the workplace. Don't do it at work. Find a way to express your feelings without swearing.

Ask Yourself...

1. Does your workplace have a dress code? Why do you think appearance is so important to success?

2. Have you ever had a bad first impression of someone? What was it about the person that created the bad impression? Did the impression last?

3. How many of the etiquette rules discussed in this section have you missed on occasion? Which ones were new to you?

12.4   CUSTOMER AND ASSOCIATE RELATIONS

Your interactions with customers and associates (whether coworkers or others) call for strong social skills. How you treat them is a crucial factor in your success and the success of your company.

Customer Relations

Poor service or bad treatment will lose customers. Moreover, it loses more than just the customer who was treated badly, because while customers will seldom tell the company about the treatment, they do tell their friends and

> " *It takes 20 years to build a reputation and five minutes to ruin it. If you think about that, you'll do things differently.*
>
> —*Warren Buffet, investor, businessman, and philanthropist* "

others. Effective customer relations, then, is an important part of an organization's marketing strategy.

If you come in contact with customers in person, by mail, or through communication technologies, the most important guideline to remember is this: "Do unto others as you would have them do unto you." The ways that employees should treat customers seem so obvious that mistreatment seems almost unthinkable, yet it occurs every day. For example, simply wearing ear buds hooked to an MP3 player while talking to a customer may make the customer feel ignored, even if the music is turned off.[9]

One rude employee can do untold damage to a business, whereas one helpful employee is worth thousands in marketing dollars. Consider the following three examples of customer treatment:

Incident 1

- *Poor Treatment.* About five minutes before Arnold was to leave for the day to start a two-week vacation, a customer came in to submit an application for credit. When Arnold was told that the customer was in the outer office, his loud response was, "Well, she'd better hurry. I have things to do." When Arnold's supervisor said, "Shhhh," with a finger to her lips, Arnold replied, again loudly, "Oh, she didn't hear me."
- *Correct Treatment.* Arnold should have either handled the application or politely asked someone else to help take his place. He should not have made comments about leaving in front of the customer.

Incident 2

- *Poor Treatment.* Wanda has been taken off telephone duty so that she may handle in-store customers. However, when all of the other clerks are busy on the telephone, the calls are forwarded to Wanda's station. Wanda dislikes answering customers on the phone so much that when her phone rings, she is abrupt with her "Hello" and snaps out answers to the callers' questions.
- *Correct Treatment.* Wanda should treat each call with professionalism, patience, respect, and consideration.

Incident 3

- *Poor Treatment.* Ronald is busy waiting on a customer in the eyeglass shop when another customer, Angie, walks in. He continues to help the first customer, assuming that Angie can look around while she is waiting. After five minutes of standing nearby and waiting for his attention without even getting a glance from Ronald, Angie leaves the shop.
- *Correct Treatment.* Ronald should have acknowledged Angie as soon as she walked into the store. He could have done this with a friendly, "Hello, I'll be with you shortly. Would you like to look around in the meantime?"

KeyPoint
Never say anything negative about customers that they might hear or learn; give them your full attention; acknowledge them immediately, and use good manners.

The following guidelines for good customer relations will be helpful in your day-to-day interactions:

- Never say anything negative about a customer when the customer might hear you or learn what you've said.

- When serving a customer by phone or in person, give that person your full attention. Don't shuffle papers or try to do other work at the same time.

- Immediately acknowledge every customer who walks into your place of business. Your manner should be pleasant and helpful. The customer should not be left unattended long.

- Don't chew gum or eat in front of customers. Your demeanor should be professional. A ready smile, eye contact, correct posture, and smooth voice are helpful in client relations.

- Remember to say "please," "thank you," "thank you for your interest in our company," and "please come again." When possible, call people by name. It's an easy way to make them feel important.

- Never conduct personal telephone calls or carry on personal conversations in front of clients or customers.

- If you must answer a phone while working with a customer who is with you, ask that person, "Will you excuse me, please, while I take this call?" Remember to take care of the first customer first by asking the second whether he or she can hold or would like you to call back. Use the additional telephone guidelines presented later in this chapter.

Associate Relations

Associate relations pertain to the way you interact with your networks, mentors, coworkers, and other business associates through courtesy and etiquette. The importance of networking has been discussed in this book. To be effective when networking, you must make a good personal appearance and sincere personal connection. A friendly "So what do you do?" can help start the connection. Use your networks appropriately. Members of your network will come to resent you if you abuse the process, for example, by trying to solicit free advice from professionals such as doctors, lawyers, and accountants.

A *mentor* is an experienced person who will give you objective career advice. Such a person can give you pointers, offer advice concerning sensitive situations, and help you avoid mistakes. A mentor can be someone inside or outside your organization but in your profession. Your choice of a mentor should be someone you respect. Therefore, act professionally so that your mentor will admire both the way you behave and the way you handle your job. Don't abuse your mentor's time or position.

In interactions with your coworkers, be careful about office politics. While impossible to avoid, they can be troublesome. Use discretion and courtesy. Participating in or even listening to gossip is not only ill-mannered, but can also have serious consequences for your career. When confronted with

> **KeyPoint**
> Associate relations pertain to the way you interact with your networks, mentors, coworkers, and other business associates through courtesy and etiquette.

gossip, avoid the discussion by simply saying, "Oh, I never pay attention to things like that."

A potentially stressful situation involving coworkers that requires strong human relations and etiquette skills can occur as employees assume greater workloads because of the economy. To maintain good relationships with coworkers, be willing to collaborate and take on additional responsibilities, share credit and accolades, meet deadlines and commitments, and get to know your colleagues on a personal level.[10]

Should conflict develop between you and a coworker, use kindness and courtesy to try to restore your relationship. If you did something that offended the other person, you need to apologize. If you don't know why the person is upset, ask in a concerned manner. Refrain from making critical comments, and remember that everyone wants to feel important. Your goal is a win–win resolution of the conflict.

A little envy among coworkers may be normal and can frequently be deflected by a sense of humor and sensitivity and, therefore, may not be a cause for concern. However, excessive competition can become disruptive. Almost half of the senior executives recently surveyed by Robert Half International,[11] a large global staffing firm, said that they believe employees are more competitive today than ten years ago—which can hinder collaboration and team work.

Suggestions for working with overly competitive coworkers include those in Figure 12.3.

> *Always do right—this will gratify some and astonish the rest.*
> —Mark Twain, American author and humorist

Figure 12.3

Suggestions for working with overly competitive coworkers.

- Try to avoid a person who is willing to hurt others to get ahead.
- If you think someone has misrepresented you or your work or is withholding information you need, discuss this with your supervisor.
- Try not to be too concerned, as others usually see through this kind of person.
- Concentrate on doing a good job, making sure your supervisor is aware of your contributions.

Another occurrence that will require your understanding, strong human relations skills, and sensitive etiquette is a coworker's loss. Accept that people feel loss for different events and that their suffering may vary in degree and duration. Difficult events (even some that are positive, such as leaving home and moving to a new state to start a new job) can trigger a natural grieving process.

Obvious examples of when a coworker might experience a loss and feel grief include death of a loved one; loss of a pet; or loss of personal belongings through fire, natural disaster, or theft. Perhaps not so obvious but still very real is grief a coworker may feel related to divorce, transfers/moving, retirement, or job loss.

If you've ever had a friend or coworker lose a job while you were still working, you may have felt unsure or awkward (or even guilty) in dealing with the person. A particularly painful period for displaced workers is after the initial shock and before they have found new jobs, which may take a while. This is the time when they may need your most sensitive understanding and actions. An example is continuing to include them in your social activities but tactfully mentioning unusual costs that may be involved.

Individuals respond to grief differently. For example, don't be surprised if a friend or coworker tries to avoid you. Understanding this will help you respond sensitively and patiently to coworkers who have suffered a loss. Simply saying, "I heard what happened, and I'm sorry" will go a long way. Other suggestions for responding to grief include the following:[12]

> **KeyPoint**
> A part of associate relationships is dealing patiently with persons who may be grieving because of job or other losses.

- Don't avoid bereaved people because you feel awkward.
- Don't expect them to be over their loss too soon.
- Don't be inappropriately cheery.
- Don't make remarks such as "I know exactly how you feel," try to explain why the loss occurred, or attempt to minimize it.
- Give them an opportunity to talk about their loss if they want, but don't pressure them.
- Offer concrete, specific ways to help them, such as doing yard work, preparing a meal, or babysitting.

If you're the one who has suffered a loss, give yourself time to grieve. Be patient with your associates, as some of them may have difficulty expressing their sympathy to you or initiating discussion with you about your loss.

Ask Yourself...

1. Do you consider yourself effective in handling customer or associate relations? How could you improve?
2. What kinds of networking opportunities are available to you?
3. What has been your experience in dealing with others' grief in the workplace?

12.5 ELECTRONIC COMMUNICATIONS

With the 21st century came a burst of new technologies advancing communication capabilities globally—wireless Internet, cell phones with cameras, text messaging, web conferencing, and others as discussed in earlier chapters. Even the Federal Bureau of Investigation, some police and fire departments, and the Coast Guard are using Twitter and YouTube, embracing social media for outreach and public relations.[13,14] These tools help them recruit and make online connections with people. They can also speed up the process of disseminating information (regarding, for example, missing children, wanted criminals, major traffic accidents, bomb threats, fires, and explosions).

Technology has made information readily available and communication easier across boundaries of time zones and great distances. However, the use of communications technologies has brought a new set of etiquette problems.

The following incidents portray only a few of the common blunders. Have you ever been guilty of any of these?

- The person who makes or answers cell phone calls in front of other meeting attendees, making them wait until he or she finishes talking
- The person who leaves excessively long voice mail messages or sends unnecessarily long e-mails
- The person whose voice mail or e-mail indicates he or she will respond shortly and doesn't
- The people who roll their eyes with a "here we go again" look before suddenly realizing they are in a videoconference and in full view of the monitor

Your fellow employees, supervisors, and customers are busy people, and it's good etiquette to be considerate of their time. Here are four ways to do this:

- Write e-mails that are brief and to the point.
- Use a voice mail greeting that tells people clearly and directly where you are and what they need to know to get in contact with you or leave a message.
- Plan voice mail messages before you leave them.
- Use the communications technology your recipient prefers.

> " *Technological progress is like an axe in the hands of a pathological criminal.*
> —Albert Einstein, physicist "

Ethics CONNECTION

To help its 65,000 worldwide employees become more aware of actions that can be unethical or inappropriate, Cisco Systems recently rewrote its code of conduct, making it easier to understand. It also created "Ethics Idol," a take-off of "American Idol" and placed it on its intranet. The training module presents various employee situations (for example, with clients), some of which may be ethically questionable. Employees vote and can then see how their votes compare to their coworkers' votes. The purpose is to encourage employees to raise concerns. Apparently, it's working. Employees are asking questions and seeking ethical and behavioral guidance.[15]

1. Have you ever worked anywhere that had a code of conduct? If so, were the guidelines easy to understand? What kinds of behaviors did the code cover?

2. Without a written code of conduct, what actions within a company do you think might create problems for you and other employees?

Use the same ethical standards, communication correctness, and respect for others' time in your communication technologies as you do in other interactions. For example, employees are acting inappropriately when they send personal messages over the company e-mail or fax, spend excessive time on personal telephone calls, or violate confidentiality of information they receive through computer usage.

Just as communications technologies are constantly changing, so are etiquette and protocol rules governing them. Make a concerted effort to stay on top of these changes, and be understanding of others.

Telephone Etiquette

As an employee, you portray the image of your company each time you use the telephone for a business purpose. Effective human relations and etiquette are just as important on the telephone as in person.

The suggestions in Figure 12.4[16] can help you present the best possible impression for your company and do an efficient job at the same time.

> **KeyPoint**
> You represent the company each time you answer the telephone at work. Your voice and attitude should present a friendly and professional image.

Figure 12.4

Tips for using the telephone.

- Answer promptly, on the first ring if possible, using a friendly, enthusiastic voice.
- On an outside line, give your company name. On an inside line, use your first and last names in answering instead of the company name.
- If you're answering for someone else, identify the office and then explain that you are answering for the expected person and add "May I help you?"
- Transfer calls only when necessary and with permission.
- When the caller asks for someone you don't know, politely ask for more information, such as the person's department.
- If you must place someone on hold, ask the person to whom you're talking for permission to do so.
- If you have calls on hold and must interrupt a call to answer, give the caller the option of holding, calling back, or being called back.
- If the requested party is busy, courteously explain and offer the caller the option of waiting on the line or being called back.
- If the desired person is out, politely explain and ask whether someone else can help or whether the caller would like to leave a name and number.
- In taking messages, have a pad and pen handy, request the information courteously, verify spelling of unusual names, and repeat the number.
- In ending calls, graciously thank the party for calling and say goodbye.

Your voice and manner should be professional, efficient, and friendly. Cultivate a good telephone personality—be alert, and keep a smile in your voice. Speak clearly and distinctly, and greet the caller pleasantly. Use the caller's name, treat every call as important, be tactful, apologize for errors or delays, take time to be helpful, and say "please," "thank you," and "you're welcome."

Call-Waiting Etiquette   The call-waiting feature on your telephone signals you while you are on the phone that another call is coming in. Except in emergencies, etiquette requires you to give the first caller your complete attention. Politely excuse yourself for a moment and check with the second caller. Once you've determined that no emergency exists, politely ask the second caller to call back or offer to return the call yourself, stating when you will be free.

Voice Mail Etiquette   The best advice in using voice mail is to leave a brief straightforward message about your reason for calling and the information you desire. Include your name (and its spelling if necessary), your company, and your phone number. Use a friendly, professional tone of voice and speak confidently, slowly, and clearly. If you are calling with a negative message, rather than leaving the message, ask for a call back by a specific time.

Cell Phone and Text Messaging Etiquette   Many workers must use their cell phones and text messaging in conducting their work, particularly when they have meetings outside the office. To be a considerate user of these technologies, consider the following prohibitions:

- Don't create danger for yourself or others (by texting while driving, for instance).
- Don't ignore the people you're with.
- Don't disturb people around you. Keep at least ten feet away from others and speak quietly and briefly.
- Don't discuss sensitive, personal subjects in front of others.
- Don't have an offensive ringtone (for example, loud, disturbing music).

Specific etiquette guidelines during meetings include setting your cell phone to silent or vibrate mode and letting others know at the beginning of the meeting that you may have to step out to take a call. If you are presenting or chairing the meeting, try holding your calls until after the meeting.

Using your cell phone quietly while waiting for an appointment or meeting is usually acceptable, but be prepared to say "gotta go" and hang up immediately once the person you are seeing is available.

E-Mail Etiquette

Two areas of concern for employers regarding e-mail are employees' personal use of it on company time and inappropriate e-mail content that may cause competitive or legal complications. E-mail may be a popular form of communication, but it's not a very private one, and messages can be intercepted or in

Technology CONNECTION

The tide is turning on rude cell phone users. Business patrons, including restaurant-goers, are rebelling and asking for cell phone free zones, much like no smoking sections. With sensitivity to their needs, the Brooklyn Café in Atlanta installed a red antique telephone booth, brought from the streets of London, as a conversation haven for cell phone users.[17] And at the request of commuters, Amtrak added a Quiet Car to each of its trains in the Northeast Corridor. These cars are free and clear of cellular and any other electronic sounds.[18]

1. What do you think about this trend? Would you be willing to use an enclosed phone booth to make your personal calls?

2. Why do you think this situation has become such an issue? In what other ways could the problem be solved?

3. Are you sensitive to the feelings of others when using your cell phone? Discuss your thoughts on this subject.

4. Have you been in a situation—perhaps at a movie or café—where someone's cell phone ring and/or conversation was a serious annoyance? What would you suggest as a possible solution to the problem?

some way compromised. A good rule of thumb is not to send anything by e-mail that you wouldn't want to see posted on an office bulletin board.

The following etiquette guidelines (in addition to those discussed in earlier chapters) can help you use e-mail in ways that are considerate of the recipients:

1. Reply promptly, using proper salutations, such as "Dear Robert" or "Hello, Susan."

2. Refrain from using emoticons, those little facial-expression symbols in e-mails, as most people find them annoying and unprofessional.

3. Don't write anything in all capital letters, which is the on-screen equivalent of yelling and is inconsiderate.

4. Avoid using slang, abbreviations, or acronyms that may be confusing to other people.

5. Re-read your message to make sure that it sounds professional and is clear, correct, concise, complete, and courteous.

6. Never express anger or other strong emotions in an e-mail or use it to convey bad news.

7. Write about just one subject. If you have another subject, write another e-mail.

8. Use "thank you" appropriately; that is, when someone has already done something. Using it when you've just asked for a favor, for example, appears that you are assuming the recipient will do as you wish.

9. Don't forward jokes, chain letters, and other such e-mails to others.

10. If you create and use a signature file for e-mailing, limit its use to e-mails you compose and send. Normally, leave it off replies to save everyone's paper, time, and patience.

11. Exercise discretion in your out-of-office message by omitting extraneous and personal details.

12. Know and follow your company's policies on e-mail transmissions.

Virtual Meeting Etiquette

In the workplace, many technologies help form the virtual office, as discussed in Chapter 4. According to Wainhouse Research,[19] virtual meetings now outnumber in-person meetings. Teleconferencing is the most familiar of these meetings, while web conferencing is the most popular one because of the flexibility it offers.

While virtual meetings may save money and time, they create whole new areas of etiquette to remember. Just as most face-to-face meetings begin with shaking hands, virtual meetings have their own etiquette for introductions and other etiquette standards.

Different virtual meeting technologies require different etiquette. According to the Emily Post Institute, etiquette rules for sound and camera technologies include speaking clearly and distinctly and making eye contact with the camera and with other participants. Don't speak over people or leave the room unless absolutely necessary. All formats require that you turn off cell phones, PDAs, and watch alarms.

Figure 12.5 provides additional etiquette guidelines for virtual meetings.

KeyPoint
Virtual meeting etiquette includes speaking clearly and distinctly, making eye contact with the camera and with other participants, and turning off cell phones, PDAs, and watch alarms.

● **Figure 12.5**

Virtual meeting etiquette guidelines.

Teleconferencing

- State your name and introduce each participant by name, title, and location.
- Limit background motion and sounds.
- Avoid interrupting.

Web Conferencing

- Write clearly, use a large font and brief/clear language, and proofread before sending.
- Listen carefully; pay attention to your meeting.
- Limit graphics; keep presentation materials to a manageable size.
- Limit chatter and note passing.

Videoconferencing

- Dress appropriately. Avoid white, black, plaids, stripes, or busy prints.

Workplace Surveillance

Workplace surveillance, although not new, has taken on new methods and meanings that warrant some discussion. Gadgets and sensors (such as small or hidden cameras, listening bugs or microphones, detectors/taps on phones, and security monitors) are being used to look at, listen to, or track workers. Employee abuse of e-mail has prompted employers to begin using systems that can read, track, and archive all company e-mail records. They can also monitor your text messages and the web sites you visit. Advances in global positioning systems (GPSs) tracking help some companies track their company vehicles' movements—and the driver—in very close detail. The availability of such devices should remind you of the importance of following established guidelines within your organization.

Employers have many reasons for exercising workplace surveillance. These include competition; protection of proprietary information; protection against hackers, viruses, or other intruders; and maintenance of a safe working environment.[20]

As discussed in the Jump Start of this chapter, most companies agree that employers have the right to monitor employee use of communications technologies at work. The same survey cited in the Jump Start found that 72 percent of them actually do track or monitor Internet use, 70 percent computer use, 57 percent e-mail use, and 56 percent telephone use.[21]

Be sure you understand your employer's policies regarding the use of e-mail and other communications technologies. Some employers ask employees to sign a statement at the time of employment agreeing to surveillance policies.

> **KeyPoint**
> Employers may use workplace surveillance because of competition; protection of proprietary information; protection against hackers, viruses, or other intruders; and maintenance of a safe working environment.

Ask Yourself...

1. How do you handle the overload of messages occurring in your life? What suggestions can you make that might be helpful to others?

2. Which real-time communication method would you prefer using for your meetings? Why?

3. How do you feel about workplace surveillance? What problems do you see for the future, if any? What suggestions can you make to avoid problems in the future?

KEY TERMS

workplace etiquette

professional presence

assertiveness

mentor

CHAPTER SUMMARY

Etiquette, acting appropriately in social and business situations, is becoming ever more important in business for many reasons, including changes in technology, growth of the global economy, more diversity, and the increasing use of teams and group decision making. Etiquette involves following rules and using courtesy. What is appropriate will depend to a certain extent on where, when, and with whom the interaction occurs.

How well you practice etiquette depends on your behavior. Assertive behavior will bring you the best results.

Appearance is an important form of etiquette because it communicates respect for the situation and the people involved. Following basic rules of table etiquette can make business meals more relaxed and enjoyable and may also improve your professional opportunities. Using etiquette in making introductions and introducing yourself will help put people at ease and show them proper respect. Never swear at work.

Effective customer relations can make or break a business. Remember that to customers, you are the company.

Associate relations are important. Networking and mentoring can help your professional development if you use your network appropriately and treat your mentor with respect. Discretion and courtesy should be your guidelines in participating in office politics. Dealing with competition and others' grief is a part of associate relations.

Many technologies have helped make our work lives easier yet more complex, and etiquette is important.

Most companies agree that employers have the right to monitor employee use of communications technologies at work. Be sure you understand your employer's policies regarding the use of e-mail and other communications technologies.

REVIEW

1. Why do many business experts believe that knowledge of etiquette is more important than ever today?

2. List three basic guidelines for table manners.

3. Name two points to be remembered in making introductions.

4. List at least one etiquette guideline for correct use of each communication technology discussed in this chapter.

5. How can you use networking, mentoring, and office politics to help your career? Why must you be careful when using them?

6. Explain how assertive behaviors can help you.

7. Discuss two uses of technology that require users to exercise caution.

CRITICAL THINKING

1. Think of times when someone showed poor manners toward you. What rule of etiquette was violated? How did the person's action make you feel? How did you respond to it?

2. Name some examples of etiquette in your daily life or work.

3. Name some instances of workplace surveillance of which you are aware through personal experience, the media, or friends. Do you see any potential problems? What do you think about this potential problem, and how would you solve it?

4. Are you a member of a professional network? If so, describe it. How do you use it? How do you contribute to it?

CASE STUDIES

In small groups, analyze the following situations:

1 **Invitation to Go Elsewhere**   "So, what do you want?" Marge gruffly asked the elderly man on the other side of the counter at the ice cream shop.
"Well, I'm not sure yet," Howard said, as he looked at his grandson and granddaughter, who were trying to make up their minds. Marge rolled her eyes and frowned, went off to visit with a coworker, and ignored the group.
"Why won't she get our ice cream?" asked the granddaughter after making up her mind. "Did we do something wrong?"
"No, sweetie," said Howard. "I think we'll just go to the ice cream shop down the street."

1. Was Marge displaying effective customer relations? Explain your answer.

2. How should Marge have behaved?

3. What has Marge cost her company?

2 **Telephone Tales** Martin had just received an invitation for his band to perform at a community event next week and was busy telling his buddy, Jose, about it on the phone. Things were slow in the plant, and Martin was bored. As Martin was telling the story, the other line blinked. He picked up the phone and mumbled quickly, "Rock Mountain Chemicals."

The caller on the other end of the line didn't speak at first, and Martin said, "Hello?" again in an impatient tone.

The caller, Martinez, said, "Oh, is this Rock Mountain Chemicals?"

"Yep, that's what I said. What do you need?" Tom said impatiently.

"Is Ms. Bailey in?" asked Martinez.

"Yeah, hang on," Martin replied and then switched back to his friend. "Sorry about that, Jose. I had to catch the other line. Let me tell you what we're going to play..." When he went back to the caller's line ten minutes later, it was dead.

Later, the president of the company called Martin into her office. "Martin," she said, "I'm going to have to write you up. My best client was trying to reach Ms. Bailey and finally gave up in frustration. If we lose that contract, our business is ruined."

1. What telephone etiquette rules did Martin violate?

2. How should Martin have handled the telephone call?

3. What might Martin's behavior have cost the business?

HUMAN RELATIONS IN ACTION

1. In two groups, go online and find two representatives from a local company to visit your class to discuss one or more topics in this chapter. These persons may, for example, discuss the company guidelines for use of electronic technologies. Or, a classmate may know someone who works for a multinational corporation and would be willing to share some valuable work experiences with the class. Alternatively, invite a worker from another country to share the customs of his or her culture. In pairs, properly introduce one another to the speaker. Prepare written thank you notes to the speaker indicating your grasp of sound business etiquette.

2. As a group, hold a mock networking meeting to practice your etiquette skills. You may want to designate certain individuals as "titled" or "dignitaries" or as different levels of management in your company. Participants should dress appropriately. A sit-down meal would add an excellent dimension if appropriate. Perhaps a short test of those skills would be appropriate.

For additional resources, refer to the web site for this text:
www.cengage.com/management/dalton

RESOURCES

1. Society for Human Resource Management. (2005, January). "Workplace Privacy Poll Findings."

2. NECN.com health. (2009, May 11). Swine flu awareness and etiquette. Retrieved from: http://www.necn.com/Boston/Health/2009/05/10/Swine-flu-awareness-and/1242008291.html

3. Kranz, Gene. (1998, November 16). Presentation at San Jacinto College, Pasadena, TX.

4. Charlesworth, Edward, and Ronald Nathan. (1980). *Stress Management*. Tallahassee, FL: Anhinga Press.

5. Doing business in Hong Kong. (nd). Kwintessential. Available http://www.kwintessential.co.uk/etiquette/doing-business-in-hondkong.html. Retrieved January 11, 2009.

6. Bixler, Susan and Dugan, Lisa S. (1991). *5 Steps to Professional Presence*. New York: G.P. Putnam's Sons.

7. Lorenz, Mary. (2008, July 15). Do you dress for the corner office or the mail room? Careerbuilder.com. [on-line]. Available: http://www.careerbuilder.com/Article/CB-930-The-Workplace-Do-You-Dress-for-the-Cor.... Retrieved June 26, 2006.

8. Murago, Greg. (2009, April 3). "Does the queen get a hug? Yes, experts say." *Houston Chronicle*, E1,9.

9. Tyler, Kathryn. (2008, January). "Generation gaps." [on-line]. *HR Magazine*. Society for Human Resource Management. Available: http://www.shrm.org/hrmagazine/articles/0108/0108Agenda_Training.asp. Retrieved January 9, 2009.

10. Associated Press. (2009, June 22). "Camaraderie alive and well." *Houston Chronicle*, B6.

11. Competition: Is it helping or hurting your career? (2009). Robert Half International. [on-line] Available: http://ca.hotjobs.yahoo.com/career-articles-competition_is_it_helping_or_hurting_your_career

12. "Responding to grief and loss." (nd). Swedish Family Medical Residence-First Hill. Available: http://www.fammed.washington.edu/network/sfm/grief.htm. Retrieved February 7, 2009.

13. Reed, Allen. (2009, June 23). "A new way of networking." *Houston Chronicle*, B1,5.

14. Antlfinger, Carrie. (Associated Press). (2009, April 14). "Tweeter lengthens arm of law." *Houston Chronicle*, A6.

15. Wright, Aliah D. (2008, September 8). "Cisco introduces 'ethics idol' to enhance ethics culture." [on-line] Society for Human Resource Management. Available: http://www.shrm.org/hrdisciplines/ethics/articles/Pages/CiscoIntroduces'EthicsIdol'.asps. Retrieved April 14, 2009.

16. Southwestern Bell Telephone Company. (nd). UPDATE: Telephone Manners—A guide for using the telephone.

17. Sims, Amy. (2003, July 23). Businesses encourage mobile manners. *Fox News*. Available: http://www.foxnews.co/story/0%2C2933%2C92660%C00.html. Retrieved August 20, 2004.

18. Charny, Ben. (2001, November 16). Shhh? Cell phone carriers call for etiquette. CNET News.com. Available: http://news.cnet.com/Shhh-Cell-phone-carriers-call-for-etiquette/2100-1033_3-275931.html. Retrieved August 10, 2001.

19. Wooley, David R. (nd). Real-time conferencing: An independent guide to software & services enabling real-time communication. Available: http://thinkofit.com/webconf/realtime.htm. Retrieved August 13, 2004.

20. Society for Human Resource Management. (2005, January). "Workplace Privacy Poll Findings."

21. Ibid.

ORGANIZATION SAVVY:
STRUCTURE, CULTURE, AND CLIMATE

OBJECTIVES

After studying this chapter, you should be able to:

13.1 Discuss what organizational structures are and why they exist.

13.2 Explain who has authority in an organization and how authority originates.

13.3 Describe how organizational structure affects communication.

13.4 Identify signs that signal future organizational changes.

13.5 Explain corporate cultures and climates and their importance.

Jump Start

Nortel, founded in 1895 to supply telecommunications equipment for Canada's fledgling telephone system, presently provides communication solutions to companies in over 150 countries worldwide and employs over 32,000 people. Lately the company has been struggling to find an organizational structure that works, having already restructured five times in the past decade. In 2009 the corporation announced yet another restructuring to help it emerge from creditor protection. Nortel has cut costs by laying off employees and by freezing both salaries and hiring. The company also plans to decentralize corporate functions and focus on vertical units aimed at enterprise customers and service providers.[1-3]

- How would you feel if you worked for an organization that restructured this often?
- What do you think will happen if Nortel does not make changes?

13.1   WHY ORGANIZATIONS NEED STRUCTURE

Structure is the relationship among parts. In the case of a business or other organization, structure helps the organization divide its work and delegate tasks. Without structure, employees do not know what their jobs and responsibilities are, which can result in frustration, low morale, conflict, and other human relations problems. An effective structure also helps people avoid duplication of work and delays that occur when work must be reviewed by numerous layers of management.

> " *No institution can possibly survive if it needs geniuses or supermen to manage it. It must be organized in such a way as to be able to get along under a leadership composed of average human beings.*
>
> —Peter F. Drucker, American management guru "

Besides the structure of an organization you can see, another extremely important structural component you can't see exists in an organization: its culture and climate. No single correct way exists to structure an organization, and organizations have a variety of cultures and climates. These aspects affect productivity, quality, employee morale, customer satisfaction, and, ultimately, the success of the entire business. Because of this, many organizations study their structure on an ongoing basis and make changes to boost efficiency. Increasingly, companies are experimenting with radical new ideas concerning structure and culture in order to spark innovation and allow a more rapid response to changing market demands.

An understanding of organizational structure and culture will help you function more effectively within any type of organization and understand and adjust to organizational changes. Organizational structure greatly impacts organization and human relations systems, dictating managerial style, leadership, power, protocol, goals, diversity, decision making, teamwork, conflict management, and ethics. Likewise, organizational structure affects learning and innovation skills as well as life and career skills and is a part of your response in the 21st century organization.

Ask Yourself...

1. Describe the structure of an organization to which you belong, such as your workplace, your school, or a volunteer group.
2. How did you learn about the structure of the organization?
3. What would happen if there were no structure? Why?

13.2 AUTHORITY AND HOW IT ORIGINATES

An organization's structure defines who has authority. Originally, organizational structure developed around the *chain of command*. The chain of command is the direction in which authority is exercised, and policies and other information are communicated to lower levels. Authority begins at the top, and each level gives commands, delegates authority, and passes information to lower levels. Information and requests beginning in lower levels of the organization follow the chain upward. The idea of the chain of command developed in the military and is prevalent in today's organizations. It forms the classic pyramidal hierarchy, illustrated in Figure 13.1.

Employees and members of an organization must respect the chain of command and exercise great caution in skipping levels. Because organizations differ on when it is acceptable for you to skip levels of the chain of command, you need to learn the practice in your organization. Such respect and caution will reduce the potential for human relations problems. One of the few occasions when you can safely ignore the chain is in emergencies or when time is crucial and your immediate supervisor is not present. You should also skip levels in the chain of command if your superiors are engaging in illegal activities or violating the organization's ethics policies.

A variety of new structures have developed as organizations have become larger and more complex. The basic *pyramidal hierarchy* no longer meets all organizational needs. However, no one specific type of organizational structure is best. The most efficient structure depends on the size of the organization, whether it provides a service or produces a product, and the number of different products or services it offers.

The formal structure can be organized by function (what each department does), geographic area, customer, or product. Large, complex organizations may use a variety of these structures, depending on their needs. Figure 13.2 represents various ways of structuring an organization.

KeyPoint
Failing to follow the chain of command can be hazardous to your career.

KeyPoint
Organizational structures are changing to fit the complex needs of modern organizations.

In The News[4,5]

As General Motors (GM) struggled financially, it reported to Congress in December 2008 that it would restructure by focusing on its four core brands—Chevrolet, Cadillac, Buick, and GMC—that account for 83 percent of current sales. In spring 2009, it discontinued the Pontiac brand. By 2010 GM expects to reduce the number of dealer locations by 42 percent. GM intends to have the right number of brands, sold by the right number of dealers, in the right locations to obtain maximum profitability for GM and the retailer network.

1. How do you think restructuring will affect current employees of GM and its dealerships?

2. Why do you think it's risky for an auto manufacturer to have so many different brands of its cars?

Figure 13.1

Chain of command.

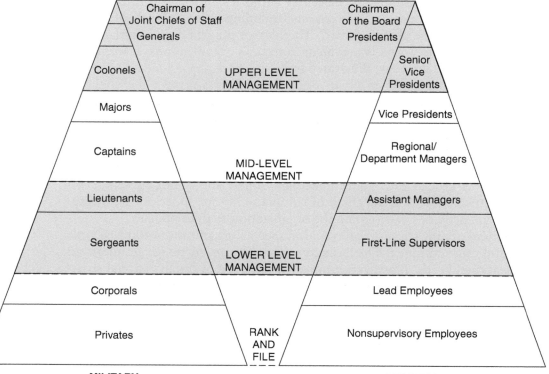

Figure 13.2

Organizational structure examples.

Function-oriented organizational structure

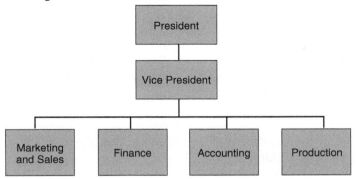

Geographical organizational structure

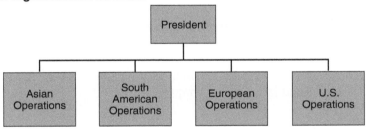

Customer-oriented organizational structure

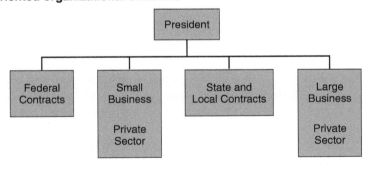

Product-oriented organizational structure

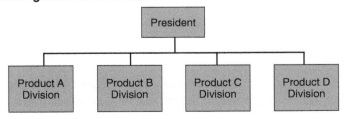

Figure 13.2

Organizational structure examples (continued).

A company using a variety of organizational structures

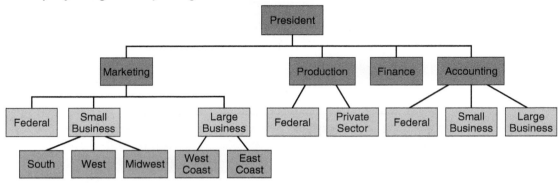

Developing an organizational structure is a complicated process and is a whole study in itself. Complex organizations have developed other structures to enhance organizational effectiveness. Some use a line and staff structure, others use a matrix structure, and still others mix the two. Additionally, organizations are trending toward modular and virtual organizations. These will be explained later in this chapter.

Line and Staff Structure

In the *line and staff structure*, line employees are directly involved in production activities. The staff employees support line employees through advice and counsel on a variety of subjects in their areas of expertise. This support may be in the form of legal, safety, personnel, or computer assistance, or may involve maintenance of equipment or facilities.

Many problems can arise from line and staff relationships. One common complication is that staff members usually have no authority to force line employees to cooperate. Staff people must frequently rely on their skills of persuasion to convince line workers that staff instructions should be followed. For this reason, some staff members are given *functional authority*—the authority to make decisions in their area of expertise and to overrule line decisions.

Matrix Structure

Matrix structures are frequently used by organizations that manage many projects. Therefore, a matrix structure is sometimes called a project structure. A *matrix structure* uses groups of people with expertise in their individual areas that are temporarily assigned full or part time to a project from other areas of the organization. The project has its own supervisor and can last a few weeks or a few years.

For instance, an engineering firm may pull together a group of engineers to oversee the design and construction of a new plant and dissolve the group as

Technology CONNECTION[6]

Web 2.0 technology is finding its way into the workplace. Increasing productivity by improving communication and global collaboration is driving this trend. Larger companies are especially attracted to the ability to personalize messages.

For instance, many companies now operate intranets. Intranets work like the Internet but are available only to the members of an organization. Information can then be distributed to employees by using web-based portals. Portals are gateways through which employees can gain information they need to perform their jobs. Portals can be designed so that employees are able to freely access only the information they need. The sales manager, for instance, would have access to all sales information for his or her group while individual sales persons could access only their own data. Employees can share information and receive training through the use of Web 2.0 technology such as blogs (a site run by one person who posts information, allowing others to add commentary), wikis (database pages that can be edited live), online video (video watched on the Intranet), podcasts (digital audio or video files that can be downloaded for later use), and RSS feeds (web feed formats used to alert subscribers of updates to web sites of interest).

1. Have you ever used Web 2.0 technology in a work setting? If so, describe your experience. Did you find it useful?

2. Are you more comfortable communicating via technology or face to face? Explain your reasoning.

soon as the plant is finished. The employees then return to their original supervisors, and the plant continues operation under its own management. Some companies utilize the matrix structure to develop products or operate in markets where decisions need to be made quickly. These groups are given the power to make decisions to speed their work, and they may be assigned experts on a number of fronts.

Matrix structures can cause difficulty. The individual assigned to head the temporary team may have no formal authority or control over the rest of the group, and power struggles may erupt as a result. If you find yourself in this type of situation, the best approach is to discuss it with the person who delegated the project to you and ask for formal authority. Someone higher in the chain of command than the participants should instruct them to cooperate and emphasize that they will be appraised on their participation and performance.

Modular Organization

In a *modular organization* a company keeps all the business activities it can perform faster, better, and more cheaply than other organizations and outsources its remaining business activities.[7] The National Aeronautical and Space

Administration (NASA) uses a modular organization. In 2008, the space shuttle workforce included approximately 15,000 contractors and 1,700 civil servants in locations across the country.[8]

The advantage of this type of organization for NASA is that it pays only for services or equipment actually needed. One disadvantage is that some loss of control occurs. Additionally, suppliers can sometimes become competitors. For example, URS Corporation, a long-time contractor for NASA, has produced, along with another firm, the winning design for New Mexico's Spaceport America. This spaceport will serve as the primary operating base for the Virgin Galactic suborbital spaceliner. NASA will no longer be the only organization with the ability to launch space vehicles on the North American continent.[9,10]

Virtual Organization

In contrast to modular organizations, *virtual organizations* are part of a network in which companies share costs, skills, capabilities, and markets. Members of a virtual organization may come together to satisfy the needs of a specific customer and, when the job is finished, go their separate ways.[11] Relationships with customers tend to be more fluid and less stable than those formed in the modular organization. This organizational arrangement, however, is not without its disadvantages. The quality of work product or deliverables is harder to control. Unless work agreements are carefully defined beforehand, opinions on what a quality work product is will likely differ. Additionally, coordinating the work of independent organizations can be a challenge. Because virtual teams form and dissolve quickly, the project manager may have to develop working relationships repeatedly as virtual team members change.[12]

Distribution of Authority

As organizations grow in size and complexity, their leaders find that making every decision has become impossible. Company presidents with thousands of employees cannot possibly make every decision and supervise everyone. Additionally, an organization's components may be scattered around the globe, with field teams in remote locations. Decision-making methods have had to change, and authority has had to be delegated to lower levels.

Two forms of authority distribution are common. An organization is said to be *centralized* when those high up in the organization closely hold authority and are responsible for making all major decisions. When important decisions are made at a lower level and authority is delegated, the organization is *decentralized*.

Both centralization and decentralization have positive and negative aspects. A centralized purchasing function, for instance, can ensure that quality of supplies remains consistent among locations. Additionally, buyers of large quantities frequently receive discounts. A drawback to centralization is that decision making can be slow and innovation can be difficult. Having to route decisions through several layers of management instead of being able to make and act on decisions immediately can add costly time to the process.

KeyPoint
Modular and virtual structures allow organizations to keep overhead costs low by paying only for the manpower needed.

> " How do you induce innovation? Simple: Decentralize! What's the problem with decentralization? It almost never works.
>
> —Tom Peters, author and business guru "

Weak managers who may not have the maturity or expertise to make effective decisions can be a problem in a decentralized organization. However, to create the type of innovative, creative, fast-paced global company this new millennium requires, organizations must work collaboratively and draw on the strengths of the entire employee base. The decision-making capability needs to be delegated up, over, around, and throughout the organization.

Span of Control

The authority given to a supervisor varies. The number of employees that can be supervised effectively by one person generally ranges from about 12 to 21, but this varies based on the industry and type of work. More people can be successfully supervised at one time if the employees are capable of working independently and their tasks are similar. However, the higher up in the organization you go, the more complex jobs become, and the fewer people you can supervise.

The number of people that an individual can supervise is called the *span of control*. The span may be either tall or flat as shown in Figure 13.3.

Figure 13.3

The span of control can be tall or flat.

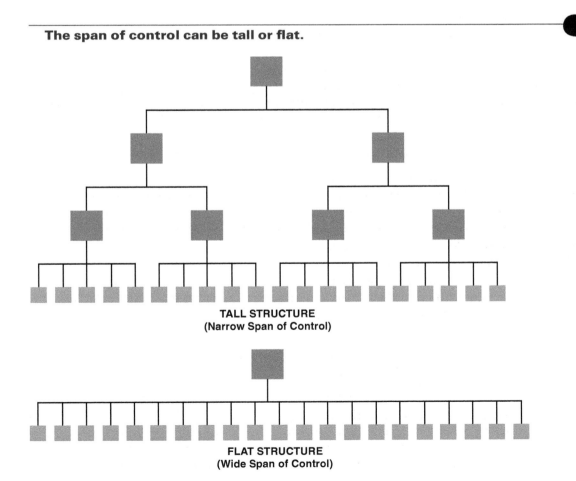

TALL STRUCTURE
(Narrow Span of Control)

FLAT STRUCTURE
(Wide Span of Control)

Not having the appropriate span of control can sometimes result in behavioral or performance problems. Employees may feel unnoticed. Good performance may be unrewarded and bad performance may go uncorrected.

One way a supervisor can broaden his or her span is by delegating authority to others within the group. Broadening the span can lessen red tape and increase morale. Individuals allowed to perform higher-level tasks feel heightened job satisfaction. Using "lead" employees to oversee the work of others might expand the span of control. These could be senior-level individuals who would continue to perform their work but who would also monitor the performance of others. While lead people generally do not have the authority to discipline or appraise performance, they are given authority to direct workflow and give orders.

For your delegation of authority to be successful, you must communicate fully. The person receiving the authority must understand the new role and be willing to act accordingly. Likewise, the other employees must be informed of what is expected of them and of the person receiving the authority. Without this communication, serious human relations problems can develop. If you are the one being given such authority, ask your supervisor whether coworkers are aware of your new responsibilities. If they are not, suggest that your supervisor inform them. If that does not happen, you should probably communicate this information to your coworkers as early as possible in your new role.

Ethics CONNECTION

In order to improve systems and processes, managers look for problems and bottlenecks. In some organizational cultures, however, striving for excellence turns into a blame game and employees invest time and energy in avoiding or deflecting fault. They develop alibis, prepare back-up explanations, and are always trying to cover themselves. The blame game only makes one person feel better by making others feel worse, destroying motivation and replacing it with antagonism and anger.

Other organizational cultures, while still holding employees accountable, focus on what has gone right. These cultures uncover and recognize good work, leaving employees free to concentrate on what they were hired to do in the first place. This focus ultimately energizes employees and increases motivation.[13]

1. Have you ever worked in an organization where coworkers played the blame game? Was it a pleasant place to work? Why or why not?

2. How can you slow the blame game mentality in an organization?

Ask Yourself...

1. Do you think organizations will begin to use virtual organizational structures more often? Why or why not?

2. Think back to a job you've had. How many people reported to one supervisor? Was this arrangement effective? Why or why not?

13.3   HOW STRUCTURE AFFECTS COMMUNICATION

Organizational structures frequently dictate how communication flows so it is important to understand the types of communication present in an organization as well as their upsides and downsides.

Formal communication, communication that flows up or down the formal organizational structure, is controlled by the chain of command. This type of communication varies in (1) the direction it flows, (2) whether it's one-way or two-way, and (3) its chance of distortion.

In any organization, communication will flow downward, upward, or horizontally (sideways). *Downward communication* consists of messages that begin at higher levels of the organization and flow downward. Typical forms of downward communication are meetings, memoranda, policy statements, newsletters, manuals, handbooks, telephone conversations, and e-mail.

Downward communication can become distorted for a variety of reasons. Long messages not in writing tend to be forgotten or misinterpreted. Furthermore, sometimes so many messages are received that a communications overload results. For example, the employee receiving 50 e-mails a day may not be able to read all of them carefully.

Upward communication consists of messages that begin in the lower levels of the organization and go to higher levels. Upward communication can be in the form of memos, grievances (presented formally or informally), meetings, attitude surveys, or suggestion systems.

Upward communication can also become distorted. Frequently, subordinates who must deliver unpleasant messages misrepresent situations for fear the receiver may blame the messenger who delivers the bad news. When you must talk about a problem that no one wants to talk about, Michael Warshaw of *Fast Company* magazine suggests the following:[14]

1. Spend time identifying the problem. Explore your motivation for bringing up the issue. Imagine how others will react.

2. Work to overcome your fear of presenting the problem. Use visualization to assist.

3. Be direct but tactful. Give the listener time to react.

4. Stay with the message. Continue to seek support for your point of view.

Horizontal communication occurs between individuals at the same level in an organization. These messages typically take the form of telephone

> " *You never really hear the truth from your subordinates until after 10 in the evening.*
> —*Jurgen Schrempp, former CEO of DaimlerChrysler*
>

KeyPoint
Two-way
communication
is effective
because it
provides an
opportunity for
feedback.

conversations, memos, meetings, informal gatherings, texting, or e-mail. Horizontal communications, too, can suffer from distortions whenever messages are not clear, perceptions differ, or attitudes get in the way.

Communication within organizations is either one-way or two-way. *Two-way communication* is one in which feedback is received. Although two-way communication is slower and less orderly than one-way communication, in general it is more accurate. The receiver of the message is able to provide feedback, and the sender is able to evaluate whether the message has been correctly interpreted.

One-way communication takes place with no feedback from the receiver. Examples include memos and videotaped lectures. Although one-way communication can present problems, it is used frequently because it is quick, easy to generate, and orderly. Can you imagine the president of a corporation of thousands of employees attempting to communicate a new benefits program using two-way communication? In addition, one-way communication is less threatening for the sender because no one is present to give negative feedback.

Informal communication is another type of communication that occurs in organizations. This form of communication, the most common type, can either help or hinder an organization's efforts. If you discuss a new company policy with someone in another department, you are using informal communication. Informal communication does not follow the formal channels of communication but travels through a channel often called the grapevine. The *grapevine* is an informal, person-to-person means of circulating information. It serves several functions for both employees and management. Many managers have learned to respect and even use the grapevine because of its speed. However, because of its unreliability, it must be used with caution. As an employee or organization member, you can satisfy some of your social needs through the grapevine, clarify formal orders, and use it as a release for your feelings and concerns. When employees feel that upward communication will be threatening, blocked, or ineffective, they frequently turn to the grapevine.

The problem with grapevines is that often messages are distorted, exaggerated, incomplete, or even totally wrong. Grapevines are the primary means for transmitting rumors. The chance of misinterpretation increases with the number of individuals through whom the messages pass. Because downward communication is sometimes ambiguous and upward communication is often nonexistent, rumors too often occur. Such situations are fertile soil for problems in human relations. Grapevines exist in every organization, and you should understand how grapevines work and respect their potential, both good and bad. Be careful that you don't contribute incorrect or inappropriate information to the grapevine. Information can easily be introduced into the grapevine or garbled once it is in, but correcting it is almost impossible.

Figure 13.4 illustrates what you may know from playing the telephone game, in which a message is relayed along a long line of people; by the time the message reaches the end of the telephone line, its content has probably changed quite a bit. The best way to receive a message clearly is to get the message from its original source.

Figure 13.4 ●

Repetition of messages.

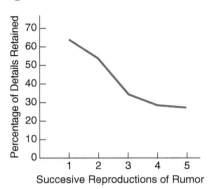

Percentage of Details Retained

Succesive Reproductions of Rumor

> If you reveal your secrets to the wind, you should not blame the wind for revealing them to the trees.
>
> —Kahlil Gibran, writer and artist

Communications authors Barry L. Reece and Rhonda Brandt developed the following guidelines and cautions concerning the grapevine to keep you out of trouble.[15]

• No one can hide from the grapevine, even though it may know only part of the truth. Our reputations are created by the grapevine and are hard to change. Be careful about what information about you makes its way into the grapevine. Watch what you tell others about yourself, choose carefully those with whom you share information, and use discretion in your behavior.

• The message (gossip) of the grapevine tends to be negative. People who consistently communicate negative information about others ultimately become distrusted or shut out. Exercise discretion about information you contribute to the grapevine. Would you want others to know what you said?

• Several grapevine networks operate in every organization. Each one is composed of people who have common experiences and concerns. In a particular network, usually only a few people pass on most of the information and that is usually downward or horizontally. Do you want to be labeled one of these people?

• The role you play in the grapevine will reflect your ethics, decision-making skills, and maturity. Mature people anticipate the consequences of their actions and words. Think about the image that you create of yourself before you participate in grapevine communication.

Ask Yourself...

1. Think of an organization in which you have worked. How was communication handled? How could communication have been improved?

2. What problems can occur if organizations do not formally release information and most of the information comes through the grapevine?

3. Can you name a time when you heard information through the grapevine? How accurate was the information? Were you able to correct inaccurate information?

13.4 WHY STRUCTURES CHANGE

Organizations change for many reasons. Products complete their *life cycles*, meaning they become obsolete and disappear as fresh products enter the market. New markets open and old markets fade away, competition or its lack increases or decreases demand—even personnel changes may necessitate adjustments. To respond to these types of changes, businesses frequently reengineer. ***Business process reengineering*** is the fundamental rethinking and radical redesign of business processes to achieve dramatic improvements in critical, contemporary measures of performance, such as cost, quality, service, and speed.[16]

During the process of reengineering the business system, an organization's structure often has to be modified. Mike Myatt, Chief Strategy Officer of N2growth, says reengineering is needed when a number of the following indicators are present:[17]

- Your revenues, margins, market shares, and/or customer loyalty greatly decline or does not grow.
- You cannot keep or hire talented employees.
- You are currently experiencing or anticipate changes in market conditions that will hurt your business.
- Your intellectual property, products, services, or solutions are outdated.

As our economy becomes increasingly global and technology is changing constantly, the need to reengineer will become more common. In *The Boundaryless Organization: Breaking the Chains of Organizational Structure,* the authors emphasize that today's organizations must learn to adjust quickly, proactively, and creatively to the changing times by sweeping away the boundaries of hierarchy, turf, and geography that they believe get in the way of outstanding business performance. They advocate an open flow of knowledge, ideas, resources, and talents up and down, across, and in and out of the organizational structure, a paradigm shift for success in the 21st century.[18]

So what does this mean for the 21st century worker? It means we can expect to see new ways of getting things done within an organization because there is a limit on how often organizational structures can be changed. In an article entitled "The Limits of Structural Change," authors Brian Smith and Jeffrey Oxman point out that, rather than being given one specific job to do, you may find yourself responsible for process and workflow while performing multiple tasks throughout the day. The speed of change will mean that you will have to be more flexible as you move to different projects; order and structure will be less common in the organization. Sharing knowledge will be critical, and employees will be expected to distribute it to everyone with a need to know.[19]

Workers are becoming increasingly self-managed, choosing with whom they will work. Skill—not position title—will be more important in getting an assignment than position title. Promotions will become less frequent, and individuals will seek out challenging or comfortable roles depending on their needs. Being more proactive and seeking training to maintain or improve marketable skills will be a must.[20]

Ask Yourself...

1. Name three products that have completed their life cycles.

2. Name a product you use that will soon be on the decline of its life cycle. Why is it on the way out?

3. Why can't you afford to say "that's not my job" anymore?

> " *The bottom line for leaders is that if they do not become conscious of the cultures in which they are embedded, those cultures will manage them. Cultural understanding is desirable for all of us, but it is essential to leaders if they are to lead.*
>
> —Edgar Schein, professor, MIT Sloan School of Management "

13.5   THE IMPORTANCE OF CULTURE AND CLIMATE

Organizational culture is defined as the combined beliefs, values, ethics, procedures, and atmosphere of an organization.[21] It's mostly an unspoken mix of the beliefs and values of society at large, the individuals who participate in the organization, and the organization's leaders and founders. The culture determines what goals the organization wants to accomplish and how it will go about accomplishing them. Important to remember is that subcultures may exist in an organization in different departments or functions.

Some organizations have strong values that are expressed, such as the Girl Scouts' "Do a good turn daily," the Boy Scouts' "Be prepared," and Google's "Don't be evil." Other organizations have well-known, although less specifically stated cultures, such as Southwest Airlines' employees having fun with passengers. Other cultural norms may not be as openly communicated but must be learned. Organizations, for instance, may have heroes—people with the beliefs, attitudes, and behaviors that the organization wishes to reinforce. These people with the "right stuff" are identified as role models for employees. Disney Productions, for example, reflects Walt Disney's values.

Barry Phegan, PhD, president, Meridian Group, has identified five levels of an organization's culture.[22] They are as follows:

1. Equipment and Other Physical Objects

   This level of culture defines the dress as well as the structures in which members work and live. This level can be readily observed. For instance

Digital Vision/Getty Images

at Google's corporate headquarters in Mountain View, California, employees work in high-density clusters with three or four staffers sharing spaces with couches and dogs.[23] Paying close attention to this level of culture is vital. Dressing incorrectly or decorating your office in a way that is frowned upon can cause problems. Bringing a dog to work may be perfectly acceptable at Google, for instance, but would get you in trouble in most other organizations.

2. The Systems that Coordinate Equipment

This level includes operating systems, processes, procedures, and methods. One restaurant, for instance, might use a sophisticated computer system in which the server types in the order, which is immediately transmitted to the kitchen for processing. In another restaurant, the server might simply write out a ticket and attach it to a wire in the kitchen. Learning the system when you first enter an organization is important so that you may efficiently accomplish your work. Not only should you pay careful attention to the activity around you, but you should also ask questions to assure you understand the procedures.

3. The Authority Structure that Connects Systems with People

The key aspect of this level is power and control. Authority, competition, organizational structures, markets, information, productivity, and

Global CONNECTION[24]

The founder and president of Cincom Systems Inc., Thomas Nies, has adopted a set of common values based on the foundation of the principles of character, competence, and commitment. Cincom, which provides software for business operations and customer communication, serves thousands of clients on six continents. Headquartered in Cincinnati, Ohio, with offices in every leading country of the world, the company derives half of its revenues from outside the United States.

The company has adopted Don Quixote, from the novel by Miguel de Cervantes written in the 17th century, as its unofficial patron saint. Quixote had values the company wants to promote, such as imagination, compassion, and discipline. He also enjoyed what he did. The company honors 10 percent of its global workforce each year for its commitment to core values. Quixote Club winners get gold diamond rings as well as corporate recognition.

Despite sharing common values, Cincom's policy is to allow local control within the framework of the shared values. Local offices are mostly managed by leaders developed from within that market, which allows the offices to be self-sufficient and self-directed.[25]

1. Don Quixote is Spanish. Do you think it's significant that the "hero" of this company is not American? Why or why not?

2. Why do you think it is difficult for global companies to allow local control?

---

profits are included. Decision making at this level is competitive. Indications of the authority structure include:

- Who has the authority to sign off on purchases?
- Who can hire and fire?
- What is considered good performance and who makes that determination?

Make it a point to learn your organization's power structure. A good place to start is by asking your supervisor what power has been delegated to you. For instance, authorizing a purchase for which you have no authority or ordering a new piece of equipment without permission can lead to trouble.

4. Communication that Connects People

Communication includes listening, understanding, dialogue, relationships, and teamwork. It also includes empathetic forms of decision making, such as consensus and win–win. Things to look for include:

- What is the preferred means of communication? E-mail? Text messages? Instant messages? A phone call? Memos? Verbal updates?

> *Culture is a way of coping with the world by defining it in detail.*
>
> —Malcolm Bradbury, British writer and academic

- How are coworkers and superiors addressed—informally? Mr./Ms./Dr.?
- Do persons in authority have an open door policy, or are you to go through your supervisor before speaking to them? Whom do you need to keep in the loop while communicating?
- Is it permissible to socialize outside of work with a superior?

Rather than acting on how you think communication should be carried out, listen to those around you in the environment and analyze how situations are handled.

5. Experience—Creating Motivation and Trust

This includes feelings such as trust, caring, safety, satisfaction, pride, and engagement. American Express works to create this type of experience with a commitment to service. The company defines that as taking pride in providing world-class service not only to its customers, but also to its employees.[26] The experience a culture produces will be evident as you continue to work in its environment.

Organizational climate, on the other hand, is the environment created by the managerial style and attitudes that pervade an organization.[27] Climates can fluctuate like moods, going from anger and depression to optimism or anxiety. Internal as well as external factors can affect climate. Organization leaders, in particular, set the tone for the climate.[28] The climate, in turn, can affect many things such as productivity and creativity.

The *Charlotte Business Journal,* for instance, reported a panicky climate at Wachovia Plaza after the announcement in September 2008 that Citigroup Inc. would buy Wachovia Corporation's banking operations. Many employees reported being concerned about the future of their jobs as well as of their friends' and coworkers'. One employee described the environment as everyone walking around like zombies.[29]

Ask Yourself...

1. Describe the differences in culture of two different organizations with which you have been affiliated. Which did you prefer and why?

2. How can you learn about a culture that is not explained in writing?

3. What might happen if you do not quickly master the culture at your workplace?

KEY TERMS

chain of command

pyramidal hierarchy

line and staff structure

functional authority

matrix structure

modular organization

virtual organization

centralized organization

decentralized organization

span of control

formal communication

downward communication

upward communication

horizontal communication

two-way communication

one-way communication

informal communication

grapevine

life cycle

business process reengineering

organizational culture

organizational climate

CHAPTER SUMMARY

Structure is the relationship among parts. Organizations require structure to arrange their workload and allow smooth operations. Organizational structure originally developed around the chain of command, the direction in which authority and communication are utilized within the organization.

Organizational structure can take many forms besides the classical pyramidal hierarchy. Work can be organized according to function, geography, customer, product, or a mixture of these. Some structures, such as the matrix and line and staff structure, while offering advantages, are multifaceted and can cause difficulties for the employees involved. Complexity of today's organizations has ushered in the modular and virtual organizations.

Authority in an organization can be either centralized or decentralized. Each option has advantages and disadvantages. An organization must also consider the most effective span of control for its particular situation. The span of control indicates how many employees a supervisor manages.

Communication in an organization can be either formal or informal. Formal communication can travel upward, downward, or horizontally and can be either one-way or two-way. Each type of communication and flow has its positive and negative aspects. Informal communication ranges from conversations among employees to rumors that travel through the grapevine.

Organizational structures often change as organizations go through product life cycles, technology upgrades, market fluctuations, and business process engineering. Understanding why structural changes are needed can help you thrive in the organization.

Lastly, organizations vary in both culture and climate. Your ability to identify key components of a culture is vital to your ability to work effectively within it.

REVIEW

1. What is the purpose of organizational structure and why is it important?

2. What is the hierarchical pyramid and where are its roots?

3. Describe the types of structures used by businesses today.

4. How is power assigned in an organization?

5. How many employees can be supervised effectively at one time?

6. What is formal communication and in which directions can it flow?

7. What factors decrease the effectiveness of formal communication?

8. What is informal communication and what are the dangers of the grapevine?

9. Why might an organization's structure change?

10. What are the components of organizational culture?

11. What is organizational climate?

CRITICAL THINKING

1. Should all firms attempt to decentralize authority? Why or why not?

2. Why are we usually more willing to accept authority of those above us than those at our level or below?

3. Have you ever received an inaccurate message through the grapevine? What happened as a result of this misinformation?

4. Identify a company in your community and describe where you believe it is in its product life cycle.

5. Think of several organizations with which you are familiar. Describe their culture.

6. Has the climate changed in an organization to which you belong? How? Why?

CASE STUDIES

In small groups, analyze the following situations.

1 **Nowhere to Run, Nowhere to Hide** As restaurant manager, Gina is responsible for the performance of her team. Yesterday her server Veronica spilled a plate of food on the mayor while serving him lunch. Unfortunately, Gina's boss Hernando was in the restaurant at the time. Hernando immediately ordered Gina to fire Veronica. Before terminating her, Gina talked to the human resource manager who said he felt termination would not be a good idea, since Veronica otherwise had a good work record. When Gina relayed this to Hernando, Hernando exploded. "I don't care what HR says! Fire her anyway!"

1. Whose orders should Gina follow? Why?

2. What type of organizational structure is being used in this scenario?

3. What problem has the structure caused?

4. Could this problem have been avoided if the human resource manager had been given functional authority? How?

2 Order from Chaos   Reginald's custom muffler business has taken off. Sales are rising and so are his problems. He currently has a factory with 60 employees as well as two small retail outlets where he sells his mufflers and other auto accessories. Additionally, he has a team of four outside sales representatives that markets his products to other retailers.

Despite the fact that Reginald has a factory manager and two lead clerks who manage the stores when he is not there, things are not running smoothly. Reginald is responsible for the bookkeeping, purchasing, and hiring as well as general management and product development. Recently inventory has disappeared from one of the stores, supplies are arriving late, and production is behind because Reginald has not had time to hire another employee. Additionally, Reginald forgot to mail a tax payment to the IRS and is now being charged penalties and interest.

1. Does Reginald need to restructure his organization? If so, how?

2. Should he add more layers of management? Why, or why not?

3. Should management decisions be decentralized? Why, or why not?

4. In which areas should he add management?

5. What would be a better span of control?

HUMAN RELATIONS IN ACTION

Visit an organization in your community and learn the organizational structure. Draw an organizational chart based on your findings. Then, see how many ways you can restructure the organization and portray your findings in chart form. Determine which structure you think will work best. Explain your reasoning.

For additional resources, refer to the web site for this text: **www.cengage.com/management/dalton**

RESOURCES

1. Dignan, Larry. (2008, November 10). Will yet another restructuring solve Nortel's problems? Retrieved December 18, 2009, from http://seekingalpha.com/article/105133-will-yet-another-restructuring-solve-nortel-s-problems.

2. Nortel Networks Corporation Profile. (n.d.). Retrieved on February 25, 2009, from http://www.smartbrief.com/news/ctia/companyData.jsp?companyId=3894.

3. Nortel: News releases: Nortel announces workforce reductions (2009, February 25). Retrieved May 26, 2009, from http://www2.nortel.com/go/news_detail.jsp?cat_id=8055&oid=100252808&locale=en-us.

4. General Motors Corporation. (2008, December 2). *Restructuring plan for long-term viability submitted to senate banking committee & house of representatives financial services committee.* Detroit, MI: Author.

5. GM to discontinue Pontiac brand, announces major restructuring plans. (2009, April 27). Retrieved May 26, 2009, from http://www.foxnews.com/politics/2009/04/27/gm-discontinue-pontiac-brand-announces-major-restructuring-plans/.

6. Web 2.0 initiatives continue to gain acceptance at companies, Watson Wyatt survey finds. (2009, May 21). Retrieved May 26, 2009, from http://ca.news.finance.yahoo.com/s/21052009/31/link-f-prnewswire-web-2-0-initiatives-continue-gain-acceptance-companies.html.

7. Williams, Chuck. (2008). *MGMT.* Cincinnati, OH: South-Western Cengage Learning.

8. National Aeronautics and Space Administration. (2008, March). *Workforce transition strategy initial report, space shuttle and constellation workforce focus.* Washington, D.C.: Author.

9. URS awarded contract at NASA's Marshall Space Flight Center—Contract has maximum value of $153 million to URS. (2008, July 10). Retrieved on December 19, 2008, from http://www.spaceref.com/news/viewpr.html?pid=25923.

10. David, Leonard. (2007, September 4). *Spaceport America: First looks at a new space terminal.* Retrieved December 19, 2008, from http://www.space.com/businesstechnology/070904_virgingalactic_spaceport.html.

11. Williams, Chuck. (2008). *MGMT.*

12. Ibid.

13. *Culture shift: Overcoming the corporate blame game.* (2008, June 02). Retrieved January 2, 2009, from http://www.managesmarter.com/msg/content_display/publications/e3ie29ff31c80c6e3df79d503250ea67a91.

14. Warshaw, Michael. (1998, December). Open mouth, close career? *Fast Company*, 240.

15. Reece, Barry L., Brandt, Rhonda. (2001). *Effective Human Relations in Organizations.* Boston: Houghton Mifflin.

16. Hammer, Michael, Champy, James. (2001). *Reengineering the Corporation.* New York: HarperCollins.

17. Myatt, Mike. (2008, September 19). When to consider corporate restructuring. Retrieved December 18, 2008, from http://cpnmhn.typepad.com/management_matters/2008/09/when-to-conside.html.

18. Ashkenas, Ron, Ulrich, Dave, Jick, Todd, Kerr, Steve. (2002). *The Boundaryless Organization: Breaking the Chains of Organizational Structures, Revised and Updated.* Hoboken, NJ: Jossey-Bass.

19. Oxman, Jeffrey A., Brian D. Smith. (2003, Fall). "The limits of structural change." *MIT Sloan Management Review*. 45, no.1.

20. Ibid.

21. *Business definition for: Corporate culture*. (n.d.). Retrieved December 30, 2009, from http://dictionary.bnet.com/definition/Corporate+Culture.html?tag=col1;trackDictionary.

22. *The five levels of company culture*. Retrieved on January 1, 2009, from http://www.companyculture.com/basics/fivelevels.htm.

23. *The Google culture*. (n.d.). Retrieved on January 2, 2009, from http://www.google.com/corporate/culture.html.

24. Nies, Tom. (n.d.). *Instilling common values in a diverse corporate culture*. Retrieved on January 2, 2009, from http://www.zeromillion.com/business/common-values-diverse-culture.html.

25. Cicom Systems Inc. (2006). *Cincom's core values* [Form CW040209-2]. Cincinnati, OH: Author.

26. *Culture overview*. (n.d.). Retrieved on January 2, 2009, from http://www212.american express.com/...t/campus/campusrecruitmenthome/workingwithus/ourculture.do?vgnextoid= e34e0681b88ec110VgnVCM100000cef4ad94RCRD.

27. *Business definition for: Corporate climate*. (n.d.). Retrieved on December 30, 2008, from http://dictionary.bnet.com/index.php?d=corporate+climate.

28. McCrimmon, Mitch. (2007, December 5). *Organizational culture and climate: The personality and mood of organizations*. Retrieved on December 19, 2008, from http://businessmanagement.suite101.com/article.cfm/organizational_culture_and_climate.

29. O'Daniel, Adam. (2008, September 29 modified 2008, October 7). *A somber mood envelops uptown Charlotte*. Retrieved on January 2, 2009, from http://www.bizjournals.com/charlotte/stories/2008/09/29/daily9.html.

14

CAREER ADVANCEMENT STRATEGIES:
REINVENTING YOURSELF

OBJECTIVES

After studying this chapter, you should be able to:

14.1 Describe the forces that are shaping careers.

14.2 Demonstrate skills needed to maintain a healthy career.

14.3 Use behaviors that can boost or damage your career.

14.4 Explain how jobs begin and end.

Jump Start

The state of Michigan is looking to the future through its No Worker Left Behind program. This program is designed to move its economy from manual labor into one that is knowledge-based. The state wants its workforce to have the right skills and education level necessary to land jobs in the emerging economy.[1,2]

The program features up to two years of free tuition at any state community college, university, or other approved training program for those willing to pursue a degree or certificate in a high-demand occupation or emerging industry or in an entrepreneurship program.

One of the program's success stories is that of Steve York, a 50-year-old worker laid off from the auto industry. York, who had formerly repaired machines at Delphi Saginaw Steering Systems, returned to school to become a chemical process technician. That training led to a job processing chemicals to make silicon, which is used in semiconductor chips, solar panels, computers, and cell phones.

- Have you or someone you know had to reinvent yourself professionally? If so, please explain.
- What were the upsides and downsides of reinvention?

14.1 FORCES SHAPING TODAY'S CAREERS

The ability to reinvent yourself is the key to a successful career in the 21st century. Because of its rapid change, the work world has become a fast-paced environment that requires flexibility, self-motivation, and lifelong learning.

Reinvention is driven, in part, by external factors. Demographics, technology, and globalization can both destroy careers and create new opportunities.[3] Additionally, you may find personal changes such as illness, divorce, or your spouse's transfer forcing you to reinvent yourself in ways you never imagined possible.

Internal factors also play a role in the need to reinvent yourself.[4] With the possibility of working 50 years or more, you're likely to find your values, interests, and lifestyle preferences changing more than once. A job you once found exciting or challenging may now bore you. Burnout is always an issue.

Life and career skills that help you adjust and reinvent yourself greatly impact organization and human relations systems. In fact, the 21st century organization demands that you are flexible and adapt to change, all the while managing your goals and time, working independently, being a self-directed learner, and acquiring skills organizations want.[5]

> **KeyPoint**
> Demographics, technology, and globalization will force you to evolve continually and learn new skills over the course of your lifetime.

If you keep track of external forces that drive careers, you'll be better able to spot career trends early. This will give you a chance to develop new skills in your industry or enter an emerging field. External forces to watch are demographics, technology, and globalization.

Demographics

Demographics are statistics showing population characteristics about a region or group, such as education, income, age, marital status, ethnic makeup, and other factors. Through the use of demographics, experts have determined that the composition of the U.S. population is changing, which will in turn affect the composition of the labor supply. By 2050, the country will be older and more diverse. Projections are as follows:

- The minority population is expected to be 54 percent of the total population[6] with Hispanics making up one-third of it.
- The working age population, individuals aged 18 to 64, is projected to decline from 63 percent to 57 percent of the population.
- By 2030, 1 in 5 Americans will be over 65 years old and the population of individuals 85 and over will triple.
- Immigration is expected to continue at record rates, with nearly one in five residents being an immigrant.[7]

With the pool of those in the working age population declining, organizations will be forced to offer more flexible scheduling, part-time work, and telecommuting in order to attract parents, the disabled, and older workers to fill the gap.

Other changes will result from the shifting demographics. Products and services catering to minorities and immigrants are expected to flourish. Older people, for instance, have different needs and are expected to spur the demand for health-care-related products and services. As family members who are responsible for caring for children or elderly parents enter or remain in the workforce, they are expected to "outsource" many routine household chores. Because of these needs, the lower-skill-level jobs in sectors such as retail trade, eating establishments, health care, child care, and other personal services are expected to be strong.

Technology

Ray Kurzweil, who studies and predicts the future, believes that the 21st century will have 1,000 times more technological changes than the 20th century had. The RAND Corporation, a nonprofit institution that addresses global challenges facing the public and private sectors, says that converging and interdependent trends in information technology, biotechnology, nanotechnology, and other technology areas have led experts to conclude that the pace of technological change will accelerate in the next 10 to 15 years.[8]

Technological advances bring with them emerging industries. The geospatial industry is an example. This industry acquires, integrates, manages, analyzes, maps, distributes, and uses geographic, temporal, and spatial information and knowledge. Within geospatial technology, remote sensing specialists use pictures and other information from satellites, planes, and ground sensors to plot and gather data about where things are on Earth. Geographic information systems analysts then review and turn this data into maps and decision-making tools.[9]

Nanotechnology is another emerging field. It is the group of emerging technologies in which matter is measured on the nanometer scale—down to individual atoms in size—and manipulated to produce unique materials and products. Within the next 10 years, the National Science Foundation estimates that the worldwide need for nanotechnology workers will rise from the current 20,000 to two million![10]

These types of technological advances increase the demand for highly skilled workers who stay current on the latest technologies. Businesses, in order to respond to market needs and utilize these latest technologies, will need to become more decentralized. This may result in more workers being independent contractors and performing project work. The cyber society will put a high premium on such entrepreneurship. Imaginative and energetic self-starters who can recognize emerging needs and create ways to fill them will be in high demand.

> *Somewhere, something incredible is waiting to be known.*
> —*Carl Sagan, American scientist and astrochemist*

Global CONNECTION

A job that requires a foreign language is not found only oversees anymore. The federal government has a high demand for those fluent in another language to work within the United States. The Federal Bureau of Investigation and the National Security Agency (NSA) are among the agencies eagerly searching for workers skilled in foreign languages.[11,12]

The NSA, for instance, is seeking those fluent in Arabic, Chinese, Pashto, Persian-Farsi, Russian, Turkish, Urdu, and other languages of the Sub-Saharan Africa region.

1. Are you fluent in other languages? If not, what stopped you from pursing this skill?
2. If you were going to develop or improve your foreign language skills, which language would you choose and why?

Globalization

Container ships, jets, satellite communications, and the Internet have made the business world truly international. Manufacturing is relocating overseas, and workers now move around the world with increasing ease. The cost of transporting goods and communicating globally has dropped so dramatically that distance is no longer an issue. Buyers in Dallas are able to communicate daily business needs with sellers in South Africa, for example. This trend toward making goods and services worldwide in scope, with no national boundaries or trade barriers on where they are produced or sold, is called *globalization.*

Globalization of manufacturing means that a metal bolt produced in Malaysia must precisely fit a nut made in Thailand and hold together parts made in Brazil and Chile. Electronic components might be bought from Japan, assembled in Mexico, and sold in the United States. Gone are the days when "Made in China" or "Made in America" truly identified a product's origins. Globalization of services means that the individual who takes your telephone call at a help desk may be located in India or Ireland.

While globalization has resulted in jobs being outsourced, it has also created new jobs in the United States. Globalization expands markets for U.S. goods and services as well as makes available a wider variety of goods and services to those living in the United States. Research suggests that more jobs are created in the United States than are lost through globalization. However, what this means is that employees who are in the manufacturing or service sectors whose jobs are lost because of globalization will be forced to develop other skills and move into sectors of the economy that have not been affected. This might require employees to move to other regions of the country in search of these jobs.[13]

© 2009 Ted Goff

"It was the only job I could find that didn't require computer skills."

Ask Yourself...

1. What technologies have been developed in your lifetime? How have they changed your life?

2. Can you name at least five products that were in demand in some part of the 20th century that are no longer produced at all?

3. What must the United States do to ensure that its workforce has the skills necessary to perform jobs of the future?

14.2   NURTURING STRATEGIES

Rapid change means that you need to take a number of steps to ensure that you are prepared for whatever may come. Specifically you should maintain a professional network, recognize and track job trends, continue your education, and stay current in your job-seeking skills.

Maintaining a Network

One of the most helpful practices you can do for your career is to develop and maintain a strong network of friends and colleagues. According to Kathy Zerner of ABBA Consulting, *networking* is the way that most individuals find employment, particularly in the hidden market. In fact, some estimates are that up to 80 percent of the jobs available are in the hidden market.[14] This market consists of jobs yet to be created as well as jobs in which vacancies are anticipated.

The key to a strong network, according to Zerner, is developing relationships. By meeting people and doing something for them—either providing information, sharing ideas, or helping them with personal or professional problems—you develop a strong network. Being sincere and giving to others first is the key. This network can include not only others in your profession, but also neighbors, friends, teachers, physicians—anybody with whom you have a relationship.[15]

Don't wait until you're unemployed or hoping to obtain a new position to begin developing your network—start now. Finding a job through your network will be much more successful if you have tended and cultivated it like a garden even when you are employed.

Actually getting out and meeting people in person is the best way to network. People tend to remember you more when you meet them personally. Make it a point to attend professional meetings and company social events, volunteer in your church or community, or perform other activities that will bring you in contact with other individuals with whom you share an interest.

Additionally having an online presence is important. As discussed in other chapters, LinkedIn and Facebook are popular ways of networking, but many other networking sites exist such as Twitter, MySpace, Ning, Bebo, and Plaxo. While you probably won't use all of them, it's important to realize that they exist.

> *Networking is an essential part of building wealth.*
>
> —Armstrong Williams, columnist and radio host

Recognizing and Tracking Job Trends

Recognizing job trends can help nurture your career. Job openings occur from both employment growth and replacement needs. Many new jobs are surfacing as technologies advance, and the shift to services continues to influence the workplace. Replacement needs arise because workers leave occupations, retire, return to school, or quit to assume household responsibilities. Replacement needs are expected to account for 68 percent of job openings between 2006 and 2016.[16]

The Bureau of Labor Statistics (BLS) projects that service-providing industries are projected to have the largest number of total job openings, 12.2 million, with 60 percent of those being replacement needs. Generally, those jobs with relatively low pay or limited training requirements such as food preparation and other service occupations have the highest replacement needs.[17]

Additionally BLS believes that the education and health service industries will grow by 18.8 percent, adding more jobs than any other industry grouping. Professional and business services, scientific and technical services, information technology, leisure and hospitality services, retail, finance, insurance, and government are also expected to have strong growth.[18]

Employment in the goods-producing industries has been relatively stagnant in the United States since the early 1980s. Overall, this sector is expected to decline 3.3 percent over the 2006–2016 period. The one bright spot in this industry is pharmaceutical and medicine manufacturing, which is expected to grow by 23.8 percent. Agriculture, forestry, fishing, hunting, and mining are expected to decline.[19]

Organizations continue to outsource functions that are not central to their business, such as security and cleaning, industrial design, manufacturing processes, business-processing tasks, human resources, information technology, and other business tasks that companies previously performed internally.[20] This outsourcing trend causes an increasing number of workers to become independent contractors, on-call workers, temporary-help agency workers, self-employed individuals, workers employed by contract firms, and part-time workers. This trend is expected to continue.[21]

Technologies that allow work products, data, and information to be transmitted quickly and inexpensively and the need for firms to respond rapidly to changing technological and market forces will increasingly result in decentralized businesses. More and more, organizations are providing frontline employees with greater authority and decision making. Instead of serving as a command and control function, corporations of the future may exist to provide rules, standards, and cultures that define how more autonomous employees operate.[22]

Knowledge will be valued to a greater extent. This also includes understanding technology, markets, customers, suppliers, business processes, and best practices. These changes mean that just doing your job will not be enough—you will need to understand the forces impacting your position intimately.[23]

KeyPoint
The shift to outsourcing means self-motivation, networking, and strong communication skills are becoming more important than ever.

It is only a step from boredom to disillusionment, which leads naturally to self-pity, which in turn ends in chaos.
—Manly Hall, Canadian philosopher

Even if you are employed, you should scan job trends every several years.[24] Ask yourself these questions:

- Is the company I work for healthy and in good financial shape?
- Is the industry I work in solid and growing, or is it shrinking?
- Are there new skills I need to learn to stay competitive where I am?
- Do I have skills that are transferable to another industry that is healthy?
- Am I bored or burned out?
- Do I need to change employers or learn new skills in an entirely different industry?

A good place to research careers and trends is the CareerOneStop web site supported by the U.S. Department of Labor. This site lets you explore careers as well as education and training. The Career Voyages web site sponsored by the U.S. Department of Labor will help you explore occupations in which employees are in demand and will advise you of what skills and training are needed for those jobs.

The *Occupational Outlook Handbook* is another excellent source. It lists major occupations and explains what the future of those careers looks like, the nature of the work, earnings, working conditions, and usual training required.

If you are still unsure, try an informational interview. Start with your instructors. If you know they are familiar with a profession that interests you, ask to discuss it with them. They may know people in the profession who would be willing to talk with you about their jobs.

By keeping track of emerging changes, you will be better able to determine when you need to transition into a new job, industry, or career. You can spot new skill sets you need to develop and master them early on.

With the advance of technology, the sky is the limit on new job creation.

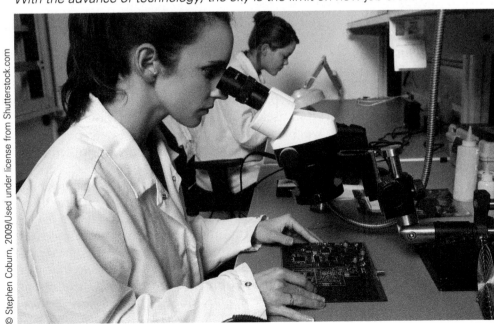

Continuing Your Education

According to *Occupational Outlook Handbook* and the *Career Guide to Industries,* the 30 fastest growing occupations for the 2006–2016 decade require advanced education. For 19 of these occupations, the most significant source of postsecondary education or training is an associate or higher degree. Computer- and health-related occupations also account for a large number of these fast-growing occupations. In fact, the higher your level of education, the more you earn and the less likely you will be to find yourself unemployed, as Figure 14.1 indicates.[25]

● Figure 14.1

The effect of education on earnings.

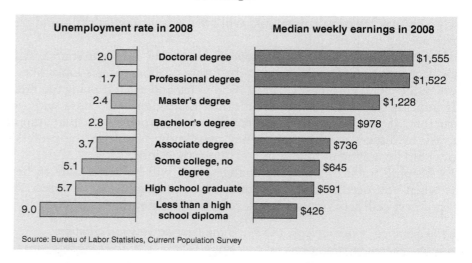

Unemployment rate in 2008		Median weekly earnings in 2008
2.0	Doctoral degree	$1,555
1.7	Professional degree	$1,522
2.4	Master's degree	$1,228
2.8	Bachelor's degree	$978
3.7	Associate degree	$736
5.1	Some college, no degree	$645
5.7	High school graduate	$591
9.0	Less than a high school diploma	$426

Source: Bureau of Labor Statistics, Current Population Survey

Education has become more important than ever as technology provides more information. For the most part, machines can't tell bad data from good, valuable information from useless, or accurate information from inaccurate. Employees who can work with computers and who can also filter the incoming information, discern it, make decisions, and address problems are in great demand.

Don't wait for your employer to train you. Realize that you must take control of your own career and personal development and take advantage of courses at your community college. Get a degree or certificate. Learn a foreign language. Sign up for any optional training offered by your employer, and volunteer for assignments that allow you to gain new knowledge. Associate with supercharged experts or stimulating conversationalists so that you can learn from one another. Learn a new software application. Read about the cultures of countries where your company does business. Read books, magazines, newsletters, newspapers, and online articles in areas that will help you at work. Watch meaningful television features. Research interesting topics on science, technology, and professional interests.

The more you understand about how business operates and what is going on in the world, the more effective you will be as an employee. Gain information that won't become obsolete—topics that deal with life and human nature or that sharpen your problem-solving skills (many CEOs love reading mysteries, for example)—as well as keeping up with business topics and changing trends.

Knowing your learning style is important so that you can design or choose learning experiences that best suit you. Felder and Soloman of the University of North Carolina have identified four types of learners as shown in Figure 14.2.

Figure 14.2

Learning styles.[26]

Active and reflective learners—Active learners have a need to explain or demonstrate what they have learned while reflective learners want to think about it. At times, you may use both methods to learn but may find that you tend to lean in one direction.

Sensing and intuitive learners—Sensing learners are patient individuals who enjoy solving problems in set, established ways. Memorizing facts is their strong suit. On the other hand, intuitive learners enjoy grasping new concepts and are more comfortable with unexpected twists and turns. In general they work faster and dislike memorization and rote activities. While you should be aware of which style is the most comfortable for you, realize that good problem solvers and learners are able to take advantage of both methods.

Visual and verbal learners—Visual learners do better when they see what they need to learn, whether it's a simulation of an activity, a picture, a video, or a diagram. Most individuals are visual learners. Verbal learners, on the other hand, do better when they have spoken or written explanations.

Sequential and global learners—Sequential learners take one step at a time, building on the material they have previously learned. Global learners are able to see the big picture and can put together seemingly random facts to solve complex issues. Unfortunately, being too sequential or too global can cause problems. Global learners may have difficulty with the details while sequential learners may have mastered the material in a shallow way and may not be able to relate it in other areas.

The key to surviving in a knowledge-based economy, then, is learning. Maintain a hunger for learning. Continue your education at any level to keep your momentum.

Staying Current with Your Résumé

The odds are that you will be spending some time in your career looking for a new job. Some people lose jobs because of layoffs, terminations, or downsizing, while others simply want to find positions that are more suitable with working conditions, location, wages, or job duties that more nearly match their needs or interests. The BLS reported that in January 2008, the median number of years that wage and salary workers had been with their current employer was 4.1 years.[27] Keeping an updated résumé as well as a reference list will enable you to begin seeking a new job immediately.

Résumés   A *résumé* is a sales tool designed to assist you in obtaining an interview. It provides a prospective employer with a brief summary of your skills, education, and job experience. A résumé does not get you a job. However, a poorly written résumé that doesn't identify your skills and abilities, contains typographical errors, and is unattractive will probably keep you from even getting an interview. By keeping track of your professional accomplishments, you can quickly update your résumé.[28]

Here are some tips and guidelines to keep in mind while you're developing your résumé:

- Limit the résumé to one page unless you have extensive work experience.

- Target your résumé to specific employers. With word processing software, you can easily customize objectives and emphasize skills that fit the job or company for which you are applying.

- Play down job skills you don't enjoy using.

- Be specific about your accomplishments. Use action verbs such as earned, planned, wrote, achieved, completed, increased, and improved when describing your accomplishments and achievements.

- Avoid the use of "I." The résumé is a formal document and starting every accomplishment with "I" detracts from the action verb you want to highlight.

- Don't enclose a photograph or provide your marital status, number of children, height, weight, race, or other personal information. This information may disqualify you from the interview. Religion, too, should not be listed, unless it's specifically related to or required for the job.

- List extracurricular activities or hobbies if they are relevant to the position for which you are applying, or highlight skills that could be useful in that position.

- Expect to complete several rough drafts. Ask someone else to read your draft critically, reviewing it for clarity, spelling errors, and format. Some employers will refuse to consider a candidate with errors in a résumé, so be sure your résumé is error free.

Technology CONNECTION

In today's volatile economy, you should keep an up-to-date résumé that is ready to be sent out at a moment's notice. Susan Ireland, author of *Complete Idiot's Guide to the Perfect Resume,* says having a résumé you can e-mail and post online is essential. She recommends both a résumé in Microsoft Word and one in plain text. In the plain text résumé you should (1) delete any indications of page breaks, such as page numbers, (2) use all CAPS for words that need special emphasis, (3) replace each bullet point with a standard keyboard symbol such as a dash, asterisk, or plus sign, (4) use straight quotes in place of curly quotes, and (5) limit your line lengths to no more than 65 characters.[29]

When e-mailing a résumé, Ireland recommends that you compose a short note to the targeted individual and then copy your plain text résumé into the body of the e-mail. She also suggests cutting and pasting the plain text résumé you have developed when submitting résumés online.

Additionally, be sure that you have an appropriate e-mail address that you check often—nothing cute or suggestive.

1. Have you ever posted a résumé online? What difficulties, if any, did you have posting it?
2. Why is it so important to send an error-free résumé?

> ❝ *Resume: a written exaggeration of only the good things a person has done in the past, as well as a wish list of the qualities a person would like to have.*
> —*Bo Bennett, businessman and author* ❞

References   Professional references are individuals who can vouch for your work abilities and personal qualities. They include former bosses, coworkers, teachers, and fellow professionals or occasionally acquaintances who know you socially. Employers expect applicants to have references but differ in their preferences regarding when and how they want to see a reference list.

Experts recommend omitting references from your résumé. Instead, do research to learn whether your target employer wants you to submit a list of references. Prepare a reference sheet that includes names, titles, addresses, and contact information for each reference, and be ready to provide it to an employer who may request it.

KeyPoint
Strategically choose your references so that different areas of your expertise can be verified.

Family members are not considered good references, as most employers do not view them as unbiased. Offer references such as former employers and teachers who can attest to your performance first. You should provide only the names of others if you are asked for character references. Never use individuals' names for a reference without obtaining permission. Tell them about your job search plans and the type of work you're seeking. Be sure that you have their complete mailing addresses, daytime telephone numbers, e-mail addresses, and correct spelling of their names.

It's standard to include between three and five references. Be sure to express appreciation to references for their willingness to assist you in your job search. Call them after an interview to let them know that they can expect a telephone call from your prospective employer.

Ask Yourself...

1. How many contacts do you have in your network? What specific plans do you have to broaden it?
2. What is your learning style? How can you strengthen your ability to learn in other ways?

14.3   CAREER BOOSTERS AND KILLERS

Think carefully before you act at work. Some seemingly small things you do can come back to help or hurt your career development. Remember, your performance is often viewed as the sum of the little things you do.

Career Boosters

Ensuring Accomplishments Are Recognized   Assuring others know of your goals as well as accomplishments is an important ingredient in nurturing your career. If you are interested in learning something new at work, let your supervisor know. When the opportunity presents itself, volunteer for extra assignments.

While you shouldn't brag about your accomplishments, your superiors do need to know if you have completed a difficult assignment or accomplished something out of the ordinary. If you receive a thank-you note from a customer for something you did to help them, be sure that your supervisor gets a copy. If you produce training materials or other reports that will make the office shine, be sure that your name is on them as the creator. However, never take credit yourself for something a group has accomplished. Be sure to recognize those who have helped you achieve something above and beyond the ordinary assignment.

Asking Questions   Don't be afraid to ask questions.[30] It's far better to ask if you don't understand something than to pretend you do. Before asking, determine whether you can find the answer yourself. If not, check with your supervisor using communication skills learned in Chapter 4 to clarify what you don't understand.

Controlling Your Behavior   In its *Job Search Handbook,* the Georgia Department of Labor recommends the following behaviors for starting and keeping a job:[31]

- Show a positive attitude and project a positive, competent image and appearance.
- Be on time for work, and ask your supervisor for the proper method of notifying him or her if you are going to be unavoidably tardy or absent.
- Follow the rules and be dependable.
- Accept criticism as constructive and show appreciation for training, support, input, and feedback.
- Keep your emotions under control and your personal life and problems at home.
- Show initiative. Meet and exceed your employer's expectations.
- Try to solve problems before asking for help. Admit mistakes and learn from them.
- Be a team player and be willing to help.

> **KeyPoint**
> You control the success of your career with actions such as initiative, honesty, and a can-do attitude.

Ethics CONNECTION

It's a dog eat dog world out there, but how far do you go to get ahead? A survey of 358 high-level employees and directors at 53 publicly traded companies uncovered seven individuals who claimed to have college degrees that could not be verified.[32] A number of high-level executives such as RadioShack's president and chief executive officer (CEO) and Herbalife's chief operating officer (COO) have been forced to resign over embellishments to their résumés.[33] The problem not only encompasses padding the résumé but leaving out specific, relevant facts.

In the case of Gregory Probert, Herbalife's COO, he performed well and was respected within the industry despite the fact that he did not have an MBA from UCLA as he had claimed.[34] So why was he forced to resign? It's an issue of trust. If he lied on his résumé, what else might he have lied about?

1. Have you or someone else you know ever used a résumé that was less than truthful? If so, were there any repercussions?
2. If you don't pad your résumé and must compete with someone who has, how would you feel?

- Be respectful and treat others the way you want to be treated.
- Treat everyone with courtesy and respect, and avoid negative, critical, and gossiping coworkers.
- Volunteer for projects and committees if your work is completed and your supervisor approves.
- Don't try to change things right away. For at least the first month on a new job, focus on listening and learning.

Career Killers

Not Keeping Confidences Gossiping can be fun. Being the first person to spread good or bad news can make you feel important. Revealing confidences, however, can put a damper on your career. Regardless of your position, you need to be able to keep quiet about things you're told in confidence. Not being able to keep a secret can block your movement into a position of responsibility.

If you are unsure whether information being passed to you should be kept confidential, ask. If you accidentally overhear something you feel would be damaging if passed on to others, keep it to yourself.

Drama Queen and King Behavior A drama queen or king is a high-maintenance individual who is always seeking some sort of attention. These people occupy center stage in the office by getting everyone involved in their issues. Blowing situations out of proportion is a hallmark of the drama queen or king.

These types of individuals require extensive supervision and absorb the valuable time of their colleagues. If you behave in this way at work, you can expect to find yourself out of a job even if you are good at what you do.

In The News

The chance of a lifetime ended in disaster for a Delaware woman. After being on the job as an innkeeper at a bed and breakfast for only three months, Natalie Smith was chosen to be featured in a show on TLC that transforms an individual's appearance after the hosts have lived the individual's life.[35]

Camera crews followed Smith for five days at work and around the streets of Rehoboth Beach, Delaware. After the film crews left, Smith was terminated. Her employer did not elaborate but stated that Smith and her friends had made derogatory comments about the owner during the taping.[36]

1. Do you think Smith should have been fired? Why or why not?
2. What sort of impact do you believe the film crew's presence had on Smith's demeanor and personality? The operation of the business?

Helicopter Parents and Significant Others   Helicopter parents are a phenomenon of Generation Y. Because of texting and cell phone technology, Gen Y members and their parents have stayed in closer communication than parents and children of other generations. Many Gen Y's rely on their parents for guidance and support into their adult years. Some Gen Y parents, however, tend to "hover," smothering their grown children with advice and direction. These helicopter parents have been known to call and inquire about why their children weren't hired or why they were fired or to interfere in other ways in the workplace.

Significant others can also be a problem. The boyfriend who goes to the office to confront his significant other's coworker or the wife who barges into a meeting between her husband and human resources can spell disaster.

Remember, at work you are expected to handle your own issues. Don't allow your parents or significant others to interfere in workplace issues, even if they are well meaning.

Other behaviors that can damage your career are:

- Consuming too much alcohol at company functions
- Surfing or shopping on the Internet during working hours
- Having an affair with a coworker or superior
- Twittering or texting during working hours
- Using company time and resources for volunteer activities without permission
- Posting pictures on sites such as Facebook or MySpace that show you engaged in unprofessional behavior or inappropriately clothed
- Bringing your family problems to work by talking about them or taking out your family stress on your coworkers
- Taking company equipment or supplies home for personal use
- Abusing sick leave

> ### Ask Yourself...
>
> 1. Review your personal behavior, whether on a job or in a volunteer organization. Which career-nurturing behaviors do you need to improve?
> 2. Do you have helicopter parents or know someone who does? If so, how can you help these parents refrain from interfering in the workplace?

14.4 STARTING AND ENDING JOBS

Starting and ending jobs can be equally stressful. If you know what to expect, you can better handle the situation.

> **KeyPoint**
> Some behaviors that you engage in off the job can affect your job both positively and negatively.

Starting a Job

The first week on the job can be a frightening affair. Although you are excited to have the position, you have much to learn, everything from people's names to where the restroom is. These adjustments can be stressful even though you looked forward to beginning the new job. Be patient with yourself and the job. Give yourself time to adjust before you make any judgments concerning your new position.

Most positions have an introductory period of 90 days. During this time you have an opportunity to learn about the company, and company members can learn about you. In general you can be terminated for any reason during this period.

Spend this introductory period learning the work culture, as described in Chapter 13. Don't make any big changes or important decisions until you're sure that what you are doing is acceptable inside the organization's culture.

Work to establish relationships with individuals who appear to be successful in the environment. A mentor relationship is the most important one you can establish. Choose someone who has a position in the company you would eventually like to have and has a good reputation within the company and the profession.[37] A good mentor will listen to your goals and objectives and give you feedback.[38] He or she will be available to coach you on difficult situations and give you insight into the company culture and industry.

Work to establish a good working relationship with this individual. Then, make an appointment with the person you have chosen to talk about becoming your mentor. Let him or her know what you would like from the relationship.

Ending a Job

At the opposite end of the spectrum is leaving a position. Most jobs don't last forever. Individuals may become bored and find no opportunity for growth. Companies lay off workers because of economic conditions, mergers, or buyouts. Sometimes people are terminated because of ethical misconduct, poor work performance, or personal chemistry that isn't right. Whatever the cause, almost everyone leaves a job for one reason or another. Warning signs of impending termination abound. Some of them are listed below:

- You dislike your job and spend excessive time thinking about what you will do after work. You find getting out of bed in the morning difficult. These attitudes tend to show at work, and others on the job realize how you feel about your job.

- You lose your influence. Your ideas and opinions are not heard, and others around you pull back and quit communicating with you, perhaps because they realize your job is in danger. You see others being promoted around you as you stay in the same position.

- You begin to hear about layoffs because of a recession or a potential takeover.
- You're not personally productive, which appears in the form of missed objectives, poorly managed time, or confused priorities.
- You fail to change. You feel unwilling to adapt and learn new skills and ways of doing things.

If you see the handwriting on the wall and feel you will soon be terminated, or if you feel ready for a job change, you need to make some decisions. Just how bad is the job? Can you hang in there until you find another position? How will you support yourself if you resign? Can you draw unemployment if you resign? Will the company pay severance pay if you resign?

Finding another job is usually easier while you still have one. In fact, approximately one-third of all job seekers are looking for another position while employed. However, never use company time to conduct your job search. Do research in the evenings or on weekends and schedule telephone calls on breaks and interviews during your lunch period. Many times, prospective employers will agree to see you late in the evening or even on Saturdays.

If you decide to resign, give two weeks' notice of your resignation. This length of notice is standard and proper. Your new employer will usually allow you time to give notice. Sometimes a company may ask you to leave immediately once your resignation is submitted, especially if you deal with trade or strategy secrets or if they feel that your immediate removal is in the best interests of other employees.

No one is ever totally prepared for termination from a job. However, if you've been reading the warning signs and suspect that it is a possibility, start preparing yourself. Expect to feel anger, shame, fear, sadness, and self-pity. Try to control these emotions during the termination interview and remain as professional as possible.

During the termination interview, find out what benefits, if any, the company may give you. If you think you will need it, ask for a reference that is positive or at least neutral. If you feel too emotional to discuss benefits, ask if you can return the next day to do so.

Be aware of the unemployment laws in your state. Some states will not pay unemployment if you resign but will if you are terminated. If you are asked to resign rather than be terminated, this may be important.

> " *You got to know when to hold 'em, know when to fold 'em, know when to walk away and know when to run.* — *The Gambler.*
>
> —*Kenny Rogers, American singer* "

> " *When one door closes, another door opens; but we so often look so long and so regretfully upon the closed door, that we do not see the ones which open for us.*
>
> —*Alexander Graham Bell, American scientist and inventor of the telephone* "

Remember the Following Dos and Don'ts of Termination:

- Do try to have a calm conversation with your supervisor to clarify the reason for your termination. Don't make things worse by verbally (or physically) attacking your supervisor or coworkers.
- Don't focus on how unfairly you were treated. Analyze objectively what you may have learned. Make it an opportunity for change and growth.
- Do seek assistance and support from your support system and professional network.
- Do use the term "separated" rather than "fired" or "laid off" when asked about your past job experience.
- Don't lie about being terminated, particularly at a job interview. Remember that many people who have been fired from their jobs in the past have gone on to enjoy successful new jobs and careers.

Never burn your bridges. Throwing a tantrum while being terminated, destroying computer files, tearing up documents, or damaging company property may make you feel better temporarily but will hurt you in the long run. You may need a reference or want to return to the company under different circumstances.

Don't be surprised if your supervisor or a member of security escorts you to your work area to remove articles. This procedure is a standard practice in a number of companies because of the terminated employees who have destroyed company property.

Many employees react with disbelief after being terminated. Some are relieved to be out of an uncomfortable situation; others turn to violence or substance abuse. Many experience a combination of reactions. Whatever your reaction, you can expect to grieve because of the loss of a job.

Ask Yourself...

1. Recall a first day on a job or at a new school. How did you feel? How long did it take to become comfortable with your new surroundings?
2. Have you ever been laid off or terminated from a job? How did that make you feel? Did you learn any lessons that would make you a better employee in the future?

KEY TERMS

demographics   networking
globalization   résumé

CHAPTER SUMMARY

Working in the 21st century is all about reinventing yourself. Changing demographics, technology, and globalization are altering not only the composition of the workforce of the future, but the way work is performed as well as the types of goods and services produced. These changes, in turn, are transforming the nature of work.

Finding work in this dynamic environment will depend greatly on your ability to network. Through networking you will be able to zero in on jobs that have yet to be created or vacancies that are expected.

The speed of change means that you must keep an eye on work trends. You must know where future jobs will be so that you can begin to update your skill set to meet new workplace demands. In order to keep your skills fresh, you must engage in continual learning, whether it is through formal or informal means. You must know your preferred learning style so that you can ensure that you design ongoing educational experiences that are right for you. Along with updated skills, you need to maintain an updated résumé and references.

Your career hinges mostly on the small things you do every day—both positive and negative. Things you do off the job may impact your career so it is important to think through everything you do and weigh the consequences of your behavior.

Lastly, beginning and ending jobs can be stressful. Knowing how to get a good start on a new job is just as important as knowing how to leave gracefully.

REVIEW

1. What are the major forces shaping our careers? Explain their effects.

2. What must you do to nurture your career?

3. Describe a network and how you would develop one for yourself.

4. Why should you track job trends?

5. How do you go about tracking job trends?

6. Describe some different ways you can learn new skills.

7. What are the basic learning styles?

8. What should go in a résumé?

9. What behaviors can boost your career?

10. What behaviors can kill your career?

11. What are some good strategies for the first 90 days on a new job?

12. How should you leave a job?

CRITICAL THINKING

1. Imagine yourself in the year 2020. What job do you expect to be performing? From what age and ethnic groups do you expect your coworkers to be? What types of equipment do you expect to be using?

2. Which of the major forces shaping our careers do you think is the most important? Why?

3. Are you fluent in another language? Why or why not? What would be the advantages of learning another language?

4. What is the economic situation in your community? Are jobs plentiful or scarce? What new skills do you believe you need to learn because of the economy?

5. What is your learning style?

6. How many organizations have you worked for and how long did you stay on that job? Do you believe jumping from job to job can make future employers shy away from hiring you? Why or why not?

7. Have you ever been terminated from a job? What happened? Could you have better handled the termination interview?

CASE STUDIES

In small groups, analyze the following situations.

1 **No Man Is an Island**   Cecilie frantically looked around the room. Her eye was drawn to a gray-haired gentleman who was deep in conversation with a woman Cecilie did not know. Drawing up her courage, Cecilie approached the couple, stuck her hand out, and introduced herself.

"Hi, I'm Cecilie McMillan. I'm looking for a job. I'll do anything; I don't care what it is."

She shook both of their hands and shoved one of her business cards at them. Both of them greeted her and handed her a card. Distressed and not knowing what else to say, Cecilie excused herself, got some more cards out of her purse, and headed to the next group of people.

During the next week she sent frantic e-mails and made telephone calls to the gentleman asking if he knew of any jobs at his company she could do.

Several weeks later she told her friend Babbette that networking was highly overrated as a way to find a job. Cecilie thought she'd do better posting her résumé on the Internet.

1. What is wrong with the way Cecilie was networking?

2. If you were her career coach, what would you tell her to do?

3. If you had been the gentleman, would you have returned her telephone calls or e-mails? Why or why not?

2 **Joe Cool**   Joe listened as his coworker Devon asked their supervisor if there were any extra projects he could take on. His supervisor said there were, but warned Devon to finish his own work first and understand that he could not work any overtime. Devon readily agreed, and the supervisor handed him a large folder full of account reconciliations that needed to be completed.

Later that afternoon, Joe was having lunch with another team member, Lucy.

"What a suck up Devon is," Joe laughed. "I can't believe he actually goes and asks for extra work. I've got everything figured out around here. If I ignore the supervisor when she comes by, she usually passes me up and dumps the extra work on Devon. That way I have a bit of time to download new music and check my e-mail before going home."

1. What do you think about Joe's avoidance of extra work? Why?

2. If you were the supervisor, whom would you recommend for promotion, and why?

3. If you had to lay someone off, whom would you lay off first? Why?

HUMAN RELATIONS IN ACTION

Working in small groups, brainstorm a workplace of the future. You may choose any industry and bring in outside source materials for reference, check web sites for additional materials, or rely on the diverse ideas of your group members. Design an office setting of the future. You are encouraged to take photos, draw pictures, or present items. What kind of furniture will be there? What computer connectivity will be required?

Present your design to the class with a verbal briefing on what is represented and why. Describe how it will work and who will be in it.

Develop a résumé for a position at this workplace. Use the form of your choice. Share it with classmates for critiquing.

For additional resources, refer to the web site for this text:
www.cengage.com/management/dalton

RESOURCES

1. State of Michigan. (2009, March). *No worker left behind*. [Fact Sheet]. Lansing, MI: Author.

2. Zielenziger, M. (2009, July–August). Fresh start: Laid off, but on track. *AARP Bulletin, 50*(6), 18–20.

3. Ongoing career planning. (n.d.). Retrieved on October 23, 2008, from the University of Wisconsin Milwaukee Web site http://www.uwm.edu/Dept/CDC/ongoing_planning.html

4. Ongoing career planning. (n.d.). Retrieved on October 23, 2008, from the University of Wisconsin Milwaukee Web site http://www.uwm.edu/Dept/CDC/ongoing_planning.html

5. Partnership for 21st century skills. (n.d.) *Life and career skills*. Retrieved on June 27, 2009, from http://www.21stcenturyskills.org/route21/index.php?option=com_content&view=article&id=11&Itemid=11

6. United States Census Bureau. (2008, August 14). *An older and more diverse nation by midcentury*. Retrieved on July 12, 2009, from http://www.census.gov/Press-Release/www/releases/archives/population/012496.html

7. Pew Hispanic Center. (2008, February 11). *U.S. population projections: 2005–2050*. Retrieved on July 12, 2009, from http://pewhispanic.org/reports/report.php?ReportID=85

8. Karoly, L. A. & Panis, C. W. A. (2004). *The 21st century at work: Forces shaping the future workforce and workplace in the United States*. Retrieved on August 29, 2004, from http://www.rand.org/pubs/monographs/2004/RAND_MG164.pdf

9. *Geospatial technology—Industry overview*. Retrieved on June 27, 2009, from http://www.careervoyages.gov/includes/incsmallwindow-allindustries-industryoverview.cfm?industrynumber=12

10. *Nanotechnology—Industry overview*. Retrieved on June 27, 2009, from http://www.careervoyages.gov/includes/incsmallwindow-allindustries-industryoverview.cfm?industrynumber=13

11. *Foreign languages jobs in the federal government*. Retrieved on July 15, 2009, from http://www.makingthedifference.org/federalcareers/foreignlanguage.shtml

12. National Security Agency career fields. Retrieved on September 3, 2009, from http://www.nsa.gov/careers/career_fields/foreignlang.shtml

13. Karoly, L. A. & Panis, C. W. A. (2004). *The 21st century at work: Forces shaping the future workforce and workplace in the United States*. Retrieved on August 29, 2004, from http://www.rand.org/pubs/monographs/2004/RAND_MG164.pdf

14. Thompson, K. (2008, October 12). How to cope with changing workplace. *Houston Chronicle*.

15. Kathy, Z. (Interviewee). (2009, July 13). *ABBA Consulting* (abbacoach@aol.com).

16. Bureau of Labor Statistics. (n.d.). Tomorrow's jobs. *Occupational outlook handbook*, 2008–2009 Ed. Retrieved on July 12, 2009, from http://www.bls.gov/oco/oco2003.htm

17. Bureau of Labor Statistics. (n.d.). Tomorrow's jobs. *Occupational outlook handbook*, 2008–2009 Ed. Retrieved on July 12, 2009, from http://www.bls.gov/oco/oco2003.htm

18. Bureau of Labor Statistics. (n.d.). Tomorrow's jobs. *Occupational outlook handbook*, 2008–2009 Ed. Retrieved on July 12, 2009, from http://www.bls.gov/oco/oco2003.htm

19. Bureau of Labor Statistics. (n.d.). Tomorrow's jobs. *Occupational outlook handbook*, 2008–2009 Ed. Retrieved on July 12, 2009, from http://www.bls.gov/oco/oco2003.htm

20. Karoly, L. A. & Panis, C. W. A. (2004). *The 21st century at work: Forces shaping the future workforce and workplace in the United States*. Retrieved on August 29, 2004, from http://www.rand.org/pubs/monographs/2004/RAND_MG164.pdf

21. Karoly, L. A. & Panis, C. W. A. (2004). *The 21st century at work: Forces shaping the future workforce and workplace in the United States.* Retrieved on August 29, 2004, from http://www.rand.org/pubs/monographs/2004/RAND_MG164.pdf

22. Karoly, L. A. & Panis, C. W. A. (2004). *The 21st century at work: Forces shaping the future workforce and workplace in the United States.* Retrieved on August 29, 2004, from http://www.rand.org/pubs/monographs/2004/RAND_MG164.pdf

23. Karoly, L. A. & Panis, C. W. A. (2004). *The 21st century at work: Forces shaping the future workforce and workplace in the United States.* Retrieved on August 29, 2004, from http://www.rand.org/pubs/monographs/2004/RAND_MG164.pdf

24. *Ongoing career planning.* (n.d.). Retrieved on October 23, 2008, from the University of Wisconsin Milwaukee Web site http://www.uwm.edu/Dept/CDC/ongoing_planning.html

25. Bureau of Labor Statistics. (2009, March 6). *Education pays.* Retrieved on September 3, 2009, from http://www.bls.gov/emp/emptab7.htm

26. Felder, R. M. & Soloman, B. A. (n.d.). *Learning styles and strategies.* Retrieved on September 3, 2009, from http://www4.ncsu.edu/unity/lockers/users/f/felder/public/ILSdir/styles.htm

27. Bureau of Labor Statistics. (2008, September 26). *Employee tenure summary.* Retrieved on July 13, 2009, from http://www.bls.gov/news.release/tenure.nr0.htm

28. Ireland, S. *Electronic resume guide: How to format resumes for email, posting online.* Retrieved on June 29, 2009, from http://susanireland.com

29. Ireland, S. *Electronic resume guide: How to format resumes for email, posting online.* Retrieved on June 29, 2009, from http://susanireland.com

30. Freeman, S. (2009, January 13). *Ask the 'dumb' questions.* Retrieved on September 3, 2009, from http://blogs.usatoday.com/oped/2009/01/ask-the-dumb-qu.html

31. Chapter 12—Keeping your job. (n.d.). *Georgia Department of Labor job search handbook.* Retrieved on August 29, 2004, from http://www.dol.state.ga.us/js/replace/chapter12.htm

32. Winstein, K. J. (2008, November 13). Inflated credentials surface in executive suite. *Wall Street Journal online.* Retrieved on June 29, 2009, from http://online.wsj.com/article/SB122652836844922165.html

33. RadioShack CEO resigns amid resume questions. (2006, February 20). *USA Today.* Retrieved on July 12, 2009, from http://www.usatoday.com/money/industries/retail/2006-02-20-radioshack-ceo_x.htm

34. Rachel. (2008, May 6). Gregory Probert resigns as president and COO of Herbalife. Retrieved on July 12, 2009, from Optree http://optree.com/gregory-probert-resigns-as-president-and-coo-of-herbalife

35. Ostroski, A. (2009, July 2). Makeover contestant fired from Rehoboth innkeeper job. *Delaware Coast Press.*

36. Shockley, M. D. (2009, July 2). TLC makes over Rehoboth innkeeper. *Delaware Coast Press.*

37. *You can participate in SHRM's e-mentor program.* (2007, November 28). Retrieved on July 16, 2009, from http://moss07.shrm.org/Communities/volunteeropportunities/Pages/mentor.aspx

38. *How can I get a mentor when my employer doesn't have a mentoring program?* (2008, December 17). Retrieved on July 16, 2009, from http://moss07.shrm.org/TemplatesTools/hrqa/Pages/HowcanIgetamentorwhenmyemployerdoesn%E2%80%99thaveamentoring program.aspx

SETTING GOALS:
STEPS TO SUCCESS

OBJECTIVES

After studying this chapter, you should be able to:

15.1 Explain why people strive to achieve.

15.2 Describe the relationship between goals and planning.

15.3 Define how to set goals and develop plans.

15.4 Explain approaches in working toward goals.

15.5 Discuss the importance of monitoring and reevaluating goals.

15.6 Explain the role of goals in performance appraisals.

Jump Start

Online retailer Amazon.com is known for establishing and attaining pioneering goals. Jeff Bezos, founder of the company, attributes its success to focusing on customers, accepting risk as a part of innovation, persisting in the face of criticism, and thinking long term.[1]

• What personal or professional goals have you set for yourself?

• How do you think your approach to attaining your goals compares to the factors identified by Bezos? Explain.

• Are you familiar with other innovative companies? If so, do you think their approach is similar to Amazon's? Explain. '

15.1   WHY PEOPLE STRIVE TO ACHIEVE

> High expectations are the key to everything.
> —Sam Walton, founder of Wal-Mart and Sam's Club

In a speech entitled "The Real Reasons We Explore Space,"[2] Michael Griffin, former top administrator of NASA, acknowledged the usual reasons of scientific discovery, economic benefit, and national security. But he said the actual reasons go further. He pointed out that Charles Lindbergh didn't cross the Atlantic to win the $25,000 prize and that Burt Rutan and Paul Allen didn't develop a private spacecraft to win the $10 million Ansari X-Prize. (The X-Prize was a competition to develop, launch, and fly the first nongovernment manned spacecraft into space twice in two weeks. Rutan and Allen actually spent twice as much as they won.) Griffin believes that the real reasons people strive to accomplish such goals include the desire to be the first or the best in some activity, to stand out, to satisfy curiosity, and to leave something behind to show what they did with their time.

Do you see yourself in Griffin's comments? If you are self-motivated, you've probably recognized that you generally set goals for yourself, follow through on them, and monitor your own progress. You're also probably good at working on a task without someone watching over you and finding ways to reward yourself once you've met a goal. If this is you, give yourself a pat on the back, as these are behaviors valued by employers. In fact, Frances Coombes, author of *Teach Yourself Self-Motivation,* said, "The art of conscious goal setting is one of the most invaluable mental tools you will ever possess."[3]

Dr. Phillip McGraw, author of *The Life Strategies Workbook,*[4] suggests that to attain success in your life, you must differentiate between your real desire and what only symbolizes that desire. For example, while you might say you want a degree from a particular university, if you look more closely and honestly, you may find that what you truly desire is the prestige, self-esteem, and sense of belonging that a degree from that school will bring you.

Understanding Maslow's Hierarchy of Needs, discussed in Chapter 3, will help you to do this. You must first ask yourself which needs you truly want to satisfy. Such insights will help you sharpen your view of your future self, refine your focus, and clarify your goals.

A *goal* is the objective, target, or end result expected from the completion of tasks, activities, or programs. In your personal life, your goals may include becoming a college graduate, a successful businessperson, or a respected community leader.

Consider what an unknown philosopher once said: "In the absence of clearly defined goals, we become strangely loyal to performing daily acts of trivia." Defining your goals will help you direct your energies.

Being successful is almost never a matter of luck or fate. When you want to accomplish a certain goal (for example, running a marathon or finding a job), do you think about the steps you must take? Planning increases your chances of success. Failure to plan can be described as taking a road trip to a strange place without a map. You may reach your destination, but getting there will probably take longer time and cost more. And you may never arrive.

In thinking about why and how to achieve, aim to be a self-starter. Your employer will be able to depend on you to motivate yourself, to accomplish your objectives in line with the company's mission or goals, and to stay focused without close supervision. To develop a self-starter attitude, first decide what you want to accomplish and then think about how you can make it exciting for yourself. Define a sequence of goals so that as you achieve one, another naturally takes its place. This sequence will help you determine what you should have accomplished and by when. Continually assess your progress, and make commitments to help yourself stay on task.

> " *Winners can tell you where they are going, what they plan to do along the way, and who will be sharing the adventure with them.*
> —Denis Waitley, author of "The Psychology of Winning" "

Example of a Self-Starter Approach to Planning and Goal Setting

Suppose that your supervisor asks you to prepare a marketing report for the department's last month sales.

- You might first decide that you want a report within two weeks that will show how many contacts each sales person made last month, how many of those resulted in sales, the quantity of sales, the kinds of businesses that bought your products, and how they are using them.

- Since you like to create computerized charts and graphs, you might make this project more exciting for yourself by thinking of the interesting charts you could include in the report and the fun you'll have while visiting with the other staff and perhaps the representatives of the businesses that are using your products.

An important part of motivating yourself to achieve at work is to find or arrange work so that it's fun or personally rewarding, as this will increase your intrinsic motivation. When students from the University of Houston attended a speech by billionaire Warren Buffett (businessman, investor, philanthropist, and Berkshire Hathaway's leader), they remembered these two suggestions from him in particular:[5]

1. Follow your true passion—this enables you to wake up each morning and be excited about what you're doing at work.

2. Don't procrastinate—you're only sabotaging yourself by hampering your chances of success.

In motivating yourself, setting goals, and achieving them, Coombes (the author of *Teach Yourself Self-Motivation*) suggests that you consider the following:[6]

- Do you have the means or requirements to attain your goals and, if not, to acquire them? Items to consider are your knowledge, skill, time, money, and connections.

- What is your motive? Do you want your outcome enough to pay the price, exercise self-discipline, and persist to completion?

- Do you have the opportunity to pursue your goal and enough control over the process to influence its outcome?

Other important factors in motivating yourself and developing your goals and plans are increasing your expectations of yourself, developing a strong work ethic, and embracing challenges and commitments.[7]

If you are not yet at the self-motivated stage of goal accomplishment, learning about planning and goal setting will help you achieve this, as goals help bring purpose into your life. In fact, working toward a goal has been found to make people more satisfied with their lives and more likely to feel positive about themselves.[8]

> " *A goal without a plan is just a wish.*
>
> —*Antoine de Saint-Exupery, French aviator and writer* "

Ask Yourself...

1. Why do you strive to achieve?

2. How do you motivate yourself to strive for a goal or complete a task when the motivation doesn't come naturally?

3. Cite examples of what you've done to gain the skills needed to motivate yourself to achieve something (for example, taken tennis lessons or an SAT preparation course).

15.2 PLANNING FOR YOUR GOALS

Planning is important for organizations and individuals—and in both your personal and professional life—as it helps make things happen. *Planning* is an attempt to prepare for and predict the future. It involves goals, programs, policies, rules, procedures, and decisions about what resources to commit to future action. These resources can include time, money, supplies, material, and labor.

> " *Apathy can be overcome by enthusiasm, and enthusiasm can only be aroused by two things: first an ideal, which takes the imagination by storm; and second, a definite intelligible plan for carrying that ideal into practice.* "
>
> —Arnold Toynbee, English historian and philosopher

Your planning should be ongoing and flexible. Priorities and goals will change as you or your organizations grow or face new situations, and you don't want to become inflexible[9] or have conflicts in priorities with your boss or coworkers. This may sometimes mean that you analyze your tasks daily to reassess your current priorities.[10]

Having specific goals provides a better chance of making things happen and achieving success. In fact, researchers have found that if you want to increase your chances of success, you should focus on achieving certain outcomes.[11]

If you don't have goals, you're likely to watch things happen, wonder what happened, or criticize what happened. Goals help motivate you because they provide you with direction, encourage you to take on difficult challenges, reinforce persistence, and help you create a plan of action.[12]

© 2009 Ted Goff

"Our plan has two parts. First, we make our first sale. Next, we dominate the market."

This plan, in turn, assists you in selecting your strategies, communicating your intentions, and evaluating the effectiveness of your actions.

An example of a typical personal planning activity is finding a job. You'll probably search for a job several times during your career. The reasons range from finding a first job, to being laid off, to desiring greater opportunity. The job search is discussed in another chapter. Generally, though, when developing and executing your plan, consider the following steps:

- Determine your goal (such as finding a beginning job in the information services field).

- Develop a plan for marketing yourself (for example, creating a resume and identifying contacts).

- Plan your job search (where, when, and how you will proceed).

- Interact professionally with potential employers (for example, through your manners, appearance, and attitudes in networking and interviews).

- Be realistic about your expectations and willing to compromise on the job you'll accept.

> " *Failure to prepare is preparing to fail.*
>
> —John Wooden, member of Basketball Hall of Fame as a player and a coach "

Saving for a new car or other major purchases or events is an example of planning in personal life.

© Monkey business Images 2009/Used under license from Shutterstock.com

> **"** *No problem can be solved until it is reduced to some simple form. The changing of a vague difficulty into a specific, concrete form is a very essential element in thinking.*
>
> —*J.P. Morgan, most powerful American banker of his time* **"**

Examples of things that require planning in organizations are shown in Figure 15.1.

Consider the last item in Figure 15.1—coping with economic changes. A business owner wrote a management consultant, asking what could be done to survive a flagging economy. The business owner had already reduced staff, capital spending, and inventories. The consultant suggested that the owner redefine the company's business plan to seek out future opportunities. To do this, the owner should review the business's product or service and customer base, concentrate on customer retention and marketing, and analyze the competition.[13]

Figure 15.1

Organizational planning.

Examples of things that require planning in organizations

Appropriate use of facilities	Time conservation
Care of materials and supplies	Schedules
Conservation of energy and power	Quality management
Cash and credit management	Cost reduction and control
Workforce management	Productivity
Information collection and processing	Coping with economic changes

Psychologists suggest that lack of planning is a subconscious desire to create crises or even to fail. In your personal life, lack of planning may make you feel more spontaneous and alive because of the temporary heightened emotion that results from scrambling to deal with unplanned events. In an organization, managers may feel more important because they have immediate decisions to make. It should be clear that such attitudes are ultimately harmful.

Why Organizations Must Plan

Without planning, organizations have no sense of direction and are ultimately unable to manage resources effectively. No planning or poor planning can result in crisis decisions and employee frustration. Employees spend their time on emergencies and must often move from one task to another as emergencies arise. Then, too, coping with change is more difficult without planning.

Planning is the difference between being reactive and being proactive. When organizations and employees are reactive, they tend to be caught off guard when problems arise. If they are proactive, they look ahead, anticipate problems, and determine solutions to potential problems before they develop. This requires goal setting by individuals within the organization.[14]

Planning in organizations is most effective when all levels of the organization pull together, beginning at the top with the company vision and ending at the bottom with the execution of operational plans. Top managers are responsible for developing the mission and middle managers the tactical plans. First-level managers and other employees are responsible for carrying out operational plans.[15]

A *vision* is a statement of an organization's purpose or reason for existing. A *mission* is the organization's overall goal, which links all efforts toward the vision, stretches and challenges the organization, and has a finish line and timeframe. *Tactical plans* show how the organization will use its resources, budgets, and people to accomplish goals within its mission. *Operational plans* are the day-to-day plans for producing or delivering products and/or services.[16,17]

Planning helps organizations and individuals identify their directions, stay on course, and manage resources effectively. Yet, people differ in their planning.

> " *Vision without action is a daydream. Action without vision is a nightmare.*
> —Japanese proverb "

How People Differ in Planning

People generally fall into three broad categories when planning and taking risks. Consider the following: Imagine three people playing a game of horseshoes. While people's actions may differ with the difficulty of situations, here is how people may approach planning in general. Where do you see yourself? Where would you like to be?

If you are realistic in your planning and risk taking, you've probably recognized that you have a positive self-image and generally plan and set goals for yourself that are challenging but attainable and involve some stretching or risk taking. In the horseshoe game, you would stand back just far enough to feel challenged. You're probably mostly successful in your endeavors,

Technology CONNECTION

To cope with a tough economy and keep up with competition, many companies are logically looking at newer ways of using e-commerce (business conducted over the Internet to assist customer shopping). They are trying to expand their customer base and improve service using such features as online credit approval, blogs, Facebook pages, customer ratings, and their own social network. Their goals are to reach more customers, make shopping easier and even fun, establish personal linkages with customers, provide product information, increase their competitive strength, and thus grow their businesses.

One such company is Conn's, an electronics, appliance, and furniture retailer based in Texas. Another is Sun & Ski Sports, a Houston-based sporting goods company. Both companies report high initial expenses but increased sales and revenues. Such companies must analyze expenses and revenues carefully to determine whether the investment is paying off and they are achieving their goals, normally using additional technology and software to do such analyses.[18]

1. What has been your experience with e-commerce?
2. If you were to start a retail business, would you consider online marketing and sales? If so, what features would you include?
3. What kinds of tactical and operational plans would you make?

> *Take risks. Ask big questions. Don't be afraid to make mistakes. If you don't make mistakes, you're not reaching far enough.*
>
> —David Packard, cofounder of Hewlett-Packard

which gives you the self-confidence to take on other and even more challenging activities. If this is you, give yourself another pat on the back, as these, too, are behaviors valued by employers.

Some people, on the other hand, tend to set goals that are lower than their abilities. Afraid that they will make a mistake or fail in the horseshoe game, they would tend to stand close to the target, thereby reducing their risk and challenge. Because these individuals seldom, if ever, push themselves, they limit how much they achieve for themselves and their organizations.

A third group of people will generally take on goals beyond their current abilities, hoping to perform better or achieve more success than expected. These individuals, uncertain of what they can expect of themselves but unable to admit this fact, would stand so far back from the target that hitting it is unlikely. Because they may aim for unrealistic goals, they may find achieving them or feeling satisfied difficult. Some risk taking is an essential part of growth; the key is to keep it reasonable.

When you are realistic in your planning, goal setting, and risk taking, your successes will give you the self-confidence to take on other and even more challenging activities and become a ***high achiever.***

Consider the following questions in relation to your own goals:

- Do you set moderate, attainable goals?
- Do you become involved in situations so that you may influence what is happening rather than just going with the flow?
- Do you arrange your tasks to be free from interruptions?
- Do you set a realistic timeline for achieving your goals?
- Do you persevere and not procrastinate?
- Are you receptive to feedback about your behavior and performance?

If you answered "yes" to these questions, you're probably already a high achiever or well on your way to becoming one. If you answered "no," analyze what you might do to increase your chances for success. If you think back on times when you did practice these behaviors, you'll probably find that you were more productive.

High achievers share the general characteristics shown in Figure 15.2.

Figure 15.2

Ten characteristics of high achievers.[19,20]

1. They like to control situations and take responsibility for their behaviors.
2. They take reasonable risks.
3. They visualize their accomplishments in advance and let their goals determine their behavior.
4. They tend to be driven and focused on the job to be done.
5. They manage their time wisely and prioritize their work effectively.
6. They use effective communication techniques.
7. They value diversity and increase productivity through teamwork.
8. In negotiations, they are fair and seek solutions that are mutually beneficial.
9. They take time to renew themselves physically, spiritually, emotionally, mentally, and socially.
10. They like immediate feedback about their performance.

> *It is the nature of man to rise to greatness if greatness is expected of him.*
> —*John Steinbeck, American author*

People procrastinate for a number of reasons. Some people procrastinate because they have an unrealistic view of what is needed for success. They don't recognize the great amount of planning, organizing, and hard work that is required to make success seem easy.

Other people procrastinate because they have poor coping skills, aren't good at handling problems, or have a low tolerance for disappointment. Instead of analyzing situations to determine alternative actions when complications occur or steps are blocked, they give up and do nothing. You can do a reality check to determine how serious a problem is by doing the following:

- Measure the difficulty. Rate it on a scale of 1 to 10. Measuring the difficulty may be as simple as writing it down.

- Bring the past into the present. Think of similar situations and remember your successes. Analyze them. What were the actions, feelings, and thoughts that led you to success?

- Imagine the worst. Ask yourself, "What is the worst that can happen if I fail in this endeavor? Will I die, lose my job, or lose my spouse?" Because the consequences are not usually that dire, such a reality check will immediately boost your confidence.

- Visualize yourself accomplishing your present goal. In doing your reality check, be careful of false confidence, which can lead to your being unprepared. If the reality check shows that the problem is indeed major, you can at least now concentrate on dealing with it rather than on being anxious about it.

Still others procrastinate as a way of rebelling against expectations, not recognizing the immaturity of such a response. A more effective approach to handling expectations that you may consider unfair or inappropriate for you is to discuss the situation with the person who holds those expectations. Then, you can decide for yourself what is best and proceed accordingly.

However, many procrastinators lack assertiveness. They are uncomfortable addressing a difficult situation, hoping perhaps that the problem will go away. This lack of assertiveness can create additional delays if people are reluctant to ask others for the resources or help necessary to perform a task.

> **KeyPoint**
>
> If you procrastinate, examine your perceptions, coping skills, tolerance for disappointment, assertiveness, and task organization.

Steps to Help You Achieve Your Goals

1. Set your goals, thinking carefully about what you want to accomplish or change, your motivation, and your purpose.
2. Develop a plan that includes the steps, activities, and materials necessary to achieve your goal. Include whatever information you need (for example, certification requirements for a career you may desire) and what you may need to change in your environment (such as setting aside specific time to study).
3. Set out to achieve your goals.
4. Periodically monitor your progress and reevaluate your goals, making any needed adjustments.

Some people create problems for themselves by thinking that they can complete a task with one big charge, forgetting the importance of a series of actions. When you find yourself putting off work on a task or goal, examine yourself and the situation closely to see why. Then, decide what you want to do. If you feel overwhelmed, dividing a large task into several smaller ones may be the answer. Don't try to do everything at once. The best way to attack giant projects is to start with small steps and remember that the key to achievement is to think big but act now. A small success can motivate you to move on to the next step. Small, steady steps are the key.

Another factor that may help you overcome procrastination is the support of someone who believes in you, such as a friend, relative, or coworker. Developing these supportive relationships takes effective human relations skills.

If procrastination is a problem for you, think about the pride you feel when you accomplish a task successfully. Giving yourself credit for your accomplishments can push you toward attempting other goals.

Ask Yourself...

1. Think back to something that you planned recently. What steps did you plan to take?

2. Did the plans go as expected? Why, or why not? Did anything unforeseen happen?

3. Would your planning have been more effective if several people had been involved? Why, or why not?

15.3   SETTING GOALS AND DEVELOPING A PLAN

Throughout your life, you'll be involved in various kinds of goal-setting and planning activities. As an employee, you'll be responsible for supporting organizational goals and helping establish and carrying out your work goals. On a personal level, you will need to choose goals appropriate to you.

> *The best leaders create high-performance cultures. They set demanding goals, measure results, and hold people accountable.*
>
> *—Louis V. Gerstner, Jr., former chair of the board and CEO of IBM*

Organizational Goals

Two management authors, Ramon Aldag and Timothy Stearns, have identified three broad categories of goals in organizations: official, operative, and operational goals. Most employees are directly involved in operational goals. However, all employees are impacted by official and operative goals.

Official goals are developed by upper management, are formally stated, and pertain to the overall mission of the organization. You may find them in your company's annual reports or newsletters. Of the three types of goals, they are usually the most abstract ones. They tend to be open-ended; that is, the goal itself may not include information about quantity, quality, or deadline. A common example in business today is "to provide excellent service"—which you would be expected to help deliver no matter at what level you are working.

Operative goals are those goals for which middle management is responsible. They concern the operating policies of the organization. These goals tend to be more specific than the abstract official goals, usually include a mix of open-ended and close-ended goals, and are normally redefined on a yearly basis. Common examples of operative goals in business today are "to increase the company's share of the market" and "to build a more diverse workforce." Your work contributions and human relations skills will help achieve these goals.

Operational goals are the responsibility of first-line supervisors and other employees. They are statements of the expected results of the efforts of the various units of the organization. They include built-in standards of behavior, performance criteria, and completion time. They are concrete and close-ended. An example of an operational goal is "to increase sales of XYZ chemical by 2012 by 20 percent over the current year by installing a new process." Notice that the goal includes a specific date for completion and specifies how much. As an employee in this company, you may be directly affected by helping to install the new process, learning how to use it, and carrying it out. Your flexibility and willingness to learn may make the difference in whether this goal is achieved.

Figure 15.3 shows the three categories of organizational goals with other examples.[21]

Figure 15.3

Categories of organizational goals.

Type of Goal	Whose Responsibility	What Pertains to	Example	
Official	Upper management	Overall mission of the organization	Become the global leader in fruit juice brands	Broad
Operational	Middle management	Operating polices and plans of the organization	Increase the company's share of the fruit juice market by 10%	
Operative	Supervisors and employees	Expected results of the efforts of the various parts of the organization	Increase global sales of fruit juice by 20% by hiring ten new sales representatives in Latin America	Specific

Understanding the three categories of goals will provide you with greater understanding of the organization and the importance of your role, work, and contributions.

Work Goals

In an organization, goals should involve participation of many levels of employees. Your most frequent participation and communication will usually be between you and your supervisor. Ideally the two of you will set mutually agreeable goals, in that you determine them together and agree that they are the focus of your work. When you participate in setting goals pertaining to the work you perform, you're more likely to understand their importance and your role and to feel committed to accomplishing them.

As an employee participating in the goal-setting process, your goals should reflect your understanding and support of the goals of your company and department. Of course, the goals should be challenging but attainable, specific, and interesting to you.

Consider the following example, using the operational goal discussed in the previous section. Your responsibility is to help the company increase sales of XYZ chemical by 2012. Therefore, your work goals might include the following: Within the next two months, I will attend training offered by the process designer to learn how to install the new process. Within the next four months, I will participate in training offered by my company to learn how to use the process effectively and safely. Within the next six months, I will work with my supervisor and team members to develop a plan for analyzing improvements in quality and quantity provided by the new process, monitoring sales, and gaining customer feedback.

Personal Goals

Choosing goals in life requires that you examine your wants and needs. Consider, for example, how important these life factors are to you:

- *Expertise.* If this is important to you, you must become an authority in some area and possess the human relations skills to communicate your expertise to others and have it received. Which area? Do your human relations skills need developing?

- *Happiness and contentment.* Without human relations skills, your life can be in constant turmoil, which can interfere with personal happiness and contentment.

- *Independence.* Being independent may require time and at least some money. When will you have that time, and how will you obtain the necessary finances to be independent?

- *Leadership.* To be a leader, you must gain influence. Where? At work? In the community? How?

- *Parenthood.* Parenthood requires a tremendous investment of time, finances, and physical and emotional energy. How will you afford that investment now? Later?

- *Personal development.* Personal development means personal growth, through hobbies, talents, expanded knowledge, or other means. It implies continuing to learn throughout your life. How will you feed this desire in

> **KeyPoint**
> In choosing your personal goals, honestly determine the relative importance of expertise, contentment, independence, leadership, parenthood, personal development, prestige, security, and service to others.

yourself? Where can you find the necessary direction, guidance, and instruction?

- *Prestige.* Prestige differs for different people. How will you measure it—by the house in which you live, the organization for which you work, or where you vacation?

- *Security.* Security may be financial or emotional. If you require financial security, how much money do you need to consider yourself financially secure, and how will you acquire it? If emotional security is important to you, what does that mean—a supportive supervisor? A caring spouse? Concerned friends?

- *Service to others.* Helping others, through a career or in different ways, is personally satisfying for many people. If you desire to serve others, where and how would you like to use your energy and abilities?

Considering these questions objectively can help you set your personal goals. Notice that all these factors, which are the means people use to measure their own personal success, require high levels of human relations skills.

A S.M.A.R.T. Approach

To set effective goals for your job or yourself, use the *S.M.A.R.T. guidelines*. S.M.A.R.T. goals are specific, measurable, attainable, realistic, and timely.[22,23] For example, your specific goal might be to increase your personal sales by 20 percent this summer. You could measure this by counting the units you sell. You would consider this goal attainable and timely if summer is a time when people and organizations are likely to buy what you're selling. And you could consider the goal realistic if you believe that with a little extra push you can exceed the 18 percent increases of the last two summers.

In The News

When General Motors (GM) filed for bankruptcy protection on June 1, 2009, Chief Executive Fritz Henderson outlined a written goal and plan to restructure the company. He set a goal to "break even on a cash-flow basis when total U.S. vehicle sales hit 10 million cars a year." Strategies for meeting this goal included offloading some dealerships, brands, and overseas units and reducing plants and employees. Apparently, numerous parties had input into the plan, including the United Auto Workers.[24]

1. Compare the GM plan to the S.M.A.R.T. guidelines. How many of the characteristics do you think the GM goal includes? Which ones?

2. If you were an employee in a GM dealership or plant, do you think the plan as described earlier provides adequate operational goals to let you know what is likely to happen to your unit? Why or why not?

Two other factors need to be considered in setting goals:

1. Goals should be written. Writing down goals increases understanding and commitment and makes reviewing them easier.

2. Your goals may need to be coordinated with other people's goals and with your personal responsibilities. For example, assume that you currently live in Los Angeles but have a personal goal to move to the New York office of your company. You will need to consider your family—your spouse may be under consideration for a major promotion in her job and your daughter excited about graduating with her classmates next year.

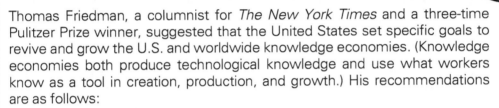

Global CONNECTION

Thomas Friedman, a columnist for *The New York Times* and a three-time Pulitzer Prize winner, suggested that the United States set specific goals to revive and grow the U.S. and worldwide knowledge economies. (Knowledge economies both produce technological knowledge and use what workers know as a tool in creation, production, and growth.) His recommendations are as follows:

- Build a flexible economy with workers that can creatively produce knowledge and use it.
- Attract diverse, smart, and energetic immigrants from around the world to add to this economy through their knowledge and expertise.[25]

1. Think about companies with which you are familiar. What have you observed or heard about them that would suggest they may have goals similar to those suggested by Friedman?

2. In Chapter 1, you learned that creativity and innovation are needed 21st century skills in the United States. Do you think that Friedman's suggested goals would help meet this need? Explain.

Developing a Plan

As listed earlier, the second step in achieving your goals is to develop a plan that outlines the necessary sequence, activities, and materials. In doing this, consider information and credentials you may need (for example, certification requirements for a career you may desire) and what you may need to change in your environment (such as setting aside specific time to study). Allow adequate time to plan the project and, for projects that affect or will involve others, obtain feedback from all concerned.

For each goal that you set, establish a time by which the goal will be completed. Divide larger, complex goals into manageable steps. For example, suppose that you are a college freshman and have decided that your goal is to become a Certified Public Accountant (CPA). Your steps might include the following:

1. Decide on the state where you would like to practice, as requirements vary in some states. This may involve discussions with significant others in your life and a consideration of financial implications (for example, costs of moving to and living in that state).

2. Research online and/or discuss with a college counselor the requirements to become a CPA in the state where you plan to practice. The discussion should include both educational and experience requirements.

3. Develop appropriate steps within your education plan. For example, some states require a bachelor's degree, 24 hours in accounting, and 24 additional hours in business-related topics while others require the equivalent of a master's degree. How, when, and where you will obtain this education become steps in your plan. In fact, if your finances prohibit your attending school full time, you may also have to add finding a job to the plan and establish timelines for completion of specific numbers of courses.

4. Some states also require at least 2,000 hours of work experience under a registered CPA before you can be licensed. Do you have the time, money, and commitment needed to acquire this experience? You will need to develop intermediate goals for acquiring this experience, pertaining to where, how, and when.

5. After meeting the education and work requirements, you will still need to devote additional time and money for the CPA exam review course. This requires creation of additional goals, such as how and when.

6. After you are licensed, will you likewise have the commitment to continue your education to remain certified? This will require setting additional goals, all of which may be affected by other goals, persons, and responsibilities in your life.

While such detailed consideration in your planning may seem daunting, don't let complex goals divert you from your dreams. Advance planning and organizing and effective work habits enable most people to accomplish even the most complex goals.

Part of effective work habits is managing your time. If you frequently overload yourself with too many tasks because you can't say "no" to your friends and family members when you are asked to take on additional chores or responsibilities, you may ultimately become bogged down on your path toward success. Staying focused on the big picture and asking for what you need (for example, time and resources) are important.

You will be involved in various kinds of goal-setting and planning activities throughout your life and career. Using the suggestions provided here will help you understand and support organizational goals and establish and address your personal goals, thereby making you more successful in both parts of your life.

Ethics CONNECTION

For numerous reasons, many Americans are taking on second jobs. They may have student loans to repay, car and credit card payments to make, increased rents and car payments to meet, or possible layoffs to anticipate.

Nancy Trejos, a writer for *The Washington Post,* points out that primary employers may become concerned about second jobs interfering with fulfilling responsibilities in employees' primary jobs.[26] Obviously, the primary job is more important, but what happens when both employers request overtime work? Or if working two jobs creates family, rest, or social life complications?

1. If you know someone who works two jobs, what has been that person's experience in fulfilling responsibilities to each employer while meeting his or her financial goals?

2. What has been that person's experience in balancing competing demands—work vs. family/friends/rest/social life?

3. What would you say to a friend who tells you he or she is working a second job and keeping it secret from the primary employer?

> *Desire is the key to motivation, but it's determination and commitment to an unrelenting pursuit of your goal—a commitment to excellence—that will enable you to attain the success you seek.*
>
> —Mario Andretti, successful race car driver

Ask Yourself...

1. What was the last personal goal you reached successfully? What steps did you take to reach the goal?

2. If you work, do you know what your company goals are and how your work supports them? If so, state those goals. If not, how can you find out? (If you don't currently work, think of jobs you or a friend may have held.)

3. If you work, what goals can you set for yourself to better demonstrate your support of company goals? (If you don't currently work, think of jobs you or a friend may have held.)

15.4   WORKING TOWARD GOALS

Your attitudes and personality can determine how successful you are in working toward your goals. Staying focused on the big picture and prioritizing your goals will help you achieve them.

A Positive Attitude

As discussed in previous chapters, a positive attitude is a major contributor to your human relations skills. It can also help you attain your goals. Research has shown that people with a positive attitude are more successful than those with a negative attitude. With a positive attitude, you believe that you have both the will and the way to accomplish your goals. You can motivate yourself and find ways to accomplish your goals. If you are having difficulty, you can reassure yourself that things will be better. As a person with a positive attitude, you are flexible enough to find different approaches or change goals if necessary, and you know to break down a daunting task into smaller, more manageable steps.[27,28]

A Versatile and Adaptive Personality

A versatile and adaptive personality will enable you to perform at your peak and feel energetic in working toward your goals. Two psychologists, Robert Kriegel and Marilyn Harris Kriegel, suggest that most people have the potential to perform in this way by maintaining an attitude that combines commitment, confidence, and control.[29]

Identifying what you want, knowing your innermost desires, and translating them into action will result in harmony between your goals and actions. The more committed you are to a goal, the less difficult it seems. Initiative and perseverance are important components of commitment and are particularly important behaviors and attitudes in a shifting economy and competitive marketplace.

Confidence in your own worth and ability to achieve a goal means that, while you might hate to fail in pursuing a goal, you don't fear it, because you know that with risks come mistakes and failures but also the possibility of learning and greater gain.

KeyPoint
A versatile and adaptive personality and an attitude that combines commitment, confidence, and control will help you reach your goals.

How to Handle Fear in Pursuing Your Goals

- Be alert to your own inner signals of fear.
- When you notice them, stop, take a few deep, slow breaths, hold each to the count of three, and exhale slowly.

This practice can help put matters back into perspective.

In pursuing your goals, concentrate on what you can control to improve your performance and effectiveness. This includes your thoughts, feelings, attitudes, and actions.

Robert Land, executive vice president of a large national human resources management consulting firm, pointed out that successful people are generally those who strive to maintain control over their work environment and a myriad of unanticipated events.[30] In other words, these people are proactive rather than reactive. He advises that we be responsible for our careers and ourselves. We can't expect our bosses to take charge of our careers because bosses seldom have the time or interest to help us plan where we should be and how to get there.

Prioritizing Your Goals

You've probably noticed that you seldom have the luxury of pursuing one goal at a time. Both organizations and individuals are always working toward multiple goals. This means you must prioritize and reassess as you go.

Aldag and Stearns, authors of management books, have identified four techniques that managers can use to decide which goals to emphasize during periods of conflict. You can apply them to your personal goals and plans as well. They include satisficing, sequential attention, preference ordering, and goal changes.[31]

Satisficing (a combination of the words *satisfy* and *suffice*) is a term created to define situations in which one perfect and unique solution may not be possible. It refers to solutions that offer good results under the circumstances. When you're faced with numerous goals, you can reduce your stress by identifying a satisfactory rather than optimum level of performance for some of them. Some tasks simply need to be done, and you may often have several acceptable ways in which they might be performed. For example, in your personal life, satisficing might consist of light housecleaning when you're pressed for time, so as not to sacrifice other goals. In many situations, perfection, or even excellence, may not be important, and can actually be costly or stressful. The desire for perfection can create havoc with goal accomplishment and people's lives if carried too far. Save your energy for the things that really do need to be as close to perfect as possible.

When you have multiple priorities, you may need to shift your attention from one goal to the next over periods of time. This is called *sequential attention*. Successful working parents frequently adopt this tactic. Work priorities sometimes take precedence over family activities, and at other times the reverse is true. The main point is to keep the overall quality of performance in each area acceptable.

If you have several goals you want to pursue, you may need to rank them according to preference. This is called *preference ordering*. For example, a company may decide to maximize profit over expansion, or you may decide to save for a new car rather than take a vacation.

You may change goals because they become outdated or inappropriate, such as when you complete a degree or buy the car for which you've been

> *Whether you are successful at work depends not on how well you do all the tasks assigned, but on how well you choose which are the important tasks to do.*
> —Charles McCloud, business author and consultant

saving. An example of *goal changing* is that of the Foundation for Infantile Paralysis. Its original goal was to develop a vaccine for polio. Once the vaccine was developed, it changed its goal to conquering birth defects and became the March of Dimes.

Ask Yourself...

1. Describe a time you had to attempt satisfaction rather than perfection.

2. In what situations might it be acceptable to do a satisfactory job rather than an excellent one? When might excellence be important?

3. Do you consider yourself a versatile and adaptive personality? If not, what would you need to do to become more so?

15.5 MONITORING AND REEVALUATING GOALS

Goals are not just a writing exercise to be put aside until the time comes to write goals for another period. Review your goals from time to time to check your progress, modify your strategies if necessary, or perhaps discard the goal if it is no longer important or possible—and then set new ones.

Monitoring Your Progress

Periodically review your goals, reevaluate their importance, and monitor your progress in achieving them. Such frequent review is important to make certain you are still on track toward obtaining your ultimate desire. If not, be flexible and willing to adjust your approach. In the final analysis, persistence will guarantee success in your life.

You and your organization will use your goals to monitor your progress. This may be done simply through observation or more formally through written progress reports. These progress checks help identify changes that may be needed while time still remains. Seek and welcome feedback from your supervisor on how you are doing in meeting your goals. Make these checks of goals in your personal life as well, recognizing that you are responsible for your own monitoring and your own progress.

You will find that this kind of feedback is not only helpful but also essential, as knowing how you are doing will help keep you on track. Further, when feedback is positive, it can build up your self-confidence and help you do better in this task or other tasks.[32,33]

Reevaluating Goals

Goals can become obsolete once you've achieved them. They can also become less important as you grow. Think of how your own goals have changed over the years. You can probably recall various ways in which you answered the

KeyPoint
Review your goals periodically to check your progress, modify your strategies if necessary, reevaluate your goals, and set new ones.

traditional question, "What do you want to be when you grow up?" At four years of age, you may have wanted to be a cowboy or princess, at six Superman, at ten an astronaut, and in your teens a professional athlete or musician. Somewhere along the line, you may have lost interest in some of these, decided you lacked the natural ability necessary for others, or found something else that appealed to you. Recall your early wish; today you may have a different career goal in mind, one that probably combines dreams and practicality. Then, after you have been working awhile, you may decide to set other career goals. Mid-career switches, for instance, are fairly common.

You may find that you sometimes have difficulty completing your long-range plans because you grow tired, forget them, or allow short- or mid-range plans to interfere. Because long-range plans cover a greater period of time, situations and circumstances may change, making the long-range plans impractical. In that case, you may need to change them.

15.6   GOALS AND PERFORMANCE APPRAISALS

The *performance appraisal* is a measurement of how well an employee is doing on the job. Performance appraisals can be performed by:

- Supervisors rating their employees
- Employees rating their superiors
- Team members rating one another
- Outsiders rating employees
- Employees rating themselves
- A combination of techniques

Because of the increasing use of workplace teams and a concern about customer feedback, appraisals by team members and outsiders are growing rapidly. The most common type of appraisal, however, is that done at least annually by an immediate supervisor.

> **KeyPoint**
> Organizations appraise employees to encourage good performance; let them know how they are doing; and gain information for raises, promotions, transfers, and terminations.

Why Organizations Appraise Employee Performance

Organizations may appraise your performance as an employee for a number of reasons:

- *To encourage good job performance, discourage unacceptable performance, and correct inappropriate behavior that interferes with good performance.* If it is conducted correctly, the appraisal session can facilitate communication. It can help you grow, increase motivation, or at least provide a better understanding of what is expected of you.

- *To let you know how you are doing.* Positive feedback will let you know what you are doing well so that you can continue to do it. Negative feedback will allow you to learn about and correct weaknesses in your behavior and performance. Such feedback will assist you in making plans for professional improvement.

- *To give the organization information about employees that can be used for raises, promotions, transfers, and terminations.* Appraisals can help move your career forward or help identify areas that need more work. They also help managers identify the need for training individuals and groups of employees.

If performance appraisals are to be effective, both the supervisor and the employee must prepare for them.

Preparing for a Performance Appraisal

You can take steps ahead of time and during the appraisal session to help make your appraisal a positive process. Using a proactive, assertive approach is to your advantage.

> *Being busy does not always mean real work. The object of all work is production or accomplishment, and to either of these ends there must be forethought, system, planning, intelligence and honest purpose, as well as perspiration. Seeming to do is not doing.*
>
> —Thomas A. Edison, inventor

An appraisal is a bit like a job interview in that you need to prepare. Spend a little time anticipating what items your employer will raise and preparing responses, as well as listing any questions you want to ask and points you want to be sure are considered. Also spend some time before the evaluation considering what you'd like your goals for the upcoming period to be.

Before your appraisal, remember that feedback through appraisal of your performance is not a disciplinary session. Rather, it will help keep you on track to pursue goals and activities that are valued by your organization or to indicate where you may be falling short. Additionally, feedback can be motivational, as it will help you identify where to sharpen your skills and when to celebrate success.

Make sure that you understand what is expected of you. Effective supervisors will be preparing for the appraisal session throughout the entire appraisal period. They will know what is expected of you, will make sure you also know, will observe you frequently, and will tell you how you are performing.

You can also prepare for it throughout the period. If you participated in the establishment of goals for your job, you understand what is expected of you. If you didn't, don't wait until the appraisal session to ask questions. Keep checking that your understanding of what you are to do is the same as your supervisor's expectations. You can also take the initiative and ask for feedback during the period. This way, you will eliminate surprises in the appraisal session. Open communication with your supervisor is extremely important.

Still considering actions before your appraisal session, become familiar with the evaluation or appraisal technique to be used. Throughout the period between evaluations, note what you consider to be your important accomplishments, with dates and other details. Whenever you accomplish something, put a brief write-up in a file, either a file based on the evaluation instrument or, if you don't have that, a simple word processing file. When the time for the appraisal draws near, you can then review the material in this file to prepare for the evaluation.

Before the session, take the time to conduct a self-appraisal by completing the instrument as objectively as you can. This activity will help you remember accomplishments that you want to bring up if your supervisor overlooks them. It also can increase communication and understanding during the session. Identify the areas that you believe need improvement also.

During the appraisal session, you can help make your appraisal a positive process by going into it willing to listen and participate, identifying obstacles to your performance, and making sure that you understand what is expected of you at the conclusion of the appraisal. If you go in with a defensive, closed mind, you will sabotage the session before it even starts. The appraisal is a good opportunity to share your career goals with your supervisor.

If obstacles have been in the way of your performing satisfactorily, you should have made them known to your supervisor before now. However, if you have not, certainly share them at this time. Are you frequently late in completing a weekly report because the sales department is late in submitting figures to you? If so, let your supervisor know what you need to perform better.

At the conclusion of the appraisal session, know what you are to do. For instance, should you continue as you have been, assume other responsibilities, or focus on performing current responsibilities better? Plan to set new goals at the conclusion of your appraisal.

Taking these steps will help make the session more effective. Strong human relations skills are extremely important in each step of this process. The greater your skills and those of your supervisor, the better will be the outcome of an appraisal. This outcome, in turn, will benefit you, your supervisor, and the organization.

The Supervisor's Role

If you know and understand the steps typically followed by an effective supervisor in conducting an appraisal, you can use them to prepare better. Lester Bittel, the author of *What Every Supervisor Should Know*,[34] suggests that the supervisor will:

1. Schedule the appraisal in advance and ask you to think about achievements and areas for improvement to be discussed during the session.

2. Read your personnel file and any other performance information available.

> **KeyPoint**
> To prepare for an appraisal, realize it can help you grow. Anticipate what items your employer will raise, prepare responses, list your questions and the points you want to be covered, and identify the goals for the upcoming period.

3. Be prepared and will plan in advance what to say.

4. Choose a quiet location for the session, free of interruptions; allow plenty of time; and give you opportunities to speak.

5. Focus on performance. (Salary is typically discussed in a separate meeting.)

6. Explain the purpose of the meeting, ask your opinion, discuss total performance, reach agreement on standards of performance, document the agreement, and have you sign the completed appraisal form.

If you accept these actions as part of the effective appraisal process, each step will seem less threatening to you.

Ask Yourself...

1. Have you ever been appraised in a job? What was it like?

2. In what ways do job appraisals differ from grades in school? In what ways are they similar?

3. How might an appraisal help you identify areas for your personal development (such as improving your written communication skills)? Is this likely to help your career development? If so, how?

KEY TERMS

goal	operative goals
planning	operational goals
vision	S.M.A.R.T. guidelines
mission	satisficing
tactical plans	sequential attention
operational plans	preference ordering
high achiever	goal changing
official goals	performance appraisal

CHAPTER SUMMARY

Planning can benefit both people and organizations by improving the chances of success. Having goals provides targets. Without planning, organizations tend to become reactive rather than proactive, creating frustration for employees.

The three broad categories of organizational goals are official, operative, and operational. They differ in how specific they are, what activities are included, and which level of employee has responsibility for them.

To be most effective, goals should be written, measurable, specific, and challenging, but attainable. In an organization, for the greatest understanding and motivation to occur, an individual's goals should be developed with the participation of both the supervisor and the affected individual. When goals conflict, four techniques can be used to prioritize them: satisficing, sequential attention, preference ordering, and goal changing.

In setting personal goals, consider your priorities in life. These can include expertise, contentment, independence, leadership, parenthood, personal development, prestige, security, and service to others.

Apply four guidelines in setting goals: (1) be realistic, (2) openly commit yourself, (3) coordinate your goals with people who are important to you professionally and personally, and (4) visualize success.

An attitude that combines commitment, confidence, and control can improve your chances of personal success.

The employee performance appraisal is a measurement of how well the employee is doing on the job. Employees should take steps to make appraisal a beneficial experience.

420   Part 3   Career Development

REVIEW

1. Explain how planning can benefit people and organizations.

2. What are the three categories of organizational goals? Whose responsibility is each category? What kinds of activities are included in each category?

3. List the characteristics of well-formulated goals.

4. Name and describe the four techniques for prioritizing goals.

5. Why do organizations conduct performance appraisals? What steps should employees take to prepare for an appraisal?

CRITICAL THINKING

1. Identify some negative situations in your personal life and at work that developed because of a lack of planning. What happened? How could the situations have been avoided?

2. Has procrastination ever been a problem for you? If so, what is the usual result of your procrastination? How might you eliminate this problem?

3. Briefly review your goals so far in life. Analyze why the goals have or haven't been accomplished. How has their status affected where you are today and your current goals?

4. Again considering situations in your personal life and at work, think about periods of conflicting goals. How was the conflict resolved? How might the four techniques for prioritizing goals described in this chapter have helped you?

5. Think about times when you received appraisals, at work or anywhere else. How did you react to the feedback? Were some of your reactions negative? Why? How did you use the feedback? Did it help you grow in some way? How?

CASE STUDIES

In small groups, analyze the following situations:

1 You Can't Have It All at Once   Roberto is a part-time student at the local community college. He is afraid that he will once again have to drop his courses even though he wants an associate degree in management very much. Roberto's wife works full time at a fast food restaurant. However, the cost of child care for their two children, normal living expenses, and assistance to his elderly parents are such that he must work full time as a shoe salesman in the nearby mall. Additionally, he feels that he should serve as coach for his children's sports activities each season. Plus, he helps his wife around the house, does all household maintenance and yard work, and helps care for his parents' yard. (The appearance of his home is an area of special pride for him.) Needless to say, all this activity leaves little time for social events with friends or evenings out with his wife—or even studying as much as he needs to.

Roberto did not go to college immediately after graduating from high school and feels that he is falling even farther behind by going part time. For the last four semesters, he has tried to catch up by registering for three or four courses even though his counselor advised against such a heavy load. By the middle of each semester, he feels so overwhelmed that he drops all or most of his courses. It is now midway through the fall semester, and Roberto once again recognizes that feeling of hopelessness.

1. What is wrong with Roberto's plans?

2. What advice would you give him in setting long-range, mid-range, and short-range goals?

3. How might he prioritize his goals?

2 **Planning Gone Awry**   Ann Aston is a new employee in a large firm. Recently she was asked to participate in setting departmental and individual goals for the next year. She spent hours in her office alone, determining her own goals and activities for the next year.

After a lot of hard work, no information about company and departmental goals, and no discussion with her supervisor, Emily Rodriguez, Ann submitted her goals to Emily, who passed them on to the corporate office.

Six weeks later, the corporate office issued the overall company goals for the next year. Ann was astonished to see no resemblance between the company's goals and activities and those she had submitted. Emily asked her to re-do her goals to support the goals issued by the corporate office, which she did. Again, there was no discussion of departmental goals.

1. Is this the correct approach that companies should use in planning and setting goals? Why or why not?

2. What happened to create the need for Ann to prepare a second set of goals?

3. What could Emily and Ann have done to make sure that Ann's goals and activities were in line with those of the company and department?

HUMAN RELATIONS IN ACTION

Go online and locate a test that assesses your ability to set goals or work toward success. Take the test, review your results, and indicate whether you agree with them. If you don't agree, why not? Is there something you can do to improve your ability to set goals and achieve different results on the test?

Next, in a one-page essay, describe what goals you want to have achieved by the year 2030 in the following areas of your life: professional life, personal relationships, and social life. Then, draw up a plan to move yourself from your current status to your desired achievements.

For additional resources, refer to the web site for this text:
www.cengage.com/management/dalton

RESOURCES

1. A willingness to be misunderstood. (2008, December 8). *U.S. News & World Report*, 51.

2. Griffin, M. (n.d.). The real reasons we explore space. *Air & Space* (Smithsonian).

3. Coombes, F. (2008). *Teach yourself self-motivation*. Ohio: McGraw-Hill.

4. McGraw, P. (Ph.D.). (2000). *The life strategies workbook*. New York: Hyperion.

5. Sixel, L. M. (2009, May 16). UH students heed advice from 'Oracle of Omaha.' *Houston Chronicle*, p. D4.

6. Coombes, F. (2008). *Teach yourself self-motivation*. Ohio: McGraw-Hill.

7. DuBrin, A. J. (2008). *Human relations for career and personal success* (8th ed.). Upper Saddle River, NJ: Pearson/Prentice Hall.

8. Krueger, R. (1998). The status of perceived dream fulfillment in midlife males. Ph.D. dissertation, California School of Professional Psychology. Cited in Niven, D. (Ph.D.) (2005). *The 100 simple secrets of the best half of life: What scientists have learned and how you can use it.* New York: HarperCollins.

9. DuBrin, A. J. (2008). *Human relations for career and personal success* (8th ed.). Upper Saddle River, NJ: Pearson/Prentice Hall.

10. Heller, R., & Hindle, T. (1998). *Essential manager's manual.* New York: DK Publishing, Inc.

11. Reece, B., & Brandt, R. (2008). *Effective human relations: Personal and organizational applications* (10th ed.). New York: Houghton Mifflin Company.

12. Ibid.

13. Consolino, R. (2009, April 19). Long-term strategy key for survival. *Houston Chronicle*, p. D4.

14. Heller, R., & Hindle, T. (1998). *Essential manager's manual.* New York: DK Publishing, Inc.

15. Williams, C. (2008). *MGMT.* Mason, OH: South-Western/Cengage Learning.

16. Ibid.

17. Collins, J. C., & J. I. Porras. (1991, Fall). Organizational vision and visionary organizations. *California Management Review*, *34*(1), 30–52.

18. Hem, B. (2008, December 17). Virtual step, real gain. *Houston Chronicle*, p. D1.

19. McClelland, D. C. (1965, November–December). Achievement motivation can be developed. *Harvard Business Review*, 43, 68.

20. McClelland, D. C. (1961). Methods of measuring human motivation. In J. W. Atkinson (Ed.), *The achieving society* (pp. 41–43). Princeton, NJ: D. Van Nostrand.

21. Aldag, R. J., & Stearns, T. M. (1987). *Management.* Mason, OH: Thomson/South-Western.

22. Williams, C. (2008). *MGMT.* Mason, OH: South-Western/Cengage Learning.

23. King, A., Oliver, B., Sloop, B., & Vaverek, K. (1995). *Planning & goal setting for improved performance: Participant's guide.* Cincinnati, OH: Thomson Executive Press.

24. Zimmerman, M. (*Los Angeles Times*). (2009, June 2). A greener GM, but will it get out of red? *Houston Chronicle*, p. A1.

25. Friedman, T. (*The New York Times*). (2009, February 11). Now is not the time to close our borders or minds. *Houston Chronicle*, p. B9.

26. Trejos, N. (*Washington Post*). (2009, January 11). Many taking second jobs to make ends meet. *Houston Chronicle*, p. D4.

27. Goleman, D. (1995). *Emotional intelligence*. New York: Bantam Books.

28. Snyder, C. R. (Interviewee) (1991). Cited in Goleman, D. (1995). *Emotional intelligence*. New York: Bantam Books.

29. Kriegel, R., & Marilyn, H. K. (1986, March). How to reach peak performance—naturally. *The Secretary*, 22–24.

30. Burdick, T. E., & Charlene, A. M. (1988, April 4). Executives face freeze on fast track. *The Houston Post*, p. C1.

31. Aldag, R. J., & Timothy, M. S. (1987). *Management*. Mason, OH: Thomson/South-Western.

32. Goleman, D. (1998). *Working with emotional intelligence*. New York: Bantam Books.

33. Quinones, M. D. (1996). Contextual influences on training effectiveness. Washington, American Psychological Association. Cited in Goleman, D. (1998). *Working with emotional intelligence*. New York: Bantam Books.

34. Bittel, L. (1985). *What every supervisor should know*. New York: McGraw-Hill.

PART 4

WORK AND LIFE

"The people who get on in this world are the people who get up and look for the circumstances they want, and, if they can't find them, make them."

—George Bernard Shaw, Irish playwright

16

CHANGE:
A CONSTANT IN AN INCONSTANT WORLD

OBJECTIVES

After studying this chapter, you should be able to:

16.1 Identify who usually recommends and implements organizational changes.

16.2 Describe significant forces that are driving change in today's workplace.

16.3 Explain several effective methods of planning and implementing change.

16.4 Understand common reasons for resistance to change.

16.5 Describe the leader's role in the change process.

16.6 Cite methods of helping employees cope with change.

Jump Start

If you own an iPhone, chances are you've downloaded some of the tens of thousands of applications available at Apple's App Store. From reminding you where you parked to transforming your phone into an ocarina, there are applications for almost any use you can imagine, designed by big companies, small ones, and even ordinary consumers. This is *end-user innovation,* modifying a product to adapt it to one's needs, and maybe in the process enhancing its value for other users and the product developer.

Time magazine writer Steven Johnson points to Twitter as another example of end-user innovation. It was designed as a bare-bones microblogging tool for posting and reading messages on a phone or online. Almost as soon as Twitter debuted in 2006, users began expanding it. They invented ways to group discussions by topic, reply to other users, and search a stream of live posts (Tweets). They've also developed thousands of third-party applications.[1]

Johnson sees such products as ushering in a new style of innovation at which the United States excels, citing other "lifestyle-changing hit products" such as the iPod, Facebook, Google, eBay, Xbox, and Amazon. In their best-seller *Wikinomics,* Don Tapscott and Anthony Williams see forward-looking organizations changing their approach to product development to make room for customers as co-innovators, as these "prosumers" form web-based communities and as companies increasingly recognize the appeal of their creations for mainstream markets.[2]

- Can you name some other examples of end-user innovation?
- If you were to add an application to the iPhone, Twitter, or another product, what would you want it to do?

16.1   THE IMPERATIVE FOR CHANGE

To survive and thrive, organizations have to change. The imperative for change comes from both outside an organization and within. Companies must change in response to external forces, such as consumer demand, the economy, globalization, technology, and demographics. They must also change in response to internal forces. For example, as a company grows, it may need to reorganize itself. As the demands of its workforce change, it may need to adopt new procedures such as telecommuting or flexible work time.

Change involves much more than keeping products and services current. For instance, organizations may have to diversify their workforces, refigure inefficient production processes, adopt new technology, shift management styles, or cut costs. At times, a company's entire organization may need to be restructured.

Some changes can be anticipated well ahead of time. For example, a company may plan years ahead to move to a new headquarters. Many others cannot be planned for in this way. Think, for instance, of new laws, competition arising from an unexpected quarter, and sudden shifts in the economy, such as the economic crisis that began in 2007. Successful organizations are adept at managing both expected and unanticipated changes.

For organizational change to succeed, it must be carefully planned and implemented. In the language of organizational change, a *planned change* is a

> **KeyPoint**
> To survive and thrive, organizations and individuals must change.

method of helping people develop appropriate behaviors for adapting to new methods while remaining effective and creative. A key to a positive transition is getting people involved in and committed to the change from the beginning. During any transition, the application of sound human relations skills will make adapting easier.

Change can be difficult. People are often unwilling to step out of their comfort zones or abandon routines to which they have grown accustomed and that they see no reason to alter. But no person or company will function long or well without deliberate and intelligent planning for change.

Many organizational experts believe that the capacity for productive change must be a continual, functioning part of organizations. That was the conclusion of Kathy Cloninger, CEO of Girl Scouts of the USA, reflecting on her recent successful efforts at restructuring the group:

> [T]he fundamental challenge for an organization of the future [is] *adaptability*. To succeed over time, an organization must somehow institutionalize the ability to change, yet in the process continue to be itself. There is no sure recipe for that, but it seems to me absolutely essential, and I believe the key to it is *strategic learning*—to observe change, learn from it, and use what you learn as the basis of an evolving strategy.[3]

Recommendations for change in organizations originate from a variety of sources. They include professional planners, outside consultants, special task forces or teams of representatives from within the organization, CEOs, and other top-level managers. A growing number of organizations solicit suggestions for change, particularly regarding products, services, and processes, from lower-level managers and front-line employees.

KeyPoint
Professional planners, outside consultants, special task forces, and top executives plan most change.

Technology CONNECTION

When consumer products giant Procter & Gamble (P&G) wanted to put out a new line of Pringles potato chips printed with animal pictures and trivia questions, it turned for the printing technology to its ideagora. Named by the authors of *Wikinomics* for the agora, a place for assembly and commerce in ancient Greek cities, these web sites match technologies with organizations that have a use for them and vice versa. P&G found a small bakery in Italy run by a university professor who had devised an ink-jet process for printing edible images on cakes and cookies. P&G acquired the technology in less than a year and at a fraction of what in-house research and development (R&D) would have cost. The Swiffer Duster, Crest SpinBrush, and Mr. Clean Magic Eraser are examples of more than 100 products that P&G's ideagora has helped bring to fruition.[4,5]

1. How might ideagoras benefit organizations?

2. Moving from almost complete in-house R&D toward a goal of 50 percent of innovation from outside meant that P&G had to change its internal culture. What might such a change involve?

Mid-level managers and their subordinate first-line managers usually carry out change using the unilateral, participative, and delegated methods:

- With the *unilateral method*, employees have little or no input in the process. Supervisors dictate the change—what it is, when and how it will be accomplished, and who will be involved.

- With the *participative method*, employee groups are used in the problem-solving and decision-making processes that precede implementation of the change. Both supervisors and employees share in bringing about the change.

- With the *delegated method*, employees are given the responsibility and authority to effect the change. They diagnose, analyze, and select the best method for implementation. This method is used most when employees are closest to the situation that needs to change. It is being used more frequently as organizations push decision making farther down into the ranks.

Ask Yourself...

1. What are some external forces that have caused change in your life?

2. Think about a change that affected you at work or in a group outside work. Which method of carrying out the change was used? Explain why it was, or wasn't, the best choice.

16.2 FORCES PROMPTING CHANGE

Several external and internal forces are strongly impacting organizations and employees and prompting change. They include the economy, globalization, science and technology, transportation, the workforce, and the work itself. The emerging organizational environment is characterized by three principal trends: intense global competition, rapid technological advancements, and continuing turbulence and uncertainty.

Economy

The most significant force impacting the workplace today is the economy. A severe economic crisis began in 2007, spreading across the world and leading to a lengthy recession. The far-reaching effects of this economic downturn, which many compared to the Great Depression, are still being felt today.

The problems that led to the recession began in 2001, when the housing industry took off in response to sharply lowered interest rates. Demand and prices rose, and lenders issued increasingly risky mortgages. In 2006, rates of foreclosures and delinquent payments began rising.

Events began to accelerate in the summer of 2007, when large, respected investment companies that had invested heavily in these risky mortgages

> " Not everything that is faced can be changed. But nothing can be changed until it is faced.
>
> —James Baldwin, American writer "

started to fail. The federal government stepped in, engineering sales of some companies and taking over or shoring up others. In October 2008, the government passed an unprecedented $700 billion bailout plan to buy up toxic assets and restore stability to the economy.

Still, banks refused to lend and stock markets worldwide fell, leading to a global recession. Stronger organizations bought up their weaker competitors, prompting a wave of restructuring. Shortly after taking office, President Barack Obama overhauled and expanded the bailout plan. The government followed with a $275 billion plan to help families with troubled mortgages and a $787 billion economic stimulus package. By the fall of 2009, two years after the crisis began, experts began seeing the first signs of what they predicted would be a prolonged recovery.[6]

A mere recitation of events fails to convey just how bad the economic downturn was. As of July 2009, 6.5 million jobs had been lost—almost 5 percent of all U.S. jobs—and the unemployment rate was at its highest in a quarter-century. Nine million workers were reduced from full-time to part-time hours, wages were frozen or cut, and the average workweek declined to 33 hours.[7] Deutsche Bank forecasted that by 2011, about half of U.S. homeowners would owe more for their homes than the home was worth.[8] In a single year, personal bankruptcies rose 34 percent.[9] Some economists predicted that one in four businesses would eventually close.

KeyPoint
The recession shed massive numbers of jobs and shook up employment projections.

In The News

The recent recession saw sharp reductions in hires, including temporary workers. But staffing company Robert Half International (RHI) saw opportunities for growth when large numbers of baby boomers who'd lost their jobs or been shorn of savings began applying. RHI's labor pool consists mostly of low- to mid-level workers. The company could charge more for the services of its new highly skilled workers, who typically had 10 to 15 years of experience. More important, it could expand beyond its base in accounting and finance jobs to areas such as technology, law, and marketing. RHI's consulting division, Protiviti, proved equally resourceful, adding services for bankruptcy, cost control, and restructuring. RHI started Protiviti in 2002 with 700 professionals hired from faltering accounting firm Arthur Andersen.[10]

1. How does this story demonstrate the importance of attitude and creativity when faced with serious, unanticipated problems?

2. In what ways (besides getting a paycheck) would skilled employees benefit from doing temporary work during tough economic times?

Government statisticians and economists could not be certain where the next generation of jobs would be. Jobs were cut across industries, with manufacturing, construction, and retail shedding the most. Health care continued to grow robustly; government employment kept climbing; and despite budget cuts, education fared well, with a boost from the economic stimulus package.

This package allocated $71 billion for energy and environmental initiatives that would create 5 million green jobs. It provided funds for a wide range of investments, including energy efficiency, cleanups, renewable energy, public transportation, and research. According to a study by the Pew Charitable Trusts, clean energy jobs grew almost 2.5 times faster than any other type of job between 1998 and 2007.[11] Some experts predicted the emergence of a green-collar economy from the blue- and white-collar economies of the past. *Fast Company* identified conservation biologist, green MBA and entrepreneur, sustainable systems developer, and urban planner as among the ten best green jobs in this economy.[12]

The recession emphasized the importance of flexibility for both organizations and employees. "In a fast-changing economy," wrote MSNBC senior writer Allison Linn, "experts say job seekers should be flexible because it's hard to say where the new growth fields might be in the next 10 or 20 years."[13]

Globalization

The opening of eastern and western European markets in the early 1990s caused an explosion in free trade and created a vast array of entrepreneurial opportunities. Goods, services, people, and capital began moving across national borders in Europe as easily as Americans cross state borders in the United States, creating a major impact on the world market.

The 1994 North American Free Trade Agreement (NAFTA) opened trade and employment opportunities among countries. Its main objective was to promote fair competition, increased investments, and enhanced trade cooperation among the United States, Mexico, and Canada. Other agreements followed.

As time passed, more nations entered the global marketplace, as trade barriers were lowered, transportation got cheaper, and telecommunications and information technologies improved and became less expensive. In recent years, small, mid-sized, and startup companies have joined the ranks of large corporations and multinational companies in selling and buying products and offering and receiving services globally. Though global trade contracted sharply during the recent economic crisis, few economists believed that, in the long run, globalization would proceed anywhere but forward.

> ❝
> *We must ensure that the global market is embedded in broadly shared values and practices that reflect global social needs, and that all the world's people share the benefits of globalization.*
>
> —*Kofi Annan, United Nations secretary-general*
> ❞

Outsourcing   A major part of the global trade revolution is outsourcing. U.S. companies began outsourcing manufacturing to Asian countries, and later, Central and South American nations, because of lower labor costs. In the late 1990s, companies started outsourcing services as well. Call centers were moved to India and other English-speaking countries. Soon U.S. firms were outsourcing tax return preparation, office functions such as billing, architectural designs and blueprints, basic legal work, and software coding and development.[14]

Today, it's possible to outsource almost any service function, from market research to medical care, to an overseas company. Increasingly, companies are also outsourcing high-tech design and services and research and development.

The purpose of outsourcing has also expanded. Companies still outsource to save costs. Blue-collar and, increasingly, white-collar jobs go overseas. But some companies are bringing certain functions back to the United States, as they discover which functions outsource well for them and which do not. Tapscott and Williams assert that "executives are discovering outsourcing is really about corporate growth, making better use of skilled staff, and even job creation." Small and mid-size companies can pick and choose the services they need to run their business.[15]

How Globalization Affects Organizations
Global competition drives organizations to produce goods and services more cheaply and target them carefully. It prompts them to be flexible and move more quickly, particularly in innovation and reacting to events.

Organizations that want to sell their products and services globally need to know their market thoroughly, which means, in part, building diverse workforces. Outsourcing may call for radical restructuring and the adoption of new management methods for people and assets. Both global marketing and outsourcing require the development of effective systems, both technological and human, for working collaboratively across cultures.

How Globalization Affects Employees
In the new global economy, employees compete in a much broader field. A Valparaiso University student, on a summer program in China, read a book about globalization, thought things over while helping a Chinese student practice his English, and changed his major to pursue three bachelor's degrees, in international business, economics, and Mandarin.[16]

Employees who will work internationally need exceptionally good human relations skills. They should be flexible, tolerant, open, sensitive to people from other cultures, at ease collaborating, and able to listen actively. To compete in a global environment, employees should plan to be flexible, continue learning, and keep their skills current.

TIME: 12:01
TEMPERATURE: 70°
NUMBER OF TIMES THE WORLD HAS CHANGED TODAY: 13

Science and Technology

Discoveries in science and their practical application through technology continue to change the work we do and the way we do it.

For employees, new technology often makes tasks easier, but it sometimes makes them more complicated and challenging, and it always involves learning. The health care industry provides examples. New medicines, tools, equipment, and procedures are produced constantly, and their use must be mastered by nurses, surgical technologists, physical therapists, cardiovascular technologists, and other professionals. For most health care occupations, licensing and certification requirements include continuing education to ensure workers keep up.

Organizations introduce new technologies to improve productivity and efficiency. Chapter 1 asked you to consider technology adoptions from a systems standpoint. Besides the investment in training, getting the most out of new technology may require new management styles, new office processes, and maybe even new structures. As Chapter 1 noted, companies expect their employees to adapt and participate in any change to new technology, work with others to help solve problems related to it, learn it, and use it effectively.

Computer and communications technologies continue to evolve rapidly, becoming more powerful, efficient, and quick and adding functions. The trend is toward portability, wireless access, and convergence of features. Teleconferencing, web conferencing, and videoconferencing have allowed businesses to span the world and have caused a revolution in how information flows and how people are managed.

When employees bring communications media such as social networks, wikis, blogs, and cell phones into the workplace, organizations see gains in productivity, connection, and collaboration. But they also grapple with issues such as wasted time, privacy, and security. One way organizations are addressing these problems is to make these technologies part of the workplace—a business version of online phone service Skype, for example, with increased security or a company-owned group in LinkedIn. They are also adopting similar products that are specifically designed for business, with special tools and security features, or building their own applications.

Companies are finding web-based social media and private networks valuable for their own purposes, such as communication, project management, training, recruitment, and information gathering.[17] For example, uses of Yammer, a Twitter-like product for business, have included asking employees to suggest a tagline for a new ad campaign (thousands did) and enabling them to comment and ask questions during a company webcast.[18]

Wikis, blogs, and social networking sites have proven to be especially rich collaborative tools. The Army set up a wiki for soldiers to rewrite training manuals.[19] The federal government uses a wiki for collaboration across offices and agencies to create the federal budget.[20] P&G maintains a Facebook-like site for its more than 138,000 employees. There they can use wikis, blogs, and other media to form groups who wouldn't normally work together but who share similar work-related interests.[21] Such tools encourage horizontal

KeyPoint
Organizations are adapting social media for their own purposes.

collaboration, enabling employees to reach across hierarchical or department lines. They provide a venue for marshaling the collective expertise of employees. In large or far-flung companies such as P&G, they are a means of forging and maintaining valuable connections.

Popular technologies will continue to make their way into the workplace. Jackie Fenn, an analyst at Gartner, a respected research company, suggests that organizations create an ongoing strategy to take advantage of them.[22]

Transportation

As a result of the bad economy, Americans drove substantially less. The Federal Highway Administration reported a decline in driving for 16 consecutive months beginning in December 2007; job losses, high fuel prices, and a steep drop in new-car purchases contributed to this change.

Although only a small percentage of Americans use public transportation, the American Public Transportation Association reported that from 1995 to 2008, ridership rose 38 percent. In 2008, despite falling fuel prices, ridership was the highest it had been in 52 years.[23] *The Washington Post* reported that nearly 60 percent of those using public transportation use it to get to work.[24]

The number of Americans who are telecommuting is increasing. According to Forrester Research, as of 2008, more than 34 million Americans telecommuted at least occasionally, and the company projected that by 2016, 43 percent of U.S. workers would telecommute.[25] Among factors driving this increase are across-the-board worker demands for more flexible schedules, high fuel costs, and the growth of high-speed and wireless Internet access.

The number of Americans who telecommute is growing every year.

morganl/iStockphoto.com

The recession prompted cutbacks in business travel, including internal meetings and professional conferences and training seminars for rank-and-file employees.[26] At the same time, interest in videoconferencing, web conferencing, and other electronic alternatives rose markedly. In a 2009 survey of corporate travel executives, they were the number-one priority.[27]

Workforce

Earlier chapters described how the composition of the workforce is changing. For many years, white, non-Hispanic males were the largest portion of the U.S. labor force. By 2016, according to Bureau of Labor Statistics projections, they will make up just 65 percent. Hispanics will compose 16 percent of the workforce, African Americans 12 percent, and Asians 5.3 percent. Women, who were 34 percent of the labor force in 1950, today make up nearly half, a proportion that is likely to stay about the same. Four generations—more than at any time in the past—are together in the workplace. By 2016, nearly a quarter of the labor force will be age 55 and older.[28]

As employers draw from this labor pool, workplaces are becoming correspondingly more diverse. Plus, organizations are intentionally diversifying their workforces for a variety of reasons. As a result, people of different cultures, backgrounds, and generations are bringing their own sets of values and beliefs into the workplace, requiring different methods of leadership, motivation, and other human relations skills. Chapters 3 and 11 presented some of these values and beliefs. Chapters 3 and 9 discussed how to motivate and lead different types of workers.

The recession stoked a trend away from traditional full-time jobs to contract and part-time work. In 2009, 31 percent of the U.S. workforce was freelance, part-time, or self-employed. Experts predict that by 2019, the figure will reach 40 percent. Contracting is already increasing in professions that haven't traditionally lent themselves to temping, such as accounting, engineering, health care, law, and sales, and is expected to continue to do so.[29]

Even before the economic crisis, workers felt less strongly about long-term employment security than in the past. Many want opportunities for job improvements, training and retraining, and career development. Those most likely to succeed will be flexible, well honed in human relations skills, and adaptable to changing conditions.

The changing demographics of the workforce place a heightened value on human relations skills such as getting along well with others, active listening, and tolerance. In an interview, the CEO of a diversity consulting firm commented, "Organizations say to me that colleges need to do a better job of preparing workers for the real-world diversity they will encounter when they come into the workplace."[30]

The Nature of Work

Work in the United States has continued to shift from industrial manufacturing and production to information and knowledge-based goods and services.

> **KeyPoint**
> The workforce will continue to include more women, members of minority groups, and older workers.

The research firm McKinsey & Co. reported that between 1998 and 2006, 85 percent of new jobs called for complex "knowledge work" such as solving problems.[31]

The recent recession reinforced trends toward work that requires education and a higher level of skills. Industries that typically employ workers lacking specialized skills shed large numbers of jobs, with either slow or poor prospects for recovery. According to Nigel Gault, chief U.S. economist at forecasting company IHS Global Insight, the new jobs appearing during the recession were not jobs requiring physical labor. They called for "education, skills, math ability, [and] probably computer literacy."[32]

While many manufacturing jobs have gone overseas, those that remain typically require fewer workers who are better educated and more highly skilled. For example, workers in a California business that produces artificial heart valves must be trained for up to a year to hand-sew the valves, each of which requires some 1,800 stitches done under a microscope.[33]

Work performance in many organizations is taking a new shape, with decisions being pushed to the lowest level possible. Employees tend to have more responsibility and authority. They make decisions and solve problems at a higher level, often as part of a team.

Computer and communications technologies continue to evolve and make people and information almost instantly available. As a consequence, work can be done almost anywhere and at almost any time. The divide between work and private life has been permanently blurred. Employees can communicate more quickly and easily, with the result that they communicate more often, work more with others, and get more done.

Ask Yourself...

1. In what ways have you been (or do you think you will be) affected by the economic downturn?
2. Which communications technologies described in this section do you use at school or work, and how do you use them?

16.3 HOW CHANGE IS PLANNED

KeyPoint Because changes in any environment are continual, planning must be ongoing and flexible.

The goals in managing change are to anticipate the need for change and bring it about effectively. The most common methods for achieving these results include strategic planning, organizational development, job redesign, and force field analysis.

Strategic Planning

The essence of planning is designing a desired future and identifying ways to bring it about. Plans must be designed to fit the unique characteristics of each organization. *Strategic planning* is the systematic setting of organizational goals, defining strategies and policies to achieve them, and developing detailed plans to ensure that the strategies are implemented—always taking into account the unique character of the organization. The process helps determine what is to be done, when and how it is to be accomplished, who is going to do it, and what is to be done with the results. Because changes in any organization's environment are continual, strategic planning must be ongoing and flexible.

Strategic planning is not simply forecasting based on trends, nor is it a set of plans that can be carved in stone to be used day after day. This type of planning for change is more a thought process than a prescribed set of procedures and techniques. A formal strategic planning system links three major types of plans: (1) strategic plans, (2) medium-range programs, and (3) short-range budgets and operating plans. Figure 16.1 illustrates the information flow and steps in a typical strategic planning process.

Figure 16.1

The strategic planning process.

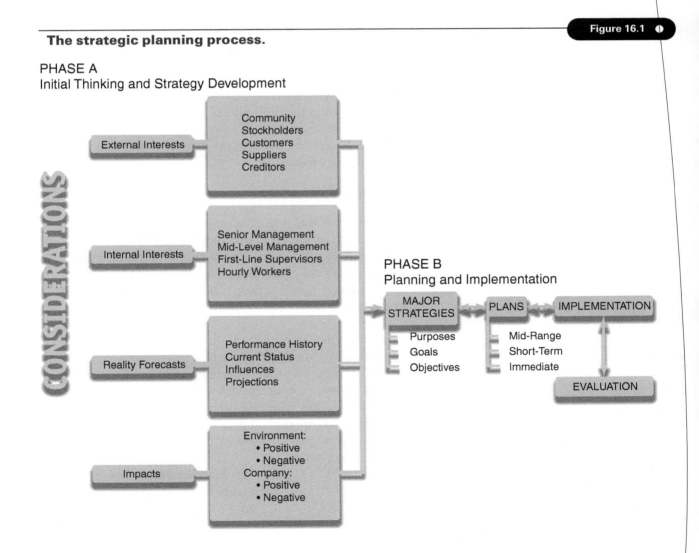

In the initial steps, consideration is given to the concerns of outside and inside interests and how they may be affected by the planned goal. For example, as a manager you may ask how the local community will react to the proposed building site for a new factory near the downtown area. Will this expansion please the stockholders by increasing profits and better serving our customers? Will it generate revenue to pay our creditors and increase orders to our suppliers? Will Joe Chang agree to leave his current foreman job to manage and operate the new facility? What has our past performance capability been in the area of pipe manufacturing, and how will the new factory change that performance? Can we forecast with reasonable accuracy the outcome of making this major investment?

What effects will this plan for expansion have overall on the environment and the company? Careful thinking is needed to initiate strategic planning.

Once all the questions are favorably answered, the next step is to design a master strategy for implementation. The purposes and objectives are clearly defined and policies are established. Then medium- and short-range steps are developed and the plan begins to take shape. With a step-by-step program plan in place, implementation can start. The land may be purchased and cleared, building specifications drawn to scale, and contractors hired to build the facility. As construction begins, each phase is carefully reviewed and evaluated to ensure maximum efficiency upon completion.

The thought process continues throughout the year that building the facility takes. If new variables arise, changes may be made to accommodate them. No plan is absolute. It may best be described as a fluid or dynamic process that allows change to occur as warranted.

Organizational Development

Organizational development (OD) is a planned change process for meeting organizational needs through employee participation and management involvement on a continuing basis. It is similar to strategic planning in concept but not in practice. OD involves the entire organization—its people, structures, culture, policies and procedures, and purpose. OD is built on the belief that any planned change process must continuously adapt to the ever-changing environment.[34]

Because OD is strongly rooted in human relations management theories, it involves a number of methods to identify degrees of concern for people as well as tasks. Methods might include sensitivity training, team-building exercises, and goal-setting activities to bring about the desired changes in both the employee and the organization. Other methods used in the OD change process include survey and feedback techniques and confrontation meetings. These methods involve a high degree of participation by employees and management to improve organizational effectiveness.[35]

Total quality management (TQM) and *benchmarking* are two new means of accomplishing an old goal—effectively implementing change in organizations. Each has roots in OD, and many high-powered companies are still using these techniques to deal with changing business environments.

KeyPoint
OD methods involve a high degree of participation by employees and management to improve organizational effectiveness.

TQM focuses on involving employees in continuous process improvements to keep the organization on the cutting edge. TQM has its roots in the theories of the American statistician and educator Dr. W. Edwards Deming, who became interested in methods of achieving better quality control in the 1930s. Deming's ideas were put to the test in the 1950s, when Japanese business leaders invited him to teach quality control as they tried to rebuild after World War II. In addition to statistical analysis of production as it related to quality, Deming advocated involving employees at all levels in the pursuit of quality. In the 1980s, American companies began to adopt Deming's ideas to compete more effectively against foreign manufacturers. Today, employee involvement in improving quality has become the vanguard of progressive companies.[36]

Benchmarking involves comparing the company's practices—among internal divisions, against those of outside competitors, or both—to determine which are the best. For example, Johnson & Johnson compared financial report filing in its internal branches and discovered ways to streamline the processes. Xerox matched prices and procedures with those of a Japanese competitor and improved its bottom line. This method involves employees in analyzing information, taking action, and reviewing the results for effectiveness.

The *change agent* is instrumental in bringing about any of these change processes. Also known as an OD practitioner, the change agent diagnoses problems, provides feedback, helps develop strategies, and recommends interventions to benefit the organization as a whole. The challenge is to develop a creative, innovative organization that easily adapts in an ever-changing world, yet remains competitive. For this type of flexibility to be fostered, employees must be made to feel part of a team. Change should be perceived as an opportunity for growth among team members as they accept new challenges and learn new skills.[37]

Actions of a Change Agent

- Be open and honest about why the change is happening.
- Encourage participation and solicit feelings.
- Allow negative comments but not negative actions.
- Explain benefits of change.
- Involve others in initiation/implementation phases.
- Acknowledge loss of the old method.

Job Redesign

Job redesign is a method of bringing about gradual, low-risk changes in an organization by changing tasks performed by individuals to make them more interesting and challenging. The goals are to relieve boredom, create interest,

KeyPoint
Job redesign changes the makeup of an employee's tasks.

and make workers more satisfied and productive. The most common methods used in job redesign are job enrichment, job enlargement, and job rotation.

- *Job enrichment* builds greater responsibility and interest into task assignments and adds tasks that encourage and motivate employees. It has proven to be an excellent means of bringing about positive change within an organization.

- *Job enlargement* increases the complexity of a job by adding tasks that are similar to those already being performed. Job enlargement may not motivate employees, but it may appeal to their desire for creative and challenging work.

- *Job rotation* shifts employees from one job to another in hopes of reducing boredom and stimulating renewed interest in job performance. The content of a particular job is not affected. Job rotation is also used to prepare an individual for permanent assignment to a higher-level position.

Reengineering

Reengineering takes redesign to the next level: Instead of simply redefining jobs, the organization retools whole divisions or corporations. Management expert James Champy defines *reengineering* as the fundamental rethinking and redesign of business processes to achieve dramatic improvements in critical, contemporary measures of performance, such as cost, quality, service, and speed. Organizations around the world have implemented this form of change with dramatic results. Microsoft, UPS, General Electric, General Motors, IBM, Intel, Levi Strauss, Germany's Siemens, Brazil's Semco, and the U.S. government are only a few of those organizations that have undertaken some form of reengineering.

KeyPoint
Reengineering means retooling whole divisions or corporations; force field analysis works with opposing forces in a change.

Force Field Analysis

Force field analysis is a technique used to analyze the complexities of a change and identify the forces that must be altered. This useful tool, developed by psychologist Kurt Lewin, views any situation in which change is to be made as a dynamic balance of forces working in opposite directions.

The forces that move the situation in the direction of the anticipated change are called driving forces. The opposite forces, those that tend to keep the situation from moving in the direction of the anticipated change, are called restraining forces. These two sets of forces working against each other create a dynamic equilibrium or balance that can be disturbed at any moment by altering either the driving forces or the restraining forces.

A change agent who uses force field analysis to determine how opposing forces operate in an organization can predict the consequences of altering either set of forces or can alter the forces to create the desired change. The forces may include people, tasks, technology, equipment, or the organization's basic structure. Planning for change is important to ensure a smooth transition with the least resistance possible. Each situation should be analyzed to anticipate the consequences of the change process.

Ask Yourself...

1. Describe a situation in which you may have been a change agent, helping to bring about change.

2. Think about your current job, a past job, or a job held by someone you know. How might you change the content if you were asked to redesign it?

16.4 RESISTANCE TO CHANGE

People sometimes resist change. Their feelings and actions create barriers to effective change. Understanding how people feel about change can help in removing barriers and making change easier. The following are four common reasons for resistance to change:

- *Fear of the unknown.* When situations remain constant, people know what to expect, how to respond, and how things fit together. They have stability and security. Change confronts them with an unknown and uncertain situation. Not having control and not knowing what will happen frequently arouse anxiety, fear, and stress.

- *Fear of power loss.* Often, people's power and status are so tied to the existing situation that any change means a potential personal loss. The change may cost them too much.

- *Fear of economic loss.* People may feel threatened by potential reductions in salary or benefits or possibly the ultimate loss of their jobs.

- *Conflict of interest.* The change may threaten the traditions, standards, values, or norms of a person or group. Social affiliations may also be jeopardized.

Resistance to change can have benefits. It can signal a problem with the change itself. For instance, sometimes the change isn't really needed. In a blog at her web site Manage to Change, Ann Michael cites examples of executives who try to implement every new management theory or people who attempt to adopt practices that worked in their previous job without stopping to think about whether they're appropriate for their current job.[38]

A more common problem that resistance to change can identify is inadequate planning. For instance, the change may be poorly timed. All the right people may not have been involved in planning it. The change may affect more people than the initiator anticipated or may affect them in unexpected ways. It may have consequences that didn't occur to the initiator. Part of planning for change is to anticipate resistance and to be prepared to address it. Resistance frequently arises when a change has been poorly communicated. Often, it provides clues for the prevention of failure.[39]

If you see problems with a planned change or don't think it's necessary, raise your concerns with your supervisor or other appropriate persons. You may learn there are reasons for the change you weren't aware of because

> **KeyPoint**
> Resistance often provides clues for the prevention of failure.

they weren't communicated properly. Even if your concerns are legitimate, they may be disregarded. But you have an obligation to try.

If a change is necessary or if administration and management want it, then the change is going to happen, regardless of whether employees consider it necessary, see problems with it, or are concerned about how it will affect them. The following suggestions might help you when facing change:

Suggestions for Dealing with Change

* Remember that change is inevitable and that fear of change is normal.

* Analyze why you're resisting the change. What fears do you have? How can they be addressed?

* Search for the positives. How could the change constructively affect your work?

* Seek assistance if you are having difficulty adjusting to the change. A supervisor or a more experienced employee may be able to help.

* Learn how to learn. The most important skill to acquire for the future is learning to keep abilities fresh and desirable in the job market.

Ask Yourself...

1. What are some ways in which you, fellow employees, or fellow students resist changes that aren't wanted?

2. Suppose you lost your job. What positive outcomes might you find in the situation?

16.5 THE LEADER'S ROLE

When change is needed, leaders are often called upon to act as change agents to make it happen. (Conversely, those who are able to act as change agents are more likely to attain positions of leadership.) If you are in a position of leadership at work or in your personal life and are asked to implement change, the process in Figure 16.2 may help you.

Modifying or changing an alternative (Step 7 in Figure 16.2) is appropriate if the expected results are not achieved or if they prove undesirable. However, making changes too frequently may cause you to appear indecisive.

For a smooth transition, open communication about the change process is essential. According to business writers Jack Welch and Suzy Welch:

> A leader creates change by clearly explaining why change is necessary to compete, painting a vivid picture of the future of the changed company, describing in gritty detail the upside of change for the employees, and then talking about the incontrovertible need for change, constantly and incessantly, until the change is widely accepted and implemented.[40]

Figure 16.2

Steps in the change process.

1. *Conduct a present state assessment (PSA).* Diagnose the situation. Where are you now, and what are the current conditions? Examine why you need to change.

2. *Conduct a future state assessment (FSA).* Determine the desired results. Where do you want to be, and how will the conditions change? Visualize the desired results.

3. *Generate alternatives.* Identify possible approaches through the use of "What if" questions. Consider probable outcomes and reactions. Who will be involved, and how will they be affected?

4. *Select one alternative.* Choose one of the alternative solutions. Decide which method will best achieve the desired results.

5. *Implement the change.* Put a plan in motion to ensure that the change occurs. Alter whatever conditions are necessary or introduce the change method. Anticipate resistance and be prepared with ways to overcome it.

6. *Evaluate the change.* Allow time for implementation and acceptance. Carefully evaluate the results to see whether you have achieved the desired outcome.

7. *Modify the change.* Modify as required. You may make only a minor revision or repeat the entire process with a different alternative.

Keeping people informed about each step and telling them how it will affect them help to garner commitment and ensure that change is embraced. The more individuals feel involved, the more likely you will be able to keep change moving in the right direction. Communication can also contribute to the ongoing evaluation of both the process and the results.

Creating a climate conducive to change is vital. At the beginning of the change process, find allies who will be supportive of your ideas, people who are respected and good communicators. Introduce processes carefully, with special attention to timing. Have vision—foresee the future and raise the expectations of those involved. Model the behavior you expect by demonstrating your commitment to the change. Transformational leadership, discussed in Chapter 9, is especially suited for achieving positive change.

The following guidelines can help you minimize resistance and smooth the change process:

- *Discuss the change.* Communicate early in the process with those who will be affected. Educate them in how, why, and when the change will occur.

- *Invite participation.* Ask people who will be affected by the change to take part in formulating it. Involvement will create ownership, a sense of empowerment, and commitment to success.

- *Be open and honest.* Share facts and information with those who will be affected. Stick to the facts and avoid what you hope or think will happen.

- *Accent the positives.* Stress the benefits. In a work environment, increased pay, fringe benefits, a lighter workload, less-hectic deadlines, or more flexible hours may be some of the positive outcomes. Although individuals are interested in how the change will affect them, they are even more interested in how it will benefit them.

- *Do not insult past methods.* A mistake often made when introducing change is to tear down old or existing methods. If you imply that the old or existing method is inadequate, individuals may resent the implication that they have not been doing a satisfactory job.

- *Follow up on the process.* Frequently, resistance to change is hidden, only to surface later. Follow up to see whether individuals are having problems accepting or implementing the change, and provide help.

- *Allow time for adjustments.* Changing longstanding habits and attitudes can take time. Give individuals a chance to adjust to the change. Be prepared to make adjustments of your own if you hit a snag in the process.

Sometimes, it's beneficial to try the change first on a small scale. Begin the process with some small segment of the group that will be affected. Other individuals will see the advantages and importance of the change, and their uncertainties will be reduced.

If the change initiative is successful, most individuals will eventually accept the change. People may pass through these four stages on their way to accepting change:

Stages in Accepting Change

1. *Recognition.* The individual must recognize the need for change.
2. *Choice.* The individual must decide that the change is beneficial and act to make it happen.
3. *Plan.* The individual must think through the change process to develop a specific approach.
4. *Support.* The individual must seek the understanding and assistance of others to help implement the plan.

Ask Yourself...

1. Think of a change you would like to have happen at work, in a group you belong to, or for yourself. Referring to Step 3 of the change process, make a list of "What if" questions to identify possible approaches to the change.

2. "Habit," wrote Mark Twain, is "not to be flung out of the window by any man, but coaxed downstairs a step at a time." Are habits so difficult to break? Based on your experience, what are the best ways to break a habit?

16.6   HELPING EMPLOYEES WITH CHANGE

Unwelcome change often results in low morale or motivation, apathy, uncertainty, instability, frustration, and stress. Even change that is welcome can cause some of these symptoms. Additionally, changes that tend toward restructuring, compressing, or reducing the workforce may result in a mismatch of skills and jobs. In this case, managers may notice performance problems and a decrease in productivity while change is being implemented.

Coaching and counseling employees are the most effective means of dealing with behavioral problems, performance and productivity problems, and employee training and development concerns brought on by change. Open communication, which is stressed in these methods, is always a good way to cope with problems.

Coaching

Coaching is a method of employee development that closely resembles on-the-job training. Typically, a skilled and experienced employee is assigned to develop or train a junior employee with lesser skills and abilities. A coach may help identify career paths, help define career goals and objectives, explain the organization's culture and norms, or simply share expertise for skills development. Coaches provide immediate and ongoing feedback.

Mentoring is a popular form of coaching. The mentor is usually a manager with political savvy and an interest in helping employees achieve both career goals and the objectives of the organization. Many companies are recognizing the benefits of establishing formal mentoring programs for both the company and the employer. Some provide mentors to help new employees rapidly enter the corporate culture. A mentor and protégé are often matched on the basis of backgrounds, interests, and work style.

In *reverse mentoring,* a junior-level employee mentors a senior employee in areas such as technology, new information in the field, diversity, and risk taking. Reverse mentoring not only boosts the mentored employees' skills but also helps improve understanding and smooth out differences between generations.[41]

If you are not assigned a mentor, you should attempt to find one either within your organization or within your profession. A mentor is often selected on the basis of being a kindred soul. You can best achieve the close rapport necessary in this relationship when the ethics, values, and operating styles of both participants mesh. A foundation of mutual respect must exist. A mentor will listen to you empathetically, invite you to discuss your concerns, assist with problem-solving and decision-making challenges, and offer specific suggestions regarding training and development opportunities. The selection of a mentor can be a wise investment in career planning and development.

Counseling

In most organizations, *counseling* is a technique used to assist employees with problems affecting performance on the job. These problems may be personal or work-related. Employee problems may result in unacceptable quality and

> **KeyPoint**
> Coaching by a senior-level employee is a good employee development method.

> **KeyPoint**
> Counseling is generally used to assist employees with performance problems.

quantity of work, absenteeism, and low morale, which cost companies millions of dollars.

The National Institute of Mental Health estimates that one in four adults suffers from a diagnosable mental disorder in any given year.[42] Problems of this nature affect not only an individual's performance but also the behavior of others in contact with that person. Of course, the problem may not be related to any particular disorder but rather to such situations as personality conflicts, being overwhelmed by the job, or uncertainty engendered by company changes.

If the problems are not easily resolved, a counselor may be needed. A counselor may be a supervisor or a trained professional capable of dealing with a wide variety of employee problems. Once a counselor identifies the problem and documents the specifics to be addressed, counseling may be scheduled. Any of three basic types of methods may be used: directive, nondirective, or cooperative.

Basic Types of Counseling Methods

Directive counseling	The counselor listens to the individual's problem, allows emotional release, determines an action plan, and advises the person on what needs to be done.
Nondirective counseling	This method requires the individual being counseled to participate more actively. Through a technique known as reflective listening, the counselor mirrors feelings and statements back to the person and allows the person to define the problem, develop solutions, and choose an action plan.
Cooperative counseling	In this method, both parties work together to explore and resolve the issues. Sharing ideas and evaluating suggested approaches can make this a time-consuming process. The person with the problem is expected to develop the ultimate solution to increase ownership and commitment.

Some supervisors find counseling a difficult part of the human relations skills required in leadership positions. They prefer to have a professional staff counselor take the responsibility. An alternative is to refer the employee to an employee assistance program.

KeyPoint
EAPs are designed to help employees with personal problems.

Employee Assistance Programs

Employee assistance programs (EAPs) are designed to aid employees with personal problems such as substance abuse, depression, stress, or family tensions that affect their job performance and disrupt their lives. These personal problems often result in undesirable behaviors at work, such as absences, errors, tardiness, decreased productivity, or accidents.

The immediate supervisor generally identifies problems. In some companies, the supervisor is expected to take immediate action. In many companies, an employee has the option of seeking confidential help before a problem affects his or her job or is even noticed by coworkers.

Most companies have specific guidelines for handling situations in which employees' personal problems have started to affect their work. The supervisor is usually required to document incidences of unsatisfactory behavior or performance, counsel the employee on performance expectations, and reach an agreement with the employee on a specific time for improvement. If appreciable improvement is not shown within the time limit, a supervisor is expected to refer the employee to the EAP for assignment to a qualified professional counselor.

Whether an employee seeks help or is referred by an employer, the counselor to whom he or she is assigned will recommend treatment to aid the employee in coping with the problem. Sometimes the rate or type of change in a company creates the problem. During the recession, financial difficulties and job troubles topped the list.

Employees are guaranteed confidentiality when entering an employee assistance program. In most cases, the employee begins to handle the problem and job performance improves. In fact, these programs have been so successful that EAPs have virtually exploded, with almost every major U.S. corporation now offering assistance to its employees.

Any planned change must give as much attention to the emotional or psychological dimensions as to the practical and informational aspects of the change process. The most important condition for effective change management is the certainty that the climate is conducive to the change being introduced, implemented, and accepted.

Ask Yourself...

1. How could you use your skills to be a reverse mentor?
2. If you were experiencing a personal problem that affected your work, would you be likely to use an EAP? Why, or why not?

KEY TERMS

planned change	job enlargement
unilateral method	job rotation
participative method	reengineering
delegated method	force field analysis
strategic planning	coaching
organizational development	reverse mentoring
total quality management	counseling
benchmarking	directive counseling
change agent	nondirective counseling
job redesign	cooperative counseling
job enrichment	employee assistance program

CHAPTER SUMMARY

To survive and thrive, organizations must change. External and internal forces, both expected and unexpected, prompt change. Professional planners, outside consultants, special task forces, and top executives plan most change. Mid-level and first-line managers usually carry it out using the unilateral, participative, and delegated methods.

Several external and internal forces are strongly impacting organizations and employees and prompting change. They include the economy, globalization, science and technology, transportation, the workforce, and work itself. In the future, the organizational environment will be intensely competitive, technologically advanced, and filled with turbulence and uncertainty. Because change can be difficult for employees, organizations must use sound human relations skills to facilitate necessary changes.

The most common methods of planning for change include strategic planning, organizational development, job redesign, and force field analysis. OD strategies include total quality management and benchmarking. Change agents are instrumental in bringing about any of these change processes.

Four common reasons for resistance to change are fear of the unknown, fear of power loss, fear of economic loss, and conflict of interest. Resistance often provides clues for the prevention of failure.

Leaders are often called upon to implement change. A seven-step change process can be useful. Open communication is essential. Creating a climate conducive to change is also vital.

Coaching and counseling are used to help individuals cope with change. Coaching and mentoring are methods of developing employees to their maximum potential. Counseling is a method of assisting employees with personal or work-related problems affecting their performance. EPAs are formal programs provided to help employees with personal problems that affect their work performance and disrupt their lives.

REVIEW

1. Who usually recommends and implements organizational changes?

2. Write six sentences to summarize the six external and internal forces described in the text that are prompting change in today's workplace.

3. Write four sentences describing the four most common methods for managing change.

4. Name four common reasons for resisting change and a way that resistance benefits employers.

5. List the seven steps in the change process, and identify three guidelines for facilitating change.

6. Explain the roles of coaching and counseling in the change process.

CRITICAL THINKING

1. Why is adaptability essential for organizations?

2. Name a force other than those discussed in the text that is prompting change at school, at work, or in society. Describe the changes being made in response to this force.

3. Compare and contrast two of the methods of managing change described in Section 16.3.

4. Give examples for each of the four reasons for resistance to change described in the text. They can be real or imagined examples.

5. How would you describe the leader's role in effecting change?

6. Why is communication essential to successful change, and at what stage(s) in the change process should it occur?

7. Explain what it means to create a climate conducive to change.

8. Give one example each of situations in which coaching, counseling, or an employee assistance program would be appropriate. They can be real or imagined examples.

CASE STUDIES

In small groups, analyze the following situations.

1 Change at the College   As assistant dean for administration at Willmeth College, Marc was charged with making budget cuts. He thought he had hit upon a good strategy in switching the custodial staff from day to night hours. The staff could complete their work much more quickly and efficiently at night when no students or faculty were in the buildings, saving time and money. He announced the change a week before he wanted it to be implemented and told the staff supervisor to set the hours.

In the next several weeks, the student newspaper ran a series of articles about the change. It profiled members of the custodial staff anonymously. Single parents were struggling to find someone to stay with their children. People were having trouble arranging transportation. Spouses working different jobs weren't seeing each other. Everyone was exhausted, and two people quit. Administrative staff and faculty, also anonymously, spoke of missing familiar faces and complained that when cleaning was needed during the day, there was no one to do it. The paper's editorial page characterized the change as unfeeling and unnecessary. The city newspaper and a radio station picked up the story, and his office had been flooded with calls.

Security, too, it turned out, was unhappy with the change. The head of security said she didn't have adequate resources to cover the custodial staff in addition to security's other night duties. She expressed strong concern about security's ability to respond to emergencies in a timely way. Night escorts for students were taking considerably longer. They complained to their parents, who were raising security concerns.

Marc was frustrated. Didn't people understand that cuts had to be made somewhere? He hadn't cut staff or services. He didn't understand what he had done wrong.

1. Considering what you have learned about managing change effectively, what do you think Marc did wrong?

2. What do you think Marc should do next? Why?

2 Kobe's Fitness Center   After six years in business, Kobe has decided to expand his fitness center, which occupies two floors of an old factory downtown. One floor has freestanding weight equipment and cardio machines, and the second is a large space for classes. There is a small juice bar at the entrance.

Kobe is taking over the third floor, which will be occupied by a dozen pieces of fitness equipment operated on a key system. The system has a generic workout that can be adapted by a fitness trainer for a particular client and then programmed into a key. After an initial session, clients can go from one piece of equipment to the next, inserting their key, and do the workout on their own. Clients can have follow-up sessions with a trainer every six weeks or so to upgrade their routines.

Kobe has some other ideas as well. He plans to divide the class space into two so that he can accommodate more classes. He wants to expand the juice bar a bit. Right now he sells water, juice, energy drinks, granola and energy bars, and t-shirts with "Kobe's Fitness Center" printed on them. He wants to update his web site so that clients can book and pay online. He's looking for promotional ideas, and he's interested in using social media to publicize the business.

Currently, Kobe has two personal trainers on staff besides himself and two people who run exercise classes.

1. Make a plan for Kobe for managing this change. Think about what you learned in Section 16.5 on leading change.

2. Take the roles of Kobe's staff members (adjust the number of members to your group). Imagine Kobe has asked you to sit down with him and help plan. What suggestions do you have for the juice bar? The social media? What classes should the gym offer? How should he publicize the change? What roles would you like to have at the fitness center? Do you have any other suggestions? Can you think of any potential problems Kobe should consider?

3. Based on your discussion in Step 2, revise the plan.

3 **Culture Shock**   The Crosbeck County Court of Appeals consists of six judges, a court administrator, eight staff attorneys, and an eight-member secretarial pool. The members of the secretarial pool are a close-knit group who, over time, have developed their own system for typing and formatting cases and correspondence. The staff attorneys, who research the cases the court hears and draft decisions, are generally friendly with one another, but a few are competitive. Both the secretaries and the staff attorneys have word processing skills, but the judges do not.

The judges have decided to rearrange the staff system. Each judge wants his or her own personal secretary and staff attorney. The judges will pick the attorneys and secretaries they want. The two extra secretaries will be transferred to other county offices. One of the two extra staff attorneys will be trained as a mediator. The other will be responsible for consulting, helping with heavy workloads, and covering during vacations.

With two fewer secretaries, you (the court administrator) realize that the judges will sometimes need to do their own word processing.

1. Consider the types of resistance to change that you learned about in Section 16.4. Which of these types of resistance are you likely to encounter? Why do you say so?

2. What are some ways in which you can minimize the resistance?

3. Where you can't minimize the resistance, what are some ways in which you could help the various employees deal with this change?

HUMAN RELATIONS IN ACTION

1. Working in groups, update the Economy or Science and Technology discussion in Section 16.2. Prepare a presentation for the class on what you learn.

   • If you choose the economy, find out how economic conditions have changed since the section was written. What is the jobless rate (national, state, and local)? Which industries are experiencing the strongest growth? What are the fastest-growing occupations? Which occupations will have the largest numerical increases? Use the Bureau of Labor Statistics web site and respected research and news sources.

   • If you choose Science and Technology, update the discussion of communications media, including web-based social media. What new media have become popular with employees? How are organizations now using social media?

2. Working in groups, do a case study of a company that is undergoing or has undergone change. It can be a local company or one that you have read about. What kind of change is it? Why was it undertaken? How was it planned? Was there resistance? How was it overcome? What have the effects of the change been for the company? How have employees adjusted to it? Present your case study to the class.

3. Do you have a mentor? If so, prepare a brief, one-page written description of why you selected that individual as a mentor for your career. If not, think of someone in your organization whom you might select and describe why you would choose that person. Be specific about the advantages you feel might result from this alliance. What skills and information might you exchange? Using the Internet, investigate a few large companies in your career area to see whether they have programs that assist new employees to more easily enter that organization. You may find one that interests you and you may want to apply.

4. Many popular books have been written about managing change. Choose one of these books and write a report on it. Compare what you have learned in this chapter to what the book presents. In this text's companion web site, you'll find a list of books in the Additional Readings and Resources section, such as *Our Iceberg Is Melting,* that are good resources.

For additional resources, refer to the web site for this text:
www.cengage.com/management/dalton

RESOURCES

1. Johnson, S. (2009, June 15). How Twitter will change the way we live. *Time, 173*(23), 37.

2. Tapscott, D., & Williams, A. D. (2008). *Wikinomics: How mass collaboration changes everything*. New York: Penguin, 128.

3. Cloninger, K. (2009). Refounding a movement: Preparing a one-hundred-year-old organization for the future. In F. Hesselbein & M. Goldsmith (Eds.), *The organization of the future 2*. San Francisco: Jossey-Bass, 215.

4. Tapscott, D., & Williams, A. D. (2008). *Wikinomics: How mass collaboration changes everything*. New York: Penguin, 107–108.

5. Huston, L., & Nabil, S. (March 2006). Connect and develop: Inside Procter & Gamble's new model for innovation. *Harvard Business Review, 84*(3), 58, 60–61, 65–66.

6. Credit crisis: The essentials. (2009, August 25). *The New York Times*. Retrieved from http://topics.nytimes.com/top/reference/timestopics/subjects/c/credit_crisis/index.html?ref=business

7. Lowenstein, R. (2009, July 26). The new joblessness. *The New York Times Magazine*, 11–12.

8. Yoon, A. (2009, August 5). About half of U.S. mortgages seen underwater by 2011. Reuters. Yahoo! News. Retrieved from http://www.reuters.com/article/businessNews/idUSTRE5745JP20090805

9. Trejos, N. (2009, August 14). Personal bankruptcy surges 34 percent. *Washington Post*. Retrieved from http://www.washingtonpost.com/wp-dyn/content/article/2009/08/13/AR2009081303399.html

10. McConnon, A. (2009, June 1). For a temp giant, a boom in boomers. *BusinessWeek*, 54.

11. Cheney, A. (2009, July 14). Green economy blooms: A recent study reveals substantial growth in green energy jobs. *Inc*. Retrieved from http://www.inc.com/news/articles/2009/07/green.html

12. Kamenetz, A. (2009, January 13). Ten best green jobs for the next decade. *Fast Company*. Retrieved from http://www.fastcompany.com/articles/2009/01/best-green-jobs.html

13. Linn, A. (2009, March 24). Changing economy has many changing jobs. msnbc.com. Retrieved from http://www.msnbc.msn.com/id/29640225

14. Outsourcing. *Encarta*. Retrieved from http://encarta.msn.com/encyclopedia_701702628_2/Outsourcing.html

15. Tapscott, D., & Williams, A. D. (2008). *Wikinomics: How mass collaboration changes everything*. New York: Penguin, 62.

16. How to keep your job onshore. (2007, August 20). *BusinessWeek*. Retrieved from http://www.businessweek.com/magazine/content/07_34/b4047417.htm?chan=top+news_top+news+index_businessweek+exclusives

17. Proust, M. (2009, August 27). Using social networks for training. Human Resource Executive Online. Retrieved from http://www.hreonline.com/HRE/story.jsp?storyId=246750617

18. Yammer: Success stories. Retrieved from https://www.yammer.com/about/case_studies

19. Proust, M. (2009, August 27). Using social networks for training. Human Resource Executive Online. Retrieved from http://www.hreonline.com/HRE/story.jsp?storyId=246750617

20. Ramienski, D. (2009, May 29). MAX federal community wiki helps shape budget. Federal News Radio 1500 AM. Retrieved from http://www.federalnewsradio.com/?nid=35&sid=1684861

21. Swanborg, R. (2009, August 24). How Procter & Gamble got employees to use social networking at work. CIO. Retrieved from http://www.cio.com/article/500363/How_Procter_Gamble_Got_Employees_to_Use_Social_Networking_at_Work

22. Mollman, S. (2008, October 25). Putting Facebook and Twitter to work. CNN.com. Retrieved from http://www.cnn.com/2008/TECH/10/23/db.workwikis

23. 10.7 billion trips taken on U.S. Public Transportation in 2008–Highest level in 52 Years; ridership increased as gas prices decline and jobs were lost. (2008, August 13). American Public Transportation Association. Retrieved from http://www.apta.com/mediacenter/pressreleases/2009/Pages/090309_ridership.aspx

24. Sun, L. H. (2009, March 9). Public transit ridership rises to highest level in 52 years. *The Washington Post*, p. A02.

25. Schadler, T. (2009, March 11). U.S. telecommuting forecast, 2009 to 2016. *Forrester Research*. Retrieved from http://www.forrester.com/Research/Document/Excerpt/0,7211,46635,00.html

26. Short-sighted austerity measures regarding professional conferences could spawn corporate intellectual depression. (2009, April 9). Association of Corporate Travel Executives. Retrieved from http://www.acte.org/resources/press_release.php?id=418

27. ACTE business travel survey shows stronger negative economic impact on global travel industry than expected. (2009, February 9). Association of Corporate Travel Executives. Retrieved from http://www.acte.org/resources/press_release.php?id=400

28. Toossi, M. (November 2007). Labor force projections to 2016: More workers in their golden years. *Monthly Labor Review*, 130(11), 44.

29. Revell, J., Bigda, C., & Rosato, D. (2009, June 12). The rise of freelance nation. CNNMoney.com. Retrieved from http://money.cnn.com/2009/06/11/magazines/moneymag/entreprenuerial_workplace.moneymag/index.htm

30. Pope, P. (CEO), Pope & Associates, & Langlois, E. (personal interview), 2006.

31. Altman, A. (2009, May 25). High tech, high touch, high growth. *Time*, 173(20), 40.

32. Linn, A. (2009, March 24). Changing economy has many changing jobs. msnbc.com. Retrieved from http://www.msnbc.msn.com/id/29640225

33. Von Drehle, D. (2009, May 25). Yes, we'll still make stuff. *Time*, 173(20), 49.

34. Zatz, D. A. (February 1994). Harnessing the power of cultural change. *The OD Papers*.

35. Ibid.

36. Ibid.

37. Ibid.

38. The change resistors: The good. (2006, June 25). *Manage to Change*. Retrieved from http://managetochange.typepad.com/main/2006/06/the_change_resi_3.html

39. Ibid.

40. Welch, J., & Welch, S. (2009, May 25). Transforming the family business. *Business Week*, 72.

41. Piktialis, D. How 'reverse mentoring' can make your organization more effective. (2009, January 26). Encore Careers. Retrieved from http://www.encore.org/find/advice/how-reverse-mentoring-ca

42. The numbers count: Mental disorders in America. (2008). National Institute of Mental Health. Retrieved from http://www.nimh.nih.gov/health/publications/the-numbers-count-mental-disorders-in-america/index.shtml#Intro

EMPLOYEE RIGHTS:
WORKING TOWARD MUTUAL RESPECT

OBJECTIVES

After studying this chapter, you should be able to:

17.1 Identify and discuss federal employment laws concerning discrimination, fair wages, and family and medical leave.

17.2 Understand the origins of the labor movement and what federal rights workers have to organize.

17.3 Explain how OSHA protects employees from safety and health hazards.

17.4 Name benefits available to employees and distinguish between those that are required and those that are optional.

17.5 Identify and discuss other employee rights at work.

Workers' rights are protected by federal and state regulations, and companies that do not comply with those regulations are subject to severe penalties.

Wal-Mart agreed to pay at least $352 million and possibly as much as $640 million in 2008 to settle 63 lawsuits pending in federal and state courts in 42 states. The plaintiffs alleged that the company forced employees to work off the clock.[1]

In fiscal year 2008, the Occupational and Safety Health Administration conducted almost 39,000 worksite inspections and logged 87,687 violations of its standards and regulations for worker safety and health, with 67,052 of these violations cited as "serious."

Additionally the agency made 12 criminal referrals for wrongdoing in that fiscal year.[2]

Merrill Lynch, the international financial services firm, agreed to pay $1,550,000 in 2008 to settle a 2005 discrimination lawsuit under Title VII of the Civil Rights Act on behalf of an Iranian Muslim former employee who was fired because of his religion and national origin. Majid Borumand, a quantitative analyst, was not promoted and was then terminated. A less qualified individual was retained and promoted.[3]

- Should federal and state governments do more to protect workers?
- Are you willing to pay extra taxes to increase compliance efforts? Why or why not?

17.1 FEDERAL LAWS PROTECTING WORKERS

Local, state, and federal laws regulate various aspects of employment. These regulations cover employment discrimination, family and medical leave, fair labor standards, the right to bargain collectively, employee safety and health, employee benefits, and miscellaneous employee rights. Both individuals and organizations need to understand and abide by these regulations.

Individuals should understand what their rights are and how to take appropriate action when those rights are violated. Understanding and abiding by workplace regulations fall under Life and Career Skills for the 21st century, and they are your responsibility.

Sometimes employees assume they have rights on the job that they, in fact, do not have. Problems may arise when employees act on these assumptions. The consequences can range from lost promotions or raises to disciplinary action or termination.

Organizations also need to be aware of, and respect, employee rights. Violating employee rights can lead to costly investigations by federal and/or state agencies. These investigations require the submission of paperwork and can disrupt the workplace by removing employees from the job to provide witness statements. In addition, employees may spend time discussing or worrying about the impending investigations rather than working. Violations may require payment of fines or back pay and reinstatement of employees. Payment for damages may be required as a result of a lawsuit. More important, employees whose rights are abused will be unhappy and less productive. Ideally, organizations will treat employees well and fairly because it is a smart business tactic and it is the right thing to do.

Because laws in the area of employee rights change rapidly, both employees and organizations must keep track of changes. Consult a lawyer for recent changes in legislation discussed in this chapter and for an explanation of state and local laws.

Employment Discrimination

Abraham Lincoln abolished slavery on January 1, 1863, by signing the Emancipation Proclamation. However, in the late 19th and early 20th centuries, freed slaves and their descendants continued to be deprived of their liberty and blocked in their pursuit of happiness through *discrimination*, or a difference in treatment based on a factor other than individual merit. A grassroots civil rights movement began in the 1950s, demanding that these inequities be corrected. As a result, several acts were passed to protect blacks and other groups against discrimination in the workplace.

Title VII of the Civil Rights Act of 1964, the Pregnancy Discrimination Act, the Equal Pay Act, the Age Discrimination in Employment Act, and the Americans with Disabilities Act were enacted to stop discrimination in the workplace. The *Equal Employment Opportunity Commission* (EEOC) is the federal agency responsible for enforcing these laws. These acts are briefly summarized next.

Title VII of the Civil Rights Act of 1964, as Amended   *Title VII of the Civil Rights Act of 1964* prohibits discrimination by companies that have 15 or more employees. Discrimination based on race, color, religion, sex, or national origin is forbidden.[4] All terms, conditions, and privileges are covered—hiring,

KeyPoint
Federal law requires equal treatment of workers, regardless of their race, religion, sex, national origin, age, color, or disability.

> *Injustice anywhere is a threat to justice everywhere.*
> —*Martin Luther King, Jr., American clergyman and civil rights leader*

In The News[5]

In November 2008, citizens of the state of California voted to deny recognition of same-sex marriages. African-American columnist Leonard Pitts responded to the vote by pointing out that African-Americans voted in support of the measure by a 2–1 margin. While he was adamant that the black experience and the gay experience were not the same, he did note that homosexuals, like African-Americans, were subjected to similar types of treatment. Both groups know what it's like to be beat down, left out, and denied basic freedoms.

Pitts pointed out how seductive intolerance is and how difficult it is to resist ridiculing or marginalizing others who are different. "We continue to struggle," he says, "to overcome the crippling legacy of bigotry and injustice."

1. What difference has the civil rights movement made in your life? The lives of your parents?
2. Why do you think it is so easy to see wrongs committed against ourselves and so hard to see those committed against others?

placement, training, promotions, transfers, layoffs, compensation, and terminations. This act also prohibits sexual harassment.[6]

In the past, some employers attempted to get around Title VII by setting specific qualifications for a position. For instance, some police departments set height and weight requirements that effectively eliminated females from the position of officer. Requiring a bona fide occupational qualification (BFOQ) curbed these practices. The employer must show a legitimate business necessity for eliminating certain groups of individuals from a job. Requiring proof that restrictions are bona fide has limited the use of discriminatory occupational qualifications by employers. However, some restrictions have been found to be valid. For instance, a producer may hire only women for female roles in a movie. Legitimate age limitations may be placed on some occupations, such as airline pilot. The courts have ruled, however, that preferences such as females for airline attendants are not BFOQs.[7]

Pregnancy Discrimination Act   The Pregnancy Discrimination Act amended the Civil Rights Act of 1964 in 1978. An employer cannot refuse to hire a woman because of pregnancy as long as the woman is able to perform the job. A pregnant woman may work as long as she is able to perform the job and may not be required to stay out a certain length of time after the baby is born. Federal law does not require that special considerations, such as light duty, be made for pregnant women. It does, however, require that pregnant women be treated the same as other employees who are temporarily disabled. If nonpregnant temporarily disabled individuals are given light duty, pregnant individuals must be allowed the same privilege.

A company is required to hold a job open for a woman on maternity leave the same length of time that jobs are held open for other employees who are on sick leave or disability leave but are not pregnant. This law does not guarantee a position upon return from maternity leave. If the company routinely fills positions of individuals who are sick for other reasons, it may legally fill positions of women who are on maternity leave. Some states, such as California, require that a position be held open for a certain length of time after the start of maternity leave.[8]

Sexual Harassment   The Civil Rights Act of 1964 prohibits sexual harassment in the workplace. *Sexual harassment* includes any unwelcomed sexual advances, requests for sexual favors, or verbal or physical conduct of a sexual nature. Examples are telling sexually oriented jokes, standing too close, touching and making physical contact, displaying sexually oriented material, and making sexual comments about a person's body if these actions are unwelcome.

Either sex can commit sexual harassment. Men can harass women, and vice versa. Additionally, men can harass men, and women can harass women. Harassment can be from a coworker, supervisor, an agent of the employer, or a nonemployee such as a repair person who comes on the company premises to perform work. Organizations are responsible for stopping the harassment from a coworker, a nonemployee, or an agent of an employer as soon as a management official becomes aware of it.

KeyPoint
Both men and women can commit sexual harassment.

President Lyndon Johnson signs the Civil Rights Act into law.

AP Photo

The Americans with Disability Act is signed into law by President George H.W. Bush.

AP Photo/Barry Thumma

Furthermore, organizations are always responsible for harassment by a supervisor even if the organization is not aware of the harassment.[9]

The law requires that employers provide an atmosphere free of sexual harassment. However, employees must make clear that the harassment is unwanted. The individual being harassed should tell the harasser in no uncertain terms that the comments or actions are not appreciated and to stop. If the harassment continues, the victim should immediately report the harassment to a management official or the human resources department.

Equal Pay Act of 1963   The *Equal Pay Act* requires that men and women be paid the same for equivalent work. For instance, a male and a female teacher with similar backgrounds and experience are to be paid equal salaries.[10]

Age Discrimination in Employment Act of 1967   The *Age Discrimination in Employment Act* prohibits employers with 20 or more employees from discriminating based on age. The law covers individuals 40 years of age and older. As long as employees are able to perform their jobs, they cannot be forced to retire. However, an exception for highly paid corporate executives does exist.[11]

The Americans with Disabilities Act of 1990   The *Americans with Disabilities Act* (ADA) prohibits discrimination against individuals who are disabled working in companies with 15 or more employees. Disabled individuals are those whose impairment (physical or mental) is severe enough to affect a major life activity. The individual with the disability must be able to perform the essential functions of the job, with or without reasonable accommodation. *Reasonable accommodation* is action that assists the disabled employees without imposing undue hardship on the company. It may include making existing facilities accessible to them; job restructuring; part-time or modified work schedules;

reassignment to a vacant position; acquisition or modification of equipment or devices; appropriate adjustment or modifications of examinations, training materials, or policies; the provision of qualified readers or interpreters; or similar accommodations for them.[12]

Genetic Information Non-Discrimination Act of 2008   The *Genetic Information NonDiscrimination Act* (GINA) prohibits employers from discharging, refusing to hire, or otherwise discriminating against employees on the basis of genetic information, which might show that they have a propensity to develop diseases such as cancer and diabetes. It applies to employment agencies and labor unions as well. This law not only bans using information gained from genetic testing but also prohibits using information on illnesses obtained through family histories. Additionally, it prohibits use of genetic information to discriminate against participants in health-care plans. The employment portion of the law went into effect on November 21, 2009, and the health-care portion went into effect for calendar year health plans in January 2010.[13,14]

Responding to Discrimination

When determining whether you are being subjected to discrimination, remember the following:

KeyPoint
Unfair treatment is not always illegal treatment.

- The law covers differences in treatment based on specific characteristics (such as race or gender). Adverse treatment because your boss "doesn't like you" or because you smoke is not covered by federal law.
- Anyone can discriminate! Just because you are a female or minority does not mean you are not capable of treating somebody who is of a different race, religion, sex, national origin, age, or disability differently. White males can also be the target of differences in treatment.
- Civil rights laws do not promise good treatment or even fair treatment, only equal treatment. You can be treated badly yet still equally.
- If someone of your own race/sex/age is treated better than you, it will be difficult to prove that your race/sex/age was the cause of your treatment.
- A disability or pregnancy does not give you permission to be less productive than other individuals in the workplace.
- Whether you have been sexually harassed depends on whether the behavior was "unwelcome." For example, you cannot laugh at off-color jokes or join in telling them and then complain that you have been harassed.

After reviewing your situation, if you still think you have been the victim of discrimination, you should attempt to settle difficulties within your organization before resorting to outside sources. If your company has a grievance or complaint procedure, use this process. If such a procedure is unavailable, approach your supervisor or a responsible individual in the human resources department. Explain your concerns and difficulties in a calm, clear manner. Listen carefully to the explanations of the company officials. External circumstances of which you are not aware may exist. Work with your organization in good faith, giving the company a chance to correct the problem.

KeyPoint
You should attempt to work issues out through company channels first.

Such action on your part demonstrates a belief that a person, not the company, is the problem.

If the company will not take action, you should file a charge of discrimination with the EEOC or your state commission on equal employment. Employers, by law, cannot retaliate against individuals who have filed a charge of discrimination with the EEOC. However, companies can continue disciplinary action that is reasonable and expected and is administered to other employees not filing charges.[15]

Trends in Employment Opportunity   *Affirmative action*, a practice originally designed to correct past discriminatory practices against minorities and women in the workplace by setting goals for hiring and upward mobility, has become increasingly controversial. Companies who do business with the federal government as well as many who do business with the state and local entities are still required to develop and implement an affirmative action program.[16] Currently, the Supreme Court has ruled that these types of programs are constitutional only if they are "narrowly tailored" to remedy the lingering effects of past discrimination. However, the justices have not clearly defined how serious the effects must be to warrant favoring women and minorities in employment and contracting decisions. Some are calling for a shift in the focus of affirmative action to help those of all races and ethnicities who are poor and disadvantaged.[17]

In 2009, amendments to the Americans with Disabilities Act went into effect that significantly extend the definition of a disability. Employers are expected to more frequently enter into dialog with employees regarding reasonable accommodations.[18]

Lastly, current federal laws do not prohibit discrimination in employment against lesbians, gays, bisexuals, and transgenders. Because President Obama's agenda includes amending the federal civil rights laws to ban discrimination based on sexual orientation and gender identity, we can expect activity on this aspect of discrimination in the future.[19]

> *Democracy arises out of the notion that those who are equal in any respect are equal in all respects.*
> —Aristotle, Ancient Greek philosopher

Fair Labor Standards

The Industrial Revolution saw a major shift in the workforce from farms to factories. Unfortunately, this rush to fill the rapidly multiplying factories with workers often meant that children and women were exploited. Young children worked the same hours as adults, sometimes 12 to 14 hours a day or all night, and they often worked in conditions unsafe for a minor. They were paid less than adults, which tended to lower the adult wage. Women were also subjected to lower wages than men and long hours of work. Public concern mounted, and states began to pass laws restricting child labor and providing a minimum livable wage.

The mass unemployment during the Great Depression of the 1930s brought a public outcry to regulate hours of work in order to allow more individuals to be employed. The result was the first national legislation to regulate working hours, wages, and child labor, which is known as the *Fair Labor Standards Act*.

> **KeyPoint**
> The Fair Labor Standards Act sets minimum wage and overtime pay requirements.

The Fair Labor Standards Act of 1938, as Amended   The Fair Labor Standards Act of 1938 sets the minimum wage, equal-pay, overtime, and child-labor standards for several types of employers and employees. These include employers who are engaged in and employees who are employed in interstate commerce or the production of goods for commerce. Employers in retail and services whose sales volumes exceed a certain amount and agricultural workers are also covered.[20] The minimum wage has slowly increased over the years. Effective July 24, 2009, the minimum wage is $7.25 per hour. A subminimum training wage allows employers to pay individuals under the age of 20 a training wage of not less than $4.25 an hour for the first 90 days.

Overtime provisions require payment of time and one-half of the employee's regular rate for all hours worked in excess of 40 hours per week except for those employees who are exempted from overtime[21] (see Figure 17.1). To qualify for exemption, employees generally must meet certain tests regarding their job duties and be paid on a salary basis at not less than $455 per week. This base rate must include incentive pay or bonuses received in that week. A workweek is considered to be seven consecutive days and may begin on any day of the week.[22] State and local governments are allowed to pay compensatory time in lieu of overtime.

● **Figure 17.1**

Fair Labor Standards Act exemptions from overtime.[23,24]

The following employees are exempt from the requirement that overtime be paid:

1. White-collar workers—executives, administrators, professionals, computer professionals, and outside sales personnel

2. Workers in specific industries—transportation, bulk oil distributors, hospitals, seasonal business, communications, and agriculture

3. Workers performing specific types of work—commissioned retail salespeople, family members, fishermen, taxicab drivers, newspaper delivery people

4. Employees working under special certificates—full-time students, learners, student learners, apprentices, employees with disabilities, and messengers

If you are uncertain whether someone is exempt, you can contact the Department of Labor regarding the application of current regulations.

Individuals under 18 years of age are not allowed to work in hazardous occupations. Individuals of 14 and 15 years old are allowed to work in a limited number of industries and occupations, but work hours are restricted and duties cannot conflict with school. Exceptions to the age limitations are for actors and actresses, newspaper carriers, and those who work in the family business.[25]

If you feel that your rights to fair wages and hours have been violated, attempt to work it out with your employer first. If this attempt fails, contact the Wage and Hour Division of the U.S. Department of Labor.

Future Trends in Wage and Hour Issues   Issues concerning payment of overtime are developing as companies are forced to become more competitive in the workplace and respond to new federal legislation. Additionally, because of technology, work is becoming "virtual," enabling many employees to put in work hours away from the job.

Many organizations are finding that even with requirements to pay overtime, working skilled employees more than 40 hours a week is less expensive than hiring and training new workers. Also, employers, always eager to reduce costs, want to be able to offer compensatory time (time off for hours worked in lieu of pay) as state and local governments are allowed to do.

Furthermore, some professionals who are exempt from overtime are routinely putting in 70 to 80 hours a week. Many feel individuals working excessive hours are being exploited.

Lastly, the idea of a livable minimum wage will continue to be an issue. Stories surface regularly of the working poor, who work 40 hours a week but earn so little that they are unable to afford decent housing or other basic necessities of life. Periods of inflation will further fuel this debate, as we search for a balance between the need for employers to remain competitive in the global economy and that of the worker to survive.

> **KeyPoint**
> Wage and hour laws, passed in the 1930s, do not well fit the way we work today.

© 2009 Ted Goff

"Who wants permission to stay late all next month?"

Family Medical Leave

As the workforce in the United States expanded with women, single mothers, and dual income families during the 1960s through 1980s, the need to balance work, health, and family responsibilities became more pressing. Many states began to pass laws designed to provide some sort of job-protected family or medical leave. Then, in 1993, the federal government addressed this need by passing the *Family Medical Leave Act* (FMLA). The FMLA provides that eligible employees be allowed up to 12 workweeks of unpaid, job-protected leave within a 12-month period for:[26,27]

- The birth or adoption of a child
- The placement for foster care of a child under 18 if not disabled, or over 18 if child is incapable of self-care
- The care of a child, spouse, or parent with a serious health condition
- An employee's own serious health condition
- Certain qualifying exigencies arising out of a military member's covered active duty status, or notification of an impending call or order to covered active duty status, in support of a contingency operation

The act also provides for a spouse, son, daughter, parent, or next of kin to take up to 26 workweeks of leave in a single 12-month period to care for a covered service member recovering from a serious injury or illness incurred in the line of duty on covered active duty. Lastly, family members of some veterans with service-related injuries or illnesses are entitled to a leave under FMLA.

The leave can be taken consecutively or on an intermittent basis. Upon returning from leave, the employee, unless deemed to be a key employee, is entitled to return to the same position held before the leave or to a position that is equivalent in pay, benefits, privileges, and other terms and conditions of employment.

To be eligible for a job-protected leave under FMLA, you must:

KeyPoint
Employees who work for businesses with less than 50 employees are not entitled to FMLA.

- Be an employee who has been employed for a total of at least 12 months by the employer on the date on which any FMLA leave is to commence

- Have been employed, on the date on which any FMLA leave is to commence, for at least 1,250 hours with the employer granting the leave during the previous 12-month period

- Be employed in any U.S. state, the District of Columbia, or any U.S. territory or possession

- Be an employee who is employed at a work site at which the employer employs more than 50 employees, within a 75 mile radius, measured by the shortest route using surface transportation.

Ask Yourself...

1. The federal government has passed legislation that restricts whom employers can hire and how much time off they must give employees. Should the government intrude on the decisions businesses make? Why or why not?

2. Do you think discrimination regulations are still needed? Why or why not?

3. Many employees are not covered by FMLA due to restrictions of company size and the requirement that they have worked at least 1,250 hours in the past year. Do you think these restrictions should be loosened? Why or why not?

17.2 WORKERS' RIGHT TO ORGANIZE

Prior to the 1930s, working conditions for many of America's workers ranged from unpleasant to truly awful. Early in the Industrial Era, factories were little more than sweatshops, exploiting the worker with long hours, unsafe work conditions, and low wages—and even using child labor—as factories sprang up and the demand for goods exploded. Management emphasis was placed on the scientific approach popularized by Frederick W. Taylor (as discussed in Chapter 1). However, while Taylor's ideal was to make work efficient for the benefit of both management and labor, many adopted only the concept of maximizing productivity output, and workers' needs were ignored. Employers showed little concern for human relations, and workers had no voice in influencing their work environment.[28]

In an attempt to protect themselves, employees began to form associations to bargain collectively with employers over wages, hours, and working conditions and to protect themselves from unfair or arbitrary treatment. These organizations were known as *unions*.

> *[Our mission is] to protect the workers in their inalienable rights to a higher and better life; to protect them, not only as equals before the law, but also in their health, their homes, their firesides, their liberties as men, as workers, as citizens; to overcome and conquer prejudices and antagonism.*
>
> —Samuel Gompers, American labor leader

These attempts by workers to unionize were resisted by management and routinely brought before the courts, which customarily ruled against labor union activities. Companies habitually used injunctions to halt strikes and boycotts to inhibit union activity. Other antiunion techniques used by management included firing labor agitators, blacklisting, yellow-dog contracts (in which employees agreed, as a condition of employment, not to join a union), and lockouts.[29]

Labor agitators, once identified by company management, were immediately fired and their names placed on a blacklist. Company managers would pass these lists of potential troublemakers around to assure that the union organizers were denied employment. The threat of unemployment had the desired result of discouraging active support for the labor movement.

When workers made demands for improved conditions or threatened early forms of strikes, company management could simply impose a lockout. Because companies could economically outlast the now unemployed worker, it was another effective means of discouraging union activities. The yellow-dog contract was also used until the *Norris-LaGuardia Act* of 1932 outlawed it, as a softening of antiunion attitudes began in the early 1930s. Occasionally, management of some shops even resorted to brutal and blatantly illegal methods to stop pro-union activities of employees.[30]

However, mounting public and congressional disfavor of these activities gave rise to the trend toward legalizing unions. Several key pieces of congressional legislation laid the framework for the labor movement and the unionization rights of workers. The Wagner Act of 1935 and the Taft-Hartley Act of 1947 are of primary interest.

The National Labor Relation Act, passed in 1935, established the right of employees to form unions and bargain collectively with management on employment issues. More popularly known as the *Wagner Act*, this legislation ordered management to stop interfering with union organizing efforts and defined what constituted an unfair labor practice by management.[31]

The Wagner Act established the *National Labor Relations Board (NLRB)* as well. The NLRB is a government agency responsible for enforcing the

KeyPoint
The Wagner Act gives employees the right to bargain with management on employment issues.

In The News[32,33]

Union membership in the United States rose for the first six months of 2008 for the first time since 1979, accounting for 12.6 percent of U.S. workers, according to the UCLA Institute for Research on Labor and Employment. At its peak, organized labor represented 32.5 percent of the workforce in 1953. Union organizers are concentrating on service industry jobs that can't be exported by targeting retail and health-care establishments as well as hotels and restaurants. Additionally, companies that employ security guards, janitors, and other low wage workers are seen as ideal targets for union organizing.

Unions are hopeful that the Employee Free Choice Act will become law in the near future and boost their ranks. This law would, among other actions, eliminate the employer's right to demand a secret ballot election before union certification and empower an arbitrator to impose a contract if the parties don't reach agreement in 100 days.

1. Do you believe American workers still need traditional union protection? Why or why not?

2. Would you join a union? Why or why not?

provisions of the Wagner Act. Regional offices throughout the United States are often called to help resolve disputes and police strike activities for violations of federal legislation.

The *Taft-Hartley Act*, also known as the Labor Management Act of 1947, was a series of amendments to the Wagner Act. It imposed certain controls on union organizing activities, internal union activities, and methods used by unions in collective bargaining attempts.[34]

In a union shop, the worker need not be a union member at the time of hiring but is required to join the union within 60 to 90 days after employment. An agency shop requires workers to pay union membership dues whether or not they actually choose to join the union. This rule serves to protect the union from would-be free riders, employees who receive the same benefits as union members without paying dues. The group represented by the union, those for whom the union negotiates, is called a *bargaining unit*, and it is in the union's interest to have as many paying members as possible.[35] The Taft-Hartley Act also contains a provision that individual states may pass right-to-work laws. The *Right-to-Work Law* allows states to give the worker the choice of union membership without compromise. State designation is indicated in Figure 17.2.

> **KeyPoint**
> If you work in a union bargaining unit, you are covered by agreements the union makes with the employer even if you are not a union member.

The Right-to-Work Law grants states the option of imposing union membership.[36]

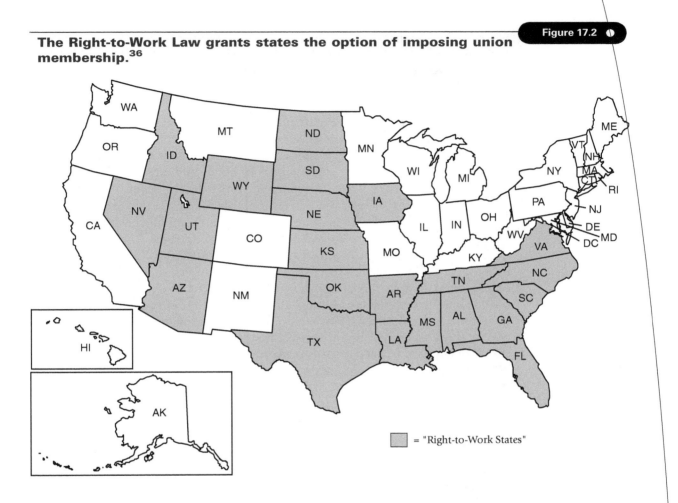

Figure 17.2

⬜ = "Right-to-Work States"

Ask Yourself...

1. Have you (or someone you know) been in a union or worked in a unionized environment? Was it positive or negative? Explain your answer.

2. In a right-to-work state, if a union wins a raise or other favorable working conditions for the bargaining unit, the employees who are not in the union but in the bargaining unit benefit even if they have paid no union dues. Do you think this is fair? Explain your answer.

17.3 REGULATING SAFETY AND HEALTH

More than 14,000 workers were killed and over 2 million were injured in industrial accidents in 1970. Estimates suggested that 300,000 new cases of occupational disease were being discovered annually. These work-related injuries had steadily increased since the 1960s, and no end to this trend could be seen. Although many companies were concerned with safety and taking actions to provide their employees with a safe environment, these individual actions were not considered sufficient. The public demanded action, which came in the form of the Occupational Safety and Health Act.[37]

The *Occupational Safety and Health Act* was passed in 1970 to "assure so far as possible every working man and woman in the nation safe and healthful working conditions and to preserve our human resources." The act sets health and safety standards for U.S. businesses. *Safety standards* address hazards that can result in a direct injury, such as broken bones and cuts. *Health standards* address the role of the work environment in the development of diseases and illnesses, such as asbestosis and black lung. (Black lung, or pneumoconiosis, is a disease that coal miners acquire from breathing air filled with coal dust.) These types of diseases are known as occupational diseases.[38]

The *Occupational Safety and Health Administration (OSHA)* was established as a federal agency to ensure that each employer provides a place of employment free of recognized hazards causing or likely to cause death or serious harm to employees. Almost all businesses that affect commerce (except government) are covered. However, only businesses with ten or more employees, or those in certain retail, service, finance, real estate, or insurance industries, are required to keep records concerning occupational illnesses or injury.

OSHA establishes standards for safety and health in the workplace. These standards cover many facets of the work environment, such as training and safety procedures for operating hazardous machinery and equipment, instructions for handling dangerous chemicals, permitted noise levels, designation of protective equipment and clothing, and sanitation regulations.

In order to enforce the act, OSHA makes inspections of company sites. These visits may be unscheduled. Unscheduled visits may be in response to complaints of imminent danger or to deaths or catastrophes.

OSHA further requires that companies give employees access to certain information about the physical and health hazards of chemical substances produced, imported, or used in the workplace. This right-to-know regulation is known as Hazard Communication Standard (HCS).[39]

Working Safely

Every employee has a responsibility to follow OSHA and company rules concerning safety. Even though *workers' compensation* helps support an employee who has been injured, payment in any amount can never make up for a lost hand or a damaged back. Specific tips for on-the-job safety are listed in Figure 17.3.

Accidents can be caused by incorrect lifting of equipment or supplies; careless operation of saws, lathes, or machinery with gears, pulleys, and belts; inattention while using hand tools; negligence while working with electricity; or falls on stairs, ladders, and scaffolds.

Office workers also need to be alert to safety. Time has been lost from injuries that occurred when file cabinets tipped over because too many drawers were opened at once. Falls on floors made slick by spilled coffee are another source of injury.

KeyPoint OSHA is a federal law mandating safety and health standards for employees.

Better a thousand times careful than once dead. —Proverb

KeyPoint Safety is your responsibility whether you work in a factory, an office, or a health-care setting.

Figure 17.3

Tips for working safely.

1. Be aware of and follow the specific safety rules at your workplace.

2. Wear personal protective equipment correctly.

3. Know how to operate all equipment properly. If you do not know, ask.

4. Check equipment before using to be sure that it is in proper working condition.

5. Be alert for unsafe conditions.

6. Report any hazardous conditions or malfunctioning equipment immediately to your supervisor.

7. Do not participate in or condone horseplay while working in hazardous areas or while using equipment.

Those in the health-care industry and those who deal with individuals in a variety of public settings need to follow guidelines on handling blood and other potentially infectious materials in order to minimize exposure risks to blood-borne pathogens such as hepatitis or human immunodeficiency virus (HIV).

OSHA also gives employees rights under the law. An employee may request an inspection and have a representative, such as a union member, accompany the inspector. Employees may talk to the inspector privately. In addition, regulations must be posted regarding employee rights under the act, and employees can have locations monitored for exposure to toxic or radioactive materials, have access to those records, and have a record of their own exposure.

Employees may have company medical examinations or other tests to determine whether their health is being affected by an exposure and have the results furnished to their personal doctors. Furthermore, employers may not retaliate against employees for exercising their rights under the Occupational Safety and Health Act.

If you ever feel unsafe on the job, you should discuss the problem immediately with your supervisor or the safety committee if your facility has an active one. Should you feel that the danger is life threatening, you have the right, by law, to refuse to work. If the problem cannot be resolved by working within the company, you should contact OSHA.

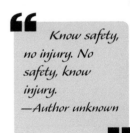

Know safety, no injury. No safety, know injury.
—*Author unknown*

Future Health and Safety Issues

Health and safety will continue to be areas of concern for both employers and employees. Employers, faced with spiraling insurance and worker compensation premiums, will be searching for ways to reduce employment-related injuries and diseases, usually through the use of protective equipment and/or training in safe work habits. Furthermore, fit employees are more productive employees, adding incentives for organizations to provide a healthy work environment.

Because workplace violence and motor vehicle accidents are the top causes of death in the workplace, accounting for 52 percent of occupational fatalities in 2007, health and safety experts will continue to focus on these areas. Less obvious hazards such as injuries caused by ergonomic factors and exposure to dangerous substances as well as a high death rate among foreign-born workers will remain a concern.[40]

Ask Yourself...

1. Have you ever done anything unsafe at work? If so, what was it and why did you not follow safety regulations?

2. What are some potential safety hazards at your organization? How could they be remedied?

3. What is your responsibility when you see someone working unsafely or notice an unsafe working condition?

17.4 BENEFITS AVAILABLE TO EMPLOYEES

Traditionally, care of those who are too infirm or too old to work was left to charitable organizations or families. This method of caring for those who are unable to help themselves worked fairly well in an agrarian society where an extra mouth could be supported by planting another row of crops or raising extra livestock. However, urbanization and industrialization began to put a strain on the ability of individuals to care for extended families. Some organizations initiated benefit programs for their employees, but the majority of employees were left without assistance.

The Great Depression intensified the crisis, leaving a great many individuals without work and unable to provide the basics for themselves, much less for their dependents. As a result, legislation was enacted that required organizations to provide retirement benefits, benefits to those who became unemployed, and compensation to those who injured on the job.

Federally Mandated Benefits

KeyPoint
The federal government mandates that employees are covered by Social Security, workers' compensation, and unemployment compensation.

Most employers must provide Social Security, unemployment compensation, and workers' compensation.

Social Security The *Social Security Act* was passed in 1935 and has been amended many times since. Social Security benefits include retirement insurance, survivor's insurance, disability insurance, and Medicare. Today one in six Americans receives a Social Security benefit, and about 98 percent of all workers are in jobs covered by Social Security.[41]

The benefits are summarized in Figure 17.4. Social Security was created to replace a portion of earnings lost as a result of old age, disability, or death—not all lost wages. Social Security is funded through payroll taxes. Employees contribute 7.65 percent of their salary up to a maximum of $106,800 as of

2009. The company matches this contribution. Regardless of the number of companies for whom an employee works, benefits will accumulate in the employee's account. Anyone who is self-employed must pay both the employee's portion and the company match for this tax.[42]

Figure 17.4

Summary of Social Security benefits.

Who May Draw Retirement Benefits?[43]

Individuals who are fully insured (have 40 credits or 10 years of work) and are at least 62 years old

Wife or husband of retiree if age 62 or older

Wife or husband under age 62 if he or she is caring for retiree's child who is under age 16 or disabled

Children of retiree if under 18 or up to 19 if they are full-time students and have not graduated from high school

Disabled children even if they are over 18

Divorced spouse of age 62 or over, unmarried, and married 10 years or more

Who May Draw Disability?[44]

Individuals who have a physical or mental impairment that lasts or is expected to last one year or more or expected to end in death and who meet the requirements for being insured

Dependents of the disabled individual

Who May Draw Survivor's Benefits?[45]

Widow or widower at 60 (50 if disabled) or any age if caring for entitled children, under 16 or disabled, of a fully insured wage earner

Divorced widow or widower if married over ten years or if caring for entitled child

Children of deceased if under 18 or disabled before age 22

Dependent parents of age 62 or over

Who May Be Covered by Medicare?[46]

Insured individuals of age 65 and over

Disabled individuals with Lou Gehrig's disease

Disabled individuals who have been entitled to Social Security benefits for 24 or more months

Insured workers and their eligible family members who need dialysis or kidney transplant because of permanent kidney failure

Consult your local Social Security office or search the Social Security Administration web site for details concerning wage credits needed to be fully insured and specific requirements for drawing benefits.

The Social Security Administration manages the Social Security program. You may contact the administration to review your earnings statement to be sure that your earnings have been correctly recorded and to inquire about the details of benefit programs.

Job Loss Compensation *Unemployment compensation* was created by the Social Security Act of 1935 to assist those who became unemployed until they find another job.

The federal government sets minimum standards for unemployment compensation, and the states developed their own standards around the minimums. For this reason, the state agency governing unemployment compensation should be contacted concerning specific benefits and qualifications.[47]

In most instances, employees who quit voluntarily are unable to receive unemployment compensation. Employees are also denied benefits in most states if they have been discharged for misconduct.

Individuals receiving unemployment compensation must be actively seeking employment and must accept suitable employment when offered. States may interpret these terms differently; therefore, you should consult your local unemployment agency when you have specific questions.

The unemployment compensation system is funded through employer taxes. The amount of tax depends on the total wages and the number of former employees drawing unemployment compensation. For this reason, employers have an incentive to keep undeserving former employees from drawing unemployment benefits.

Compensation for Injury on the Job Workers' compensation is a system that compensates individuals who have been physically or mentally injured on their jobs or who have developed an occupational disease. The compensation can include cash payments, reimbursement for medical costs, and, in some cases, the costs of rehabilitation for the employee or compensation for survivors of an employee killed on the job.

Employers are required to either purchase insurance to cover workers' compensation or become self-insured, and state regulations vary on how they can acquire coverage. Employers do, however, have an incentive to reduce injuries, because injuries mean not only lost time from the job but also higher premiums.

Each state has its own compensation laws. The Federal Employees' Compensation Act covers federal employees, and federal coverage is extended to maritime workers on navigable waters of the United States. As with unemployment insurance, the state agency should be contacted for specific details.[48]

Benefits Employers Voluntarily Offer

Employers typically offer a number of benefits voluntarily. They have found that attractive benefit packages help draw and keep qualified employees, allowing them to remain competitive in the workplace. The variety of benefits

> **KeyPoint**
> If you voluntarily quit your job, you are unlikely to receive unemployment benefits.

Ethics CONNECTION

During fiscal year 2007, the Fraud and Abuse Division of the Kansas Division of Workers Compensation received the following complaints of fraud, abuse, or failure to comply with workers' compensation regulations allegedly committed by claimants, employers, insurance entities, and self-insured employers, as well as by health-care givers and attorneys. During that year, the division collected $244,006.24 in restitution and civil penalties.[49]

Kansas Division of Workers Compensation, Fraud and Abuse Division

Type of Fraud, Abuse & Compliance Referrals FY 2007	Total
Obtaining or denying benefits by making false statements	58
Failure to confirm benefits to anyone providing treatment to a claimant	5
Refusing to pay compensation when due	12
Refusing to pay any order awarding compensation	5
Employer's duty to report accidents	454
Receiving temporary or permanent total disability benefits while working	6
Failure to maintain workers' compensation insurance when required	121
All other fraud and abuse practices	18

1. Workers' compensation benefits do not come close to replacing the salary of an injured individual. Is working while receiving benefits justified?
2. If competition is tough, is it justified for businesses to cut corners by not filing timely accident reports or failing to maintain workers' compensation insurance?
3. Are you willing to pay more for products so that workers have compensations for on-the-job injuries?

that may be offered by employers is listed in Figure 17.5. The employer may pay in part or in full for these benefits. An employer may give employees a choice of benefits so that they can design their own benefit packages. All benefits together, mandatory and optional, averaged 30.3 percent for the U.S. civilian workforce in 2008.[50]

KeyPoint
Voluntary and mandatory benefits can average as much as 30.3% of salaries.

Figure 17.5

Examples of voluntary company benefits.

Financial Plans	Other Benefits or Services
Pension plans	Housing or moving assistance
Profit sharing	In-house health services
Thrift plans	Flexible work hours
Employee stock ownership plans	Parental leave
Individual retirement accounts	Child care programs
Bonuses	Social or recreational services
	Long-term care/elder care
Insurance	Educational assistance
Health—hospital, medical, dental, vision, prescription drug	Employee-assistance plans
	Legal services
Life insurance	Financial planning
Disability insurance	Assistance or discounts on purchasing food or other goods and services
	Credit unions
Payment for Time Not Worked	Financial and retirement planning
Vacation	Medical savings accounts
Holidays	Transportation services
Sick leave	Wellness programs
	Concierge and personal benefits services
	Phased retirement programs
	Casual dress
	Bring your dog to work

In 1974, the federal government enacted the Employee Retirement Income Security Act (ERISA). This act regulates benefit plans for health insurance, group life insurance, sick pay, long-term disability income, pension plans, profit-sharing plans, thrift plans, and stock bonus plans. It sets legal standards around which employee benefit plans must be established and administered. In addition, ERISA requires that employees be given a summary plan description and have access to plan financial information.

Plan termination insurance, which guarantees benefits if certain types of retirement plans terminate, is another provision of ERISA.[51]

If you have questions concerning your benefits or options, consult your supervisor or the human resources department. The company will have literature or other information that will explain the benefits available in detail.

The Future of Benefits   Employee benefits will continue to be a controversial topic in the 21st century. With private companies dropping pensions at an ever-increasing rate, retirees will be relying more heavily on Social Security benefits and personal savings to fund their retirement. Funding of Social Security will continue to be an issue because of the large number of individuals who will be drawing benefits. As of 2008, the Social Security Administration estimates that by 2017 benefits owed will outweigh what's been collected, and the Social Security trust fund will be exhausted in 2041 unless changes are made.[52]

Continuing medical benefits offered by employers is now a crisis. Many companies are hiring only part-time workers in an effort to avoid paying medical insurance premiums. Others are shifting the burden of rising premiums to employees or even dropping coverage altogether. In an effort to further reduce medical costs, some insurance carriers are dropping the amount of coverage allowed on some claims, which leaves the employee paying an increasing share of medical bills. On the positive side, employers are offering more wellness programs as a way to reduce medical costs, which is better for both employees and the health-care system.

Ask Yourself...

1. Have you noticed the insurance premiums increasing in your workplace? How do you feel about it?

2. If your employer was forced to do away with paid vacation time to save the company money, how would you feel?

3. Do you take advantage of any voluntary benefits that your employer offers?

> " The liberty of the individual must be thus far limited; he must not make himself a nuisance to other people.
> —John Stuart Mill, English philosopher and author "

17.5   OTHER EMPLOYEE RIGHTS

In general, our rights as employees differ from those we have away from the workplace. Understanding our rights as employees is crucial to functioning in the work world. Using sound communication and human relations skills is important as we attempt to work out problems on the job.

The rights of employees of governmental bodies and union members are usually better defined than those of other employees. Some of the rights discussed in the following sections are controversial at this time. Many areas are gray and subject to change. Changes in rights evolve from court and arbitration decisions. At times, court cases can be inconsistent, with one court deciding for an issue while another court rules against it.

As an employee, you should be aware that standing on principle over some of the following issues discussed might result in termination. A court case may be needed, and years may pass before the case comes to trial.

State and local law varies in the areas discussed next. Consult a local legal expert for additional details in these areas of the law.

Employment at Will *Employment at will* means that an employee serves at the discretion of an employer and can be terminated at any time for any reason even if the employee is performing well. The employee also has the right to quit at any point. Presently, the legality of this practice is in question, and the law is rapidly changing in this area. In general, most states support the concept of employment at will. However, employees who have contracts or implied contracts should consult an attorney, since recent decisions have favored employees in cases where "at will" statements in employee handbooks or on contracts have been unclear.

The exceptions to employment at will are individuals who assert their rights under certain federal legislation, such as the equal employment laws, Occupational Safety and Health Act, Fair Labor Standards Act, Vietnam Era Veterans Reemployment Act, Clean Air Act, and Federal Juror's Protection Law. These people cannot be terminated for exercising those rights.

Courts have also ruled that employees cannot be terminated for filing for workers' compensation benefits, obeying a subpoena, leaving for jury duty, refusing to participate in an employer's lobbying efforts, or reporting an employer's illegal acts.

Proof of Eligibility to Work The Immigration Reform and Control Act (IRCA) of 1986 bans employment of unauthorized aliens and requires employers to document the identity and authorization to work for all new employees. Employers are required, within three days of hire, to complete an employment eligibility verification form called an *I-9* on all new employees. The documents that may be used for identification are listed in Figure 17.6.[53] All individuals seeking employment should be sure that they have the correct documentation to provide proof of authorization to work in the United States. If you have any questions concerning your documentation, consult the Department of Homeland Security.

Freedom of Speech Public employees, in general, cannot be terminated for speaking on matters of public concern. This right, however, can be limited if the speech interferes with the efficient operation of the government. They can be terminated for speaking on matters of personal interest. Public employees are not allowed to campaign for people who will become their bosses. The Hatch Act was passed in 1940, limiting the political activity of federal civil servants.[54] Many states and large cities have passed their own Hatch acts.[55] Some states offer broad protection, whereas others offer little or none. In general, individuals in high positions in a company have fewer rights than those at lower levels. The potential impact of statements coming from individuals in higher positions of authority or prestige is greater.

Acceptable documents for I-9.[56]

Figure 17.6

LISTS OF ACCEPTABLE DOCUMENTS
All documents must be unexpired

LIST A Documents that Establish Both Identity and Employment Authorization OR	LIST B Documents that Establish Identity	LIST C Documents that Establish Employment Authorization
1. U.S. Passport or U.S. Passport Card	1. Driver's license or ID card issued by a State or outlying possession of the United States provided it contains a photograph or information such as name, date of birth, gender, height, eye color, and address	1. Social Security Account Number card other than one that specifies on the face that the issuance of the card does not authorize employment in the United States
2. Permanent Resident Card or Alien Registration Receipt Card (Form I-551)		
3. Foreign passport that contains a temporary I-551 stamp or temporary I-551 printed notation on a machine-readable immigrant visa	2. ID card issued by federal, state or local government agencies or entities, provided it contains a photograph or information such as name, date of birth, gender, height, eye color, and address	2. Certification of Birth Abroad issued by the Department of State (Form FS-545)
		3. Certification of Report of Birth issued by the Department of State (Form DS-1350)
4. Employment Authorization Document that contains a photograph (Form I-766)	3. School ID card with a photograph	4. Original or certified copy of birth certificate issued by a State, county, municipal authority, or territory of the United States bearing an official seal
	4. Voter's registration card	
5. In the case of a nonimmigrant alien authorized to work for a specific employer incident to status, a foreign passport with Form I-94 or Form I-94A bearing the same name as the passport and containing an endorsement of the alien's nonimmigrant status, as long as the period of endorsement has not yet expired and the proposed employment is not in conflict with any restrictions or limitations identified on the form	5. U.S. Military card or draft record	
	6. Military dependent's ID card	5. Native American tribal document
	7. U.S. Coast Guard Merchant Mariner Card	
	8. Native American tribal document	6. U.S. Citizen ID Card (Form I-197)
	9. Driver's license issued by a Canadian government authority	
	For persons under age 18 who are unable to present a document listed above:	7. Identification Card for Use of Resident Citizen in the United States (Form I-179)
6. Passport from the Federated States of Micronesia (FSM) or the Republic of the Marshall Islands (RMI) with Form I-94 or Form I-94A indicating non-immigrant admission under the Compact of Free Association Between the United States and the FSM or RMI	10. School record or report card	8. Employment authorization document issued by the Department of Homeland Security
	11. Clinic, doctor, or hospital record	
	12. Day-care or nursery school record	

Employment and Military Service   The dependence on the Reserve/National Guard to assist in military actions has increased in recent years. In 1994, Congress passed the Uniformed Services Employment and Reemployment Rights Act. The act protects members of the uniformed services from discrimination and provides for reemployment rights as well as protection of certain benefit rights.[57]

Defamation of Character   Defamation is the open publication of a false statement about a person tending to harm his or her reputation. Truth is considered a defense in defamation charges. Most courts consider a statement protected if it is made in good faith in the discharge of a public or private duty to someone else who has a corresponding interest, right, or duty. For instance, if a security guard reported to the managers that an employee had attempted to steal property, the courts would most likely not consider this defamation of character.

> If you tell the truth, you don't have to remember anything.
> —Mark Twain, American author

Smokers' Rights   At present, an employer may totally forbid smoking on the job and, in some states, discriminate against smokers by not hiring them. Some companies that do not totally ban smoking may identify smoking and nonsmoking areas.

Medical Benefits   The Health Insurance Portability and Accountability Act (HIPAA) was passed in 1996 to provide increased privacy for employee health information and greater portability of employee health-care coverage, allowing employees who are leaving an employer health plan to have access to the new employer health plan without waiting periods or limitations because of preexisting conditions or health status.[58]

In addition, the Consolidated Omnibus Budget Reconciliation Act (COBRA) requires employers with 20 or more employees to extend health-care coverage to employees and dependents for 18 to 36 months in situations where they would no longer be eligible for coverage. The individual must pay 102 percent of the premium, at a minimum.[59]

Personnel Files   Employers are compelled to protect themselves from charges of discrimination and unjust punishment or termination. Many rely on documentation in the personnel file to protect themselves in this area. Employees can expect to find reprimands, warnings, or write-ups concerning performance or behavior in their files. Most states allow access to personnel records by employees at reasonable times. Some states allow employees to correct documents or remove erroneous materials or insert explanations of disputed materials. Employees should consult their employee handbook and state laws to determine whether access to their personnel files is allowed.[60]

Drugs on Personal Time   Currently, the courts do not give employees in private enterprise many rights in this area. Terminations of employees who test positive for drugs whether used on or off the job are upheld. Governmental employees have more rights concerning drug testing than those in private industry. Even though some drugs can stay in the system seven days or more after use, the courts have made no allowances for use of drugs on personal time.[61]

Global CONNECTION

Companies around the world have vastly different views of employee rights. Some countries, for instance, do not support employment at will. The European Union has enacted strict employee privacy regulations that prohibit employers from using personal information without permission or tracking computer usage through software. In addition to limiting the freedom of the employer to fire employees, the freedom of employees to change jobs is also often limited.[62,63] Many countries mandate that companies offer long vacations. In some countries, political power is tied up in issues of employee rights.

Countries worldwide will have to weigh the pros and cons of maintaining local traditions versus competing globally. Although many will choose the higher profits offered by global opportunities, some will choose to protect their cultures.

1. What problems can different employment rights cause for companies operating globally?

2. Should employment practices be standardized worldwide? Why or why not?

Search of Work Areas   In general, employers have the right to search employee packages, files, desks, and cars in order to prevent theft and control operations. Court restrictions on search and seizure are limited, particularly if the employer has warned employees that they are subject to search.

> **KeyPoint**
> Employers have a right to search your desk without your permission.

Polygraphs   The Employee Polygraph Protection Act of 1988 prohibits most private employers from using lie detector tests to screen applicants. The tests cannot be the sole reason for discharge and can be used only if a reasonable suspicion of guilt exists. Because polygraph use is limited, some employers have turned to the use of pencil and paper tests concerning honesty and substance abuse in order to screen job applicants.[64]

Plant Closings   The Worker Adjustment and Retraining Notification Act of 1988 requires that plants with 100 or more workers give a 60-day advance notice of a shutdown affecting at least 50 workers. Layoffs of more than one-third of the work site employees for more than six months must also be announced in advance.[65]

Dress Codes   Dress codes that are reasonably related to the business needs of the company and that are clear, consistently enforced, and communicated have generally been upheld by courts and arbitrators. Some reasonable accommodation, however, must be made if the employee asks to deviate from the dress code for religious reasons.

> **KeyPoint**
> Employers have a right to enforce business-related dress codes.

Blowing the Whistle on Illegal Activities Federal and state employees who report illegal activity in their organizations have varying amounts of legal protection from retaliation.[66] In the private sector, the Sarbanes-Oxley Act protects officers, employees, contractors, subcontractors, or agents of publicly traded companies from adverse employment-related actions.[67] If they report conduct they reasonably believe involves a violation of federal securities laws, the rules or regulations of the Securities and Exchange Commission, or "any provision of federal law relating to fraud against shareholders," they are covered by this act. Additionally a variety of laws offer protection to those in nuclear energy, ground transportation, defense, and manufacture and sale of some 15,000 retail products.[68]

Technology CONNECTION

Technology allows employers to monitor employees' locations in the workplace—or on the road, if the employee is, for example, driving a delivery truck—at all times. Companies are rapidly turning to GPS as well as biometric scanners that indicate an employee's presence through fingerprint, eye, or palm prints. In addition, today's technology allows monitoring of telephone conversations, keystrokes on the computer, and Internet access.[69]

1. Should employers have a right to monitor the activities of workers? Why or why not?

2. Why do you think an employer might feel the need to monitor employees?

3. Would you work for an employer that required you to wear a badge to track your location on the work site? Why or why not?

Electronic Surveillance of Employees Currently, employers may legally survey employees electronically, particularly if they have advised the employees that surveillance may occur without the employees' knowledge and that refusal to permit it may be grounds for discipline. Some companies have employees sign waivers; others post copies of search policies. Some companies perform electronic surveillance to prevent theft and reduce unproductive time of employees who are not closely supervised.

Employers may eavesdrop with hidden microphones and transmitters attached to lockers or telephones that pick up office conversations or spy with pinhole lenses in walls and ceilings. Some companies record the length of telephone calls, when the calls were made, and where the calls were placed. They may also monitor the content of the telephone calls.

E-mail Privacy   Currently, e-mail communications are not private and can be subject to subpoena. Even e-mails that have been erased can be retrieved.

Future Rights   The future will most likely bring extensive changes in the area of miscellaneous employee rights. As technology becomes more sophisticated and inexpensive, enabling companies to perform even more thorough surveillance on employees, a push to curb this "big brother" type of activity will most likely occur. States are beginning to adopt legislation banning companies from requiring employees to have a microchip tag (RFID) inserted under their skin.[70]

The courts are expected to continue to move away from the employment-at-will doctrine, granting employees even more rights. For instance, a movement is growing to protect employees from bullying and concerns are being raised as companies and their insurance carriers increasingly commit lifestyle discrimination. This practice targets employees who engage in risky behaviors and hobbies that are legal during their off time such as smoking, scuba diving, hang gliding, and riding motorcycles.[71,72]

Ask Yourself...

1. Have you benefited from any of the rights listed in this section? In what ways did you benefit?

2. How can strong human relations skills help you avoid having problems with any of the elements covered by these rights, either as an employee or as an employer?

KEY TERMS

discrimination
Equal Employment Opportunity
  Commission
Title VII of the Civil Rights Act of
  1964
Pregnancy Discrimination Act
sexual harassment
Equal Pay Act
Age Discrimination in Employment
  Act
Americans with Disabilities Act
reasonable accommodation
Genetic Information
  Nondiscrimination Act
Affirmative action
Fair Labor Standards Act
Family Medical Leave Act
union

Norris-LaGuardia Act
Wagner Act
National Labor Relations Board
  (NLRB)
Taft-Hartley Act
bargaining unit
Right-to-Work Law
Occupational Safety and Health
  Act
Safety standards
Health standards
Occupational Safety and Health
  Administration (OSHA)
Social Security Act
unemployment compensation
workers' compensation
employment at will
I-9

CHAPTER SUMMARY

Various federal, state, and local laws regulate the workplace. Federal laws protect employees from discrimination based on race, religion, sex, color, age, national origin, and disability. Employees may form unions legally in order to bargain collectively with employers over wages, hours, and working conditions. The health and safety of workers is regulated through the Occupational Safety and Health Act. Federal laws also mandate fair labor standards, family and medical leave, retirement, disability, survivor's benefits, and unemployment compensation through the Social Security Act. State laws control compensation for employees injured or killed on the job.

Many employers offer additional benefits, such as health insurance, retirement, savings plans, or child care, in addition to federally mandated benefits. These benefits, along with required benefits, can average up to 30.3 percent of an employee's salary.

In general, miscellaneous employee rights at work differ from those enjoyed away from the job. Public employees tend to have better-defined rights than private employees. Employees should learn what they can and cannot do in their locale.

REVIEW

1. Which federal laws regulate discrimination in the workplace? What types of discrimination do they prohibit?

2. Which major laws regulate fair labor standards? Explain them.

3. What is a union? What is a union allowed and not allowed to do?

4. What is OSHA? How does it protect employees' safety and health?

5. Identify three benefits that are required by law and five that may be offered voluntarily to employees.

6. What miscellaneous rights do employees have at work?

CRITICAL THINKING

1. Review the employee rights discussed in Section 17.5. Do you think employees should have more rights or fewer rights?

2. Have you ever been confronted by an unsafe working condition on the job? What did you do about it?

3. Should an employer have the right to search your work area? Why or why not?

4. Social Security was not intended to support fully individuals who have lost income through death, disability, or retirement. Explain what other benefits companies provide to help fill the gap. Have you begun to plan for your retirement? Why or why not? If so, how?

5. Do you agree with the subminimum training wage for individuals under 20? Why or why not?

6. Should employers be able to tell you what to wear to work? Why might an employer care about what you wear?

7. What are your feelings about electronic surveillance in the workplace? Should employers have the right to monitor employees to see that they are working during business hours and assess the quality of their work?

CASE STUDIES

1 **Gossiping Can Lead to Trouble**   Dora and her supervisor, Herbert, had been at odds for months. Dora thought that he was obnoxious and disliked his ordering her around and making demands.

Dora began to complain about Herbert to others in her group. She criticized his decisions to Manuel and made fun of his clothes when talking to Chen Lee. Other workers began to pick up on this behavior and made fun of Herbert behind his back.

One evening, Dora noticed Herbert in the café across the street from the office. A young woman was with him. The next day she reported this scene to the group, and they began to speculate concerning the woman's identity and why she and Herbert were together. Dora and the group were standing in front of the water fountain, laughing and talking, when Herbert walked up.

"Dora, I want to see you in my office right now," he said abruptly. Dora followed him in and Herbert shut the door. "Dora, I'm going to have to let you go. You're a troublemaker. Every time I turn around, you're in someone else's office gossiping and interrupting work. You're causing too much trouble."

1. What employer right did Herbert exercise?

2. Should Dora have been allowed freedom of speech? Was the issue really about freedom of speech? How would you have felt if you were Dora? How would you have advised Dora to behave?

3. How would you have felt if you were Herbert? What might happen to a company if employees were allowed to disrupt business and undermine authority? What are some other actions Herbert might have taken, even if he still ended up having to fire Dora?

4. How do you think the other members of the group will react?

2 Equal and Fair Are Two Different Things   "I've had it," Carmelita said as she sat down next to Emilio. "That Elvin is a real monster. He yells at me, returns my work, and makes me do it over. He's always telling me that I'm stupid when I make mistakes. He makes me so nervous that I can't think straight. I'm tempted to go to the EEOC and file charges on him. I don't think he likes Hispanics."

"I know what you mean," Emilio said. "He chewed me out in front of the whole office. I was so embarrassed that I felt like hiding."

Just then Jan walked up and joined the conversation.

"You can try EEOC if you want," Jan said. "But he treats everyone that way. I was in Alice's office yesterday when Elvin told her what a fool she was because she had added some figures incorrectly. He threw the report on her desk, yelled 'Do it right or else!', and stormed out. Alice is white and she gets that treatment. I guess he treats everybody equally!"

1. What discriminatory treatment do federal laws prohibit? Would they be applicable to Carmelita and Emilio?

2. Does being treated equally mean that you will be treated fairly or as you would like to be treated?

3. How do you think Carmelita and Emilio might handle the situation?

4. Do any governmental regulations dictate the type of treatment to be received by employees?

HUMAN RELATIONS IN ACTION

Divide into two groups. Debate the following statements, one side supporting the statement and the other side opposing it. Support your arguments with information from the chapter and from information you find on U.S. Department of Labor and government web sites.

1. Unions are no longer needed. Employers treat employees fairly.
2. An employee has no obligation to report discrimination.
3. Employees should have the right to say anything they wish at work.

For additional resources, refer to the web site for this text:
www.cengage.com/management/dalton

RESOURCES

1. Greenhouse, S., & Rosenbloom, S. (2008, December 23). Wal-Mart settles 63 lawsuits over wages. *The New York Times*. Retrieved on January 6, 2009, from http://www.nytimes.com/2008/12/24/business/24walmart.html

2. *U.S. Labor Department's OSHA highlights another successful enforcement year in FY 2008*. (2008, December 19). Retrieved on January 6, 2009, from http://www.dol.gov/opa/media/press/osha/osha20081859.htm

3. *Merrill Lynch to pay $1.55 million for job bias action against Iranian Muslim former employee*. (2008, December 31). Retrieved on January 6, 2009, from http://www.eeoc.gov/press/12-31-08a.html

4. U.S. Equal Employment Opportunity Commission. (n.d.). *Discriminatory practices* [Fact Sheet]. Washington, DC: Author.

5. Pitts, L. (2008, November 17). *In historic election, blacks embrace discrimination*. Retrieved on January 30, 2009, from http://www.dailycamera.com/news/2008/nov/17/in-historic-election-blacks-embrace/

6. U.S. Equal Employment Opportunity Commission. (n.d.). *Discriminatory practices* [Fact Sheet]. Washington, DC: Author.

7. Bona fide occupational qualifications. (n.d.). Retrieved on March 3, 2009, from http://en.wikipedia.org/wiki/Bona_fide_occupational_qualifications

8. U.S. Equal Employment Opportunity Commission. (n.d.). *Discriminatory practices* [Fact Sheet]. Washington, DC: Author.

9. U.S. Equal Employment Opportunity Commission. (n.d.). *Discriminatory practices* [Fact Sheet]. Washington, DC: Author.

10. U.S. Equal Employment Opportunity Commission. (n.d.). *Discriminatory practices* [Fact Sheet]. Washington, DC: Author.

11. U.S. Equal Employment Opportunity Commission. (n.d.). *Discriminatory practices* [Fact Sheet]. Washington, DC: Author.

12. U.S. Equal Employment Opportunity Commission. (n.d.). *Discriminatory practices* [Fact Sheet]. Washington, DC: Author.

13. Bush signs measure banning genetic bias in workplace. (2008, May 27). BNA HR and Payroll Store Human Resources Professional Information Center, 59, 22. Retrieved on January 6, 2009, from http://subscript.bna.com/pic2/hr2pic.nsf/id/BNAP-7F3P5P?OpenDocument

14. Leonard, B. (2008, December). The stealth statute. *HR Magazine, 53*(12), 47–49.

15. U.S. Equal Employment Opportunity Commission. (n.d.). *Retaliation* [Fact Sheet]. Washington, DC: Author.

16. Conrad, P. J., & Maddux, R. B. (1988). *Guide to affirmative action: A primer for supervisors and managers*. Los Altos, CA: Crisp Publications.

17. Eubanks, R. W. (2009, Winter). Affirmative action and after. *The American Scholar*. Retrieved on December 4, 2009, from http://www.newamerica.net/publications/articles/2009/affirmative_action_and_after_9706[1/7/2009 10:02:34 AM]

18. Postol, L. P. (2009, January). *ADAAA will result in renewed emphasis on reasonable accommodations*. Retrieved on January 19, 2009, from http://www.shrm.org/hrresources/lrpt_published/CMS_027438.asp

19. *The Obama-Biden plan to strengthen civil rights.* (n.d.). Retrieved on January 7, 2009, from http://change.gov/agenda/civil_rights_agenda/

20. *Elaws Fair Labor Standards Act Advisor: What is the minimum wage?* (n.d.). Retrieved on January 7, 2009, from http://www.dol.gov/elaws/faq/esa/flsa/001.htm

21. *Elaws Fair Labor Standards Act Advisor: What is the minimum wage?* (n.d.). Retrieved on January 7, 2009, from http://www.dol.gov/elaws/faq/esa/flsa/001.htm

22. Department of Labor. (n.d.). *Exemption for executive, administrative, professional, computer & outside sales employees under the Fair Labor Standards Act (FLSA)* [Fact Sheet #17A]. Washington, DC: Author.

23. Department of Labor. (n.d.). *Exemption for executive, administrative, professional, computer & outside sales employees under the Fair Labor Standards Act (FLSA)* [Fact Sheet #17A]. Washington, DC: Author.

24. *Employment law guide: Minimum wage and overtime pay.* Retrieved on February 2, 2009, from http://www.dol.gov/compliance/guide/minwage.htm

25. *What jobs can youths do?* Retrieved on January 7, 2009, from http://www.youthrules.dol.gov/jobs.htm

26. *Family & medical leave.* (n.d.). Retrieved on January 7, 2009, from http://www.dol.gov/dol/topic/benefits-leave/fmla.htm

27. *Revised final regulations under the Family and Medical Leave Act (RIN 1215-AB35).* Retrieved on January 7, 2009, from http://www.dol.gov/esa/whd/fmla/finalrule.htm

28. Ahern, E., Bernstein, I., Cohen, W. J., Goldberg, J. P. Jr., Jones, J. E., & Mangum, G. L. et al. (1976). *Federal policies and worker status since the thirties.* Madison, WI: Industrial Relations Research Association.

29. Dutton, W. N., Rabin, R. J., & Lipman, L. R. (1994). *The rights of employees and union members.* Carbondale, IL: Southern Illinois University Press.

30. Dutton, W. N., Rabin, R. J., & Lipman, L. R. (1994). *The rights of employees and union members.* Carbondale, IL: Southern Illinois University Press.

31. Dutton, W. N., Rabin, R. J., & Lipman, L. R. (1994). *The rights of employees and union members.* Carbondale, IL: Southern Illinois University Press.

32. US union membership up substantially in 2008, study shows. Retrieved on January 7, 2009, from http://www.eurekalert.org/pub_releases/2008-08/uocuum082808.php

33. Grossman, R. J. (2008, January). Reorganized labor. *HR Magazine, 53*(1), 37–41.

34. National Labor Relations Board. (1995). *The first sixty years: The story of the National Labor Relations Board 1935–1995.* Washington, DC: Author.

35. National Labor Relations Board. (1995). *The first sixty years: The story of the National Labor Relations Board 1935–1995.* Washington, DC: Author.

36. *Right to work states.* (n.d.). Retrieved on January 30, 2009, from http://www.nrtw.org/rtws.htm

37. *About OSHA.* Retrieved on August 29, 2004, from http://www.osha.gov/about.html

38. *About OSHA.* Retrieved on August 29, 2004, from http://www.osha.gov/about.html

39. Occupational Safety and Health Administration. (n.d.). *Hazard communication standard* [Fact Sheet No. OSHA 93-26]. Washington, DC: Author.

40. *Census of fatal occupational injuries summary, 2007.* (2008, August 20.) Retrieved on January 13, 2009, from http://www.bls.gov/news.release/cfoi.nr0.htm

41. Social Security Administration. (2007, October). *Social Security, a brief history*. (No. 21-059). Social Security Administration: Author.

42. Social Security Administration. (2009, January). *Update 2009* [Publication No. 05-10003]. Baltimore, CA: Author.

43. Social Security Administration. (2008, October). *Retirement benefits* [Publication No. 05-10035]. Baltimore, CA: Author.

44. Social Security Administration. (2008, November). *Disability benefits* [Publication No. 05-10029]. Baltimore, CA: Author.

45. Social Security Administration. (2009, January). *Survivors benefits* [Publication No. 05-10084]. Baltimore, CA: Author.

46. Social Security Administration. (2009, January). *Medicare* [Publication No. 05-10043]. Baltimore, CA: Author.

47. *Excerpted from the 2000 house ways and means green book, "unemployment compensation."* Retrieved on January 9, 2009, from http://www.policyalmanac.org/social_welfare/archive/unemployment_compensation.shtml

48. Kilgour, J. G. (2007, August). *A primer on workers' compensation laws and programs.* Retrieved on January 9, 2009, from http://www.shrm.org/hrresources/whitepapers_published/CMS_000039.asp

49. Kansas Division of Workers Compensation. (2008, January). *Annual statistical report 2007*. Topeka, KS: Author.

50. *Employer costs for employee compensation—September 2008*. (2008, December 10). Retrieved on January 9, 2009, from http://www.bls.gov/news.release/ecec.nr0.htm

51. *Employee Retirement Income Security Act—ERISA*. (n.d.). Retrieved on January 9, 2009, from http://www.dol.gov/dol/topic/health-plans/erisa.htm#doltopics

52. Social Security Administration. (2008, April). *The future of Social Security* [Publication No. 05-10055]. Baltimore, CA: Author.

53. *Immigration Reform and Control Act of 1986 (IRCA)*. Retrieved on January 9, 2009, from http://www.uscis.gov/portal/site/uscis/menuitem.5af9bb95919f35e66f614176543f6d1a/?vgnextchannel=b328194d3e88d010VgnVCM10000048f3d6a1RCRD&vgnextoid=04a295c4f635f010VgnVCM1000000ecd190aRCRD

54. *Hatch Act for federal employees*. (n.d.). Retrieved on January 13, 2009, from http://www.osc.gov/ha_fed.htm#may

55. *Questions & answers on speech in the workplace*. (2007, January 24). Retrieved on January 13, 2009, from http://www.ala.org/ala/aboutala/offices/oif/ifgroups/cope/copeinaction/explanatory/ALA_print_layout_1_388278_388278.cfm

56. *Form I-9, employment eligibility verification*. (2009, February 2). Retrieved on January 9, 2009, from http://www.uscis.gov/portal/site/uscis/menuitem.5af9bb95919f35e66f6141765 43f6d1a/?vgnextoid=31b3ab0a43b5d010VgnVCM10000048f3d6a1RCRD&vgnextchannel= db029c7755cb9010VgnVCM10000045f3d6a1RCRD

57. U.S. Department of Labor program highlights, Veterans' Employment and Training Service. (n.d.). *VETS USERRA* [Fact Sheet 3]. Washington, DC: Author.

58. *HIPAA: Your rights to health insurance portability*. (n.d.). Retrieved on January 13, 2009, from http://www.insure.com/articles/healthinsurance/HIPAA.html

59. U.S. Department of Labor, Employee Benefits Security Administration. (2006, September). *An employee's guide to health benefits under COBRA* [Brochure]. Washington, DC: Author.

60. *Who has a right to view personnel files?* (n.d.). Retrieved on January 13, 2009, from http://smallbusiness.findlaw.com/employment-employer/employment-employer-other/employment-employer-other-policies/right-to-view-personnel-files.html

61. *Drug testing and other possible conditions of employment.* (n.d.). Retrieved on January 13, 2009, from http://www.collegegrad.com/book/New-Job-Preparation/Drug-Testing-And-Other-Possible-Conditions-Of-Employment

62. Society for Human Resource Management Workplace Trends Program. (2002). Key european employment legislation. *Workplace Visions, 1,* 21.

63. Smith, J. J. (2008, November 14). *U.S. lawyers risk jail for seeking EU workers' data without permission.* Retrieved on February 6, 2009, from http://moss07.shrm.org/hrdisciplines/global/Articles/Pages/USLawyersRiskJail.aspx

64. U.S. Department of Labor, Employment Standards Administration Wage and Hour Division. (n.d.). *Employee Polygraph Protection Act of 1988* [Fact Sheet #36]. Washington, DC: Author.

65. *The Worker Adjustment and Retraining Notification Act (WARN) Act.* (n.d.). Retrieved on February 6, 2009, from http://www.dol.gov/compliance/laws/comp-warn.htm

66. *The law: An overview.* (n.d.). Retrieved on January 13, 2009, from http://whistleblowerlaws.com/protection.htm

67. Berkowitz, P. M. (2005, July–August). *Sarbanes-Oxley whistleblower claims: The meaning of 'fraud against shareholders'.* Retrieved on January 13, 2009, from http://www.shrm.org/hrresources/lrpt_published/CMS_013084.asp

68. Devine, T., & Maassarani, T. (2008, September). *Running the gauntlet: The campaign for credible corporate whistleblower rights.* Washington, DC: Government Accountability Project.

69. Caruso, D. B. (2008, March 26). *Growing number of companies use scanners to track employees.* Retrieved on January 13, 2009, from http://www.mindfully.org/Technology/2008/Scanners-Track-Employees26mar08.htm

70. Shtuhl, O. (2008, January 12). *California could become third state to ban forced microchip tag implants (RFID).* Retrieved on January 13, 2009, from Global Research, http://www.globalresearch.ca/index.php?context=va&aid=7781

71. *The U.S. campaign for workplace bullying laws.* (n.d.). Retrieved on January 13, 2009, from http://www.bullyfreeworkplace.org/id29.html

72. *The rights of employees: ACLU briefing paper number 12.* (n.d.). Retrieved on January 11, 2009, from http://www.lectlaw.com/files/emp08.htm

18

MAINTAINING WORK AND LIFE BALANCE:
THE KEY TO A HEALTHY LIFESTYLE

OBJECTIVES

After studying this chapter, you should be able to:

18.1 Appreciate the importance of work–life balance.

18.2 Understand stress and its side effects.

18.3 Describe the effects of substance abuse on job performance.

18.4 Develop a plan for effective time management.

18.5 Carry out sound health practices.

Jump Start

Neuroscientists, who study the brain, are reporting that work–life balance is important if we wish to remain effective and productive on the job. Chronic stress, for instance, causes us to think unclearly, shrinking the brain mass and knocking at least ten years off our life. Lack of sleep can also have an impact on our performance. Sleep occurs in cycles of about 90 minutes, with the rapid eye movement (REM) cycle coming nearly 60 minutes into the cycle. If you do not have REM sleep, you can lose what you learned the day before. Another feature of the brain, researchers point out, is that it is a social animal that needs interaction with others.[1]

- On a scale of 1 to 10, with 10 being the greatest amount of stress, where do you rate the amount of stress in your life today?
- Do you get enough sleep? If not, what can you do to improve the amount and quality of your sleep?

18.1   THE IMPORTANCE OF WORK–LIFE BALANCE

A number of trends are occurring that are causing organizations and employees to focus on issues of work–life balance. *Work–life balance* is defined as the comfortable equilibrium between what you do at work and what you do outside of work for yourself and with friends and family. Profound shifts in who works and the ways we work are creating stress, ultimately leading to rising costs for organizations in the form of lower productivity and increased health-care benefits.

Part of your responsibility to develop 21st century life skills includes learning to be productive and accountable. Developing a work–life balance, avoiding substance abuse, learning to manage your time, and maintaining a healthy lifestyle are important to your success.[2]

> **KeyPoint**
> Achieving work–life balance is one of the most difficult tasks of a successful career.

Forces Affecting Work–Life Balance

Demographics   The traditional American family with a stay-at-home mother and working father no longer dominates the U.S. workforce. Today more than half of mothers with infants work.[3] Because of the large number of working parents (couples, single fathers and mothers, and grandparents caring for children), maintaining a balance between work and home has become more important than ever.

The aging population is also putting a strain on American workers. Currently 65 percent of those over 65 live with relatives, who no doubt become at least partly responsible for their care.[4]

Technology   Technology has enabled many employees to perform their work in places other than the office. Employers can now be more flexible in terms of the places and times work is performed without worrying about a decrease in productivity. However, this breakthrough is causing many workers to find themselves working all the time and blurring the lines between work and home. The barriers between work and home are expected to continue to dissolve.[5] The downside of this flexibility can be longer work hours, increased stress, and lack of time to exercise or maintain a proper diet.

The Meaning of Work   Flexibility to balance work–life issues was recently rated as very important to 44 percent of U.S. workers.[6] Economist Charles Handy says that work is a fundamental part of life. However, he divides work into several areas, the first being paid work. Outside of paid work, he identifies three other types of work. These include home work (caring for home and family), gift work (volunteering), and study work (keeping abreast of developments in your area of expertise and upgrading skills). Some workers, he says, are trading security for independence to perform all types of work, interspersed with leisure time. Organizations, in order to entice the next generation of talent, will need to allow employees an opportunity to perform all types of work.[7]

Costs of Work–Life Imbalance

While employees can suffer from the lack of balance in their lives, companies also pay the price for failing to assure that their employees are able to achieve stability.

Costs of Health Insurance   Rising health-care costs, for instance, are an area of concern for many organizations. Estimates are that 75 percent of health-care spending goes to chronic illnesses[8] such as diabetes, muscular dystrophy, bipolar disorder, asthma, cardiovascular disease, obesity, and cancer. Aging workers are particularly vulnerable to chronic diseases. Although chronic diseases are among the most common and costly health problems, they are also among the most preventable. Adopting healthy behaviors, such as eating nutritious foods, being physically active, and avoiding tobacco use can prevent or control the devastating effects of these diseases.[9]

Absenteeism   Unhealthy employees miss more days of work. Studies indicate that employees with one health risk will likely miss six days of work while those with four or more health risks will miss 12 days.[10]

Presenteeism   Unhealthy employees who actually go to work may not perform at their peak. Those with allergies, mental health problems, respiratory difficulties, musculoskeletal issues, or diabetes, for instance, often have difficulty maintaining a high level of performance.[11]

While almost half of the companies surveyed by Watson Wyatt Worldwide, a global consulting firm focused on human capital and financial management, were aware that stress was killing their productivity, only 5 percent of the companies were actually doing something about it.[12]

Those organizations that are addressing the problem have developed *health and productivity programs*. These programs commonly address safety and emotional health as well as physical health and wellness. A focus on prevention is a key strategy of an effective program. While effective programs

> **KeyPoint**
> Presenteeism costs are difficult for organizations to control and measure.

Examples of Work–Life Benefits

- Dependent care flexible spending account
- On-site vaccinations (e.g., flu shots)
- Flextime
- Wellness program, resources, and information
- Health screening programs (high blood pressure, cholesterol, etc.)
- Gym subsidy
- Family leave above required FMLA leave
- Compressed workweeks
- Casual dress days (every day)
- Bring child to work in emergency
- Weight loss program
- Relocation services
- Smoking cessation
- Legal assistance
- Sabbatical leave
- Job sharing

- On-site fitness center
- Club memberships
- Career counseling
- Food services/subsidized cafeteria
- Elder care referral service
- Adoption assistance
- On-site child care center
- Company supported elder care center
- Career counseling
- Travel planning services
- Massage therapy at work
- Self-defense training
- Bring your dog to work
- Pet sitting
- Concierge services
- Telecommuting
- Training and educational benefits
- Extended maternity/paternity leave
- Discounted products or tickets

---

boast 20 percent more revenue per employee,[13] many organizations fail to find and eliminate the root cause of stress within the organization.[14]

Ask Yourself...

Employers want employees who are willing to devote themselves body and soul to the company, according to Jeffrey Pfeffer, Professor of Organizational Behavior at Stanford Graduate School of Business.[15]

1. Why do you think this attitude exists today despite the demand for balance between home and work?

2. What barriers do organizations face in initiating work–life benefits?

3. Do you think those who work part time or those who do not to put in extra hours deserve the same career advancement as those who do?

18.2 DEFINING STRESS AND ITS SIDE EFFECTS

Stress is a physical response to environmental pressures. Any challenge, physical or psychological, can trigger a stress reaction. The body reacts the same to both physical and psychological challenges—the mind actually prepares the body for some activity in response to the external stimuli. Stress is an unavoidable effect of living. However, if stress is too powerful or our defenses are inadequate, physical or mental disorders may result. Generally, the problem today is that, with the rapid pace of daily life and the pressures that seem to be ever present, we are almost constantly under stress and have no time to reenergize.

Origins of Stress

Stress is not a new phenomenon, although the term "stress" was applied relatively recently to humans. The reaction now called stress was first recognized on the battlefield in the Civil War. Nervous and anxious reactions in the form of heart palpitations were so common among fearful soldiers that they became known as "soldier's heart." Stress was called "shell shock" during World War I and "battle fatigue" during World War II.

These reactions, in fact, existed in prehistoric times. When faced with possible danger, the autonomic nervous system responded by preparing early humans to face the situation with additional strength, energy, and endurance. Stored sugar and fat poured into the bloodstream to provide fuel for quick energy, breathing speeded up to provide more oxygen, and blood-clotting mechanisms were activated to protect against injury. Muscles tensed for action, digestion slowed to allow blood to be directed to the muscles and brain, pupils dilated to allow more light to enter the eye, and hormone production increased to prepare them either to fight or to run for safety. This response to anxiety is commonly known as the "fight or flight response."[16]

Modern humans respond similarly to the pressures and demands of daily events. For example, you may worry or feel anxious about juggling family and job responsibilities, the local school board election, a career-limiting mistake you made at work, or an accident you nearly had on the freeway. In each of these instances, your body reacts in much the same way that early humans reacted to a wild animal or attacking enemy. A series of biochemical changes occurs, and the body's system is thrown out of balance.

In today's society, you can seldom fight or flee in these situations. The physiological responses are turned on without being used for the intended purpose. The body is unable to release its stored energy because aggressive behavior would not be appropriate in most social situations. Repeated or chronic preparation for action that does not occur can lead to stress-related diseases and disorders.

KeyPoint
Stress is a key part of life, but too much stress can be destructive.

KeyPoint
Many organizations offer benefits to help employees ease the stress of work.

Stress Overload

Stress can be caused by either good or bad events. Holidays, weddings, births, and moving into a new house are examples of events that are both pleasant and stressful for most people. The death of a loved one, divorce, being fired from work, and just experiencing trouble on the job are negative events that cause stress.

Since stress is, by definition, a challenge, then challenges such as exams, sports contests, or anything that includes competition can induce a stress response. Even simple daily stressors have an effect on your body.

Unruly kids, a missed bus, a flat tire, traffic, and a rush job at work are all small stressors that add up. And those are just the emotional stressors. Physical stressors, which can range from poor nutrition to allergies to illness, add to the load. Chemical stressors, such as excessive caffeine, cigarette smoke, or any other substances that affect the body's response systems, can also contribute to becoming stressed out.

"You'll experience a certain amount of stress in your new job, but don't worry. We keep a defibrillator here on my desk."

© 2009 Ted Goff

> *The perfect no-stress environment is the grave. When we change our perception we gain control. The stress becomes a challenge, not a threat. When we commit to action, to actually doing something rather than feeling trapped by events, the stress in our life becomes manageable.*
>
> *—Greg Anderson, American author*

Some experiences are obviously more stressful than others. Often, the same type of experience will be more stressful to one person than to another. Regardless of the varying intensities of the experience, each person has a limit, or a stress threshold, to the amount of stress that can be handled physically and psychologically.

As stress builds up, people will experience an overload, which results in negative symptoms or behaviors. Thinking can become imprecise.[17] Overeating, loss of appetite, overindulgence in alcohol, ulcers, temper tantrums, headaches, hypertension, and heart disease are common results of stress overloads. Additionally, a decrease in the ability to concentrate, memory problems, insomnia, anxiety, depression, and other personality changes may accompany stress overloads. In fact, estimates are that as many as 90 percent of all medical complaints are, in part, stress-related illnesses. Additionally, stress accounts for 40 percent of job turnover.[18]

KeyPoint
Because the lines between work and home are blurred, stress reduction efforts need to be focused on both home and work.

News Headlines

In The News[19]

The National Institute for Occupational Safety and Health (NIOSH) has begun a new work–life initiative aimed at addressing health risks from work (both physical and organizational factors) and individual risk factors (such as smoking and diet). The agency believes that this approach is more effective in protecting and improving worker health and well-being than traditional isolated programs. Several trends are prompting this approach:

- Health-care costs are rising faster than wages or profits; many employers are cutting back on health benefits; and families are paying more out-of-pocket costs for health care.

- Corporate mergers, restructuring, and job insecurity are leading to increased work hours, greater job responsibilities, and added risks to employee health.

- Chronic disease rates are high and treatment is costly, highlighting the importance of effective prevention and disease management programs.

- The distinction between illness and injury from work and off-work risks is eroding.

- Work is one of the most important determinants of people's health. Up to 70 percent of health determinants can be addressed in workplace programs.

1. In 2008 over 5,071 people died from work-related injuries.[20] Do you believe stress from home could have played a part in any of these deaths? If so, explain your answer.

2. Do you change your eating pattern in times of high stress? If so, how? Do you believe this change could eventually affect your on-the-job performance? Explain your answer.

Learning to deal with stress, then, can literally be a matter of life and death. A healthy lifestyle can help you deal with stress and other health-related matters. It should include not abusing substances, effective time management, proper diet, exercise, relaxation, other leisure activities, sufficient sleep, and no smoking. It also involves reducing stressful thoughts, attitudes, and behaviors.

Ask Yourself...

1. Stress seems to be a way of life in today's society. Do you believe modern technology has increased stress on the job? Why or why not?

2. Do you expect stress at work to continue to increase or begin to decrease?

3. Can companies lower stress and still be competitive?

18.3   SUBSTANCE ABUSE AND JOB PERFORMANCE

Substance abuse is the misuse of alcohol, illegal drugs, or prescription drugs. It causes great concern for organizations because of the millions of dollars lost each year through decreased productivity, absenteeism, theft, industrial accidents, and excessive benefits use.

Estimates of the total overall costs of substance abuse in the United States—including health- and crime-related costs as well as losses in productivity—exceed half a trillion dollars annually. This includes approximately $181 billion for illicit drugs, $168 billion for tobacco, and $185 billion for alcohol. As staggering as these numbers are, however, they do not fully describe the breadth of deleterious public health and safety implications, which include family disintegration, loss of employment, failure in school, domestic violence, child abuse, and other crimes.[21]

> " *People who drink to drown their sorrow should be told that sorrow knows how to swim.*
> —Ann Landers, U.S. newspaper columnist "

Alcohol and Its Abuse

Alcohol is the most abused drug in the United States. Alcohol abuse and alcoholism cut across gender, race, and nationality. In the United States, 17.6 million people—about 1 in every 12 adults—abuse alcohol or are alcohol dependent. In general, more men than women are alcohol dependent or have alcohol problems. And alcohol problems are highest among young adults aged 18–29 and lowest among adults aged 65 and older. People who start drinking at an early age are at much higher risk of developing alcohol problems at some point in their lives than someone who starts drinking at age 21 or after.[22] A depressant, alcohol slows down the activity of the brain and spinal cord, impairing judgment and coordination. Although it may produce feelings of well-being, it can lead to sedation, intoxication, blackouts, unconsciousness, and death. Heavy consumption of alcohol may cause immediate physical problems, such as inefficiency, low energy, weight loss, lethargy, sleeplessness, accidents, and memory loss. Emotionally, it can cause a person to feel jealous, sexually aroused, impotent, moody, easily angered, guilty, depressed, worthless, despondent, and even suicidal.

Over a period of years, the effects of heavy drinking include malnutrition, brain damage, cancer, heart disease, liver damage, ulcers, gastritis, and birth defects in children whose mothers abused alcohol during pregnancy.[23,24]

Although alcohol is a legal substance, some people should not drink it at all. Abstinence is usually the only way that recovering alcoholics and individuals from alcoholic families are able to prevent abusing substances. More information can be obtained from the National Council on Alcoholism, Alcoholics Anonymous, or other organizations that deal with alcohol abuse.

KeyPoint
Find healthy activities you can do in place of drinking alcohol.

Do You Have a Problem with Alcohol?[25]

Answering the following four questions can help you learn if you or your loved one has a drinking problem:

- Have you ever felt you should cut down on your drinking?
- Have people annoyed you by criticizing your drinking?
- Have you ever felt bad or guilty about your drinking?
- Have you ever had a drink first thing in the morning to steady your nerves or to get rid of a hangover?

One "yes" answer suggests a possible alcohol problem. More than one "yes" answer means it is highly likely that a problem exists. If you think that you or someone you know might have an alcohol problem, seeing a doctor or other health-care provider right away is important. They can help you determine whether a drinking problem exists and plan the best course of action.

To assure you control your alcohol consumption, follow these tips from the National Institute on Alcohol Abuse and Alcoholism:[26]

1. *Write your reasons for cutting down or stopping.* Looking at this list frequently will remind you why changing your behavior is important.

2. *Set a drinking goal.* Choose a limit for how much you will drink. You may choose to cut down or not to drink at all. If you are cutting down, keep below these limits:

   Women: No more than one drink a day.

   Men: No more than two drinks a day.

   A drink is:

   a 12-ounce bottle of beer;

   a 5-ounce glass of wine; or

   a 1 1/2-ounce shot of liquor

   These limits may be too high for some people who have certain medical problems or who are older. Talk with your doctor about the limit that is right for you.

3. *Keep a diary of your drinking.* During the week, write down every time you have a drink. Do this for a month. This will show you how much you drink and when. How different is your goal from the amount you drink now?

4. *Watch it at home.* Keep a small amount or no alcohol at home. Don't keep temptations around.

5. *Drink slowly.* When you drink, sip your drink slowly. Take a break of one hour between drinks. Drink soda, water, or juice after a drink with alcohol. Do not drink on an empty stomach! Eat food when you are drinking.

6. *Take a break from alcohol.* Pick a day or two each week when you will not drink at all. Then, try to stop drinking for one week. Think about how you feel physically and emotionally on these days. When you succeed and feel better, you may find it easier to cut down for good.

7. *Learn how to say NO.* You don't have to drink when other people drink. You don't have to take a drink that is given to you. Practice ways to say "no" politely.

8. *Stay active.* What would you like to do instead of drinking? Use the time and money spent on drinking to do something fun with your family or friends.

9. *Get support.* Ask your family and friends for support to help you reach your goal. Talk to your doctor if you are having trouble cutting down.

10. *Watch out for temptations.* Watch out for people, places, or times that make you drink, even if you don't want to. Stay away from people who drink a lot or bars where you used to go. Plan ahead of time what you will do to avoid drinking when you are tempted.

11. *DO NOT GIVE UP!* Most people do not cut down or give up drinking all at once. If you don't reach your goal the first time, try again.

> **KeyPoint**
> Even though alcohol is a legal substance, its misuse can lower your productivity at work and lead to physical and emotional problems.

Global CONNECTION[27]

Employees on overseas assignments need to be aware that the penalties for substance abuse in foreign countries can be vastly different—and usually far more severe—from those in the United States. Failure to respect the differences can result in jail time or worse consequences.

The U.S. Embassy in Seoul, South Korea, for instance, has seen an increase of Americans working in South Korea who have been jailed for drug use. In that country marijuana is classified as a dangerous narcotic. American citizens are subjected to that country's laws and are not given a break because they are Americans. Additionally, the U.S. Embassy cannot assist American prisoners with legal matters; their only job is to assure that Americans get fair treatment under the South Korean laws.

1. Should Americans working overseas be protected from foreign laws? Why or why not?

2. How can you get information concerning views about alcohol and illegal drugs in other countries?

Commonly Abused Drugs

The National Institute on Drug Abuse has identified the following as the most commonly abused drugs.[28]

Cannabinoids　*Cannabinoids* include marijuana and hashish. Side effects include euphoria, slowed thinking and reaction time, and confusion as well as impaired balance and coordination. Users can experience a cough, frequent respiratory infections, impaired memory and learning, increased heart rate, anxiety, and panic attacks. The body can develop a tolerance to cannabinoids and become addicted to it.

The tetrahydrocannabinol carboxylic acid (THC) in cannabinoids can be detected by standard urine testing methods several days after a smoking session. In heavy users, however, traces can sometimes be detected for weeks after they have stopped using marijuana.[29]

> **"**
> *Dope never helped anybody sing better or play music better or do anything better. All dope can do for you is kill you—and kill you the long, slow, hard way.*
> —Billie Holliday, American singer
> **"**

Depressants　As a class, *depressants* can reduce anxiety, deliver a feeling of well-being, and lower inhibitions. However, they can also be particularly dangerous because of their ability to slow your pulse and breathing; lower blood pressure; cause poor concentration, fatigue, and confusion; and impair coordination, memory, and judgment. These drugs can lead to addiction, respiratory depression and arrest, and death.

Commonly abused depressants are:

- Barbiturates (Amytal, Nembutal, Seconal, phenobarbital: barbs, reds, red birds, phennies, tooies, yellows, yellow jackets)
- Benzodiazepines (Ativan, Halcion, Librium, Valium, Xanax: candy, downers, sleeping pills, tranks)
- Flunitrazepam (Rohypnol: forget-me pill, R2, Roche, roofies, roofinol, rope, rophies)
- Gamma-hydroxybutyrate (GHB; G, Georgia home boy, grievous bodily harm, liquid ecstasy)
- Methaqualone (Quaalude, Sopor, Parest: ludes, mandrex, quad, quay)

Dissociative Anesthetics　*Dissociative anesthetics* include ketamine (known as Ketalar SV: cat Valiums, K, Special K, vitamin K) as well as PCP and analogs (known as phencyclidine, angel dust, boat, hog, love boat, peace pill). These drugs can cause increased heart rate and blood pressure, impaired motor functioning and memory loss, numbness, nausea, and vomiting. At high doses ketamine can cause delirium and depression as well as respiratory depression and arrest. PCP can cause panic, aggression, violence, and loss of appetite.

Hallucinogens   Lysergic acid diethylamide (LSD: acid, blotter, boomers, cubes, microdot, yellow sunshines), mescaline (buttons, cactus, mesc, peyote), and psilocybin (magic mushroom, purple passion, shrooms) make up the class of *hallucinogens*. These drugs, while altering states of perception and feeling, can cause nausea and persisting flashbacks.

Opioids and Morphine Derivatives   Addiction, tolerance, nausea, respiratory depression and arrest, unconsciousness, coma, and death are the side effects of *opioids and morphine derivatives* that induce drowsiness, confusion, and sedation. The following are classified as opioids:

- Codeine (Empirin with Codeine, Fiorinal with Codeine, Robitussin A-C, Tylenol with Codeine: Captain Cody, schoolboy (with glutethimide), doors & fours, loads, pancakes and syrup)
- Fentanyl and fentanyl analogs (Actiq, Duragesic, Sublimaze: Apache, dance fever, friend, goodfella, jackpot, murder 8, TNT, Tango and Cash)
- Heroin (diacetylmorphine: brown sugar, dope, H, horse, junk, skag, skunk, smack, white horse)
- Morphine (Roxanol, Duramorph: M, Miss Emma, monkey, white stuff)
- Opium (laudanum, paregoric: big O, black stuff, block, gum, hop)
- Oxycodone HCL (Oxycontin: Oxy, O.C., killer)
- Hydrocodone bitartrate, acetaminophen (Vicodin: vike, Watson-387)

> **"** *The basic thing nobody asks is why do people take drugs of any sort? Why do we have these accessories to normal living to live? I mean, is there something wrong with society that's making us so pressurized that we cannot live without guarding ourselves against it?*
>
> —*John Lennon, British singer and songwriter* **"**

Stimulants   *Stimulants* increase the heart rate, blood pressure, and metabolism, leading to feelings of exhilaration, energy, and increased mental alertness. They also, however, cause rapid or irregular heartbeat, reduced appetite, weight loss, heart failure, nervousness, and insomnia. Drugs in this category are as follows:

- *Amphetamine* (Biphetamine, Dexedrine: bennies, black beauties, crosses, hearts, LA turnaround, speed, truck drivers, uppers). The drug can specifically cause rapid breathing and tremor, loss of coordination, irritability, anxiousness, restlessness, delirium, panic, paranoia, impulsive behavior, aggressiveness, tolerance, addiction, and psychosis.
- *Cocaine* (cocaine hydrochloride: blow, bump, C, candy, Charlie, coke, crack, flake, rock, snow, toot). Increased temperature and chest pain, respiratory failure, nausea, abdominal pain, strokes, seizures, headaches, malnutrition, and panic attack are a hallmark of cocaine.

- *Methylenedioxy-methamphetamine* (MDMA; Adam, clarity, ecstasy, Eve, lover's speed, peace, STP, X, XTC). It produces mild hallucinogenic effects, increased tactile sensitivity, empathic feelings, impaired memory and learning, hyperthermia, cardiac toxicity, renal failure, and liver toxicity.

- *Methamphetamine* (Desoxyn: chalk, crank, crystal, fire, glass, go fast, ice, meth, speed). Side effects of this drug are aggression, violence, psychotic behavior, memory loss, cardiac and neurological damage, as well as impaired memory and learning. The substance is addictive and you can develop a tolerance for it.

- *Methylphenidate* (Ritalin: JIF, MPH, R-ball, Skippy, the smart drug, vitamin R). While this drug is safe and effective for treatment of attention deficit hyperactivity disorder, it can be abused and be dangerous if used incorrectly.

- *Nicotine* (cigarettes, cigars, smokeless tobacco, snuff, spit tobacco, bidis, chew). Nicotine use can lead to chronic lung disease, cardiovascular disease, stroke, and cancer. It is addictive, and the body can develop a tolerance to it.

Other Compounds   Other compounds that are commonly abused include anabolic steroids, dextromethorphan, and inhalants.

Anabolic steroids (Anadrol, Oxandrin, Durabolin, Depo-Testosterone, Equipoise: roids, juice) have no intoxication effects but can be quite damaging to the body. The side effects include hypertension, blood clotting and cholesterol changes, liver cysts and cancer, kidney cancer, hostility and aggression, and acne. Adolescents can experience premature stoppage of growth while males can develop prostate cancer, reduced sperm production, shrunken testicles, and breast enlargement. Menstrual irregularities as well as the development of a beard and other masculine characteristics are common in females.

Dextromethorphan (DXM) (Robotripping, Robo, Triple C) is found in some cough and cold medications. It causes distorted visual perceptions as well as complete dissociative effects. At higher doses, its side effects are similar to those listed for dissociative anesthetics.

Inhalants are solvents (paint thinners, gasoline, glues), gases (butane, propane, aerosol propellants, nitrous oxide), and nitrites (isoamyl, isobutyl, cyclohexyl). When inhaled they can cause stimulation, a loss of inhibition, headache, nausea or vomiting, slurred speech, loss of motor coordination, wheezing, unconsciousness, cramps, weight loss, muscle weakness, depression, memory impairment, damage to cardiovascular and nervous systems, and sudden death.

Fighting Substance Abuse at Work

Organizations are using a variety of techniques, such as drug testing, employee assistance programs (EAPs), and employee education, in an effort to curtail substance abuse at work. Testing can be performed on potential as well as current employees.[30]

KeyPoint
Employers use a variety of drug testing schedules to assure that their environments are safe and productive.

Pre-employment drug testing requires job applicants to be tested for drugs in their system prior to employment. Applicants who do not pass or refuse to take the examination are not hired.

A growing number of organizations are also testing current employees for substance abuse. A variety of testing schedules are used, depending on the preference of the organization. One type of schedule is known as *expected interval testing*. Under this method, employees are informed ahead of time when testing will occur. It is then performed at the same time on a continuous basis. For example, the test may be scheduled for the first workday after each payday.

Random interval testing involves giving tests at random to a particular group of employees. For instance, all employees in the accounting department may be informed that they are to report immediately for a drug test. This testing is most often used for job categories involving public safety or security.

A third type of testing schedule is called *"for cause" testing*. With this method, individual employees may be tested when they appear to exhibit signs of substance abuse, such as slurred speech or dilated pupils. Testing is sometimes done after industrial accidents or for reasonable cause.

Employees may also be expected to submit to *treatment follow-up testing*. This type of testing is used to monitor an employee's success in remaining drug free after being allowed to complete a substance abuse treatment program rather than be terminated.

Other organizations test only employees who are transferred or promoted or those who are in critical positions. Examples of those who are in critical positions are factory employees who work with dangerous equipment and airline pilots.

Company policies and procedures vary on what happens to an employee who fails or refuses to submit to a substance abuse test. Many companies require termination on the spot. Others may require mandatory enrollment in a substance abuse program. Generally, the policy will be more lenient for legal substances than illegal. Employees should be familiar with their company policy on this matter.

Most companies reserve the right to search all areas and property over which the company maintains control without the consent of the employee. On occasion, organizations have been known to call local law enforcement agencies or use dogs trained to locate illegal substances in an effort to curtail substance abuse.

Besides utilizing drug detection programs, many firms have established employee assistance plans to provide short-term counseling to employees and assist them in obtaining appropriate treatment for substance abuse. Employee education programs are also used to alert employees to the dangers of substance abuse and encourage those who are abusing to seek treatment.[31]

> *Just Say No.*
> *—Partnership*
> *for a Drug-Free*
> *America*

Coming to Terms with Substance Abuse

If you are abusing substances, you need to take action before their use interferes with your current job, prevents you from obtaining a job, disrupts other major areas of your life, destroys your health, or kills you.

Check the telephone book or Internet for treatment and counseling centers. If you are employed and your company has an EAP, use it. The program is designed to help employees with substance abuse and other personal problems. It is confidential and usually free.

Substance Abuse Affects Many Life Areas[32]

Relationships Individuals who abuse substances have difficulty in maintaining healthy family relationships. Friends who do not abuse substances may avoid contact with the abuser, particularly at social functions, because the abuser often behaves in a fashion that causes embarrassment. Many substance abusers drop nonusing friends in favor of those who also abuse substances.

Finances Abusing substances is expensive, and an abuser may spend more than he or she earns to support the habit. In addition, the abuser may not pay attention to finances and may become careless with money.

Work Performance may deteriorate, resulting in disciplinary action or termination. Friction with coworkers may become a problem as coworkers become irritated at the abuser for not doing a fair share of the work.

Health Abusers develop health problems such as high blood pressure, deterioration of brain cells, depression, malnutrition, cancer, and cirrhosis of the liver.

Many individuals are reluctant to use an EAP for fear that their employer will learn that they have a problem. Most plans ensure confidentiality and do not reveal to the employer which employees have used the services. Employers will eventually find out about untreated substance abuse problems when performance declines.

If you don't take action to correct your substance abuse problem, it's quite likely your supervisor will. Most organizations that operate drug testing programs have trained their supervisors to recognize behavior that signals substance abuse.

> People always want to ask me about my drug problem. I never had a drug problem; I had a self-esteem problem.
>
> —Gloria Gaynor, American singer

Seeking help is the first step in controlling a substance abuse problem.

JeanellNorvell/iStockphoto.com

Many substance abusers deny having a problem and fail to realize that the problem is interfering with their work. Because of employee denial, organizations usually instruct their supervisors to do the following if they suspect an employee of substance abuse:

- Judge only on performance and do not accuse the employee of having a substance abuse problem.
- Do not accept excuses for ongoing poor performance or absenteeism.
- Document all poor performance.
- Assist employees in obtaining treatment if asked.
- Do not preach or moralize.
- Begin action up to and including discharge if the employee does not satisfactorily perform the job.

Employees with substance abuse problems should recognize that supervisors have support from higher management in taking these actions. Abusers should address their problem if they wish to remain employed. Two federal laws can assist substance abusers in getting treatment and keeping their jobs.

The Americans with Disabilities Act requires that employers with 15 or more employees give a reasonable accommodation to individuals with disabilities. Under the act, alcoholism is treated as a disability. However, employees who abuse alcohol may be disciplined and discharged when their alcohol use adversely affects job performance. Users of illegal drugs are not protected and can be discharged for drug use. Former drug addicts, however, are covered.

Individuals who voluntarily check themselves into a drug treatment center prior to being identified by the company as a substance abuser will most likely be protected by the act and be allowed a reasonable amount of time to pursue treatment.[33]

The Family Medical Leave Act (FMLA) requires employers with 50 or more employees within a 75-mile radius to provide employees who have worked for the company at least 1,250 hours in the past 12 months 12 weeks of unpaid leave during a 12-month period for a serious health condition. Absence for treatment of substance abuse does qualify for FMLA leave.[34]

As these laws and their interpretations rapidly change, anyone wanting protection for treatment under these laws or any state laws should check with the company's human resource department or obtain legal counsel.

Dealing with Abusers at Work

Becoming aware that a coworker or supervisor is abusing drugs or alcohol presents a dilemma. If you allow such people to operate machinery or perform any activity that might injure themselves or others, or destroy equipment or property, and something actually happens, living with yourself will be difficult. If you report the individual to management, he or she will most likely resent you, which will cause you future difficulties in working with this person.

Others in your work group may feel uncomfortable around you, thinking that you will report their activities to management. Covering up for coworkers or supervisors by doing their work or making excuses for their tardiness or absence is called *enabling*. Enabling behavior includes:[35]

Covering up—providing alibis, making excuses, or doing an impaired coworker's work rather than allowing it to be known that he or she is not meeting his or her responsibilities

Rationalizing—developing reasons why the person's continued use is understandable or acceptable

Withdrawing—avoiding contact with the person with the problem

Blaming—becoming angry at the individual for not trying hard enough to control his or her use

Controlling—trying to take responsibility for the person's use by throwing out his or her drugs or cutting off the supply

Threatening—saying that you will take action (e.g., turning the person in) if he or she does not control his or her use, but not following through when he or she continues to use

Enabling behavior allows substance abusers to continue this conduct and avoid confronting the problem. Enabling may keep peace in your work group. However, you will continue to perform extra work while the abuser carries on the pattern of missed hours and substandard performance. Resentment on your part will soon build.

Additionally, you may wish to assist the individual in trouble. You may give advice, preach, or moralize. This action generally doesn't help because substance abusers typically deny that they have a problem. The more you attempt to help, the more resentful the substance abuser will become, frustrating both of you.

KeyPoint You don't have to be the victim of coworkers who abuse substances—you can take direct action by not enabling their behavior.

KeyPoint Denial that substance abuse is a problem is a classic behavior for a substance abuser.

Ethics CONNECTION[36]

The hangover—headache, nausea, sensitivity to light and noise, lethargy, and unpleasant mood—is a frequent side effect of drinking too much. It can affect the light to moderate drinker who does not have a problem with alcohol. While signs of alcohol in your blood may be gone, your productivity is not 100 percent. In fact, it is estimated that almost 10 percent of employees nurse a hangover at work. Hangover-related absenteeism and lowered productivity cost the American economy billions annually.[37]

1. While almost everyone recognizes the toll alcoholics and drug addicts take on productivity, almost no one notices the loss of productivity caused by light to moderate substance abuse. Do you agree? Why or why not?

2. Are you being fair to your employer if you abuse alcohol after work regularly? To yourself?

3. Should organizations be allowed to dictate substance avoidance during nonwork hours? Why or why not?

Dealing with substance-abusing coworkers and supervisors, then, requires human relations skills. Use tact and diplomacy, involving only those who need to know. Tell abusers that their behavior is making your working with them difficult. Point out a specific behavior, such as absence, that is causing you difficulty. Offer support by showing concern that they don't appear to be their old selves and asking what you can do to help. Be supportive if they decide to enter treatment.

Not allowing impaired employees to operate equipment, refusing to "enable" by covering for them, and not preaching or moralizing are the best ways to help yourself and your fellow employees. Both of you benefit: the abuser is forced into treatment quicker, and you won't be worried about a potential disaster or feel that you're being used or taken advantage of.

Ask Yourself...

1. Most employees do not seek EAP assistance on their own but get help only when forced to do so by their employer. Why do you think this is?

2. Do you believe EAPs keep information confidential? Why do you feel this way?

3. What other methods of treatment are available in your community?

4. Why is denial a problem when dealing with substance abuse? Review the definition of *enable* in this chapter and the defense mechanism *denial* in Chapter 2.

5. Name some specific actions that are enabling.

18.4 EFFECTIVE TIME MANAGEMENT

Time is a precious commodity. Every individual has the same amount of time each day to be wasted or spent well. How we choose to use our time makes the difference in whether we achieve our goals. Effective **time management** is simply maximizing the time that we have to our greatest advantage. When we are in control of our time, we perform better, feel better about ourselves, and suffer fewer stress-related illnesses. We can develop better time management by assessing how we use time, identifying how we waste it, and implementing a plan to use it better.

Assessing How You Spend Your Time

The first step in assessing whether you are managing your time wisely is to assess your time management skills using the test in Figure 18.1.

If you want to make good use of your time, you've got to know what's most important and then give it all you've got.

—Lee Iacocca, American auto executive

Now, determine if you are suffering from any of the negative symptoms of poor time management. These negative symptoms are:

Indecision. You have so much to do that you cannot decide what to do first. You end up doing nothing and getting nowhere.

White rabbit habit. "I'm late, I'm late, for a very important date" accurately describes your life. Like the rabbit in Lewis Carroll's *Alice's Adventures in Wonderland,* you are always in a hurry, running late, and missing appointments and deadlines.

Stress illnesses. Responses to the pressures of poor time management include headaches, backaches, insomnia, and hives.

Irritability and anger. You stay angry and upset and have a tendency to take your frustration out on others.

Don't say you don't have enough time. You have exactly the same number of hours per day that were given to Helen Keller, Pasteur, Michelangelo, Mother Teresa, Leonardo da Vinci, Thomas Jefferson, and Albert Einstein.

—H. Jackson Brown, American author

Negative symptoms may make you look "out of control" and keep you from getting results. Good time management tends to be reflected in a confident and controlled approach to activities.

Figure 18.1 ◑

Time management skills assessment.

Answer the following with a "yes" or "no."

_____ 1. Do you have a plan for the day's work before you begin?

_____ 2. Do you frequently interrupt your work to return IMs, text messages, or e-mail?

_____ 3. Do you tackle important assignments when you know your productivity is at its best?

_____ 4. Do you procrastinate, putting off work because you feel you don't have time to do it correctly?

_____ 5. Do you know how to get people off the telephone or out of your office politely?

_____ 6. Do you have so much to do that you can't decide what to do first?

_____ 7. Is your work space organized? Can you find everything you need?

_____ 8. Are you always in a hurry, running late, or missing appointments and deadlines?

_____ 9. Do you break big projects up into manageable pieces?

_____ 10. When pressured to meet deadlines, do you get headaches, backaches, or suffer from insomnia?

Answers to Even Numbered Questions		Answers to Odd Numbered Questions	
Yes	No	Yes	No
2.		1.	
4.		3.	
6.		5.	
8.		7.	
10.		9.	
Give yourself 1 point for every "no" answer		Give yourself 1 point for every "yes" answer	

Scoring Guide

8–10 points   You manage your time well.

5–7 points   You have room for improvement.

1–4 points   You need to work on your time management skills immediately!

Another valuable step in assessing your time usage is to keep a time log, as illustrated in the sample time log in Figure 18.2. Use a log for at least a one-week period. Logging your daily activities for this length of time will allow you to identify your major time wasters. You may be surprised at the amount of time you spend on innocent activities that rob you of using your precious commodity more productively.

Figure 18.2

Sample time log.

Time	Planned Work	Telephone	Interruption	Meeting	Unplanned/New	Reports	Other	Subject	Originator (Person)	Priority A	B	C	Other	Comments
7:30														
7:45														
8:00														
8:15														
8:30														
8:45														
9:00														
9:15														
9:30														
9:45														
10:00														
10:15														
10:30														
10:45														
11:00														
11:15														
11:30														
11:45														
12:00														
12:15														
12:30														
12:45														
1:00														
1:15														
1:30														
1:45														
2:00														
2:15														
2:30														
2:45														
3:00														
3:15														
3:30														
3:45														
4:00														
4:15														
4:30														
4:45														
5:00														

Priority Definitions:

A—Very important; high priority item

B—Important; have more time to complete

C—Less important; could be delegated or rescheduled for later time

Other—Could "not do"; wasted time

Start Identifying Time Wasters

Lack of planning, drop-in visitors, telephone games, procrastination, electronic communication addiction, meetings, overcommitment, fighting brushfires, personal disorganization, the inability to say "no," television, and Internet surfing are among the most frequent time wasters at work. You may recognize some of them as being at the top of your list. Methods of handling some of the biggest time wasters are described as follows.

Lack of Planning   An old adage appropriate to this situation states, "If you fail to plan, you plan to fail." Planning a course of action is crucial in accomplishing your goals. One of the easiest methods of planning is to make a list of tasks to be accomplished. Ideally, you will have a daily list of five to ten major actions in the order of importance. Limiting your list to five to ten items enables you to add unexpected or forgotten items while keeping the list manageable. The important point is to stick to your list and not overcommit. Carry over any unfinished tasks to the next day and integrate them into that day's priority list. An effective way of handling your priority list is to keep it on a calendar throughout the year. This practice also provides you with an excellent record of your activities.

Another useful method of planning is to use your "peak times" for tough tasks. You may be a morning person or a night person. Our body clocks, or biological rhythms, do tick strongest at different times of the day for each person. Recognizing your peak performance time may assist you in planning your more difficult tasks for that time to maximize your effectiveness. For instance, if you are a morning person, you will want to complete a difficult report early in the morning rather than waiting until late afternoon when you are not as alert.

Another timesaving tip is to plan certain activities for your nonpeak times. For example, banking on Friday afternoons will most certainly cost you more time than a midweek visit. Attempting postal business during your lunch break will find you in long lines with other individuals who had the same idea. A midmorning or afternoon visit to the post office will probably save you time.

Drop-in or Casual Visitors   Friends and colleagues may unwittingly rob you of precious time needed to meet personal or professional commitments. That drop-in visit from the coworker down the hall to discuss the Monday night football game may disrupt your concentration on an important report due by noon to your boss or throw your daily schedule completely off track. The following phrases can be useful in controlling the length of visits:

"I appreciate your stopping by, but..."

"I have a tight schedule; could we talk about this on..." (and set a time and date).

"I have about ten minutes before I have to go..." "How can I help you?"

> **KeyPoint**
> Making a "to do" list is one of the most important things you can do to stay on track.

> **KeyPoint**
> In order to manage your time effectively you must understand and confront your time wasters.

Technology CONNECTION

You're having lunch with a customer who wants to meet with you and your boss to finalize a contract. You have your calendar handy in your smart phone. But when is your boss free? No problem—just log into his or her calendar via your smart phone using iCal. (iCal or iCalendar is the standard internet calendar format that allows Internet users to share tasks and meeting requests with one another as well as share files.) Seeing a free space of time, you book the appointment for that day, and send an electronic invitation to the boss.

Need a reminder about the meeting? iCal will send you a text or email, so you won't forget that important event.

1. What is helpful about using an online calendar?
2. What problems could you possibly have using this type of technology?
3. Can technology keep you from missing the meeting? Explain your answer.

Procrastination   One of the most difficult time wasters to control is your own procrastination. *Procrastination* is defined as putting off or intentionally delaying activities that need to be done. Once you understand the problem, you can develop methods of overcoming it. Chapter 15 presented some of the reasons we procrastinate.

We occasionally find ourselves saying and meaning two different things:

Saying:		Meaning:	
	I really should…		I don't really want to…
	I can't do…		I won't do…
	I might…		I won't…
	I'll try to…		I won't…
	Could we discuss this some other time?		I really don't ever want to talk about it.

> One worthwhile task carried to a successful conclusion is worth half-a-hundred half-finished tasks.
>
> —Malcolm S. Forbes, American magazine publisher

You can deal with procrastination by using the following suggestions:

1. Tackle tough problems at your body's peak performance times.
2. Break large tasks into smaller segments so that they will not seem overwhelming.
3. Use daily "to do" lists and set specific goals.
4. Fight perfectionism. Realize that in today's fast-paced world of work, many things can be done satisfactorily. Perfection is not always necessary.
5. Seek help if needed.
6. Let go of low-priority tasks in order to focus and concentrate on high-priority ones.
7. Schedule appropriate blocks of times to do specific tasks.
8. Establish a reward system for positive reinforcement.

Major Causes of Procrastination

Inappropriate Causes

- *Perfectionism:* You put off tasks until you can do them exactly right, the very best you can. You fear they won't be right or good enough.

- *Abdication:* You wait for things to "happen" rather than make them happen; you make panic decisions; you let someone else make the decision; you do nothing at all.

- *Overwhelmed:* Job/task appears too big to handle. It seems threatening.

- *Uncertainty:* You are unsure how to do the task.

Appropriate Causes

- *Stressed/exhausted:* You are too tired to think through the problem effectively. You might make a poor or wrong decision. You tend to use bad judgment and may wind up doing it over again.

- *Impulsive/emotional:* You might make snap judgments or might do things in a fit of anger and regret them.

- *Lack of information:* You need more facts to make a good decision.

- *Feel cautious/concerned:* You heed a subconscious message that you should not do that activity.

Telephone Games   You may have been involved in a game of phone tag or screened your calls to avoid someone who talks for too long. Phone tag—two people calling numerous times, leaving messages but never reaching each other—can take hours of unproductive time. Instead, leave a message specifying what you want or leave instructions concerning required actions. If someone you need doesn't return your call, you might try leaving a message such as, "Unless I hear from you by close of business today, I plan to..." This warning will normally prompt action by the other party. If all else fails, try to get your information elsewhere.

What if you get a call from someone who wants to discuss everything but the important purpose of the call? The following phrases may help control the length of time you spend on these calls:

"I appreciate your call, but..."

"I'm working on a term paper due this week. Can we visit later when I'm not so pressed for time?"

"Could you call back when we might have more time?"

Addiction to Electronic Communication   A compulsion to check your voicemail, e-mail, text messages, or Facebook feed can waste an enormous amount of time. One study estimated that 44 percent of the time employees worked on a PC was spent doing these activities.[38]

The impulse to check electronic messages the moment they arrive is distracting. Time is lost switching from one activity to another. Failure to concentrate for even 10 minutes at a time can cause you to lose anywhere from 20 to 40 percent of your efficiency.[39]

When you need to concentrate on a task, limit digital interruptions. Close your e-mail and instant messaging programs. Turn off your cell phone. Schedule to check them at certain points during the day.

Keep a record of what you instant message or Twitter. Is it really important to tell your friends what you had for lunch or what TV show you plan to watch later on? Limit your messages to important activities.

Meetings   Endless, nonproductive meetings are some of the biggest time wasters in the workplace. Practicing a few important meeting strategies can help all attendees manage their time and get the most out of the meeting.

A *planned agenda* is an outline or list of what is to be discussed or accomplished during the meeting. The agenda is a valuable tool for controlling your meeting. Ideally, an agenda should be distributed several days prior to the meeting time. People will be able to schedule their time to support the meeting and prepare information that may be needed.

The agenda will serve as your guideline for a smooth transition from topic to topic and prevent the introduction of hidden agendas. A *hidden agenda* consists of topics that attendees wish to discuss that have no relevance to the purpose of your meeting. A hidden agenda can be disruptive because it often sidetracks the meeting and forces attendees to focus on topics other than those originally scheduled to be discussed. This can lead to lengthy meetings that fail to focus adequately on the topic at hand.

As the meeting leader, you have the responsibility for adhering to the planned agenda. A successful meeting should move quickly, sufficiently cover all scheduled topics in the shortest possible time, and accomplish the planned meeting objectives.

Try these guidelines for running an effective meeting:

1. Provide advance agendas reflecting timed subjects.
2. Invite only those people who are needed.
3. Start on time.
4. Set clear goals/purposes for the meeting.
5. Set time limits on the meeting and discussion topics.
6. Adhere strictly to your agenda.
7. Record and assign action items during the meeting.
8. Distribute meeting minutes within 48 hours.
9. Schedule an action-item follow-up.

Putting It All Together

Once you have analyzed how you spend your time, you may want to develop some definite action plans. The sample time management action plan in Figure 18.3 provides you with a format and brief example of an action plan.

Figure 18.3

Sample time management action plan.

Desired Result:	Quit watching excessive TV.
Change Required:	Be more productive; read more, watch less.
Target Date:	Within a week.
Actions Required:	Schedule TV time ahead, and don't deviate.
Key People Involved:	Family—they won't like it.
Evaluate/modify:	Did I achieve desired results? If not, try another approach.

Once you've made an action plan, you need to stick with it. As with any plan, you must develop the habit of sticking with the action plan for it to work.[40]

Ask Yourself...

1. Often, we spend time *efficiently* but are not *effective*. What is the difference between efficient and effective?

2. Do you take time to determine what really matters and concentrate on that activity? Why or why not?

18.5   SOUND HEALTH PRACTICES

Sound health practices are vital to a successful career. You can take responsibility for your own health by eating a balanced diet, maintaining an appropriate weight, limiting alcohol consumption, not smoking, and developing a mindset that allows you to relax and enjoy leisure time while limiting stressful thoughts, attitudes, and behaviors.

> " *The way you think, the way you behave, the way you eat, can influence your life by 30 to 50 years. Most people believe that aging is universal but there are biological organisms that never age.*
>
> —*Deepak Chopra, Indian physician and author* "

Weight Management

A third of Americans are obese, accounting for approximately 9 percent of the medical spending in the country. Generally, medical spending averages $1,400 more per year for an obese person than for someone who is of healthy weight.[41]

In order to control costs and stay healthy, the United States Department of Agriculture (USDA) and Health and Human Services recommend that we eat a balanced variety of foods to get the nutrients we need and at the same time the right amount of calories to maintain a healthy weight. In their

Dietary Guidelines for Americans, 2005, they encourage consumption of the following food groups:[42]

- Consume a sufficient amount of fruits and vegetables while staying within energy needs. Two cups of fruit and 2 1/2 cups of vegetables per day are recommended for a reference 2,000-calorie intake, with higher or lower amounts depending on the calorie level.

- Choose a variety of fruits and vegetables each day. In particular, select from all five vegetable subgroups (dark green, orange, legumes, starchy vegetables, and other vegetables) several times a week.

- Consume three or more ounce-equivalents of whole-grain products per day, with the rest of the recommended grains coming from enriched or whole-grain products. In general, at least half the grains should come from whole grains.

- Consume three cups per day of fat-free or low-fat milk or equivalent milk products.

Being overweight or obese has been associated with increased risk of developing conditions such as high blood pressure, Type 2 diabetes, and coronary artery disease. To decide whether you are at risk because of your weight, determine your body mass index (BMI) by using the chart that follows in Figure 18.4. Then, using your BMI, gauge your health risk relative to normal weight.[43]

> **KeyPoint**
> You should ultimately consult a physician to determine your health risks relative to your weight.

Figure 18.4

Are you at a healthy weight?

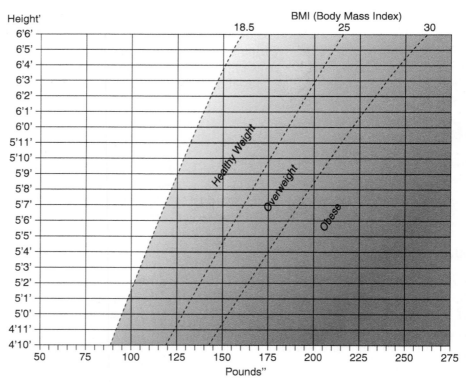

SOURCE: Report of the Dietary Guidelines Advisory Committee on the Dietary Guidelines for Americans, 2000, page 3. Retrieved on October 23, 2009 from http://www.cnpp.usda.gov.

In The News[44]

In 2010 Alabama State employees are eligible for a monthly $25 wellness discount off single coverage health insurance. To qualify, they must supply their employer with baseline readings for blood pressure, cholesterol, glucose, and BMI. In order to continue getting the discount in 2011, state employees who are health risks must prove that they are working to reduce their risk factors or that they have a condition that does not allow them to improve those factors.

1. The state of Alabama has the second highest rate of obesity in the nation. Do you believe it's fair to charge those who are obese more for their insurance than those who aren't? Explain your answer.

2. What other things do you think employers could do to help their employees become healthier?

Making Healthy Choices

Cutting back on harmful substances and learning to practice stress management techniques can contribute greatly to overall health.

Limit the Consumption of Caffeine   Regular consumption of caffeine (over 350 mg/day) through coffee or caffeinated soft drinks may not only cause dependency but chronic insomnia, persistent anxiety, restlessness, heart palpitations, upset stomach, and depression. Eliminating caffeine intake after 2:00 PM will help you sleep better, which is necessary for the body to produce high energy.[45]

Stop Smoking   Smoking is the single most important preventable cause of death in our society. Cancers of the lung, larynx, oral cavity, esophagus, pancreas, and bladder; heart and blood vessel diseases; chronic bronchitis; and emphysema have all been linked to smoking. Additionally, involuntary or passive inhalation of cigarette smoke can cause or worsen symptoms of asthma, cardiovascular and respiratory diseases, pneumonia, and bronchitis. Smoking during pregnancy has been associated with premature births, small or underweight babies, and respiratory and cardiovascular problems in infants. Besides these physical implications, smoking is a major contributor to death and injury from fires and other accidents.

In an effort to curb smoking-related problems, most states have passed legislation limiting or forbidding smoking in enclosed public places.

Smoking has been banned on domestic and many international air flights, and more nonsmokers today are demanding and obtaining smoke-free environments at work and in public areas. Asking someone not to smoke around you should be done tactfully, however.

> **KeyPoint**
> You alone control whether you make healthy choices.

Giving up smoking takes determination. Smoking often serves as an outlet for nervousness. Smoking can become psychologically addictive. Nicotine, a key ingredient in cigarette smoke, is physiologically addictive, making it even more difficult to stop. Many programs designed to help people stop smoking are available, and some are covered by medical insurance.[46]

Cut Back on Multitasking   Today's workers find themselves bothered, constantly being interrupted, and moving from one task to another. In fact, one study found that workers spend an average of 11 minutes on a project and, during that time, may change activities every three minutes. This leads to the feeling of overwork and frustration. These interruptions and the time it takes to get yourself back on task can eat up about 2.1 hours of your day. Trying to do two tasks at once, such as talking on the telephone and writing a memo, leaves you more likely to make mistakes and decreases your efficiency.

Learning to create blocks of uninterrupted time for yourself and teaching yourself to focus can greatly improve your creativity, productivity, and efficiency. Busyness does not necessarily make you effective.[47]

Exercise   Exercise is one of the most effective methods known for reducing stress. Although it is not a cure-all, exercise releases the stored energies of the "fight or flight" response. Moderate running, swimming, biking, racquetball, and basketball are all good forms of exercise for reducing stress. Regardless of which type of exercise you choose, fitness experts recommend a minimum of 20 minutes of continuous exercise, three or four times a week.

However, lighter forms of exercise can be equally effective stress reducers. Working in the garden, mowing the yard, playing ping pong or pool, or taking a brisk walk can disengage you from the sources of stress. These exercises provide you a mental break.

Exercise need not be dull or seem like a chore. Its benefits, such as relieving tension, helping control weight, and lowering cholesterol, can be obtained through small changes in your personal routine. You don't have to be an accomplished athlete or a physical fitness expert to achieve desired results through exercise. In addition to establishing a regular exercise program at home or a gym, you might consider changing simple daily habits. The following small changes in your lifestyle can increase your physical activity:[48]

1. Use the stairs rather than the elevator.

2. Park your car at the back of the parking lot and walk to the store.

3. Put more vigor into everyday activities.

4. Take a walk each day at lunchtime or after work, and keep walking shoes in your car for these occasions.

5. Go dancing.

6. Use the restroom on a different floor at work and take the stairs.

Before starting any exercise program, however, you should consult a physician to determine what is appropriate for your age and physical condition.

> "
> *The only exercise some people get is jumping to conclusions, running down their friends, side-stepping responsibility, and pushing their luck!*
> —*Author unknown*
> "

Relaxation   Learning the art of relaxation is crucial to controlling stress. Headaches, backaches, and nervousness can be reduced or eliminated by using progressive relaxation techniques. Nervousness wastes energy, making us more fatigued and less alert.

To relax, spend 20 to 30 minutes twice a day applying some of the various relaxation techniques. All that is necessary is a quiet place where you won't be disturbed. Mini-relaxation breaks of five minutes throughout the day can also be invaluable in reducing stress. Only a comfortable chair or sofa is necessary.

Leisure   Leisure time is important. It allows us a chance to relax and get away from daily stresses, permitting us to return refreshed and ready to work. Unfortunately, obtaining that time often seems to be difficult. Although we live in what is often called the "short-cut society," we still have less time to enjoy stress-free activities. With the advent of fast foods, virtual offices, fax machines, smart phones, pagers and similar electronics, laptop computers, microwaves, satellites, and robotics designed to make our lives easier, the pace of life has simply increased, and we are part of the frenzy.

This inability to make time for leisure activity is part of the pattern of a workaholic. *Workaholics* are individuals who are consumed by their jobs and derive little pleasure from other activities. These people are likely candidates for heart attacks, depression, hypertension, insomnia, and other physical ailments. They often view their lives as one long, continuous workday reaching well into the night and are rarely able to enjoy even the thought of leisure time. They are known to carry a briefcase full of work along anywhere they go and frequently check for communications from the office, adding to their stress level. For workaholics, even vacations are seldom restful because they take thoughts and worries of their jobs with them, compounding the stress.

Personality traits can also contribute to stress conditions. Two well-known personality types have been identified by extensive psychological research on behavior patterns. *Type A personalities* tend to be highly competitive, aggressive, achievement-oriented, and impatient. They typically appear pressured, rushed or hurried, and volatile, and dislike waiting in lines or for traffic lights to turn green.

Type B personalities exhibit an opposite behavior pattern. They appear more relaxed, easy-going, and even-paced in their approach to life in general. The Type B individual seldom overcommits, can say "no" without feeling guilty, and takes time to smell the roses along the way.

Type A individuals are more likely to experience high stress levels and exhibit stress symptoms than Type B individuals. Type A personalities are twice as prone to cardiovascular diseases, such as heart attacks and clogged arteries, as Type B personalities. An important step in developing a healthy lifestyle may be to identify these patterns in your personality and strive to reduce negative Type A tendencies you may have.

> "
> *If you look at what you have in life, you'll always have more. If you look at what you don't have in life, you'll never have enough.*
> —*Oprah Winfrey, American talk show host*
> "

Tips for Leaving Stress at the Office

1. Try to end the day as smoothly as possible. Start unwinding about one-half hour before you leave. Save easier jobs for last to assist you in unwinding.

2. To cut down worry about unfinished items, make a list of what needs to be done, imagine successfully completing these items, and leave them until the next morning.

3. Maintain a perspective. Remember that today's disasters are not the end of the world and will be of little importance in the future.

4. Use your commute to unwind. Listen to soothing music, read a good book, or enjoy a picturesque magazine if you are not driving.

5. Arrange with your family to be allowed a small bit of quiet time. This will help ease the transition between work and home.

6. Don't make dinner an ordeal with fancy meals. Turn off the television and limit interruptions. Limit work-related conversations at mealtime.

7. Don't overschedule your leisure hours. Don't bring work home on a routine basis, and discourage colleagues from calling in the evenings with work-related questions.

KeyPoint
Focusing on changing your own behavior and not that of others will reduce your stress and allow you to develop strong relationships with others.

In addition to making the most of our leisure time, you should choose activities carefully. For highly competitive individuals, sports such as softball and tennis can be as stressful as work.

Reducing Stressful Thoughts, Attitudes, and Behaviors   Setting realistic goals, learning to take risks, raising self-esteem, practicing positive self-talk, using communication skills, understanding the grieving process, and developing assertive behavior are discussed in other chapters. All of these skills can assist you in changing stressful thoughts, attitudes, and behaviors.

Another important skill that reduces stress is the ability to be self-focused. Harriet Goldhor Lerner, in her book, *The Dance of Intimacy,* states that individuals who are not self-focused see others as the problem and believe the solution is for the other person to change. These individuals are unable to achieve intimacy with those around them, which increases stress. The best idea is to focus on our own problems and work on resolving them rather than trying to change the behavior of others.[49]

Lerner also suggests avoiding what she calls "triangles." A triangle occurs when one person brings you into a problem that he or she is having with a third person. Refusing to be drawn into a problem between others is a healthy behavior to learn.[50]

You can cultivate other healthy attitudes and behaviors in these ways:

1. Don't try to change others; accept them as they are.
2. Don't expect actions from others. Thoughts such as "they should" and "they must" can cause anger and frustration.
3. Clarify what you want and firmly state your wants in an assertive manner.
4. Recognize situations in which you have no control. A traffic jam will unclog at the same time whether you are angry at the inconvenience or attempt to relax and spend the time productively.
5. View situations realistically. What will failure in this situation mean next month? Next year? In ten years?
6. Recognize that you do have options and control of many situations.
7. Develop a support system of friends and relatives with whom you can discuss stressful events and situations.
8. When choosing a relationship, ask whether it will be good for you or whether it will increase your stress.
9. Take coffee and lunch breaks away from the office.
10. Schedule some quiet time to be alone, during which you may dream, relax, or think.

Accepting and applying some of these attitudes and behaviors will ease feelings of stress that complicate your daily routine.

> " Happiness is an attitude. We either make ourselves miserable, or happy and strong. The amount of work is the same.
> —Francesca Reigler, unknown "

Ask Yourself...

Many individuals consciously participate in activities that are potentially harmful to their health.

1. Should companies have the right to refuse to hire individuals who smoke, even if they don't smoke at work? If not, what alternatives might companies have to keep insurance rates lower for others?
2. Should companies have the right to refuse to hire those who are overweight or who participate in dangerous activities such as skydiving and mountain climbing?

KEY TERMS

work–life balance
health and productivity programs
stress
substance abuse
alcohol
cannabinoids
depressants
dissociative anesthetics
hallucinogens
opioids and morphine derivatives
stimulants
anabolic steroids
dextromethorphan (DXM)
inhalants

pre-employment drug testing
expected interval testing
random interval testing
"for cause" testing
treatment follow-up testing
enabling
time management
procrastination
planned agenda
hidden agenda
workaholics
Type A personalities
Type B personalities

CHAPTER SUMMARY

The composition of the workforce, changing technology, and changing attitudes about the meaning of work are causing both employees and employers to try to balance work and life. While many organizations are aware of the need for work–life balance, few are taking action to resolve the issue. Those that develop effective programs see an increase in their revenue per employee.

Stress is the physical state of the body in response to environmental pressures that produce emotional discomfort. Stress can result from good or bad causes. When the body reaches its stress threshold, certain physical and mental reactions occur. Excessive stress can be harmful to your health and reduce your productivity at work.

Organizations are concerned about substance abuse because abusers cost them money in the form of lost productivity, industrial accidents, and excessive use of benefits. Individuals who are abusing substances need to take action to control their problem. If they do not, their supervisors may take action.

Lastly, a healthy lifestyle can help manage stress and prevent disease. Hallmarks of a healthy lifestyle include the ability to manage time effectively; a healthy diet; not smoking; and changing stressful thoughts, attitudes, and behaviors. Relaxation and leisure activities also contribute to a well-rounded way of life.

REVIEW

1. What is work–life balance? Why is balance good for both employer and employee?

2. What are organizations doing to promote work–life balance?

3. What are the physical and mental results of stress overload?

4. What are companies doing to combat substance abuse?

5. What substances are commonly abused? What are the effects of these substances?

6. What actions can an abuser of substances expect from a supervisor who has been trained to deal with substance abusers?

7. What are the most effective methods of time management?

8. What is the importance of proper diet in minimizing stress effects?

9. How do exercise and relaxation help you stay healthy?

10. How can you change stressful thoughts, attitudes, and behaviors?

CRITICAL THINKING

1. If you work, does your organization provide work–life benefits for employees? If so, what are the obvious benefits of these programs?

2. What symptoms of stress do you feel? What do you believe are the major causes? What do you do to reduce the stress?

3. Should employers have the right to administer drug tests to employees? Why or why not?

4. What difficulty would you have in handling a coworker and good friend who is abusing substances? What might happen to the coworker if you became an enabler, allowing him or her to continue in the abuse? What might happen to you? To others? To the company?

5. What method of time management do you use? What benefits do you realize from your method? How might you improve your method?

6. Do you procrastinate? Why? How might you overcome your procrastination?

7. Do you have a problem finding leisure time in your daily schedule? Do you exhibit symptoms of being a workaholic? How might you better plan for leisure time?

8. Which of your thoughts, beliefs, or behaviors contribute to your feelings of stress? How might you reduce these sources of stress?

CASE STUDIES

In small groups, analyze the following situations:

1 **A Lack of Focus** Alice checked her e-mail and then sent a text message to her boyfriend, Larry, asking him what he was going to wear to the party Saturday. She then opened the folder her supervisor had left on her desk. He wanted her to get pricing for 60 new workstations for the teleservice center—quickly. She read the purchasing parameters and then heard a beeping from her computer. She answered the IM from Gloria, wanting to know the e-mail address for the vendor who would be supplying new chairs.

About that time, Mark stopped by her cubicle. "Hey, you missed a good concert last night," he said and began to tell Alice all about it.

After Mark left, Alice checked her e-mail and responded to a survey from her women's group about what outings she would like to attend in the fall. She then responded to Larry's text message about the party. Glancing at her watch, she wandered over to the kitchen to get a cup of coffee and go to the restroom. When she returned, she picked up the job parameters and began to query the Internet. However, an article about workstations and ergonomics caught her eye and she spent a few minutes reading it.

About 15 minutes later her boss called, wanting the numbers. He fussed and fumed when Alice told him she hadn't quite finished. Hurriedly she finished the project and e-mailed it to him, without time to double-check her work.

1. Do you believe that Alice is managing her time effectively? Explain your answer.

2. What suggestions do you have for Alice to improve her work habits?

3. Do you believe being more organized would change Alice's attitude toward her job? Why or why not?

2 **Getting Sidetracked** Carey called a meeting of the design team for the new XM engine two weeks in advance. Prior to the meeting, he asked participants what issues they wanted to address and then put out a memo listing the agenda items. He promised the meeting would end promptly at 11 A.M.

The meeting was to begin at 10 A.M., but one coworker, Frank, was 10 minutes late. When the group had covered half the agenda items, Frank mentioned that he was having difficulty with the modulator and wanted everyone's opinion. The modulator was not on the agenda, but the group discussed it anyway.

By 11 A.M., three of the other group members indicated they had to leave for a lunch engagement with a customer. Four of the agenda items had not been discussed.

1. What caused Carey's meeting to get off track?

2. How might Carey have prevented this problem?

3. Do you believe Frank had a hidden agenda? What do you think it could have been? How would you have handled Frank's action?

HUMAN RELATIONS IN ACTION

Review the section on healthy choices. Pick one area in which you have been making poor choices. Research options for improving that area, and write an action plan. The action plan should have goals and objectives, as well as a way to measure and chart your progress. Share your plan with the class.

For additional resources, refer to the web site for this text:
www.cengage.com/management/dalton

RESOURCES

1. Fox, A. (2008, March). The brain at work. *HR Magazine*, 37–42.

2. Partnership for 21st century skills. (n.d.). *Life and career skills*. Retrieved on June 27, 2009, from http://www.21stcenturyskills.org/route21/index.php?option=com_content&view= article&id=11&Itemid=11

3. Facts for features & special editions. (2009, March 10). *Mother's day: May 10, 2009*. Retrieved on July 24, 2009, from http://www.census.gov/Press-Release/www/releases/ archives/facts_for_features_special_editions/013412.html

4. Facts for features. (2008, March 3). *Older Americans month: May 2008*. Retrieved on July 24, 2009, from http://www.census.gov/Press-Release/www/releases/archives/facts_for_ features_special_editions/013384.html

5. Conley, D. (2009). *Elsewhere, U.S.A.* New York: Pantheon.

6. Society for Human Resource Management. (2008). *2008 Job satisfaction*. Alexandria, VA: Author.

7. Wagner, C. G. (2002, September). *The new meaning of work. Futurist, 36*(5, 6), 2p, 3c.

8. Gurchiek, K. (2008, July 15). *More employers committing to wellness initiatives*. Retrieved on January 21, 2009, from http://www.shrm.org/hrnews_published/archives/ CMS_026132.asp

9. *Chronic disease prevention and health promotion*. (n.d.). Retrieved on July 24, 2009, from http://www.cdc.gov/nccdphp/index.htm

10. Killian, M. J. (2008, May). *Integrating health and productivity management: A 360-degree view of employee health and organizational wellness*. Retrieved on January 21, 2009, from http://www.shrm.org/rewards/library_published/benefits/nonIC/CMS_025546.asp

11. Ibid.

12. Watson Wyatt Worldwide. (2007/2008). *Staying@work report: Building an effective health & productivity framework executive summary*. Retrieved on January 21, 2009, from http://www.watsonwyatt.com/research/resrender.asp?id=2007-US-0216&page=1

13. Ibid.

14. Pallarito, K. (2008, August). *Employers take steps to relieve workers' stress*. Retrieved on January 18, 2009, from http://www.workforce.com/archive/feature/25/69/08/index.php

15. Pfeffer, J. (1998, Spring). The real keys to high performance. *Leader to Leader, 8*. Retrieved on October 11, 2009, from http://www.leadertoleader.org/knowledgecenter/journal. aspx?ArticleID=155

16. Cavanagh, M. E. (1988, July 1). What you don't know about stress. *Personnel Journal*, 53–59.

17. Fox, A. (2008, March). The brain at work. *HR Magazine*, 37–42.

18. Killian, M. J. (2008, May). *Integrating health and productivity management: A 360-degree view of employee health and organizational wellness*. Retrieved on January 21, 2009, from http://www.shrm.org/rewards/library_published/benefits/nonIC/CMS_025546.asp

19. *NIOSH worklife initiative*. (n.d.). Retrieved on October 11, 2009, from http://www.cdc. gov/niosh/worklife/

20. *Worker fatalities*. (n.d.). Retrieved on October 11, 2009, from http://www.osha.gov/

21. *NIDA infofacts: Understanding drug abuse and addiction*. (n.d.). Retrieved on July 26, 2009, from http://www.drugabuse.gov/infofacts/understand.html

22. *NIAAA*. (n.d.). Retrieved on October 11, 2009, from http://www.niaaa.nih.gov/FAQs/General-English/default.htm#groups

23. The Partnership for a Drug-Free America. (n.d.). *Alcohol*. Retrieved on October 12, 2009, from http://www.drugfree.org/Portal/drug_guide/Alcohol

24. Moelker, W. (2008, September 6). *Long term alcohol abuse effects*. Retrieved on October 12, 2009, from http://www.web4health.info/en/answers/add-alcohol-longrun.htm

25. NIAA. (n.d.). *Rethinking drinking: Alcohol and your health*. Retrieved on October 12, 2009, from http://rethinkingdrinking.niaaa.nih.gov/

26. Ibid.

27. VanKoughnett, H. (2008, February 27). *Drug arrests, English teachers, and the role of the U.S. Embassy in South Korea*. Retrieved on March 10, 2009, from http://www.korea4expats.com/news-drug-arrests-english-teachers.html

28. NIDA. (n.d.). *Commonly abused drugs*. Retrieved on July 26, 2009, from http://www.drugabuse.gov/DrugPages/DrugsofAbuse.html

29. NIDA. (n.d.). *Marijuana: Facts for teens*. Retrieved on July 27, 2009, from http://www.drugabuse.gov/MarijBroch/teenpg3-4.html#long

30. Drug-free workplace kit. (n.d.). *Identify issues: Test for drug use*. Retrieved on October 12, 2009, from http://www.drugfreeworkplace.gov/WPWorkit/drugtesting.html

31. Ibid.

32. Maddux, R. B. & Voorhees, L. (1986). *Job performance and chemical dependency*. Menlo Park, CA: Crisp Publications.

33. *Disability discrimination*. (n.d.). Retrieved on October 12, 2009, from http://eeoc.gov/types/ada.html

34. Find it! By topic. (n.d.). *Leave benefits: Family & medical leave*. Retrieved on October 12, 2009, from http://www.dol.gov/dol/topic/benefits-leave/fmla.htm

35. Addiction (dependence). (n.d.). Retrieved on July 26, 2009, from http://www.dol.gov/asp/programs/drugs/workingpartners/sab/addiction.asp#q6

36. U.S. Department of Health and Human Services. (n.d.). *Workplace substance abuse statistics fact sheet*. Washington, DC: Author.

37. EAP series part II: EAP's: Targeting substance abuse and alcohol. (September 1, 2004). Retrieved on October 12, 2009, from http://www.shrm.org/Research/Articles/Articles/Pages/EAP_20Series_20Part_20II_20-_20EAP%27s__20Targeting_20Substance_20and_20Alcohol_20Abuse.aspx

38. Ricadela, A. (2009, March 9). *High-tech time management tools*. Retrieved on July 27, 2009, from http://www.businessweek.com/managing/content/mar2009/ca2009039_010841.htm

39. Grensing-Pophal, L. (n.d.). *Efficiency boosters: Making the most of your time resources*. Retrieved on July 28, 2009, from http://www.shrm.org/hrdisciplines/consultants/Articles/Pages/CMS_014426.aspx

40. *Why high-tech solutions don't help with time management*. (n.d.). Retrieved on July 27, 2009, from http://www.rockyourday.com/why-high-tech-solutions-dont-help-with-time-management/

41. Neergaard, L. (2009, July 28). *9.1% of health costs linked to obesity: Medical spending doubles in the past decade.* Retrieved on October 12, 2009, from http://www.chron.com/CDA/archives/archive.mpl?id=2009_4770803

42. U.S. Department of Health and Human Services & U.S. Department of Agriculture. (2005). *Dietary guidelines for Americans 2005.* Washington, DC: Authors.

43. U.S. Department of Health and Human Services & U.S. Department of Agriculture. (2005). *Dietary guidelines for Americans 2005.* Washington, DC: Authors.

44. *Wellness premium discount program.* (n.d.). Retrieved on October 12, 2009, from http://www.alseib.org/HealthInsurance/SEHIP/HealthWatch/WellnessWatch.aspx

45. Gestl, J. (n.d.). *Coffee, caffeine, and fitness.* Retrieved on August 29, 2004, from http://www.mamashealth.com/exercise/caf.asp

46. *Tobacco and cancer.* (n.d.). Retrieved on October 12, 2009, from http://www.cancer.org/docroot/PED/ped_10.asp?sitearea=PED&level=1

47. Jackson, M. (August 1, 2008). Quelling distraction. *HR Magazine*, 43–46.

48. Dreyfuss, I. (1999, February 22). Wellness, exercise programs may save companies some money. *The Desert News.*

49. Lerner, H. G. (1990). *The dance of intimacy.* New York: Perennial/HarperCollins.

50. Ibid.

Glossary

5 Cs of communication. Reminders to improve writing; complete, concise, correct, courteous, and conversational/clear.

80-20 Rule. Rule that says 20 percent of your problems will account for 80 percent of your losses or gains.

A

Accountability perspective. View that businesses are accountable for their actions, with a responsibility to individuals and the general public to be fair and considerate.

Active listening. A conscious effort to listen to both the verbal and nonverbal components of what someone is saying, without prejudging.

Ad hoc committee. A committee that has a limited life and serves only a one-time purpose.

Arbitration. An employment dispute is submitted to an impartial person or panel that makes a final decision, which may be voluntary or involuntary.

Assertiveness. The process of expressing your thoughts and feelings while asking for what you want in an appropriate, calm, and confident manner.

Affirmative action. A practice originally designed to correct past discriminatory practices against minorities and women in the workplace by setting goals for hiring and upward mobility.

Age Discrimination in Employment. Act Federal legislation that prohibits discrimination against individuals age 40 and over in the workplace.

Alcohol. The most commonly abused drug in the country. Alcohol is a depressant that slows the activity of the brain and spinal cord.

Americans with Disabilities Act. Federal legislation that prohibits discrimination against individuals who are disabled.

Anabolic steroids. Legal, man-made drugs that are designed to build muscles.

Autocratic leadership. Leadership style that is task oriented and highly directive and involves close supervision and little delegation.

B

Bargaining unit. The group represented by the union; those for whom the union negotiates.

Behavioral school of management. Study of management that focused on techniques to motivate workers.

Benchmarking. A method of organizational change that involves comparing the company's practices, among internal divisions and/or against those of competitors, to determine which are best.

Bias. An inclination or preference either for or against an individual or group that interferes with impartial judgment.

Binding. A type of decision to which the parties must adhere. It cannot be appealed.

Brainstorming. Group problem-solving technique that involves the spontaneous contribution of ideas from all members of the group.

Business ethics. Rules of conduct that apply to businesses and their employees; they allow you to put many of your values into play in a business setting.

Business process reengineering. The fundamental rethinking and radical redesign of business processes to achieve dramatic improvements in critical, contemporary measures of performance, such as cost, quality, service, and speed.

C

Cannabinoids. These abused drugs include marijuana and hashish. Side effects of their use include euphoria, slowed thinking and reaction time, and confusion as well as impaired balance and coordination.

Caucus. When a mediator discusses issues with one party in private.

Centralized organization. An organization where those high up in the organization closely hold authority and are responsible for making all major decisions.

Chain of command. The direction in which authority is exercised and policies and other information are communicated to lower levels.

Change agent. Person who diagnoses problems, provides feedback, assists in developing strategies, or recommends interventions to benefit the organization as a whole. Also known as an Organization Development practitioner or an OD consultant.

Classical perspective. Belief that businesses need not feel responsible for social issues and should concentrate on being profitable.

Classical school of management. Study of management that focused on the technical efficiency of work as a way to maximize production.

Coaching. A method of employee development that closely resembles on-the-job training where a senior experienced and skilled employee helps develop or train a junior employee.

Code of ethics. List that requires or prohibits specific practices by employees in a particular organization or by all members of a professional group.

Coercive power. Power based on fear and punishment.

Cohesiveness. Degree to which group members are of one mind and act as one body.

Communication. Process by which we exchange information through a common system of symbols, signs, or behavior.

Compensation. A defense mechanism in which individuals attempt to relieve feelings of inadequacy or frustration by excelling in other areas.

Competency. A practical, useful way in which we handle emotions on the job or in life.

Concentration. Focusing intensely on a problem to the exclusion of other demands.

Conceptual skills. Administrative or big picture skills; ability to think abstractly and to analyze problems.

Conflict. Disagreement between individuals or groups about goal accomplishment.

Conflict management. A process in which the parties cooperate and work together to reach a solution that is agreeable to everyone.

Consensus. A solution that all members of the group can support.

Context. Conditions in which something occurs that can throw light on its meaning.

Conversational rituals. Things we say without considering the literal meaning of our words.

Cooperative counseling. A mutual problem-solving effort involving both parties in exploring and solving issues.

Corporate social responsibility. The idea that corporations have an ethical obligation to consumers beyond their economic, profit-driven purpose to stockholders and owners.

Counseling. A discussion technique used to assist employees with problems affecting performance on the job.

Creativity. Thinking process that solves a problem or achieves a goal in an original and useful way; the ability to come up with new and unique solutions to problems.

Critical thinking. the process of evaluating what other people write or say in order to determine whether to believe their statements. A critical thinker gathers all available information and takes into consideration what others have stated or discovered about the issue as well as his or her own observations and experiences.

Cross-functional work teams. Teams composed of individuals from two or more different functional areas; commonly used to design and bring a new product to market and ensure its long-run success.

D

Decentralized organization. An organization where important decisions are made at a lower level and authority is delegated.

Decision support systems (DSS). Computer applications that help sort through large amounts of data and pick among a variety of choices.

Defense mechanisms. Unconscious strategies that serve to protect our feelings of self-worth as well as help us avoid or reduce threatening feelings, although they may keep us from confronting the real problem.

Delegated method. Giving employees the responsibility and authority to effect change.

Delegation. Assigning tasks to subordinates and following up to ensure proper and timely completion.

Democratic leadership. Leadership style, also described as participative, that is usually preferred by modern management and involves showing concern for followers, sharing authority with them, and involving them in decision making and organizational planning.

Demographics. Statistics showing population characteristics about a region or group, such as education, income, age, marital status, or ethnic makeup.

Denial. A defense mechanism in which a person refuses to believe something that creates anxiety or frustration.

Depressants. These drugs can reduce anxiety, deliver a feeling of well-being, and lower inhibitions; they can also be particularly dangerous because of their ability to slow your pulse and breathing; lower blood pressure; cause poor concentration, fatigue, and confusion; and impair coordination, memory, and judgment. These drugs can lead to addiction, respiratory depression and arrest, and death.

Derivative power. Power obtained from close association with a powerful person.

Deviance. Not conforming to group norms.

Dextromethorphan. (DXM) A drug found in some cough and cold medications. It causes distorted visual perceptions as well as complete dissociative effects; at higher doses, its side effects are similar to those listed for dissociative anesthetics.

Direct communication style. Style of speaking that reflects a goal orientation and a desire to get down to business and get to the point.

Directive counseling. A method of counseling that involves the counselor's listening to the employee's problem, allowing emotional release, determining an action plan, and advising the employee on what needs to be done.

Discrimination. A difference in treatment based on a factor other than individual merit.

Displacement. A defense mechanism by which an individual acts out anger toward a person who does not deserve it but who is a "safe" target.

Dissociative anesthetics. These drugs include ketamine as well as PCP and analogs; they can cause increased heart rate and blood pressure, impaired motor functioning and memory loss, numbness, nausea, and vomiting. At high doses, ketamine can cause delirium and depression as well as respiratory depression and arrest, while PCP can cause panic, aggression, violence, and loss of appetite.

Diversity. Refers to differences. In people, it refers to differences such as race, religion, sex, age, disability, sexual orientation, national origin, educational levels, area in which you live, occupation, and job title.

Downward communication. Communication that begins at higher levels of the organization and flows downward.

E

Emergent leader. An informal leader who emerges without formal appointment and can exert as much or more power than the formal leader.

Emotional intelligence. Your ability to recognize and manage your feelings and those of others; it relates to keeping your emotions in check and using them in a thoughtful way.

Emotions. Your feelings, impulses to act, and mind and body reactions; examples include anger, sadness, fear, enjoyment, love, surprise, disgust, and shame.

Empathy. The action of understanding, being aware of, being sensitive to, and vicariously experiencing the feelings, thoughts, and experience of another.

Employee assistance program (EAP). A formal company program designed to aid employees with personal problems, such as substance abuse or psychological problems, that affect their job performance.

Employment at will. A philosophy that states the employee serves at the discretion of an employer and can be terminated at any time and for any reason, even if the employee is performing well.

Empowerment. Allowing others to make decisions and have influence on outcomes.

Enabling. Covering up for or making excuses for the behavior and performance of individuals who are abusing substances, allowing them to continue their disruptive conduct.

Equal Employment Opportunity Commission (EEOC). Federal agency responsible for enforcing laws related to employment discrimination.

Equal Pay Act. Federal law that requires men and women be paid the same salary provided they perform the same job and have the same experience and education.

Esteem needs. Level of Maslow's hierarchy that includes the need for respect from self and others and that can be met by increased responsibility, recognition for work well done, and merit increases and awards.

Ethical dilemma. Conflict of values that arises when our sense of values or social responsibility is questioned internally or challenged externally.

Ethics. As defined by *The American Heritage Dictionary,* "the study of the general nature of morals and of the specific moral choices to be made by a person; the rules or standards governing the conduct of a person or the members of a profession"; the study of what is good, right, and proper for people.

Ethnocentrism. A specific form of stereotyping in which one believes that one's own nationality, religion, or cultural traditions and customs are superior to others.

Expected interval testing. A type of schedule employers use to test current employees for substance abuse. Under this method, employees are informed ahead of time when testing will occur. It is then performed at the same time on a continuous basis.

Expert power. Power based on having specialized skills, knowledge, or expertise.

F

Fact. Something that is known to be true, to exist, or to have occurred; a statement presented as fact may actually be untrue.

Fair Labor Standards Act. Federal legislation that sets the minimum wage, equal pay, overtime, and child labor standards.

Family Medical Leave Act (FMLA). Federal legislation that provides eligible employees with up to 12 weeks of job-protected family or medical leave.

Feedback. Information given back to a sender that evaluates a message and states what the receiver understood.

"For cause" testing. Drug testing of employees only when they are suspected of being under the influence of drugs or alcohol.

Force field analysis. A technique used to analyze the complexities of a change and identify the forces that must be altered.

Foreign Corrupt Policy Act. Law requiring companies to operate ethically in their worldwide dealings.

Formal communication. Communication that flows up or down the formal organizational structure along the chain of command.

Formal group. A group designated by the organization to fulfill specific tasks or accomplish certain organizational objectives.

Formal roles. Roles that are assigned; people in these positions have a specific, recognized set of responsibilities.

Free-rein leaders. Allow employees to more or less lead themselves; they may integrate some activity or close out some assignment with a signature but generally remain uninvolved with directing or controlling tasks.

Functional authority. Authority given to staff personnel to make decisions in their areas of expertise and to overrule line decisions.

Functional group. Groups made up of managers and subordinates assigned to certain positions in the organizational hierarchy.

Functional work teams. Employees from one particular function, such as accounting or human resources, who work together to serve various groups.

G

The Genetic Information Nondiscrimination Act (GINA). Prohibits employers from discharging, refusing to hire, or otherwise discriminating against employees on the basis of genetic information, which might show that they have a propensity to develop diseases such as cancer and diabetes.

Globalization. Making goods and services available worldwide with no national boundaries or trade barriers on where they are sold or where they are produced.

Goal. Objective, target, or end result expected from the completion of tasks, activities, or programs.

Goal changing. You may change goals because they become outdated or inappropriate, such as when you complete a degree or buy the car for which you've been saving.

Grapevine. An informal person-to-person means of circulating information or gossip.

Great man theory. A theory of leadership based on the belief that certain people are born to become leaders and will emerge in that role when their time comes.

Grievance procedure. Provides a formal structure and outlines the steps an employee should take to resolve an issue; it often gives timelines for lodging a complaint and receiving a response.

Group. Two or more persons who are aware of one another, interact with one another, and perceive themselves to be a group.

Group norms. Shared values about the kinds of behaviors that are acceptable or unacceptable to the group.

Groupthink. Process of deriving negative results from group decision-making efforts as a result of in-group pressures.

Groupware. Computer software that has been developed to facilitate the use of groups and teams; technology that relies on modern computer networks, such as e-mail, newsgroups, videophones, or chat to improve group interactions.

H

Hallucinogens. Drugs that produce chemically induced hallucinations.

Halo effect. A process by which an individual assumes that another's traits are all positive because one trait is positive.

Hawthorne effect. The idea that the human element is more important to productivity than the technical or physical aspects of the job. The effect was identified through experiments conducted by Mayo.

Health and productivity programs. Programs that commonly address safety and emotional health as well as physical health and wellness; a focus on prevention is a key strategy of an effective program.

Health standards. These address the role of the work environment in the development of diseases and illnesses, such as asbestosis and black lung.

Herzberg's two-factor theory. A popular theory of motivation that says two sets of factors or conditions influence the behavior of individuals at work: one set to satisfy and the other to motivate.

High achiever. The culmination of being successful in planning, taking risks, and setting and achieving goals; your successes give you the self-confidence to take on other and even more challenging activities.

Hidden agenda. Topics that meeting attendees wish to discuss that have no relevance to the purpose of the current meeting.

High context groups. Groups that value long-term relationships, communicate in a less verbally explicit fashion, and strongly define who is accepted and who is considered an outsider.

Horizontal communication. Communication that occurs between individuals at the same level in an organization.

Hoteling. Sharing an office space in your company's building through reservations.

Human relations. Study of relationships among people.

Human relations skills. Ability to deal effectively with people through communicating, listening, being empathetic, inspiring and motivating, being perceptive, and using fair judgment.

Hygiene factors. Factors identified by Herzberg that are necessary to maintain a reasonable level of satisfaction, such as working conditions, job security, quality of supervision, and interpersonal relationships on the job.

I

I-9. Employment eligibility verification form all new employees are to complete within three days of hire.

Illumination. The "Aha!" stage of the creative process; when solutions break through to conscious thought.

Incubation. Stage of the creative process that is mysterious and below the surface and involves reviewing ideas and information.

Indirect communication style. Style of speaking that reflects a focus on the relationship and is used to develop a rapport before getting down to business.

Influence. Ability to change the attitude or behavior of an individual or group; the application of power through actions we take or examples we set that cause others to change their attitudes or behaviors.

Informal communication. Communication that does not follow the chain of command.

Informal group. A group created to satisfy the needs of individual members that are not satisfied by formal groups.

Informal roles. Roles that members take on when they perceive a need.

Information overload. An inability to continue processing and remembering information because of the great amount coming at us at one time.

Inhalants. Hydrocarbon-containing substances that are inhaled for their intoxicating effects.

Innovation. The end product of creative activity.

Intellectual properties. The knowledge or confidential business information an employee may have about that company; examples include protecting a prototype design; keeping the names of a client list from competitors; making certain a new invention is safely guarded until the patent lawyers can register the item; or assuring that the financial records of your company aren't given to your competitor.

Intercultural competence. Measures your effectiveness when you interact with others who are different from you, whether they work next to you or in different parts of the world.

Internal dispute resolution (IDR). A wide variety of methods used by organizations to deal with conflicts that employees are not able to resolve on their own.

J

Job enlargement. Increasing the complexity of a job by adding similar tasks to those already being performed.

Job enrichment. Building greater responsibility and interest into task assignments.

Job redesign. A method of bringing about change within the organization aimed directly at the tasks performed by individuals.

Job rotation. Shifting employees from one job to another in hopes of reducing boredom and stimulating renewed interest in job performance.

L

Leadership. The process of influencing the activities of individuals or organized groups so that they follow and do willingly what the leader wants them to do.

Legitimate power. Power derived from formal rank or position within an organizational hierarchy.

Life cycle. Stages of a business, consisting of start-up, expansion and growth, stability, decline, and phase-out or revitalization.

Line and staff structure. A complex organization structure in which the line (production employees) is given support by staff in such areas as law and safety.

Linguistic styles. characteristic speaking patterns, such as directness or indirectness, pacing and pausing, and word choice, and the use of elements such as jokes, figures of speech, stories, questions, and apologies.

Low context groups. Groups that value the written or spoken word, are task-oriented and results-driven, and generally adopt a direct linguistic style.

M

Management science school. Branch of management that began after World War II and was used to solve complex management problems. The computer has played an important part in this school.

Managerial Grid®. Leadership theory developed by Blake and Mouton that uses a grid to plot the degree to which leaders show concern for people and concern for production.

Maslow's hierarchy of needs. Motivation theory that recognizes five levels of needs. Individuals are motivated by the needs within each specific level. When these needs are met, individuals are no longer motivated by that level and move upward.

Matrix structure. A complex organization structure that uses groups of people with expertise in their individual areas who are temporarily assigned full or part time to a project from other parts of the organization.

McClelland's acquired needs theory. A motivational theory that states that through upbringing, individuals acquire a strong desire for one of three primary needs: achievement, affiliation, and power.

Mediation. The voluntary process in which a neutral third party presides over a formal resolution session.

Medium. The form in which a message is communicated.

Mentor. An experienced person who will give you objective career advice. A senior-level manager or retired professional with political savvy and an interest in helping employees achieve both career goals and the objectives of the organization.

Message. The content of the communication sent or received; may be verbal, nonverbal, or written.

Mission. An organization's overall goal that links all efforts toward the vision, stretches and challenges the organization, and has a finish line and timeframe.

Modular organization. The structure in which a company keeps all the business activities it can perform faster, better, and more cheaply than other organizations and outsources its remaining business activities.

Monochronic style. Consists of doing one thing at a time and following plans closely.

Motivation. Needs or drives within individuals that energize behaviors.

Motivational factors. Factors identified by Herzberg that build high levels of motivation, such as achievement, advancement, recognition, responsibility, and the work itself.

Motivational source fields. Forces that motivate; can be outside, inside, or early.

N

National Labor Relations Board (NLRB). A government agency responsible for enforcing the provisions of the Wagner Act, established in 1935.

Networking. (1) Process whereby you give and receive moral support, career guidance, and important information by developing contacts with people in your place of employment and in other professional organizations. (2) Method of finding employment that involves telling all individuals you know that you are seeking a job and asking them to contact you if they hear of any openings.

Non-disclosure agreement. A legal contract between you and the company that forbids you from disclosing certain information defined in the document; this agreement allows companies to hire individuals, expose them to sensitive data on projects, and then feel comfortable that that the information shared will not passed on to unauthorized persons when that employee leaves.

Nondirective counseling. A method of counseling viewed as a mutual problem-solving effort involving both parties in exploring and solving issues.

Nonverbal communication. Meaning conveyed through the body, the voice, or position.

Norris-LaGuardia Act. A federal law enacted in 1932 to abolish the use of yellow-dog contracts by companies as an antiunion technique.

O

Occupational Safety and Health Act. Federal legislation that sets safety and health standards and ensures that they are observed in the workplace.

Occupational Safety and Health Administration (OSHA). Federal agency that regulates safety and health in the workplace.

Official goals. Formally stated, abstract goals that are developed by upper management.

Ombuds. Provide informal, confidential help for those who want their problems addressed but not advertised; they often report directly to the head of the organization and maintain a neutral stance.

One-way communication. Communication that takes place with no feedback from the receiver.

Ongoing committee. A committee that is relatively permanent, addressing organizational issues on a standing or continuous basis.

Open door policies. The freedom to talk with any level of management at any time; this method is the one most often used to resolve conflict.

Operational goals. Concrete and close-ended goals that are the responsibility of first-line supervisors and employees.

Operational plans. The day-to-day plans for producing or delivering products and/or services.

Operative goals. Goals that are developed by middle management and are more specific than official goals.

Opinion. A view about a particular issue that is not necessarily true.

Opioids and morphine derivatives. Addiction, tolerance, nausea, respiratory depression and arrest, unconsciousness, coma, and death are the side effects of opioids and morphine derivatives that induce drowsiness, confusion, and sedation. These drugs include codeine, morphine, and opium.

Organization climate. The environment created by the managerial style and attitudes that pervade an organization; like moods, climates can fluctuate going from one extreme to the other.

Organizational culture. A mix of the beliefs and values of society at large, the individuals who work in the organization, and the organization's leaders and founders.

Organizational development. A holistic approach to organizational change involving the entire organization—its people, structures, culture, policies and procedures, and purpose.

P

Participative method. A method of implementing organizational change that uses employee groups in the problem-solving and decision-making processes preceding the actual change.

Passive power. Power source that stems from a display of helplessness.

Peer review process. Typically involves volunteer employees who sit on a panel and determine whether a policy or procedure was properly and fairly applied.

Perception. (1) Way in which we interpret or give meaning to sensations or messages; (2) the first stage in the creative process requiring that we view objects or situations differently.

Performance appraisal. A measurement of how well an employee is doing on the job.

Physiological needs. A level of Maslow's hierarchy of needs that includes the desire for food, sleep, water, shelter, and other physiological drives.

Planned change. A method of helping people develop appropriate behaviors for adapting to new methods while remaining effective and creative.

Planned agenda. An outline or list of what topics are to be discussed or what is to be accomplished during a meeting.

Planning. An attempt to prepare for and predict the future; it involves goals, programs, policies, rules, and procedures.

PODSCORB. An acronym for the functional abilities required of leaders—planning, organizing, directing, staffing, coordinating, reporting, and budgeting.

Polychronic style. Consists of doing many things at once, changing plans easily, and tolerating interruptions.

Power. The ability to influence others to do what we want them to do even if we are not a formal leader.

Power-compulsive. Power personality with a lust for power; seldom satisfied with the amount of power achieved.

Power politics. Developing opportunities for success.

Power positioning. Conscientious use of techniques designed to position an individual for maximum personal growth and gain in an effort to develop power.

Power-positive. Power personality that genuinely enjoys responsibility and thrives on the use of power.

Power-shy. Power personality that tends to avoid being placed in position that requires overt use of power.

Power symbols. Physical traits, personality characteristics, and external physical factors that are associated with those who are perceived to be powerful.

Pregnancy Discrimination Act. Federal law that prohibits discrimination against pregnant women in the workplace.

Pre-employment drug test. A test given to job applicants to determine whether they have drugs in their systems. Applicants who do not pass the test or who refuse to take it are not hired.

Prejudice. The act of prejudging or making a decision about a person or group of people without sufficient knowledge.

Preparation. Acquiring skills, background information, and resources for sensing and defining a problem.

Preference ordering. Ranking the goals you want to pursue according to preference; for example, a company may decide to maximize profit over expansion or you may decide to save for a new car rather than take a vacation.

Primary needs. Basic needs required to sustain life, such as food, water, air, sleep, and shelter.

Problem. Disturbance or unsettled matter that requires a solution if the organization or person is to function effectively.

Professional presence. Combines the poise, self-confidence, control, and style that empowers you to command respect in any situation.

Procrastination. The intentional putting off or delaying of activities that need to be done.

Project teams. Groups that come together to accomplish a specific project, frequently used in the engineering and construction industries to design and construct buildings or plants. Upon completion, the team disbands and team members are generally assigned to other teams.

Projection. A defense mechanism whereby individuals attribute unacceptable thoughts or feelings about themselves to others.

Public perspective. View that links businesses with the government and other groups to solve social and environmental problems actively.

Pygmalion effect. Psychological phenomenon whose premise is, "You get what you expect."

Pyramidal hierarchy. Triangular shape of an organization with the single head of the organization at the top. Smaller pyramids appear within the larger.

R

Random interval testing. The process of giving drug tests to employees at varying and unannounced times.

Rationalization. A defense mechanism by which a person explains away a problem.

Reality checking. Exploring the consequences of possible solutions by developing and honestly answering probing questions about what you want as a resolution and what might happen if you chose that option.

Reasonable accommodations. Actions that assist people with disabilities to perform the essential function of their jobs without imposing an undue hardship on the company.

Receiver. One to whom a message is transmitted; one who receives the message.

Reengineering. The fundamental rethinking and redesign of business processes to achieve dramatic improvements in critical, contemporary measures of performance, such as cost, quality, service, and speed.

Referent power. Power based on respect or admiration.

Regression. A defense mechanism whereby a person reverts to an earlier behavior pattern.

Repression. A defense mechanism by which an individual cannot remember an unpleasant event.

Résumé. Sales tool designed to assist in obtaining an interview. It provides a prospective employer with a brief summary of a job seeker's skills, education, and work experience.

Reverse halo effect. A process by which an individual assumes that another's traits are all negative because one trait is negative.

Reverse mentoring. A system in which a junior-level employee mentors a senior employee in areas such as technology, new information in the field, diversity, and risk taking; this can boost the mentored employee's skills as well as help improve differences between generations.

Reward power. Power based on the ability to give something of material or personal value to others.

Right-to-Work Law. A provision of the Taft-Hartley Act that allows states to prohibit both the closed and the union shop contract agreements, thereby giving the worker the choice of union membership.

Role ambiguity. Confusion that occurs when individuals are uncertain about what role they are to fill or what is expected of them.

S

S.M.A.R.T. guidelines. Use this approach to set goals that are specific, measurable, attainable, realistic, and timely.

Safety and security needs. A level of Maslow's hierarchy of needs that reflects the desire for physical, economic, and emotional security, such as safe working conditions, job security, and periodic salary increases.

Safety standards. These address hazards that can result in a direct injury, such as broken bones and cuts.

Sanctions. Actions taken to force compliance with established norms.

Sarbanes-Oxley Act. A set of complex regulations that protects investors and enforces corporate accountability and responsibility by requiring accuracy and reliability of accounting and disclosures in publicly traded corporations. The act grants the Securities and Exchange Commission increased regulatory control, imposes greater criminal and compensatory punishment on executives and companies that do not comply, and establishes procedures for handling whistleblower complaints.

Satisficing. Defines a situation in which one perfect and unique solution may not be possible; combines the words *satisfy* and *suffice.*

Saving face. Refers to maintaining a good image; you can help someone save face by giving minor concessions or stating your feelings without making a judgment about the other person.

Scapegoating. A defense mechanism that relieves anxiety by blaming other persons or groups for problems.

Secondary needs. Needs that include security, affiliation or love, respect, and autonomy; developed as a result of an individual's values and beliefs.

Self-actualization needs. A level of Maslow's hierarchy that includes the need for personal growth, freedom of creative expression, and using one's abilities to the fullest extent.

Self-awareness. Knowing yourself on an emotional level to recognize and understand your moods, emotions, and drives and how they affect you and others.

Self-confidence. A competency for self-awareness that is essential for success; it reflects how sure you are about your self-worth and capabilities.

Self-directed work teams. Teams that, to a certain extent, manage themselves; they may or may not have a leader. Often these teams are responsible for selecting and hiring their members, reviewing member performance, and making decisions regarding corrective action.

Self-disclosure. Revealing information to others about yourself.

Self-esteem. Feelings about yourself that can be positive or negative. These affect your daily outlook.

Self-regulation. Entails your ability to control or redirect impulses and moods that are disruptive as well as to stop and think before acting.

Self-talk. Making positive statements to ourselves.

Semantics. The study of the meanings and the changing meanings of words.

Sender. Person who transmits, or sends, the message.

Sequential attention. If you have multiple priorities, you may need to shift your attention from one goal to the next over periods of time.

Sexual harassment. Unwelcome sexual advances, requests for sexual favors, or verbal or physical conduct of a sexual nature found in the workplace.

Social needs. A level of Maslow's hierarchy that centers on the desire for meaningful affiliation with others, such as love, affection, and acceptance.

Social responsibility. Obligation we have to make choices or decisions that are beneficial to the whole of society; involves issues such as environmental pollution and welfare.

Social skill. The ability to get along well with others as well as to manage relationships and build networks; this also includes finding things in common with others and building rapport.

Social Security Act. Federal legislation that mandates retirement, Medicare, disability, and survivors' benefits.

Span of control. Number of people that an individual supervises.

Spoken communication. Any message sent or received through oral words; effective spoken communication is clear, direct, and to the point.

Statistical models. Mathematical models that assist managers with planning and controlling factors such as inventory, product mixes, and sales forecasts.

Stereotypes. Fixed or distorted generalizations made about members of a particular group.

Stimulants. These drugs increase the heart rate, blood pressure, and metabolism, leading to feelings of exhilaration, energy, and increased mental alertness; they can also cause rapid or irregular heartbeat, reduced appetite, weight loss, heart failure, nervousness, and insomnia.

Strategic planning. The systematic setting of organizational goals, defining strategies and policies to achieve them, and developing detailed plans to ensure that the strategies are implemented.

Stress. The physical state of the body in response to environmental pressures that produce emotional discomfort.

Sublimation. A defense mechanism by which an individual directs unacceptable impulses into socially accepted channels.

Substance abuse. The misuse of alcohol, illegal drugs, and prescription drugs.

Synergy. Interaction of two or more independent parts, the effects of which are greater than they would attain separately.

System. A group of interrelated items or parts that act as a whole; all parts are connected to all other parts and are affected by at least one other part, and each part affects the whole.

T

Tactical plans. Show how an organization will use its resources, budgets, and people to accomplish goals within its mission.

Taft-Hartley Act. A series of amendments to the Wagner Act that imposes controls on unions' organizing activities and methods used in collective bargaining attempts.

Task group. A group formed for a specific reason with members drawn from various parts of an organization to accomplish a specific purpose.

Team. An identifiable group of people who work together toward a common goal and who are dependent upon each other to realize that goal.

Team building. A series of activities designed to help work groups solve problems, accomplish work goals, and function more effectively through teamwork.

Technical skills. Skills required to perform a particular task.

Telecommuters. Term coined to describe people, frequently based at home, who use technology networks to send and receive work and information to and from different locations, locations (such as offices) to which they would once have needed to commute.

Theory X and Theory Y. Two sets of assumptions that leaders hold about followers, as outlined by Douglas McGregor; Theory X is a pessimistic view and Theory Y an optimistic view.

Third-party conflict manager. Uses conflict management skills to help others who are in conflict defuse an issue and then resolve it.

Time management. Using the time available to the greatest advantage.

Title VII of the Civil Rights Act of 1964. Federal law that prohibits discrimination based on race, color, religion, sex, or national origin in the workplace. This law also prohibits sexual harassment.

Total quality management. An organizational change method that focuses on involving employees in continuous process improvements to keep the organization on the cutting edge. TQM is rooted in the theories of American statistician Dr. W. Edward Deming.

Trade secret. A certain type of confidential business information that is protected by law under the Uniform Trade Secrets Act (UTSA),

Transactional leadership. Leadership style in which leaders determine what followers need to achieve their own and organizational goals, classify those needs, and help followers gain confidence that they can reach their objectives.

Transformational leadership. Leadership style that motivates followers to do more than they originally expected to do by raising the perceived value of the tasks, by getting them to transcend self-interest for the sake of the group goal, and by raising their need level to self-actualization.

Treatment follow-up testing. Drug testing used to monitor an employee's success in remaining drug free after being allowed to complete a substance abuse treatment program rather than be terminated.

Two-way communication. Communication between two or more parties in which feedback is given and received both ways.

Type A personalities. Persons who tend to be highly competitive, aggressive, achievement oriented, and impatient, and typically appear pressured, hurried, and volatile.

Type B personalities. Persons who tend to be relaxed, easygoing, and even-paced in their approach to life.

U

Unemployment compensation. Benefits paid to those who have become unemployed involuntarily.

Unilateral method. A method of implementing organizational change that allows supervisors to dictate change with little or no input from the employees.

Union. An association of employees formed to bargain collectively with employers over wages, hours, and working conditions and to protect themselves from unfair or arbitrary treatment.

Upward communication. Communication that begins in the lower levels of the organization and goes to higher levels.

V

Value systems. Sets of values that provide road maps for our behavior in a variety of situations.

Values. Principles, standards, or qualities considered worthwhile or desirable; those things (as a principle or quality) intrinsically valuable or desirable.

Verification or elaboration. Last stage of the creative process; testing, evaluating, revising, retesting, and reevaluating an idea.

Virtual office. Computer and information networks that link people in different ("remote") locations, so that they can interact and share work as if they were located in one office building.

Virtual organization. Is part of a network in which companies share costs, skills, capabilities, and markets; members of this may come together to satisfy the needs of a specific customer and, when the job is finished, go their separate ways.

Virtual teams. Task- or project-focused teams that meet without all members being present in the same location or at the same time.

Vision. A statement of an organization's purpose or reason for existing.

Visualization. A thought process by which you view yourself being successful.

Vroom's expectancy theory. A theory that views motivation as a process of choices and says people behave in certain ways based on their expectation of results.

W

Whistleblower. A person who identifies organizational wrongdoing or unethical practices to officials who have the authority to enforce appropriate sanctions on any inappropriate behavior.

Win–win options. Those that satisfy the interests of both parties.

Wagner Act. A federal law enacted in 1935 that ordered management to stop interfering with union organizing efforts and defined what constituted unfair labor practices; established the right of employees to form unions and collectively bargain with management on employment issues; established the National Labor Relations Board.

Workaholics. People who are consumed by their jobs and derive little pleasure from other activities.

Workers' compensation. Compensation to those who have been physically or mentally injured on the job, or who have developed an occupational disease.

Work–life balance. The comfortable equilibrium between what you do at work and what you do outside of work for yourself and with friends and family.

Workplace etiquette. Deals with commonly accepted rules for good behavior in workplace interactions; this includes acting appropriately, being considerate, making other people feel comfortable in your presence, and trying not to embarrass others.

Index